Canadian Retailing

Fourth Edition

Michel Laroche
Concordia University

Gordon H. G. McDougall
Wilfrid Laurier University

Toronto Montréal New York Burr Ridge Bangkok Bogotá Caracas Lisbon London Madrid
Mexico City Milan New Delhi Seoul Singapore Sydney Taipei

McGraw-Hill
Ryerson Limited

A Subsidiary of The McGraw-Hill Companies

CANADIAN RETAILING
Fourth Edition
Laroche and McDougall

ISBN: 0-07-086044-0

1 2 3 4 5 6 7 8 9 0 QPD 0 9 8 7 6 5 4 3 2 1 0

Printed and bound in USA

Editorial Director & Publisher: Evelyn Veitch
Sponsoring Editor: Lenore Gray Spence
Developmental Editor: Denise McGuinness
Supervising Editor: Julie van Veen
Copy Editor: Gail Marsden
Senior Marketing Manager: Jeff MacLean
Marketing Manager: Bill Todd
Production Co-ordinator: Nicla Dattolico
Art Direction: Dianna Little
Cover and Interior Design: Greg Devitt
Cover Photo: Rodney C. Daw
Cover Location: Mountain Equipment Co-op, Toronto
Typesetter: Visutronx
Printer: Quebecor

Canadian Cataloguing in Publication Data

Laroche, Michel, 1945-
Canadian Retailing

4th ed.
Previous eds. by J. Barry Mason... [et al.]
Includes bibliographical references and index.
ISBN 0-07-086044-0

1. Retail trade – Canada. I. McDougall, Gordon H.G., 1942- . II. Title

HF5429.6.C3C347 2000 658.8'7'00971 C99-932367-9

This book is dedicated to Anne H. Laroche,
and to Betty, Michael, and Sandy McDougall.

TABLE OF CONTENTS

LIST OF CASES

PREFACE

Since the third edition was published, Canadian retailing has experienced many significant events, from the explosive development of electronic commerce to the continuing impact of the North-American Free Trade Agreement (NAFTA) and the continuing invasion by huge American retailers such as Wal-Mart. These events have had a substantial impact on Canadian retailers, including the demise of one of Canada's oldest department store chains, Eaton's. Inefficient retailers were forced out of business, and many others were prompted to rethink their basic strategic approach, including the opening of big-box outlets, a better focus on good customer service, and the development of Web sites on the Internet.

The first decade in the new millennium will bring even more challenges and opportunities, particularly for the astute entrepreneur who understands retailing in the Canadian environment within a globalized economy. What kinds of new retailing concepts will be introduced, particularly to lower distribution costs? How far will the concept of controlled environment be extended, and will the future bring more megamalls, or will new types of malls be designed and developed? How far will electronic commerce go, what new technologies will be introduced, and how will this affect the management of retail institutions, or create new ones? Will the big-box phenomenon continue its strong growth, or will it decline? How will consumer environmental concerns affect retailing in Canada?

Answers to these and other questions will determine which retailing institutions will survive in a highly competitive and globalized economy. This text emphasizes a managerial, practical approach to retailing, focusing directly on the strategic issues faced by the owner, the manager, or the employee of a retail institution for the beginning of the new millennium. It assumes no prior knowledge of retailing, and it covers the conceptual and analytical foundations necessary to understand all aspects of retail management in the current Canadian environment. This is done from a pragmatic, practical point of view, and in simple straightforward language, with many real-life examples. All chapters contain information relevant to the resources available through the Internet.

Each chapter starts with an introduction that sets the stage for the following material. Throughout the chapter, numerous examples and *Retail Highlights* reflecting recent events have been added to provide an in-depth look at important issues and applications. It ends with detailed chapter highlights, a list of the key terms, discussion questions, application exercises, and suggested cases. The complete package is intended to maximize learning while doing. Enhanced pedagogical features have been added to improve student access to important details: page references for end-of-chapter key terms, suggested cases keyed to each chapter, and an end-of-text glossary, as well as new figures, tables, and exhibits.

The book follows a logical sequence towards strategy development for the retail firm.

In *Part 1, The World of Canadian Retailing,* three chapters provide a broad perspective on the institutions, the economy, and the markets in the Canadian environment. Chapter 1 introduces the reader to retailing in Canada, its evolution, structure, and trends. Chapter 2 covers the critical environmental factors affecting retail strategy development (legal, economic, social, and technological). Understanding the retail customer, including individual factors and social influences (Chapter 3), is critical to the success of the retail strategy.

In *Part 2, Developing the Retail Strategy,* the conceptual and organizational aspects of the retail strategy are logically developed. Chapter 4 deals with the development of strategic planning as a method of defining the objectives of the firm and deciding how to compete. Franchising as a means of owning and operating a retail firm is examined in detail (Chapter 5). Chapter 6 discusses the critical issues in the recruitment, selection, training, and motivation of retail employees, as well as organizing the retail firm.

In *Part 3, Designing the Retailing Mix—Location and Merchandising Decisions,* the decisions on some key variables of the retailing mix related to location and merchandising are discussed. The important issues in the retail location decisions are covered in Chapter 7. Store design, layout, and merchandise presentation decisions are covered in Chapter 8. Merchandise and expense planning decisions are the subject of Chapter 9. Buying, handling, and inventory management decisions are explained in Chapter 10.

In *Part 4, Designing the Retailing Mix—Pricing, Promotion, and Customer Service,* the remaining critical aspects of the retail mix are covered. Determining retail prices is the topic of Chapter 11. In order to successfully promote their products or services, retailers need to: help their employees develop methods of successful selling (Chapter 12); design effective programs in retail advertising, sales promotion, and publicity (Chapter 13); and instill in their employees a customer-focused culture (Chapter 14).

In *Part 5, New Dimensions in Retailing,* Chapter 15 is devoted to the developing fields of services retailing and nonstore retailing. Finally, Chapter 16 covers the important topic of electronic commerce.

In *Part 6, Evaluating Retail Performance,* the tools used to determine how well the retail strategy is doing are explained in Chapter 17. Internal financial evaluation is critical to the retail manager.

Finally, three appendices are provided: Appendix A covers careers in retailing to help students make informed decisions about the many facets of working in retailing. Knowledge of markets is essential to succeeding in Canadian retailing, and the retail research methods used to obtain this knowledge are covered in Appendix B. To compete successfully retailers need to understand how to start and finance a retail business (Appendix C).

Another strong feature of the text is the set of cases and exercises that follow the appendices. These are among the best case materials available in Canada, and they cover all aspects of the text. The cases are keyed to each chapter, and some cases can be used to cover several topics. Some cases were contributed by Canadian academics and the others by the authors of the text. The mix of cases provides the instructors with some that are very comprehensive, others that are of more restricted scope, and the remainder can be used to focus on very specific issues. Thus, a wide range of teaching material is provided to maximize learning.

At the end of the text, a glossary of terms, arranged alphabetically, is provided for the convenience of the reader.

The text includes a colour insert—pictures of advertisements, Web sites and retail scenes that highlight the impact of colour in retailing. Internet exercises and Web links related to the text's content will enhance students' learning experiences.

The following supplements accompany *Canadian Retailing, Fourth Edition* and provide further resources to instructors:

- Printed Instructor's Manual (ISBN 0-07-086382-2)
- Printed Test Bank (ISBN 0-07-086383-0)
- CD-ROM for Instructors (ISBN 0-07-086384-9) containing the following:
  - Instructor's Manual
  - Test Bank (questions in MS-Word format to print and use in your own tests)
  - PowerPoint slides
  - Computerized Test Bank (questions and software for constructing customized tests)

Visit our Web site (http://www.mcgrawhill.ca/college/laroche) for: http://www.mcgrawhill.ca/college/laroche

- Internet Application Questions and Quiz Questions
- Resource links
- Password-protected downloadable files for the supplements (available to instructors only)

In the preparation of this edition, many people have provided encouragement, suggestions, and material, and we are most grateful for their assistance. The following instructors provided many helpful comments and insights on the fourth edition of *Canadian Retailing:*

Robert MacGregor, Bishop's University
Cheryl Pollmuller, Lethbridge Community College
Lynn Ricker, University of Calgary
Donna Smith, Ryerson Polytechnic University

Development of the fourth edition owes much to the thoughtful and thorough reviews of:

Carla Furlong, Kwantlen University College
Linda Hoffman, Northern Alberta Institute of Technology
Alison MacCallum, Sheridan College
Bryan MacKay, Confederation College
Cheryl Pollmuller, Lethbridge Community College

Many thanks also to the case contributors who provided material for the book.

The production of this manuscript involved other individuals to whom we are most grateful. Many thanks to Lenore Gray Spence, Denise McGuinness, Julie van Veen, Gail Marsden, and Greg Devitt for the great job they did in the production of this book, and to Isabelle Miodek and Anne H. Laroche who helped find and develop new material. As well, the financial support of McGraw-Hill Ryerson is very gratefully acknowledged.

Finally, we hope this revised edition of *Canadian Retailing* will provide you with a useful and rewarding learning experience for many years to come.

January 2000

Michel Laroche
Gordon H.G. McDougall

Part 1

The World of Canadian Retailing

The three chapters in *Part 1, The World of Canadian Retailing* provide a broad perspective on the types of retailers, the economy, and the markets in the Canadian environment. Chapter 1 introduces the student to retailing in Canada, its evolution, structure, and trends. Chapter 2 covers the critical environmental factors affecting retail strategy development (legal, economic, social, and technological). Understanding the retail customer including individual factors and social influences, as discussed in Chapter 3, is critical to the success of the retail strategy.

CHAPTER 1

CANADIAN RETAILING TODAY

STRUCTURE AND TRENDS

CHAPTER OBJECTIVES

After reading this chapter you should be able to:

1. Relate retailing to the marketing discipline.
2. Explain and describe the strategic classifications of retailing.
3. Explain and describe the descriptive classifications of retailing.
4. Review the explanations of retail structural change.
5. Understand the major trends in retailing.

Canadian retailers operate in a dynamic, exciting, competitive environment. The deep recession of the early 1990s led to bankruptcy for thousands of Canadian retailers, from small independents to large, well-known chains like Woodwards. The major department store, the Bay, is under siege from U.S. and Canadian category killers like Wal-Mart, Price/Costco, Future Shop, Chapters, and Home Depot. For many retailers the major threat is electronic commerce where consumers shop on-line over the Internet. It is the most rapidly growing form of retailing in the world.

New types of retailers are constantly evolving, from "big box" stores to "stores-within-stores," to "power centres" as retailers seek to deliver value and convenience to consumers whose needs are constantly changing depending on economic, family, and personal circumstances. The goal is to survive and prosper in these ever-changing times.

And some retailers do survive and prosper. Whether times are good or bad, there is a group of retailers who continually outperform their competitors. Canadian Tire reinvented itself, moved to large store formats, and focused on three retail lines of merchandise. Tim Hortons merged with Wendy's, added soups, salads and bagels, and continuously added stores in attractive locations. Sears Canada revitalized its stores and product lines, focused on the female market, and introduced a separate furniture retail concept. These and other retailers identified the changing competitive and consumer scene, revised their strategies, and grew.

To set the stage, we offer the following overview of retailing in Canada:

- Retailing employs more Canadians than any other industry. More than 1,400,000 people work in retailing, which is approximately 11 percent of Canada's work force.
- Total retail sales in Canada are more than $260 billion annually; on average, each Canadian spends more than $8,600 on retail goods and services in stores from Prince George (population 78,000, with annual retail sales of more than $840 million) to Corner Brook (population 29,000, with annual retail sales of more than $300 million).
- More than 200,000 stores dot the Canadian landscape. Although independent retailers account for the majority of total retail sales (because of their sheer numbers), much of the buying power is in the hands of a few large chains that are well known to most Canadians (Table 1-1).
- Canadians spend approximately 50 percent of their retail dollars in shopping centres. From regional malls like the MicMac Mall in Dartmouth, Nova Scotia, with 150 stores serving a trading area of 93,000 households, to community malls like the St. Albert Centre in St. Albert, Alberta, with 58 stores serving 15,000 households—more than 1,800 shopping centres, with over 73,000 stores, are the shopping destinations for many Canadians.
- Canadians respond to new retailing concepts. Category specialists, often referred to as category killers, like Chapters, Home Depot, Business Depot, and Future Shop are gaining a greater share of the retail market as they meet the needs of Canadians who are seeking a deep assortment of products in specific categories (e.g., books, office supplies). The most appealing new concept for many Canadians is on-line shopping or

Retail Highlight 1-1 The Retailing Challenges Beyond Year 2000

- *Economic environment.* Small increases in annual incomes and high consumer debt means a low growth economy. The challenge is to manage a retail business where consumers have become more value conscious.
- *Demographic environment.* The Canadian population is aging, non-traditional household groups are emerging, and ethnic markets are increasing. The challenge is to respond to the diverse needs of these new market segments.
- *Competitive environment.* New forms of competition including foreign retailers entering the Canadian market, category specialists, and other new retail formats are changing the competitive landscape. The challenge is to revise retail strategy to reflect this new retailing era.
- *Technology environment.* The Internet and electronic commerce will have the most significant impact on retailing. The challenge for retailers is whether to enter, if they enter, how to enter, and how to make money. Many retailers may not have the capabilities to respond to this challenge.
- *Customer satisfaction.* Many consumers have expressed dissatisfaction with the merchandise, value, and service offered by retailers. The challenge is to address these consumer concerns by focusing on customer satisfaction through the merchandise mix and services offered, including retail staff training.
- *Store location.* Shopping centres have lost their glamour for a number of Canadians who are now shopping in power centres. The challenge is to rejuvenate these centres by rethinking the store mix, store cluster, and physical design.
- *Positioning.* A number of Canadian retailers do not have a clear image in the consumer's mind. The challenge is to design and implement a positioning strategy that presents an image that matches the needs of target markets.

electronic commerce that meets needs of convenience, choice, and price.

- Canadian retailers face many challenges and opportunities including the economic environment, new forms of competition, and shifting demographics (Retail Highlight 1-1).

Retailing in Canada is a competitive, dynamic business. As the above examples show, retailers must continually adjust to an environment where consumers, segments, and competitors are constantly changing. Success in retailing is not easy but it's always exciting.

Retailing consists of all activities involved in the sale of goods and services to the ultimate consumer. A retail sale occurs whenever an individual purchases groceries at a Sobey's supermarket, a compact disc at Sam the Record Man, a coffee at Tim Hortons, a haircut at Magicuts, or a membership at a fitness centre. Not all retail sales are made in stores. Some are made by retailers selling though the Internet, by mail-order firms such as Eddie Bauer, by telemarketers such as the Canadian Home Shopping Network, by the use of automatic vending machines, or by farmers selling produce at the roadside.

Marketing is the process by which individuals and groups obtain what they need and want through creating and exchanging products and value with others. Retailing is the final part of that process, satisfying individual and organizational objectives through exchanges.

Table 1-1 Canadian Retail Chains

Department and Warehouse Stores	Revenue ($000)	Characteristics
Hudson's Bay Company	$7,100,000	Comprises two chains, the Bay (over 100 stores) and Zellers (350 stores).
Sears Canada	5,000,000	Has 110 retail stores and 1,752 catalogue units across Canada.
Wal-Mart Canada	4,200,000	World's largest retailer, with over 130 stores in Canada.
Price/Costco Canada	2,600,000	Warehouse club chain, with locations across Canada.
Eaton's	1,700,000	Was Canada's best known department store chain, went bankrupt in 1999.
Clothing Stores		
Dylex	1,100,000	Operates a number of chains including Fairweather, Tip Top, Thrifty's, Braemar and BiWay. Has over 650 stores.
Reitmans	424,000	Operates more than 700 stores under various banners including Reitmans, Smart Set, Penningtons, Dalmys, Antels, and Cactus.
Mark's Work Wearhouse	417,000	Calgary-based chain of more than 150 corporate and franchise stores.
Suzy Shier	328,000	Operates over 400 Suzy Shier, L.A. Express, and La Senza stores.
Chateau Stores	161,000	Operates stores under the Le Chateau name.
Specialty Stores		
Canadian Tire	4,400,000	A Canadian landmark, with over 430 stores.
Shoppers Drug Mart	4,200,000	Part of the Imasco Group, including more than 820 franchised Shoppers Drug Mart and Pharmaprix stores across Canada.
Future Shop	1,800,000	A dominant force in computer and electronics products with over 110 stores.
Chapters	457,000	Operates Chapters, Coles, Smith Books and Classic Bookstores.
Leon's Furniture	351,000	Operates over 50 company-owned stores.

Source: Various annual reports and *The Globe and Mail, Report on Business: Top 1000 Companies*, July 1999.

Structure is the arrangement of parts, elements, or constituents considered as a whole rather than a single part. Thus, the **retail structure** comprises all the outlets (organizations, establishments) through which goods or services move to the ultimate consumer. The structure is complex and can be classified in various ways to help understand its components.

ALTERNATIVE WAYS TO CLASSIFY THE RETAIL STRUCTURE

The complexity and dynamics of retailing can best be understood by analyzing its structure. Analyzing retail structure and understanding competition is critical to developing and implementing retail strategies. By analyzing the structure, better ways of serving consumer needs through new types of retailing organization may be revealed. These new approaches can serve as a competitive advantage that may be difficult for competitors to copy in the short run.

The retailing structure can be classified in various ways, and for two broad purposes: for strategy assistance (strategic classifications) and for describing and understanding (descriptive classifications).

Strategic Classifications

The following strategic classifications help to explain retailing and they also assist retailers in achieving differential advantages in the market. The classifications include strategic dimensions that may provide helpful ideas for achieving a competitive advantage.

Variety and Assortment

The major characteristic of a retailer is its retail mix—the strategy a retailer uses to satisfy its customers' needs. Central to this is the variety and assortment of merchandise offered. **Variety** is the number of lines of merchandise carried; **assortment** is the choice offered within a line. Variety can be thought of as the width or breadth of a store's merchandise selection, and assortment can be thought of as the depth of a store's selection, including sizes, colours, and types of material. Figure 1-1 illustrates the concept of width and depth for sports shoes carried in a specialty store, a department store, and a discount department store.

In this example, the number of items reflects the models offered by each manufacturer. The specialty store carries more types of shoes (width) and more depth (brands and items) within each type than either the department store (e.g., the Bay) or the discount department store (e.g., Zellers). The width of the Bay's and Zellers' sports shoe lines are the same but Zellers offers more depth, including a store brand (Venture). The specialty store, with its wide and deep line, provides a wider choice, which is appealing to customers but requires more inventory. The strategy is to attract more customers and hopefully generate more sales because of the greater choice offered.

Figure 1-1

Types and Brands of Sports Shoes Offered

Types of Sports Shoes	Specialty Store	Department Store	Discount Department Store
Running	Reebok Nike Brooks Adidas Asics Saucony New Balance Avia (47 items)	Reebok Nike Brooks (18 items)	Nike Brooks Venture (22 items)
Basketball	Nike Reebok Adidas Converse Asics (26 items)	Nike Reebok (4 items)	Nike Adidas Converse Venture (19 items)
Cross-training	Nike Reebok Avia (30 items)	Nike Reebok (12 items)	Nike Venture (14 items)
Tennis	Adidas Nike Reebok (14 items)		
Volleyball	Asics Kangaroo (3 items)		
Soccer	Reebok Nike Mitre Adidas (32 items)		
Golf	Nike Reebok (4 items)		

The Margin-Turnover Classification

The margin-turnover framework for retail structure may be applied to all types of outlets. The framework is useful for understanding basic strategic choices along financial dimensions.

Margin is defined as the difference between the cost and the selling price or as the percentage markup at which the inventory in a store is sold. **Turnover** is the number of times the average inventory is sold, usually expressed in annual terms.

A specialty store carries a deep range of jogging shoes to target serious runners as well as casual joggers.

Photo by James Hertel

Figure 1-2 diagrams four quadrants, defined by margin and turnover, into which any retail outlet can be placed. Typically, the low-margin, high-turnover retailer focuses on price, offers few services, and carries a large variety of merchandise. Three leading retailers—Wal-Mart, Zellers, and Sears Canada—have adopted this strategy. The high-margin, high-turnover retailers focus on convenience by having numerous locations and extensive open hours, charge prices above the market, and provide a large variety of merchandise, considering the store size. Mac's Milk, 7-11, and a host of convenience stores pursue this strategy. The high-margin, low-turnover stores focus on service, charge above the market, and offer a limited variety of merchandise, often on an exclusive basis. Holt Renfrew, the exclusive women's wear chain, typifies this category. The low-margin, low-turnover retailers have a poor strategy that requires adjustment to regain profitability.

Retail Price and Service Strategy Classification

A third classification utilizes two major value dimensions—price and service. In Figure 1-3, quadrants I and IV are not viable in the long run and are in fact "traps." Quadrants II and III are promising strategic options.

In Quadrant I, even though customers would be pleased with high service/low prices, the strategy would be unwise for the retail firm because it is unlikely to generate sufficient profits. Customers would not be interested in Quadrant IV's poor value of low service at high prices. Retailers must monitor this strategy carefully as they reduce service in an attempt to be more price competitive. A popular strategy recently has been that illustrated by Quadrant III and represented by such firms as Price/Costco, Zellers, and Wal-Mart.

Quadrant I, high price/high service, illustrates the business practices of firms such as Birks, Holt Renfrew, Liptons, Talbots, and Lands' End in catalogue retailing.

Figure 1-2 The Margin-Turnover Classification

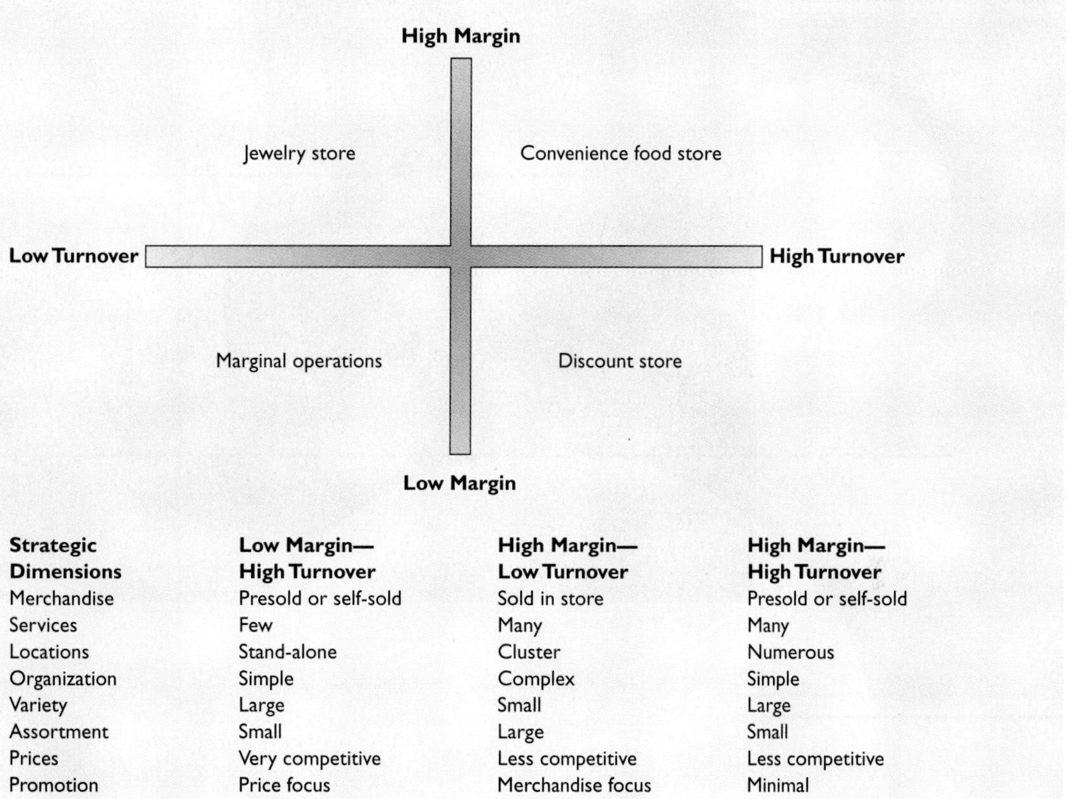

Strategic Dimensions	**Low Margin—High Turnover**	**High Margin—Low Turnover**	**High Margin—High Turnover**
Merchandise	Presold or self-sold	Sold in store	Presold or self-sold
Services	Few	Many	Many
Locations	Stand-alone	Cluster	Numerous
Organization	Simple	Complex	Simple
Variety	Large	Small	Large
Assortment	Small	Large	Small
Prices	Very competitive	Less competitive	Less competitive
Promotion	Price focus	Merchandise focus	Minimal

Figure 1-3 The Retail Price/Service Strategy Classification

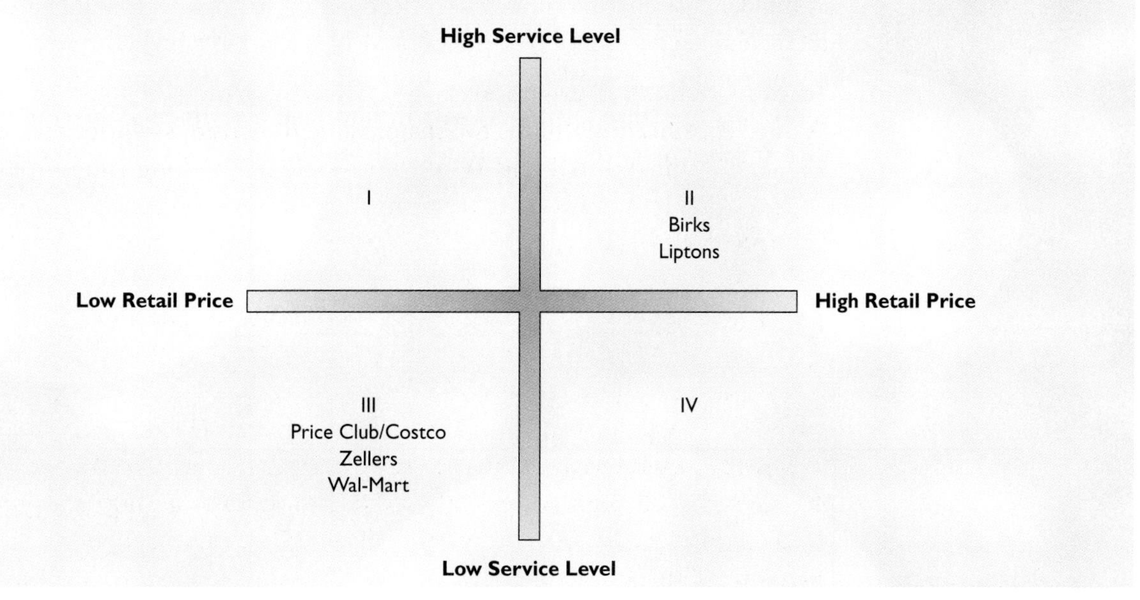

Holt Renfrew focuses on consumers who value exclusive quality merchandise and excellent service.

Courtesy Holt Renfrew

Table 1-2 combines a number of these strategic dimensions (variety, assortment, service, margins, and turnover) to illustrate some of the types of retailers that pursue each strategy. Department stores, like the Bay, carry a broad variety and deep to average assortment, offer services, have average to high margins/prices, and average turnover. Discount stores, like Wal-Mart and Zellers, reduce their assortment, offer lower levels of service but charge lower prices. Specialty stores, like Holt Renfrew, the Gap, and Pier 1 Imports, have a narrow but deep assortment, strong service, and higher prices. Category specialists, sometimes referred to as category killers, include Chapters, Business Depot, and Home Depot. They offer narrow and very deep assortments, and service can vary depending on the specific retailer. Warehouse clubs, like Price/Costco, offer a wide but shallow assortment, little service, and low prices, and typically have high turnover. The electronic commerce retailers appear to be the wave of the future. While they currently are specialized, offering narrow but deep assortments, they are constantly evolving and may create new strategies based on variations of the strategic dimensions.

Table 1-2

Characteristics of Retailers Based on Strategic Dimensions

Type	Variety	Assortment	Service	Margins/ Prices	Turnover
Department stores	Broad	Deep to average	Average to high	Average to high	Average
Traditional discount stores	Broad	Average to shallow	Low	Low	High
Traditional specialty stores	Narrow	Deep	High	High	Low
Category specialists	Narrow	Very deep	Low to high	Low to average	High
Warehouse clubs	Average	Shallow	Low	Very low	High
Off-price stores	Average	Deep, but varying	Low	Low	High
TV home shopping	Average	Shallow	Average	Average	Average
Electronic retailing	Narrow	Deep	Average	Average	Average

Descriptive Classifications

The two main descriptive ways of classifying retail structures are (1) type of ownership and (2) location.

Type of Ownership

The most common classification is based on ownership, and the two major types are independent and chains. The independent with a single store constitutes over 60 percent of total retail sales. Single-unit organizations tend to be small businesses operated by family members.

The small independent store can compete with chains because: (1) the store's cost of doing business is usually low due to low rents, location in a lower traffic neighbourhood or rural area, and ownership by the proprietor; (2) the store is often located closer to customers than are larger chain stores; (3) a personal relationship between customers and the manager is more likely to occur, allowing the smaller store to develop a unique personality; and (4) the manager can be very flexible in meeting the needs of customers. Still, the failure rate among small, independent retail stores remains high. Such failures can be attributed to inexperience, incompetence, or other management shortcomings.

A **chain** is a retail organization consisting of two or more centrally owned units that handle similar lines of merchandise. In food retailing and the general merchandising field, chain stores control a substantial proportion of the market. The five largest department and discount store chains—the Bay, Zellers, Sears Canada, Wal-Mart, and Eaton's—have total sales exceeding $14 billion

Retail Highlight 1-2 Canadian Department Stores: The Originals

Two of Canada's department store chains, the Bay and Eaton's, have considerable importance from an historical perspective. The Hudson's Bay Company is Canada's oldest enterprise. The original charter, granting them trading rights in Hudson's Bay, was given on May 2, 1670. During its first century of operation the company established forts and the Bay and traded with the First Nations. The merger of the company with a rival trading firm in 1821 led to the Hudson's Bay Company. The company played an important role in Canada's development from its inception to today. It is now a conglomerate with sales exceeding $6.5 billion annually.

Timothy Eaton, generally acknowledged in Canada as the "father of the department store," opened his first store in 1860 in St. Mary's, Ontario. Nine years later he opened a store on Yonge Street in Toronto, and in early 1870 he added a slogan to his handbills and advertisements that was to revolutionize Canadian retailing: "GOODS SATISFACTORY OR MONEY REFUNDED." By 1929, three chains, one being Eaton's, accounted for 80 percent of all department store sales. [Eaton's long struggle for survival ended in bankruptcy in 1999.]

Sources: *Hudson's Bay Company, Annual Report, 1998; Eaton's, Annual Report, 1999;* William Stephenson, *The Store That Timothy Built,* McClelland & Stewart, Toronto, 1969.

annually. Two of the chains—the Bay and Eaton's—have operated in Canada for over 100 years and have historical importance (Retail Highlight 1-2).

The large supermarket chains, including Safeway, Loblaws, Provigo, Atlantic & Pacific, Sobey's, and the Oshawa Group, have achieved dominance in food retailing through vertical integration and buying power. The merger of these chains into four groups creates even more buying power and opportunities for increased profitability through economies of scale.

A number of specialty retail chains have become major forces in Canadian retailing—Reitmans and Dylex in the clothing field, Home Depot in the home improvement area, Sport Chek in sporting goods, Lewiscraft in leisure products,

Future Shop offers an exciting environment with its creative visual displays and listening posts where customers can "try" before they "buy."

Courtesy Future Shop

Future Shop in home entertainment and consumer electronics, and Canadian Tire in the automotive and hardware business. The size of these chains provides them with many opportunities including buying power, advertising economies, and in-store specialists. Overall, these chains can use their size to create efficiencies in distribution, management, and purchasing.

Retail stores can be owned by manufacturers, such as Bata Shoes; by governments, such as provincially-owned liquor stores; or by consumers. **Consumer co-operatives** are retail stores owned by consumers and operated by a hired manager. Co-ops have prospered in some rural areas of Canada where the benefits of group buying are more important than in larger communities. However, some co-ops have been successful in larger communities, such as Co-op Atlantic with its reduced prices to members and its slogan "It Pays to Belong."

Location

An analysis by location is helpful in establishing long-term trends in regional levels of retail sales. The three major types of locations are the central business district, shopping centres, and stand-alone locations. As mentioned earlier, shopping centres account for about 50 percent of all retail sales in Canada but many retailers do very well by locating in the downtown area or in a stand-alone location. The characteristics of these locations and trends within these locations are discussed in Chapter 7. Trading area, another concept dealing with location, is also discussed in Chapter 7.

RETAIL STRUCTURAL CHANGE

The **life cycle** describes the stages a retail institution goes through from its beginning to its decline and possible disappearance from the retailing scene. In general, the life cycle has four stages: (1) introduction, where the new form begins (e.g., the West Edmonton Mall that combined retail and amusement concepts in 1981), (2) growth, where new competitors enter the market (e.g., the current situation with wholesale clubs), (3) maturity, where intense competition is often the major characteristic (e.g., warehouse retailers with their advertising and price wars), and (4) decline, where the store type slowly fades from the landscape (e.g., variety stores).

THEORIES OF RETAIL CHANGE

In response to changing consumer needs, increased competition, and other environmental factors, new types of retailers enter the market to capture new opportunities, and existing retailers modify their merchandise and service mix to match the changing market requirements. A number of theories have been proposed to help explain and understand these changes in retail structure.

The Wheel of Retailing

The **wheel of retailing** hypothesis is the best-known explanation for changes in the retail structure (Figure 1-4). This theory states that new types of retailers enter a market as low-margin, low-priced, low-status, low-service firms. Gradually, they add to their operating costs by providing new services and improving their facilities in the trading-up phase. Over time, they become high-cost merchants and are vulnerable to new types of competition that enter the marketplace as low-cost, no-frills competitors. When the warehouse club format (Price/Costco) entered Canada in the low-priced, low-status area it proved to be a formidable competitor, resulting in a strong reaction from many existing competitors including Canadian Tire and Loblaws.

The theory has been criticized because not all institutions begin as low-margin outlets with few services.[1] Upscale fashion stores did not follow the model and have never fit the wheel of retailing.

Figure 1-4 The Wheel of Retailing

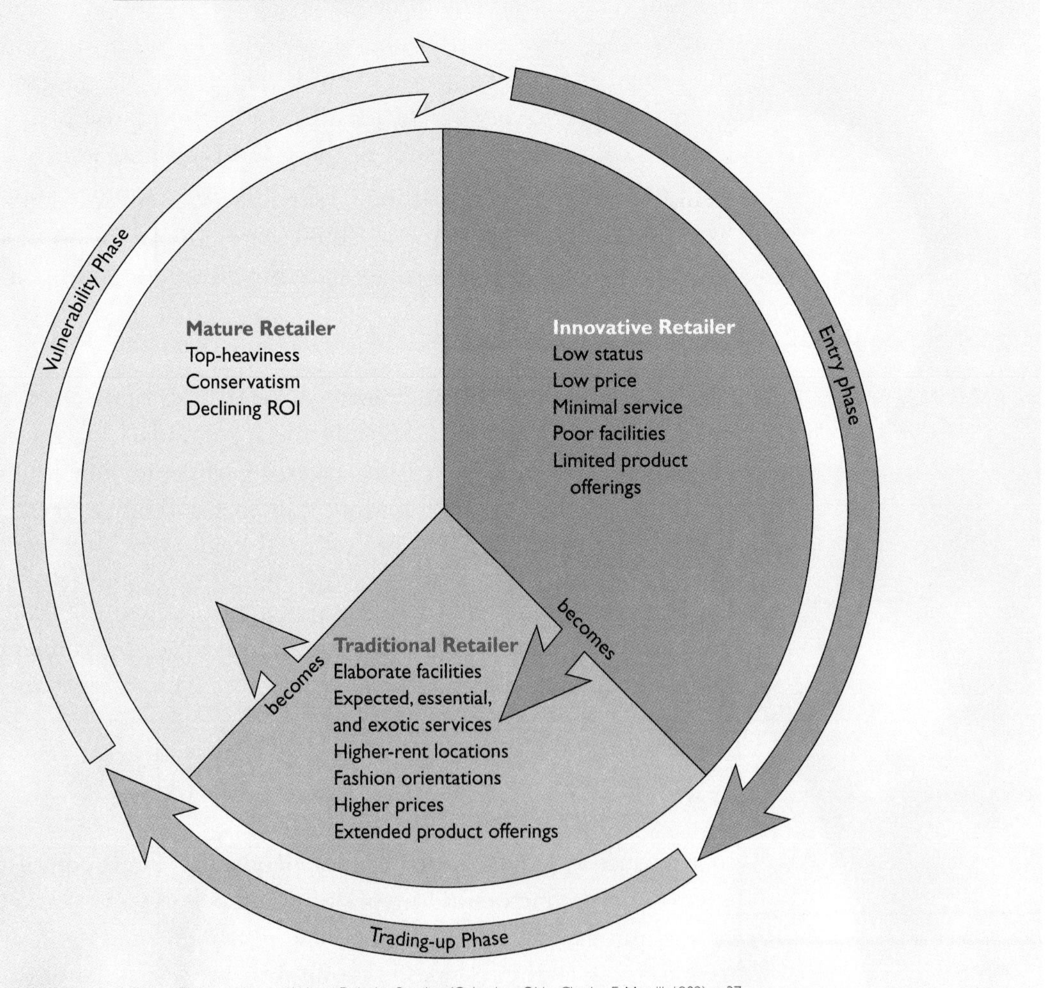

Source: Dale Lewision and Wayne Delozier, *Retailing* (Columbus, Ohio: Charles E. Merrill, 1982), p 37.

The Retail Accordion

An alternative explanation for change is the concept of the **retail accordion** (see Figure 1-5). Proponents of the theory argue that changes in the merchandising mix, not prices and margins, are a better explanation for changes in retail institutional structure than the wheel of retailing. The accordion theory is based on the premise that retail institutions evolve over time from broad-based outlets with wide assortments to outlets offering specialized, narrow lines. Over time the outlets again begin to offer a wide assortment, thus establishing a general-specific-general pattern. Retailers contract their lines to focus on more specific target markets, higher margin lines, and higher turnover merchandise. Then, the retailers expand their lines to attract more customers to increase overall sales. Then, the explanation is that the retailer makes the decision to focus again. This evolution suggests the term *accordion*, which reflects a contraction and expansion of merchandise lines.

For example, modern retailing in Canada began with the general store, a one-stop outlet with wide assortments of merchandise. Then came the urbanized department stores, more specialized than the general store. As urbanization continued, single-line and specialty stores (e.g., bookstores, drugstores) emerged. Over time, the single-line and specialty stores added complementary lines. For example, grocery stores over time added faster-moving merchandise to the traditional lines. Some stores added small appliances, convenience food items, and paper products. Many supermarkets now offer nonfood items such as drugs and cosmetics, and discount stores offer a variety of soft goods. More recently, a new form of specialty store has emerged. These retailers, referred to as category killers or category specialists, such as Toys "Я" Us and Sport Chek, offer consumers deep selections of a limited number of merchandise categories.

Two further theories have been proposed to explain changes in retailing. One theory, the **dialectic process**, is based on the adage, "If you can't beat them, join them."[2] As a new store, for example the discount store, gains a share at the expense of existing stores, for example department stores, a new form emerges that is a blend of both stores, for example the discount department store such as Wal-Mart and Zellers. The second theory, the **adaptive behaviour** explanation, suggests that the retailing institutions that can most effectively adapt to economic, competitive, social, technological, and legal environmental changes are the ones most likely to survive.[3] The variety store is often cited as an institution that failed to adapt to the changing environment and is seldom

Figure 1-5 The Retail Accordion

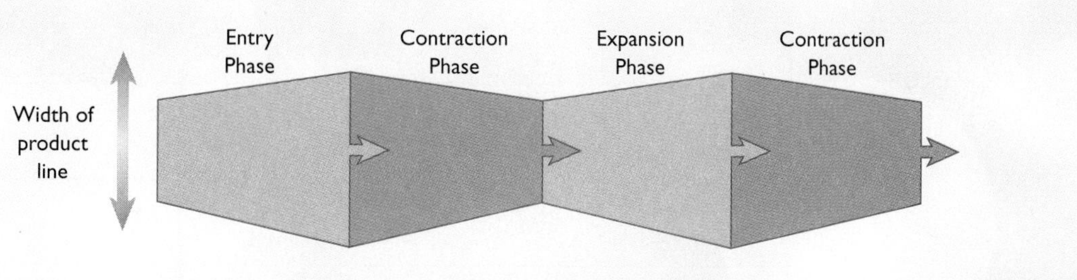

seen today. On the other hand, video stores grew rapidly with the advent of video-cassette recorders.[4]

TRENDS IN CANADIAN RETAILING

The final section of this chapter discusses the major trends that are likely to affect retail strategies in the future. Retailing strategies probably change more quickly than any other component of the business structure. The reason is that retailing is closer to the consumer than any other part of the corporate world. As a consequence, retailing strategies are constantly changing in response to shifts in the external environment and as new forms of competition are developed to meet consumer needs.

The major trends that retailers are facing are (1) the globalization of markets, (2) new retail formats, and (3) technology changes.

The Globalization of Markets

There has been a continuous trend to reduce trade barriers around the world to encourage more international trade. As well, a number of economic communities have been formed to eliminate all trade barriers and create a common market among a group of nations. As one example, the European Community, a group of the major Western European nations, has created a "common market" with a population exceeding 320 million people. In 1994, the North American Free Trade Agreement (NAFTA) established a free trade zone between Canada, the United States, and Mexico, which will eliminate most trade barriers between the three countries over the next 15 years. The agreement creates a market of 360 million people who produce and consume over $8 trillion worth of goods and services.

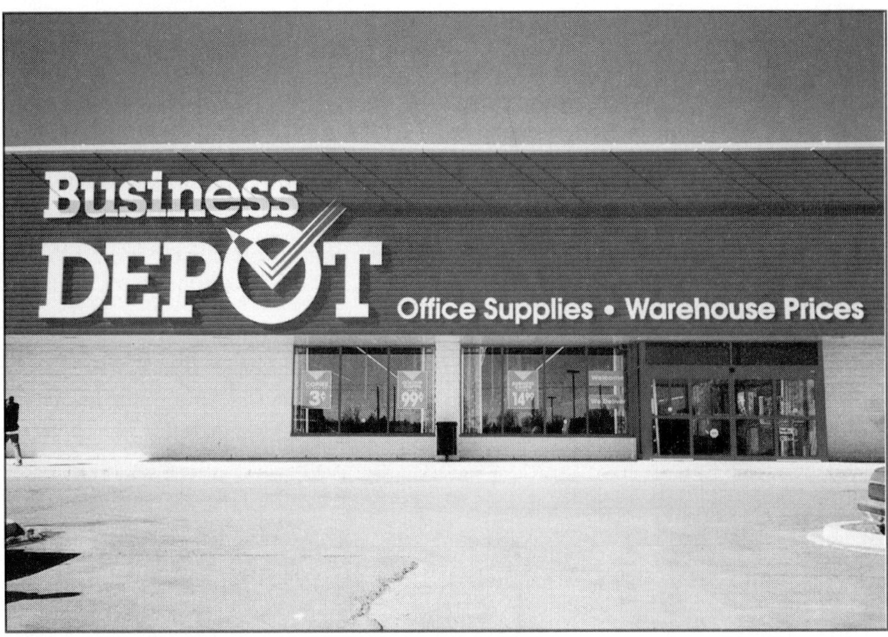

A U.S. category killer opens another store in Canada; Business Depot offers a wide and deep product mix at very competitive prices.

Photo by Betty McDougall

To date, the major impact for Canadian retailers has been the influx of U.S. retailers into Canada. The list is extensive, U.S. retailers are now in Canada, and they include Wal-Mart, Home Depot, Business Depot, Price/Costco, Lenscrafters, Michaels, PetSmart, The Office Place, Payless Shoes, and Gap Canada. These retailers have captured a significant market share in Canada and are forecast to gain an even greater share. Canadian retailers have to improve their competitive strategies to defend their markets in the face of this strong competition from U.S. retailers. The major response has been to reformat their stores (Canadian Tire is moving to the big box format), realign their merchandising mix (the Bay has moved away from hard goods like appliances and into soft goods like women's fashion), and reposition (BiWay moved slightly upmarket). The challenge for Canadian retailers will continue as the foreign invasion increases.[5]

The strategy pursued by Zellers when Wal-Mart entered the Canadian market in 1994 illustrates one approach to a major competitive challenge. In response to Wal-Mart's entry, Zellers renovated 62 stores, reconfigured stores to provide for broader, more competitive merchandise assortments, and revised its pricing to maintain its dominant price position against all competitors, including Wal-Mart. The result led to increased sales and market share but a decline in profits.[6] More recently, Zellers has moved upmarket with more brand names including a Martha Stewart line. Zellers is no longer competing directly with Wal-Mart on a price basis.[7] Even with the competitive responses of retailers like Zellers, Wal-Mart has had a substantial impact since its arrival in Canada (Retail Highlight 1-3).[8]

New Retail Formats

In the late 1980s a new retail format, commonly called big boxes, began appearing in Canada. By the late 1990s this format, now referred to as **category killers**, superstores, big boxes, and warehouse clubs was the fastest growing format in Canada. Today, the format is being refined, moving from single standing units to clusters called power centres or destination centres. The sheer size of some of these retailers—Chapters is 12 times larger than a traditional bookstore, Home Depot is 18 times larger than a traditional department store—offers consumers a depth of merchandise assortment that is unmatched by the traditional stores. As well, these retailers incorporate new information technologies that include on-line inventory tracking systems, direct connections with suppliers through electronic data interchange, and sophisticated shipping systems. This provides these retailers with significant cost and inventory advantages over traditional retailers. With their focus on price, selection, service, and quality, these category killers have gained market share at the expense of the traditional retailers, many of whom have gone out of business.[9]

Retail Highlight 1-3 Wal-Mart: The Impact on Competitive Retailers

In a study of Wal-Mart's impact on the Canadian retail environment, Stephen Arnold, a marketing professor at Queen's University School of Business, found that in the first year that Wal-Mart was in Kingston it had a large impact. In surveys before (1994), one year after (1995) and three years after (1997) Wal-Mart arrived (it took over the Woolco store), Dr. Arnold found the following:

First Choice to Shop in Kingston

	1994	1995	1997
• Zellers	40%	39%	33%
• Woolco/Wal-Mart	7%	22%	30%
• Sears	19%	10%	12%
• The Bay	16%	13%	10%
• S&R Dept. Store	9%	8%	8%
• K mart	9%	7%	7%

Which Store Has the Lowest Prices?

	1994	1995	1997
• Zellers	55%	37%	29%
• Woolco/Wal-Mart	8%	44%	51%
• Sears	2%	1%	1%
• S&R Dept. Store	19%	10%	11%
• K mart	9%	6%	7%

His report noted that the dramatic gains on the dimension "Wal-Mart having the lowest prices" did not bode well for any of its competitors. The report also mentioned that Wal-Mart quadrupled its share of shoppers in three years.

Source: Stephen J. Arnold, "Shopping Habits at Kingston Department Stores: Wave III," Research Report #3, Queen's University, 1997.

The main weapons retailers are using in response are enhanced customer service, the formation of alliances (e.g., supermarkets and banks), creating new mega-malls, and rejuvenating existing malls to add more entertainment. Whether these strategies will succeed remains to be seen but what is certain is that retail formats will continue to evolve.

Technology Changes

As noted earlier, electronic commerce, which includes all transactions completed on-line, will have the greatest impact on retailing in the future. We are just starting this new retail revolution and how it will unfold remains to be seen. We will devote a chapter to this phenomenon and suggest, throughout the text, the possible implications on strategy, merchandising, and the other elements of the retail mix. For now, consider the implications for location. Where once the three major decisions in retailing were location, location and location, electronic commerce needs no physical location. Electronic retailers do not need a physical presence when setting up a store; they have a "site" where shoppers "come" to them without leaving their home or office. Location may be replaced, in part, by retailers who offer attractive, easy to use Web sites.

Courtesy Chapters

Chapters' retailing strategy is on the cutting edge; offering customers a choice of visiting its category killer stores or shopping on-line.

www.chapters.ca

Whatever the result, we know that retailing tomorrow will be different from retailing today. We also know that to succeed, retailers will have to respond to these and many other changes taking place in the Canadian environment.

CHAPTER HIGHLIGHTS

- Marketing is the process by which individuals and groups obtain what they need and want through creating and exchanging products and value with others. Retailing is the final part of the process, satisfying individual and organizational objectives through exchanges.
- The dynamics of retailing can best be understood by analyzing its structure, which also helps illustrate the strategies by which retailers compete in the marketplace.
- Strategic classifications include variety and assortment, margin-turnover, and price and service.
- Descriptive classifications of retailing structure include ownership and location.
- The retail structure is dynamic. Retail types appear to follow a pattern of evolution, but no single theory explains the evolution of all types of retail outlets. The existing theories are, at best, descriptive and perhaps somewhat explanatory.
- The wheel of retailing theory is based on the premise that retailers evolve through three phases: entry, trading-up, and vulnerability. A second explanation for change is the retail accordion where retail institutions evolve from broad-based outlets with wide assortment patterns to specialized narrow lines and then return to the wide-assortment pattern.
- Two further theories are the dialectic process ("If you can't beat them, join them.") and adaptive behaviour (those that most effectively adapt to the changing environment will survive).

- Retailers are facing three major trends: (1) the globalization of markets, (2) new retail formats, and (3) technology changes.

KEY TERMS

adaptive behaviour	15	marketing	4
assortment	6	retail accordion	15
category killers	17	retail structure	5
chain	11	retailing	4
consumer co-operative	13	turnover	7
dialectic process	15	variety	6
life cycle	13	wheel of retailing	14
margin	7		

DISCUSSION QUESTIONS

1. Explain the following concepts: retailing, marketing, and retail structure.
2. Why is it important to classify the retail institutional structure?
3. Discuss the margin-turnover classification model (Figure 1-2). Give an example of a retail outlet that may exist in each of the four quadrants of the margin-turnover model.
4. Identify Canadian retailers that are in each category of Table 1-2. Which one(s) do you think will be most profitable over the next ten years? Why?
5. How might the owner of an existing store benefit from a study of retail structure in a given market area?
6. Which retail change theory best describes the growth of category killers?
7. What are the major reasons for the success of the new retail formats?
8. What share of the Canadian retail market do you think electronic commerce will have in the next five years? Why?
9. Summarize the major trends that are projected beyond the year 2000 in the competitive structure of retailing.

APPLICATION EXERCISES

1. Select a full city block or a shopping centre in your city. Classify each store according to its margin-turnover classification scheme.
2. Place five different stores in your community in each quadrant of the margin-turnover figure (Figure 1-2). Explain the reasons for their placement.
3. Using the strategy classification schemes in the text, choose the major stores in the retail structure in your community and make a complete classification chart. Then draw some strategy conclusions.

SUGGESTED CASES

1. The Independent Bookstore
2. Ralph's Optical

CHAPTER 2

THE CANADIAN RETAIL ENVIRONMENT

CHAPTER OBJECTIVES

After reading this chapter you should be able to:

1. Describe the major federal legislation affecting retailers.
2. List the key economic indicators that impact on retailing.
3. Evaluate the demographic environment.
4. Discuss how changes in competition affect retailing.
5. Describe trends in technology and its impact on retailing.

The new century is bringing dramatic changes to the Canadian retail environment. Where once Sunday shopping was a major political issue, now Canadians can shop on-line 24 hours a day, seven days a week. They buy everything from books to cars, from groceries to computers, and they are purchasing more on-line every month. While Canadians still go to the malls, many are now shopping in power centres, sprawling open-air locations that offer a huge selection of goods and services at everyday low prices. These power centres are adding entertainment components, such as multi-screen theatres, restaurants, and bookstores as a way of offering consumers a more complete shopping experience. These centres offer the merchandising mix to cover the needs of Canadians in the 21st century.

In addition to on-line shopping, technology has had a tremendous impact on retailing. Point-of-purchase scanners allow firms to evaluate tactical decisions on a daily basis and to optimize the merchandising mix. Electronic data interchange provides the basis for quick response delivery systems, which can improve customer service and reduce inventory and distribution expenses. Loyalty programs provide retailers with the opportunity to better understand and meet the needs of their customers. Retailers can fine tune targets and deliver product assortment and services that are customized to profitable segments.

Canadian retailers have experienced intensive competition from foreign firms entering the market. Beginning with the giant warehouse clubs, like Price/Costco, and followed by others such as the Gap and Home Depot, these firms brought new capabilities and services to Canada. But the major new entrant is Wal-Mart, the world's largest discount retailer who is defining the retail experience in Canada. Wal-Mart has, and will continue to have, a substantial impact on Canadian retailing.

Progressive retailers know that change is continuous. These retailers constantly monitor the environment so they can anticipate and react to these changes. New strategies are developed to capture opportunities and avoid threats in the retail environment. These strategies, as discussed in Chapter 4, emerge after an analysis of both the internal and external environments facing the firm. Careful analysis of shifts in the economy, in competitive behaviour, in demographics, in the legal environment, and in technology are important in order to base planning efforts on realistic assumptions about the future. Consumer responses to economic and social trends are complex, and they reveal themselves in changing patterns of consumption.

The ability to anticipate and respond to such changes is the key to strategic success in retailing. Forward-thinking managers have established approaches to monitor trends and determine their impact. This chapter discusses the major environmental forces affecting retailers, beginning with the legal environment.

THE LEGAL ENVIRONMENT

Retailing decisions are affected by the legal environment, which is made up of legislation (federal, provincial, and municipal), government agencies, and various action groups. These laws, agencies, and groups regulate and influence retailers' strategies and tactics.

Table 2-1

Major Federal Legislation Affecting Retailers

1. Trade Practices

- **Competition Act:** encourages competition in the marketplace and benefits consumers by reducing upward pressure on prices, rewarding innovation and initiative, increasing choice and quality of goods offered, and preventing abuses of market power by ensuring that firms compete with each other on a fair basis.
- **Bankruptcy Act,** intellectual property laws (e.g., **Copyright Act, Trademarks Act, Labelling Act** and **Industrial Design Act, the National Trade Mark and True Labelling Act**, and the **Canada Business Corporation Act**): make rules for the marketplace that impact on consumers.
- **Tax Rebate Discounting Act**: protects consumers who use tax discounting services.
- Other legislation involving trade practices include **Broadcasting Act, Canadian Human Rights Act, Income Tax Act, Official Languages Act, Small Loans Act, Employment Equity Act**, and **Multiculturalism Act**.

2. Health and Safety

- **Food and Drug Act** (partly administered by Health and Welfare Canada): protects consumers from hazards to health, and from fraud or misleading representations associated with the sale of foods.
- **Hazardous Products Act**: protects the health and safety of consumers by prohibiting or regulating the sale, advertisement, and importation of products considered to be dangerous to the public.

3. Product Standards and Grades

- **Consumer Packaging and Labelling Act**: specifies what product information must be made available to consumers on prepackaged products, and how it must be displayed.
- **Weights and Measures Act**: sets national standards for fair measure in trade for most measured commodities.
- **Textile Labelling Act**: requires that information on fibre content and dealer identity be provided on the labels of consumer textile articles.
- **Precious Metals Marking Act**: protects consumers from false claims for articles containing adulterated or substandard precious metals.

Legislation Regulating Retailers

More regulations affecting retailing have been introduced in the past two decades than in the previous 100 years. Devising effective ways to regulate the marketplace while sustaining an environment of healthy competition, innovation, and economic growth is a major challenge confronting retailers, the government, and consumers. A description of the major federal legislation affecting retailers is provided in Table 2-1.

Table 2-2

The Competition Act

Mergers:	Section 33 prohibits mergers by which competition is, or is likely to be, to the detriment of, or against the interest of the public.
Pricing:	Sections 34 and 35 prohibit a supplier from charging different prices to competitors purchasing like quantities of goods (**price discrimination**); and prohibit price cutting that lessens competition (**predatory pricing**).
Pricing and Advertising:	Section 52 prohibits prices that misrepresent the regular selling price (misleading price advertising). Section 53 prohibits advertising activities that misrepresent warranties, guarantees, and testimonials. Provisions for double ticketing (if two prices are shown on a product, the lower price is the price to consumers) and pyramid selling are included in Sections 54 and 56. Pricing and advertising are also covered under Section 37, which prohibits "bait and switch" selling (the nonavailability of advertised bargains) and prohibits selling above the advertised price.
Pricing:	Section 38 prohibits suppliers from requiring subsequent resellers to offer products at a stipulated price (**resale price maintenance**).
Distribution:	Section 48 prohibits consignment selling if the purpose is to control prices or discriminate between dealers. **Exclusive dealing**, when retailers agree to handle the products of only one supplier, is prohibited where the result is that competition is, or is likely to be, substantially lessened. Tied selling, where a supplier will sell a line of merchandise only if the retailer also agrees to purchase other merchandise from the supplier, is also prohibited if competition is lessened.

In 1986, the federal government enacted the Competition Act—the major legislative act regulating marketing and retailing practices in Canada. The Act is designed to protect companies, consumers, and the interests of society. It does this by prohibiting mergers that reduce competition to the detriment of the public. The important sections of the Competition Act that directly affect retailers are shown in Table 2-2, and examples of the types of activities that retailers have been prosecuted for are shown in Retail Highlight 2-1.

At the provincial level, each province has business practices acts that are similar to or extend the federal legislation. For example, all provinces regulate the activities of door-to-door retailers and allow for "cooling-off" periods, ranging from two to ten days, when consumers can cancel contracts with this type of seller.

Retailers operating in Quebec need to comply with language requirements for their signs and displays. For example, all outdoor signs must be in French, but within the store English signs and messages are allowed. Quebec retailers are also governed by regulations concerning advertising to children and roadside advertising.

Retail Highlight 2-1 Examples of Prosecution of Retailers under Section 36 of Competition Act

- A Winnipeg sporting goods retailer stated in newspaper advertisements that a discount of "30–40 percent off" the ordinary selling price was available for golf clubs. Investigation revealed the statements were untrue and the retailer was fined $2,000.
- A national paint and wallpaper retailer was fined $225,000 because, for certain stains, paints, and wallpaper, most of the sales were at the discount sale price, not the ordinary sale price.
- A furniture retailer compared its sale price to a regular price in advertising matters. It was found that the regular price was substantially exaggerated and the retailer was fined $115,000.
- A national womenswear retailer was offering its clothing at discount prices, with price tags indicating the original amount, the special price, and the amount of the discount. It was found that the clothing was never sold at the original price as the clothing was already tagged "special" before even entering the store. The retailer pleaded guilty and was fined $300,000.
- A department store chain distributed more than a million "scratch-and-win" cards, which gave the impression that consumers had one chance in four of winning a 25 percent discount on merchandise. It was established that over 90 percent of the cards offered only a 10 percent discount and the chain was fined $100,000.
- A department store chain compared its sale price to its regular price in advertising tires. It was established that the chain had systematically misled the public in misrepresenting the regular price and it was fined $135,000.
- A department store chain misled consumers by claiming that bicycles would be on sale for a limited time only, when in fact the sale continued for a much longer period of time. It was fined $600,000.

Source: Competition Bureau, Industry Canada (various publications)

Action Group Activities

www.bbb.org

Various consumer groups also affect the activities of retailers. On a formal basis, groups like the Consumers Association of Canada (CAC) lobby governments, manufacturers, and retailers for changes that safeguard and protect consumer interests. The Better Business Bureau, which operates branches in 20 Canadian cities (www.bbb.org), provides a strong voice for consumers who have complaints against specific retailers.

Consumer concern over environmental issues is reflected in retailer actions. Although recent studies show a decline in the percentage of Canadians expressing a willingness to pay more for environmentally safe products, a segment of Canadians is committed to improving the environment. Retailers such as Loblaws and The Body Shop have been actively marketing environmentally safe products to these individuals.

Conclusion

Various government regulations affect both growth strategies and marketing plans. More than ever, managers must be sensitive to the liabilities they can face from various actions or lack of action. Management needs to develop a positive response to the regulations and consumer concerns. Simply put, government regulations are designed to provide consumers with useful and honest information that makes it easier for them to function as rational shoppers.

THE ECONOMIC ENVIRONMENT

Retailers need to monitor the economic environment to anticipate the conditions that are likely to occur in the future. This is done by paying close attention to the key economic indicators that reflect the state of the economy. These indicators include the gross domestic product, personal saving rates, unemployment rates, the consumer price index, the prime interest rate, new housing starts, and the foreign exchange rate.

In the early 1990s Canada's economy was in a recession with high unemployment and reduced consumer expenditures. During that time, retail sales and profits declined and retail bankruptcies increased dramatically. A number of well-known retail chains went out of business during these times including Woodwards, Woolworth, Steel, Town and Country, and Bargain Harold's. Recently, the Canadian economy has improved but the ravages of the recession, increased taxation, and high consumer debt loads (on average, consumer credit and mortgage debt are at 100 percent of annual household disposable income) have led to modest gains in the growth of the retail sector.[1] Today retailers have to continually focus on offering value to Canadians because of the slow growth and competitive pressures. Proactive retailers are better positioned than others to respond to changing economic conditions. Through monitoring the economic environment, retailers can take a proactive position and adjust both strategies and tactics to maximize opportunities and minimize threats.

Economic conditions vary considerably across Canada. For example, the Maritimes, particularly Newfoundland, has experienced greater unemployment than most other areas of Canada. The income rating index (per capita income per population) and the market rating index (retail sales per population) for Newfoundland are typically below the national average. On the other hand, Ontario often has a favourable economic climate and both indices are above the national average. In response, many retailers modify their merchandise mix depending on the economic conditions by region across Canada.

THE DEMOGRAPHIC ENVIRONMENT

Changing demographics are important because of their impact on retail strategy and responses to competition. Recent changes in the population's age distribution, in the rate of household formation, geographic shifts in the population, relative income gains among selected market segments, and increasing ethnic markets all can affect retail strategy.

The Changing Age Distribution

The 35-to-49 age group now constitutes the largest segment of the population and is dominated by baby boomers (persons born between 1946 and 1966) who are in the middle of their careers, raising children, and paying into investment plans (Table 2-3). The baby boomers are aging; in 2001 the oldest are 54 and the youngest are 35. Boomers have created high growth markets for retailers who offer all kinds of entertainment, luxury cruises, and health food additives.[2] They have major implications for retailers as they move through life. Boomers are responsible for the "Echo Boom," the children of the boomers, and will eventually join the "Countdown Generation" (Retail Highlight 2-2).

As one example of the impact of the baby boomers, in terms of outdoor recreation activities, the highest forecasted growth rates will be in natural environment activities (e.g., hiking, pleasure walking) followed by general recreation (e.g., picnicking, sightseeing). These growth rates are fueled by the large number of baby boomers reaching middle age. For recreational sports, golf and cross-country skiing will lead the way, again reflecting the boomers' interests. For retailers specializing in leisure products, this will have significant implications for their merchandising mix.

Table 2-3 Population Age Distribution (1996–2016)

	Thousands				Percent Change	
Age Group	**1996**	**2001**	**2006**	**2016**	**1966–2006**	**2006–2016**
Children (0–9)	3,970	4,010	3,940	4,130	0	5
Youth (10–19)	4,020	4,250	4,380	4,300	9	(2)
Young adults (20–34)	6,900	6,660	6,840	7,400	0	8
Early middle age (35–49)	7,220	7,780	8,000	7,610	10	(5)
Late middle age (50–64)	4,220	5,090	6,120	7,790	45	27
Retirees (65 and over)	3,650	4,090	4,480	5,900	23	33
	29,980	31,880	33,760	37,130	13	10

Source: Statistics Canada

Canadian Tire offers an extensive line of sporting goods for the growing leisure market.

Courtesy Canadian Tire

The changing age mix of the population will result in different growth rates for various age groups. Between 2006 and 2016, the fastest growing segment will be the 65 and older group, followed by the late middle age group. Declines will be experienced by the youth and early middle age segments. These shifts will have significant impacts on the purchase of many products and services.

In the longer term, the 50-plus age group market will represent over one-third of all Canadians. An important fact is that this population segment will account for about three-quarters of all of Canada's population growth in the next 20 years. Proactive retailers are developing strategies now to capitalize on the future potential of the 50-plus market. Research has shown that these Canadians, who control most of the personal wealth in Canada, are active shoppers with an intense interest in specials. They want to believe they are saving money whenever they spend and they have a strong value orientation that is based on "getting your money's worth," a reflection of the economic hardship many experienced in their youth.[3]

Retail Highlight 2-2 The Echo Boom and the Countdown Generation

In 1987, the birth rate in Canada dropped to an all-time low. But that is changing as the baby boomers (those Canadians born between 1946 and 1966) who are in their early 30s to mid 50s are now making the decision to have children (more than one-third of babies born in 1990 were born to women 30 and over). Called the "Echo Boom," the birth rate in Canada has been increasing since 1987 and now over 400,000 live births are recorded each year. Opportunities are now available for retailers who target this group. Many couples with new babies change residences, buy cars, and change brands to ones best suited for their babies. They need products such as car seats, playpens, baby foods, and diapers. The kids are the first generation to be raised with computers, the Internet is an important medium to sell to them, and they exert a strong influence on the purchase of electronic products.

The Countdown Generation is at the other end of the age spectrum. Canadians over 50 control over 75 percent of the personal wealth and 55 percent of the discretionary spending power in Canada. This group is mature, secure, and relatively rich. The Countdown Generation is used to saving because of economic hardship in their youth. They have paid off their mortgages and now have considerable wealth, mainly in the value of their home. This group will provide many opportunities to retailers who can satisfy their needs for experiences (e.g., travel, entertainment), quality products, and personal growth (e.g., recreational activities). Retailers who deliver excellent customer service will appeal to the group that remembers when store personnel were there to serve customers.

Sources include: David K. Foot and Daniel Stoffman, *Boom, Bust and Echo 2000*, Macfarlane, Walter & Ross, Toronto, 1998 and Klaus Rohrich, "Life After 49," *Marketing*, February 3, 1998, p. 18.

The interesting group for many retailers is the Echo Boomers or Y Generation, those teens and "tweens" between the ages of 9 and 19 who number over 4.1 million. Advertisers and retailers see them as two distinct age groups, 9 to 14 and 15 to 19, because their interests and buying behaviours differ. In total, they spend over $14 billion annually and are an attractive market for many retailers. Consider the "tweens," the 9 to 14 group, who are trend watchers, ready to spot and buy the latest music, fashion, or pop culture. They spend most of their money on food, entertainment, and clothing and most make their own decisions on what shoes and clothes to buy. Over 60 percent of them have bank accounts and 20 percent have their own ATM cards. Retailers from Le Chateau to the Royal Bank have targeted the "tweens" with products and services designed to appeal to their latest fad or fashion. At one time, these retailers would direct their campaigns to the "tweens'" parents, on the assumption that the parents controlled both the money and the products bought. Now they focus directly on the group, using the media and the messages that relate to this brand-conscious, fad-loving, peer-influenced group. Because most of the group has access to the Internet, retailers include this media in their efforts to be relevant for the "tweens."[4]

The 15 to 19 group has greater spending power, is slightly less fad driven, and has more independence than the "tweens." They want clothes that are in style and choose their clothes with great care. They are suspicious of advertising, rejecting any claims that don't ring true. Retailers need to "talk" to teens honestly with messages that are relevant to them. Lifestyle advertising is often used to capture the interest of this group. Independent retailers can attract this group by offering unique labels, such as Fubu and Roxy, that are not carried by the chains. They can offer personal service and create a store atmosphere that may be difficult for the chains to copy.

Rate of Household Formation

The rate of household formation has been increasing slightly faster than the growth in population. Among the reasons for this is an increase in non-family households. The number of one-person households has increased while the number of households with more than four people has declined. Now, about one-quarter of all Canadian households are people who live alone and about 44 percent of all households are non-family or single-parent households. This group includes singles, widows, empty nesters, childless and unmarried couples living together, and younger couples planning to have children later. These small households are prime prospects for townhouses, condominiums, kitchen mini-appliances, and packaged goods in single servings. SSWDs (single, separated, widowed, and divorced) spend more money on travel and entertainment, but they save less and tend to buy more services.

A recent trend is for more young adults to continue to live with their parents. Currently 56 percent of unmarried men and 47 percent of unmarried women, age 20 to 34, live with their parents. Often due to economic circumstances, this phenomenon reduces household formation and slows retail growth across a number of sectors including big ticket items (e.g., appliances, furniture).

Skewed Income Distribution

Income distribution in Canada is very skewed. Both the higher income and lower income groups are growing, while the middle income group is declining. The higher income group, the top 25 percent of households, account for more than 50 percent of all income earned; while the bottom 45 percent of households account for only about 20 percent. The 35 percent in the middle income group account for about 30 percent of total income earned.

Retailers need to consider the size and spending power of these income groups when making strategic decisions. For example, BiWay is a chain of stores retailing lower-price men's and women's casual wear to price- and value-conscious shoppers. Wal-Mart has captured a substantial share of the lower income market plus many of the value-conscious middle income consumers with its "every day low pricing" strategy. On the other hand, Harry Rosen menswear stores target the upper-income professional man, and one location in the heart of downtown Toronto features three levels of shopping, including an entire floor of designer boutiques. Holt Renfrew is another retailer that has achieved success by meeting the needs of the higher income consumer with high fashion offerings and excellent service.

One of Canada's department stores, the Bay, has had some difficulty with the skewed income distributions. It has found its middle income market shrinking and, with increased competitive pressures, has struggled to find a strong position in the marketplace.

Increasing Ethnic Markets

Canada has become an ethnically diverse nation. Now, over 12 percent of Canada's population are visible minorities (non-Caucasian and non-First Nations) and about 30 percent of the total population are members of ethnic heritages other than Canadian (English or French). Canada is a multicultural society, with varied tastes and needs, and presents many opportunities for retailers. Some of the larger ethnic groups are:

German-Canadians They number about one million, and are mostly concentrated west of Ontario, comprising 14 percent of the population of Kitchener, 13 percent of Regina, and 12 percent of Saskatoon. They maintain their ethnicity through celebrations and rituals, but only 11 percent speak German at home. The four major values of this group are a strong sense of family, work ethic, drive for education, and sense of justice.

Italian-Canadians The vast majority of the 750,000 Italian Canadians are concentrated in the metropolitan areas of Quebec and Ontario. They represent 9 percent of the population of Toronto and 5 percent in Montreal. They have maintained a strong culture by developing a community with their own stores, cinemas, newspapers, radio stations, and TV programs, and about 37 percent speak Italian at home. Their primary relations are with people of their own background, and as their level of affluence increases, they become more status-conscious, want to own their own homes, buy new cars, and send their children to university.

Chinese-Canadians They number over one million. They have unique behavioural patterns and needs, high levels of education, high incomes, and, thus, present interesting opportunities for many retailers. For example, 70 percent of the Chinese in Toronto are exposed to Chinese TV and 78 percent to Chinese newspapers, so retailers advertising in Chinese may get more business from this group. Only 10 percent of the Chinese in Toronto consider themselves truly bilingual.

Ukrainian-Canadians About 500,000 strong, they are mostly concentrated west of Ontario, including 7 percent of the population of Winnipeg. Although Ukrainian is the mother tongue of 46 percent of them, only 10 percent speak it at home. They are known for their distinct types of food, crafts, clothing styles, techniques for building and decorating homes, and leisure activities.

Other Significant Groups Other significant groups are First Nations people (500,000), South Asians (900,000), Polish (300,000), Portuguese (260,000), and Filipinos (220,000).[5]

Retail Highlight 2-3 The Ethnic Market—A Challenge for Retailers

It is estimated that by 2001 over 5.7 million ethnic consumers, including over 1.3 million Chinese and 1.1 million South Asians, will comprise over 17 percent of Canada's population. While these groups are very attractive to many retailers (for example, four ethnic populations—Chinese, Italian, Portuguese, and South Asian—spend over $13 billion in Toronto alone), it is often a challenge for retailers to effectively reach and market to these groups. While the overall ethnic population is large, it is comprised of many different communities. In many instances, the cost of designing a retail strategy to reach these markets does not justify the potential return. Retailers may have to focus on the two most concentrated areas, Toronto and Vancouver, to achieve acceptable returns. In these markets, ethnic media are available to target particular groups more easily than in other regions of Canada. For example, in British Columbia's lower mainland, Indo-Canadians are served by two radio stations, two consumer magazines, and several newspapers.

To increase their effectiveness, retailers need to be flexible to change their mix; products should reflect the dominant segment of the ethnic shoppers in the area, authentic brands from the countries will have to be included, and pricing needs to reflect the price sensitivity of these shoppers.

As noted, many of these ethnic groups are concentrated in metropolitan areas. It has been estimated that visible minorities comprise 32 percent of Toronto's population, 31 percent of Vancouver's, and 16 percent of Calgary's. About 54 percent of Canada's visible minority population live in Ontario, 21 percent in British Columbia, and 14 percent in Quebec. This concentration is favourable to retailers (Retail Highlight 2-3). For example, the major Canadian banks are targeting Asian Canadians, particularly Chinese-speaking ones in Toronto, Vancouver, and other Canadian cities, using Chinese-speaking employees and other services to make these consumers feel as comfortable as possible.

Malls have been developed that specifically target ethnic groups. As one example, malls in Richmond and Toronto include stores and products that are focused on Chinese consumers. In Toronto alone, there are more than ten large Chinese theme malls. The merchandise mix in these malls offers everything from exotic foods to high quality, tailored clothing for this target market.

THE COMPETITIVE ENVIRONMENT

Understanding Competition

Competition among retailers is a fact of life. The most familiar type is intratype competition. **Intratype competition** is competition between two retailers of the same type, such as two drugstores. Examples include the Bay and Sears Canada (traditional department stores), Zellers and Wal-Mart (discount department stores), McDonald's and Harvey's (fast-food retailers), and Reitmans and Braemar (women's specialty stores).

A second competitive model is **intertype competition**, which is competition between different types of retail outlets selling the same merchandise. Intertype competition is a common type of retail competition today. For example, Loblaws competes with Sears Canada in many of the nonfood lines sold by Loblaws. The acceptance of scrambled merchandising has allowed similar merchandise to be sold by many different types of retailers. Many convenience products, such as chewing gum, candy, magazines, and soft drinks, are sold in a wide variety of stores ranging from convenience stores to supermarkets to department stores to drugstores.

The New Face of Competition

The competitive structure of retailing is changing radically. The changes are causing a rethinking of the concepts of retail competition and are also causing changes in consumer shopping habits.

Supermarket Retailing and Category Killers

The supermarket concept, long familiar in the food field, has been adopted by many other types of retailers. The key elements of **supermarket retailing** are (1) self-service and self-selection, (2) large-scale but low-cost physical facilities, (3) a strong price emphasis, (4) simplification and centralization of customer services, and (5) a wide variety and broad assortment of merchandise. This concept, with some modifications, has been successful in many lines of trade including sporting goods—Sporting Life and Sport Chek; home improvement—Home Depot; furniture and housewares—IKEA; and business office supplies—Business Depot and Staples. When successful, this strategy results in category killers, firms who dominate a specific product category, like home improvement products (Home Depot), office supplies (Office Depot), or pet food (PetSmart). One of the keys to this strategy is to offer a specialized and deep merchandise assortment that can satisfy most or all of the target market's needs.

The International Dimension

Canadian retailers now face new competition on an international basis. Foreign retailers, primarily from the United States, have entered the Canadian market in record numbers. The most dramatic impact on the Canadian retail scene was the entry of Wal-Mart. In January 1994, Wal-Mart, the world's largest discount retailer, purchased 122 Woolco stores for $300 million (U.S.) and began converting them to Wal-Mart stores. Since that time, the major Canadian department store chains, including the Bay, Zellers, Sears Canada, and other large merchandisers, like Canadian Tire, have changed their strategies to meet the Wal-Mart challenge. These changes include efforts to streamline operations, reduce costs, or focus on satisfying defined customer segments. As well, they have improved merchandise quality, lowered prices, offered better customer service, and instituted loyalty programs. One of the major impacts of Wal-Mart in Canada is that it has changed consumer preferences for store selection. After Wal-Mart has entered a community, more consumers select a store based on attributes such as "lowest everyday prices." This makes it more difficult to compete with Wal-Mart because it is known for this attribute.[6]

Many other international retailers, such as Price/Costco, HMV, the Gap, Tiffany, Lenscrafters, Disney, Pier 1 Imports, IKEA, The Body Shop, Toys "Я" Us, Home Depot, and Business Depot have successfully entered the Canadian market in recent years. Among the reasons for the success of foreign retailers in Canada is their experience in highly competitive markets, their high operating efficiency, their clearly defined target markets, and their focus on hiring, training, and motivating salespeople to provide quality customer service. Many of the weaker Canadian retailers have been driven out of business by the intense competition of foreign retailers, particularly the "big box" stores and category killers (e.g., Wal-Mart, Home Depot, and Business Depot), with their emphasis on price and selection.

THE TECHNOLOGY ENVIRONMENT

Changes in technology are affecting virtually every dimension of the retailing outlet. Detailed information that can aid retailers in making decisions ranging from merchandise elimination to credit authorization is now available on a timely basis through point-of-sale (POS) technology and electronic data interchange (EDI). This information forms the basis of the management information system, the structure necessary to gather, analyze, and distribute information needed by management. Other technology changes include new methods of merchandising presentation ranging from video kiosks to home video shopping through such channels as the Canadian Home Shopping Network.

Future Shop uses technology to enhance merchandise presentation.

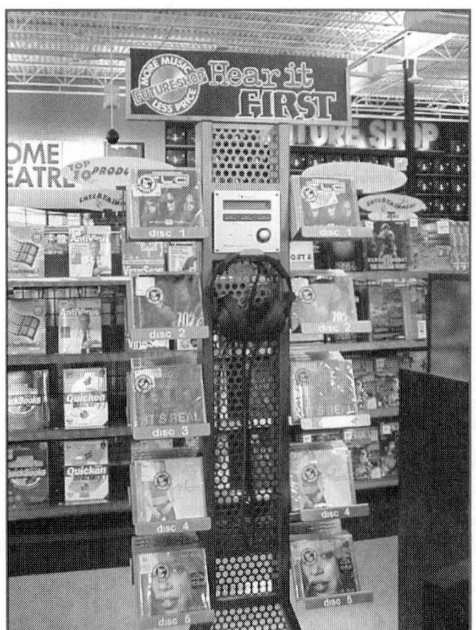

Courtesy Future Shop

Point-of-Sale Technology

A **point-of-sale (POS)** cash register (or terminal) is the key input device for many retailing systems. POS terminals record a variety of information at the time a transaction occurs. The terminals are usually connected to the retailer's computer information system, which provides on-line information on which merchandise, styles, and colours of various manufacturers are selling most rapidly and allows buying staff and managers to effectively manage the store's merchandise. POS information provides the basis for the sales reports, which are key to inventory control, sales forecasting, and scheduling sales staff. As an example, The Body Shop Canada has created an information technology system that makes it possible to analyze sales data from its 120 stores. It can determine what's hot and what's not and which products should be bundled together in its gift baskets.[7]

POS information, combined with customer information from credit and debit cards and loyalty programs, can be of assistance in identifying target groups for promotional activities and reward programs. For example, by knowing the buying patterns of various target groups, retail managers can design promotions that can be directed, through personal letters, to these groups. More retailers are using direct targeting to encourage their customers to continue shopping with them.

Electronic Data Interchange

Electronic data interchange (EDI) is the computer-to-computer transmission of data and business documents between retailers and suppliers. EDI allows retailers to instantly transmit purchase orders to their suppliers, reducing inventory costs for both parties. Other benefits include reduced administrative costs such as filing, storing, and retrieving documents and productivity gains because data are entered only once.

EDI has allowed retailers to develop quick response (QR) delivery systems, a form of inventory management system that lowers inventory investment, reduces lead time, improves customer service through improved product availability, and reduces distribution costs. Both the retailer and its vendors share the inventory, sales, and marketing data (in most cases, the vendors have access to the retailer's POS terminal data so they can track sales of their products) and they use the EDI system to transmit orders. QR will be discussed further in Chapter 10 (Buying, Handling, and Inventory Management).

Universal Vendor Marking

Universal vendor marking (UVM) is an identification system for marking merchandise at the vendor level. The need to mark the items when they are received at the store level can be eliminated largely by the use of such a standardized format. Stores like Price/Costco and Canadian Tire are using vendor marking. The major advantage is the ability of the retailer to "handle" incoming merchandise through the use of computers and electronic data input, leading to major increases in productivity.

Price/Costco lowers costs by using universal vendor marking.

Courtesy Price/Costco

Other Technology Advances

Other new technology advances will include wireless telephones, microwave communications, communication satellites, and fibre optics, all of which are bringing in an era of low-cost, convenient, universal communications. These devices are already transforming many forms of retailing as a result of the electronic information links that allow retailers to break out of building walls and shopping malls. Increasingly, the new technology will go directly into households and present images, comparative data, and product descriptions. Electronic bulletin boards will provide the latest information to in-store customers. Similarly, technology will allow shoppers to try on outfits electronically (see how they look on screen) before deciding on the one to purchase.

Artificial intelligence will also provide devices that can listen, understand, and respond to customer queries. Smart cards (credit cards with a memory chip) will allow retailers to tailor product lines to precise consumer demand since life and family histories of each customer can be recorded on the card. Retailers are also considering other technologies for today and for the future (Retail Highlight 2-4).

Emerging Technologies

Other changes are occurring in the way technology is used in retailing. These changes involve **electronic commerce**, customer communications, and similar activities.

Retail Highlight 2-4 The Technology Adoption Continuum for Retailers

Retailers continue to invest in leading edge technology. For example, in a survey of Canadian retailers here is what they are doing and planning for the future:

- What's here today—most common are local-area networks, mainframe systems, traditional POS terminals, client/server technologies, and wide area networks. The acceptance of these technologies is consistent with retailers' traditional operational concerns.
- What's on the horizon—piloting radio-frequency devices for warehouses, data warehousing, and executive information systems. These tools will become critical competitive components over the next few years.
- What's leading edge—virtual reality, neural networks, and pen-based computing applications are being researched for future use. Now, their benefits have not proven to outweigh their costs and other risks.

Source: 1998 Canadian Retail IT Survey, Ernst & Young and the Retail Council of Canada.

Electronic Commerce

Through the Internet consumers can shop from home and literally search the world for products and services (Retail Highlight 2-5). The **Internet** is a worldwide network of computers linked to facilitate communications between individuals, companies, and organizations. Because it is changing the face of retailing, we have devoted a chapter (Chapter 16) to discussing the challenges and opportunities created by the Internet. Briefly, the Internet is reducing the importance of location, increasing the knowledge of consumers in making purchase decisions, and allowing retailers to customize consumer preferences on an individual basis. Estimates are that electronic commerce will account for over 20 percent of all retail sales within 10 years.

Video Technology

Home television shopping began in Canada in the late 1980s. The Canadian Home Shopping Network combined traditional merchandising with modern technology to offer consumers a wide variety of products via cable television. While television shopping has grown rapidly in the United States, consumer acceptance has been slower in Canada. Cable marketing is also being used by real estate firms to interest potential home buyers in various properties and by automobile traders to sell used cars. Two or more channels in many Canadian communities are devoted to cable marketing shows.

Retail Highlight 2-5 Electronic Commerce

Today consumers have many choices in deciding where and when to purchase a product or service. If they want a mortgage, they can go to a bank, trust company, supermarket, or the Internet. For example, at I Money (www. imoney.com) they can arrange for a mortgage on-line within a day. If consumers want a book, they can go to a convenience store that has a limited selection, a supermarket that has a larger selection, a traditional bookstore that will carry 10,000 titles, a category killer like Chapters that has up to 100,000 titles, or go on-line to Chapters (www.chapters.ca) that has even more titles and provides reviews of many books. If consumers want to buy a house, they can search on-line by city across Canada (www. mls.ca) and find houses in a price range and neighbourhood they prefer. And they can check out the houses before they ever contact a real estate agent. The Internet offers consumers convenience, product and service knowledge, and offers the potential for more informed purchase decisions.

www.imoney.com

www.chapters.ca

www.mls.ca

Interactive In-Store Video Sales Aids

Increasingly, retailers are turning to the use of in-store videos to provide prerecorded answers to questions frequently asked by customers. The devices help increase productivity because they reduce the need for salespersons to provide basic information. HMV uses in-store videos and "listening posts" to allow consumers to see and hear musicians and music before they make their purchase.

Moving to Alberta? Consumers can find the neighbourhood and houses they like in Calgary on the Internet.

www.mls.ca

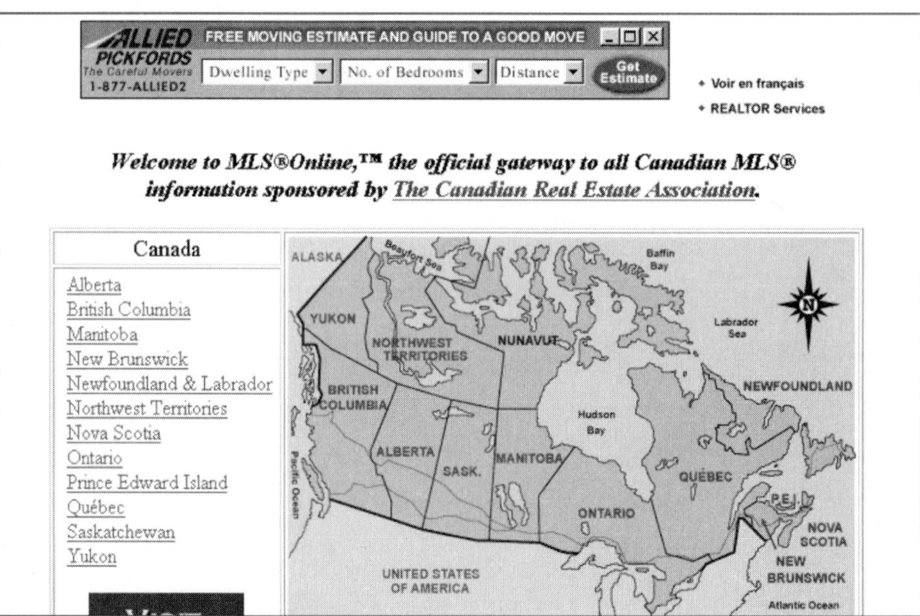

Retailers are also experimenting with interactive, electronic in-store couponing. In one form, a kiosk in a supermarket dispenses coupons in 15 to 20 grocery categories, which are valid only the same day at the same store. In another form, a kiosk displays nine retailer categories and, after the consumer has selected a category, it displays the names of up to six retailers. The consumer can then select coupons for products from these retailers.

CHAPTER HIGHLIGHTS

- The major federal regulations affecting retailers include acts dealing with trade practices (Competition Act, Bankruptcy Act), health and safety (Food and Drug Act, Hazardous Products Act), and product standards and grades (Consumer Packaging and Labelling Act, Textile Labelling Act). In particular, the Competition Act is important as it regulates unfair trade practices such as misleading price advertising.
- The economic environment can be understood, in part, by paying close attention to key economic indicators, such as interest rates, unemployment rates, and the consumer price index.
- The primary demographic factors of importance to retailers include the changing age distributions, the rate of household formations, changing family relationships, skewed income distribution, regional differences, and increasing ethnic markets.
- The primary types of competition include intratype competition and intertype competition. The competitive structure of retailing as a whole is undergoing change including supermarket retailing and the international dimensions.
- Changes in technology that have impacted on retailing include the use of point-of-sale technology and electronic data interchange to improve merchandising and reduce costs and new emerging technologies that offer new ways of shopping. The major technology change is the advent of electronic commerce, made possible by the Internet.

KEY TERMS

electronic commerce	36	point-of-sale (POS)	35
exclusive dealing	24	predatory pricing	24
Internet	37	price discrimination	24
intertype competition	33	resale price maintenance	24
intratype competition	32	supermarket retailing	33

DISCUSSION QUESTIONS

1. What are some retail activities covered by the Competition Act?
2. List four key economic indicators that retailers should monitor. What type of retailer is most likely to be affected by changes in each indicator?
3. Why is competition so intense in retailing today? Does this competitive intensity have an impact on retailers' needs to monitor and forecast environmental changes? Explain your answer.

4. Summarize the changes that are occurring in the demographic profile of consumers and households in our society, and the likely impact on retail operations.
5. Summarize the information presented in the text relative to changes in the competitive environment. Explain how these changes are impacting retailing.
6. Why is the Canadian market so attractive to many foreign-based retailers?
7. What are the major benefits of electronic data interchange (EDI) to retailers? to suppliers?
8. What are the major technological advances occurring today that are impacting non-store shopping?

APPLICATION EXERCISES

1. Visit the managers of two or three of the retail stores in your city. Find out their major problems, if any, with government regulations. Which aspects of the business seem to be most affected? Does the manager think the regulations serve a useful purpose?
2. Develop a sample of fast-food outlets, sit-down restaurants, coffee shops, and supermarkets, and determine which of the outlets are offering breakfast menus. Compare and contrast the offerings and seek to identify the demographic characteristics of the primary customer base.
3. Review the Statistics Canada catalogue and identify the publications that would be of primary interest to department store managers who want to understand the most significant trends that will influence their businesses in the next five years.
4. Go to four Canadian retailers' Internet sites and evaluate them in terms of ease of use, useful product knowledge, and entertainment value.

SUGGESTED CASES

1. The Independent Bookstore
2. Ralph's Optical
3. The Bay—A Question of Survival

CHAPTER 3

UNDERSTANDING THE RETAIL CUSTOMER

CHAPTER OBJECTIVES

After reading this chapter you should be able to:

1. Describe the retail consumer as a problem solver.
2. Explain the motives for shopping other than buying.
3. Discuss where consumers buy, how they buy, what they buy, and when they buy.
4. Explain the role of image in affecting consumer buying decisions.
5. Emphasize the importance of responding to dissatisfied consumers.
6. Understand the decision-making process within a family and the role of reference groups and opinion leaders.
7. Explain the influence of social class, culture, and subculture on retail strategy in Canada.
8. Understand the concept of lifestyle and describe the role of lifestyle merchandising in the retail strategy mix.

While the target of preference of retailers has traditionally been the **baby boomers**, another group has been gaining in importance—"baby busters," also called "**Generation X**," which is the group between 22 and 33 years old in 1998. (They number 5.3 million and compose 17.5 percent of the population.) The key characteristics of the Xers are: (1) they are *demanding* that products live up to their claims and their expectations; (2) they are *suspicious* of product claims, and will scrutinize the product, the company that makes it, and the retailer that sells it; (3) they are *knowledgeable and savvy*, requiring clean stores to examine products and trained salespeople to answer questions; (4) they are *value conscious*, always looking for the best deal; and (5) they are looking for *honesty and simplicity* in products, store layout, and advertising, and they are turned off by hype, preferring soft sell messages telling the simple truth in an interesting way (with humour or a touch of irony). The children of the baby boomers, between 11 and 22 years in 1998, are called "**Generation Y**" and they love to shop, which should be of interest to many retailers. They are 4.5 million strong (14.8 percent of the population), they have more than $8 billion a year to spend, and are the first generation to grow up within a multi-media, computer-literate environment at home and at school.[1]

Recent patterns of immigration to Canada, particularly from Hong Kong, have boosted the Asian population to over 900,000 by 2000. They have settled mostly in Toronto or Vancouver, which have strong established Chinese communities. Most of the new immigrants are young, they are starting families, and they need houses, major appliances, and cars, which they tend to buy with cash. They are highly educated and have high incomes (the average annual household income for those living in Toronto is $52,800). They are status conscious and prefer prestige brands, like Courvoisier cognac (used as an aperitif). Retailers need to understand what kinds of products they need, and how to appeal to them, in terms of store displays, signs, advertising media and copy, as well as service quality. For example, in the past five years, Leon's Furniture has used advertising in Chinese, adapted or created specifically for that market, using television (CFMT) and Chinese newspapers. Leon's has also been advertising in Italian and Portuguese for the past ten years.[2]

Development of retail strategies begins with an understanding of the consumer. An old saying is that "nothing happens until a sale is made." Sales only occur when the retailer understands and responds to how consumers buy, what they buy, where they buy, and when they buy. Retailers must also understand the consumer as a problem solver and seek to develop merchandise offerings to address unmet needs. An additional critical dimension is knowing how consumers form images of retail outlets and how to develop merchandising and marketing strategies compatible with the desired image. In addition, demographics alone are not enough to understand and serve markets. Individual consumers are also influenced by others including family members, friends and colleagues, other members of their social class, or their cultural or subcultural group. Finally, the concept of lifestyle, as a customer's pattern of living, is introduced as a major influence on retail merchandising.

TYPES OF CONSUMER DECISIONS

You might like to keep in mind the following points about consumers when studying this chapter:

- *Consumers are problem solvers.* The role of the retailer is to help them solve their buying problems.
- Consumers try to *lower their risk* when buying merchandise by seeking information. They also seek information for reasons other than risk reduction.
- Store choice and merchandise choice depend on variables such as location, image, hours, and price, which are under the influence of the retailer.
- Many other factors, such as store atmosphere and courtesy of sales personnel, affect the in-store behaviour of consumers.

MOTIVES FOR SHOPPING

Consumers shop for reasons other than buying as shown in Figure 3-1. These reasons can be grouped into **personal motives** and **social motives**. Careful planning by a retailer can influence shoppers to make purchases even when the primary purpose of the trip is for social or personal reasons.

Personal Motives

Personal motives result from internal consumer needs, which are different from the needs that are fulfilled in purchasing a good or service.

Role Playing Consumers often engage in activities that they perceive as associated with their role in life. Familiar roles include those of housewife, student, husband, or father. For example, a husband may perceive that in his role he should purchase only high-quality gifts from prestigious outlets for his wife; or that he should be able to fix things in the house when they break or need adjustment (and proper advice from well-trained retail personnel may prove invaluable for someone who is not too handy).

Diversion Shopping often provides the opportunity to get a break from the daily routine. Simply walking through a shopping centre can allow a person to keep up with the latest trends in fashion, styling, or innovation. Similarly, malls often schedule antique or craft shows in an effort to attract consumers. Regional shopping malls are popular browsing sites because of their comfortable surroundings and appealing atmosphere. Research has shown that many consumers derive multisensory and emotional enjoyment from the activity of shopping for goods or services. This enjoyment is the **hedonic value of shopping**, in contrast with the *utilitarian* value (acquiring goods).[3] Stores that carry deep product assortments and unique brands are especially attractive to browsers because of the novelty and stimulation inherent in such outlets. Heavy browsers are more involved with the merchandise, more knowledgeable, and more likely to be opinion leaders than are other consumers. Recent trends toward *experiential retailing* underline the importance of making sure that shoppers have fun while they shop.[4]

Figure 3-1 Motives for Shopping

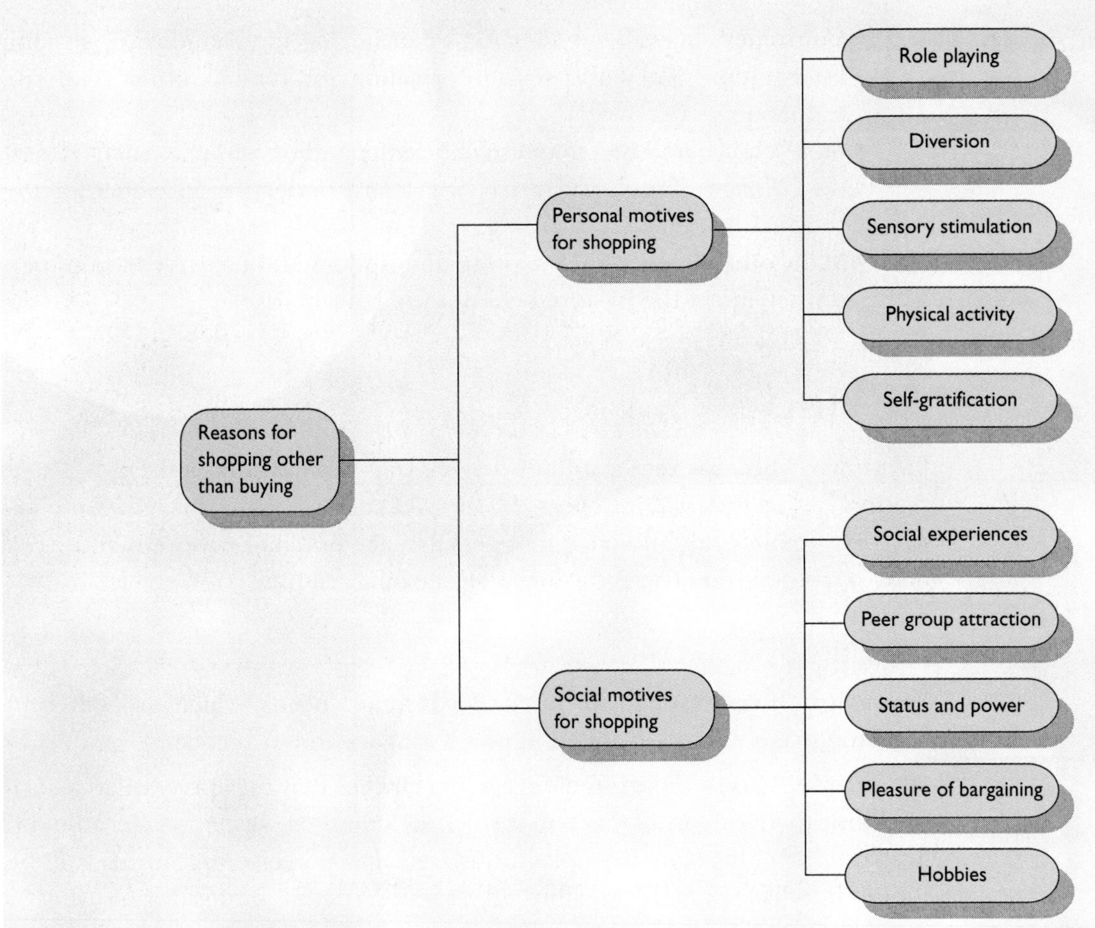

Sensory Stimulation Shoppers often respond favourably to background music, scents, and other types of sensory stimulation as part of the shopping process. Research has shown that customers feel more at ease, spend more time, and shop more often in a store that plays soft background music, compared to no music or loud music.[5]

Physical Activity Many people, particularly older people, welcome the opportunity to walk for exercise in a safe, temperature-controlled environment. Thus, some malls have organized walking and health clubs in response to such needs. The malls are opened for walking before the shops are opened for business. Large cities such as Toronto or Montreal have extensive underground malls, often connected to each other in the downtown areas. These large malls have often replaced, particularly in the winter months, the 'main street' as the favourite strolling areas for the whole family or friends.

Self-Gratification Shopping can alleviate loneliness or other emotional stress. It has been shown that shopping is often used to compensate for negative moods and complement positive ones, with the act of shopping displacing cigarettes or chocolate bars. In addition, people in a good mood are more likely

The pleasure of shopping is as much a personal experience as a social one. Excellent service in a pleasant environment is essential today.

Courtesy Hudson's Bay Company—Corporate Collection

to buy if they are involved in the shopping experience and when the experience itself is a good one.[6]

Social Motives

Social motives for shopping are also illustrated in Figure 3-1. These motives include the desire for group interaction of one sort or another.

Social Experiences For many people shopping has become a social activity. They take advantage of such opportunities to meet friends or to develop new acquaintances. Some malls feature morning promotions especially designed to serve mature consumers.

Peer Group Attraction Individuals may shop so as to be with a peer or reference group. One will often find teenagers at a music store that offers music styles that appeal to their tastes.

Status and Power Some consumers seek the opportunity to be served and catered to as part of the shopping experience. Such an activity may be one of their primary ways to get attention and respect.

The Pleasure of Bargaining Some persons enjoy the opportunity to negotiate over price. They get ego satisfaction as a result of bargaining.

Hobbies Interest in a hobby may bring people together, as it is a common desire to meet people like oneself. Thus, retailers can provide a focal point for persons with similar interests or backgrounds. For this reason, retail computer outlets sponsor hobbyist clubs, Home Depot runs various seminars, and PetSmart offers dog training classes.

A MODEL OF THE CONSUMER DECISION PROCESS

The decisions facing shoppers seeking to make a buying decision differ widely and depend on their past experiences with the merchandise to be bought. Many decisions, such as buying a loaf of bread, are routine because consumers have made similar purchases many times before. Such activities are known as **low-involvement decisions**. Other decisions, such as buying an automobile, may be difficult for some consumers because of their lack of experience or the risk involved in making a wrong decision. Consumers exhibit **high involvement** in such situations.

When making these more difficult purchases, the consumer normally goes through six decision stages, shown in Figure 3-2. The stages are: (1) problem recognition, (2) search for alternatives, (3) evaluation of alternatives, (4) risk reduction, (5) the purchasing decision, and (6) post-purchase behaviour. Retailers can influence consumer choices and actions at each stage of the decision process. Such efforts by retailers are key components of their segmentation and positioning strategies.

Figure 3-2 A Model of the Consumer Decision Process

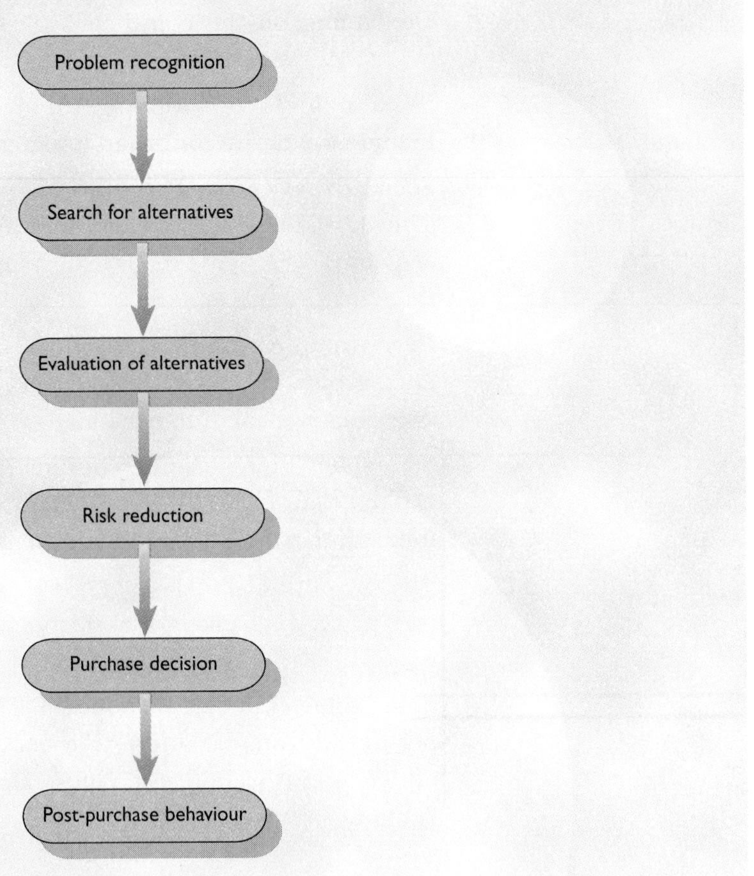

Step 1: Problem Recognition

The decision process begins when the consumer realizes that a difference exists between an existing and a preferred state of affairs. Sometimes, consumers may simply discover that they need to purchase gasoline for their automobile. Other things that may trigger problem recognition are: a lack of satisfaction with an existing product or service; a raise; a spouse begins to work (more money is now available); the need to purchase a gift for someone; or a change in fashions. Retailers can also trigger problem recognition through advertising, in-store displays, or through the creative use of sight, sound, or smell.

Step 2: Search for Alternatives

The consumer seeks and evaluates information after problem recognition occurs. The search may be physical or mental. Mental search means drawing on past experience for information. The consumer may need up-to-date information about products, prices, stores, or terms of sale. Physical or mental search may be required to obtain the needed information. The search may occur for the merchandise or for the preferred store at which the purchase will be made. Consumers evaluate the store on the basis of factors important to them and choose the outlet that most closely matches these factors.

Problem-Solving Behaviour

Depending on the consumer's background and experience, he or she may exhibit extensive, limited, or routinized response behaviour (Table 3-1). Each type of problem solving requires a different response by the retailer.

Extensive Problem Solving Consumers engage in **extensive problem solving** when faced with a first-time purchase in an unfamiliar product category, perhaps during the introductory or early growth stages of the life cycle of the product or service class. Examples include cellular phones and personal computers. Retailers should provide consumers with information on uses of the product or service, reasons why they need it, and characteristics of the product or outlet important to consider in the purchase.

Table 3-1 Problem-Solving Behaviour

Level Required	Typical Products	Retailer Response
Extensive	Personal computers Cellular phones	Provide information on the following: Uses of product or service Reasons consumer needs product Important characteristics
Limited	Small appliances Clothes Breakfast cereal	Facilitate brand-to-brand comparisons Target features important to consumer
Routinized response	Health and grooming aids Food items Automobile gas	Convenience of location

Limited Problem Solving The consumer who is familiar with the class of product or service engages in **limited problem solving**; the decision becomes a choice between brands or outlets. An example for many of us would be small appliances. Shoppers evaluate brands by comparing prices, warranties, after-sale service programs, or similar features. At this stage, facilitating brand-to-brand comparisons is often a key element of the retail marketing plan.

Routinized Response Behaviour Many consumers reach a stage of **routinized response behaviour** after they become familiar with a product class, the brands within the class, or an outlet. Such buyers tend not to engage in any kind of information search before a purchase. They exhibit low-involvement behaviour. Low-involvement products are of limited interest to the consumer, carry little risk of a wrong choice, and are not socially visible. Low involvement typifies the purchase of a loaf of bread or a tank of gasoline at the most convenient outlet. Neither the brand nor the outlet is important to the customer.

Information Sources

The retailer can make information available to consumers in a variety of forms to help them in their search. Consumers are normally exposed to (1) marketer-dominated sources, (2) consumer-dominated sources, and (3) neutral sources of information, as shown in Figure 3-3.

Figure 3-3 Sources of Consumer Information

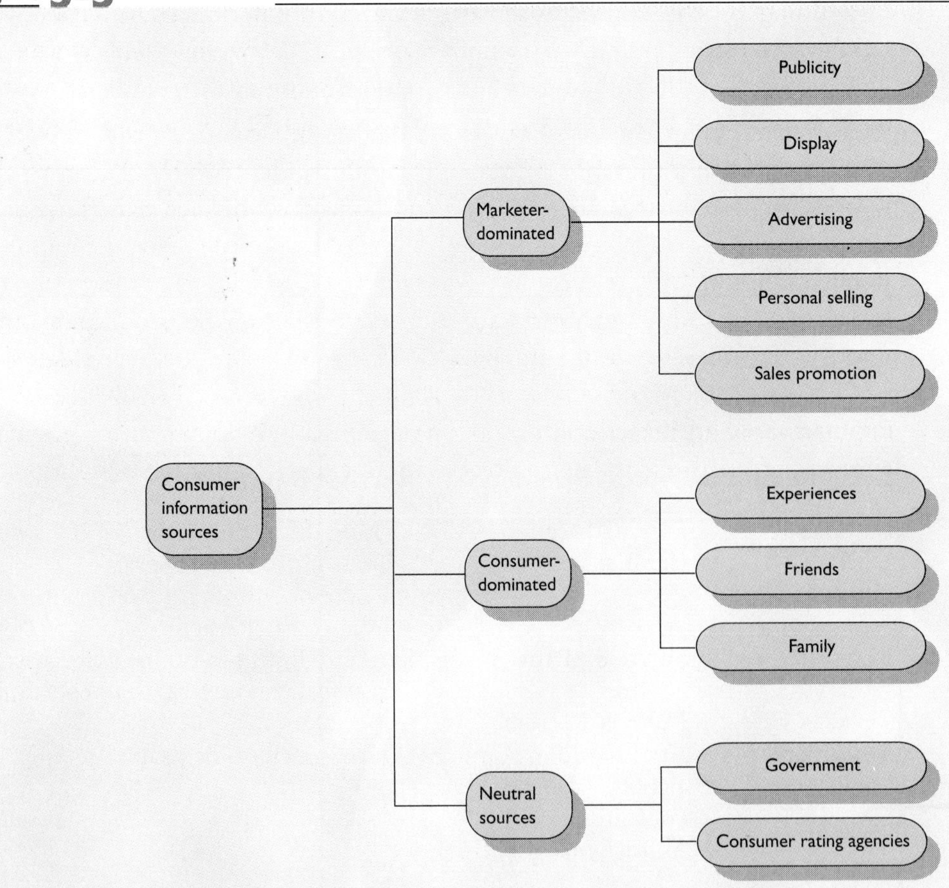

Marketer-Dominated Sources **Marketer-dominated information sources** include advertising, personal selling, displays, sales promotion, and publicity. The retailer exercises control over their content. Typically, the retailer provides information on price, product features, and terms of sale.

Consumer-Dominated Sources **Consumer-dominated information sources** include friends, relatives, acquaintances, or others. Consumer-dominated information is normally perceived as trustworthy. Satisfied consumers become especially important since they tend to talk to others about their shopping experiences. Additional consumer-dominated sources of information are persons who are known and respected by their peers. Consumers are likely to respect information from such individuals. Retailers may therefore be able to use such groups as sports leaders, college class presidents, and other socially active persons to convey product and store information. Word of mouth information from such persons is likely to be received favourably.

Dissatisfied customers can have a negative impact on an outlet. They often talk to as many as nine people about their bad experiences.[7] Satisfied consumers typically are less vocal. Dissatisfied consumers in positions of influence can also have a damaging impact on an outlet because of their role as influentials.

Neutral Sources of Information **Neutral sources of information** are also likely to be perceived as accurate and trustworthy. The Consumers' Association of Canada and federal and provincial consumer protection agencies are examples of neutral information sources. Government agencies, for example, provide information on gasoline consumption for autos and energy efficiency ratings for appliances.

Typically, most information is provided by commercial sources even though consumers may rely more on personal sources. Marketer-dominated sources may serve to create initial awareness while personal and neutral sources are then used to help evaluate specific outlets or brands of merchandise.

Step 3: Evaluation of Alternatives

After background information is acquired, the consumer evaluates the outlet and product attribute alternatives. Examples of these attributes are shown in Table 3-2. Attribute importance varies among consumers. Knowledge of the importance of attributes is critical to management in helping consumers make choices compatible with their personal preferences. Product trial and demonstration, for example, is one way of reducing risk.

Table 3-2 Factors Influencing the Choice of Merchandise and the Choice of Retail Outlet

Factors Affecting Merchandise Choice		**Factors Affecting Store Choice**	
Product Features	*Service Features*	*Store Characteristics*	*Employee Characteristics*
Fashion	Credit terms	Hours	Knowledge
Brands	Installation	Layout	Friendliness
Quality	Accessories	Cleanliness	Helpfulness
Styles	Delivery	Displays	Courteousness
Colours	Layaway	Decor	
Assortments		Image	

Step 4: Risk Reduction

A desire to reduce the risk of a poor decision influences the evaluation of alternatives. Six types of risks that affect the consumer's choice of outlet and merchandise have been identified:

- **Performance risk**—the chance that the merchandise purchased may not work properly.
- **Financial risk**—the monetary loss from a wrong decision.
- **Physical risk**—the likelihood that the decision will be injurious to one's health or likely to cause physical injury.
- **Psychological risk**—the probability that the merchandise purchased or outlet shopped will not be compatible with the consumer's self-image.
- **Social risk**—the likelihood that the merchandise or outlet will not meet with peer approval.
- **Time loss risk**—the likelihood that the consumer will not be able to get the merchandise adjusted, replaced, or repaired without loss of time and effort.

The task of the retailer is to minimize each of the risks for the consumer. For example, performance risk and financial risk can be addressed by money-back guarantees or exchange privileges. Performance risk can also be addressed by offering instruction in training programs. Psychological and social risks can be minimized by focusing on the brands carried, national advertising programs that support the merchandise, and the individuals serving as advisors to the outlet. Time loss risk can be addressed by stressing the chainwide applicability of warranties for repair, availability of on-site repair or replacement, and similar services.

Step 5: The Purchasing Decision

After evaluating some of the alternatives available, a substantial percentage of shoppers make their final decision while in the store. For example, research has shown that 80 percent of grocery shoppers make their final buying decision while in the store, and that 60 percent of grocery purchases are unplanned or impulse decisions, so layout, displays, and merchandise presentation are critical (see Chapter 8).[8]

Hard Rock Café is an example of a store as theatre.

Courtesy Hard Rock Café

Choosing the outlet and the merchandise does not end the purchasing process. The consumer has to decide on the method of payment, accessories for the merchandise (such as a camera lens for a camera or a belt for a pair of trousers), whether to purchase an extended warranty, and delivery of bulky merchandise. Retailers often offer a variety of options designed to meet a diverse array of consumer preferences.

Step 6: Post-Purchase Behaviour

Retailers need to reassure consumers after the purchase that they made the right decision. When making a major purchase, consumers are often afraid that they may have spent their money foolishly. This feeling is called **cognitive dissonance**,[9] and retailers must find ways of reducing this level of dissonance. A follow-up letter from the retailer or a phone call often can help reassure and satisfy the customer. As well, a policy of "satisfaction guaranteed or your money back" provides customers with the assurance that stores, such as Holt Renfrew, stand behind their merchandise.

The level of consumer satisfaction also influences whether the store and its merchandise will be recommended to a friend. Satisfied customers help to generate stronger customer loyalty, repeat business, reduced vulnerability to price wars, the ability to command a higher relative price for merchandise without affecting market share, lower marketing costs, and growth in market share.[10] Retailers need to be sensitive to the uncertainties in the minds of the consumers, then work to alleviate their concerns.

In conclusion, understanding the decision-making process of consumers is essential for retailers because of the implications for strategy development. How retailers can influence consumers is detailed in the next part.

UNDERSTANDING THE WHERE, HOW, WHAT, AND WHEN OF SHOPPING

Retailers may have the most influence on the behaviour of consumers during the information search and evaluation stages of the decision process. An understanding of the *where, how, what,* and *when* of consumer shopping behaviour can help retailers respond to consumer needs for information during their search and evaluation efforts.

The retailer needs to have the right merchandise at the right place, at the right time, and at the right price and quality to match consumer decisions on where to buy, what to buy, how to buy, and when to buy, as shown in Figure 3-4.

- *Where* means the choice of a downtown location, a free-standing location, a shopping centre, the specific outlet, the Internet, or any other pattern.
- *How* includes decisions on whether to engage in store or nonstore shopping.
- *What* includes consumer decisions on merchandise price and quality, whether to purchase store brands or national brands, and criteria used in evaluating merchandise.
- *When* includes decisions on such matters as time of day and day of week to shop.

Where Do Consumers Shop?

Consumers have a large variety of places at which to shop, some of which are discussed next. (See a more complete discussion of this topic in Chapter 7.)

Shopping Centres Consumers may choose shopping centres because of convenience, a controlled climate, and the merchandise assortment available. Others go to shopping centres because they can meet friends there, as shopping

Figure 3-4 Retailers Must Match Their Merchandising to the Consumer Decision Process

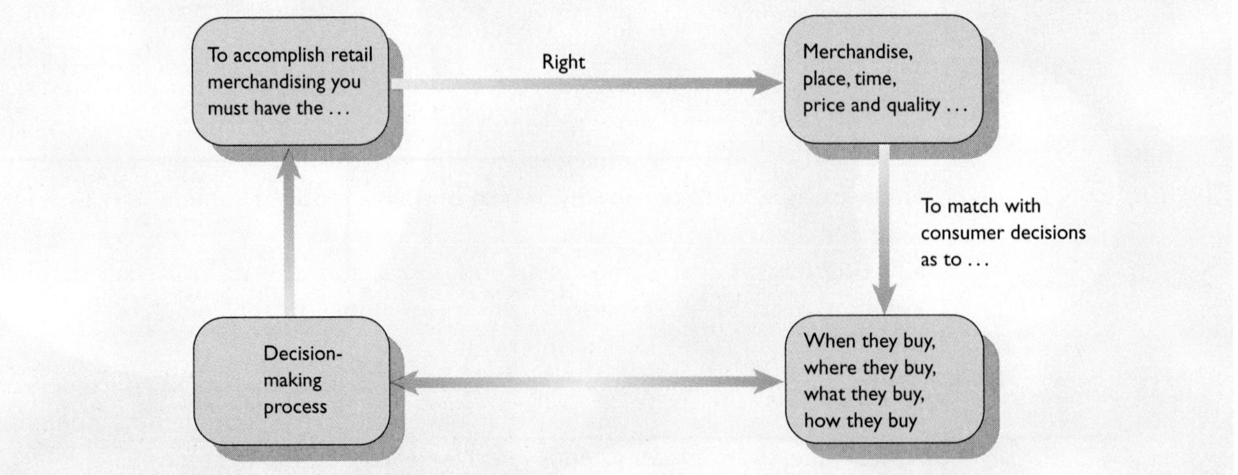

centres provide a festive atmosphere and a convenient way to keep up with the latest trends in fashion. Some people prefer shopping at "strip" shopping centres as opposed to the enclosed malls. Strip centres require less walking and generally involve less hassle in shopping. Additionally, access is typically easier than to major enclosed malls, but the merchandise selection is limited in comparison.

Downtown Some people prefer to shop downtown because of convenient public transportation and the availability of nonshopping facilities, such as financial institutions. Others work downtown and find it convenient to shop there. Finally, some consumers, often those with lower incomes and no transportation, live near the downtown area and shop in the outlets closest to their homes. In most large Canadian cities, the downtown area has seen the opening of *urban centres* such as the Eaton's centres in Calgary, Edmonton, Winnipeg, Toronto, and Montreal; Midtown Plaza in Saskatoon; Pacific Centre in Vancouver; Confederation Court Mall in Charlottetown; Barrington Place in Halifax; Atlantic Place in St. John's; Brunswick Square in Saint John (NB); or the underground centres like Les Promenades de la Cathédrale in Montreal, built underneath a church!

Outshopping Some consumers go out of town to shop (**outshopping**) because (1) the selection may be better, (2) they may want to get out of town for a visit, including, perhaps, a good meal, (3) they may work out of town and do their shopping after work, and (4) store hours, store personnel, and services such as repair may be better in the other community. Outshopping (also called **cross-border shopping** when applied to the U.S.) activities are particularly important in Canada for a number of unique reasons:[11] (1) the concentration of a large percentage of the Canadian population along the American border, and near some large U.S. cities (about 80 percent of Canadians live within 200 km of the U.S. border); (2) the large distances between Canadian cities, particularly on an east–west axis; (3) economic variables such as price and currency differentials, as well as promotional enticements; (4) the lessening of border controls under the North American Free Trade Agreement; (5) the severe climatic conditions in Canada, particularly during the winter months; and (6) the tendency to travel south for vacations ("Canadian snow birds").[12]

Nonstore Shopping Catalogue, telephone, and electronic shopping are the primary types of **nonstore shopping** (see also Chapter 16, which covers electronic commerce). Nonstore shopping is popular because it allows consumers to make purchase decisions at their leisure without leaving home. Nonstore shoppers tend to have higher incomes and higher education. Higher incomes allow them to make more discretionary purchases, and education often widens the opportunity for selling merchandise to these individuals. Because they have more education, nonstore shoppers often see less risk than other consumers in buying in a nonstore setting. Direct merchants can stress several important factors in nonstore purchases by consumers. Making purchases from their homes is a great convenience to consumers. Good product guarantees are important in assuring consumers that risks in nonstore purchases are not unreasonable.

Choosing a Store

Consumers make decisions about outlets at which to shop after deciding whether to shop downtown or at a shopping centre if in-store purchases are to be made. The *image* of a retail outlet is important in such a decision. The major attraction characteristics include the type and quality of merchandise and services offered, physical facilities, employees, and other shoppers. For example, consumers may be seeking a particular brand or quality of merchandise, specific services such as credit or delivery, an attractive outlet, courteous employees, and an outlet where consumers with similar lifestyles are likely to shop. All of these characteristics other than the characteristics of other shoppers are under the direct influence of retailers. Research has shown that quality customer service has a greater effect on sales than any other variables under the control of the retailer.[13]

Research is often necessary to help management develop an understanding of the importance of these characteristics to shoppers. The information may help retailers do a better job of meeting consumer needs. Most of Canada's foremost retailers, such as the Bay, are spending hundreds of millions of dollars remodelling all their stores across Canada in order to improve their image and withstand the competition of the discount stores. The idea is to project a strong image of quality, fashion, and sophistication.[14]

There are a number of useful methods for measuring store image from using open-ended questions, semantic differential scales (using bipolar adjectives such as "helpful/unhelpful"), or a multiattribute model. The **multiattribute model** of consumer choice is one that is frequently used to help retailers understand the importance of various outlet features to consumers.[15] The model can be applied as follows:

$$As = \sum_{i=1}^{n} B_i W_i$$

where As = Attitude toward the store; B_i = Belief by a consumer that a store possesses a particular attribute; W_i = The importance of the attribute to consumers; n = Number of attributes important to consumers in their choice of a store.

Example Assume that the four attributes shown in Table 3-3 are important in the consumer's choice of a store at which to shop. The *belief* about each attribute in store choice is rated on a scale of 1 to 5, with a score of 5 indicating that the store rates high on that attribute, and 1 indicating that it rates low. Consumers rate the *importance* of each attribute on a scale of 1 to 5, with 5 reflecting a very important one to consumers, and 1 a very unimportant one.

As shown in Table 3-3, the importance and belief scores are multiplied for each attribute and summed to develop a measure of the consumer's attitude toward each of the three stores being evaluated. Scores could range from 4 to 100 ($5 \times 5 \times 4$) with 4 being the least favourable score and 100 the most favourable.

Table 3-3 The Multiattribute Model of Store Choice

Attributes	Importance (W_i)	Beliefs (B_i) Store 1	Store 2	Store 3
Low prices	4	1	3	5
Wide merchandise assortment	5	5	3	3
Courteous personnel	2	4	3	2
After-sale service	4	4	3	1
Attitude toward the store		53	45	43

Store attributes clearly vary in importance to consumers. Store 1 (for example, a sporting goods store) may offer the widest selection of merchandise and the most qualified salespersons. Store 3 (for example, a discount store) on the other hand may offer little, if any, advice and stock only the fastest-moving items. However, its prices are likely to be lower than at other outlets. Store 2 (for example, a junior department store) rates average on all the attributes.

Based on the customer's stated importances in Table 3-3, it is likely that she or he will shop in the first type of store, since the attitude is the highest among the three (i.e., 53 versus 45 and 43). Other types of consumers may express different importances that may lead to different attitudes toward the three stores.

Understanding Store Image

The above model is one way to determine a consumer's image of a retail outlet. **Image** is the way consumers "feel" about an outlet. The image is what people believe to be true about an outlet and how well those beliefs coincide with what they think it should be like. The image may be accurate, or it may be quite different from reality. Knowing how consumers feel about an outlet is important in developing strategies for attracting them.

Why Think About Store Image?

The retailer should be concerned about store image because the flow of customer traffic depends on it. Management may have what they think is the right merchandise, at the right price, in the right style, and in the desired size, colour, and quality. But it is what the customer thinks of the price, the quality, and the service that is important. Also important is the impression that customers have of the employees. If they like the employees, they are more apt to have favourable impressions of what the outlet offers.

How Are Images Formed?

Specific features of an outlet provide the elements that make up its image. By examining each of the elements management can determine the importance of these elements to consumers.

Price Policy *An outlet's price line influences the way people think of its other aspects.* Therefore, prices must be consistent with the other elements of the retailing mix. To illustrate, a supermarket learned that when it installed carpeting, it created a higher price image. Customers felt that prices had gone up even though they had not. Yet, it isn't always necessary for an outlet to give the impression that it is a "bargain centre." A low-price policy may create an unfavourable image. Some customers feel that low quality goes with low prices and will not shop at these outlets. Yet, other customers like bargain stores. The importance of price varies with a number of factors such as the type of product, family income, and competitive offerings.

Two questions that can be helpful in image building efforts are:

- What price do the customers expect to pay?
- Do the customers consider price as important as quality, convenience, dependability, and selection?

Merchandise Variety Image improves when customers find a product that they like but don't find in other outlets. On the other hand, failure to carry certain items may give a retailer's whole product line a bad name. Similarly, when customers find one product that displeases them, they are apt to become more critical of the rest of the offering. The key is in knowing the preferences of the customers.

Employees Salespeople and other employees who are seen by customers affect the outlet's image. Customers may react negatively if the educational level of an outlet's personnel is different from theirs. Whether an outlet appeals primarily to professional or working class people, salespeople should dress and speak in such a way that the customers feel comfortable talking to them. Telephone personnel should be knowledgeable, friendly, and efficient, as should back-office personnel.

Outlet Appearance What people see as they pass by an outlet is another important element in its image. Even people who never enter an outlet form an impression from its outside appearance, including the window displays. That impression may be the reason they don't break their stride when they go by the outlet. Consumers form images of nonstore retailers based on their reliability in filling orders, the knowledge of employees, the ease of resolving complaints, the quality of their Web site and similar attributes.

Inside the outlet, the layout and the decor reinforce customers' impressions about the products and salespeople. For example, classic design fixtures usually appeal to older and more conservative groups. The new redesigned department stores (e.g., the Bay and Sears Canada) with polished, richly-decorated emporiums are meant to create excitement and project an image of quality.[16] Plain, inexpensive-appearing fixtures help to build a good image with young families whose incomes are limited. Low ceilings may make the store more personal, and indirect lighting usually makes the customer think of higher quality. Some colour schemes are considered masculine, feminine, or neutral, which may be important in displaying certain types of merchandise.

Type of Clientele The image that some people have of an outlet is influenced by the type of people who shop there. Some people, for example, think of a shop as one where professional people usually shop. They think of other outlets as ones where blue-collar workers usually shop.

The image (or feel) of the store reflects the values and lifestyles of its customers. Club Monaco's minimalist approach is carried out through its product line, selection of housewares, and furniture.

Courtesy *Marketing Magazine*

Advertising Advertising tells people whether the outlet is modern or old-fashioned, low-price or high-price, small or large. It also communicates other things of both a physical and psychological nature.

For example, when printed ads are full of heavy black print, customers get an image of low prices. Conversely, white space often connotes quality. A food store could improve its image by including a personal interest feature in its weekly ad of special prices. The outlet could feature a recipe, perhaps with the picture of the chef who originated it.

www.sears.com

Catalogues and Web sites are also very useful in forming a store image. Major department stores like Sears Canada produce beautiful catalogues and Web pages (www.sears.com), in particular during the Christmas season.

Changing the Outlet's Image

An image is a complex affair, and managers should not try to change an outlet's image without careful thought and planning. However, if a retailer is dissatisfied with the store image customers seem to have, three questions should be asked:

- What kind of image will best serve the existing market?
- What kind of image does the store have now?
- What changes can be made to improve the image?

A store cannot be all things to all people. In fact, one of the competitive strengths in retailing is that each outlet can be different. Many outlets are successful because they specialize and their owner-managers build an image around that particular specialty. The recent spending by the leading department stores builds on this theme.[17]

Keeping the Image Sharp

Maintaining an outlet's image can be handled in the same way as other management problems. Managers should review the image periodically just as they periodically review financial statements.

Listen to Customers Management can ask customers what they like about an outlet and why they prefer it to others. Their answers give an idea of the strong points in the marketing mix and its image. They can also indicate what products and services should be advertised and promoted. All customers speak in sales. What they buy, or don't buy, speaks louder than words. Keeping track of sales by item can help to determine what customers like or don't like.

Customer complaints can help deal with reluctant customers—those who shop for one or two items that they can't get elsewhere. In most cases, their reluctance is caused by the image they have of the store. Management can change that image only by learning its cause and making adjustments.

Management should also look at competitors. They can do some comparison shopping with the goal of trying to find out the strong points competitors use to create attractive images, starting with their Web sites.

Listen to Noncustomers Management often finds there are more people in their neighbourhood who don't patronize them than who do. Why? Often only one or two aspects of an operation irritate and keep some people from having a good image of it. Because of a grouchy cashier, for example, such potential customers think poorly of the whole store.

How Do Consumers Shop?

The way in which consumers select products and services and the distance they will travel to shop also affect merchandising decisions.

The Costs of Shopping Many consumers try to minimize the costs of shopping when making a shopping trip. The costs of shopping are money, time, and energy. *Money costs* are the cost of goods purchased and the cost of travel. *Time costs* include the time spent getting to and from the store(s), time spent in getting to and from the car, and time spent paying for merchandise. *Energy costs* include carrying packages, fighting traffic, parking, waiting in line, and various psychological costs as shown in Table 3-4.

Management can be responsive to these problems by having the proper store hours and by offering shoppers credit, delivery, and similar services.

Consumers are willing to travel farther for specialty goods than for either shopping goods or convenience goods because they believe the satisfaction they obtain from getting exactly what they want more than offsets the cost of the extra effort.

Table 3-4 Costs in Shopping and Buying

- **Cost of merchandise**
- **Other monetary outlays**
  1. Parking fees
  2. Automobile gasoline and wear and tear
  3. Installation
  4. Credit
  5. Repairs
  6. Wrapping
  7. Babysitting fees
  8. Warranties
- **Nonmonetary costs**
  1. Time away from other activities
  2. Waiting in line or on-line
  3. Comparison of merchandise between stores
  4. Comparison of alternative merchandise offerings
  5. Travel or delivery time
- **Emotional costs**
  1. Frustration from out-of-stock items
  2. Dealing with surly or indifferent sales assistance
  3. Bargaining over price and terms of sale
  4. Concern over a wrong decision or over security on the Internet
  5. Effects of crowding in the store or on the Internet

- **Convenience goods** are frequently purchased items for which consumers do not engage in comparison shopping before making a purchase decision. Among convenience goods are staple goods, (e.g., bread and fruits), impulse goods (e.g., a chocolate bar), and emergency goods (e.g., batteries).
- **Shopping goods** are products for which consumers make comparisons between various brands in a product class before making a purchase.
- A **specialty good** is a product that consumers know they want and for which they are willing to make a special effort to acquire.

It is not possible to generalize as to what types of merchandise can be described as convenience, shopping, or specialty goods. Consumers view merchandise differently. What is a shopping good to one consumer may be a convenience good to another one. However, typical examples of convenience, shopping goods, and specialty goods can be identified.

Household salt is a convenience good for most shoppers. They will make the purchase at the nearest available outlet. Household durables or appliances are shopping goods for many persons. A lawnmower is an example of such a product. Consumers often do not have strong brand preferences for such an item. As a result they will compare price, warranties, and various features before

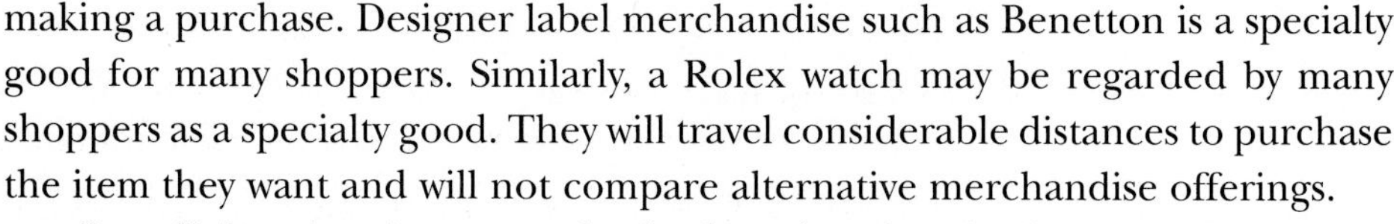

making a purchase. Designer label merchandise such as Benetton is a specialty good for many shoppers. Similarly, a Rolex watch may be regarded by many shoppers as a specialty good. They will travel considerable distances to purchase the item they want and will not compare alternative merchandise offerings.

Overall, less time is spent today in shopping than in the past. The reasons include: (1) advertising, which makes information more easily available, (2) the higher cost of gasoline, (3) the increase of women who now work outside the home and have less time for shopping, (4) increasing nonstore (including the Internet) alternatives for purchases, and (5) availability of Internet product-comparison services (example: www.compare.net). Many shoppers do not visit more than two stores even when buying items such as TV sets.

www.compare.net

How Far Are Consumers Willing to Travel? Most shoppers at grocery stores live within a kilometre of the store. Shoppers usually will travel 10 minutes or so to shop for higher-priced merchandise. Typically, 75 percent of the persons travelling to a large shopping centre live within 15 minutes of the centre. However, shoppers will travel much further to purchase specialty goods, particularly to the new **big-box** or **warehouse-style stores** such as Wal-Mart, Zellers Plus, Price/Costco, Home Depot, or Future Shop.

What Do Consumers Buy?

Price and brand are two major attributes that affect consumer purchases. Price is important because it is often a measure of worth and quality. Brand is often relied on as a measure of quality. Other factors that are important in merchandise choice include shelf displays, shelf location, and coupons.

Price Consumers ordinarily do not know the exact price of a merchandise item. But they usually know within well-defined ranges. The higher-income consumer usually is less price conscious than the lower-income consumer seeking the same merchandise. The more of a shopper's income that is spent on an item, the greater price awareness there is likely to be. Also, price is not as important to the nondiscount shopper as to the discount shopper.

Brands Some consumers purchase only well-known brands of manufacturers such as Sony. These **national brands** are the brands of a manufacturer such as Procter and Gamble that are sold through a wide variety of retail outlets. Purchasing these brands helps consumers avoid unsatisfactory purchases. Many stores, such as Sears Canada, Canadian Tire and Loblaws, sell their own brands. Known as **private brands**, they are brands of merchandise that retailers develop and promote under their own label.

Private brands have been especially important to department stores and specialty stores in recent years. During much of the previous decade these outlets had relied heavily on designer labels such as Calvin Klein to develop upscale, somewhat exclusive images. However, as the sales volume of the designer labels levelled off due to the rather exclusive pattern of distribution through department and specialty stores, suppliers began selling the merchandise through mass market outlets. The merchandise thus lost its exclusivity and in many instances was heavily price discounted. Department and specialty stores as a defensive strategy began developing their own private labels to maintain desired margins on the merchandise and to protect the integrity of their image.

Shelf Displays and Location Retailers tend to give the most shelf space to merchandise with the highest profit margins. Profits tend to drop, however, if managers shift store displays and layout too often. Point-of-sale materials, even simple signs, can increase item sales by as much as 100 percent. End-of-aisle and special displays can have even larger effects on consumer buying behaviour. Today with computerized cash registers, managers know exactly how often a product sells. As a result they often will stock only the two or three best-selling brands in each product category. The subject of shelf space allocation is discussed in greater detail in Chapter 8 on layout and merchandise presentation.

Shelf location becomes especially critical for low-involvement products since consumers are likely to purchase the first item that catches their attention. Examples include cleaning supplies or paper products. Conversely, consumers are likely to make brand comparisons in a high-involvement product class such as salad dressings in which shoppers may compare products on such bases as content or number of calories. Shelf location may be a less critical factor for high-involvement products since consumers will be making a more concerted effort to compare alternative offerings. Merchandise located on the lowest shelves may present difficulties for elderly or infirm consumers, and merchandise on the higher shelves may be difficult for some individuals to reach. The ideal shelf location depends on the consumer. For example, merchandise directed primarily at children should be on a lower shelf where they can easily see it.

Coupons and Other Sales Promotions[18] **Coupons** can be used to draw new customers to a store and to increase purchases by regular consumers. They can also be used to offset the negative features of a store by drawing customers to a poor location. Coupons can be issued by manufacturers (*manufacturer coupons*) or by retailers (*store coupons*). Retailers may provide coupons in a variety of ways, the most popular ones being: in their weekly advertisements (*retailer-initiated coupons*), on the shelves (*in-store-shelf coupons*), or in booklets. The coupon users tend to have slightly higher incomes than the average household and normally have children. They are especially good customers for retailers. Trading stamps, rebate offers, and similar strategies also can be used to attract new consumers and to retain the loyalty of current customers.

When Do Consumers Buy?

Sunday, 24-hour openings, and Internet shopping are attractive to many shoppers. Sunday is often the only time some families can shop together, and working women are more likely to shop in the evenings and on Sunday.[19] Many retailers do not like Sunday openings or long hours, but consumer preference for these hours and competitive pressures are making these openings very common. Retail Web pages allow consumers more flexibility to shop when they want and provide retailers with additional sales at a lower cost.

Retailers may also experience great seasonal variations. Some retailers make one-third or more of their annual sales in November and December. Spring dresses sell well just prior to Easter. Picnic supplies sell best in the summer, and ski equipment during the fall and early winter.

SOCIAL INFLUENCES ON THE RETAIL CONSUMER

Retail consumers make decisions based on input from family members, friends, other members of their social class or their cultural group (Figure 3-5).

Family Buying Behaviour

Buying decisions may be influenced by one or several members of a family (Figure 3-5). Shopping behaviour may involve the husband, the wife, and some of the children. This pattern of influence evolves also over time, both in terms of family life cycle and in terms of changing roles within the family.

Figure 3-5 Social Influences on the Retail Consumer

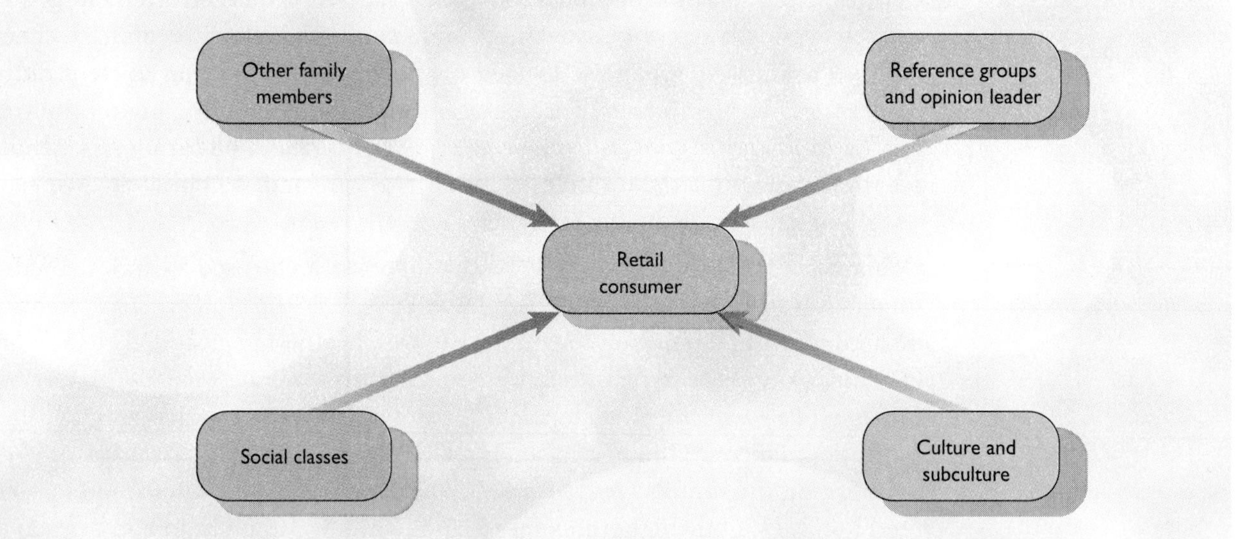

Family Life Cycle

The concept of **family life cycle** reflects the combined effect of several demographic factors: marital status (legal or common-law), age of the adult(s), employment status, and number and age of the children. Although 13.7 percent of Canadian couples are living in common-law relationships, and 47.2 percent include children, Statistics Canada counts these common-law couples as families, and in the following discussion, we will use the same convention.[20]

The various stages of a family life cycle are represented in Figure 3-6, which takes into account some recent family patterns in terms of divorces (others could be added as need be). As families pass through some of these stages, their financial resources and needs vary in fairly predictable ways. For instance, the

Figure 3-6 Family Life Cycle Stages

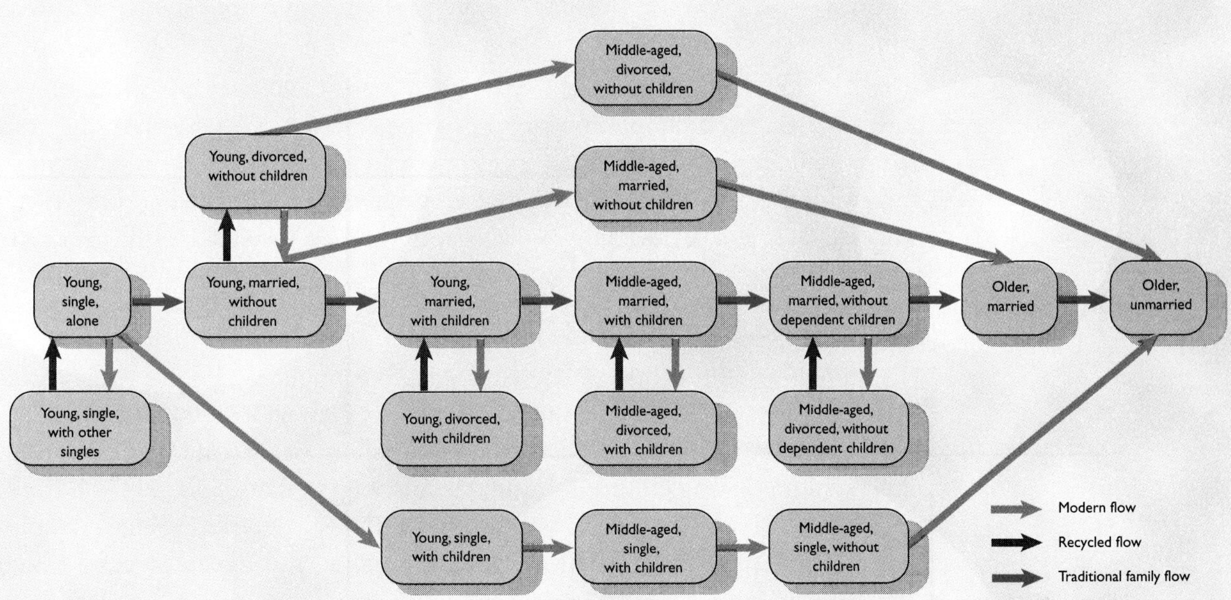

arrival of children for young couples will change their financial situation due to the expenses incurred in terms of housing, appliances, toys, and other child-related costs.

Retail strategies can be based, in part, on the size and location of families in a given stage of a family life cycle. For example, 2.7 million childless couples live in Canada, and many of them are choosing to be childless. These are often two-income households with a large disposable income, and needs that are very different from other couples of the same age. For retailers, these customers represent an attractive market for fine furniture and appliances, travel, and luxury products.[21] Similarly, other stages or subgroups within a stage (for example, higher income groups), may be targeted by retailers.[22]

Decision Making Within the Family

For many products, such as cars or homes, several family members play a role in the purchase decision. There are four basic types of decisions within a family.[23]

Wife-dominant A decision is said to be **wife-dominant** when the decision to purchase a product is made most of the time by the wife. For example, this might be the case for the wife's and children's clothing.

Husband-dominant A decision is said to be **husband-dominant** when the decision is made most of the time by the husband. For example, this might be the case for life insurance.

Autonomous A decision is said to be **autonomous** when the decision is made over time independently by the husband or the wife. Thus, on one occasion, it may be the husband, and in another, it may be the wife. For example, this might be the case for savings, alcohol, and the husband's clothing. Contrary to the previous two types of decisions, the retailer should target both spouses in advertising or in-store selling.

Syncratic A decision is said to be **syncratic** when the decision is made jointly by both spouses. For example, this might be the case for vacations, housing, and living-room furniture. As in the previous type of decision, the retailer must make sure that the needs of both spouses are met. In selling living-room furniture, the salesperson must interact with both spouses, instead of only one or the other.

Role of Children in Decision Making

There are 5.1 million children 12 years old and younger in Canada. After reaching a high of 406,000 in 1990, the birthrate has fallen to 365,000 births in 1996. The earlier "echo boom" has led to the launching of new magazines, and an interest in marketing children's products, such as car seats, toys, and children's clothing. However, this pattern may be affected by the decision of many couples to remain childless for a variety of reasons. Retailers must keep abreast of such changes.[24] In addition to influencing the family decision process, children are also consumers. These kids represent a major market for many retailers of cereal, candy, chewing gum, soft drinks, clothing, toys, and video games (e.g., the Nintendo craze).

The Changing Roles of Men and Women

The last thirty years have seen major changes in the respective roles of men and women within the family, and these have important implications for retailers.

First, more women are now working than at any time in the past; about 60 percent of the 10 million women of working age are now in the labour force, and two out of five working women consider themselves career women, i.e., they are mostly interested in developing their careers.[25] By contrast to this group, the other working women enter the work force primarily for generating additional income for the family. Different job orientations within the family have been found to lead to different behaviours.

Some implications of these changes for retailers are that shopping is viewed as a chore by working women, and that the emphasis should be on convenience, in terms of location and opening hours (evening and Sunday shopping). Another implication is that the additional income puts the family in a higher income group and social group, allowing the purchase of time-saving products and services such as microwave ovens, freezers, convenience foods, and vacation packages.[26] Also, these families spend their time differently, and must be reached with different kinds of media (e.g., prime time television, weekend newspapers, and billboards). Finally, a study shows that women *still* have the major role for planning for grocery shopping, meal planning, and meal preparation, but that the men who actually carry out these plans may decide on where to shop, what brand to buy, and how much to spend.[27]

Men have reacted in different ways to this new reality. Four distinct types have been identified:[28]

Progressives (13 percent) They are young, educated, with above-average incomes, and support their wives' employment. About two-thirds do the main food shopping.

All Talk, No Action (33 percent) Their attitudes, but not their behaviour, are similar to the progressives. About 20 percent do the main food shopping.

Ambivalents (15 percent) Because of economic pressures, they reluctantly accept their wives' employment. About 60 percent do the main food shopping.

Traditionalists (39 percent) Older, less educated, they believe that their wives' place is at home.

Some of the implications of these changes for retailers are in terms of targeting both spouses for store loyalty, merchandise selection, pricing, and promotion. In particular, the increase in food shopping by men may affect store layout and placement of impulse products.[29]

Reference Groups and Opinion Leaders

A **reference group** is any group for which a consumer is a "psychological participant," that is with which he or she will identify and accept its norms or judgment. Examples of reference groups are family, relatives, friends, colleagues, professional or religious associations, celebrities, and salespersons.

Retailers can use their knowledge of reference groups' influences in various ways. For example, they may use recognized members of a group (such as a local celebrity) in their advertisement or in their direct selling, or they may indicate to the customer that members of a certain reference group routinely patronize their store. They may also post letters from or photographs of such persons.

When retailers can identify persons whose product-specific competence is recognized by others (called **opinion leaders**), they can attempt to influence them in a number of ways. These individuals may be consulted when new products are introduced and they may receive free samples or trial use of a product. The objective is to win over the opinion leader, who through positive word-of-mouth will generate traffic and sales.

Finally, a good salesperson may act as a reference person for several customers, if they have come to trust and depend on this salesperson. Some customers may be unsure about their choice, either because they do not have the expertise, or do not trust their own judgment. When they find a salesperson who is credible and sincere, and has made the "right" choice for them in the past, they will continue to depend on that person for what may be a very long time.

Influence of Social Classes

Social classes are divisions of society that are relatively homogeneous and permanent, and in which individuals or families often share similar values, lifestyles, interests, and types of behaviour. This applies also to shopping behaviour and, as such, is of great importance to retailers, since a large number of studies found that social classes affected the consumption of products, services, the selection of a retail outlet, and the use of credit cards.

In practice, social class membership is measured using major components such as how prestigious the occupation of the family head is, the area of residence of the family and the type of dwelling (e.g., detached house or apartment), the source of family income (e.g., salary, investment, or welfare), and/or the level of education.

Social Classes in Canada

A study provides the distribution of the Canadian population among four major social classes:[30]

Upper classes (11 percent) These include self-employed and employed professionals, and high-level management. They tend to shop at the better retail outlets, buy high quality goods and clothing, jewelry, luxury cars, appliances, and furniture. They represent the best market for luxury goods and status symbol products.[31]

Middle class (28 percent) These include semi-professionals, technicians, middle managers, supervisors, forepersons, and skilled clerical-sales-service. With the working class, they represent the mass market for most goods and services. They tend to shop at department stores, buy good quality goods, clothing, and furniture. They tend to be price sensitive while selecting quality items.

Working class (41 percent) These include the skilled tradespeople, the farmers, the semi-skilled manual and clerical-sales-service. They tend to shop at discount stores and promotional department stores, they spend less than the middle class on clothing, travel, and services, more on sporting goods and equipment. They tend to prefer national brands.

Lower classes (20 percent) These include the unskilled clerical-sales-service, and manual and farm labourers. They tend to spend most of their income on the basic necessities of life, little on luxury products. They purchase second-hand cars and used furniture, and less expensive goods and clothes.

Many implications for retailers are based on social class structure including merchandise mix, store image, design and layout, pricing, and advertising.

Influence of Culture and Subculture

Culture

As individuals grow up within a cultural group, they learn a set of values, attitudes, traditions, symbols, and characteristic behaviours. In a sense, **culture** affects and shapes many aspects of consumption behaviour, including shopping behaviour. In looking at the Canadian "salad bowl" and its cultural groups, retailers should recognize that the differences among them stem from a variety of sources, including:

- The system of inherited values, attitudes, symbols, ideas, traditions, and artifacts that are shared by the members of the group. These differences will affect the merchandising mix, the pricing policy, and the promotional strategies of the retailer, depending on the group(s) targeted.

- The dominant religion of the group, which may be confounded with culture, and which may affect some values and attitudes, for example, toward Sunday shopping.
- The dominant language spoken by the group, which may also be confounded with culture, and which may require different promotional or selling strategies; for example, advertising in French or Italian, or using salespeople with certain language skills.

Cultural Groups in Canada

A brief overview of the two major cultural groups in Canada, and their characteristics of interest to retailers is as follows (for the other significant groups, see Chapter 2):

English Canadians They represent the largest group in Canada with about 12 million people. They are present in all major markets in Canada, although they are not a homogeneous group, with regional differences, and differences among those of Scottish descent, Irish descent, and recent immigrants from England. However, as a group they exhibit consumption and shopping behaviour that is different from that of other groups. Compared to the French Canadians, they consume more frozen vegetables, less beer and wine, more hard liquor, shop at more stores, and purchase furniture more at department or furniture stores than discount stores.[32]

French Canadians They represent the second largest market in Canada, with about 7.5 million people, and they account for over $56 billion in retail sales. French Canadians reside mostly in Quebec, Ontario, and New Brunswick. In many respects, their consumption and shopping behaviour may be vastly different from that of the English Canadians, not only in terms of degree, as illustrated in the previous paragraph, but also in terms of approach. Many retailers, including Burger King, have developed specific campaigns to meet the needs of French Canadians. Retail Highlight 3-1 provides additional characteristics of this major group.

Conclusion on Ethnic Groups in Canada What can be gathered from this brief discussion is that Canadian retailers must thoroughly understand the ethnic origins of their customers, and adjust their strategies accordingly, particularly in the areas of merchandise mix, advertising and sales promotion, store location and design, in-store selling, and pricing. This is especially important in major metropolitan areas where the ethnic markets are large.

Retail Highlight 3-1 How Are French Canadians Different?

Compared to English Canadians, French Canadians in general:

- are more willing to pay premium prices for convenience and premium brands;
- buy few "no-name" products but make greater use of cents-off coupons;
- patronize food warehouses less, and convenience stores and health food outlets more;
- are less likely to consume tea, diet colas, jam, tuna, cookies, and eggs, but more likely to consume pre-sweetened cereals, regular colas, instant coffee, and butter;
- give more importance to personal grooming and fashion, and visit more specialized clothing boutiques;
- are less likely to use medicated throat lozenges, cold remedies, and nasal sprays;
- have a higher propensity to drink wine and beer and smoke cigarettes, but a lower one for hard liquor;
- are less likely to play golf, jog, garden, go to the movies, and entertain at home;
- buy more lottery tickets, subscribe to book clubs, and make fewer long distance phone calls; and
- have more life insurance but fewer credit cards.

Compared to English Canadians, Mature Quebecers (55-plus):

- go to the supermarket more often, and seldom to food warehouses;
- consume fewer canned foods, cranberry-based items, frozen vegetables, ginger ale, boxed chocolates, and bran cereals;
- drink more milk, fresh orange juice, prune nectar, bottled water, cognac, gins, French wines, and vermouth;
- are less active, travel less, but are more likely to go dancing; and
- are less likely to use automatic banking machines, credit cards, to own cats, dogs, or cars.

Source: François Vary, "Sizing up 55-plus," *Marketing,* October 5, 1995, pp. 13-14; François Vary, "Quebec Consumer Has Unique Buying Habits," *Marketing,* March 23, 1992, p. 28.

LIFESTYLE MERCHANDISING

Lifestyle and Psychographics

Lifestyle is a customer's pattern of living as reflected in the way merchandise is purchased and used. **Psychographics** are the ways of defining and measuring the lifestyles of consumers. They can be measured with a series of questions called the lifestyle (or AIO) inventory, which includes questions on various *a*ttitudes (e.g., I find shopping enjoyable), *i*nterests (e.g., I often go to the movies), and *o*pinions (e.g., all retailers are honest businesspeople). The respondent is asked to agree or disagree with these types of statements.

Lifestyle concepts influence almost every dimension of merchandise presentation in retailing. Why has lifestyle merchandising become so important? We live in an age in which large differences exist in the behaviour of people with similar demographic profiles. This diversity makes it hard to offer merchandise to consumers based only on an analysis of their age, income, and education. Instead, retailers need to know how people (1) spend their time, (2) spend their money, and (3) what they value, so that they can serve the customers better. Market segmentation based on lifestyle characteristics (as measured by the AIO inventory) gives retailers a more realistic picture of the customers they want to serve.

Lifestyle retailing has grown in importance since the early 1970s. Previously, retailing had been characterized by a sameness in operations. Large retailers such as Sears Canada and the Bay had few significant differences in strategy. Managers could be shifted from one store to another across the country and would find few differences between the stores.

Lifestyle Merchandising

Retailers quickly realized that defining consumers in terms of demographics alone was not sufficient for fast growth. The concept of lifestyle merchandising thus evolved. The new focus was on understanding and responding to the living patterns of customers rather than making merchandising decisions primarily on the basis of consumer demographics, and in doing so integrating all the social dimensions discussed in the first part of the chapter.[33]

A portfolio of lifestyle-oriented outlets then emerged as the next evolutionary stage for some retailers. Management recognized that a portfolio of outlets is likely to be more profitable than focusing on only one or two target groups. Even such a traditional mass merchant as K mart has opened a variety of lifestyle-oriented retailing specialty outlets, such as Builders Square targeted to the do-it-yourself market (also served by Home Depot) and Northern Reflections, launched in Canada as a faux-country chain stocked with casual clothes. At the Toronto-based Sporting Life, the entire store format, including the salespeople and the merchandise, appeal to the individual who loves the outdoors and many kinds of sports.

Why Worry About Lifestyle Merchandising?

As just illustrated, lifestyle analysis offers retailers: (1) an opportunity to develop marketing strategies based on a life-like portrait of the consumers they are seeking to serve, (2) the ability to partially protect the outlet from direct price competition by developing unique merchandise offerings that attract shoppers for reasons other than price, and (3) the opportunity to better understand the shopping behaviour and merchandise preferences of customers.

Management is simply better able to describe and understand the behaviour of consumers when thinking in terms of lifestyle. Routinely thinking in terms of the activities, interests, needs, and values of customers can help retailers plan merchandise offerings, price lines, store layout, and promotion programs that are tightly targeted. However, lifestyle analysis only adds to the demographic, geographic, and socioeconomic information retailers need in serving markets effectively. Lifestyle analysis is not a substitute for this information. Rather, all the information sources taken together give retailers a richer view of their customers and help them recognize and serve consumer needs.

We are all a product of the society in which we live. We learn very early concepts such as honesty and the value of money. And these stay with us throughout our lives. These cultural influences, plus individual economic circumstances, produce consumer lifestyles—traits, activities, interests, and opinions reflected in shopping behaviour. Individuals can be grouped into distinct market segments based on the similarities of their lifestyles.

The lifestyles of consumers are rooted in their values. **Values** are beliefs or expectations about behaviour shared by a number of individuals and learned from society. Some of these values do not change much over time, while others can change quite rapidly. The major forces shaping consumer values include family, culture, religious institutions, schools, and early lifetime experiences.

www.polk.ca

A study of cultural and economic lifestyle influences offers some of the most important and interesting ways of understanding consumers. This information helps in serving them more effectively. The following example of such analyses will help you understand the impact of lifestyles on consumer buying behaviour. For a more complex micromarketing analysis of Canadian markets, check CompuSearch's PSYTE clustering method at www.polk.ca.

www.sri.com

Values and Lifestyles (VALS)™

SRI International (SRI: www.sri.com) developed a psychographic consumer segmentation system, **VALS** (values and lifestyles), that helps retailers understand correlations between a consumer's psychology or "mind-set" and his or her consumer preferences. The VALS consumer segments are summarized in Figure 3-7.

Figure 3-7 The VALS™ Network

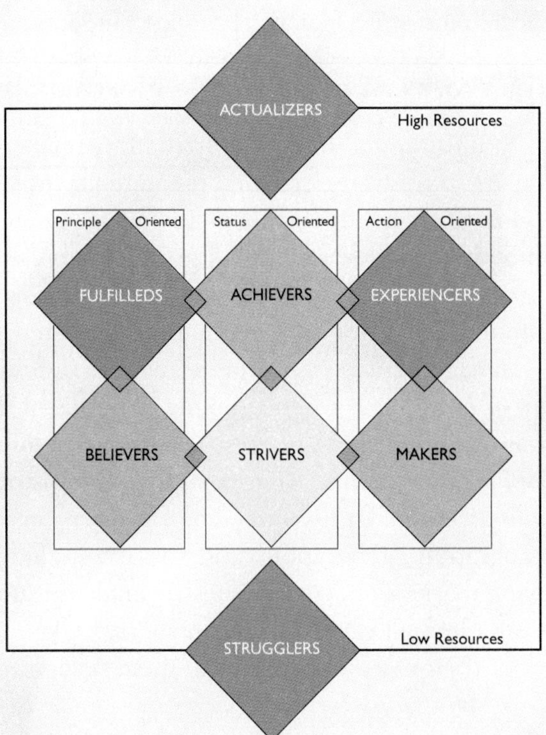

The VALS program enables retailers to predict consumer responses to merchandise or types of outlets. For example, a consumer survey about food consumption, in which the respondents were VALS-typed, showed that Fulfilleds were most likely to eat yogurt. Similarly, the Experiencers are more likely to buy imported cheese than domestic cheese. Experiencers and Strivers shop more frequently at convenience stores than Actualizers do. VALS information can also help retailers develop promotional campaigns targeted at specific groups. Fulfilled consumers read magazines and newspapers but do not watch much television. When they do, it is often an educational channel. They listen to radio on an average basis but focus on news, soft rock, and classical music.

The VALS system divides consumers into eight groups, determined by their psychological makeup or self-orientation, and resources. **Self-orientation** refers to the patterns of attitudes and activities that help people reinforce, sustain, or modify their social self-image. For VALS purposes, resources include education, income, self-confidence, health, eagerness to buy, and energy level. Resources generally increase from adolescence through middle-age and decrease with extreme age, depression, financial reverses, and physical or psychological impairment. VALS identified three self-orientations to be highly effective predictors of consumer behaviour: principle, status, and action orientations.

Principle-oriented consumers are guided in their choices by their beliefs or principles, rather than by feelings, events, or desire for approval. **Status-oriented consumers** are heavily influenced by the actions, approval, and opinions of others. **Action-oriented consumers** are guided by a desire for social or physical activity, variety, and risk taking. Each of the groups has distinctive attitudes, lifestyles, and life goals. Consumers within each group buy products and services and seek experiences characteristic of themselves.

With those factors as a foundation, a thumbnail sketch of the eight VALS segments follows:[34]

- **Actualizers** are successful, sophisticated, active, take-charge people with high self-esteem and abundant resources. Their possessions and recreation reflect a cultivated taste for the finer things in life. Image is important to them.
- **Fulfilleds** are mature, satisfied, comfortable, reflective people who value order, knowledge, and responsibility. Most are well educated, and in, or recently retired from, professional occupations. Although their income allows them many choices, they are conservative, practical consumers, concerned about functionality, value, and durability of the products they buy. Leisure activities centre around the home.
- **Believers** are conservative, conventional people with concrete beliefs and strong attachments to traditional institutions: family, church, community, and the nation. They follow established routines, organized in large part around their homes, families, and social or religious organizations. As consumers, they are conservative and predictable, favouring national products and established brands.

- **Achievers** are successful career-oriented people who like to, and generally do, feel in control of their lives. They value structure, predictability, and stability over risk, intimacy, and self-discovery. They are deeply committed to their work and their families. As consumers, they favour established, prestige products that demonstrate their success to their peers.
- **Strivers** seek motivation, self-definition, and approval from the world around them. They are striving to find a secure place in life. Unsure of themselves, and low on economic, social, and psychological resources, they are deeply concerned about the opinions and approval of others. They emulate those who own more impressive possessions, but what they wish to obtain is generally beyond their reach.
- **Experiencers** are young, vital, enthusiastic, impulsive, and rebellious. They seek variety and excitement, savouring the new, the offbeat, and the risky. Still in the process of formulating life values and patterns of behaviour, they quickly become enthusiastic about new possibilities but are equally quick to cool. They are avid consumers and spend much of their income on clothing, fast food, music, movies, and videos.
- **Makers** are practical people who have constructive skills and value self-sufficiency. They live within a traditional context of family, practical work, and physical recreation and have little interest in what lies outside that context. They experience the world by working on it (for example, building a house or canning vegetables), and have sufficient skill, income, and energy to carry out their projects successfully. They are unimpressed by material possessions other than those with a practical or functional purpose.
- **Strugglers'** lives are constricted. Chronically poor, ill-educated, low-skilled, without strong social bonds, aging, and concerned about their health, they are often despairing and passive. Their chief concerns are for security and safety. They are cautious consumers, and although they represent a very modest market for most products and services, they are loyal to favourite brands.

VALS segments are balanced in size so that each truly represents a viable target for retailers. In addition, some segments share some characteristics, so they can be combined in various ways to suit particular retailing purposes.

Internet Exercises

//future.SRI.com/

The VALS range of programs is available in the following site: //future.SRI.com/, then click on the VALS icon. Once inside, you can do the following exercises:

- By clicking on iVALS (Internet VALS), discover your VALS type by taking the iVALS survey and, once the results are in, examine the characteristics of your type and other types by looking at the iVALS profiles.
- By clicking on the Japan VALS, study the 6 (regrouped from the original 10) Japanese segments and compare them to the 8 North American segments.

What Else Do We Know About Changing Cultural Patterns?

There are a number of cultural and lifestyle trends that have important implications for retailers.

The divorce rate remains high. In the 1996 Census, there were 1.1 million single-parent families in Canada, or 17 percent of all families (83 percent were female lone parents). The divorce rate has dropped recently to around 71,500 a year.[35] As a result, the value patterns of today's children are shifting. More children are being raised without fathers in the home.

Parents are spending less time with very young children. For example, today more than 30 percent of preschool children are in day care centres, a segment of retailing that will continue to grow rapidly.

People move more often than in the past. Thus, less influence comes from grandparents and aunts and uncles as part of the extended family. Many of today's young people lack "roots" and a sense of traditional family values.

Schools are becoming more important in shaping values. More young people are staying in high school, and approximately half now go to college.[36] Young people are being exposed to a larger number of different values than in the past and are more willing to experiment and try alternative lifestyles.

Small family sizes and more single-person households. The small family size of the 1990s (at about 3.1 persons) is continuing and their lifestyle patterns continue to create new merchandising opportunities. Many of these households have high discretionary income and spend more on restaurants, educational products, and travel services than larger families. Their homes are typically smaller than in the past and the furnishings also are smaller.

Single-person households reflect lifestyles that are not impacted by family norms and the preferences of other family members. Activities are on a per person basis as opposed to a household basis. Products and services for such households are being personalized rather than standardized. Such retail services as health care, personal finance, and insurance are now offered on a per person rather than a per household basis.

The increasing emphasis on the family is being accompanied by an increase in adult-oriented lifestyles. More and more adult-oriented programming is available to households through cable television and the networks. The popularity of adult soap operas reflect this trend in society. In addition, the penetration of VCR, DVD, and videostores is making it easier to watch movies at home.

The yuppies (young, urban professionals) are getting older. The share of persons aged 35–44 will decrease to 15.6 percent by 2006, while persons aged 25–34 will decrease to 13.6 percent.[37] Such households typically have two incomes, are well educated, and have the money to spend to support their lifestyle preferences. The yuppies are placing more emphasis on their households than they did when they were in their 20s. They are purchasing more expensive home furnishings and quality art, and are major consumers of services. Banks, stock-brokerage houses, and other financial institutions are rejoicing at the opportunity to serve these markets. These consumers are conspicuous in their consumption and are willing to spend heavily to support their lifestyles. The values of aging yuppies are characterized by the term "couch potatoes" and by what is popularly described as "cocooning." They are increasingly inclined to buy things that provide control, comfort, and security against what they perceive as a harsh outside world. Domino's Pizza, capitalizing on this lifestyle, became a national force in the pizza business by providing home delivery.

Families earning more than $80,000 a year are growing and they now comprise more than 18 percent of all families. An important number of these affluent families represent retirees who have earned good pensions during the last fifty years (called the Countdown Generation).[38] Affluent buyers seek products and services that reflect their self-image and are interested in aesthetics as much as performance. From retailers, they seek the highest-quality merchandise that reflects prestige and fashion. They expect high-quality service and expert consultation. Affluent dual-income households provide strong markets for luxury products such as satellite dishes, boats, and premium cars. Retailers such as Holt Renfrew are positioned to serve these markets.

No longer are the roles of the male and the female in the household as clearly defined as in the past. More and more women are buyers of financial services and other male-oriented products. Men are increasingly becoming purchasers of household products, and young adults of both sexes are learning how to manage households and to cope with problems of school and education. Many retail promotions are universal in content and not targeted specifically to either males or females.

One of the most dramatic changes has been the effects of technology on consumer lifestyles. The development of video cassette players led to the emergence of video outlets that specialize in the rental of movies and VCR equipment. Busy consumers are responding to the opportunity to view films at their convenience in the privacy of their homes rather than go to movie houses. Microwave ovens have led to changes in the types of foods eaten, and in-home interactive shopping offered through cable services is beginning to redefine how and when consumers shop.

Not all consumers are sharing in the affluence of some demographic segments. Such consumers, as part of their lifestyles, are very responsive to coupons and other promotions. They use generic products, buy at flea markets and garage sales, are willing to accept less service in return for lower prices, and are active in seeking goods that last longer and require less maintenance. Such consumers are responsible for the growth of warehouse outlets for various types of merchandise.

There is a major shift in attitudes and values. In the last few years, there have been some subtle and important shifts in attitudes and values among consumers that will profoundly affect the economy in the future:[39]

- The return to conservative ideals, in terms of life, work, love, and family.
- The rejection of the legacy of conspicuous consumption.
- The demand for real intrinsic value, including product quality and durability.
- The growth of altruism.
- The search for balance and moderation, in particular the search for simplicity and convenience.

The more money people have to spend, the less time they have to spend it. The most affluent households typically have two wage earners, which means that they have little time for shopping. As a result, they are willing to pay for time-saving goods including lawn care services and cleaning services. They also have been responsible for the rapid growth in specialty shops, in supermarkets, and in downtown department stores. Such consumers also seek high-quality recreation because of the limited amount of time available to them. They are prone to go to fashionable ski resorts, take sun-and-surf winter vacations (Canadian snowbirds), and go to theme restaurants and expensive golf and tennis resorts.

Understanding Emerging Global Lifestyles

Global telecommunications, frequent cross-border travel, and a global economy are creating an international youth culture whereby fashion, music, and food are becoming part of a universal, international lifestyle that is essentially the same in Vancouver, Madrid, and Osaka. "It is consumer-driven: drinking cappuccino and Perrier; furnishing the apartment with IKEA; eating sushi; dressing in the united colours of Benetton; listening to U.S.–British rock while driving the Hyundai over to McDonald's."[40] Groups of consumers in Toronto and Milan often have greater similarities than consumers do in Calgary and Halifax.

Television media deliver the same images around the world. McDonald's competes for the same expensive real estate whether in Montreal's Crescent Street, the Ginza in Japan, or the Champs-Elysées in Paris. Sushi bars have flooded the Canadian cities, Tex-Mex cuisine is served in Israel, and numerous oriental restaurants operate in Canada.

Fashion, especially, is becoming international in this era of global travel and telecommunications. Italian youths today tend to dress in blue denim, and Canadians are switching to Italian suits. Fashion-conscious youth favour clothes from such international fashion retailers as Benetton, Roots, and Esprit, all outfitters of the global lifestyle. Benetton's "All the Colours of the World" oozes international flavour unmatched in history. Esprit, based in California, is also one of the world's leading sportswear merchants. Habitat, a British home furnishings merchant, operates its stores worldwide, as does IKEA, the Swedish unassembled furniture merchant, whose catalogues are published in 12 languages.

Global pricing is the result of global merchandising and global electronics. Prices are controlled electronically so that outlets around the world for any particular chain are largely immune to currency fluctuations. A Chanel suit sells for essentially the same price on Rodeo Drive, in Hong Kong, and in Paris.

The Wall Street Journal, the British-based *Economist*, and the *Financial Times* are transmitted around the world by satellite transmission. The *Economist* is read by people in more than 170 countries. Less than 25 percent of its readers live in Great Britain. Vast cultural exports from the United States essentially have conquered the world, from Disney products (theme parks, stores, and cruise ships) outside the United States, to food outlets (e.g., Hard Rock Cafés), to movies and television shows.

English has emerged as a universal language as the cultures of English-speaking countries increasingly dominate world trends. More than one billion English speakers live in the world today. English is the language of the international youth culture, who are equally comfortable singing the lyrics of Bryan Adams, U2, or Janet Jackson. Global lifestyles are slowly helping to overcome cultural nationalisms. No longer can progressive merchants think in terms of North American lifestyles only as nationalist borders become unimportant for other than political reasons.

CHAPTER HIGHLIGHTS

- Consumers shop for reasons other than buying, which can be grouped into personal and social motives. Personal motives include role playing, diversion, sensory stimulation, physical activity, and self-gratification. Social motives include the desire for social experiences, peer group attraction, status and power, the pleasure of bargaining, and hobbies. Careful planning by a retailer can influence shoppers to make purchases even when the primary purpose of the trip is social or personal.
- Consumers go through a series of stages in making a purchase decision. The stages, for other than routine purchases, include problem recognition, information search, evaluation and risk reduction, the actual purchase decision, and post-purchase behaviour. Retailers can influence consumer choices and actions at each stage of the decision process.
- Retailers can have the most influence on the behaviour of consumers during the information search and evaluation stage. An understanding of the how, when, where, and what of consumer shopping and buying behaviour can help retailers be responsive to their needs for information.
- Consumers use consumer-dominated, marketer-dominated, and neutral sources of information in making store and product choices. Marketer-dominated sources include advertising, personal selling, displays, sales promotion, and publicity. Consumer-dominated sources include friends, relatives, acquaintances, or others. Neutral sources include federal and provincial government consumer protection agencies.
- Consumers seek to minimize risks during the purchase evaluation stage. The risks they are seeking to avoid include performance risk, financial risk, physical risk, psychological risk, social risk, and time loss risk.
- Consumers may seek to go to shopping centres, downtown stores, out of town (outshopping) or out of the country (cross-border shopping), or simply shop from their own home (nonstore shopping).

- Store image is an important consideration in store selection. It is formed based on information such as price, merchandise variety, employee behaviour and appearance, store appearance, type of clientele, and advertising. Efforts must be made to improve, change, or maintain the store's image.
- Many consumers try to minimize the costs of shopping when making purchase decisions. These costs include money, time, and energy. Actual purchases by consumers are influenced by many factors, including price and brand, shelf displays and shelf locations, coupons, trading stamps, and rebates.
- Retailers must understand how decisions are made within a family, the respective roles of men, women, and children, and the changing needs during different stages of its life cycle.
- Retailers may often use reference groups and opinion leaders such as local celebrities to improve the image of their store and the credibility of their salespersons.
- Social class distinctions have often been used instinctively by retailers in defining their targets and their marketing strategies.
- Most Canadian retailers should be sensitive to the Canadian "Salad Bowl" and understand the subtleties of attitudes and behaviour of the various sub-groups.
- Retailers can more readily meet the needs of customers if they understand how people spend their time and money and what they value. The essence of this type of information is lifestyle analysis.
- Lifestyles are based on the values of people. The forces affecting consumer values are the influence of the family, religious institutions, schools, and early lifetime experiences.
- Positioning emerged in the early 1970s. Management began to target their offerings to narrow groups of consumers defined in terms of demographics. By the mid-1970s, lifestyle merchandising emerged with an emphasis on the activities, interests, and opinions of consumers.
- The VALS program offers retailers the opportunity to structure lifestyle-focused marketing programs. The SRI analysis combines the notions of psychological and material resources and shows the cultural role they play in the translation of psychological motivations into purchasing behaviour.
- Society today is characterized by parents who spend less time with young children than in previous generations, high divorce rates, and the declining influence of relatives. The increasing importance of schools in shaping the values of youth, decreasing family sizes, increasing number of single-person households, and the redefinition of the role of the male and female are affecting shopping behaviour. Similarly, health awareness, poverty of time, and lifestyle changes brought about by dramatic changes in technology are redefining shopping behaviour.
- Sensitivity to lifestyle differences affects the retailing strategist in various ways, including making him or her aware of the importance of lifestyle merchandise classifications, the psychological effects of design and layout on purchasing behaviour, and ambience on targeted consumer markets.
- Understanding global lifestyles is becoming more important to the marketing strategy decisions of many retailers.

KEY TERMS

Achievers	72
action-oriented consumers	71
Actualizers	71
autonomous decision	63
baby boomers	42
Believers	71
big-box store	60
cognitive dissonance	51
consumer-dominated information sources	49
convenience goods	59
coupon	61
cross-border shopping	53
culture	66
Experiencers	72
extensive problem-solving behaviour	47
family life cycle	62
financial risk	50
Fulfilleds	71
Generation X	42
Generation Y	42
hedonic value of shopping	43
high involvement	46
husband-dominant decision	63
image	55
lifestyle	68
limited problem-solving behaviour	48
low involvement	46
Makers	72
marketer-dominated information sources	49
multiattribute model	54
national brands	60
neutral sources of information	49
nonstore shopping	53
opinion leader	65
outshopping	53
performance risk	50
personal motives	43
physical risk	50
principle-oriented consumers	71
private brands	60
psychographics	68
psychological risk	50
reference group	65
routinized response behaviour	48
self-orientation	71
shopping goods	59
social classes	65
social motives	43
social risk	50
specialty goods	59
status-oriented consumers	71
Strivers	72
Strugglers	72
syncratic decision	64
time loss risk	50
VALS	70
values	70
warehouse-style store	60
wife-dominant decision	63

DISCUSSION QUESTIONS

1. Briefly describe each of the stages (steps) of the consumer decision process discussed in the text. What are some retailers doing to help consumers buy more effectively?
2. Provide an example of each of the personal and social motives discussed in the chapter as reasons for shopping but not buying.

3. What are some of the reasons consumers might prefer to shop downtown? Why do some people prefer to shop in shopping centres?
4. What is the importance of image to the retailer? How does it affect the shopping behaviour of consumers? Think of the two largest department stores in your community. How would you describe their images?
5. What are some of the things retailers can do to reduce each of the six types of risks discussed in the chapter? What are some of the things that retailers can do to help consumers minimize the costs of shopping?
6. What are the major changes occurring within the modern Canadian family, and what impact would these changes have on retailers?
7. Why is it important for the backgrounds of salespeople to match the lifestyles of the customers they will be serving? How does this relate to the notion of reference group?
8. Very briefly review the eight segments in VALS , and give some specific examples of the types of stores where each would shop.
9. Summarize changes occurring today in society that are shaping Canadian values and discuss the resulting effects on consumer behaviour.

APPLICATION EXERCISES

1. Visit a national supermarket in your community, a discount or warehouse grocer food outlet, and a 24-hour type of food store. Prepare a paper that points out the similarities and differences between the three types of stores. Write a brief statement that summarizes your thoughts about the image of each type of outlet. Describe the characteristics of the people whom you think are most likely to shop at each of the three outlets.
2. Interview a local retail manager of your choice and try to identify the methods used by that manager to track and understand the company's customers. Write a report presenting your results according to the framework of this chapter.
3. Examine the range of retail outlets in your community for one specific group of items (e.g., fashion clothes, jewelry, gifts). Either by personal visits or by studying their advertising, regroup the stores who tend to appeal to a similar clientele. Then define this clientele in terms of age groups, gender, social class, or ethnic origin. In each case, explain your reasoning.
4. Visit a mall or the central business district and identify one or two stores that represent lifestyle merchandising in action. Relate the strategy to the positioning that you believe management is attempting. Discuss whether you feel management of the stores you identify needs to be more alert to changes in lifestyles.

SUGGESTED CASES

4. Dave Wong—Experiences of a New Immigrant
5. Bill Greene Buys Golf Equipment

Part 2

Developing the Retail Strategy

In *Part 2, Developing the Retail Strategy*, the conceptual, financial, and organizational aspects of the retail strategy are systematically developed. Chapter 4 deals with strategic planning, as a method of defining the objectives of the firm, and deciding how to compete. Franchising as a means of owning and operating a retail firm is examined in detail in Chapter 5. Chapter 6 discusses the critical issues in the recruitment, selection, training, and motivation of retail employees, as well as organizing the retail firm.

CHAPTER 4

RETAIL STRATEGY

CHAPTER OBJECTIVES

After reading this chapter you should be able to:

1. Understand the concept of a retailer's mission statement.
2. Identify the key elements of a retail strategy.
3. Evaluate the components of a positioning strategy.
4. Identify the major growth alternatives available to retailers.
5. List the steps involved in the strategic planning process.

In the early 1990s, Christine Magee and two future business partners were researching the mattress industry and discovered a promising niche for a retail mattress chain that would promote value and service. The competition in the Canadian mattress industry was department stores, holding 50 percent of the market, and a wide variety of retailers who held the remaining 50 percent. The partners felt that little marketing effort was offered by way of the competitors in this "sleepy" industry. In their research, they discovered Sleep Country USA, a small Seattle retail mattress chain with a significant market share. Ms. Magee and her partners gained the rights to its name and jingle for Canada. The success of the similar U.S. model confirmed their strategy for Sleep Country Canada. The key elements of the strategy are:

- Their "sleep expert" staff educating customers in a friendly low pressure sales environment
- The promise to beat any competitor's price by 5 percent
- Wide selection
- Full service, including a 60-day exchange guarantee for dissatisfied customers
- Free delivery and removal of the old mattress, which Sleep Country refurbishes and donates to a local charity.
- Prompt, friendly delivery staff

Possibly the key element in Sleep Country's strategy was the decision to have Ms. Magee appear in the ad campaigns. Women usually make the final decision in mattress purchases, so it made sense to have the president appear in the ads to target its audience better. According to industry experts, Ms. Magee's personality is what makes the campaign so effective. She brands the promotion to herself so customers feel like they are buying a mattress from her. Sleep Country runs a saturation advertising campaign, spending over $10 million annually to create brand awareness, dominate the Canadian retail mattress market, and get people to visit its stores first when it comes time to buy.

Today, Sleep Country Canada has over 50 stores, sales of over $90 million, and is one of the most widely known retail outlets in Canada. Its success is based on a retail strategy that delivers what the customer wants. As Ms. Magee says: "Why buy a mattress anywhere else?"[1]

The success of any strategy depends on how the retailer implements its plan and meets the needs of customers. In a highly competitive market a well-designed and well-executed strategic plan is essential for survival and growth. Christine Magee and her partners evaluated the retail mattress industry in Canada and identified strategies that would allow the firm to prosper and grow. The strategies are implemented through the retail mix, which includes pricing, promotion, product assortment, and location in order to accomplish the overall mission of the firm.

Sleep Country Canada's success is based on a retail strategy that delivers what the customer wants.

Courtesy Sleep Country Canada

MISSION STATEMENT AND GOALS

Strategic planning includes defining the overall mission or goals of the company, deciding on objectives that management wants to achieve, and developing a plan to achieve these objectives.

The **mission statement** describes what the firm plans to accomplish in the markets in which it will compete for customers it wants to serve. Retail Highlight 4-1 provides examples of Canadian retailers' mission and goal statements, presented in their annual reports. Most of these retailers have more detailed mission statements that are provided to their employees.

The first part of the chapter focuses on retail strategy and its key elements; the target market and positioning. Next, it examines the growth strategies available to the firm. The chapter concludes with a discussion of the strategic planning process.

Retail Highlight 4-1 Canadian Retailers' Mission and Goal Statements

Many retailers today are focusing on customer satisfaction as their primary goal. Listed below are mission statements from a number of Canadian retailers. Which retailers seem to have adopted a mission of customer satisfaction?

Thriftys' (a division of Dylex) mission is to be the leading jeanswear specialty retailer, providing unsurpassed value and fashion for teens and young adults. Thriftys leads the Canadian specialty retail scene by keeping its customers in mid-priced, fashion-forward, casual clothing.

Holt Renfrew's mission is to provide our customers with a world-class retail experience, selling high quality, high value merchandise, meeting their apparel and lifestyle needs, and extending extraordinary customer care.

Canadian Tire's vision, which guides the daily activities and long-term strategy of the enterprise, is to be the best at what customers value most. From this vision is derived the mission; to be the first choice of Canadians in automotive, sports and leisure, and home products, providing total customer value through customer-driven service, focused assortments, and competitive operations.

Zellers targets the budget-minded customer with the assurance of the lowest price. Excellent values are offered in both national and private brand merchandise and these are communicated aggressively with frequent advertising. Zellers is further distinguished by Club Z, its customer rewards program.

Sources: Dylex, Holt Renfrew, Canadian Tire, and Hudson's Bay Company Annual Reports.

RETAIL STRATEGY

A **retail strategy** identifies the retailer's target market and how the retailer plans to satisfy the target market's needs and build a competitive advantage through positioning. **Target markets** are the segments that management decides to serve. **Positioning** is how management plans to compete in target markets. It

Danier Leather's positioning is delivered through a well-designed retail strategy.

Courtesy Danier Leather

includes the retailer's mix—merchandise and services offered, pricing, communications program, store design and layout and location. Here are two examples of retail strategies.

Danier Leather is a designer, manufacturer, and retailer of high quality leather and suede products. With annual sales of over $89 million through its 57 plus stores, it targets men, women, and children who seek style, fashion, and value. It positions itself by offering unique products (through its in-house design team), at competitive prices (by manufacturing its own products), at convenient locations (including its own power centres). It monitors and quickly responds to market trends and consumer preferences through its marketing research and in-house design capabilities. In summary, it offers the target customer a superior combination of style and value.[2]

Mark's Work Wearhouse targets two segments; consumers who typically do not wear a suit and tie to work and consumers who have needs for casual and outdoor clothing and footwear. With over 290 stores (under three banners) and sales of over $260 million annually it positions itself by offering a wide and deep assortment within a niche concept (work and casual clothing) of well-known brand names and private labels in attractive destination stores with helpful, well-trained employees. It pays off, as Mark's is the number one retailer in work, safety, winter, and hiking boots. As well, a high percentage of customers are loyal and they shop at Mark's an average of seven times a year.[3]

Target Markets

Selecting target markets involves analyzing consumers, identifying groups or segments with similar needs, and deciding which segment or segments the retail firm can satisfy. Typically, the retail firm is seeking segments that offer the greatest opportunity for profits, considering the strength of competitors the firm will be facing. Consider the example of Le Chateau, a leading retailer of apparel, accessories, and footwear targeted at young-spirited, fashion-conscious men, women, and kids. Its target is primarily the 15–25-year-old age group for its 140 plus retail stores. It identified a market segment, girls aged 8 to 14, that was rapidly growing (part of the Echo Boom), with more money to spend (spending power of over $1 billion), had little competition, and matched some of Le Chateau's strengths. It introduced the Young Girl brand within its stores with considerable success.[4]

Spotting the same opportunity was Nancy Dennis, an experienced retail manager. She saw the potential of this untapped market and launched her own store called Ch!ckaboom in Toronto in 1997. Her target was "tween" girls from 5 to 13 and she marketed directly to these girls, not to their parents. To compete with large competitors like Le Chateau, Ms. Dennis focused entirely on merchandise for these "tweens" and offered fashion shows and special events for the segment.[5] As more competitors enter this market the winning firms will need to match this segment's needs with the merchandise assortment, atmosphere, and locations it desires. It is all part of the never-ending process of monitoring customers and competition to determine a successful retail strategy. The never-ending process caught up with Ch!ckaboom as the retailer opened a second outlet, over-extended itself, and went bankrupt in 1999.

Positioning

After target markets are selected a positioning strategy is developed. Positioning is the design and implementation of a retail mix to create an image of the retailer in the customer's mind relative to its competitors. A positioning map is often used to portray the customer's image and preference for retailers. More information on retail image from a customer's perspective is provided in Chapter 3. A hypothetical positioning map for women's apparel retailers is provided in Figure 4-1. The two dimensions, fashion and assortment, are two criteria that consumers might use in forming images of the stores. In this example, Sarah's Classics and Fudge's Apparel are close to each other because consumers see them as similar

Figure 4-1 Hypothetical Positioning Map for Women's Apparel Retailers

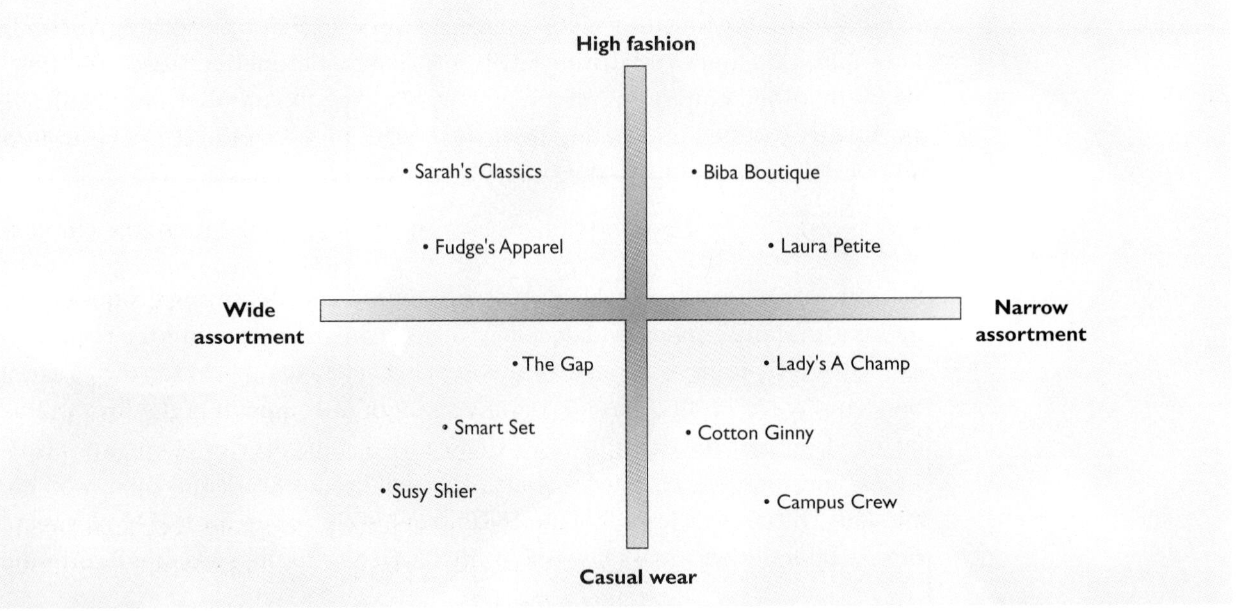

in terms of fashion and assortment. In contrast, Biba Boutique and Suzy Shier are far apart, suggesting that consumers have quite different images of them. Retailers use these maps to determine how consumers perceive them and their competition. Based on these consumer perceptions, a particular retailer can reinforce its position or consider repositioning if its current position is unsatisfactory.

Retailers can position themselves on a number of dimensions that are important to consumers, including customer service and convenience. For example, Holt Renfrew and Eddie Bauer excel at customer service, while Canadian Tire offers convenience with its numerous locations and extended hours.

The importance of developing and maintaining a positioning strategy must be stressed, especially in an era when competition in retailing is fierce. When Zellers' positioning was threatened by the entry of Wal-Mart into Canada, it reconfigured its stores to provide for broader, more competitive merchandise assortments and repriced its merchandise to maintain its dominant position against all competition. More recently, it has repositioned itself with more brand name and private brand merchandise to move slightly upmarket from Wal-Mart. It now markets the Martha Stewart Everyday home furnishings line and the Cherokee line of casual clothing as part of its repositioning strategy. It launched the Truly brand across a wide range of product categories to appeal to the Zellers' target shopper, women over 25 with a family. Again, if the Truly line is successful, it will help with the repositioning of Zellers.[6]

The positioning strategy involves the use of retailing mix variables. The **retailing mix** consists of all variables that can be used as part of a positioning strategy for competing in chosen markets. As shown in Figure 4-2, the retailing mix variables include product, price, presentation, promotion, personal selling, and customer service. Issues related to the retailing mix variables are included in Chapters 7 to 14 of the text.

The Gap, a popular and profitable specialty clothing chain, will be used to illustrate how the marketing mix variables play a critical role in positioning efforts within target markets. The Gap has over 2,100 stores in the U.S., Canada, and four other international markets, targeting consumers with a simple, yet powerful positioning strategy—quality, style, and exceptional service in an exciting and accessible atmosphere. The blend of some of the retailing mix variables in support of this position strategy is:

Product — The Gap designs its own clothes with the focus on simplicity. New collections hit the stores about every eight weeks and unpopular designs are marked down and quickly sold off. The Gap's current product strategy is "less is more," which offers more sizes and colours, but in fewer styles.

Price — Strict quality control procedures and using manufacturers in 40 countries ensures high quality, low costs, and a very good price for customers.

Presentation — Merchandise is displayed to emphasize the deep assortment of colours and is laid out on tables and shelves where it can be easily touched.

Figure **4-2** Variables of the Retailing Mix and Types of Decisions

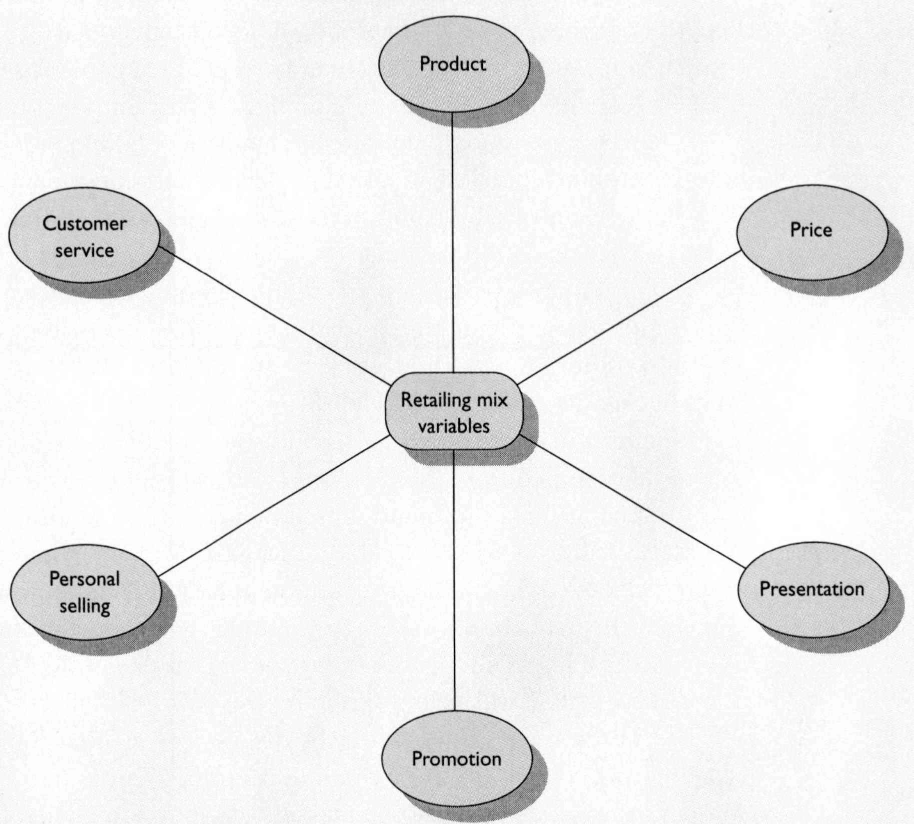

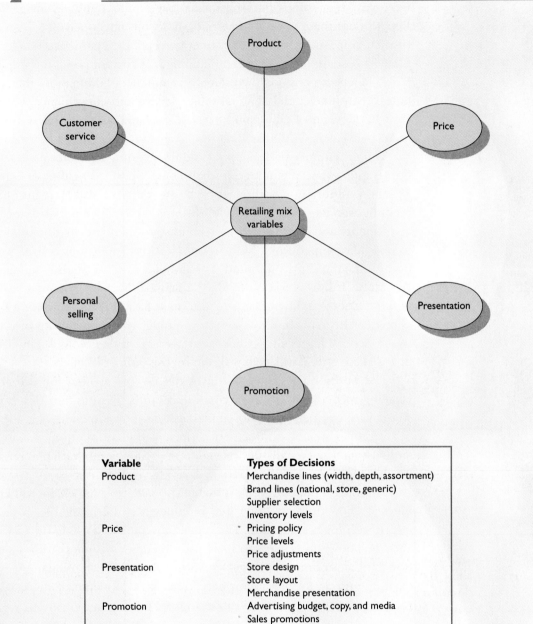

Variable	**Types of Decisions**
Product	Merchandise lines (width, depth, assortment)
	Brand lines (national, store, generic)
	Supplier selection
	Inventory levels
Price	Pricing policy
	Price levels
	Price adjustments
Presentation	Store design
	Store layout
	Merchandise presentation
Promotion	Advertising budget, copy, and media
	Sales promotions
	Publicity and public relations
	Web site
Personal selling	Sales force size, training, and compensation
	Motivation of staff
Customer service	Support services
	Credit policies
	Returns policies

Promotion — Advertising for the Gap has been striking, including award-winning campaigns that have featured Missy Elliott, LL Cool J, Lena Horne, and Aerosmith. The message communicates an individual sense of style.

Personal selling — Sales staff receive extensive training and constant contests are run to motivate the staff to provide quality service.

Customer service — The Gap has an Internet mail order business (www.gap.com) and has used technology to improve in-store service.[7]

www.gap.com

www.mec.ca

Mountain Equipment Co-op is an example of a retailer that developed a successful retail strategy and mix based on its mission statement (Retail Highlight 4-2).

Retail Highlight 4-2 Mountain Equipment Co-op—Example of a Retail Strategy

Mountain Equipment Co-op (MEC) was launched in 1971 by six experienced hikers who were frustrated by the lack of mountaineering equipment available in Vancouver. They decided to open a store that focused on the selling of good quality equipment for mountaineering, rock climbing, ski mountaineering and touring, and hiking. Later they added paddling and bicycle touring equipment. From its humble beginnings, MEC has grown to five mega stores with sales of over $130 million annually. They accomplished this by creating a mission statement in 1973 and designing and executing a retail strategy that has been consistently followed since that time.

- **Mission Statement** MEC is a member owned and directed retail consumer co-operative which provides products and services for self-propelled wilderness oriented recreational activities, such as hiking and mountaineering, at the lowest reasonable price in an informative, helpful and environmentally responsible manner.
- **Vision Statement** MEC will be recognized throughout Canada as the best supplier of quality wilderness equipment and services, as a model Co-operative, as a leader in environmental and social responsibility, and as an outstanding place to work.
- **Core Purpose** We support people in achieving the benefit of wilderness oriented recreation.
- **Retail Strategy** The target market is the consumer who is an outdoor enthusiast, seeks quality equipment, and is environmentally oriented. To date, MEC has over one million members. MEC's positioning is based on its vision statement. It offers a wide range of quality equipment and services at very competitive prices. Its store personnel are typically hiking enthusiasts who have a thorough knowledge of MEC's product line and can offer advice to beginners through to experts interested in outdoor activities. The stores are designed to reflect the four R's—reduce, reuse, recycle and reclaim. As one example, all the stores use high efficiency, low consumption energy systems. Its Web site (www.mec.ca) offers extensive information on its products, how to care for equipment, and many other "answers" to questions its customers might have. Since its beginning, MEC has granted over $2.7 million to conservation and environmental projects across Canada.

MEC is an excellent example of a retailer that followed its mission strategy in determining its target market, positioning and developing its retail mix variables. MEC is unique in that it has not wavered from its original concept—and has been successful because the concept appealed to a large segment of Canadians.

Source: www.mec.ca

GROWTH STRATEGIES

In broad terms, a retailer may consider pursuing one or more of four major growth strategies; market penetration, market development, retail format development, and diversification (Figure 4-3).

Market Penetration

Retailers following a strategy of **market penetration**, which targets existing market segments with existing formats, seek a differential advantage over competition by a strong market presence that borders on saturation. Retailers often use market penetration because it builds on the firm's existing strengths, which include knowledge of current customers and their preferences and the firm's familiarity with the merchandising lines. Such a strategy is designed to increase (1) the number of customers, (2) the quantity purchased by customers, and (3) purchase frequency.

Increasing the number of customers can be accomplished by adding stores and modifying in-store offerings. Sears Canada has added new national brands, devoted more space to apparel, and added more private labels to attract more customers to its stores. For years, Sobeys has added new stores in Atlantic Canada to increase its dominant position in this market. Sobeys also continues to remodel existing stores—making them brighter and larger—to attract more customers.

Improving the store layout and merchandise presentation can help to create an atmosphere that is conducive to more spending. Loblaws invests substantial sums to renovate existing stores to provide a comfortable shopping environment, and has expanded produce, seafood, deli, and bakery depart-

Loblaws introduces in-store pharmacies to attract new segments.

Courtesy Loblaw Companies Ltd.

Figure 4-3 Major Growth Strategies

Retail format		Market segment: Existing	Market segment: New
	Existing	**Market Penetration** • Increase number of customers • Increase quantity purchased by customers • Increase purchase frequency	**Market Development** • Reach new segments with existing formats • Expand markets
	New	**Retail Format Development** • Offer new retail formats to existing customers	**Diversification** • Develop new retail formats targeted at new segments

ments to get more customers into the stores and to increase the quantity purchased. Another approach is to encourage salespeople to cross-sell. Cross-selling involves salespeople from one department attempting to sell complementary merchandise from other departments to their customers. For example, a salesperson that has just sold a skirt to a customer would take the customer to the blouses to sell the customer a blouse that complements the skirt.

Toy supermarkets such as Toys "Я" Us, the U.S. chain with 56 stores in Canada, have been quite successful in implementing strategies designed to increase purchase frequency. The firm offers a complete selection of items that sell year-round. Customers know that when they buy a toy at Christmas they will find a good selection after Christmas to accommodate returns. Toys in the low- to medium-price ranges, often with strong licensed characters and video games, provide sales day in and day out. High-impulse items like pegboards, die-cast toys, and hobby kits lead to high customer traffic.

Market Development

A strategy of **market development** focuses either on attracting new market segments or completely changing the customer base. Market development normally involves bolder strategy shifts, more capital, and greater risk than a market penetration strategy. Examples of market development efforts include reaching new segments and market expansion.

Fast-food restaurants provide a good example of the strategy of attracting new segments in existing markets. McDonald's, through the years, has added, and sometimes dropped, chicken, breakfast items, salads, pizza, and Tex-Mex dishes to their menu. This helps attract consumers who are looking for something non-fried, less filling, with lower calories, and more nutritious than many traditional fast-food offerings. Harvey's has broadened its product line to include sandwiches to attract new segments. KFC has added potpie, crispy chicken, roast chicken, and hot wings to extend its chicken line. Wendy's has added sandwiches, fresh salads, potatoes, chili, chicken, and pitas to its hamburger line. Tim Hortons has added muffins, bagels, tea biscuits, soup, and sandwiches to its doughnuts and coffee to attract new segments. McDonald's also seeks to reach new segments by opening restaurants in unique, non-traditional sites including hospitals, subway and train stations, and tourist areas. In the Toronto SkyDome, McDonald's has four outlets, including one seating 600 people.

An effective strategy for many retailers is to expand on a geographic basis. The basic premise is that if the store concept works in one locale, it should work in another. Franchise retailers have successfully used geographic expansion for many years. Probably one of the most interesting and well-documented franchise expansions was McDonald's Canada's expansion to Moscow. With over 1,600 outlets in Canada, Tim Hortons has aggressively pursued market expansion. The takeover of Tim Hortons by Wendy's allowed for more rapid expansion for Wendy's and Tim Hortons as they continue to open a number of combo units (combining both Wendy's and Tim Hortons in one location) in both Canada and the United States.[8]

Retail Format Development

A **retail format development** is introducing a new retail format to customers. For example, Sears Canada has opened a number of freestanding furniture stores, called Whole Home, in Ontario, and plans to have up to 40 locations across Canada within a few years. At 3,252 square metres (35,009 square feet) the Whole Home Furniture Store has tripled the selling space for furniture, rugs, and decor items over what is offered by the typical Sears store. Sears Canada identified an opportunity for this kind of furniture store, which offers a wide range of value-priced and higher-end fashionable merchandise.[9] Canadian Tire is opening Auto PartSource stores, containing extensive auto parts, targeted at the "heavy do-it-yourself" customer and professional installers. Other examples are fast-food retailers like McDonald's, Tim Hortons and Subway who offer limited menus in smaller locations inside major stores (e.g., Wal-Mart) or gasoline stations.

Diversification

Diversification is a move to an entirely new retail format directed toward a market segment that the retailer currently does not serve. CIBC's strategy of selling automobile insurance through telemarketing is an example of diversification. The major Canadian banks' strategy of taking over investment firms and offering these services through the Internet is another example of diversification. Loblaws joining with CIBC and launching President's Choice Financial banking services is another example of diversification.[10]

THE STRATEGIC PLANNING PROCESS

The **strategic planning** process includes the steps a retailer goes through to develop a retail plan (Figure 4-4).

The Situation Analysis

To begin, the retailer conducts a **situation analysis**, which is an analysis of the strengths and weaknesses of the organization and the threats and opportunities in the environment. The internal or self-analysis focuses on the strengths and weakness of the firm. Strengths include what the firm is good at and its major resources and expertise. Weaknesses include the major problems faced by the firm and what it is doing poorly.

The external analysis focuses on the opportunities and threats and incorporates an examination of the external environment—legal, social, economic, and technological (Chapter 2). As well, the external includes an examination of the competitive environment. The competitive analysis assesses the abilities of competitors and the strategies they are likely to use. Retailers need to under-

Figure 4-4 The Strategic Planning Process

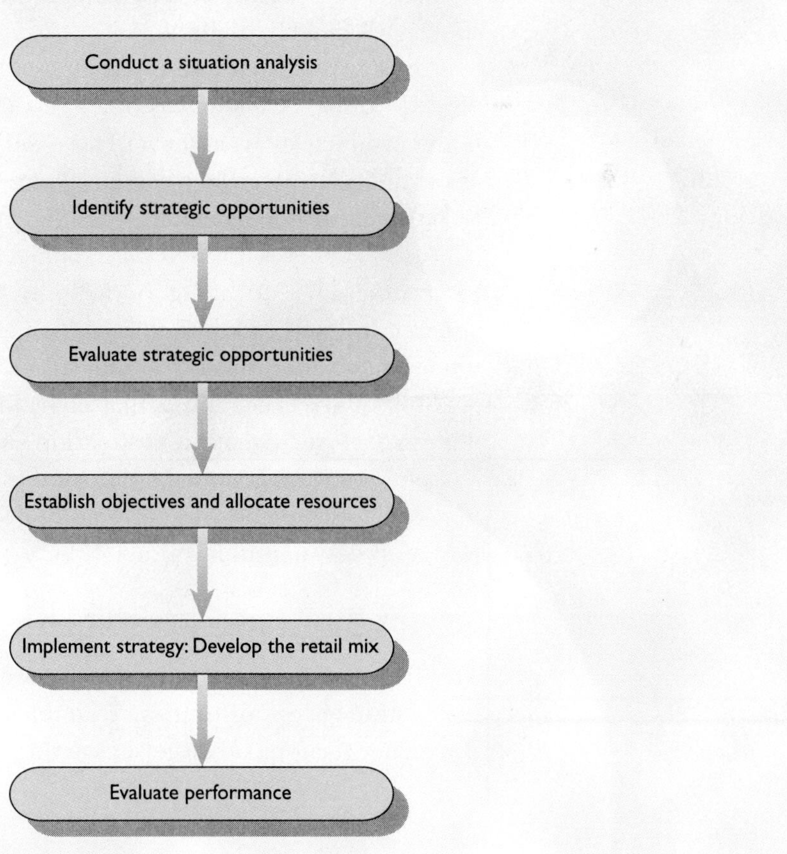

Retail Highlight 4-3 Forzani Identifies an Opportunity

The Forzani Group is Canada's largest sporting goods retailer with over 280 stores (Sport Chek and Forzani's) and sales of over $250 million. It conducted a situation analysis and found the following:

- Department stores getting out of sporting goods.
- Small regional players making little money because of the local economic and weather conditions.
- Independent retailers having to pay higher prices for merchandise because they could not obtain volume discounts.

This led them to the conclusion that a few national retailers would eventually dominate the industry. They then designed core strategies for their success including:

- Offering superior front line sales and service personnel.
- Achieving and maintaining a low-cost competitive position.
- Increasing product segment dominance in specific product categories.
- Developing and maintaining a clear differentiated retail offering.

Source: Forzani Group Ltd., *Annual Report* 1998.

stand their competitors in depth so they can develop an effective strategy to compete successfully. The Forzani Group took this approach in revising their strategy (Retail Highlight 4-3).

Mark's Work Wearhouse has identified some of its key strengths as: its people who offer excellent customer service; its ability to design quality private brand products such as Denver Hayes and WindRiver; its store format that offers assortment; and technology that allows for quick stock replacement. Mark's weaknesses include its inability to operate successfully in the U.S. market.

Mark's believes it is well placed to capture the opportunities in the external environment. The aging population means more consumer emphasis on apparel products oriented towards comfort and leisure; dressing more casually for business; and consumer values that are shifting to seeking more value in apparel. Mark's recognizes that its major competitors are moving to focused, dominant store formats in destination locations—power centres, power streets, and power strips. It anticipated this move and invested $25 million in the past five years to store improvements and now 80 percent of its stores are large store format in destination locations.[11]

Identify Strategic Opportunities

The result of the situation analysis forms the foundation for identifying the major strategic opportunities. Examples of these opportunities are provided in the earlier sections on target marketing and growth strategies.

One of Mark's Work Wearhouse's key strengths is its ability to design quality private brand products.

Courtesy Mark's Work Wearhouse

Evaluating Strategic Opportunities

The next step is to evaluate the strategic opportunities. In general, the retailer is seeking those opportunities where it can utilize its strengths and avoid its weaknesses. For example, BiWay, the 270-store discount chain, saw an opportunity develop when Zellers decided to move to slightly more upscale merchandise. It is capitalizing on that opportunity, in part, through its extensive renovation of its existing stores to make shopping easier for its customers. BiWay is also focusing on staying at the lower end of the discount market. It believes it can serve the customers who want a particular item, can come to their neighbourhood store, get their item, and be on their way in a few minutes.[12]

Establish Objectives and Allocate Resources

Next, the retailer sets specific objectives for the opportunity. The overall objectives and goals have been established within the mission statement. **Objectives** are statements of results to be achieved. Objectives may include profitability, sales volume, market share, or expansion results. Good objectives are measurable, are specific as to time, and indicate the priorities for the organization. To illustrate, Mark's Work Wearhouse's specific goals are related to profits, debt-to-equity ratio, current ratio, and other measures on an annual basis. The goals include sales per square metre, gross margin return on investment, and staff performance ratings. Examples of well-stated and poorly stated objectives appear in Table 4-1.

Table 4-1 Examples of Well-Stated and Poorly-Stated Objectives

Examples of Well-Stated Objectives	Examples of Poorly-Stated Objectives
Our objective is to increase market share from 15 percent to 18 percent in 2001 by increasing promotional expenditures 15 percent.	Our objective in 2001 is to increase promotional expenditures.
Our objective for 2002 is to earn after-tax profits of $5 million.	Our objective is to maximize profits.
Our objective is to open three new units by 2002 in each of the following provinces where the chain presently has no units: Nova Scotia, New Brunswick, and Prince Edward Island.	Our objective is to expand by adding units to the chain.

Implementing Strategy: Developing the Retail Mix

The next step is to develop the retail mix for each opportunity. The elements in the retail mix were discussed in "positioning" on pages 86–89.

Evaluating Performance

The final step is to evaluate performance. Managers need feedback on the performance of the new strategy to determine if objectives are being met. If not, the strategy will be re-evaluated and adjusted. In extreme cases, managers may have to evaluate the overall mission and goals of the firm. Chapter 17 focuses on several types of control systems that help management assess the success of operations.

The effectiveness of the long-term competitive strategy of the firm must also be evaluated periodically. This evaluation is required so that the firm's plan does not degenerate into fragmented, ad hoc efforts that are not in harmony with the overall competitive strategy of the business. Management can also use the process to decide what changes, if any, should be made in the future to ensure that the combination of retailing mix variables supports the firm's strategy.

CHAPTER HIGHLIGHTS

- To begin developing a retail strategy a firm prepares a mission statement. The mission statement tells what the firm intends to do and how it plans to do it.
- The retail strategy identifies the retailer's target market and how the retailer plans to satisfy the target market's needs and build a competitive advantage through positioning.
- Selecting target markets involves analyzing consumers, identifying groups or segments with similar needs, and deciding which segment or segments the retail firm can satisfy.
- Positioning is the design and implementation of a retail mix to create an image of the retailer in the customer's mind relative to its competitors.
- The positioning strategy involves the use of retailing mix variables. The retailing mix variables include product, price, presentation, promotion, personal selling, and customer service.
- A retailer may consider pursuing one or more of four major growth strategies; market penetration, market development, retail format development, and diversification.
- The steps involved in strategic planning are: (1) conduct a situation analysis, (2) identify strategic opportunities, (3) evaluate strategic opportunities, (4) establish objectives and allocate resources, (5) implement strategy: develop the retail mix, and (6) evaluate performance.

KEY TERMS

diversification	92	retailing mix	87
market development	91	retail format development	92
market penetration	90	retail strategy	84
mission statement	84	situation analysis	93
objectives	96	strategic planning	93
positioning	84	target markets	84

DISCUSSION QUESTIONS

1. What is meant by a retailer's mission statement? What does this statement normally include?
2. Explain the relationships between target markets, positioning strategy, and the retailing mix.
3. Discuss each of the following strategy alternatives: market penetration, market development, retail format development, and diversification.
4. Indicate the steps involved in developing a strategic plan.
5. What is a situation analysis? Which factors are evaluated in such an analysis? What is the ultimate value and use of a situation analysis?

APPLICATION EXERCISES

www.sedar.com

1. Mission statements of a number of Canadian retailers are included in the text. Go on-line (www.sedar.com) and find mission statements of other retailers from their annual reports. Be prepared to discuss if they provide a clear sense of direction for the firm.
2. Select at least three fast-food operations in your community. Indicate each firm's target market and positioning strategy and discuss how the elements of the retailing mix are combined in implementing the positioning strategy.
3. Select at least four women's clothing stores in your community. Suggest how each store might be positioned. Recommend how their positioning could be improved.

SUGGESTED CASES

1. The Independent Bookstore
2. Ralph's Optical
3. The Bay—A Question of Survival
6. Clean Windows, Inc.
7. Omer DeSerres: Artists' Supplies and Computers
8. Wing and a Prayer

CHAPTER 5

FRANCHISING

CHAPTER OBJECTIVES

After reading this chapter you should be able to:

1. Discuss the importance of franchising in the Canadian economy.
2. Evaluate the advantages and disadvantages of becoming a franchisee.
3. List the types of costs involved in becoming a franchisee.
4. Evaluate franchise opportunities.
5. Discuss the trends and outlook for franchising.

One of Canada's most successful franchises is M&M Meat Shops, which provides frozen quality meat and specialty food items to the public at reasonable prices. The first M&M Meat Shop was opened in Ontario in 1980 and today they have over 250 franchise stores across Canada, annual sales of over $180 million, and aggressive growth plans.

Mac Voisin, the co-founder, has designed a franchise strategy that includes the following components:

- *Mission*—to create a friendly food shopping experience that makes the customers say, "I'll be back."
- *Concept*—reasonably priced, high-quality meats and specialty food items. The product line includes a wide variety of flash-frozen, wholesome products including steaks, burgers, pork, chicken, and seafood. All items are ready for the oven, BBQ, or microwave. All items are flash-frozen to ensure retention of flavour and nutrition.
- *Marketing and Advertising*—continuously increase consumer awareness of stores as well as promote the dedication to store image, cleanliness, and service.
- *Selection of Franchisees*—preference is given to team players who appreciate the benefits of working within a proven system of operation. Franchisees should have good interpersonal and communication skills, be familiar with and involved in the community where the store is located, ensure success by working in and managing the store, and have the financial capacity to invest in the store as well as the financial ability to survive the first year with only a small salary.
- *Commitment to Franchisees*—M&M Meat Shops is committed to developing the strongest franchiser–franchisee relationship in the industry. To be part of the team is to be in business for yourself but not by yourself.

Mac Voisin has received numerous awards for his efforts, but he is particularly proud of the "Award of Excellence in Franchise Relations" he received from the Canadian Franchise Association. He says, "The strength of the franchise is the franchisees." He believes that communication, motivation, and trust are the prime factors that bolster the company's success and bind the franchisees together. As an example, M&M invests from $3,000 to $20,000 in its least profitable franchises to help turn them around. It also sends in consultants to develop ways to help the franchisee grow the business.

The company also returns a part of its profits back into the community. It is the largest supporter for The Canadian Foundation for Ileitis and Colitis and has raised more than $1.5 million for the foundation. All in all, it adds up to a successful franchise system that has never seen a franchisee fail and continues to outperform the competition.[1]

M&M Meat Shops, one of Canada's most successful franchises

Courtesy M&M Meat Shops

Franchising is one of the fastest growing segments of retailing in Canada with annual growth rates exceeding 20 percent. It accounts for about 40 percent of all retail sales, employs over one million Canadians, and represents over $100 billion in annual sales.

Franchises exist in virtually every line of trade today including lawn care, maid services, babysitters, dentists, tutors, funeral homes, dating services, skin-care centres, legal offices, and many others. About 1,100 franchising companies are operating in Canada today, with over 65,000 outlets across the country.

Surprisingly, even though many of the best-known franchises are the foreign giants—McDonald's, Pizza Hut, KFC—nearly 75 percent of all franchises in Canada were started in Canada. From Shoppers Drug Mart to Canadian Tire, from Provi-Soir to Harvey's, from Becker's to Uniglobe Travel, numerous franchises are owned and operated by Canadians.

Franchising has become a powerful force partly because economic factors have made growth through company-owned units difficult for many businesses. Therefore, by emphasizing independent ownership, franchising provides one method of addressing such problems as shortage of capital, high interest rates, and finding and hiring competent employees.

The formal relationship in franchising is established by a **franchise contract**, a legal document, that enables a firm (the **franchiser**) to expand by allowing an independent businessperson (the **franchisee**) to use the franchiser's operating methods, financing systems, trademarks, and products in return for the payment of a fee. Franchisers may sell products, sell or lease equipment, or even sell or rent the site and premises.

ADVANTAGES OF BECOMING A FRANCHISEE

A number of advantages exist for franchisees as part of a franchising program. The advantages include training programs and operating manuals that teach the retailer how to operate the business. Also, such programs allow individuals to enter a business with little previous experience. Management consulting and assistance may also be offered. Less cash may be required to enter the business since the franchiser may be willing to provide credit to a prospective franchisee.

The purchasing power of the franchiser can result in lower costs and higher gross profits for the franchisee. The franchisee also benefits from the national advertising and promotion by the franchiser and a recognized brand name and image already exists. Additionally, up-to-date merchandise assistance, displays, and other materials prepared by the franchiser are available.

An equally important advantage is the program of research and development that is designed to improve or add new products or services. Firms such as Wendy's and McDonald's have regular, ongoing research programs designed to identify new menu additions to help increase sales. Franchisees may also have access to a variety of fringe benefits such as dental plans at lower rates than are available to independent retailers.

The franchiser can also provide advice for handling special problems. Help is available in site selection, record-keeping, taxes, and other issues. As a result, around 90 percent of all franchises succeed in Canada, whereas around 80 percent of all new small businesses fail. However, these statistics are somewhat misleading, as the top 20 franchise operations account for over 80 percent of the business. The top ten Canadian fast-food franchises are presented in Table 5-1. More than 50 percent of Canadian franchisers have been in business for less than five years and most of these for less than two years. While the well-established franchises have excellent track records, some of the newer companies may not be as successful. Oversaturation is also a problem in the franchise area. Some of the hot franchises of yesterday, like bagel shops, are having difficulties today.

Table 5-1 Top Ten Fast-Food Franchises

Company	1998 Revenue ($millions)	Units	Business/Operations
McDonald's Restaurants of Canada	1,911	1,085	Franchiser/operator of McDonald's Restaurants
TDL Group	1,325	1,767	Franchiser of Tim Hortons, subsidiary of Wendy's International
Cara Operations	1,246	1,681	Franchiser/operator of Harvey's and Swiss Chalet; stake in Second Cup
Tricon Global Restaurants (Canada)	1,176	1,520	Operator of KFC, Pizza Hut, and Taco Bell
Yogen Fruz World Wide	645	2,516	Franchiser of Yogen Fruz; franchisee of Country Style Donuts
Subway Franchise System (Canada)	434	1,290	Franchiser of Subway Sandwiches and Salads
Burger King Restaurants of Canada	364	283	Franchiser of Burger King Restaurants in Canada
Scott's Restaurants	364	404	Operator of KFC (franchisee) and Highway Travel Centres
A&W Food Services (Canada)	341	525	Operator of A&W Restaurants
Dairy Queen Canada	298	617	Franchise/operator of Dairy Queen and Orange Julius
The Second Cup	283	669	Franchiser/operator of Second Cup

Source: Carolyn Cooper, "Canada's Top 100 Companies," *Foodservice and Hospitality*, July 1999, pp. 37–40.

DISADVANTAGES OF BECOMING A FRANCHISEE

Some disadvantages to franchising do exist. A major problem is the high cost of the franchise. Many franchisees feel they have to pay too much for supplies, fees, royalties, and other arrangements. In some cases, franchisees have found that they could purchase their supplies for less and have more favourable credit and payment terms if they dealt directly with a supplier rather than the franchiser. Some franchisers have extremely high royalty rates, sell too many franchises in a particular geographic area, and use debatable leasing contracts. The Subway franchise system has suffered from these problems. In particular, Subway franchisees are dissatisfied with the costs of the food supplied by Subway. Against the wishes of the co-owner, Fred DeLuca, the franchisees have formed a food buying co-operative to lower their food costs. As well, they have formed an association to combat what they regard as unfair practices by Subway. This includes the aggressive expansion strategy of Subway, which often means the setting up of too many franchises in an area. The result is lower sales for all franchisees in the area.[2]

The franchisee gives up flexibility in return for the right to a franchise. Operations are handled centrally at the corporate office and standard policies apply to all outlets. Individuals who want to run a business their own way would probably find a franchise unsuitable because of the inflexible nature of franchise operations. For example, in evaluating prospective franchisees, M&M Meat Shops prefer "team players" rather than "entrepreneurs" who want everything their own way. The rigidity that results from centralized operations can also be detrimental to franchisees who face unusual local market conditions. Decisions on how profits are to be shared between the franchiser and the franchisee as well as the conditions of termination typically favour the franchiser.

Conflicts occur between franchisers and franchisees. Because only one province, Alberta, has franchise legislation, franchisers are not required to disclose past failures, current performance, or audited financial statements in the rest of Canada. This has led to problems with franchisers exaggerating earnings and performance to prospective franchisees, breaking promises, and considerable litigation between franchisers and franchisees in Canada.[3]

THE COSTS OF FRANCHISING

Typically, a franchisee agrees to sell a product or service under contract and to follow the franchiser's formula. The franchiser is normally paid an initial fee for the right to operate at a particular location and a franchise fee based on monthly sales. The various costs involved in becoming a franchisee can include the following: the initial cost, the franchise fee, opening costs, working capital, premises expenses, site evaluation fees, royalties and service fees, and promotion charges. Each cost is briefly described below.

- *Initial costs.* Franchisees typically must pay an initial sum for the right to operate under the terms and conditions of the franchise. The amount may be only a down payment with the remainder financed by the franchiser or from other financing sources.
- *Franchise fee.* The right to use the trademark, licence, service mark, or other operating procedures of the franchise.
- *Opening costs.* Payments for equipment, inventory, and fixtures.
- *Working capital.* The financial resources required to meet operating expenses until the business breaks even.
- *Premises costs.* The costs of building, remodeling, and decorating.
- *Site evaluation fee.* The charge by the franchiser to determine the market potential at alternative sites.
- *Royalties.* A continuing service charge or payment based on monthly gross sales. In return for the charge, the franchiser provides such services as product research, management advice, accounting services, inventory records, and similar activities.
- *Promotion costs.* A percentage of gross sales, normally 1 or 2 percent, to support local advertising and promotion.

Typical franchise fees are structured as follows:

www.timhortons.com

- Tim Hortons—The franchise fee is $50,000 and start-up costs range between $200,000 and $245,000. Franchisees pay 4.5 percent of gross sales as royalties (www.timhortons.com).

www.mcdonalds.com

- McDonald's—Franchisees invest, on average, $700,000 to open a new outlet. The money pays for the equipment within the store and entitles the franchisees to a 20-year operating licence. Additionally, the franchisee pays fees generally totalling about 12.5 percent of annual gross sales in return for services that include training for management and crews, operating assistance, marketing, financial advice, and menu research (www.mcdonalds.com).

www.collegepro.ca

- College Pro Painters—There is no franchise fee and the start-up costs are estimated at $2,000 to $3,000. The royalty fee ranges between 14 percent and 17 percent of gross sales. All College Pro franchisees start out as university or college students (www.collegepro.ca).

www.yogenfruz.com

- Yogen Fruz—Franchisees pay a franchise fee of $25,000 and the start-up costs range between $55,000 and $130,000. They are required to pay 6 percent of gross sales for royalty fees and 2 percent for advertising (www.yogenfruz.com).

www.harveys.ca

- Harvey's—total start-up costs average around $450,000 and Harvey's Plus (i.e., Harvey's serving Swiss Chalet) average approximately $580,000 (www.harveys.ca).

IDENTIFYING FRANCHISE OPPORTUNITIES

Franchise opportunities are easy to identify. Choosing the right one is difficult. Intense competition exists among franchisers in attracting interested franchisees and advertisements for franchise opportunities are common in many newspapers. Both the *Financial Post* and *The Globe & Mail* have an advertising section devoted to franchise opportunities ranging from travel agencies to submarine sandwich shops to total body-care retail concepts. These advertising sections also include information on franchise fairs that individuals interested in getting into franchising can attend and meet representatives of franchisers. Various publications also provide information on available franchises.

The *Franchise Annual* and the *Buyer's Guide to Franchise and Business Opportunities* contain listings of Canadian franchise opportunities. *The Rating Guide to Franchises* rates a number of franchises including some Canadian operations. Each franchise is rated on six criteria; industry experience, franchising experience, financial strength, training and services, fees and royalties, and satisfied franchisees. Each criterion receives a rating between one and four stars. Business fairs are also held at which franchisers try to attract franchisees.

EVALUATING THE FRANCHISE AND THE FRANCHISE COMPANY

Alberta is the only province in Canada that has regulations governing franchising companies. Ontario is considering legislation that is similar to Alberta's. The Alberta Franchise Act is designed to protect potential franchisees by requiring the franchiser to provide complete disclosure of all the facts relating to the franchise being offered. A prospectus must be filed with The Alberta Securities Commission outlining the franchiser's financial capabilities, the history of the franchise company, its principals, and franchisees who have left the system. Potential franchisees in Alberta are entitled to a copy of the prospectus. Because most Canadian franchisees are not protected by specific legislation, individuals considering buying a franchise should proceed with caution and a lawyer should be consulted before any franchise purchase is made.

Evaluating the Company

The franchising company should have a good credit rating, a strong financial position, and a favourable reputation in the business community. The firm also should have been in business for a sufficient period of time to demonstrate expertise and the ability of its products or services to prosper in a competitive environment. The local and national offices of the Better Business Bureau should be contacted to determine if there have been complaints about the franchise company and, if so, how they were resolved. Also, the Canadian Franchise Association (www.cfa.ca) and the appropriate provincial Ministry of Consumer Affairs should be contacted about the reputation of the company and its product.

www.cfa.ca

Various books and other information sources are also available to help guide the potential franchisee through the evaluation process. The federal government provides information in newsletters and trade magazines (*Info Franchise Newsletter, The Franchise Handbook*), directories (*The Franchise Annual Directory, Opportunities Canada*), bank publications (*Buying a Franchise, Franchising—Doing it Right, Franchisor, The Franchise Commitment*), and publications designed for prospective franchisees (*Financing Your Franchise, Running a Successful Franchise, Tips and Traps When Buying a Franchise, The Complete Guide to Franchising in Canada*).[4] All of Canada's major banks offer both Web site information and guides to purchasing a franchise.[5]

Evaluating the Product or Service

Interested buyers should make sure the product or service has been tested in the marketplace before signing a franchise agreement. An independent investigation to determine the likelihood of the franchise's success in a local market is also in order. Equally important is an evaluation of the product warranties as part of the franchise agreement. The prospective buyer should understand the terms and conditions of the warranty, who is issuing the warranty, and the reputation of the company for keeping its promises. The buyer should also determine the legitimacy of claimed trademarks, service marks, trade names, and copyrights.

Understanding the Franchise Contract

The franchise contract varies by franchiser. The contract is a legal document that specifies the rights and responsibilities of the franchiser. The advice of a lawyer should be sought before signing the document. The critical areas to be considered in deciding whether to sign a franchise agreement include the nature of the company, the product, the territory, the contract, and assistance available.

All franchise contracts contain a variety of provisions to which the franchisee must agree. For example, the franchisee typically must agree to abide by the operating hours established by the franchiser. The franchisee often must also agree to use a standardized accounting system, follow company-wide personnel policies, carry a minimum level of insurance, use supplies approved by the franchiser, and follow the pricing policies established by the franchiser.

The franchiser often retains the right to require the franchisee to periodically remodel his or her establishment(s) and to allow the franchiser to conduct unscheduled inspections. Territorial restrictions are typically stated in the contract agreement and provisions for expanding into additional territories are carefully stated.

Some contracts impose sales quotas that are designed to ensure that the franchisee vigorously pursues sales opportunities in the territory. Most contracts also prohibit a franchisee from operating competing businesses and prohibit an individual whose franchise has been terminated from opening a similar type of business for a specified period of time.

Most franchise contracts cover a minimum period of 15 years. They typically contain provisions for termination and renewal of the contract, the franchisee's right to sell or transfer the business, and a provision for arbitration of disputes between the franchiser and franchisee.

Franchisee Advisory Councils

Some franchisees have established franchisee advisory councils to represent individual owners in dealing with the franchiser. The purpose of joining together is to allow the franchisees to accomplish common goals and to exert greater power over the franchiser in resolving issues that are of concern to the individual franchisees. The franchisees as a group can also support needed legislation, exchange ideas, and generally work to strengthen their position relative to the franchiser.[6]

TRENDS AND OUTLOOK

All trends indicate that franchising will continue to expand, creating great opportunities for existing and new businesses, developing new entrepreneurs, new jobs, new products, and new services. With long-term prospects for franchising bright, growing numbers of smaller companies, operating in local or regional markets, are turning to franchising for new ways to distribute their goods and services. Continuing economic improvement, stable prices, a slower-growing population, and increased competition for market share are turning many companies, both large and small, to franchising. Franchising can enable these firms to cover existing markets or penetrate new markets at minimal cost.

Although the overall trend for franchising is positive, some caution is warranted. Many markets are crowded with franchise outlets and new entrants have difficulty surviving. As well, whereas many of the large franchise markets, such as car dealerships, fast-food outlets and auto-service shops, are profitable, often the newer franchises are operating in markets that are considerably smaller and have limited opportunity. For example, franchises in home inspection, portable shelter, custom closets, and flavoured shaved ice have limited profit potential because the overall market size is relatively small.

Two new trends in franchising that are growing in popularity are "minifranchising" and "twinning." *Minifranchising* is a smaller version of a franchise, often located in a unique setting, such as a McDonald's in Wal-Mart. These McDonald's offer limited menus and rely on the store traffic to generate their business. Silcorp, which operates the Mac's and Mike's Mart chains in Canada, has entered franchise agreements with Subway and Pizza Hut to open limited menu versions of these franchises in a number of its locations. The advantage for the franchiser, like McDonald's or Pizza Hut, are the franchise fees and royalties from locations that would not be available with their existing formats. For the franchisee, the advantages are reduced dependence on existing product lines, increased sales from new product lines, and increased traffic because of the well-known franchises like McDonald's. The disadvantage for the franchiser may be some customer disappointment because the minifranchise does not offer the complete product line and for the franchisee, the possibility of a low return on investment because of the location.

Twinning is a concept that puts two different franchise operations under the same roof. The idea is to find a combination where consumers shop for two different types of product at different times of the day or to offer consumers more choice and thereby attract a wider market segment. For example, combining doughnut and ice cream franchises may lead to a more balanced and profitable operation. The $400 million merger of Wendy's and Tim Hortons is probably the most well-known example of twinning, but a number of franchise firms have pursued this option (Retail Highlight 5-1). Harvey's, one of Canada's largest restaurant chains, is adding Church's Chicken franchises into some of its Harvey's restaurants and Swiss Chalet into others. The strategy of twinning has improved sales and profits for Harvey's.

Business and personnel franchise services in particular are expected to continue to rise significantly for the next few years. In particular, the small office/home office (SOHO) market is growing rapidly as more individuals start their own home-based businesses. One franchise service that is directly targeting this market is Mail Boxes Etc. (MBE), which is the world's largest franchiser of retail business, communication, and postal services (over 3,700 MBE centres worldwide). MBE provides the SOHO market with extensive services including packing and shipping, a business address, and a one-stop source for copies, faxes, office supplies, and other services. As one example, MBE provides customized on-line services that help small businesses complete many business tasks such as marketing their products or services, finding employees, or researching the competition. These services provided by MBE allow a small business to operate like a big business without investing in office space and equipment or other overheads.[7]

Companies will also need additional business and management consulting services to provide innovative marketing ideas geared to a better-educated and more affluent consumer in highly segmented markets. The continued drive by businesses and governments to cut costs has led to increased franchising in areas like document shredding, cleaning services, sign and graphic shops, copying services, and print shops.[8]

In summary, major changes are in progress in the economy as a whole. As we move into the new century, creativity and imagination in the treatment of goods and services will be richly rewarded. The continuing trend toward a service economy and the desire of individuals to "be their own boss" suggest that franchising will be a growing method of doing business in the future.[9]

Retail Highlight 5-1 Wendy's and Tim Hortons: The Fast-Food Alliance

In late 1995, when Wendy's and Tim Hortons merged, it was the largest example of "twinning" or alliances in the fast-food business in Canada. The benefits to combination restaurants like Tim Hortons–Wendy's are:

- More product offerings to meet different tastes.
- Combo units cost less to build, thereby improving profitability.
- More use of dining areas throughout the day (Tim Hortons for breakfasts and snacks, Wendy's for lunches and dinners).
- More cost savings by pooling supplies, staff administration, and real estate.
- Entry into smaller towns because of the added draw of both restaurants.

Other franchise chains have purchased twinning so consumers can have:

- Frozen yogurt and donuts (Yogen Fruz and Country Style Donuts).
- Fried chicken and burgers (Church's or Swiss Chalet and Harvey's).
- Pizza and chicken (Pizza Delight and Le Coq Roti).
- Cookies and fries (Mrs. Field's Cookies and New York Fries).

Industry experts see these firms as trying to create a new market and draw more people into their stores at a time of day when the stores usually don't attract customers. As well, many consumers prefer to buy food from familiar and trusted brand names.

Twinning gives the consumer three choices in this location.

Sources: Marina Strauss, "Marriage All the Rage in Fast-Food Field," *The Globe & Mail*, August 10, 1995, p. B7 and Wendy's *Annual Report*, 1998.

CHAPTER HIGHLIGHTS

- Franchising is a way of doing business that allows an independent businessperson (the franchisee) to use another firm's (the franchiser) operating methods, financing systems, trademarks, and products in return for payment of a fee.
- Franchising is one of the fastest-growing segments of retailing in Canada and accounts for about 40 percent of retail sales. Experts predict continued growth in new franchises and sales. About 1,100 franchising companies are operating in Canada today with over 65,000 outlets across the country.

- The overriding advantage of a franchising program is the ability to quickly expand a company with limited capital. Another advantage of franchising is the training programs that are available that allow an individual to enter a business with no experience. The franchisee can also benefit from the purchasing power of the franchiser. Equally important are the programs of research and development that many franchisers have established to improve their product or service.
- A major disadvantage of a franchise is the high initial fee. The franchisee also gives up some flexibility in return for the right to purchase a franchise. Complaints may arise over the nature of the franchise contract.
- The various costs involved in becoming a franchisee can include the initial cost, the franchise fee, opening costs, working capital, premise expenses, site evaluation fees, royalties and service fees, and promotion charges.
- Evaluating franchise opportunities includes determining the credit rating, financial position, and reputation of the franchiser. As well, the product or service offered should be market tested and the franchise concept should be thoroughly understood.
- The typical franchise contract gives the franchisee the right to sell a product or service under an arrangement that requires the individual to follow the franchiser's formula. The franchiser is usually paid an initial fee for the right to operate at a particular location and a franchisee fee based on monthly sales.
- Trends indicate that franchising will continue to expand, creating opportunities for new businesses, jobs, and products and services.

KEY TERMS

franchise contract	101	franchiser	101
franchisee	101		

DISCUSSION QUESTIONS

1. Discuss why franchising has become a powerful force in retailing.
2. What are the major disadvantages of franchising?
3. Write a brief essay on the cost elements that are typically included as part of a franchising contract.
4. What are the issues a prospective franchisee should evaluate in deciding whether to purchase a franchise?
5. What are the ingredients of a typical franchise contract?
6. Highlight the advantages and disadvantages of becoming a franchisee and of franchising as a way of doing business.
7. What are the legal restrictions on franchising?
8. Discuss the trends and outlook for franchising.

APPLICATION EXERCISES

1. Review the various sources cited in the chapter (these typically are found in your library and on the Internet) to establish the initial opening costs for the following types of franchises: A national food franchise such as Tim Hortons Donuts, a personal service franchise such as Weed Man, a retail cosmetics franchise such as Faces, and a car rental business such as Rent-A-Wreck.
2. Talk to the owner/managers of three fast-food franchises in your community and write an essay outlining the primary advantages and disadvantages they see in being a franchisee.
3. Find and evaluate ten Web sites that offer information for Canadians who want to buy a franchise (Hint: start with the Canadian Franchise Association's Web site at www.cfa.ca, then check out Web sites provided in the Notes for this chapter at the end of the book.)

SUGGESTED CASES

6. Clean Windows, Inc.
9. The Franchising Exercise

CHAPTER 6

DEVELOPING THE HUMAN RESOURCES PLAN

CHAPTER OBJECTIVES

After reading this chapter you should be able to:

1. Understand the importance and content of human resources policies.
2. Discuss how to determine needed job skills and abilities.
3. Plan and conduct an effective retail personnel recruitment and selection process.
4. Discuss the need to train employees.
5. Outline and describe the various methods for evaluating and compensating retail employees.
6. Discuss the issues involved in employee motivation and job enrichment.
7. Explain how to organize for profits.

According to a recent Angus Reid poll, 39 percent of Canadians said the level of service in retail stores had improved, and 44 percent that the level of knowledge among the sales staff is better than before. However, the main complaints of the same Canadians deal with lack of assistance (18 percent), long lines (16 percent), aggressive and rude staff (14 percent), and inexperienced staff (8 percent). Reacting to poor service, 85 percent said they would go to a competitor's store, 80 percent would go to that store less often, and 40 percent would never patronize the store again. If the product is not in stock, 52 percent said they would go to another store.[1] Also, many Canadians indicate that they like to shop in the United States because of the excellent service they receive; and the U.S. stores who entered the Canadian market, like Wal-Mart, are capitalizing on this reservoir of goodwill.

Thus, there is more to good customer service than a smiling and polite salesperson. A large part of excellent customer service is a highly trained and competent staff. Consider the following examples: [2]

- Ian Outerbridge needed new screens for his summer cottage. Once the order came in, they were too big and would not fit. Another supplier sent two right sides of another order instead of one right and one left. When he sent them back, he received in return two left sides! One retailer greeted him jokingly by saying: "What mistake can we make for you this morning?"
- When a regular customer complained that her favourite lunch selection, "black bean fried rice," was not on the menu, Christine Renner, manager of Vancouver's Fortes Seafood House, would naturally respond in a positive way. If that valued customer would call the day before her next lunch, Ms. Renner would make arrangements. And, when the customer showed up, she was handed a menu where the favourite dish was featured as the first special of the day. This level of service is no accident, but the result of lots of planning and special training by Bud Kanke, the owner of Joe Fortes Seafood House, The Cannery, and The Fish House. In 1995, company-wide training cost $200,000, and *all* employees, including bussers, have to go through the program.

The unique success of well-known retail outlets such as Joe Fortes Seafood House and Wal-Mart depend to a substantial degree on the skills, motivation, and dedication of their employees. Employees should not be regarded as throwaway assets. All dimensions of the human resources plan, ranging from selection and placement to pay and performance appraisal, should be structured to allow employees to feel they are a vital part of the organization. Sensitivity to the issues inherent in employee motivation and job enrichment are also important in progressive organizations.

THE RETAIL HUMAN RESOURCES CHALLENGES

The human resources environment has become increasingly volatile in recent years as a result of such issues as testing for illegal drug use, concern about AIDS, undocumented foreign workers, growing labour shortages for hourly employees, concerns over child care, and the impact of mergers, acquisitions, restructuring, and the North American Free Trade Agreement on human resources.

Human resources staffs, as never before, are looking for ways to motivate and empower employees. The challenges are numerous:

- Training a nontraditional work force consisting increasingly of immigrants and older people.

- Competing against other industries that normally pay more for entry level and mid-level management employees.
- Identifying innovative approaches to finding and keeping good employees.
- Meeting expectations for sales increases, productivity, and customer satisfaction.
- Finding ways to remain competitive as mid-level managers and top-level executives continue to be eliminated in downsizing programs.[3]

All managers need to understand and appreciate the importance of good human resources policies in the recruiting, training, and compensation of employees in addition to organizational issues. Understanding the goals and values of employees can also be of great benefit in avoiding unnecessary conflicts in the enterprise.

The development of a human resources plan in helping to implement competitive strategy is thus becoming increasingly important in retailing. One reason is that the age of growth through expansion seems to be almost over for many firms. More emphasis is being placed on market share management and improving productivity through better use of people, current assets, and facilities. Both of these avenues for growth put stress on human resources personnel because of the labour-intensive nature of retailing. The payroll/sales ratio runs to as much as 25 percent in the higher-price/better-service stores such as Holt Renfrew. The specialty store is the most labour-intensive type of retailer, with payroll ratios as high as 30 percent.

Success in maintaining a result-oriented focus in the organization depends on defining or enforcing performance standards at each level in the organization. The focus should always be on achievement, producing results by using the full array of rewards and punishments outlined in this chapter. Intense people orientation, constantly reinforced, is the key to getting everyone in the organization committed to the goals to be achieved. The key element is making champions out of the people who turn in winning performances. Firms such as Disney (see Retail Highlight 6-1) refer to employees as *cast members*, and McDonald's uses the term *crew member*. They all seek out reasons and opportunities to reward good performance.

The remaining portions of this chapter focus on four things:

1. What the managers are expected to do for the company
2. What the company can do for the employee
3. How the managers and employees can work together to accomplish organizational objectives
4. How to effectively organize the company

Retail Highlight 6-1 Good Employees Are a Major Part of the Retail Offering

Everyone who is "employed" by Disney, from dishwasher to monorail operator, begins with three days of training and indoctrination at Disney University. Disney never hires an employee for a job. The "actors" are "cast" in a "role" to perform in a "show." Sometimes the show is called Walt Disney World, sometimes Disneyland, sometimes The Disney Store, and so forth. Their main purpose is to look after the "guests." Disney has never had customers.

Every "cast member" is provided with a "costume," not a "uniform." That way a guest doesn't have to ask "Do you work here?" Each cast member is told not to hesitate to get a new costume if the old one gets dirty. Cast members do not work the floor; they are "on stage." The stock rooms and other nonpublic areas are "backstage."

One cast member is always designated to be the "greeter." The greeter position is a very important one. The role is to greet all guests as they enter and as they leave, and to thank them for "visiting our store," not for shopping. The greeter sets the tone for the guests' visit and also acts as a small deterrent to shoplifting because people are less likely to shoplift if they have been recognized by someone when they entered the store.

The words *no* and *I don't know* are not part of the Disney script. Everything is positive. Instead of "I don't know," cast members say, "I'll find out." Instead of, "We don't have any," cast members say, "We are out of," and instead of saying, "That item won't be available until," they say, "That item will be available on." Any response to the guest is phrased in a positive manner.

The Disney Store does not have stuffed animals; it has "plush" animals. A Disney Store cast member always points with an open palm, not the index finger. When you point with the index finger, four fingers are pointing back at you.

The Disney show is several things. It's the entire experience that is created by the environment, the merchandise, the attractions, the music, and so forth, but, most importantly, it is the people. The cast members have a certain look that includes style of hair, makeup, name tags, and so on, all of which are a part of the Disney script.

Source: Prepared by Donald Smith, a cast member at The Disney Store, a Division of Walt Disney Enterprises.

THE JOB ANALYSIS AND JOB DESCRIPTION[4]

A manager looking for someone to fill a job should spell out exactly what he or she wants in a job description. Imagine an owner/manager advertising for a "salesperson." What should the applicant be able to do? Just tally sales receipts accurately? Keep a customer list and occasionally promote products? Run the store while the manager is away? The job of salesperson means different things to different people. Retailers should determine what skills are needed for the job, what skills an applicant can get by with, and what kind of training should be given to the employee.

Good *job descriptions* and *job specifications* are excellent tools but they will not, by themselves, assure the best possible selection and assignment of employees to jobs, nor will they assure that the employees will be trained and paid properly. If good job descriptions and clear job specifications exist, however, selection, training, and salary decisions will be much easier and better.[5] Job descriptions and job specifications are written from a *job analysis.*

Job Analysis

Job analysis *is a method for obtaining important facts about a job.* Specifically, the job analysis obtains answers to four major questions that the job description and job specification require:

1. *What* physical and mental tasks does the worker accomplish?
2. *How* does the person do the job? Here the methods used and the equipment involved are explored.
3. *Why* is the job done? This is a brief explanation of the purpose and responsibilities of the job that will help relate the job to other jobs.
4. What *qualifications* are needed for this job? Here are listed the knowledge, skills, and personal characteristics required of a worker for the job.

A job analysis thus provides a summary of job (1) duties and responsibilities, (2) relationships to other jobs, (3) knowledge and skills, and (4) working conditions of an unusual nature.

Conducting a Job Analysis

An easy way to begin a job analysis is to think about the various duties, responsibilities, and qualifications required for the position and jot them down on a note pad. The ingredients of a job analysis outline are shown in Figure 6-1. Management should chat with the job supervisor or a person who now holds the job to fill in the details about the job.

When conducting a job analysis, it is important to describe the job and the requirements of the job rather than the employee performing it. (The present employee may be overqualified or underqualified for the job or simply have characteristics irrelevant for the job.) It is also a good idea to keep in mind the ultimate goals of job analysis: to simplify and improve employee recruitment, training, and development, and to evaluate jobs for determination of salary and wage rates.

Using the Job Analysis

After a job analysis has been conducted, it is possible to write a job description and job specification from the analysis. A **job description** is that part of a job analysis that describes the content and responsibilities of the job and how the job ties in with other jobs in the firm. The **job specification** is that part of a job analysis that describes the personal qualifications required of an employee to do the job.

Figure 6-1

Job Analysis Outline for a Sales Manager

Duties

Assist customers with purchases
Develop expertise of staff
Achieve sales goals
Schedule hours and assign work to subordinates
Complete performance reviews on time
Present merchandise
Manage inventory
Open and close store
Provide floor supervision

Education

University or college graduate

Relationships

Report to store manager daily
Meet daily with subordinates

Knowledge/Skills

Transaction entry
Merchandising and operating procedures
Selling skills and product knowledge
Sales analysis knowledge
Knowledge of company's human resources standards and procedures
Performance review skills
Merchandise program knowledge
Inventory control procedures
Employee training
Supervisory skills

Physical Requirements

Capable of basic manual skills
Able to work on feet all day

On-the-Job Hazards/Working Conditions

No danger if safety rules and regulations are followed.

Source: Sears Canada

Figure 6-2 demonstrates the relationship of job analysis to job description and job specification. In addition to their usefulness in explaining duties and responsibilities to the applicants, job descriptions and specifications can help with:

Figure 6-2 Relationship among Job Analysis, Job Description, and Job Specification

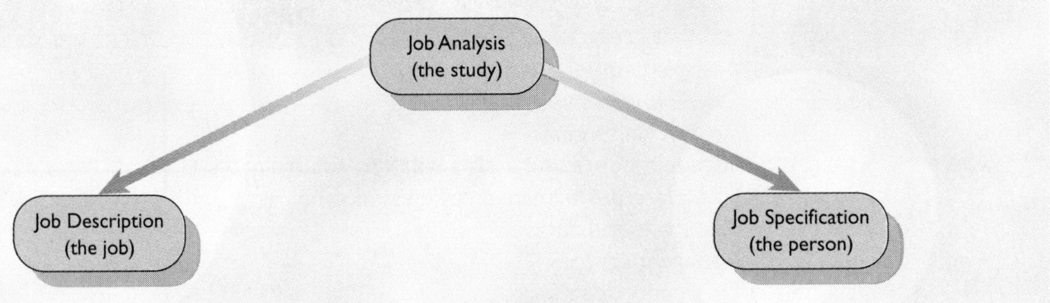

- **Recruiting.** Job descriptions and specifications make it easier to write advertisements or notices announcing the job opening, or explaining the job to an employment agency.
- **Interviewing applicants.** Since a job description provides a written record of the duties and requirements of a particular job, and a specification provides the qualifications needed for the job, they can be very helpful in planning an interview, especially as guidelines for asking the applicant questions about his or her abilities.
- **Training and development of new employees.** Having the duties of each job clearly defined can provide a basis for determining what knowledge and skills should be taught to new employees and helps to plan training so that (*a*) important skills are learned first and (*b*) the training is comprehensive.
- **Coordination.** Job descriptions, when they are available, can insure that people know what is expected of them and that their activities are coordinated.
- **Setting wage rates and salaries of employees.** By providing a perspective of the relative amounts of work required and qualifications needed for different positions, fairer wage rates and salaries may be established. Remember that the minimum wage varies with the federal government, and from province to province (the highest is British Columbia, and the lowest is Newfoundland).[6]
- **Employee relations.** The information about the job in the description can assure that fewer misunderstandings will occur about the respective duties and responsibilities of various jobs.

Job Description

A job description is a summary of the important facts about a particular job. It states in a concise, clear way the information obtained in a job analysis. A fully adequate job description should be outlined on less than one page. For instance, a job description for a buyer at Sears Canada could be written as in Figure 6-3.

Job Specification

A job specification, like a job description, is written from the job analysis and describes those personal requirements that should be expected of anyone who is placed on the job, as well as any unusual or hazardous environmental conditions that the job holder must be prepared to accept. A job specification thus describes the type of employee required for successful performance of the job. One way to prepare a job specification is shown in Figure 6-4.

Figure **6-3**

Job Description for a Buyer

JOB DESCRIPTION

JOB TITLE: Buyer Date:________

Statement of the Job

Develops a marketing plan and advocates what is best for the company—item by item, line by line—and brings forth those recommendations to the company via the department/group marketing plan.

Major Duties

1. Makes recommendations on items and/or lines. This includes private label/national brand or combination, selling plan, item price by geographic region, vendor, inventory investment, and assortment and depth by store volume.
2. Purchases goods as agreed to in the marketing plan.
3. Ensures that sales personnel and customers understand the value of the product line.

Relationships

The buyer works with other buyers and store managers in preparing the group marketing plan. The buyer works with vendors to obtain merchandise and store personnel to market merchandise.

Source: Sears Canada

Figure **6-4**

Job Specification for a Sales Manager

JOB SPECIFICATION

JOB TITLE: Sales Manager Date:____________

Education: *(List only that which is really necessary for the job, e.g., high school, college, trade school, or other special training.)*
University or community college graduate

Experience: *(The amount of previous and related experience that a new employee should have.)*
None specifically.

Knowledge/Skills: *(List the specific knowledge and skills that the job may require.)*
Must know how to:

- enter customer transactions.
- work within the merchandising and operating procedures (the list would include the elements listed in the job analysis in Figure 6-1).

Physical and Mental Requirements: *(Mention any special physical or mental abilities required for the job, e.g., 20/20 eyesight, availability for irregular work hours, ability to work under time pressure, etc.)*
Must have a good personality and be able to lead and motivate people.

Source: Sears Canada

RECRUITING APPLICANTS

When the owner/manager knows the kind of skills needed in a new employee, she or he is ready to contact sources that can help recruit job applicants. Application forms help screen and select the best candidates.

Selecting the Right Recruiting Methods

The recruiting methods used depend upon what type of employee is sought and how hard the retailer wants to search for the best available candidate.

Each recruiting method has its advantages and disadvantages. Some may be time-consuming, such as direct newspaper ads, which require screening of all who apply, or notices on college and university bulletin boards, which may be very slow in bringing in an adequate number of applicants. Others can be fairly costly, such as employment agencies, where competent applicants often expect the retailers to pick up the fee.[7] Some can be used concurrently, but it would be inefficient to use others in such a way.

In each province there is an employment service with several Canada Employment Centres. All are affiliated with Human Resources Development Canada, which operates a computerized, nationwide job databank. Local Canada Employment Centres are ready to help businesses with their hiring problems. A retailer should be as specific as possible about the skills required for a job, and notify the Canada Employment Centre, which will post the notice of a job opening with its requirements on its bulletin board. All interested applicants are interviewed by a Centre counsellor, and if the assessment is positive, a referral is made to the retailer.

www.hbc.com/careers

The Internet is a very useful method of identifying applicants quickly and inexpensively. For example, check the Web site of the Hudson Bay Company at www.hbc.com/careers.

Private employment agencies can also help in recruitment. However, the employee or the employer must pay a fee to the private agency for its services.

Another method of recruiting is a *"Help Wanted" sign* in the front window. But there are drawbacks to this method: a lot of unqualified applicants may inquire about the job, and a retailer cannot interview an applicant and wait on a customer at the same time.

Newspaper advertisements are another source of applicants. They reach a large group of job seekers, and retailers can screen these people at their convenience. But a retailer should think twice before listing the store's phone number in the ad. He may end up on the phone all day instead of dealing with customers.

Job applicants are also readily available from schools, colleges, and universities. The local high school may have a distributive education department, where the students work in the store part-time while learning about selling and merchandising in school. Many part-time students stay with the store after they finish school. Colleges and universities also provide placement services for students, and are a good source of talent for retailers.

Reviewing Recruiting Practices

It is useful to review the firm's recruiting practices from time to time to see how they can be improved. The retailer may wish to simply note what brought success, as well as the methods that did not seem to work well. For example, it could be that a Web site seems to bring better applicants than posting notices on college or university bulletin boards.

Developing Application Forms

Some method of screening the applicants and selecting the best one for the position is needed. The application form is a tool that can be used to make the task of interviewing and selection easier. An example is shown in Figure 6-5. The form should have blank spaces for all the facts needed as a basis for judging the applicant. Retailers will want a fairly complete application so they can get sufficient information. However, the form should be kept as simple as possible.

The retailer must not abuse the information from the application in hiring. The Canadian Human Rights Act prohibits discrimination in employment based on race, national or ethnic origin, religion, age, sex, marital status, family status, disability, and conviction for which a pardon has been granted.[8] This act applies to all departments and agencies of the federal government, all Crown corporations, and businesses under federal jurisdiction. The Act is administered by the **Canadian Human Rights Commission** and a Tribunal with broad powers to order an end of the discriminatory practice, some financial compensation for the victim, or to develop and implement an affirmative action program (Section 15). This last application of the Act has been strengthened by the Constitution Act of 1982, especially the Charter of Rights and Freedoms.

In areas not under federal jurisdiction, which includes most retailers, protection is given by provincial human rights laws, which are similar in contents and remedies to the federal law.

Figure **6-5** Sample Employee Application Form

APPLICATION FOR EMPLOYMENT

Name: ____ Date: __________

Last First Middle

Present address: __________________________ Social insurance no.: ______________

Telephone number: ________________________ Driver's licence no.: ______________

Indicate dates you attended school:

Elementary from ________________ to ________________

High school from ________________ to ________________

College from ________________ to ________________

Other (specify type and dates) ____

Can you be bonded? ______________ If yes, in what job? ______________________

Do you have any physical limitations that preclude you from performing certain kinds of work? ________

If yes, describe each and specify work restrictions: __________________________________

____

List below all present and past employment, beginning with most recent:

Name and address of company	From Mo/Yr	To Mo/Yr	Name of supervisor	Reason for leaving	Weekly salary	Describe the work you did

May we contact the employers listed above? ________ If no, indicate which ones you do not wish us to contact:

____

Remarks: ____

____

____

SELECTING EMPLOYEES

After recruiting a number of job candidates, the retailer has to weed out the unqualified ones and then select the best remaining candidate for the job. The main tools will be the questions asked and perhaps pre-employment tests. Answers to some questions may be obtained through a résumé, but by far the most informative answers come from a job interview and the job application form.

Many different selection methods are available. These include personal interviews, tests, and recommendations from various people who had contact with the candidates. The human resources office seeks to develop objective criteria in screening applicants to achieve the best match of person and position. One frequent approach to this problem is the development of performance criteria. Such an approach involves identifying the characteristics of those who perform the job in a superior manner. These characteristics are then sought in potential new employees. Ideally, a limited number of characteristics can be isolated. Executives can use the performance criteria in predicting which applicants will perform most satisfactorily. Such predictors may include intelligence scores, tests of manual dexterity, formal education, or past related job experiences.

One potential problem, however, is bias against some applicants because of the measures being used. Federal, provincial, and local governments actively challenge selection tools that can lead to bias in hiring. Companies can use employment tests if they can show that the tests are valid and reliable in predicting job success and that no better way exists to make such evaluations. This process is difficult and requires the use of statistics, including coefficients of correlation and other measures. Tests may also be biased because of cultural or language problems for some applicants.

The burden of proof rests with the employer. The employer must be able to show that the procedure utilized is capable of predicting job performance and does not systematically discriminate against any one group of applicants. Arbitrary job descriptions that specify minimum education levels, age, sex, marital status, or similar requirements are open to challenge. Management cannot use that "gut" feeling any more, because a rejected applicant may sue, charging unlawful discrimination on a variety of grounds.

Preliminary Screening of Applicants It is wise to ask applicants to send résumés before scheduling appointments for interviews. This has two advantages:

- Reviewing résumés will enable the retailer to screen out some unacceptable job candidates. Priorities can also be assigned to the résumés so that the most promising candidates are seen first. In this way, the retailer will run less risk of losing the best ones to job openings in other firms while going through the selection procedure.
- When the retailer decides to interview a candidate, some background information on the person will be available from the résumé and thus will enable the retailer to ask better questions and conduct a better interview.

The Job Interview

The objective of the job interview is to find out as much information as possible about the applicants' work background. The major task is to get the applicants to talk about themselves, their skills, and their work habits. The best way to go about this is to ask each applicant specific questions, such as "What did you do on your last job? How did you do it? Why was it done?" Questions that have no relationship to the ability of a person to do the job in question cannot be considered in making a hiring decision.

As the interviews go along, evaluate the applicants' replies. Do they know what they are talking about? Are they evasive or unskilled in the job tasks? Can they account for discrepancies? When conducting an interview, the following guidelines can be helpful:

- *Describe the job in as much detail as is reasonably possible*
  Give descriptions of typical situations that might arise and ask the applicant how he or she would handle it. "What would you say to a customer with a complaint?" "What colour blouse would you recommend to complement a red plaid skirt?" The interviewer shouldn't expect responses to be as expert as their own, but training could make them so. Do not be discouraged or discouraging. Offer praise such as, "That is a good way to go about it. If we hire you, we can teach you several other ways to handle situations such as that."[9]
- *Discuss the pluses and the minuses of the job*
  No job is without its minuses. If they are known initially, they are less likely to become obstacles later. If the person is expected to work nights, weekends or holidays, say so. Disclosure can prevent many misunderstandings later.
- *Explain the compensation plan*
  What is the salary? What fringe benefits are offered? What holidays are allowed? What is the vacation policy?
- *Weigh all factors in reaching a decision*
  Of all the factors mentioned above, no single one is overriding. Perhaps the most important characteristics to look for are common sense, an ability to communicate with people, and a sense of personal responsibility. Only personal judgment will tell the interviewer whether the applicant has these characteristics.

Making the Selection

When the interviews are over, the applicants should be asked to check back later if the interviewers are interested in the applicant. The interviewers should never commit themselves until they have talked with all likely applicants.

Next, the interviewers should *verify the information obtained.* Previous employers are usually the best sources. Sometimes, previous employers will give out information over the telephone that they might hesitate to put on paper for fear of being sued. But it is usually best to request a written reply.

To help ensure a prompt reply, retailers should ask previous employers a few specific questions about the applicant that can be answered with a yes-or-no check, or with a very short answer. For example: How long did the employee work for you? Was his or her work poor, average, or excellent? Why did the employee leave your employment? After the retailers have verified the information on all the applicants, they are ready to make the selection. The right employee can help the firm make money. The wrong employee will cost the firm much wasted time and materials, and may even drive away customers.

THE NEED TO TRAIN EMPLOYEES[10]

The next step is to train employees. Sales training programs will be covered in Chapter 12, so this section will discuss the evolving nature of sales training in the context of the human resources plan.

In the past, sales training programs have been related to the hiring sequence and perhaps to retraining. Today, with the evolution of retail systems, the complexity of the environment, and the need to improve the delivery of customer service, old ideas of integrating an employee into the retail operation are no longer useful. In addition, the situation is complicated by different educational or cultural backgrounds of employees.

Today, employees must deal with complicated automated systems, and retailing requires candidates with higher intellectual qualities for a successful training program. Once found and selected, they must be given a customized training program covering all modern aspects of modern retail operations. In

Helping a customer find the "right" clothes and ensuring the best fit require excellent training.

Courtesy Hudson's Bay Company—Corporate Collection

the example of Bud Kanke at the beginning of this chapter, each of the 30 managers have to fill out a two-page goal planner and all 250 staff members have to go through a rigorous training program run by Executive Development Services, at a cost of $250,000 in 1995. For example, waiters are told that they run a micro-business of six tables, and they have to succeed in that business, with daily performance sheets posted on a board.[11] Retail Highlight 6-2 further illustrates how important training employees is to excellent customer service.

An additional complication in today's environment is the changing demographic and cultural profile of the market, providing a pool of candidates who are culturally different from past employees, and from current customers. Again, the training program must try and bridge these gaps. Otherwise, the retailer may anticipate problems in terms of customer service perceptions.

Retail Highlight 6-2 Masterminding Success by Training and Good Customer Service

One important strategy for independents to beat large, often impersonal chain stores is by emphasizing *product knowledge*, i.e., knowing just about all there is to know about products, related goods and services, and how they are used. To provide it requires commitment, a trained staff, and low turnover. Jonathan Levy, co-owner of the ten Toronto-area Mastermind stores (which sell educational toys and computer and science wares) knows that salespeople have to know what's appropriate for children of different ages and interests. But sales also depend on his staff giving out reliable, on-the-spot, easy-to-understand information.

Training is a priority. Levy holds regular seminars, bringing in suppliers "to transplant as much product knowledge as possible from the source to the end-user of the knowledge." But just to be sure, he has built in a fail-safe system. When store employees can't answer a customer's question, they can call any of three designated "experts," one for books, one for science, or Levy for other subjects, who work in the combined head office and warehouse. Levy says that the trio respond to three or four calls a day from each store.

Reaching out to customers after the sale keeps the information flowing and sparks interest in new purchases. Three times a year, Levy publishes a newsletter that goes out to 20,000 customers, containing news, product reviews, and children's activities. "It's a way to reach out and touch our customers, to keep them informed about what we're doing," says Levy. What the newsletter does also is educate consumers (who are easier to sell to) *and* reinforce employee knowledge (ongoing training).

Source: Marlene Cartash, "Catching a Falling Store," *Profit*, December 1990, pp. 27–28.

DEVELOPING THE PAY PLAN [12]

Pay administration may be another term for something management is already doing but has not bothered to name. A formal pay plan, one that lets employees know where they stand and where they can go as far as salary is concerned, will not solve all employee-relations problems. It will, however, remove one of those areas of doubt and rumour that may keep the work force anxious, unhappy, less loyal, and more mobile.

What is the advantage of a formal pay plan for the firm? In business, it is good people who can make the difference between success and failure. Many people like a mystery, but not when it is how their pay is determined. Employees working under a pay plan they know and understand can see that it is fair and uniform, and that pay is not set by whim. They know what to expect and can plan accordingly. In the long run, such a plan can help to (1) recruit, (2) keep, (3) motivate employees, and (4) build a solid foundation for a successful business.

Types of Salary Plans

A formal pay plan does not have to be complex nor cost a lot of time and money. Formal does not mean complex. In fact, the more elaborate the plan is, the more difficult it is to put into practice, communicate, and carry out. The foremost concern in setting up a formal pay administration plan is to get the acceptance, understanding, and support of management and supervisory employees.

The steps in setting up a pay plan are: (1) define the jobs as discussed earlier in the chapter, (2) evaluate the jobs, (3) price the jobs, (4) install the plan, (5) communicate the plan to employees, and (6) appraise employee performance under the plan.

Job Evaluation and Compensation

The question of how much to pay an employee in a particular position is an important but complicated matter. If management offers too little pay for a particular position, the good employee will leave to perform the same work elsewhere and only the less motivated, less able employee will remain for the lower pay. On the other hand, management has very little to gain by paying an employee far more than what is being paid in other organizations for the same work.

Job Evaluation **Job evaluation** is a method of ranking jobs to aid in determining proper compensation. Figure 6-6 can now be used to demonstrate the relationship of these four basic personnel management tools.

Figure 6-6 Relationship of Job Evaluation with Respect to the Other Three Management Tools

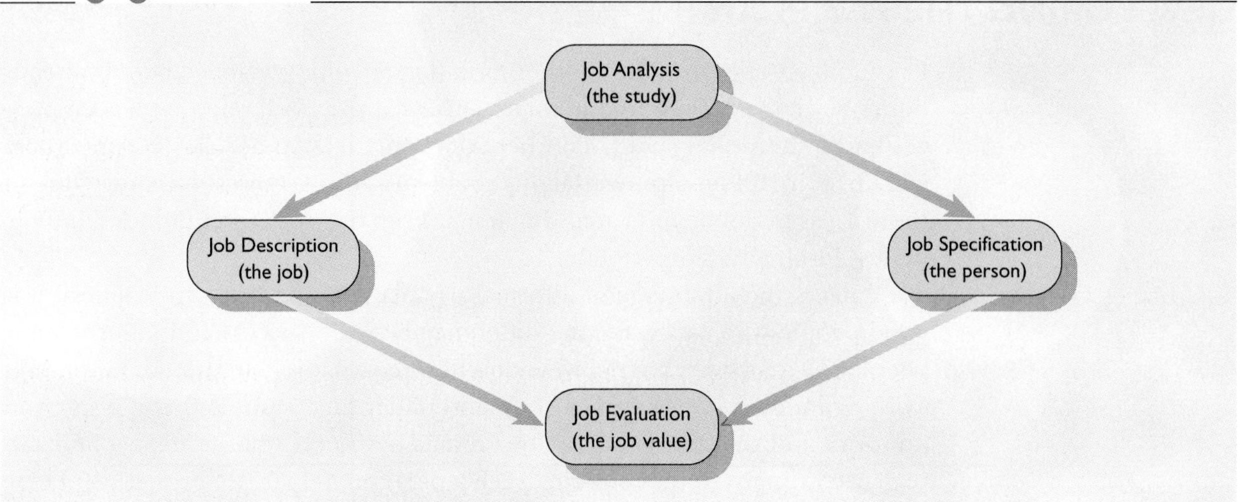

Thus, a job evaluation is obtained by evaluating both the responsibilities from a job description and the items on a job specification. The reason for job evaluation is to establish a fair method of compensating employees for their work.

Compensation In determining **compensation**, it is important to take several principles into consideration:

- Equal pay for equal work. This is a very important principle that has been slowly gaining acceptance by legislators at the federal and provincial level. The federal government and some provincial governments have some form of pay equity regulations.
- Higher pay for work requiring more knowledge, skill, or physical exertion.
- Reasonable pay, in comparison to pay for similar work in other organizations.
- Over-qualified employees are not paid more (or much more) than a qualified employee in the same position.
- After several years, very little or no extra pay for the length of time an employee has remained with the firm.
- Total earnings reflect, in some way, the employee's contribution to the organization.
- As much as possible, pay scales are known to employees.
- Fairness in application of these principles.

One general but fairly effective rule of thumb to follow when determining salaries and wage rates is to pay the most important nonsupervisory job as well as or somewhat better than the job receives elsewhere and to do the same for the least important full-time job. Rates for all other jobs can then be set in a reasonable way, in between. Job descriptions are often helpful in finding similar positions in other businesses with which to compare pay rates.

Management can obtain information on *competitive salaries* from various sources, including:

- Local surveys conducted by nearby business associations and organizations.
- Informal contacts, such as meetings with other owners/managers in social, civic, or community functions. Usually this information is useful only to get a general feel of things, since competitors may not wish to disclose salaries of jobs, and noncompetitive companies may be different from your firm.
- Industry meetings and conventions.
- Job advertisements in local newspapers and trade journals.
- National surveys, if they are available.

It is not always possible to compare salaries with pay rates in other businesses. This is especially true if some of the jobs in a business are not standard or common jobs.

Methods of Job Evaluation Another way, then, to establish salaries and pay rates for jobs is to evaluate the worth of the job to the business, so that more important jobs receive more pay. In this way, management is able to take into consideration all but one of the principles of salary administration discussed earlier. This principle concerns providing a reasonable pay level, in comparison to pay for similar work in other organizations.

There are two different ways to evaluate jobs. They are:

- Ranking—comparing a job against a job.
- Classification—comparing the jobs with the aid of a scale.

These two methods are described in detail in the next sections.

The Rank Method of Job Evaluation

Job ranking, possibly with the aid of job descriptions, is the simpler and usually more practical way to evaluate jobs. The most valuable and complex job is assigned a "1"; the job which is second in complexity and importance, a "2," and so on until all jobs have been assigned a number. Jobs that are equal in importance may be assigned the same number. If management uses this method, they know that the higher the job's position on the list, the more important the job is to the business, and can assign pay levels accordingly.

In creating new jobs, management can then place them into their proper places in the ranking.

Example: Suppose that a restaurant owner/manager who is looking for an assistant manager, a cook's helper, and a dishwasher has the situation indicated in Table 6-1. In this case, the assistant manager should be paid more than a cook, but less than a manager, somewhere between \$25,000 and \$30,000 a year. A cook's helper seems to fit in the range of less than \$8.00 per hour, but more than \$5.50 per hour. The dishwasher, being the least important job, would receive the minimum wage or only a little above it.

Table 6-1

Application of Job Ranking

Job Rank	Job Title	Salary or Wage Rate
1	Manager	$30,000 to $35,000 per year
2	Assistant manager	?
3	Cook 1	$24,000 to $26,000 per year
4	Cook 2	$8.00 to $8.50 per hour
5	Head waiter/waitress	$7.50 to $8.00 per hour
6	Cook's helper	?
7	Waiter/waitress	Minimum wage plus tips averaging $5.50 per hour
8	Dishwasher	?

The Classification Method of Job Evaluation

In the **job classification** method, jobs are evaluated and rated on two scales:

- The *complexity* of the various responsibilities and qualifications that are required on the job and their respective importance to good performance.
- The *length of time* the respective responsibility and qualification are utilized during the average day.

For each responsibility and qualification, two rating numbers are assigned—one for the complexity and importance to the job, and the other one for the length of time during which it is used. For instance, if knowledge of computer programming is required on a job, it may receive a 7 for responsibility and qualification, but if that knowledge is required only a few hours out of each week, it may receive a 2 for length of time. These two numbers can then be multiplied and averaged with all other qualifications and responsibilities of that job, to provide a classification number. Large numbers indicate the more difficult and important positions.

Planned Pay Structure In general, a planned pay structure makes it possible to tie individual rates of pay to job performance and contribution to company goals.

A *straight salary* is most likely to be paid in a small store in which employees have a variety of responsibilities other than selling. This pay plan also avoids the temptation for employees to engage in "pressure" selling. The drawback of the plan is that it does not provide an incentive for extra effort, which may lower employee motivation.

A *salary plus commission* is the most frequently administered plan in retailing, primarily because it emphasizes both selling and customer service. It provides an extra incentive for "plus sales" and also provides a stable income for employees.

The *quota-plus-bonus plan* provides for the payment of a bonus as a varying percentage of sales achieved above a quota established for each category of merchandise. The program allows unique sales incentives to be established by category of merchandise/tasks, does not encourage overly aggressive selling, and does provide a stable income during periods of slow sales. The disadvantages are that the plan can be misunderstood by employees and must be changed to reflect changes in the merchandise mix by season.

The *straight commission* pay plan provides a strong financial incentive for outstanding salespersons and thus is likely to attract strong sales personnel. The disadvantage is that the arrangement can promote overly aggressive "pressure" selling, which can antagonize customers. Employees may also be prone to focus excessive attention on high-cost goods creating ill will and tension between salespersons.

Drawing Account A **drawing account** is a cash advance paid to retail salespeople. The account is established as a "draw" for the employee as needed. The amount withdrawn is repaid to the company out of the sales commissions earned during each period. A drawing account may or may not be guaranteed. Under a *nonguaranteed* plan, the advance is a loan. The balance of the debt is carried over to the next period if the salesperson does not earn a sufficient amount in commissions to pay back the advance in a single period.

A *guaranteed* draw account is one in which the loan debt is cancelled if the salesperson's commissions are less than the draw. In effect, a guaranteed draw is much like a salary. For that reason, the nonguaranteed draw is more widely used because it is less of a financial burden on the retailer.

Drawing accounts are designed to offset some of the disadvantages of the straight commission plan. They provide both security and regularity of income. The accounts are subject to abuse, however. Salespeople may view the draw as salary rather than a loan. In addition, employees in arrears may simply quit. Drawing accounts are declining in popularity because of the problems involved in administering them. Retailers instead are more prone to supplement a commission with a salary.

Installing the Plan

At this point, employers have a general pay plan, but they do not, of course, pay in general. They pay each employee individually. They must now consider how the plan will be administered to provide for individual pay increases.

There are several approaches for administering the pay increase feature of the plan:

- **Merit increases**, granted to recognize performance and contribution.
- **Promotional increases**, given to employees assigned different jobs in higher pay levels.
- **Tenure increases**, given to employees for time worked with the company.
- **General salary increases**, granted to employees to maintain real earnings as required by economic factors and in order to keep pay competitive.

These approaches are the most common, but there are many variations.[13] Most annual increases are made for cost of living, tenure, or employment market reasons. Obviously, employers might use several, all, or combinations of the various increase methods.

Employers should document salary increases for each employee and record the reasons for them.

Updating the Plan

To keep the pay administration plan updated, the employer should review it at least annually. Adjustments should be made where necessary, and supervisory personnel should be retained in using the plan. This is not the kind of plan that can be set up and then forgotten. What matters is how the plan helps employers achieve the objectives of the business.

PLANNING EMPLOYEE BENEFITS[14]

Employee compensation includes wages or salary, commissions, incentives, overtime, and benefits. **Benefits** include holidays and paid vacations, employment insurance, Canada (or Quebec) pension, health care, company pensions, welfare benefits (life insurance, supplementary health, dental plan), disability payments, and services like credit unions, product or service discounts, legal assistance, travel clubs, education subsidies, profit-sharing plans, and food services.

After productivity, employee compensation is the most difficult employee-relations issue for management. Employee benefits can help develop a stable and productive work force, but employers must have effective cost and administrative controls. Legally required benefits (e.g., Canada Pension, employment insurance) can be managed with minimal difficulty by keeping records, submitting forms to the proper authorities, and paying for the required coverage. But when choosing and managing other types of benefits, employers should get professional advice in planning and setting up programs.

As the benefits cost increases as a percentage of total compensation, the direct pay cost percentage decreases. Employers cannot recognize outstanding achievement with direct pay increases because funds for direct pay are diminishing as benefits spending gets bigger. As a result, unfortunately, the compensation differential between the mediocre employee and the outstanding achiever is narrowing. Managers need to recognize the advantages, limitations, and cost impact that employee benefits have on business operations and net profit.

Analyzing benefits costs can be accomplished by grouping them into the following categories:

- Legally required benefits (Canada/Quebec pension plan, workers' compensation, employment insurance).
- Private pensions.
- Group insurance.
- Supplementary insurance.
- Payment for time not worked.
- Employee services such as day care.
- Perquisites such as employee discounts or merchandise.

Many employers now pay for most, if not all, of the employees' life, medical, and disability insurance. The rapid escalation of benefits cost, as compared to direct pay compensation, has caused managers to become more diligent in controlling these costs and in getting better employee relations.

Selecting Employee Benefits

Benefits should be designed with the help of an individual who is a competent planner and manager. Employers need an approach that allows them to offer employee benefits designed to meet the company's and the employees' needs. For example, employees who are older and no longer have the responsibility of a family will have different requirements from the employees who have families. Also, employees whose spouses are covered by another employer's plan might be considered in such a way as to minimize double coverage.

EMPLOYEE PERFORMANCE APPRAISAL

Many retail employees are under a merit increase pay system, though most of their pay increase may result from other factors. This approach involves periodic review and appraisal of how well employees perform their assigned duties. An effective employee appraisal plan (1) achieves better two-way communications between the manager and the employee, (2) relates pay to work performance and results, (3) provides a standardized approach to evaluating performance, and (4) helps employees see how they can improve by explaining job responsibilities and expectations.

Such a performance review helps not only the employees whose work is being appraised, but also the manager doing the appraisal to gain insight into the organization. An open exchange between employee and manager can show the manager where improvements in equipment, procedures, or other factors might improve employee performance. Managers should try to foster a climate in which employees can discuss progress and problems informally at any time throughout the year.[15]

EMPLOYEE RELATIONS AND HUMAN RESOURCES POLICIES[16]

There are many ways to manage people. The manager can be strict or rigidly enforce rules. Communications can be one-way from boss to employee. The job might get done, but with fairly high turnover, absenteeism, and low morale. Or the owner can make an extra effort to be a "nice guy" to everyone on the payroll. This management style may lead to reduced adherence to the rules, and employees may argue when they are asked to do work they do not like. Controlling the daily operation of the business may become more and more difficult. The business may survive, but only with much lower profit than if the owner followed more competent human resources policies. But there is another way. A way where employees can feel a part of the firm, where manager and employees can communicate effectively with each other, where rules are fair and flexible, yet enforced with positive discipline. The job gets done efficiently and profitably, and the business does well.

Large companies have a separate human resources department. Most managers of a small firm view this "human resources function" as just part of the general job of running a business. It is good practice, though, to think of this function as a distinct and separate part of management responsibilities—only then are human resources responsibilities likely to get the priorities they deserve. The human resources function is generally considered to include all those policies and administrative procedures necessary to satisfy the needs of employees. Not necessarily in priority order, these include:

1. Administrative human resources procedures.
2. Supervisory practices based on human relations and competent delegation.
3. Positive discipline.
4. Grievance prevention and grievance handling.
5. A system of communications.
6. Adherence to all governmental rules and regulations pertaining to the human resources function.

Administrative Human Resources Procedures

Favourable employee relations require competent handling of the administrative aspects of the human resources function. These include the management of:

1. Work hours.
2. The physical working environment:
   a. Facilities
   b. Equipment.
3. Payroll procedures.
4. Benefit procedures, including insurance matters, and vacation and holiday schedules.

Developing Job Commitment

If an employee's job satisfies his or her needs, the employee responds more favourably to the job. Such employees tend to take their responsibilities seriously, act positively for the firm, and are absent from work only rarely. There are five factors that generally cause a deep commitment to job performance for most employees. These are:

1. *The work itself.* To what extent does the employee see the work as meaningful and worthwhile?
2. *Achievement.* How much opportunity is there for the employee to accomplish tasks that are seen as a reasonable challenge?
3. *Responsibility.* To what extent does the employee have assignments and the authority necessary to take care of a significant function of the organization? Properly used, the empowerment of service workers may bring high dividends to retailers, as in the example in the introduction.[17]
4. *Recognition.* To what extent is the employee aware of how highly other people value the contributions made by the employee?
5. *Advancement.* How much opportunity is there for the employee to assume greater responsibilities in the firm?

These five factors tend to satisfy certain critical needs of individuals:

1. The feeling of *being accepted* as part of the firm's work team.

2. *Feeling important*—that the employee's strengths, capabilities, and contributions are known and valued highly.
3. The chance to *continue to grow* and become a more fully functioning person.

If the kinds of needs just described are met by paying attention to the five factors previously listed, management will have taken significant steps toward gaining the full commitment of employees to job performance. To do this, several practical strategies can be used, such as:

- Establishing confidence and trust with employees through open communication and the development of sensitivity to employee needs.
- Allowing employees participation in decision making that directly affects them.
- Helping employees to set their own work methods and work goals, as much as possible.
- Praising and rewarding good work as clearly and promptly as inadequate performance is mentioned.
- Restructuring jobs to be challenging and interesting by giving increased responsibilities and independence to those who want it, and who can handle it.

Positive Discipline

The word *discipline* carries with it many negative meanings. It is often used as a synonym for punishment. Yet discipline is also used to refer to the spirit that exists in a successful ball team where team members are willing to consider the needs of the team as more important than their own. Positive discipline in a retail firm is an atmosphere of mutual trust and common purpose in which all employees understand the company rules as well as the objectives, and do everything possible to support them.

Any disciplinary program has, as its base, that all of the employees have a clear understanding of exactly what is expected of them. This is why a concise set of rules and standards must exist that is fair, clear, realistic, and communicated. A good set of rules need not be more than one page, but can prove essential to the success of a business. A few guidelines for establishing a climate of positive discipline are given below:

1. There must be rules and standards, which are communicated clearly and administered fairly, and these must be reasonable. In addition, employees should be consulted when rules are set.
2. Rules should be communicated so they are known and understood by all employees. An employee manual can help with communicating rules. While a rule or a standard is in force, employees are expected to adhere to it.
3. There should be no favourites and privileges should be granted only when they can also be granted to other employees in similar circumstances.
4. Employees must be aware that they can and should voice dissatisfaction with any rules or standards they consider unreasonable as well as with working conditions they feel hazardous, discomforting, or burdensome.

5. Employees should understand the consequences of breaking a rule without permission. Large companies have disciplinary procedures for minor violations that could apply equally well in small companies. If the problem continues, there is a formal, verbal warning, then a written warning, and if the employee persists in violating rules, there would be a suspension and/or dismissal. In violations of more serious rules, fewer steps would be used.
6. There should be an appeals procedure when an employee feels management has made an unfair decision.
7. There should be recognition for good performance, reliability, and loyalty. Negative comments, when they are necessary, will be accepted as helpful if employees also receive feedback when things go well.

Corrective Action No matter how good the atmosphere of positive discipline in a business, rules are bound to be broken, by some people, from time to time. In those situations, corrective action is sometimes necessary. In some rare cases, the violation may be so severe that serious penalties are necessary. If an employee is caught in the act of stealing or deliberately destroys company property, summary dismissal may be necessary. In all other severe cases, a corrective interview is needed to determine the reasons for the problem and to establish what penalty, if any, is appropriate. Such an interview should include all, or most, of the following steps:

1. Outlining the problem to the employee, including an explanation of the rule or procedure that was broken.
2. Allowing the employee to explain his or her side of the story. This step will often bring out problems that need to be resolved to avoid rule violations in the future.
3. Exploring with the employee what should be done to prevent a recurrence of the problem.
4. Reaching agreement with the employee on the corrective action that should be taken.

Even in the best environment, employees will occasionally feel unhappy about something. They may not get paid on time, or may feel that the room is too hot, too cold, or too dark. They may feel that they deserve a merit increase, or that someone has hurt their feelings inadvertently. When this happens, *a written grievance procedure, known to employees, can be very helpful in creating a positive atmosphere.* It informs employees how they can obtain a hearing on their problems and it assures that the owner/manager becomes aware that the problem exists.

JOB ENRICHMENT

Too many companies today treat employees as throw-away assets. The average annual turnover rate among restaurant workers, for example, is 250 percent while management turnover is about 50 percent. Many employees leave within 30 days of employment, wasting whatever training they have been given. The retail investment is too high to take such an approach.

Forward thinking managers view the employee as a total person. Keeping employees satisfied at work is more than a matter of salary. Employees want to feel they belong and that the company cares about them as total human beings.

Careful attention to these needs will contribute to higher employee productivity and a lower turnover rate.[18]

Motivation and job enrichment cannot be separated. **Motivation** is normally related to work policies and supervisor attitudes. Motivated employees will devote their best efforts to company goals. As a result, management is recognizing the benefits of flexibility in work schedules, enrichment programs, and building employee motivation. Programs such as flex time, job sharing, on-site day care, and quality circles have emerged in retailing in recent years as management has sought ways to increase productivity and enrich the job by reducing worker stress at home and at work.

Typical Programs

Flex Time **Flex time** is a system by which workers can arrive and depart on a variable schedule. Flex time programs contribute to improved employee morale, a greater sense of employee responsibility, less stress, and reduced turnover. Retailers with flex time programs include Sears Canada and the Bank of Montreal.

Job Sharing **Job sharing** occurs when two workers voluntarily hold joint responsibility for what was formerly one position. In effect, two permanent part-time positions result from what was one full-time position. Job sharing differs from work sharing. **Work sharing** usually occurs in organizations during economic recessions where all employees are required to cut back on their work hours and are paid accordingly. Job sharing is a way to retain valuable employees who no longer want to work full-time. Management has found that the enthusiasm and productivity in such programs is high.[19]

Child and People Care Programs Young children pose a special problem for working mothers. About 53 percent of all single mothers with preschool children are now in the work force.[20] There is a growing recognition in Canada about the value of providing good day care services, with the increased assistance of governments. Some companies, such as the Bank of Montreal, are giving their employees paid time off, called "people care days," to deal with personal matters such as taking a driving test, applying for a mortgage, or doing volunteer work in the community.[21]

Employee Assistance Programs Drug abuse and alcohol are two of the most obvious areas in which employers can provide counselling and assistance. Other programs include scholarships for children of employees and encouraging community volunteer work.

Total Quality Management (TQM) TQM programs create situations in which employees at all levels have input into decisions that affect the retail organization. Employees gain an increased sense of self-worth by taking part in the process. Management also benefits from the ideas of dedicated workers at all levels in the organization. Managers and workers seek consensus on company operations instead of having orders simply passed down from above.

Improved Communications Mechanisms should be in place for regular communication between managers and hourly employees. Opportunities should be provided for the employees to communicate their concerns to management.

ORGANIZING

Decisions must also be made on how the retail firm will be organized. Most merchants are all-arounders. They do all jobs as the need arises, or assign tasks to employees on a random, nonspecialized basis. Employees are extensions of the managers to carry out the tasks they lack time to do themselves. Small merchants don't think of setting up distinct functions and lines for the flow of authority, nor do they select specialists to handle each function. As a store grows, however, specialization becomes necessary. The primary purpose of organizational structure is to "support market-driven values and behaviour and reinforce desired behaviour across the business."[22] For some thoughts on organizing from the man who built the world's largest retail chain, see Retail Highlight 6-3.

Basic Organization Principles

Before discussing organizational structure, certain management principles need to be considered in organizing the firm:

- The principle of specialization of labour.
- The principle of departmentalization.
- The span-of-control principle.
- The unity-of-command principle.

Retail Highlight 6-3 Mr. Sam's Thoughts on Organizing

Sam Walton, who died in 1992, built the world's largest retail chain, Wal-Mart, with more than 2,000 stores and sales of over $55 billion. Recognized as one of the best and brightest retailers ever, he offered these thoughts on organizing a retail firm:

- Keep your ear to the ground. Managers and buyers should spend most of their time in stores seeing what customers are and are not buying.
- Push responsibility and authority down. As companies, like Wal-Mart, get bigger, the more important it becomes to shift responsibility and authority towards the front lines, toward that department manager who is stocking the shelves and talking to the customer.
- Force ideas to bubble up. Encourage store employees to push their ideas up through the system.
- Stay lean, fight bureaucracy. If you are not serving the customer or supporting the folks who do, Wal-Mart does not need you.

Wal-Mart also has a profit-sharing plan in which all employees can participate. Sam Walton felt this was critical to Wal-Mart's success because the salespeople then feel that they are part of the company and treat customers better than salespeople in other stores do.

Source: "Sam Walton in His Own Words," *Fortune*, June 29, 1992, pp. 98-106.

Specialization

Modern organizations are built on the concept of **specialization.** More and better work is performed at less cost when it is done by specialists than when it is done by employees who shift from one job to another and who continually improvise. Specialization is of two kinds: *tasks* and *people.* Specialization of tasks narrows a person's activities to simple, repetitive routines. Thus, a relatively untrained employee can quickly become proficient at a narrow specialty. Specialization of people involves not simplifying the job, but developing a person to perform a certain job better than someone else can. Training and experience improve the quality and quantity of the work. In the smaller retail store, most of the specialization is of the second type; but in larger stores there is more need for narrow task specialization. For example, certain special records must be kept, and certain phases of merchandise handling must be done by a well-trained person.

Departmentalization

Management will probably find that it can use **departmentalization** and group jobs into classes such as the following (each demanding a certain combination of skills for good performance):

- Merchandising—buying and managing inventory for different groups of merchandise.
- Direct and general selling and adjustments—customer contact.
- Sales promotion—largely concerning advertising and display.
- Accounting and finance—records, correspondence, cash handling, insurance, and sometimes credit.
- Store operation—building, equipment, and safety measures.
- Merchandise handling—receiving, marking, storing, and delivering.

Selling computers requires highly specialized, well-trained employees.

Courtesy Future Shop

- Human resources—employment, training, employee benefits, and personnel records.

Recognizing the many functions to be performed doesn't mean that a specialist is necessary for each of them. Management can combine some functions. But management should look ahead and have an organization plan that provides for various specialized positions when they are needed.

Span of Control

Span of control addresses the question of how many subordinates should report to a supervisor. Generally, a supervisor's span of control should be small because an individual can work effectively with only a limited number of people at one time. Span of control, however, depends on factors such as the competence of the supervisor and subordinates, the similarity of the functions to be performed, and the physical location of people.

Unity of Command

The **unity of command** concept involves a series of superior–subordinate relationships. This concept states that no person should be under the direct control of more than one supervisor in performing job tasks. Thus, an employee should receive decision-making power from and report to only one supervisor. An unbroken chain of command should exist from top to bottom. Otherwise, frustration and confusion will occur.

How to Organize for Profitable Operations

The two functions that probably will be organized first are *merchandising* and *operations*, or store management. Such an organization would look like the one illustrated in Figure 6-7.

The *merchandise manager* has other functions in addition to being responsible for buying and selling. The person supervises or prepares merchandise budgets (or both); handles advertising, displays, and other promotions; and is responsible for inventory planning and control. The *operations manager* is responsible for building upkeep, delivery, stockrooms, service, supplies, equipment purchasing, and similar activities.

Figure 6-7 The Simplest Organization

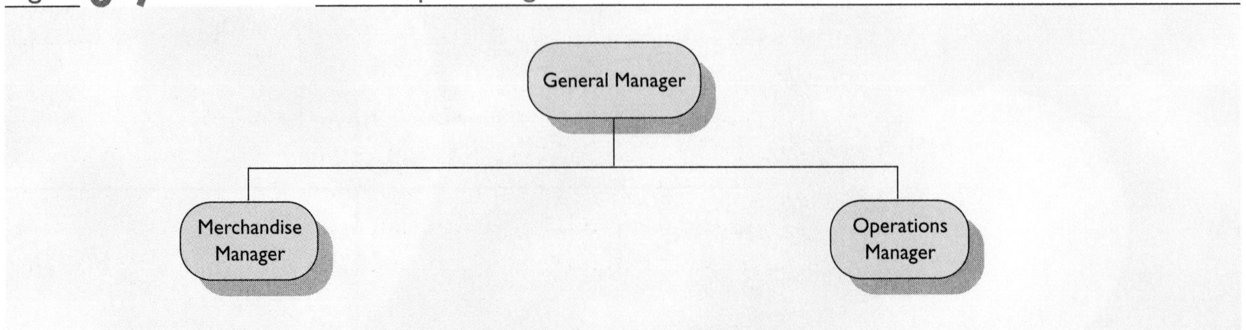

Figure 6-8 Five-Function Organizational Plan

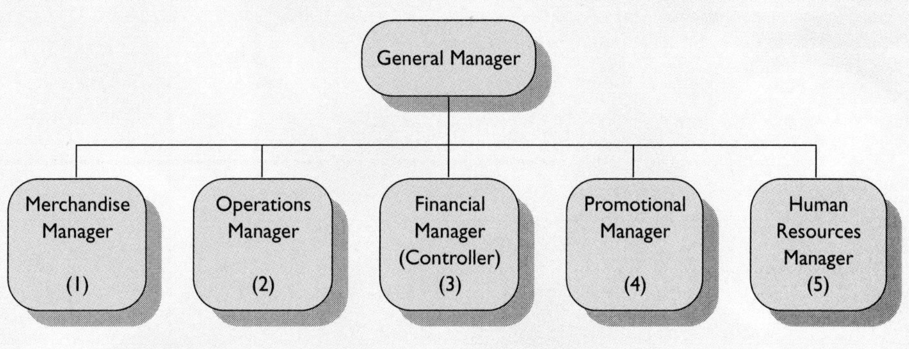

As a store continues to grow in size, specialization of labour occurs. The organization structure may begin to look like the one in Figure 6-8. The next managers who should be added are financial, promotion, and human resources managers. The financial manager, or controller, handles the finances of the firm and probably has an accounting background. The organization structure in the figure is typical of most department stores. A food operation, however, performs the same functions, as do all retail firms.

Trends in Organizing

Separation of Buying and Selling

There are arguments for and against the separation of the buying and selling responsibilities in the organization.

Those *opposing* the separation of the two functions pose the following arguments:

- The buyer must have contact with consumers to be able to understand their needs.
- Those who buy merchandise should also be responsible for selling it.
- It is easier to pinpoint merchandising successes and failures when the two functions are combined.

Those who *favour* the separation of the two functions counter their opposition as follows:

- If the two functions are combined, buying is likely to have more importance than selling.
- Buying and selling require two different types of job skills.
- With technology, reports, and so forth, it is not necessary for the two functions to be combined.
- Salespeople can be shifted more easily under this arrangement.

The arguments against separating the buying and selling functions do not seem as strong as the counterarguments. The branch store problem seems to demand separation. Thus, the trend is to separate the two. Figure 6-9 shows a department store that is organized for the separation of buying and selling. The

Figure 6-9 Organization for Separation of Buying and Selling

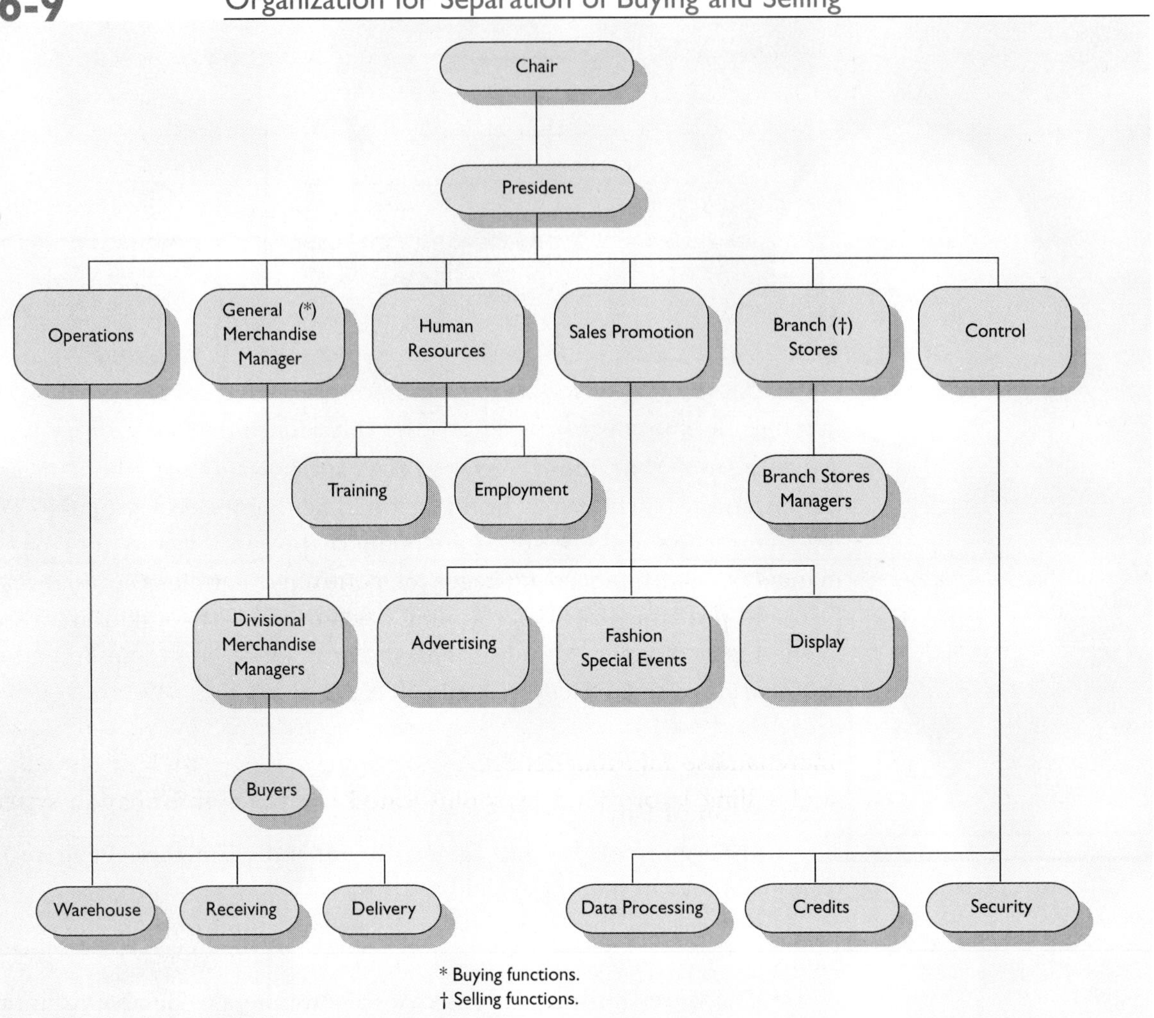

general merchandise manager is responsible for buying, and the vice-president of branch stores is responsible for selling.

Food stores could have faced the same conflict, but their expansion history actually solved their problems. Rather than branching, these companies expanded as chain-store organizations. No main stores exist in a chain organization. Buying and selling are always separated. Many Canadian retailers, including Loblaws, have buyers who focus on maximizing the rate of return on shelf space investment. Using computer analysis, Loblaws' buyers know the volume and rate of return that competitive products are delivering to a store. A new buyer/seller relationship is evolving where the buyer works very closely with the seller to develop a mutually beneficial relationship. Called **reverse marketing**, it reflects the proactive stance taken by many buyers.[23]

Centralization versus Decentralization[24]

Specialty stores historically have been highly centralized. The Limited, until around 1990, for example, consisted of roughly a dozen major fashion divisions controlled by the chairperson. The organizational philosophy was that synergies between the divisions in distribution, real estate and legal departments, and so forth could be achieved by centralization. The firm has moved to aggressively decentralize its business. Each division now has autonomy in merchandising and operations. The only issues controlled centrally are finances and reporting relationships. Toys "Я" Us made the decision to operate its Kids "Я" Us and its international divisions as separate, autonomous units.

Department stores are exhibiting a countertrend to the decentralization trend among specialty stores. Traditionally, each department store division in a multidivision holding company was allowed to operate independently and to compete not only with other department stores but also with other divisions of the parent organization. In essence, department stores have recognized that they do not need a buyer for each classification in every division to be efficient. Rather, operating information systems and electronic merchandising have made it possible for the buyers to make chainwide decisions. For example, the Hudson's Bay Company has moved to greater centralized buying, and at the same time, to provide more flexibility for individual store managers to select a merchandise mix that reflects local market needs. The link between buying and selling is provided by sophisticated computer information systems that allow managers to identify merchandise trends at the local, regional, and national levels.[25]

CHAPTER HIGHLIGHTS

- Staffing a store with the right people is a critical part of the strategic plan for a retailer. Staffing needs vary depending on the type of merchandise carried, services the store will offer, the image management wants to project to customers, and the way in which the firm wants to compete.
- The initial step in developing a human resources plan for the firm is to develop good job descriptions and job specifications. These are written after a job analysis has been undertaken to obtain important facts about the job. The job description provides the content and responsibilities of the job and how it ties in with other jobs. The job specification describes the personal qualifications required to do the job.
- Recruiting, attracting the right people, is a critical element of the plan. Recruits may be sought either inside or outside the firm. Specific guidelines exist that management must follow in administering selection tests and in otherwise screening employees.
- Simply hiring the right people is not enough. Training is often necessary for new employees and should be offered as an ongoing part of the personnel program.
- Employees need to know about their rights and responsibilities within the firm, the history of the firm, and specific information about their job respon-

sibilities. Sales personnel may also need training in technical dimensions of the merchandise for which they will be responsible.

- An equitable employee pay plan is a further important component of a human resources plan and can contribute to higher employee productivity and satisfaction. Retailers should make sure that employees understand how the pay plan was developed, how it will be administered, and how they will be evaluated for pay increases or promotions.
- Employee performance appraisal also needs to occur on a regular basis; normally employees are appraised annually.
- Employee motivation and job enrichment are also important elements of the personnel plan. Management must recognize that employees have needs such as the desire for recognition and achievement, which cannot be satisfied by money alone.
- Basic organizational principles are specialization of labour, departmentalization, span of control, and unity of command.
- The two functions that probably will first be organized in a retail store are merchandising and operations (store management).

KEY TERMS

benefits	132	job ranking	129
Canadian Human Rights Commission	121	job sharing	137
compensation	128	job specification	116
departmentalization	139	merit increases	131
drawing account	131	motivation	137
employee compensation	132	people care programs	137
flex time	137	promotional increases	131
general salary increases	131	reverse marketing	142
job analysis	116	span of control	140
job classification	130	specialization	139
job description	116	tenure increases	131
job evaluation	127	unity of command	140
		work sharing	137

DISCUSSION QUESTIONS

1. What are the key federal and provincial laws that affect recruiting, selection, and compensation of employees? What are the likely effects as a result of these regulations?
2. Assume you are the manager of a men's clothing outlet located close to a major university campus. What would be the basic elements of a training program for the outlet? How would your program likely differ from the type of training that might be offered for new employees who have been hired by Sears Canada?

3. Briefly describe the steps that must be carried out in developing a formal compensation plan.
4. What is likely to be the most effective method for compensating (*a*) a retail salesperson, (*b*) an accountant, and (*c*) a department buyer?
5. Why should retail management institute an employee performance appraisal plan? What might be some of the performance factors that are evaluated?
6. Why should an employee grievance procedure and a procedure for handling disciplinary matters be established, even in the absence of a union?
7. What are some of the things retail management can do to enhance greater job enrichment and motivation among employees?
8. Discuss the following four principles of organization: specialization of labour, departmentalization, span of control, and unity of command.

APPLICATION EXERCISES

1. Devise a format and interview at least five people who have worked in the retailing industry in some capacity. Determine the individual's honest views on wages, working conditions, superior–subordinate relationships, and so on. Prepare a report for class discussion on what you have discovered.
2. Select several different retail companies (differing in organizational arrangement, number of stores and sales volume, and product line) and make an appointment with the executive responsible for the personnel functions. Describe the employment process of each (include selection, training, and benefits including compensation) and draw comparisons among the group. See if you can explain the differences in apparent effectiveness of the programs. See if you can get them to discuss affirmative action.
3. Arrange through your college or university placement office to have a few minutes with all the recruiters coming to campus to interview people for retailing companies. Structure a questionnaire to administer to each recruiter to find out: what he or she is looking for in a student; how the interview on campus enters into the selection process; what kind of questions are asked of the interviewee; what the recruiter expects the interviewee to know about the company; what variables are considered in evaluating the student; and what the subsequent steps are in the employment process.

SUGGESTED CASE

10. Martin's Department Store

Part 3

Designing the Retailing Mix

Location and Merchandising Decisions

In *Part 3, Designing the Retailing Mix—Location and Merchandising Decisions*, the various decisions on the major variables of the retailing mix related to location and merchandising are discussed. The key issues in the retail location decisions are covered in Chapter 7. Store design, store layout, and merchandise presentation decisions are covered in Chapter 8. Merchandise and expense planning decisions are the focus of Chapter 9. Buying, handling, and inventory management decisions are explained in Chapter 10.

CHAPTER 7

RETAIL LOCATION DECISIONS

CHAPTER OBJECTIVES

After reading this chapter you should be able to:

1. Explain the strategic dimensions of the location decision.
2. Explain how to make the market selection.
3. Explain and use the various techniques and procedures for trading area evaluation.
4. Determine the volume of business that can be done in a trading area.
5. Explain and use the principles of site evaluation to assess the value of alternative sites.

How difficult the retail location decisions are can be illustrated by the following cases:[1]

- The notion that a proposed mega-shopping centre, like the one being built near the Hippodrome in Montreal (10 single-storey commercial buildings with three large-surface stores), will take away business from local merchants is not always true. The important survival ingredients for local retailers are specialization and convenience. With the attraction power of mega-malls, as is the experience of the Marché Central in North Montreal, retailers with unique offerings benefit from increased traffic.
- After pre-testing it successfully in 15 locations across Canada, Sears Canada decided to open, starting in 1996, fifty specialty stores across the country, with selling areas between 400 and 600 m^2, and with a variety of products from televisions to sewing machines. Some announced locations are Greenwood, N.S.; Sept-Iles, Quebec; and Campbell River, B.C. With these new specialty stores, Sears Canada wants to better serve markets that are currently serviced by a Sears catalogue outlet.

These examples illustrate the importance of location decisions for retailers, and how these decisions are affected by the economic situation and the competition. Building the right type of store in the right location is the key to serving a carefully targeted market. Location decisions are essential elements of the competitive strategy of any retail organization. Outlets such as Canadian Tire can succeed in a stand-alone location. Other firms such as Sears Canada seem to function best as an anchor tenant in a major shopping centre. Small specialty firms, lacking the ability to attract customers on their own, often choose a high traffic location in a shopping mall.

We cannot overemphasize the importance of a carefully developed location strategy. Such a strategy is the spatial expression of a retailer's goals. Location decisions must be made in the context of the demographics of the target market segments, the patronage behaviour of consumers within the segments, the geographic dimensions of demand, and all other dimensions of the marketing program.

The selection process begins with an assessment of the firm's strategy, followed by (1) choice of region or metropolitan area, (2) trade area analysis, and (3) site evaluation and selection. Choice of location in essence determines how goods and services are made available to the customer. Even small differences in location can have a major impact on profitability and market share because location affects both the number of customers attracted to the outlet and the resulting level of retail sales.

COMPETITIVE STRATEGY AND LOCATION DECISIONS

Differences in competitive strategy can result in different location objectives even for firms with similar types of merchandise. For example, discount stores, specialty retailers, and chain department stores sell clothing and may even feature the same national brands. Still, each firm may be targeting a different market segment as reflected in their location strategies. Firms such as Home Depot are likely to be free-standing. Major department stores will serve as anchor tenants in shopping centres. They may also locate in the downtown section of major metropolitan areas.

Competition among firms offering similar merchandise and shopping experiences occurs primarily on the basis of location, promotion, and price. Consumers, in choosing between highly similar outlets, are likely to shop at the most conveniently located outlet offering the best prices. The result is that firms such as gasoline stations are likely to be tightly clustered and include mini-markets or fast-food outlets. Frequently such retailers will be located on all four quadrants of a major high-traffic artery. Supermarkets are another example of a type of retailing with interchangeable merchandise. Grocery outlets also rely on convenience of location, and price competition is likely to occur among such outlets in a narrowly defined area.

Thus, key strategic decisions in retail location relate to (1) the type of market coverage, and (2) the type of goods sold.

Type of Market Coverage

Three primary strategies are possible: (1) regional dominance (primarily for large retail outlets), (2) market saturation, and (3) emphasis on smaller towns and communities.

Regional Dominance

The retailer may decide to become the dominant retailer in a particular geographic area rather than locate the same number of outlets over a much wider geographic area. Examples of regionally dominant retailers include Sobeys in the Maritimes, IGA in Quebec, Loblaws in Ontario, Safeway in Manitoba, Alberta, and British Columbia, and Co-op in Saskatchewan.

The advantages of **regional dominance** include:

1. Lower costs of distribution because merchandise can be shipped to all the stores from a central warehouse.
2. Easier personnel supervision.
3. The ability to better understand customer needs.
4. The likelihood of a strong reputation in the area.
5. Better economies in sales promotion since the outlets are concentrated in one region.

Retailers practising regional dominance can offset their high fixed costs by high market share. Typically, the retailers, measured on a city-by-city basis, that have the leading market shares have the highest profits. In addition, high market share increases the number of stores in an area, which in turn improves customer convenience.

Market Saturation

This strategy is similar to regional dominance. However, **market saturation** is often limited to a single metropolitan market, such as Toronto, Montreal, Vancouver, Calgary, or Halifax, where the population base is large. The advantages are the same in both instances. Dominance simply occurs on a larger scale than a single metropolitan market.

Smaller Communities

Smaller communities are popular because building codes make it more difficult to build in large cities, costs are lower, and competition is weaker. Secondary markets, communities of less than 50,000, present some advantages to retailers: (1) These communities often welcome new business, such as tourism in Whistler (B.C.), and an auto plant in Bromont (Quebec), (2) the quality of life is often higher, (3) wage rates are lower, (4) unions are less of an issue, (5) the markets are easier to serve, and (6) competition is often less intense.

Some retail chains like Stedmans and Metropolitan operate primarily in small towns (less than 50,000 population) as these companies feel that they can more effectively serve these markets. For example, the Metropolitan chain operates over 450 stores across Canada under various names (e.g., Metropolitan and Red Apple Clearance Centre) mainly in secondary markets. Others, like Sears Canada, are opening specialty stores in rural communities to better service its current catalogue markets and to increase its market share in several product categories, such as snowblowers, stereos, and dishwashers.[2] Wal-Mart reports requests from smaller communities to open a store in their town.[3]

Type of Goods Sold

Merchandise can be classified as convenience, shopping, or specialty goods based on customer buying habits. Stores can be classified in the same way as shown in Table 7-1. Understanding how consumers perceive merchandise and stores can help in evaluating the importance of location.

Table 7-1 Matrix of Consumer Goods and Stores

Goods	Stores: Convenience	Stores: Shopping	Stores: Specialty
Convenience	Consumers prefer to buy the most readily available brand and product at the most accessible store. 1	Consumers are indifferent to the brand or product they buy, but shop among different stores in order to secure better retail service and/or lower retail prices. 4	Consumers prefer to trade at a specific store, but are indifferent to the brand or product purchased. 7
Shopping	Consumers select a brand from the assortment carried by the most accessible store. 2	Consumers make comparisons among both retail-controlled factors and factors associated with the product (brand). 5	Consumers prefer to trade at a certain store, but are uncertain as to which product they wish to buy and examine the store's assortment for the best purchase. 8
Specialty	Consumers purchase their favoured brand from the most accessible store that has the item in stock. 3	Consumers have strong preference with respect to the brand, but shop among a number of stores to secure the best retail service or price for this brand. 6	Consumers have preference for both a particular store and a specific brand. 9

Source: Yoram Wind, *Product Policy: Concepts, Methods, and Strategy* (Reading, Mass.: Addison-Wesley Publishing, 1982), p. 71.

Convenience goods are often purchased on the basis of impulse at outlets such as Mac's Milk. The volume of traffic passing a site is thus the most important factor in selecting a site at which to sell convenience goods. Some convenience goods outlets such as card shops are often located close to major department stores in shopping malls and depend on the department stores to attract traffic for them. Such outlets are known as parasite stores.

Consumers purchasing *shopping goods* prefer to compare the offerings of several stores before making a buying decision. A store such as Classic Bookstores is an example of a shopping goods outlet. Thus, consumers will travel farther in purchasing shopping goods than convenience goods but will not make a special effort to reach an outlet if others are more easily accessible.

Specialty goods are items for which consumers will make a special effort to purchase a particular brand or shop at a given store. Such outlets generate their own traffic. As a result, retailers of such merchandise can choose a somewhat isolated site relative to outlets offering shopping goods or convenience goods.

In summary, if management offers "shopping goods," the best location is near other stores carrying shopping goods. Conversely, locating a shopping goods store in a convenience goods area or centre is not recommended. Stores that carry shopping goods and those that offer convenience goods often locate in the same regional shopping centre. But, it is still important to locate in a section of the centre that is compatible with the retailer's product lines. Management would want to locate a gift shop near department stores, theatres, restaurants—in short, any place where lines of patrons may form, giving potential customers several minutes to look in the gift shop's display windows.

The Process of Selecting a Retail Location

As noted above, the location strategy for the firm ultimately reflects both growth and expansion objectives. Developing the location plan after making such decisions requires a careful study of potential markets. Assessment of markets begins with *choices among regions or metropolitan areas* that appear to offer the greatest market potential in meeting the firm's growth objectives.

Choices must then be made within the regions or the cities chosen. Considerable variation within such areas can occur because of the geographic configuration of the area, housing patterns, or land use. Analysis of the different subareas of a city is known as *trade area analysis*. Finally, *site analysis and evaluation* decisions must be made. At this point, management assesses the cost of land and development, traffic flows, ingress (i.e., going in) and egress (i.e., going out or exiting), and similar issues in making specific site choices.

Thus, selection of a retail location typically follows a four-step process, as indicated in Figure 7-1: (1) choosing the region or the metropolitan area; (2) analyzing the trade area; (3) assessing alternative sites; (4) selecting the site. It must be clear that every step is a refinement of the previous one, and that the process is not necessarily linear. The remainder of the chapter will be devoted to detailing these steps.

Figure 7-1 The Four-Step Process of Selecting a Retail Location

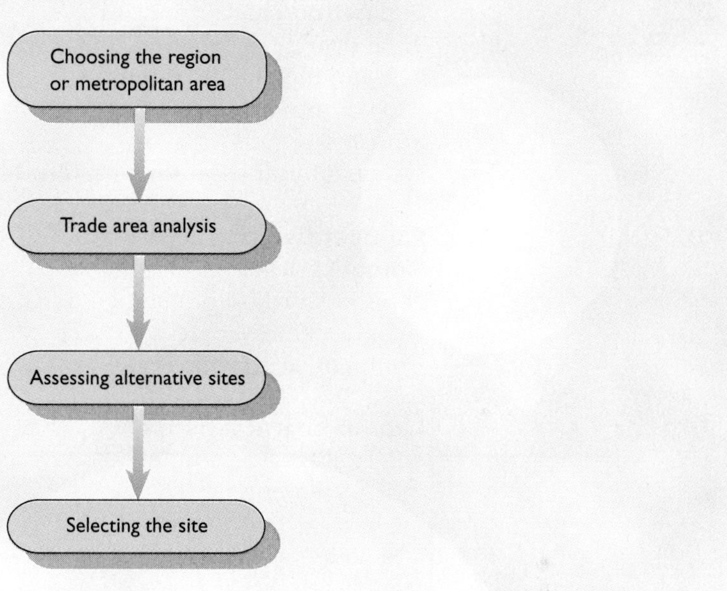

CHOICE OF REGION OR METROPOLITAN AREA

In making the market selection, management evaluates the economic base of targeted regions, the level of competition, size and socioeconomic characteristics of the population, and the overall potential of the area, as shown in Table 7-2.

Population Characteristics

For example, a retailer needs to study the number of people, their education, income, ages, and family composition, as well as probable population increases in the area. Census data is a useful source of such information, and is available for all markets in the yearly publication *Canadian Markets.* For example, the detailed listing on Moose Jaw indicates a 1999 population of 35,600, a per capita income of $18,300 (10 percent below national average), and total retail sales of $328 million (on a per capita basis, 7 percent above national average).[4]

Labour Availability

Management talent is most readily available in larger areas, but is more expensive, as is clerical help. In smaller communities, local management talent may not be available, and outsiders may not want to move to the area. However, clerical labour is less likely to be a problem.

Distribution Problems

These include the timing and frequency of delivery schedules to the store and the reliability of delivery, as well as the distance between the store and the company-owned or the distributor's warehouses.

Table 7-2

Factors to Consider in Area Selection

Population characteristics
Total size
Age and income distributions
Growth trends
Education levels
Occupation distribution and trends

Competitive characteristics
Saturation level
Number and size of competitors
Geographic coverage
Competitive growth trends

Labour characteristics
Availability of personnel
  Management
  Clerical
  Skilled
Wage levels
Unions
Training

Economic characteristics
Number and type of industries
Dominant industry
Growth projections
Financial base

Supply source characteristics
Delivery time
Delivery costs
Availability and reliability
Storage facilities

Location characteristics
Number and type of locations
Costs
Accessibility to customers
Accessibility to transportation
Owning and leasing options
Utility adequacy

Promotion characteristics
Type of media coverage
Media overlap
Costs

Regulation characteristics
Taxes
Licensing
Zoning restrictions
Local ordinances

Media Mix Issues

These include the availability of newspapers, of radio stations, and of television coverage of the market. Also, good production facilities are needed to help assure high-quality commercials.

Types of Industries in the Area

Large manufacturing plants with highly skilled union workers provide better market potential than small plants that use unskilled labour and pay low wages. However, unionized firms are more subject to strikes that can hurt retail sales.

Service organizations such as hospitals and government offices provide a stable or declining economic base, but pay low wage rates. A retailer ideally seeks a community with a more balanced economic base. They also seek a community with a history of growth and aggressiveness in seeking new industry. They tend to avoid a community with a history of labour problems or that is losing population.

Competition

Who are the likely competitors? Are any national retailers located in the area? How long have they been present? Can the market support another retailer without taking too much business from competition?

Availability of Locations

Does the community have several shopping centres with vacancies? Does the downtown area look "alive"? Are plans under way to revitalize downtown? Is land available at reasonable prices for building a stand-alone location?

Regulations

Can a business licence to operate be obtained, and how much will it cost? Can the firm be open on Sundays? Is the community aggressively seeking new retailers?

Index of Retail Saturation

One of the more commonly used measures of market attractiveness is the *Index of Retail Saturation (IRS)*. The index is based on the assumption that if a market A has a low level of **retail saturation**, the likelihood of success is higher than would otherwise be the case. The calculation of the IRS can be made as follows, and Figure 7-2 provides a concrete example of the use of the formula:

$$\text{Index of Retail Saturation}_A = \frac{\text{Demand}}{\text{Square metres of retail selling space}}$$

Thus, for market 1:

$$IRS_1 = \frac{C_1 \times RE_1}{RF_1}$$

where:

IRS_1 = Index of retail saturation for market 1
C_1 = Number of consumers in market 1
RE_1 = Retail expenditures per consumer in market 1
RF_1 = Retail facilities in market 1

Figure **7-2**

Evaluating the Saturation for Women's Clothing Stores In Fredericton

Teresa Juppe, the owner of a small chain of women's clothing stores, is interested in opening a new store in Fredericton, New Brunswick, and she is concerned about the women's clothing store retail saturation in this market. Through some research, she has been able to gather the following information:

- The 128,000 consumers in Fredericton spend an average of $314 per year in women's clothing stores.
- There are numerous women's clothing stores serving Fredericton with a total of 10,000 square metres of selling area.

This information allows her to calculate an index of retail saturation for women's clothing stores in this market:

$$IRS = \frac{128{,}000 \times 314.00}{10{,}000} = \frac{40{,}192{,}000}{10{,}000} = \$4{,}019.20$$

The revenue of $4,019.20 per square metre of selling area measured against the revenue per square metre necessary to break even provides her with the measure of saturation in Fredericton. The $4,019.20 figure is also useful in evaluating relative opportunities in different market areas.[5]

Census data, which is published every five years, can provide information on the number of potential customers within a trading area. Statistics Canada reports expenditure data by product category for households by income level. The number of competitors within the trading area can be determined by counting them, although selling areas would have to be estimated. Another very useful source is the *Canadian Markets*, published annually.

TRADE AREA ANALYSIS

Trade area analysis occurs after management agrees on a specific geographic region or a general area of a city as a possible retail location.

Understanding Trade Areas

Retail sales forecast accuracy depends on the ability to estimate the trade area for an outlet. The **trading area** is the geographic region from which a store primarily attracts its customers, and it is further subdivided into two major parts: the **primary trading area** includes the majority of the store's customers, living within a certain range of the store and having the highest per capita sales; the **secondary trading area** includes almost all of the customers, situated outside the primary area (the rest is called the fringe trading area). For example, for the Sahili Centre Mall in Kamloops, the primary area includes 75,000 customers within five minutes driving range, and the secondary area includes 95,000 customers within 25 minutes.[6]

A variety of factors determine trading area size, and they include:

1. The price of the good at one location compared to its price at another.
2. The number of inhabitants concentrated in various areas.
3. The density and distribution of the population.
4. The income and social structures of the population.
5. The proximity of other shopping opportunities.

What does this all mean for students of retailing? It means that the more highly specialized a product or service being offered, the larger the trading area must be before the service can be supported.

Population Characteristics

We earlier mentioned the importance of population in market selection. An analysis of population characteristics is even more critical when evaluating a *trading area.* Management needs to understand such features as the population profile of the trading area, population density, and growth trends. The population of a trading area may not change over time, for example, but the characteristics of the people in the area may change dramatically. Some older inner-city areas in recent years have experienced the return of young urban professionals (yuppies).

Such variables as sex, occupation, education, and age are also important, as are family size and family life cycle. An outlet selling lawn supplies would be interested in the number of single family homes in the vicinity. On the other hand, retailers seeking suitable sites for a day-care centre would be more interested in the number of families with preschool children.

Evaluating a Trade Area

Retailers differ from manufacturers because they have to be close to their target market, since consumers typically shop at the nearest retail outlet that will meet their needs. Techniques for measuring a trade area range from a simple "seat-of-the-pants" approach to complex mathematical models (for examples of commercial suppliers of these types of services, check www.dgrc.ca and www.thompsonassociates.com).

Information from Existing Stores

Retailers with existing stores have an advantage over a person seeking to open an outlet for the first time. The experienced retailers can use information that they have obtained about their existing stores in making decisions about a planned new store. If the new store is similar to the old one, the sales generated will likely be similar.

Credit Records

Credit records can be analyzed to determine the trading area of an existing store. A sample of charge accounts or debit card users is selected and customer addresses are plotted on a map. Of course, this is only possible if the retailer has developed a credit-granting procedure.

Customer Spotting

Customer spotting is a technique used for determining the location of target customers. Target customers must first be defined, say by income group, or profession. Next, a mailing list of these types of customers within a defined region may be purchased from mailing lists suppliers (such as direct marketing companies, or research companies such as CompuSearch, see www.polk.ca). Then the home addresses of the target customers are spotted on a map and a circle is drawn to define the primary trading area in the outlet.

Driving Time Analysis

Driving time analysis can also be used to define a trading area by determining how far customers are willing to travel to reach an outlet. Trading areas typically are measured in terms of time instead of distance because of problems of congestion and physical barriers. A rule of thumb is that customers will travel no more than five minutes to reach a convenience outlet. Three-fourths of the customers of a large regional shopping centre normally will drive 15 minutes to reach the centre.

Customer Survey

A good way to determine a trading area is to conduct or sponsor a customer survey. The survey can be done by mail, telephone, or by personal interview, and each method has its good and bad points. The interview can be conducted at the store if they are personal interviews. Alternatively, a sample of respondents can be chosen from customer records and called on the phone or mailed a questionnaire. Retailers may also be able to participate in surveys sponsored by the local chamber of commerce or a similar organization, or buy into an omnibus survey.

The customer survey can provide information on where people shop for items similar to the planned merchandise offering. For example, if a store interviews its own customers, the addresses can be plotted on a map to measure the store's trading area. Also, retailers can do a survey of noncustomers and establish trading areas for competitors. Drawing circles with a radius of one, two, and five kilometres makes it possible to see how far most customers travel to shop at the outlet. If a retailer is planning the first store, the information for an outlet similar to the planned one can be plotted.

A customer survey can provide other useful information as well. Such information might include: (1) *demographics* (e.g., age, occupation, number of children); (2) *shopping habits* (e.g., type of store preferred, how often consumers shop, area of town preferred); (3) *purchasing patterns* (e.g., who does the family buying); and (4) *media habits* (e.g., radio, TV, and newspaper habits).

Reilly's Law of Retail Gravitation[7]

Retail **gravity models** are an improvement over other methods of trading area analysis. They are based on both population size and distance or driving time as the key variables in the models. Reilly's Law is the oldest of the trading area models.[8] The model, as described in Figure 7-3, allows the calculation of a "breaking point" in retail trade between two communities.

These breaking points can be calculated between several cities and, when joined together, form a set of trading area boundaries for a community, as shown in Figure 7-4 for four smaller cities around city **A**.

Figure 7-3 Reilly's Law

According to Reilly's Law, the "breaking point" in retail trade between two communities a and b is calculated as follows:

$$D_b = \frac{D}{1 + \sqrt{\frac{P_a}{P_b}}}$$

where

P_a, P_b = Population sizes of centres a and b (b is the smaller community)

D_b = Break-point distance of trade to centre b

D = Distance between centres a and b

Example: In applying the formula, assume the following information:

P_a = 89,442 population, and **a** is Kelowna (from the 1996 Census)

P_b = 30,987 population, and **b** is Penticton (from the 1996 Census)

D = 65 kilometres

$$D_b = \frac{65}{1+\sqrt{\frac{89{,}442}{30{,}987}}} = \frac{65}{1 + 1.70} = 24.1 \text{ kilometres}$$

The breaking point between Kelowna and Penticton is thus 24.1 kilometres from Penticton (and 40.9 kilometres from Kelowna).

Figure 7-4 The Breaking Points Between City **A** and Each of Four Smaller Cities Help Define the Boundaries of the Trading Area for a Store in City **A**.

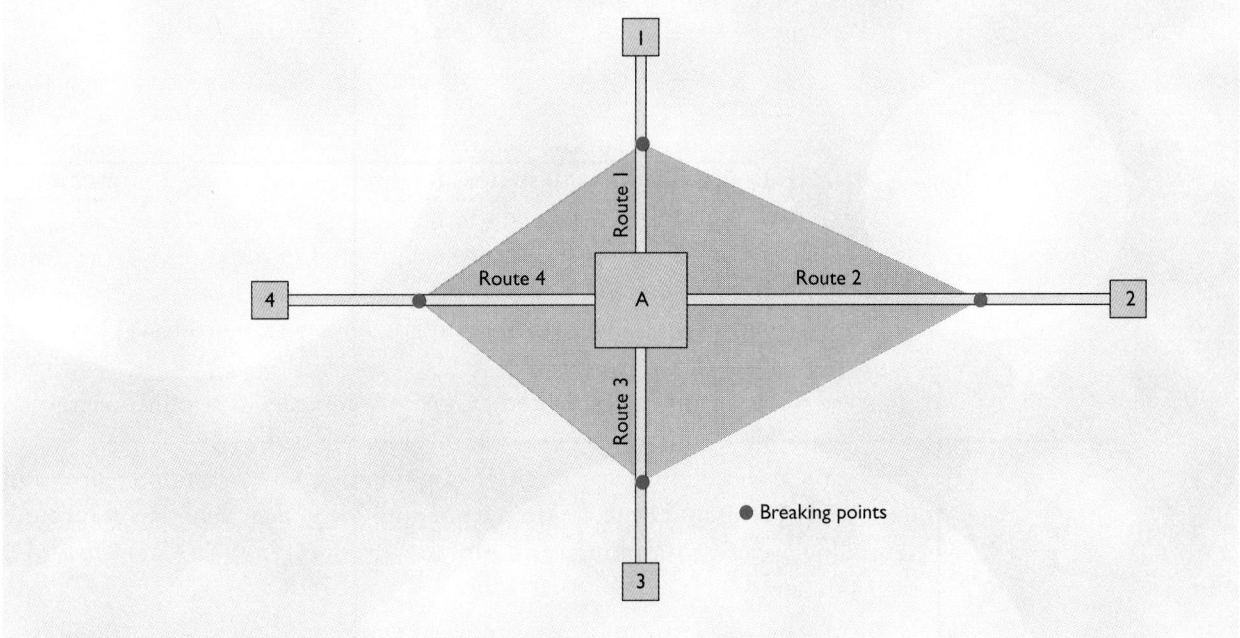

The formula can be modified in several ways including the substitution of driving time for distance, and square metres of retail floor space for population.

Reilly's Law works satisfactorily in rural areas where distance has a major impact on the choice of a community at which to shop. Breaking points do not exist in metropolitan areas, however, because consumers typically have several shopping choices available within the distance that they are willing to travel. In essence, Reilly's Law states that the size of a trading area increases as population density decreases. For example, people may travel several kilometres to shop at a small rural village. However, the same persons would only be willing to travel a few blocks in a major metropolitan area. Further, the use of Reilly's Law is appropriate only for communities of roughly similar size. Also, trade areas vary by type of good sought, a reality not reflected in Reilly's model. Patronage is also assumed to be linearly related to time or distance from the consumer's household.

The Huff Model

A model developed by David Huff helps overcome the limitations of Reilly's model. For example, Huff's models are premised on the assumption that the likelihood of consumer patronage increases with the size of a centre. Thus consumers are willing to travel greater distances when additional merchandise is available at a central location. The probability of patronage is also assumed to be linearly related to time or distance from the consumer's household.

The formal expression of the model is as follows:[9]

$$P(C_{ij}) = \frac{\dfrac{S_j}{T_{ij}^{\lambda}}}{\displaystyle\sum_{j=1}^{n} \dfrac{S_j}{T_{ij}^{\lambda}}}$$

where:

$P(C_{ij})$ = Probability of a consumer at a given point of origin i travelling to a given shopping centre j

S_j = Square metres of selling space devoted to the sale of a particular class of goods at shopping centre j

T_{ij} = Travel time involved in getting from a customer's travel base i to shopping centre j

λ = A parameter estimated empirically to reflect the effect of travel time on the various kinds of shopping trips

The most frequently used method of estimating λ is a computer program developed by Huff and Blue.[10] After estimating λ, management can determine the trading area of a shopping centre for any product class. The steps involved are as follows:

1. Divide the area surrounding a shopping centre into small statistical units within a constructed grid. Such units are represented by i in the model.
2. Determine the square metres of retail selling space of all shopping centres (j) included within the area of analysis.
3. Ascertain the travel time involved in getting from each statistical unit i to each of the specified shopping centres j.
4. Calculate the probability of consumers in each of the statistical units going to each shopping centre for a given product purchase, using the above formula.
5. Map the trading area for the shopping centre by drawing lines connecting all statistical units having the same probabilities.

A concrete example of application of the Huff model is given in Figure 7-5.

Still, the Huff model has its weaknesses. It assumes that consumers with comparable demographic characteristics will exhibit similar retail patronage behaviour. Huff's model includes all potential retail centres in the system although all centres might not be patronized. Recent research has shown that allowing consumers to specify their choice set of shopping centres as opposed to an arbitrarily imposed set in the traditional Huff model substantially improves the performance of the model and can be used for predictive and explanatory purposes.

Figure 7-5

A Numerical Application of the Huff Model

Alice Middleton, the owner of a women's clothing store, is interested in opening a new store in one of the three major shopping centres (Thorncliffe, Westmount, and Eaton Plaza) serving the West Park residential area, a high income community. After doing some research, she has been able to ascertain the following facts:

Square metres of selling space devoted to the sale of women's clothing at each shopping centre:

S_1 = 1000 m^2, for Thorncliffe Shopping Mall
S_2 = 1500 m^2, for Westmount Shopping Centre
S_3 = 2000 m^2, for Eaton Plaza

Travel time involved in getting from a customer's home in West Park to each shopping centre:

T_{i1} = 2 km, from West Park to Thorncliffe Shopping Mall
T_{i2} = 3 km, from West Park to Westmount Shopping Centre
T_{i3} = 4 km, from West Park to Eaton Plaza

$\lambda = 2$

Probability of a consumer from West Park travelling to each shopping centre:

$$P(C_{i1}) = \frac{\frac{1000}{2^2}}{\frac{1000}{2^2} + \frac{1500}{3^2} + \frac{2000}{4^2}} = \frac{250}{250 + 167 + 125} = 0.46, \text{ for Thorncliffe;}$$

Similarly, $P(C_{i2}) = 0.31$, for Westmount;
$P(C_{i3}) = 0.23$, for Eaton Plaza.

One can easily verify that 0.46 + 0.31 + 0.23 = 1.00. From this information, one can deduce that Alice would have a potential 46 percent of West Park residents if she located in Thorncliffe, compared to 31 percent for Westmount and 23 percent for Eaton Plaza.

If the population of West Park is 100,000 residents, and the average per capita sales of women's clothing is $240, each centre would generate in women's clothing sales:

Thorncliffe: 100,000 X $240 X 0.46 = $11,040,000
Westmount: 100,000 X $240 X 0.31 = $ 7,440,000
Eaton Plaza: 100,000 X $240 X 0.23 = $ 5,520,000

Next, Alice must estimate the share of these total sales that she could realistically expect, given the competition already there for each centre. By multiplying these market shares by the total sales, she will get an estimate of the sales from West Park residents in each location to be compared to the costs of opening a store in each centre. Of course, if each centre draws customers from other areas, the same calculations should be made and aggregated into total expected sales for each location.

How Much Business Can Be Done in the Trading Area?

Retailers need five sets of data to help estimate the amount of sales available in a trading area: (1) number of people in the trading area; (2) average household income; (3) amount of money spent each year by the households on the type of goods sold by the firm—i.e., groceries, drugs, or apparel; (4) the total market potential; and (5) the share of the total market potential management can expect to get.

The number of people in a trading area can be obtained from an analysis of Statistics Canada census data in almost any library, as noted above. The data are reported by **census tracts** (small areas with 2,500 to 8,000 people) for all cities with a population of 50,000 or more. There are over 5,000 census tracts in Canada, and these can be used for large shopping centre location decisions. A finer breakdown can be obtained by using **enumeration areas** that contain 100 to 200 households. There are about 40,000 enumeration areas in Canada, which are very useful for small store location decisions. Finally, distances can be entered into the analysis by using the **universe transverse mercator (UTM) system**, which gives the coordinates of every possible location in Canada, including the centre of the enumeration areas.

The average household income in each census tract is published by Statistics Canada every five years. Information about the amount of money spent each year on various types of merchandise can be found in Statistics Canada publications on family expenditures.[11]

Multiplying average annual household income by the number of families in the trading area yields total sales potential. Multiplying total sales potential by the percentage of the average annual household income spent on each type of goods (for example, groceries) yields total sales potential by type of good.

Table **7-3** Estimating Annual Sales in a Retail Store's Trading Area

	(1)		(2)		(3)		(4)		(5)
Method:	Number of households in a census tract in retail trading area	×	Median annual income of the households in the census tract	×	Proportion of a household's annual income spent on type of items sold by store	×	Proportion of money spent on item that will be spent in this store	=	Proposed store sales revenue from census tract
Census tracts in trading area:									
354XX	6,500	×	$10,000	×	.20*	×	.10†	=	$ 1,300,000
354XY	8,500	×	8,000	×	.15	×	.15	=	$ 1,530,000
Total projected annual sales									$ 2,830,000

*The proportion of .20 percent of the typical household's annual income of $10,000 is spent on merchandise sold by this store.
†The proportion of .10 means that management anticipates that 10 percent of the total merchandise purchased in this census tract will be purchased at this specific store.

Retailers then decide on the amount of the available sales potential they can get. One way to do this is by plotting competitors in the trading area on a map and trying to establish the sales levels of each. Indicators may be the number of checkouts, number of employees, square metres, and industry trade averages for sales per square metre. Retailers must also decide on the amount of business they need to make a profit. Then, they decide on whether and how much business they can take from the competition. Table 7-3 shows this five-step process.

SITE ANALYSIS AND EVALUATION

Site analysis and evaluation is the third step in the selection of a retail location. The retailer has four basic choices for a site: a strip shopping centre, a shopping mall, the central business district (the "downtown" shopping area), or a free-standing (or stand-alone) location. Even within these types, there are more categories to choose from.

Understanding the Dynamics of the Local Retail Structure

The urban business pattern is constantly changing as new retail outlets are built, inner cities decay and are rebuilt, and central business districts lose their attraction as magnets for major retailers. Understanding the shopping centre structure, the dynamics of central business districts, and the nature of stand-alone sites available is important at this stage of the analysis. The following sections describe the different types of locations and provide criteria for selecting a particular site. Table 7-4 gives an overview of the strengths and weaknesses of the basic choices.

Table 7-4 Strengths and Weaknesses of Selected Location Alternatives

Type of Location	Strengths	Weaknesses
Shopping mall	Large number of stores Drawing power of large anchor stores Parking availability Planned balanced tenant mix Entertainment available Pedestrian focus	Occupancy costs Some inflexibility (e.g., store hours, merchandise sold)
Strip shopping centre	Operating costs Shopping convenience Shared promotions	Tenant mix Facility condition High vacancy rate Susceptible to competition
Central business district	Mass transit Urban redevelopment Business/work traffic generates exposure	Parking Limited shopping hours Facility condition Suburban shift Rent costs
Solo location	Lack of close competition Lower rent More space for expansion Greater flexibility	Harder to attract customers Probably have to build instead of rent Higher promotion costs

Shopping Centres

Shopping centres are a geographic cluster of retail stores collectively handling an assortment of varied goods that satisfy one or more categories of the merchandise wants of consumers within convenient driving time of the centre. Shopping centres with a mix of stores that meet a very large variety of needs are said to have a **balanced tenancy**. The shopping centres have parking close to the store, but usually no pedestrian focus. In recent years, other types of shopping centres have emerged by catering to more narrow needs (e.g., only food, clothing, or home decoration). Retail Highlight 7-1 explains the nature of shopping centres in Canada.

What Are Shopping Centre Strengths and Weaknesses? The strengths of shopping centres are: (1) balanced tenant mix for the traditional type, depth of assortment in the category for most of the others; (2) common store hours; (3) centre-wide promotions; (4) few parking problems; (5) climate control; (6) longer store hours; and (7) a pleasant environment for attracting shoppers.

Small shopping centre stores can take advantage of the traffic-drawing ability of large mass merchandisers or outlets with national reputations. Often, people will shop in the small shops even though they came to the shopping centre primarily to shop at the large mass merchandisers. But strip shopping centres also have weaknesses. The primary problems centre around what the individual merchant can and cannot do. Specifically, tenants face restrictions on (1) what can be sold and (2) store hours. Also, the policies of the centre are often dictated by the large **anchor tenant**(s). Finally, rent will be higher than in a stand-alone location.

What Are the Choices?[12] Whether a retailer can get into a shopping centre depends on the market and management. A small strip shopping centre may need only one children's shoe store, for example, while a shopping mall may expect enough business for several.

In order to find tenants whose line of goods will meet the needs of the market to be reached, the developer-owner first signs prestige merchants as lead tenants. Then, other types of stores are selected that will complement each other. This bolsters the centre's competitive strength against other centres, as well as supplying the market area's needs. However, many malls in Canada tend to have the same types of tenants, especially the large chains such as the Bay, or the specialty chains such as Dylex. This may adversely affect new entries with this kind of sameness, and favour new malls with a special flavour, especially those who have incorporated unique entertainment outlets, as in the Mills malls described in the Retail Highlight 7-1.

To finance a centre, the developer needs major leases from companies with strong credit ratings. Lenders favour tenant rosters that include the triple-A ratings of national chains. When most spaces are filled, a developer may choose small outlets to help fill the remaining vacancies. However, a person who is considering a shopping centre for a first-store venture may have trouble. Financial backing and merchandising experience may be unproven. The problem is to convince the developer that the new store has a reasonable chance of success and will help the tenant mix.

Retail Highlight 7-1 Shopping Centres: Are They the New Town Centres?

Recent history has challenged the notion that shopping centres could be compared to the ancient city square, a meeting place for people to socialize and to be seen. When it opened its doors in 1975, the TransCanada Mall in Calgary was a shiny example of modern consumerism. It seemed ideally located, at a major intersection, dominating an established neighbourhood where no competing malls would likely be built. It obviously was not enough of an attraction for the nearby residents, and the mall was torn down to be replaced by a strip shopping centre of food and convenience stores, all facing the street. In downtown Halifax, along Spring Garden Road, malls have gone through boom and bust. According to Geri Shepard, manager of Bayer's Road Shopping Centre, "Spring Garden Road was a wonderful pedestrian place bounded by parks. It was a residential neighbourhood with seniors, young families, and university students. The developers saw that traffic and translated it into shopping centre traffic." But it does not always work, and the malls on Spring Garden Road have had a hard time.

What these examples illustrate is that the success of shopping centres is not only a function of traffic or competition, but it must correctly account for the needs of the population, and develop a competitive advantage beyond location. For example, industry analysts have pointed out that: Middle-aged couples, many juggling children and two jobs, found that they had less time and inclination to browse through the malls. The *mix* of retailers is the second most important factor after location, particularly for customers who do not want to go through several malls to find an item. Malls must provide more services, for example, day care for children and medical offices for seniors. Some developers have increased the *density* of nearby population by adding office towers, hotels, and car showrooms at mall locations. The success of a mall as a popular town centre will depend on how well it meets the needs of the population.

The answer to the new reality may have been found by a U.S. mall developer called Mills Corp. A Mills mall offers customers both fun and entertainment, including virtual reality games, fishing ponds, and football games shown on a large television screen. Bargain hunters find lots of high quality merchandise at discount prices. The first Canadian Mills mall is scheduled to open in Vaughan, Ontario in 2001, with a retail area of 140,000 m^2, dozens of factory outlets, new retailer clearing-house outlets, several category killers, hot new concepts like Rainforest Café, and other new types of retailers. It has been termed the "Disney World of retailing." In the U.S., Mills malls have become huge tourist attractions, with thousands of tour buses, and claim that customers spend twice as long and twice as much as in regional shopping centres.

Along Spring Garden Road, malls have gone through boom and bust.

Photo by Mike Harvey

Sources: Barbara Wickens, "Misery at the malls," *Maclean's*, March 23, 1992, pp. 30–31; Andrew Allentuck, "Is the mall beginning to pall?" *The Globe & Mail*, May 5, 1992, p. B23; Sean Silcoff, "Retail That Rocks," *Canadian Business*, November 27, 1998, pp. 48–58.

Strong anchor tenants, like Zellers and Canadian Tire, are critical to the success of a mall.

Photo by Anne Laroche

Factors to Consider in a Shopping Centre Choice Suppose that the owner-developer of a shopping centre asks a retailer to be a tenant. In considering the offer, the retailer needs to make sure of what he or she can do in the centre. What rules will affect the operation? In exchange for the rules, what will the centre do for the firm?

The Centre's Location In examining the centre's location, look for answers to questions such as these:[13]

1. Can the store hold old customers and attract new ones?
2. Would the centre offer the best sales volume potential for the kind of merchandise to be sold?
3. Can management benefit enough from the centre's access to a market? If so, can it offer the appeal that will make the centre's customers come to the store?

A retailer should make an analysis of the market the developer expects to reach. In this respect, money for professional help is well-spent, especially when the research indicates that the centre is not right for the type of firm planned.

Store Space Determine where the space will be. The location within a centre is important. Does the store need to be in the main flow of customers as they pass between the stores with the greatest "customer pull"? What will be the nature of the adjacent stores? What will be their effect on sales of the planned firm?

Amount of Space Using their experience, retailers should determine the amount of space needed to handle the sales volume expected. The amount of space will also determine the rent to be paid.

Total Rent Most shopping centre leases are negotiated either on a percentage basis or on a fixed fee per square metre. The contents of a lease will be covered later in the chapter. Rental expenses may begin with a minimum guarantee that is equal to a percentage of gross sales. While this is typically between five and seven percent of gross sales for nonanchor tenants, it varies by type or size of business and other factors. For anchor tenants, this percentage is usually lower.

Alternatively, fixed annual rents in most Canadian shopping centres tend to average between $150 and $300 per square metre, and may go higher in some instances; for example, in the West Edmonton Mall, the average annual rent can go as high as $650 per square metre.[14] Other charges are assessed in addition to the minimum guarantee or the monthly rent. A retailer may have to pay dues to the centre's merchant association and for maintenance of common areas.

Rent, then, should be considered in terms of "total rent."If "total rent" is more than the present rent in an existing location, the space in the centre will have to draw enough additional sales to justify the added cost.

Finishing Out Generally, the developer furnishes only the bare space in a new centre. The retailer does the "finishing out" at his or her own expense. For example, a retailer pays for lighting fixtures, counter shelves, painting, and floor coverings. In addition, heating and cooling units may have to be installed. Some developers help tenants plan store fronts, exterior signs, and interior colour schemes.

Types of Shopping Centres

Because shopping centres are built around major tenants, centres are classified, in part, according to the leading tenant and whether there is a pedestrian focus. The classification includes two major types: strip shopping centres and malls.

Strip Shopping Centres

There are three types of strip shopping centres: neighbourhood, community, and power. The typical characteristics of these are described in Table 7-5.

Neighbourhood Shopping Centre Statistics Canada defines a **neighbourhood shopping centre** as one with 5 to 15 stores, and which offers free parking.[15] The supermarket or the drugstore is the leading tenant in a neighbourhood centre.

Table 7-5

Description of the Three Types of Strip Shopping Centres

	Neighbourhood	Community	Power
Number of stores	5-15	16-30	more than 30
Leading tenant	supermarket or drugstore	variety or junior department	category killer, warehouse club, discount department
Typical leasable space	5,000 m^2	15,000 m^2	30,000 m^2
Typical site area	1.6 hectares	4 hectares	12 hectares
Minimum trade population	7,500 to 25,000	25,000 to 75,000	75,000 or more

This type is the smallest in size among shopping centres, with few stores, and caters to the convenience needs of a neighbourhood. For example, Westsyde Shopping Centre in Kamloops is anchored by Cooper's Market and Quality Bakery, has 11 stores, a gross leasable retail area of about 5,200 m^2, a primary population of 7,000, and a secondary population of 25,000.[16]

Community Shopping Centre Statistics Canada defines a **community shopping centre** as one with 16 to 30 stores, and which offers free parking.[17] Variety or junior department stores are the leading tenants. Such centres include some specialty shops, wider price ranges, greater style assortments, and more impulse-sale items. For example, Country Fair Mall in Summerside (P.E.I.) is anchored by Zellers and Sobeys, has 23 stores, a gross leasable retail area of about 14,860 m^2, and a population base of 37,700.[18]

Power Centre A **power centre** is a recent development created by the growth of new types of retailers catering to value-conscious consumers. Power centres are usually dominated by category killers (Home Depot), warehouse clubs (Price/Costco), and other discount stores (Wal-Mart). The most frequently represented power centre anchor tenants, in descending frequency, are: toy/children's superstore, off-price apparel outlet, soft lines promotional department store, discount department store, consumer electronic superstore, deep-discount drugstore, or a consumer-oriented home improvement outlet. They are usually freestanding stores with or without a specific arrangement. Everything is visible from the street, and consumers can drive directly to where they want to go. Such centres have smaller acquisition, building, and maintenance costs than shopping malls. Additionally, the developers achieve a greater merchandise depth than the typical strip centre. The strongest candidates for power centres are national, regional, and local retailers with a strong presence and name recognition. A strong value image is also important. One example of a power centre is the Marché Central in North Montreal.[19]

Shopping Malls

A **shopping mall** is a planned mix of tenants that are connected to each other so that customers can access all the stores once they have parked their cars. In addition, many malls have added restaurants (food courts), and entertainment (movie theatres, virtual reality games), and the newer types of malls have

Power Centre in Oshawa includes PetSmart, Michaels Arts and Crafts Superstore, and other big box stores.

Courtesy Blade Marketing

become the new meeting place for teenagers, older citizens, and families.[20] There are five major types of shopping malls: regional shopping centre, value and entertainment-oriented megamalls, theme or festival centres, fashion-oriented centres, and outlet centres.

When considering a mall, retailers should weigh the benefits against costs. At the outset, it may be difficult to measure savings, such as the elimination of store fronts, against costs. For example, the cost of heating and air-conditioning may be higher in the enclosed mall. In an enclosed mall centre, tenant groupings include drugstores and supermarkets in a separate building at the edge of the parking area. Relatively high-priced women's goods stores tend to cluster together. Service and repair shops are located where customers have direct access from the parking lot for quick in-and-out pickup of goods.

Regional Shopping Centre This is the oldest type of shopping mall. Statistics Canada defines a **regional shopping centre** as one with more than 30 stores, and which offers free parking.[21] The department store, with its prestige, is the leader in the regional centre. When a retailer finds that a second or third department store is also locating in such a centre, he or she will know the site has been selected to draw from the widest possible market area. The smaller tenants are picked to offer a range of goods and services approaching the appeal once found only downtown. A typical regional shopping centre is the Fredericton Mall with three anchors, 66 tenants, a gross leasable area of 22,730 m^2, and a market population of 165,310.[22] Retail Highlight 7-2 provides some interesting facts about shopping malls in Canada.

The Value and Entertainment-Oriented Megamall[23] The West Edmonton Mall has forced a reexamination of malls as a new format of retail institution. While regional malls were designed and managed to satisfy a major purpose, i.e., shopping, the **value and entertainment-oriented megamall** is a new type of shopping mall providing several additional functions, such as entertainment, recreation, eating, drinking, socializing, working, and sightseeing. The planned Mills

Mall in Vaughan, Ontario (joint venture with Cambridge) falls into the same category (see Retail Highlight 7-1).

Theme or Festival Centres[24] The **theme centres** can be quite diverse in thematic format, size, and market orientation, but all share features that distinguish them from other centres: a common architectural theme that unites a wide range of retailers who repeat the theme in their spaces; tenants who offer unusual merchandise; restaurants and entertainment that serve as anchors, rather than supermarkets or department stores; and a strong appeal made to tourists as well as local shoppers.

With a strong representation of restaurants, fast-food, specialty retailers, and entertainment facilities, **festival centres** tend to be large. Opportunities for

Retail Highlight 7-2 Edmonton: the Mall Capital of Canada

Major malls have been built in most regions of Canada, but nowhere to the extent of Edmonton, which on a per capita basis has *3.3 times* the national average of per capita square metres of mall retail area. Here is the ranking for the top 22 census metropolitan areas in Canada:

Metropolitan Area	Number	Leasable Area (000 m^2)	Area Per Capita (m^2)
Edmonton	8	806	0.89
Quebec City	6	476	0.68
Halifax	4	231	0.66
London	4	239	0.56
Regina	2	110	0.55
Sherbrooke	1	84	0.55
Calgary	7	444	0.49
Hamilton	5	322	0.48
Vancouver	14	908	0.46
Ottawa/Hull	6	465	0.45
Toronto	24	1,884	0.41
Chicoutimi	1	65	0.39
St. Catharines/Niagara	2	142	0.36
Oshawa	1	102	0.35
Sudbury	1	56	0.34
Winnipeg	3	228	0.33
Trois-Rivières	1	47	0.33
Windsor	1	89	0.29
Saskatoon	1	65	0.29
Montreal	12	947	0.28
St. John's	1	47	0.27
Kitchener	1	70	0.17
Canada	**114**	**8,274**	**0.27**

Of Canada's 114 malls, 34 can be called "super regional malls," with more than 75,000 m^2 of leasable area. Of the 114 malls, 51 were built in the 1970s, 21 were added in the 1980s, and only 7 so far in the 1990s.

Sources: *1999 Directory of Shopping Centres, vol. 1 and 2*; Statistics Canada, *Annual Demographic Statistics, 1998*, Cat. 91-213-XPB, Tables 5.1 and 5.2 (February 1998).

new growth are considered limited. A typical festival centre is Le Faubourg in Montreal, a collection of food stalls, specialty shops, and restaurants in an old warehouse building. Often these enterprises are the result of young entrepreneurial merchants who fill an indoor marketplace with boutiques selling items ranging from towels and hats to strawberry-scented soaps. Ultra-small retailers are a fixture in many such operations. Many of the urban centres built by developers as part of a commercial building offer local neighbourhood customers (including the "office crowd") and tourists a new experience.

Fashion-Oriented Centres These fashion-oriented centres consist mainly of apparel shops, boutiques, and craft shops carrying selected merchandise of high quality and price. They appeal to high-income shoppers. Growth was strongest for fashion-oriented centres in the mid-1980s but has slowed recently.

Outlet Centres In contrast to factory outlets of the past, typically found at the factory site, **factory outlet centres** consist of retail outlets owned and operated by manufacturers where goods are sold directly to the public. Factory outlet malls draw customers from a variety of income and age groups, and often include some off-price stores.[25] Vanity Fair, Burlington, and Bally are examples. *Complete centres devoted to factory outlets have become a permanent fixture in the shopping centre field because they combine two of the key draws that lure shoppers: perceived value and one-stop shopping.*[26] Add to that plenty of parking space, fast-food restaurants, a movie theatre, and a recreation store with blinking electronic games.

Specialty Centres

There are several types of shopping centres that do not fall neatly into the two main categories of strip or mall. They are a response by retailers to very specific shopping needs.

Urban Arterial Developments **Urban arterial developments** are often found in an older part of the city. The sites were initially developed to provide good locations on a busy street for shoppers. Typical examples include home repair centres, appliance stores, automobile repair shops, and office equipment firms, which serve either a commercial or consumer market. Highway-oriented strip developments occur on the outskirts of major cities and are characterized by such facilities as motels and restaurants.

Discount Centres A discount centre is usually anchored by one or more discount stores with a strong representation of discount merchants. The centres appeal mainly to lower-income groups.[27]

Service-Oriented Centres These centres depend heavily upon service-oriented retailers, such as opticians, dentists, repair services, health clinics, legal services, and so forth. Their present share is expected to grow in strip centres, the largest industry component and one with much space to fill.

Home Improvement Centres **Home improvement centres** are anchored by a large home improvement retailer or feature a concentration of home improvement and hardware specialty retailers. As yet, numbers are not significant, but this concept is expected to grow.

Single Theme Centres Zeroing in on consumer needs in a narrow range such as auto care, home decorating and design, or weddings, this new approach calls for tenanting the centre solely with retailers and services that match the theme.

Niche Malls These malls are targeted to a very specific group of customers, which is why the name *niche* was selected. In Canada, these have been targeted toward the Chinese population in areas of large concentration such as in the metropolitan areas of Montreal, Toronto, and Vancouver. In the U.S., **niche malls** have targeted working women and blacks.[28]

A Downtown Location

Central business district (downtown) locations offer several advantages:

1. Rents are lower than in many shopping centres.
2. Public transportation may be more readily available to downtown.
3. The locations are usually close to large office complexes that employ many people.
4. Entertainment districts offering theatres, restaurants, bars, and similar facilities are often available.

However, disadvantages can exist. They include the following:

1. Downtown stores are often not open in the evening.
2. Crime rates may be higher.
3. Traffic congestion is bad.
4. Downtown areas are sometimes decaying and rundown.

The high concentration of commercial buildings makes the central business district (CBD) one of the important components of urban structure. The CBD attracts people from throughout the metropolitan area, often including visitors. Mass transit also brings people into the CBD in many metropolitan areas. Such areas contain a wide variety of stores and often include the flagship of one of the leading department store chains. Examples include Sears Canada in Toronto, and Ogilvy in Montreal. Some have suggested that municipalities try to emulate the appearance of the malls to give their downtown a more inviting and exclusive look, in the same way the malls have borrowed heavily design elements from the downtown (such as parks, fountains, and plazas).[29] In addition, "Old towns" in Montreal and Vancouver are examples of revival of the CBDs. Medical districts around large hospitals also fit this description, as do streets known for their high-class fashion stores or art galleries such as Sherbrooke Street in Montreal.

A Solo Location

Statistics Canada defines a **solo location** (also called an on-street or stand-alone location) as a store or outlet located in a residential neighbourhood, commercial section, or major traffic arterial, and which is not in a shopping plaza or other type of shopping malls.[30] Superstores such as Wal-Mart, Home Depot, and Future Shop often choose solo locations. Other organizations such as Canadian Tire, Sears Canada, and Zellers have developed their own "big box" stores; for example, Sears Canada has opened in Kitchener (Ontario) a giant furniture store (3,250 m^2) called the Sears Whole Home Furniture Store, and Zellers has opened in Gatineau, Quebec, a 12,000 m^2 giant store called Zellers Plus.[31]

IKEA can use a solo-location strategy because it has strong customer loyalty and a wide assortment of merchandise in home furnishings.

Courtesy IKEA Canada

Solo locations on heavily travelled areas have several advantages including:

- The lack of close competition.
- Lower rent.
- More space for parking and expansion.
- Greater flexibility in store hours and other methods of operation.

But, disadvantages also exist. For example:

- Such stores may have difficulty attracting consumers because comparison shopping is not easy.
- Advertising costs are often higher than if the firm was in a shopping centre with other stores that would advertise together.
- The retailer will probably have to build a store rather than rent one.

The most successful stores in on-street locations are those with a strong customer loyalty and a wide assortment of national-brand merchandise from which consumers can choose. After deciding on an acceptable general location, a retailer then assesses the economic potential of the trading area to determine whether it can support the planned store.

Making the Choice

Ultimately the choice of a location depends on the retailer's strategy for growth. The choice also depends on the market to be served, the characteristics of the customers who will be shopping at the outlet, the image of the firm, the current or projected competitive position of the retailer, and the growth objectives and capabilities of the firm.

Figure 7-6 provides a checklist of specific site evaluation criteria.

Accessibility is affected by physical barriers such as rivers, ease of ingress (i.e., going in) and egress (i.e., going out or exiting) from the site, traffic congestion, and road conditions. As a generalization, the higher the volume of traffic, the higher the level of potential sales. However, the composition of traffic is also important. A high

Figure 7-6

Evaluation Checklist

Zoning
Type
Surrounding zoning patterns
Likelihood of getting changes if needed

Utilities
Water, sewer, gas
Adequacy
Cost
Location of lines

Accessibility
Quality of ingress and egress
Traffic volume and flow
Public transportation availability

Land use
Vacancies
Terrain
Parking availability
Building patterns
Amenities

Growth potential
Trends in income
Trends in number and mix of population
Trends—building permits issued
Location pattern of competitive business

volume of commercial or truck traffic, for example, is not desirable. Similarly, a high volume of pedestrian traffic with little time for browsing is also not desirable.

The amount of parking needed depends on frequency of vehicle turnover, the type of merchandise sold, and peak parking requirements. However, peak parking should be evaluated in a "normal" period as opposed to a heavy shopping period such as Christmas. Otherwise, the retailer will find excess parking spaces sitting vacant most of the year.

Traffic counts can be of critical importance in evaluating the suitability of a site. The general objective of a traffic count is to count the passing traffic—both pedestrian and vehicular—that would constitute potential customers who would probably be attracted into the store.[32] Data from traffic counts should not only show how many people pass by but generally indicate what kinds of people they are. Analysis of the characteristics of the passing traffic frequently reveals patterns and variations not readily apparent from casual observation. The season, month, week, day, and hour all have an effect upon a traffic survey. For example, during summer there is generally an increased flow of traffic on the shady side of the street. During a holiday period, such as the month before Christmas or the week before Easter, traffic is denser than normal. The patronage of a store varies by day of the week, too, as store traffic usually increases during the latter part of the week. In some communities, on factory paydays and days when social security cheques are received, certain locations experience heavier-than-normal traffic.

Management also has to decide whether they want to locate in proximity to the competition. Locating in proximity to competitors can encourage comparison shopping. Some areas of a community, for example, have a concentration of automobile dealers or furniture outlets for that reason.

Other Factors to Consider

Most first-time business owners have no idea how effective a strong merchants' association can be in promoting and maintaining the business in a given area.

Management should always find out about the merchants' association. The presence of an effective association can strengthen the business and save management money through group advertising programs, group insurance plans, and collective security measures. Some associations have induced city planners to add highway exits near their shopping centres. Others have lobbied for (and received) funds from cities to remodel their shopping centres, including extension of parking lots, resurfacing of building, and installation of better lighting.

Responsiveness of the Landlord

Directly related to the appearance of a retail location is the responsiveness of the landlord to the individual merchant's needs. Unfortunately, some landlords of retail business properties actually hinder the operation of their tenants' businesses. They are in fact responsible for the demise of their properties. Retail Highlight 7-3 provides examples of effective landlords.

By restricting the placement and size of signs, by foregoing or ignoring needed maintenance and repairs, by renting adjacent retail spaces to incompatible—or worse, directly competing—businesses, landlords may cripple a retailer's attempts to increase business. Sometimes landlords lack the funds to maintain their properties. Rather than continuing to invest in their holdings by maintaining a proper appearance for their buildings and supporting their tenants, they try to "squeeze" the property for whatever they can get.

Retail Highlight 7-3 For Effective Landlords, a Lease Agreement Is a Partnership

For a landlord, a good tenant is a steady source of revenue, particularly when the lease agreement includes a percentage of sales, and when the economy is faltering. It is, thus, extremely important for the landlord to help current and potential tenants succeed. The following example helps illustrate the benefits of this proactive approach:

When Confed Realty Services bought for $1 the Eaton Centre mall in downtown Edmonton from Triple Five Corp., the mall was doing very poorly, and tenants were asking rent concessions. Sandy McNair, a proprietor and manager of the mall, knew that rent concessions would not increase sales, which is what was needed to make the mall profitable. By using the amount of money that would have gone into rent concessions, he was able to invest it in a program that produced impressive results. Some of the elements were: (1) a complete interior renovation of the mall to make it more appealing to customers; (2) an ongoing program to advise retailers on improving their operations, including window displays and store designs (using consultants paid by Confed); (3) the Eaton Centre Retail Management Institute taught by professional consultants (again paid by Confed) giving an eight-week course on customer service, salesmanship, time management, and human resources; (4) a customer-loyalty program developed, run, and financed by Confed, which serves as a database for marketing, providing useful information to retailers about who their customers are, and serving as a basis for targeted promotion.

Source: John Southerst, "The Reinvention of Retail," *Canadian Business*, August 1992, pp. 26–31.

Leases

What Is a Lease? A lease is a legal contract that conveys property from the landlord to the tenant for a specified period of time in return for an agreed-on fee. Leases can take several forms. Under a **fixed-payment lease**, the landlord charges the tenant a fixed amount each month. In a **variable-payment lease**, the retailer pays a guaranteed minimum rent plus a specified percentage of sales. The minimum rent typically covers the landlord's expenses, such as taxes, insurance, and maintenance. The percentage of sales component of the rent allows the landlord to share in the profits the retailer makes as a result of being in a choice location.

The rent to be paid is determined by several factors. The primary factor is the sales per square metre that can be generated at the site. Retailers with high sales per square metre typically pay a lower percentage rent than retailers with lower sales per square metre. Outlets with high sales per square metre generate higher volumes of customer traffic and as a result are able to negotiate lower percentage rents because they are more desirable tenants.

SELECTING THE SITE

A perfect location rarely exists. Ideally, management can find a location with easy accessibility, high traffic flow, at a reasonable price, and in a desirable shopping environment.

Rating Sites

The final choice among alternative sites can be made after management decides on (1) the *importance* of selected factors in choosing a site and, (2) the *attractiveness* of the site based on the factors identified as important. Multiplying importance by attractiveness as shown in Table 7-6 yields a weighted score for each factor. The total score for each site allows management to compare and rank alternative sites more objectively in making a final choice.

Table 7-6 Rating Sheet for Sites

Factor	Importance*	Attractiveness+ Ranking of Site	Weighted Score
Growth potential	2	2	4
Rental conditions	6	4	24
Investment required	5	5	25
Strength of competition	1	1	1
Ability to serve target	3	6	18
Profit potential	4	3	12
Total Score for Site			*84*

* I is most important to the owner-manager.
\+ For the site considered, I is most attractive to the owner-manager.

Consider the Future

Management should look ahead. Try to picture the situation ten years from now. Try to determine whether the general area can support the firm as the business expands. Also, management must consider whether a site that fills its present needs will allow for future expansion.

Relocate for Growth?

Sometimes an owner-manager should consider relocating although the need for it is not apparent—even though the present space may seem adequate, and customers are being served without undue complaints. If a facility has become a competitive liability, moving to another building may be the most economical way to become competitive again. For example, if a new high quality shopping centre in a downtown area is expected to attract a lot of traffic away from the street merchants, the owner of a retail store situated in an old building should seriously consider relocating inside the centre.

CHAPTER HIGHLIGHTS

- Location is a key factor in the retailing mix. Retailers should consider such a decision as carefully as pricing, promotion, and other elements of the retailing mix.
- Key strategic decisions in retail location relate to the desired type of market coverage and the type of goods sold. The process of selecting a retail location goes from region or metropolitan area choice, to trade area analysis and site analysis and evaluation.
- Key factors in making the market selection include its size, composition of the population, labour market, closeness to the source of merchandise supply, media mix available, economic base of the community, existing and probable future competition, availability of store sites, and local, provincial, and federal regulations.
- Trade area analysis is done once the market has been selected. Retailers can employ a variety of techniques in assessing the size of the probable trading area (primary and secondary). These techniques include a study of existing stores, an analysis of credit records, consumer spotting, driving time analysis, gravity models, and conducting a customer survey to help understand customer shopping behaviour.
- After establishing the size of the trading area, management then has to determine the amount of business that can be done in the trading area. The amount of business is a function of the number of people in the trading area, the average household income, the amount of money spent each year by households on the type of goods sold by the firm, the total market potential available, and the share of the total market potential that management expects to attract.
- Analyzing and evaluating alternative sites within a trading area is the third step in selecting a retail location. Retailers can decide on a shopping centre, a downtown, or a solo location. The retailer has the choice of locating in a strip shopping centre (neighbourhood, community, or power), in a shopping mall (regional, value and entertainment-oriented megamall, theme or festival, outlet), or in a specialty centre (discount, service-oriented, home improvement, niche malls).

- Analyzing specific sites also involves assessing the adequacy and potential of vehicular or passenger traffic passing a site, the ability of the site to intercept traffic en route from one place to another, the nature of adjacent stores, type of goods sold, and adequacy of parking.
- Finally, there are a number of other factors to consider, including the responsiveness of the landlord and the contents of the lease agreement.

KEY TERMS

Term	Page	Term	Page
anchor tenants	164	primary trading area	156
balanced tenancy	164	regional dominance	150
census tract	162	regional shopping centre	169
central business district	172	retail saturation	155
community shopping centre	168	secondary trading area	156
enumeration area	162	shopping mall	168
factory outlet centre	171	solo location	172
fixed-payment lease	176	theme or festival centre	170
gravity models	158	trading area	156
home improvement centre	171	traffic count	174
market saturation	150	universal transverse mercator (UTM)	162
neighbourhood shopping centre	167	urban arterial developments	171
niche mall	172	value and entertainment-oriented megamall	169
power centre	168	variable-payment lease	176

DISCUSSION QUESTIONS

1. Explain why regional dominance, market saturation, and emphasis on smaller towns and communities are seen today as the best three location strategies.
2. What do you consider to be the important factors in selecting a site for a fast-food outlet? How do these contrast, if at all, with your notion of the key factors for the location of an outlet selling stereo components?
3. In deciding whether to locate in a particular shopping centre, what are the factors (questions) the retailer needs to consider?
4. Distinguish among the following: neighbourhood shopping centres, community shopping centres, and power centres.
5. What factors have led to the decline of downtown areas as desirable locations for many retail outlets? What can downtown areas do to better compete with the suburban shopping centres?
6. Distinguish among the following techniques used by retailers to determine the size of a trading area: gravity models, credit-records analysis, and customer surveys.
7. What are the various types of information a retailer needs to estimate the amount of likely sales within a trading area? What are some of the sources from which this information may be obtained?

8. Why is information about a retail store's target market an essential factor to consider when conducting a pedestrian traffic count?

APPLICATION EXERCISES

1. Devise a questionnaire to obtain the following information for the shopping centre at which a sample of consumers most frequently shop:

   a) Distance travelled to the shopping centre.

   b) Number of visits per week/month.

   c) Items usually purchased at this shopping centre.

   d) Factors most liked about the shopping centre.

   e) Dominant reason for shopping at the centre.

   f) Opinion about the prices of merchandise.

   g) Opinion about the quality of merchandise.

   h) Opinion about selection of merchandise.

   i) Opinion about salespeople.

   j) Opinion about the convenience of location.

   k) Amount spent here on the average per week/month.

   Expand this questionnaire to obtain similar information about the shopping centre frequented second most. Using the data obtained from your questionnaire, do an analysis to isolate the factors that determine the choice of shopping centres. Which factors are the most important? Which are the least important? Are greater dollar amounts spent at the shopping centre visited most frequently? What meaning does this have for the retailer? What are the similarities and differences in the reasons given for the shopping centre visited most and second most?

2. A topic of interest in many cities is the future of the central business district (CBD). If you are in a city that has gone through a downtown revitalization program, arrange to have interviews with the public servants (and volunteers) who were responsible for getting the project "going." Describe it; indicate the views of success; and indicate future directions. If you are not in such a situation, search the current literature for examples of cities that have done downtown revitalization jobs. Contact the chambers of commerce for information and indicate some of the national efforts along these lines.

3. Prepare a location and site analysis for a good-quality cafeteria (other types of service retailers or tangible goods establishments may be used) for your local community based on the information in the text. Assume that the cafeteria is a regional chain with excellent regional recognition and acceptance but that it is not in your community. Prices are higher than "fast-food" outlets but lower than "service restaurants" of comparable quality food.

SUGGESTED CASES

11. Arizona Restaurant

12. A Video Rental Store Location

CHAPTER 8

STORE DESIGN AND LAYOUT, AND MERCHANDISE PRESENTATION

CHAPTER OBJECTIVES

After reading this chapter you should be able to:

1. Discuss main dimensions of exterior and interior store design.
2. Describe typical store layout arrangements.
3. Explain how to allocate space to selling departments and nonselling activities.
4. Explain how to measure selling-space productivity.
5. Evaluate factors to consider in locating selling departments and sales-supporting activities within the store.
6. Describe the essentials of visual merchandising.

The importance of store design, layout, and merchandise presentation is illustrated with the following examples.[1]

- The Loblaws store on Toronto's Queen's Quay is modelled after the Disney concept of recreating attractive images of the past, particularly the "local neighbourhood with the butcher, grocer, and baker." On one side of the huge "big box," the produce and meat section are a recreation (although sanitized) of a European market, with Italian-style tile floor, colourful umbrellas, crates, and baskets of attractive produce. A Mövenpick Marché sells bakery items, fresh coffee, and juices from stalls. Next to this market, is a traditional supermarket with off-white floors and standard aisles. The consumer is encouraged to spend more money on high margin produce and meats. In addition, the store has a PC (President's Choice) no-fee bank, a dry-cleaner, a liquor store, a florist, and a shoe-repair store. In the overall design, all elements (lighting, flooring, colours, and signage) are used to create unique, more personal environments.

- The Seattle store of REI (Recreation Equipment Inc.) provides education as well as entertainment. It is a huge store (10,000 m^2) with 60,000 different items from bicycles (350 models), to tents (30), to kayak paddles (30). What sets this store apart is that customers can try the equipment before buying it and talk to experts. There is a 20-metre-high climbing pinnacle, a 145-metre-long biking trail, a Rain Room (to test water-resistant outerwear), and an Illumination Station (to test bicycle lights). In terms of design elements, the store has door handles made of ice axes, the aisles between departments resemble hiking trails, the entrance made of glass and wood gives strong, clean, welcoming signals. The store attracted 1.5 million visitors in its first year of operation, and the National Park Service established a station inside.

As these examples illustrate, innovative retailers take great care in the design and layout of their store, in the presentation of their merchandise and in creating a strong welcoming atmosphere. This chapter focuses on these decision areas. The end goals are to show how effective layout and presentations can lead not only to increased sales levels but also to greater space productivity. Store layout and design and merchandise presentation are critical elements of a firm's positioning strategy. At times, firms may need to redesign their stores' interiors and exteriors as part of a new image projection for the organization.

Ideally, design creates a store that invites customers to have fun shopping, makes them feel comfortable, helps them find the merchandise, and increases their satisfaction.[2] The major goal of store design and layout and merchandise presentation is to get the shopper into the store to spend as much money as possible on a given shopping trip. In many instances, identical merchandise can be found in directly competing stores. Thus, it is very important for any given store to create a general atmosphere and specific presentations that will trigger buying decisions on its own sales floor rather than that of competitors.

CREATING THE PHYSICAL ENVIRONMENT

In order to more easily discuss the important physical environment of a store, a few terms should be defined:

Figure 8-1 The Store Planning Process

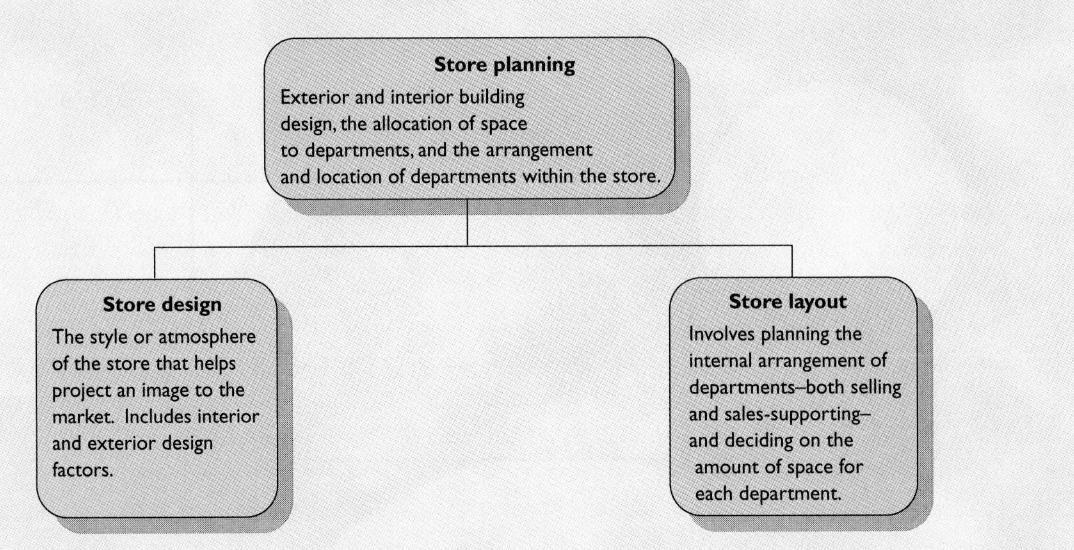

- **Store planning** includes exterior and interior building design, the allocation of space to departments, and the arrangement and location of departments within the store.
- **Store design** refers to the style or atmosphere of a store that helps project an image to the market. Store design elements include such exterior factors as the store front and window displays and such interior factors as colours, lighting, flooring, and fixtures.
- **Store layout** involves planning the internal arrangement of departments—both selling and sales supporting—and deciding on the amount of space for each department.

Figure 8-1 shows the relationships among these three terms.

STORE DESIGN

Store design is an important image-creating element and should begin with an understanding of the preferences, desires, and expectations of the store's target market. For example, store design for warehouse food stores, whose target segment is price-conscious shoppers, would feature tile floors, strong lighting, and limited in-store signing. Similarly, a design using bold colours, flashing lights, and eye-popping displays might be very appropriate for a store targeting young people, but inappropriate for a store focusing on older, conservative shoppers.

Demographic characteristics such as income and age are not the only variables of the target market to affect store design. Increasingly, store design is influenced by the lifestyles of target customers. A store that specializes in tennis equipment could reflect the lifestyle of its intended clientele by using murals with large photographs of tennis courts, and of famous tennis players.

Retailers must also constantly monitor changes occurring in the external environment and alter store design to be responsive to such changes. Retailers must use store design as a competitive weapon, appealing to the changing lifestyles of their target shoppers. For example, retail store design is being affected by the changing buying roles of men and women. With women becoming bigger buyers of hardware and automotive products, some hardware and auto-parts stores, such as Canadian Tire, are changing their store design to shed their "macho" image.

Design and Store Image

In developing an image for the store, the design should answer five fundamental questions:[3]

- Can the concept and merchandise being sold in your store be explained in one or two sentences?
- Will the customer distinguish your store from the competition?
- Can you explain the concept of your competitors that appeals to customers?
- Will your name, logo, and store design reflect the image that you want to project?
- Will your store design still look good two or five years from now?

Store design is a reflection of two elements: (1) the exterior design, and (2) the interior design, which includes everything within the store such as walls, floor, ceiling, lighting fixtures, colours, scents, and sounds. The exterior and interior designs should be in harmony with the store's merchandise and customers.

Exterior Design

Store designers indicate that many retailers make the mistake of concentrating only on the inside of the store and fail to give adequate attention to the exterior of the building. However, a store's exterior is a most important aspect of image creation.

The building's architecture and entrances, display windows, and signs are some of the image-creating elements related to exterior design.

Architecture and Entrances

A store's architecture can create image impressions in a number of ways. The architectural design may reflect the nature of the products sold in the store. A restaurant emphasizing Mexican dishes may use yellow and green colours with adobe-style walls and Mexican decorations (e.g., sombreros or piñatas).

The store's architectural style may also reflect the size of the store. For example, a huge food store may design a building on the model of a "French Market," with a large curved glass ceiling and big columns to give a feeling of space and scale.

A store's entrance should provide for easy entry into the store. However, some designers may also see entrances as a "transition zone," for example using

Courtesy Black's

Black's design and layout invite customers in. The focus on the colour reinforces name recognition and creates an image of elegance and quality.

corridors leading to courtyards, in order to ease the customer into a busy or large area, as in the REI store described at the beginning of this chapter.

Finally, some designers emphasize the importance of consistency between the exterior and interior design elements, in order to carry through the same theme associated with the design.

Display Windows

Window shopping is quite often very important for many types of retailers, and window displays should primarily be used to attract the attention and interest of the customer, leading to entering the store. Window displays are important, especially among department stores and higher-priced retailers and in cities where walking and window shopping are still in style. This is also true for stores located inside the malls, especially the large malls with many competing stores. Whether in city streets or in "mall streets," window displays may be used to enhance store image, to expose would-be shoppers to new products, or to introduce a new season.

Retailers put considerable effort into designing window displays for Christmas, since for many of them this is the best selling period. Properly decorated Christmas windows will put the customers into the right mood, bring back childhood memories, break down their inhibitions, and put them into the spirit of giving, as illustrated in Retail Highlight 8-1. For major department stores, Christmas represents the largest decorating expenditure, and is the responsibility of a special committee who works 12 months to plan and order for the upcoming season.[4]

Retail Highlight 8-1 **Especially During the Christmas Selling Season, Window Displays Put Shoppers in the Spirit of Giving**

There is much art and imagination in designing windows for the Christmas season. The general idea is well known by most: Santa Claus, the nativity scene, gift-giving, and holiday festivities and activities, such as skating on the pond. The challenge is to find an interesting execution, one that would say to the shopper: "That's an innovative retailer, let's see what's inside." Some examples from the 1994 season in Toronto are:

- At Tiffany's, on Bloor Street, the idea is to have the shopper bang his or her head into the glass trying to get a glimpse at the various tableaux. The story is developed around Santa's preparations for the big event. Santa himself is never seen, but he is there: picking up his laundry (such as his darned red socks), checking his list of who was nice and who's naughty, having tea and cookies on this cold night. Of course, all around the tableaux, tastefully arranged, are Tiffany's products.
- At the Bay, on Queen Street, the idea is to enchant the shopper by a fantastic rendition of Santa's bedroom in a Victorian style, with a twin-unicorn headboard, a carousel horse, a wonderful Victorian birdcage, an armoire, and a sleigh full of porcelain dolls, stuffed bears, and a nutcracker.
- At Grafix, an art supply store, the idea is to make fun of artists, such as Matisse, Van Gogh, and Cezanne, with "self-portraits with Santa Claus hats." The message is, "If these people can paint, you can too."

Source: Judy Margolis, "Windowonderlands," *The Globe and Mail*, December 8, 1994, p. D11.

Much art is involved in developing window displays, as illustrated in the Retail Highlight 8-1. Principles of good design—balance, proportion, and harmony—are all essential. Errors retailers sometimes make are using too much or too little merchandise, inappropriate props and lighting, or simply not changing a display frequently enough with the result that it loses its special significance. The ideal is to change the window displays about 15 to 20 times a year.

Management can evaluate the results of window displays by (1) the number of people passing the window in a certain period, (2) the number of passersby who glance at the window, (3) the number that stop, and (4) the number that enter the store after looking at the window display.

Signs

The creative use of an easy-to-read outdoor sign serves the purpose of identifying the store and providing some information about it. The sign can also be an important factor in creating a favourable image for the store. Some retailers have developed distinctive signs that are widely recognized by consumers. An example is McDonald's with its golden arches.

Interior Design

Within the store, consumers not only respond to the products or services being offered but also to their surroundings. Environmental factors can affect a shopper's desire to shop or not shop at the store and the amount of time spent in the store. The internal environment can also influence the customer's desire or willingness to explore the environment and to communicate with salespeople. Thus, retailers must consider the psychological effects of their outlets on consumer purchasing behaviour. Fast-food restaurants do this by utilizing hard chairs and fast-tempo music to encourage rapid turnover during lunch times.

As has been observed: "A subtle dimension of in-store customer shopping behaviour is the environment of the space itself. Retail space, i.e., the proximate environment that surrounds the retail shopper, is never neutral. The retail store is a bundle of cues, messages, and suggestions which communicate to shoppers. Retail store designers, planners, and merchandisers shape space, but that space in turn affects and shapes customer behaviour. The retail store ... does create moods, activates intentions, and generally affects customer reactions."[5] This observation was confirmed in a study that showed that lighting and music interact with friendliness of employees to affect customers' pleasure and willingness to buy.[6]

Some retailers view the interior of their stores as a stage in a theatre and realize that theatrical elements can be used to influence customer behaviour. They feel the customer should be entertained and excited. This principle is illustrated in Retail Highlight 8-2.

Many fast-food outlets have undergone interior design changes as a way of attracting customers in an intensely competitive environment. Many feel that a more upscale design attracts a broader range of customers, with less plastic, metal, and bright primary colours. Typically, operators are aiming for subtler lighting and are using pastel colours, marble, mirrors, brass, wood, and greenery

Retail Highlight 8-2 To Many Avid Readers, a Bookstore Is More Than a Big Box Full of Shelves

While the recent trend in the book industry has been bigger and bigger stores—some big-box stores like Chapters stock more than a million titles—serious readers always look for a store "with a sense of occasion."

Vancouverites, who have the distinction of being Canada's most avid readers, now have such a store called Bollum's Books, at the corner of Georgia and Granville. It stocks 85,000 titles in over 200 m^2 of old fir floor space, with travertine marble walls, and cherry-wood shelves. There is classical music playing, overstuffed sofas for comfort, intimate alcoves, a fireplace with a beautiful wood mantelpiece, brass lamps everywhere, and a café with free newspapers on bamboo rods.

At Bollum's Books, authors come regularly for reading and signing sessions. There is a special-orders desk, a large multimedia section, a large Chinese department, and a wide selection of magazines and newspapers (including out-of-town newspapers).

If you feel comfortable in the store, it is opened every weekday and Sunday from 8 a.m. to 10 p.m., and until midnight on Friday and Saturday!

[Ed. note: Bollum's Books has gone out of business since the publication of this article. See page 454.]

Source: John Masters, "Bookstore bravura," *The Financial Post*, May 20, 1995, pp. 26–27.

Harvey's has updated its restaurants inside and out to convey a more contemporary design.

Courtesy Cara Operations Ltd./Photo by Ron Norgrove

to create a warm, earthy environment. Other Canadian store designers use state-of-the-art fixtures as well as borrow some European flavour, particularly in designing fashion stores where the trend is on using sophisticated mannequins, "invisible fixturing," and showing less rather than more in terms of merchandise.[7]

The store's interior design should be based on an understanding of the customer and how design contributes to the strategy for reaching the target market. This is a very important decision, and the selection of a store designer should be done with a great deal of care.

Store Atmospherics

A store's interior design includes everything within the store walls that can be used to create store **ambience or atmospherics**. These elements include floor, wall, and ceiling materials; lighting; fixtures; colours; scents; and sounds. The following sections focus on colour, lighting, sounds, and scents as store atmospherics.

Colours The use of colours should be done with a great deal of thought, since colours often create an atmosphere for the store. For example, a children's store needs primary bright colours. A bookstore needs soothing and reflective colours. Traditional menswear is best set with country club colours (like forest green), and young womenswear in a pastel environment. For food services, Retail Highlight 8-3 provides a case example.

Research has determined that colour can affect store and merchandise image and customer shopping behaviour. People, regardless of colour preferences, are physically drawn to warm colours such as red and yellow. Thus, warm colours (red and particularly yellow) are good colour choices for drawing customers into a retail store, department, or display area. Warm colours are appropriate for store windows and entrances as well as for buying situations associated with impulse purchases. Think of "red tag sale" or "red dot special," for example. Cool colours (such as blue and green) are appropriate where customer deliberations over the purchase decision are necessary.[8]

Retail Highlight 8-3 The Proper Use of Colour and Lighting Can Lead to Dramatic Changes in Customer Perceptions

When Provigo decided to redesign their discount Maxi Supermarkets, it developed the unique concept of the Maxi & Co. flagship stores in both Ontario and Quebec. Starting with a big box of 8,500 m^2, with standard grocery, fresh foods, and nonfood products, the design encompassed three distinctive sections organized in a very "Cartesian" pattern. Bold, colourful, and playful designs were used, with appealing colour schemes that projected a clean, fresh, and bright feeling. Two other major design elements were a series of original three-dimensional murals along the outside walls and bold, colourful original signage that helps shoppers find departments.

Lighting was essential to create the proper, pleasant, and unique atmosphere for each specialty area: for example, in the produce area, the lighting must provide true colour rendition and not generate heat; in the cosmetics showcases, the lighting must be concealed (using fluorescent strips), to enhance the beauty products and create a dramatic effect. Effective lighting enhances the perception of space and showcases the products.

In 1997, the Maxi & Co. concept was awarded first place by the International Council of Store Planners and was well received by customers.

Source: "Supermarket design geared to big box concept," *Lighting Magazine*, vol. 12, Fall 1998, pp. 8–9.

Background colours for product presentations are also a major concern for retailers. For example, the colours white, pink, yellow, and blue should not be used in the "toddler" department. Those are the colours of most of the merchandise; thus the garments would merely "fade into the walls." Sometimes, the colour that is used to show off the product should be related to the final use of the product. Fine jewelry, for example, may look dramatic against bold colour backgrounds, but the colour fine jewelry is most often seen against is flesh. On the other hand, costume jewelry is best presented against vivid tones.

Lighting Lighting can be used to spotlight merchandise, to affect shopping behaviour, and to lower operating costs. Some supermarket retailers have chosen to make the produce area dark and then put light on the merchandise to make it stand out. Others, however, feel that customers are not comfortable in a dark area and thus are moving away from the overall dark, theatrical effect while still focusing light on the product.

Other retailers switched from a fluorescent system to high-intensity discharge (HID) fixtures, which resulted in better visibility and reduced energy costs. With HID fixtures, the light goes up and then is redistributed down at different angles. Thus, the fixtures direct the light to the ceiling and walls in addition to illuminating the merchandise on display. Improved light distribution is important when the retailer stacks its merchandise high in a warehouse-style setting. Shoppers have an easier time reading package labels. The HID units are also well suited for retailers who use up to three times more in-store signage than other retailers. Finally, the new lighting system may add to the overall appearance of the store, enhancing the store's colour scheme and making flooring and its patterns more attractive.[9] Retail Highlight 8-3 provides an example of the use of lighting for a supermarket.

Sounds Music has been found to have an impact on shopping behaviour. Research has found that shoppers spend less time in a store when music is played loudly.[10] A 30 percent increase in supermarket sales was experienced when the store played slow music compared to fast music. Also, in a restaurant, customers spent more time at their tables, consumed more alcoholic beverages, but ate no more food when slow music was played compared to fast music.[11] These improvements in sales were attributed to customers spending more time in the outlet, usually because they moved at a slower pace. Of interest is that a significant number of these customers, after they left, did not recall that music was being played. The implication is that shopping behaviour was altered by the music without their awareness.

Scents Research has shown that scents can affect consumer behaviour; for example, if a grocery store pumps in the smell of baked goods, sales in that department will increase, and scents coming out of stores like The Body Shop or Soapberry Shop can draw customers in. Some department stores pump fragrances, carefully choosing them to match their target audience.

Interestingly, scents can affect the perception of products that don't naturally smell—such as shoes. In a study sponsored by Nike, participants examined a pair of Nike gym shoes in two separate rooms. One room was completely odour free; the other was filtered with a pleasing floral scent. The scent had a direct positive effect on the desirability of the sneakers on 84 percent of the participants. The results of the study suggest that stores could boost sales by releasing scents that appeal specifically to targeted audiences. For example, retailers might use a spicy odour if they are targeting men in their thirties; a mixed floral scent would be more appropriate for females in their sixties. Furthermore, retailers should choose scents to suit the area of the store and the time of the day.[12]

STORE LAYOUT

Store layout is a very important element of store planning. Layout not only affects customer movement in the store but also influences the way merchandise is displayed. The following elements are part of layout planning:

1. The overall arrangement of the store.
2. Allocation of space to selling departments and sales-support activities.
3. Evaluation of space productivity.
4. Location of selling departments and sales-supporting activities within the store.

Arrangement of the Store

Typical layout arrangements are the grid, the free-flow or open plan, the boutique concept, and the racetrack plan.

Figure 8-2 Grid Layout

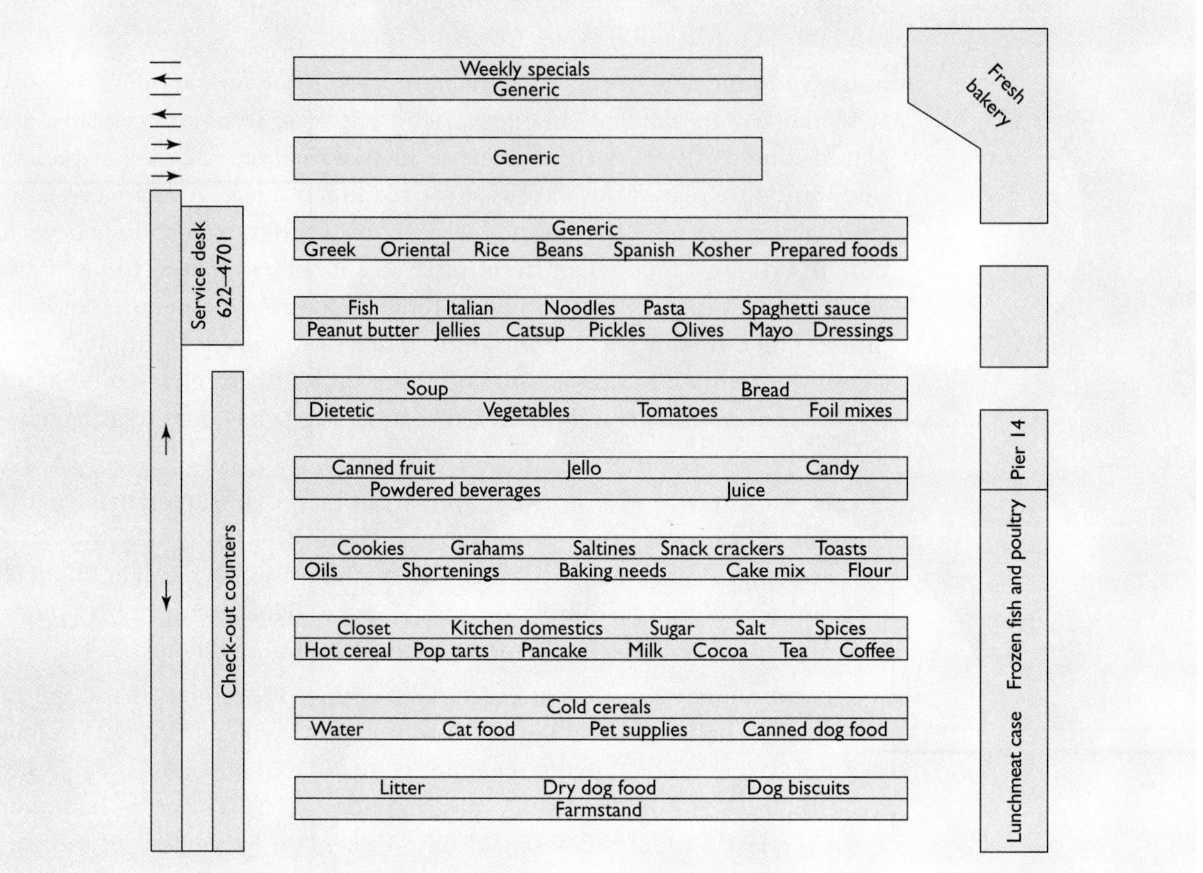

Grid Layout

In a **grid layout**, merchandise is displayed in straight, parallel lines, with secondary aisles at right angles to these. An example is shown in Figure 8-2. A supermarket typically uses a grid layout.

The grid arrangement is more for store efficiency than customer convenience, since the layout tends to hinder movement. Customer flow is guided more by the layout of the aisles and fixtures than by the buyer's desire for merchandise. For example, 80 to 90 percent of all customers shopping in a supermarket with a grid layout pass the produce, meat, and dairy counters. Fewer shoppers pass other displays, because the grid forces the customers to the sides and back of the supermarket.

In department stores, a grid layout on the main floor usually forces traffic down the main aisles. Thus, shoppers are less likely to be exposed to items along the walls. Shopping goods (highly demanded merchandise) should be placed along the walls, and convenience goods should be displayed in the main part of the store. Customer traffic then is drawn to otherwise slow-moving areas.

Free-Flow Layout

In a **free-flow layout**, merchandise and fixtures are grouped into patterns that allow an unstructured flow of customer traffic, as shown in Figure 8-3. The free-flow pattern is designed for customer convenience and exposure to merchandise. Free-flow designs let customers move in any direction and wander freely, thus encouraging browsing and impulse buying. Merchandise divisions are generally made on the basis of low fixtures and signage. The visibility of all departments is possible from any point in the store, which allows for better departmental interselling. The layout, however, is more costly and uses space less efficiently than the grid layout. A free-flow arrangement is often used in specialty stores, boutiques, and apparel stores.

Boutique Layout

A variation of the free-flow layout is the **boutique layout** where merchandise classifications are grouped so that each classification has its own "shop" within the store, as shown in Figure 8-4. The boutique concept is an outgrowth of lifestyle merchandising wherein a classification is aimed at a specific lifestyle

Figure 8-3 Free-Flow Layout

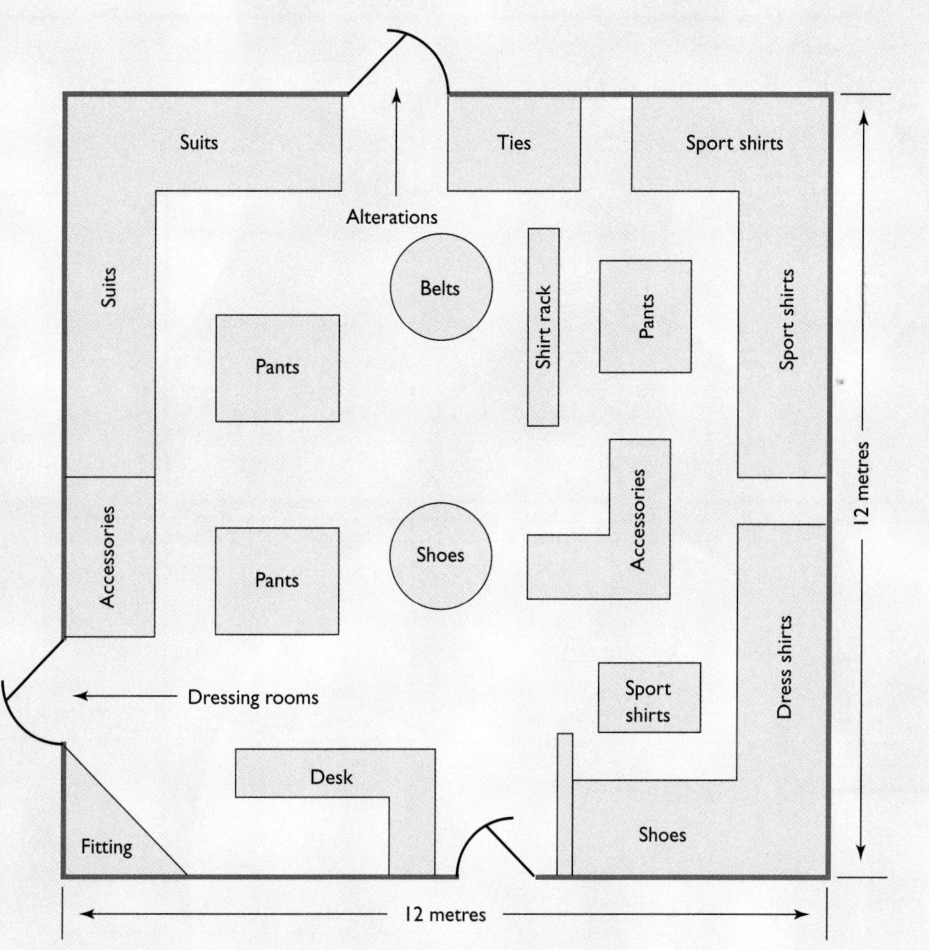

Figure 8-4 Boutique Layout

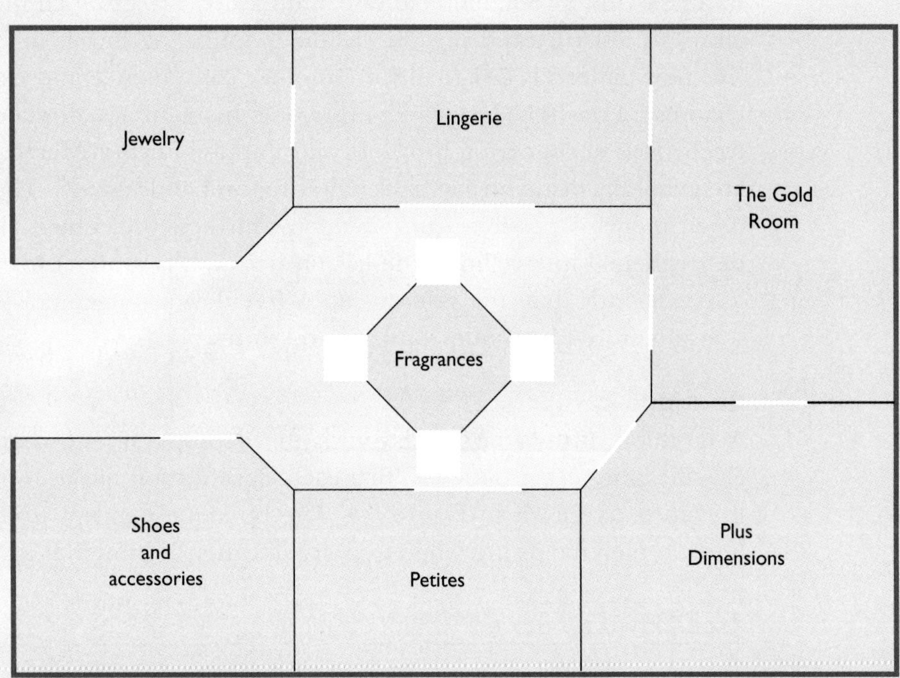

Figure 8-5 Racetrack Layout

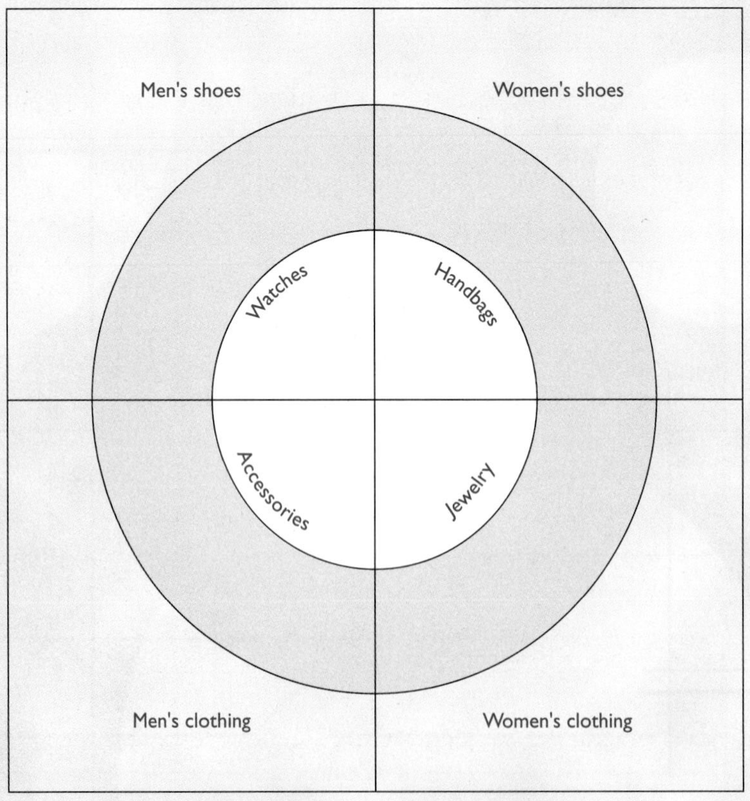

segment often featuring merchandise from a single designer or company, as shown in Figure 8-4.

Each shop has its own identity, including colour schemes, styles,and atmosphere. Even though greater flexibility is possible with this arrangement, construction costs and security costs are higher. As a result, the concept is used in high-status department stores and other outlets where the sale of higher priced merchandise allows absorption of the increased costs. However, some discounters are experimenting with the store-within-the-store concept.

Racetrack (or Loop) Layout

The **racetrack (or loop) layout** encourages customers to visit several departments (or boutiques) by providing a major aisle that loops through the store (or floor), as shown in Figure 8-5. Customers are constantly stimulated by various arrangements, and are encouraged to complete the loop.

Store Size and the Allocation of Space

Store Size

For a variety of reasons, some retailers are reducing store size. Downsizing is becoming increasingly important, for example, as the cost per square metre of retail space soars. However, retailers who are reducing the sizes of their stores are attempting to maximize space productivity so that merchandise presentation and sales will not be negatively affected by the smaller store size. Industry analysts refer to this concept as "maximizing the cube." The concept requires maximum utilization of space, especially the walls of the store: for example the use of free-standing fixtures and glass display counters; the merchandise displayed on two-tiered hangrods or on shelves that have been built into the walls; a vaulted ceiling to provide the illusion of space; a rear wall that is mirrored to make a small space appear larger.

Overseas expansion may lead to smaller stores. For example, when Talbots opened its first store in Japan the store was 200 square metres, about half the size of one of its North American stores. Two factors were at work here. One was the high cost of retail space; the other was a smaller inventory requirement owing to a smaller range of sizes. Whereas in North America the company would have a size run starting at size 4 and go up to 18 or 20, in Japan the stores have a size run of only three or four sizes.[13]

As firms move into smaller markets, smaller outlets may be needed. For example, McDonald's wants to add stores, but major markets already are at or near saturation. Thus, a key to growth is entering smaller markets, and McDonald's sees towns with populations of up to 4,000 as a revenue source it wants to tap. The company has learned, however, that its traditional outlets can't produce enough volume from smaller, rural markets to make profitable franchises. Thus, in these smaller markets, McDonald's is opening units about half the size of standard McDonald's restaurants. These units seat 50, including counter seating.[14]

Allocation of Space

Dividing total space between selling and sales-supporting areas is the first step in space allocation. In general, the larger a store, the higher its ratio of sales-supporting space to selling space. As a general rule, retailers—other than specialty or fashion outlets—devote as much space to the sales area as possible. However, the amount of sales space varies by size and type of store. In a very large department store, selling space may account for roughly 65 percent of total space. Jewelry stores need almost no sales-supporting space. A home improvement centre, however, may use more space for warehousing and storage than for selling. A warehouse-type store will put all its inventory on the selling floor, and this practice seems to have sparked a trend in the industry, with more and more stores using a larger proportion of space for selling. For example, a regular Canadian Tire store devotes just 40 percent of its space to selling, while the Canadian Tire's warehouse concept has 80 percent of its space accessible to customers.[15]

The amount of space allocated to nonselling areas may be impacted by the advent of electronic data interchange (EDI) and greater UPC vendor marketing. With EDI and UPC, merchandise moves more quickly and accurately through the distribution channel, with smaller quantities arriving at the store more frequently. Since large "cushion" stocks will not be required, backroom can be greatly reduced in size, and greater use will be made of store space by merchandising.

Management can use two basic methods for allocating selling space:

1. Industry averages by type of merchandise.
2. Sales productivity of product lines.

Industry Averages Management can use the national average percentage of selling space that a particular merchandise line occupies in a certain type of store. For example, assume that the health and beauty aids department accounts for 4 percent of total selling space as an average in a superstore. Thus, in a superstore with 3,400 square metres of selling space, management would set aside 136 square metres for the health and beauty aids department (3,400 x .04 = 136).

Sales Productivity Method **Sales productivity** is measured by sales per square metre of selling space. Assume that the planned sales for health and beauty aids is $136,000. If the national average sales per square metre for this department is $1,000, then management would allocate 136 square metres to the department ($136,000/$1,000 = 136). Table 8-1 gives an idea of the average sales per square metre for various types of stores.

Table 8-1 Average Sales per Square Metre for Selected Types of Stores

Type of Store	Average Sales per m² ($)
Pharmacies	7,880
Jewelry stores	6,872
Liquor and beer stores	6,385
Appliance, television, radio, and stereo stores	6,067
Gift, novelty, and souvenir stores	5,730
Camera and photographic supply stores	5,656
Grocery stores	5,456
Supermarkets	5,241
Opticians' shops	5,057
Record and tape stores	4,992
Luggage and leather goods stores	4,389
Shoe stores	3,932
Sporting goods stores	3,837
Men's clothing stores	3,573
Women's clothing stores	3,451
Household furniture stores (without appliances and furnishings)	3,392
Pet stores	3,175
Floor covering and drapery stores	2,693
Florist shops	2,690
Household furniture stores (with appliances and furnishings)	2,316
Paint, glass, and wallpaper stores	1,509

Source: Statistics Canada, *Retail Chain and Department Stores*, Cat. 63-210-XIB, April 1999, p. 12.

Evaluation of Space Use

Good use of space involves more than creating an aesthetically pleasing environment, although such a goal is important. Effective use of space can also translate into additional dollars of profit. Thus, retailers must evaluate whether store space is being used in the most effective way. Management can use a variety of measures to evaluate space utilization. The gross-margin-per-square-metre method is discussed below to illustrate one method retailers can employ.

To determine whether a department can "afford" the space it occupies, the gross margin per square metre of the department should be measured. Big-ticket items may ring up more sales than lower priced goods, yet the ratio of gross margin to square metre may be smaller for high-priced merchandise. As shown in Table 8-2, three calculations are involved in evaluating space utilization by the gross-margin-per-square-metre method. Sales per square metre less cost of merchandise sold per square metre yields the gross margin per square metre figure.

Table 8-2

Calculating Gross Margin per Square Metre

Three calculations are involved in figuring gross margin per square metre:

$$1.\ \frac{\text{Total sales}}{\text{Total square metres}} = \text{Sales per square metre}$$

$$2.\ \frac{\text{Cost of merchandise sold}}{\text{Total square metres}} = \text{Cost of merchandise sold per square metre}$$

$$3.\ \text{Sales per square metre} - \begin{array}{c}\text{Cost of merchandise}\\ \text{per square metre}\end{array} = \text{Gross margin per square metre}$$

Example

	Department A	**Department B**
Sales	\$50,000	\$70,000
Cost of merchandise sold	\$30,000	\$35,000
Square metres of space	50 m^2	70 m^2
Sales per square metre	\$ 1,000	\$ 1,000
– Cost of merchandise sold per m^2	\$ 600	\$ 500
= Gross margin per square metre	\$ 400	\$ 500

With this gross-margin-per-square-metre figure, departments of varying sizes selling different types of goods can be compared. Gross margin per square metre can show management which departments are doing well, which are not, which might improve if expanded, and which can be reduced in space allotment.

For example, based on the calculations shown in Table 8-2, management might be tempted to decrease the selling space allocated to department A and increase the selling space devoted to department B. However, the decision to reallocate space is not a simple one. Advertising and selling costs may rise when selling space is increased. After the reallocation, the merchandise mix may change, which can result in either higher or lower gross margins. Management thus needs to simulate the likely changes in the three variables used in the calculations as a result of possible shifts in space allocation and determine whether reallocations are likely to increase the overall profitability of the firm.

An evaluation of space utilization may not only lead to a reallocation of space among selling departments. Some stores are converting unproductive retail space to other uses.

Locating Departments and Activities

Management must decide where to locate selling and sales-supporting activities within the store. Several guidelines are available to retailers to aid in making these decisions.

Locating Selling Departments

The convenience of customers and the effect on profitability are the primary concerns of management in locating selling departments within the store. With these factors in mind, the following suggestions are offered:

- *Rent-paying capacity.* The department with the highest sales per square metre is best able to pay a high rent. Thus, this department should be placed in the most valuable, highly travelled area of the store. If a number of departments are equally good, the decision should be made based on the gross margins of the merchandise.
- *Impulse versus demand shopping.* **Impulse merchandise** is bought on the basis of unplanned, spur-of-the-moment decisions. Departments containing impulse merchandise normally get the best locations in the store. **Demand merchandise** is purchased as a result of a customer coming into the store to buy that particular item. Departments containing demand merchandise can be located in less valuable space because customers will hunt for these items.
- *Replacement frequency.* Certain goods, such as health and beauty aids, are frequently purchased, low-cost items. Customers want to buy them as conveniently as possible, so the department should be placed in an easily accessible location.
- *Proximity of related departments.* Similar items of merchandise should be displayed close together. In a superstore, for example, all household items—such as paper products, detergents, kitchen gadgets—should be placed together, so customers will make combination purchases. Similarly, the men's furnishings department—such as shirts, ties, and underwear—should be placed near the suit department in a department store. A customer wanting a new suit often needs a matching shirt and tie as well. Combination selling is easier when related items are close together. Location of related goods is even more important in a self-service store because no salesperson is around to help the customer.
- *Seasonal variations.* Items in some departments are big sellers only a few months or weeks of the year. Toys and summer furniture are examples. Management might decide to place these departments next to each other. When toys expand at Christmas, extra space temporarily can be taken from summer furniture, and vice versa.
- *Size of departments.* Management also may want to place very small departments in some of the more valuable spaces to help them be seen. A very large department could use a less desirable location in the store because its size will contribute to its visibility.
- *Merchandise characteristics.* In a supermarket, bakery products (especially bread) should be near the checkout. Customers avoid crushing these items in the carts by selecting bakery products at the end of their shopping. Products such as lettuce are usually displayed along a wall to allow more space and to better handle wiring for cooling.
- *Shopping considerations.* Items such as suits and dresses are often tried on and fitted. They can be placed in less valuable locations away from heavy traffic. Also, they are demand, not impulse, items and can be placed in out-of-the-way areas since shoppers will make an effort to find them.

- *New, developing, or underdeveloped departments.* Assume management has added a new department such as more "nonfoods" in a superstore. Management may want to give more valuable space to the new department to increase sales by exposing more customers to the items.

Locating Sales-Supporting Activities

Sales-supporting activities, such as the customer service department, can be thought of in several ways:

- Activities that must be located in a specific part of the store—Receiving and marketing areas should be located near the "dock" area, usually at the back of the store.
- Activities that serve the store only—Such activities are office space and personal services for employees of the store. These departments can be located in the least valuable, out-of-the-way places.
- Activities that relate directly to selling—Cutting areas for fresh meat need to be close to the refrigerators. Both refrigeration and cutting need to be close to the display cases. Drapery workrooms in department stores need to be close to the drapery department.
- Activities with direct customer contact—In a supermarket, customers often want to check parcels, cash a personal cheque, or ask for information about an item. Credit departments and layaway services are needed in department stores. Such activities can be located in out-of-the-way places to help increase customer movement in the store.

VISUAL MERCHANDISING

Visual merchandising is part of the so-called silent language of communication. Displays can be used to excite, entertain, and educate consumers. If effectively used, they can have a profound influence on consumer behaviour, as illustrated in Retail Highlight 8-4.

Principles of Displays

Customers in a retail store stop at some merchandise displays, move quickly past some, and smile at others. Shoppers are professional display watchers and know what they like. However, customers usually do not consciously judge displays. So the job of the retail manager is to "prejudge" for the purchaser. Managers need to be clever and creative enough to affect behaviour by display. Displays should attract attention and excite and stimulate customers. In spite of the basically artistic and creative flair needed for display, some principles do exist. The following basic principles have been developed from years of experience.

1. Displays should be built around fast-moving, "hot" items.
2. Goods purchased largely on impulse should be given ample amounts of display space.
3. Displays should be kept simple. Management should not try to cram them with too many items.

Retail Highlight 8-4 Effective and Imaginative Merchandise Displays Improve the Shopper's Experience

Retailers need to constantly rethink their displays in order to make the shopping experience a pleasant one, not a chore. Examples of innovative approaches are:

- Food retailers have known for years that proper food presentations are key to sales volume. They have used mirrors behind vegetables and empty boxes under piles of fruits to give the impression of abundance. Also, loose fragile fruits, such as strawberries, are perceived to be more fresh, and the customer who bags his own selection ends up buying more strawberries, increasing sales, and reducing spoilage. But retailers like Provigo, the third largest grocery chain, are testing other methods such as using wooden stands on wheels (some refrigerated), and placing shelves at an angle for special effects.
- The same principle is true for department stores, like the Bay store at Yonge and Bloor, which spent $10 million trying to make the customer feel happy, upbeat, and comfortable. For instance, in the men's department, the fixtures and the colours are there to direct attention to the merchandise in custom-millwork display shelving. In the women's department, an unusual iron-work tree is used to display handbags hanging from the branches; an atrium is full of mannequins, in a French Art Deco style, dressed in various designer clothes.

Sources: Jean Benoît Nadeau and Julie Barlow, "Shopping for Wow!" *Report on Business Magazine*, October 1995, pp. 58–67; Gerald Levitch, "Memories of Versailles," *The Globe and Mail*, November 30, 1995, p. D4.

4. Displays should be timely and feature seasonal goods.
5. Colour attracts attention, sets the right tone, and affects the very sense of the display.
6. Use motion. It attracts attention.
7. Most good displays have a theme or story to tell.
8. Show goods in use.
9. Proper lighting and props are essential to an effective display.[16]
10. Guide the shopper's eye where you want it to go.

Interior Displays

Interior displays can take a variety of forms, depending on the type of merchandise and image to be projected by the firm. While space does not permit an in-depth discussion of the principles of interior display, we do offer several guidelines for planning the effective arrangement of merchandise in departments.

Consider the following suggestions regarding interior merchandise display:

- Place items so that choices can readily be made by customers. For example, group merchandise by sizes.
- Place items in such a way that "ensemble" (or related-item) selling is easy. For example, in a gourmet food department, all Chinese food components should be together. In a women's accessories department, handbags, gloves, and neckwear should be together to help the customer complete an outfit.

- Place items in a department so that trading up or getting the customer to want a better-quality, higher-priced item is possible. Place the good, better, and best brands of coffee, for example, next to each other so customers can compare them. Information labels on the package help customers compare items displayed next to each other.
- Place merchandise in such a way that it stresses the wide assortments (choice of sizes, brands, colours, and prices) available.
- If the firm carries competing brands in various sizes, give relatively little horizontal space to each item and make use of vertical space for the different sizes and colours. This arrangement exposes customers to a greater variety of products as they move through the store.
- Avoid locating impulse goods directly across the aisle from demand items that most customers are looking for. The impulse items may not be seen at all.
- Make use of vertical space through tiers and step-ups, but be careful to avoid displays much above eye level or at floor level. The area of vertical vision is limited.
- Place items in a department so that inventory counting (control) and general stockkeeping is easier.

At Future Shop, all appliances are grouped together to allow consumers to compare brands, models, and prices.

Courtesy Future Shop

Use of Manufacturer-Supplied Display Fixtures

Retailers are reacting more positively to the use of manufacturer-supplied display fixtures—one reason being that manufacturers are attempting to be more sensitive to the retailers' needs when designing such fixtures. In the past, retailers complained that many displays were ineffective for inventory control, used space poorly, and did not aid consumers in shopping. Retailers also felt many of the racks were unattractive and did not fit in with their store's decor.

Today, manufacturers are attempting to design display fixtures that overcome these problems. An example is the display fixture for Raid insecticides. The in-store display features various Raid products arranged under a colour code to help consumers pick the right spray for the right bug. A flip chart gives information on the habits of insects and suggests ways to "knock 'em dead." The unit can be arranged in various configurations to accommodate various store sizes.

In the self-service environment of mass marketing, manufacturer-provided displays can be used effectively as a selling tool.[17]

Shelf-Space Allocation

A very important merchandise presentation issue is determining the amount of space that should be allocated to individual brands or items in a product category. A number of rules have been devised for allocating facings to competing brands. One rule frequently stressed by major consumer goods manufacturers is that shelf space should equal market share. Thus, a brand with 20 percent market share in a category takes 20 percent of shelf space.

For a retailer, however, this rule makes little sense. It takes no account of the profit margins or direct costs associated with each item. Some retailers thus allocate space according to gross margin. Other retailers apply the concept of **direct product profitability** (DPP). Direct product profitability equals a product's gross margin (selling price minus cost of goods sold) plus discounts and allowances, less direct handling costs (see Table 8-3). More space should be allocated to brands or items with greater DPP. The use of DPP was limited until the development of the personal computer and spreadsheet programs such as Lotus 1-2-3, which have made the calculations much easier. DPP is actually a better measure of a product's performance than the product's gross margin and is thus replacing gross margin in merchandising decisions. The greater accuracy of DPP is shown in Table 8-3, which indicates that gross margin overstated the product's financial performance by $1.36 ($2.20 - 0.84 = $1.36). As shown in Table 8-4, item A initially appeared to be more profitable than item B based on gross margin. However, in using DPP, discounts and allowances for item B were found to be higher and handling costs to be lower. The result is that DPP is higher for item B than item A.

Table 8-3

Computing Direct Product Profitability

Retail price	$9.50
Less cost of goods sold	7.30
Equals gross margin	$2.20
Plus discounts and allowances	
Merchandise allowance	.25
Payment discount	.10
Less direct handling costs	
Warehouse direct labour	.20
Retail direct labour	.75
Warehouse inventory expense	.05
Retail inventory expense	.06
Warehouse operating expense	.10
Retail operating expense	.50
Transportation to stores	.05
Equals direct product profitability	$ .84

Computer applications for shelf-space allocations are becoming commonplace. With the aid of software such as Superman III and AccuSpace, retailers can develop complete categories of products (**planograms** or shelf layouts) and experiment with efficient space use based on financial evaluation, product movement, profit yields, and other information. One area of great interest among chains is store-specific systems, whereby a retailer can identify the categories and products that best fit a specific store's customers. Retailers input information on package size, past sales history, projected sales, store deliveries, and other relevant data, and out comes an exact representation of the planogram schematic. The computer works to establish merchandising placement based on products that have the highest turnover or gross margins or other criteria that will allocate shelf space to best influence the consumer's behaviour. During the planogram simulation, adjustments can be made to the database or planogram to best serve the retailer. For example, products tied to seasonal movement can be adjusted to reflect a temporary space allocation, or several planograms can be generated revealing layouts of different heights or widths.[18]

Table 8-4

Direct Product Profitability Comparison

	Item A	Item B
Retail price	$19.00	$18.00
Less cost of goods sold	7.25	8.20
Equals gross margin	$11.75	$ 9.80
Plus discounts and allowances	.60	1.80
Less direct handling costs	3.50	1.70
Equals direct product profitability	$ 8.85	$ 9.90

A particularly thorny problem is assigning space to new products. Some manufacturers, having conducted marketing tests, are able to recommend facing levels. The new item problem is simpler for a line extension. A new flavour of potato chips, for example, is invariably located with existing products in single-carton quantities until increased sales demand otherwise. In the case of a completely new category, facings can be provided only by creating new space or by destocking one or more lines from another category. Some firms tackle the new item problem by placing it in a special display until demand has stabilized at a predictable level of trial and repurchase. Because of the numbers of new products manufacturers attempt to introduce into the market each year and because of limited shelf space, some retailers (especially food retailers) are requiring manufacturers to pay slotting fees in order to gain shelf space for new products. These fees range from $250 to $3,000 per store.[19]

CHAPTER HIGHLIGHTS

- Store layout and design and merchandise presentation are important aspects of a firm's positioning strategy. The major goal of store design and layout and merchandise presentation is to get the shopper into the store to spend as much money as possible on a given shopping trip.
- Store design is a reflection of two elements: the interior design and the exterior design. Both should be in harmony with the store's merchandise and customers. Exterior design includes the building's architecture and entrances, display windows, and signs. Today, there is a renewed interest in window displays, especially among department stores and higher-priced retailers and in cities where walking and window shopping are in style. Window displays can be used to enhance store image, to expose shoppers to new products, or to introduce a new season.
- Some retailers view the interior of the store as a theatre and realize that theatrical elements can be used to influence customer behaviour. Interior design includes everything within the store walls that can be used to create an atmosphere, such as colours, lighting, and sound.
- Store layout is a very important part of store planning. One aspect of store layout is the arrangement of the store. Typical arrangements are the grid, the free-flow or open plan, the boutique concept, and the racetrack layout.
- Another element of store layout is space allocation. Dividing total space between selling and sales-supporting areas is the first step in space allocation. Management can use two basic methods for allocating selling space: industry averages by type of merchandise and sales productivity of product lines.
- Effective use of space can translate into additional dollars of profit. Thus, retailers must evaluate whether store space is being used in the most effective way. The gross-margin-per-square-metre method is one method retailers may use.
- Management must decide where to locate selling and sales-supporting activities within the store. Several guidelines are available to aid in making these decisions.

- Merchandise displays can be used to excite, entertain, and educate consumers. If effectively used, they can have a profound influence on consumer behaviour. In spite of the basically artistic and creative flair needed for merchandise display, some guidelines and principles do exist.
- Interior displays can take a variety of forms, depending on the type of merchandise and image to be projected by the firm. A number of guidelines to the use of interior merchandise displays are offered.
- An important aspect of merchandise display is determining the amount of space that should be allocated to individual brands or items in a product category. Some retailers allocate shelf space according to gross margin; others use the concept of direct product profit. Some retailers use computer software packages to determine optimum formulas for deciding how much shelf space each item should be allocated.

KEY TERMS

ambience	187	planogram	202
atmospherics	187	racetrack layout	193
boutique layout	191	sales productivity method	194
demand merchandise	197	store design	182
direct product profitability	201	store layout	182
free-flow layout	191	store planning	182
grid layout	190	visual merchandising	198
impulse merchandise	197		

DISCUSSION QUESTIONS

1. Define store planning, store design, and store layout.
2. What are the decision areas that comprise layout planning?
3. Compare the following layout arrangements—the grid layout, the free-flow or open plan, the boutique concept, and the racetrack layout.
4. Describe the two methods retailers can use for allocating selling space in a store among the various departments.
5. Explain the gross-margin-per-square-metre method of evaluating space use.
6. What various factors do retailers need to consider in deciding where to locate selling departments and sales-supporting activities within the total store space?
7. Discuss the guidelines retailers can use relative to interior display of merchandise.
8. What information can retailers use in making the shelf-space allocation decision?

APPLICATION EXERCISES

1. Select three different types of stores (e.g., a traditional department store, a discount department store, a specialty apparel shop) and carefully observe their displays, fixturing, appearance—all the elements that make up the interior design of the stores. Write a report describing differences between the stores and how these differences relate to image projection and market segmentation.
2. Visit the following types of stores: a multilevel department store, a supermarket, a national chain, a national specialty chain outlet, and a discount department store. Describe the overall arrangement of the stores (e.g., grid, free-flow, boutique, racetrack). Evaluate the layout of each store and comment on the impact of each layout on the general image of the outlets. What changes, if any, would you suggest and why?
3. Visit several department stores and interview store management. Determine the method(s) used to allocate selling space to the various departments and how management evaluates space use. Based on what you learned in the chapter, evaluate the location of selling departments and sales-supporting activities within each store.
4. Use the following information and calculate the product's direct product profitability (DPP):

Selling price	$20.00
Cost of product	14.50
Payment discount	.40
Merchandise discount	.25
Warehouse direct labour	.10
Warehouse inventory expense	.05
Warehouse operating expense	.08
Transportation to stores	.60
Retail direct labour	.88
Retail inventory expense	.05
Retail operating expense	.20

SUGGESTED CASE

13. Today's Supermarket

CHAPTER 9

MERCHANDISE MANAGEMENT

CHAPTER OBJECTIVES

After reading this chapter you should be able to:

1. Understand the need to make merchandise decisions that support the overall competitive strategy of the firm.
2. Explain how merchandise strategies can be implemented to obtain a competitive advantage.
3. Describe the process of developing a merchandise budget to make inventory decisions.
4. Identify the issues to consider in making merchandise width and depth decisions.
5. Explain the relationship between planning and control.
6. Illustrate how to establish a dollar control and open-to-buy system to control dollar merchandise investment.
7. Explain unit control of inventory investment.

A good example of a retailer with a competitive advantage is Future Shop, the Canadian electronics chain. The chain has grown from a single store in Vancouver in 1982 to over 100 stores and $1.8 billion in sales by the end of 1999. The stores feature wide and deep inventories of electronic products, from television sets to VCRs to computers to stereo systems, to achieve assortment dominance. This retailer wants consumers to come to its shops for all their electronic needs and encourages them with extensive advertising of its products and competitive prices. Future Shop sells three things—service, selection, and price. The retailer differentiates itself by offering excellent customer service and a dominant assortment of merchandise at very competitive prices. It promises to match any lower price within 30 days of a purchase at its stores. The strategy of Future Shop has led them to be leaders in the field, the ultimate goal in retailing.[1]

High-performance retailers such as Future Shop are credited with having a "compelling competitive advantage." Consider also Shoppers Drug Mart with its "Everything you want in a drugstore" strategy, which commits the retailer to carry an extensive product assortment to satisfy customer needs. Then there is "There's a lot more to Canadian Tire," which builds on Canadian Tire's dominance in automotive products for its other major product categories. Each of these examples illustrates the important role that merchandise management plays in the overall competitive strategy of the firm.

Development of the merchandise plan is the logical place to begin a discussion about competitive advantage in the marketplace, because without merchandise (or some offering), a retail firm cannot exist.

MERCHANDISE MANAGEMENT

Merchandise planning includes all the activities needed to balance inventory and sales. The major portion of this chapter is directed toward the merchandise plan at the department classification level. Although the function of merchandise planning is somewhat technical, the concept of merchandising is not. Traditionally, merchandising has been defined as offering the right merchandise at the right price at the right place in the right quantities at the right time. We support these "rights," but we see merchandising in the 2000s as much more. We see merchandising as a part of the strategic plan—the creative positioning tactics that support the long-run mission and objectives of a firm.

Merchandise management is the management of the product component of the retailing mix; it comprises planning and control activities. Its purpose is to ensure that the inventory component of the mix supports the overall merchandising philosophy of the firm and meets the needs of target customers. Retail Highlight 9-1 illustrates the merchandising philosophy for Canadian Tire.

Retail Highlight 9-1 Canadian Tire—A Clearly Defined Merchandise Philosophy

Canadian Tire manages change through its strategic planning process. Faced with competitors like Wal-Mart and Home Depot and with environmental changes, Canadian Tire developed a new strategic direction to improve the company's growth and profits.

Components of the new strategy included: a concentration on three product categories—auto parts, sports and leisure goods, and home products; opening of new format stores—larger, brighter, more modern; improvements in customer service—including a no-hassle return policy; and improving the cost of operations—major productivity gains were achieved.

An important part of Canadian Tire's strategy is continually refining the value package they offer to their customers. Their goal is to be the best at what their customers value most; to offer the best combination of quality, service, convenience, loyalty programs, *and* price.

Canadian Tire's merchandising philosophy is based on its strategy and customer value. In focusing on the three product areas and introducing new format stores, Canadian Tire reviewed all of the chain's 50,000 "stock-keeping units," eliminated non-performing products, and added thousands of items. It significantly broadened product lines in home entertainment, pet food, personal security, and gardening supplies. Canadian Tire offers its customers a highly focused assortment (in the three product categories), a deeper and more competitive assortment (by adding product lines and more brands within each category), and the best value for the customer's dollar (through offering the best value combination).

Source: *www.canadiantire.com.*

www.canadiantire.com

Progressive retailers like Canadian Tire recognize the importance of identifying changes in its stores and merchandise to meet customers' needs. Merchandising planning requires retailers, in particular, to meet the changing needs (value changes) of customers.[2]

Another important aspect of merchandising for many retailers, like Canadian Tire, is the optimal balance between private and national brands and, in some instances, generics. **Private brands (or private labels)** are owned by a retailer (e.g., Canadian Tire's Mastercraft tools). **National brands,** often called "manufacturer" brands, are owned by a manufacturer and can be sold to whomever the owner desires (e.g., Procter & Gamble's Tide laundry detergent).

One retailer that has aggressively used a blend of generic (no-name), private, and national brands is Loblaws. To differentiate itself from its competitors, Loblaws has introduced over 1,500 "no name" and 400 "President's Choice" store-branded products. As well, it has introduced the "Club Pack" line, the environmentally friendly "Green" line, and the "Too Good to Be True" line. This merchandising strategy allows Loblaws to offer customers a product assortment that cannot be duplicated by competitors. Loblaws' executives believe that these products provide their customers with a powerful combination of excellent quality and low price. Loblaws' store brands now account for $1.6 billion in sales, of which about $500 million is in its Club Pack line, or 15 percent of Loblaws' revenues.[3]

Club Pack, one of Loblaws store brands, is positioned to compete against the warehouse stores like Price/Costco.

Courtesy Loblaw Companies Ltd.

Retailers promote private-label programs to (1) defend themselves against off-price competition, (2) offer an alternative as the upscale catalogue companies feature virtually all competitive national labels, (3) guarantee some market exclusivity, (4) achieve a degree of control over merchandising programs, and (5) protect their profit margins.

In deciding on the best mix of national, private, and generic brands to carry, the retailer should consider a number of factors. National brands are well known and are usually supported by advertising. Additionally, many consumers regard national brands as superior to either private or generic brands in terms of reliability and quality. Private brands generate higher margins for retailers, offer economic benefits to consumers because they are usually cheaper than national brands, and may assist in developing store loyalty. Private brands do require the retailer to invest time and money and could damage the store's image if the brand is viewed by consumers as having poor quality. For the retailer, generics share some of the same risks as private brands but they appeal to price-conscious customers. Generics can help to create a strong competitive price image for a retailer.

Even though many retailers are introducing private brands and others are adding to their line of private brands, some retailers have reduced the ratio of private to manufacturer brands in their stores. For example, Sears Canada's shift from private labels to a strong manufacturer brand statement has been attributed largely to its new philosophy of appealing to a broader range of consumers by offering more choices to more people. Sears Canada added BOCA, Petites by Tan Jay, Nygard Collections, and Le Chateau national brands to its clothing line, and IMAN to its cosmetics line, to broaden its appeal and respond to changing consumer tastes. Thus, the private versus national brand issue is a challenge for both retailers and manufacturers (Retail Highlight 9-2).

Retail Highlight 9-2 Private Labels versus National Brands: The Issues

From the manufacturer's viewpoint, private label products pose a serious threat for a number of reasons:

- Private label products have improved in quality.
- Retailers have developed premium private label brands that compete directly with national brands.
- New distribution channels are emerging (e.g., warehouse club/mass merchandisers) and they carry an increasing number of private label lines.
- Private labels are moving into new categories, such as clothing and beer, and creating more acceptance among consumers for private label purchases.

In response, national brand manufacturers have advantages:

- Brand names provide consumers with an assurance of quality and simplify consumers' decisions.
- Brand name firms have a solid foundation (quality, name recognition) on which to build their business.
- National brands have value for retailers—consumers expect them in stores, the brands have traffic-building power, and retailers can use them, with promotions, to create a store image.
- Retailers who carry large numbers of private brands dilute their strength because consumers have difficulty believing that a store can provide quality private brands across a wide range of categories.

From the retailer's viewpoint, private brands pose some threats:

- If the private brand varies in quality, particularly in categories where sophisticated manufacturing and automation are required, then consumers may be dissatisfied with both the brand and store.
- If the comparative quality of the private brand relative to national brands is low, then consumers may be reluctant to purchase any of the store's brands.

The retailer is likely to have success with private labels where:

- The product quality is consistent and relatively similar to national brands, thus offering consumers a high value proposition.
- The product category is large and profitable, thus attracting less competitive response from national brands.
- There are few national brands and there are relatively low advertising expenditures by those brands.

Sources: John A. Quelch and David Harding, "Brands versus Private Labels: Fighting to Win." *Harvard Business Review*, January–February 1996, pp. 99–109; Stephen J. Hoch and Shumeet Banerii, "When Do Private Labels Succeed?" *Sloan Management Review*, Summer 1993, pp. 57–67; and David Dunne and Chakravarthi Narasimham, "The New Appeal of Private Brands," *Harvard Business Review*, May–June, 1999, pp. 41–48.

MERCHANDISE PLANNING

As defined earlier, merchandise planning includes those activities needed to ensure a balance between inventory and sales. The other element of the total management process is control, the assessment of how effective the planning has been. Merchandise control is covered in the last section of this chapter.

Canadian Tire illustrates a focused and deep assortment in sporting goods, one of the three main product areas in its new strategy.

Courtesy Canadian Tire

Basic Terms

A **product** is simply a tangible object, service, or idea, such as a dress or a dress-cleaning service. A **merchandise line** refers to a group of products that are closely related because they are intended for the same end use (dishwashers), are used together (knives and forks), or are sold to the same customer group (children's footwear). Two important decisions the retailer makes are the breadth and depth of the merchandising lines carried by the store. **Breadth (or width)** is the number of different merchandising lines carried.[4] **Depth** is the number of items that are carried in a single merchandise line. Breadth and depth, illustrated in Figure 9-1, define the merchandise mix, which is the total of all the merchandise lines.

Assortment means the range of choices (selection) available for any given merchandise line. Assortment can also be defined as the number of **stockkeeping units (SKUs)** in a category. For example, a litre package of Nabob coffee is one SKU; a 500 ml bag of Maxwell House coffee is another SKU. Do not confuse, however, the number of items with a SKU. In other words, a food store might have 100 packages of the 1 litre Nabob coffee, but this represents only one SKU.

Figure 9-1 The Merchandise Mix

		Number of Merchandise Lines **Breadth**	
		Few	Many
Number of Merchandise Items **Depth**	Few	Narrow and shallow (Fast-food restaurant)	Broad and shallow (Convenience store)
	Many	Narrow and deep (Golf specialty store)	Broad and deep (Department store)

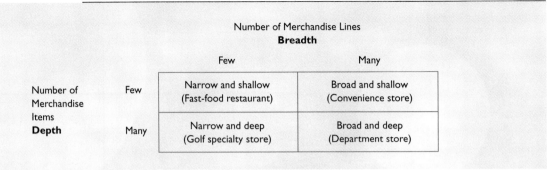

Merchandise (or inventory) **turnover** is the number of times the average inventory of an item (or SKU) is sold, usually in annual terms. Turnover can be computed on a dollar basis in either cost or retail terms, or in units.

Merchandise Assortment Planning

The major focus of this section is merchandise assortment planning, the purpose of which is to maintain *stock balance*—balance between inventories and sales. Figure 9-2 is a diagram of the merchandise planning process. Reference will be made to this diagram throughout most of this chapter.

Retailers may consider merchandise assortment in three different ways: width, depth, or dollar planning. Let's assume that we are planning for the men's sport shirt assortment in the men's clothing department of a department store.[5] The three aspects of assortment planning as shown in Figure 9-2 are (1) width or breadth, point 4; (2) depth, point 5; and (3) total dollars, point 3.

Width Width (breadth) of merchandise assortments refers to the assortment factors necessary to meet the demands of the market and to meet competition. Decisions must be made on the number of brands, sizes, colours, and the like. In our example for shirts, the following might be a planning process in terms of width:

Brands (Bugle Boy, Tommy Hilfiger, Chaps)	3 SKUs
	x
Sizes (small, medium, large, and x-large)	4 = 12 SKUs
	x
Prices ($59.95; $69.95)	2 = 24 SKUs
	x
Colours (white, grey, blue)	3 = 72 SKUs
	x
Fabrics (knit, woven)	2 = 144 SKUs

Thus, we see that there are 144 SKUs necessary to meet customers' wants and the offerings of competitors.

Figure 9-2 The Merchandise-Planning Process

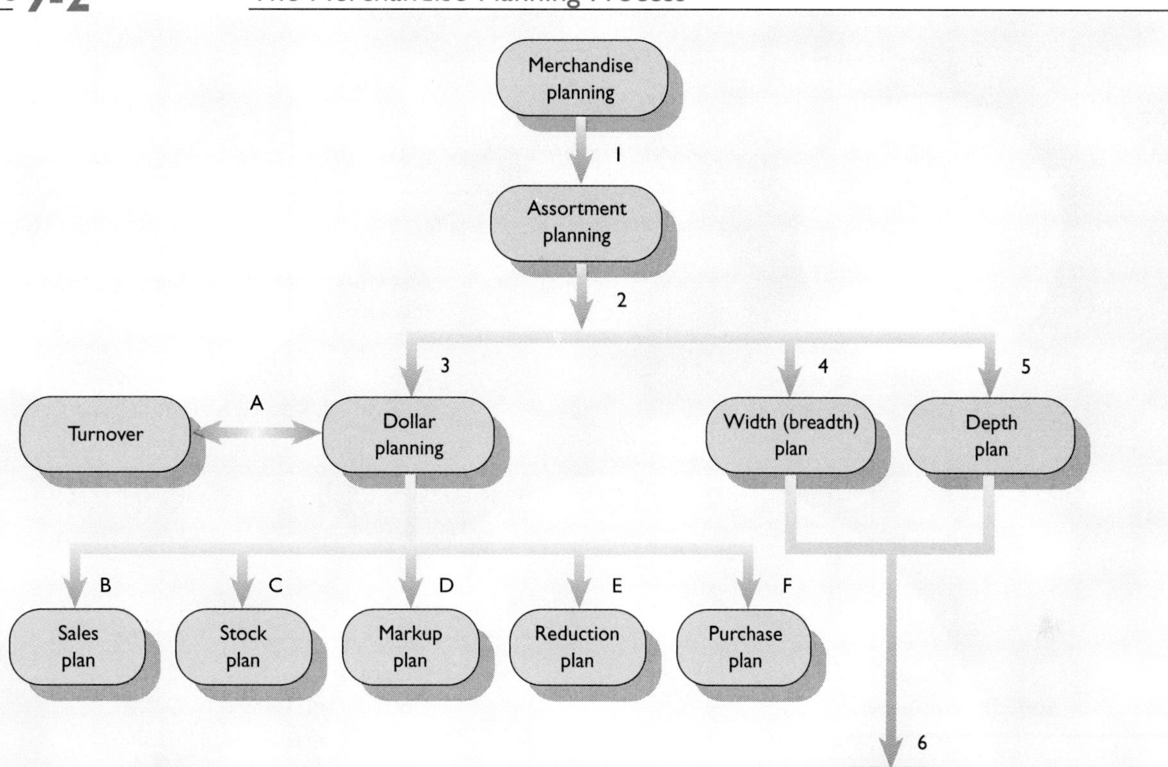

Depth The next question is: How many units of merchandise do we need to support our expected sales of each assortment factor? This decision must be based on expectations of the sales importance for each assortment factor. For example, how many small Bugle Boy shirts, at $59.95, in blue do I expect to sell? Such decisions involve the art of merchandising. Knowledge of the customer market, the segment appealed to, the image of the store and/or department, and other factors all enter into this subjective decision.

Dollar Planning of Inventory Assume that 1,000 shirts are needed for the ideal stock level. This number, however, does not tell the manager how many dollars need to be invested in stock at any one time. Thus, the total dollar investment in inventory is the final way to look at stock balance.[6] Here merchandise turnover comes into play.

Figure 9-3 shows how to calculate turnover. For turnover goals to be meaningful, they must be based on merchandise groupings, that are as much alike as possible. Planning on the basis of large, diverse merchandise groupings is unwise. Also, it is impossible to tell whether a particular turnover figure is good or bad unless it is compared to something. The retailer can compare turnover rates to average rates for various merchandise classifications or to the firm's

Figure 9-3 Stock Turnover Calculation

Based on dollars

Turnover at retail

$$\text{Turnover} = \frac{\text{Retail sales (\$100,000)}}{\text{Average inventory in retail dollars (\$25,000)}} = 4 \text{ times}$$

How to calculate average retail inventory

↓

Add together all available inventory figures and divide by the number of counts, e.g., →		
	Beginning of year	$30,000
	+Midyear	20,000
	+End of year	25,000
	= Total	$75,000
	Average = $75,000 ÷ 3 =	$25,000

Turnover at cost

$$\text{Turnover} = \frac{\text{Cost of sales (\$60,000)}}{\text{Average inventory at cost (\$15,000)}} = 4 \text{ times}$$

How to calculate cost of sales:

↓

See what was available; add purchases; subtract what is left; then see what moved out—all at cost →		
	Beginning inventory	$12,000
	+Purchases	66,000
	+Total dollars available	$78,000
	– Ending inventory	18,000
	= Cost of goods sold	$60,000

Based on units

$$\text{Turnover} = \frac{\text{Number of units sold (3,200)}}{\text{Average inventory in units (800)}} = 4 \text{ times}$$

Figure 9-4 How to Look at Assortment Planning

Ways to Look at Assortment Planning	Examples	Things to Consider in Assortment Planning
Width (or breadth)	Number of brands, sizes, colours	What customers want What competitors offer
Depth	How many units are needed to support expected sales of each size, etc.	The sales importance of each size
Total dollars	How many dollars are inventory?	Look at turnover. a. Fast enough to get good return b. Not so fast that out-of-stocks occur

own rates for past periods. The goal, however, is to have a turnover rate that is fast enough to give the retailer a good return on money invested in inventory, but not so fast that the retailer is always out of stock.

Figure 9-4 recaps what has been discussed thus far in the chapter. Readers should understand the material before proceeding to the next section, which discusses how to set up a merchandise budget.

THE MERCHANDISE BUDGET

This section of the chapter focuses on merchandise planning in total dollars. Later sections look at planning in terms of width and depth.

Approaches to Preparing the Merchandise Budget

Traditionally, merchandise planning has been structured around either a bottom-up or a top-down approach. The bottom-up approach starts with estimates at the classification level. These estimates are then combined into a departmental merchandise budget and finally into a total company plan. The **merchandise budget** is a plan of how much to buy in dollars per month based on profitability goals. The top-down approach starts with a gross dollar figure established by top management. This dollar figure is then allocated to the various merchandise classifications. A third method of merchandise planning is the interactive approach. Interactive means that management sets broad guidelines and the buying staff then follows the bottom-up approach with reviews by management. The interactive approach probably results in the most accurate merchandise plan.

The Merchandise Budgeting Process

The following items affect profit return and are included in the merchandise budget:

1. Sales: Figure 9-2, point 3B.
2. Stock (inventory): Figure 9-2, point 3C.
3. Markup: Figure 9-2, point 3D.
4. Reductions: Figure 9-2, point 3E.
5. Purchases: Figure 9-2, point 3F.

Figure 9-5 presents a diagram of these profit factors. References will be made to this diagram as each of these factors is discussed in more detail.

Sales Planning

The starting point in developing a merchandise budget is the sales plan. Note from Figure 9-5 that sales are first planned by season and then by month. In discussing sales planning by season and month, let's assume we are planning a merchandise budget for sporting goods.

By Season *A season* is the typical planning period in retailing, especially for fashion merchandise. Assume that the merchandise budget is being planned for the 2001 spring season (February, March, April, May, June, and July). The

Figure **9-5** Schematic Diagram of Merchandise Budget

	Components to Be Budgeted					
	Sales			Reductions		
	Season	Month	Stock	Season	Month	Purchases
Quantitative (factual) data						
Qualitative (subjective) data: trends and environmental factors						

retailer would start planning in November 2000. The factors the retailer needs to consider in developing this seasonal plan are given in Figure 9-6.

In planning seasonal sales, the retailer begins by looking at last year's sales for the same period. Assume sales were $15,000 for the spring of 2000. Too many retailers at this point merely use the past period's figure as their sales forecast for the planning period. However, recent sales trends should be considered. For example, if sales for the 2000 fall season have been running about 5 percent ahead of fall 1999 and this trend is expected to continue, the retailer would project spring 2001 sales to be $15,750 ($15,000 x 1.05 = $15,750).

But the retailer cannot stop here. Now one must look at *forces outside* the firm that would have an impact on the sales forecast. For example, the retailer's projections would be affected if a new sporting goods store opened next door, carrying similar assortments (especially if this new store was part of a national chain with excellent management), or a major manufacturer in the community was planning a large expansion. As well, the retailer needs to consider *economic conditions*, as noted in Chapter 2. Next the retailer must look at *internal conditions* that might affect the sales forecast. Moving sporting goods to a more valuable location within the store is an example of an internal condition.

Figure **9-6** Diagram of the Sales Budget, 2001

	Sales	
	Season	**By Month**
Information available for planning	1. Sales for spring, 2000 2. Recent trends in sales	1. Sales percentages by month, 2000 2. Check distribution against published trade data
Judgment applied in certain issues	1. Factors outside the store such as new competition 2. Internal conditions such as more space available	1. Factors outside the store such as new competitors 2. Internal conditions such as more space available

A new competitor, Golf Town, will have an impact on sales of existing sporting goods retailers in the area.

Exact numbers cannot be placed on all these external and internal factors. Retailers must, however, use judgment and incorporate all factors into the sales forecast. Assume that the retailer has decided sales should increase by 10 percent. The sales plan for the 2001 spring season is now $16,500 (15,000 x 1.10 = $16,500).

By Month

The planned seasonal sales must now be divided into monthly sales. Figure 9-6 presents those factors that must be considered.

Again, the starting point is spring 2000. Assume the following sales distribution by month for this season: February—10 percent; March—20 percent; April—15 percent; May—15 percent; June—30 percent; and July—10 percent. Further assume that the retailer has considered all internal and external factors that would affect this distribution and has decided that no adjustments need to be made. Based on this breakdown, the season's sales plan by month for spring 2001 would look like that in Figure 9-7.

Stock Planning

The next step in developing the merchandise budget is to plan stock (inventory) levels by month. In planning monthly stock needed to support monthly sales, several different techniques can be used. Because the **stock-to-sales ratio** method is often used to plan monthly stock levels for fashion merchandise and for highly seasonal merchandise, it will be used to illustrate the concept of stock planning. The formula is:

Beginning of Month (BOM) inventory = Planned monthly sales × stock-to-sales ratio.

Figure 9-7

Spring Sales Plan, 2001

Month	Percent of Total Season's Business in 2000	x	Season's Sales Forecast	=	Planned Sales for Months of 2001 Season
February	10		$16,500		$ 1,650
March	20		16,500		3,300
April	15		16,500		2,475
May	15		16,500		2,475
June	30		16,500		4,950
July	10		16,500		1,650
Total	100				$16,500

The stock-to-sales ratio reflects the relationship between the dollar amount needed in inventory at the beginning of a month (BOM) to support planned sales for that month. For example, if $30,000 in inventory is needed at the BOM to support sales of $10,000, the stock-to-sales ratio would be 3 ($30,000/$10,000 = 3).[7]

To determine the BOM inventory, the retailer multiplies the month's planned sales figure by the month's stock-to-sales ratio figure. For example, as shown in Figure 9-7, planned sales for February are $1,650. If the retailer knows from past experience and industry trade data that 4.7 times more dollars in inventory than planned sales are needed, the BOM inventory for February would be $7,755 ($1,650 x 4.7 = $7,755). The 4.7 figure is the stock-to-sales ratio figure for the month of February.[8]

In determining monthly stock-to-sales ratios, retailers can use existing stock-to-sales ratios from past performance. However, retailers must judge whether the prior periods' stock-to-sales figures need to be adjusted. To help with this judgment, trade data may be used along with the retailer's own information. Stock-to-sales ratios can also be calculated directly from the turnover goal set for the line of merchandise. To do this, the retailer simply divides the desired annual turnover figures into 12 (the number of months in a year). For example, if the turnover goal is 2.5, the average monthly stock-to-sales ratio for the year would be 4.8 (12/2.5 = 4.8). If the desired turnover rate were 4, the average monthly stock-to-sales ratio for the year would be 3 (12/4 = 3). As one can see, the lower the turnover rate, the higher the average monthly stock-to-sales ratio.

Figure 9-8 provides information on needed monthly BOM stock for spring 2001, using planned monthly sales for spring 2001 from Figure 9-7 and the monthly stock-to-sales ratios for past years. In reality, the retailer would use judgment in deciding whether to use last year's monthly stock-to-sales figures or whether any conditions exist that would require them to be changed.

The end-of-the-month (EOM) inventory for a particular month would be the BOM inventory for the following month. For example, as shown in Figure 9-8, the BOM inventory for February is $7,755. The EOM inventory for February would be $13,860, which is also the BOM inventory for March.

Figure 9-8 BOM Stock, Spring 2001

Month	Planned Sales	x	Stock to Sales	=	Planned BOM Stock
February	$ 1,650		4.7		$ 7,755
March	3,300		4.2		13,860
April	2,475		4.3		10,640
May	2,475		4.4		10,890
June	4,950		3.2		15,840
July	1,650		6.9		11,385
Total	$16,500				$70,370

Reductions Planning

Reductions are anything other than sales that reduce inventory value.

Employee Discounts Are Reductions If an item sells for $100 and employees receive a 20 percent discount, the employee pays $80. The $80 is recorded as a sale. The $20 reduces the inventory dollar amount but is not a sale. It is an employee discount—a reduction.

Shortages (Shrinkage) Are Reductions A shoplifter takes a $500 watch from a jewelry department. Inventory is reduced by $500 just as if it were a sale. But no revenues come from shoplifting. If a salesperson steals another watch (internal pilferage), the results are the same. A $1,000 watch is received into stock and marked at $500 because of a clerical error. Fewer inventory dollars are in stock than the retailer thinks.

Markdowns Are Reductions For example, assume a $50 tennis racket does not sell during the season and is marked down to $30. The $20 markdown is counted as a reduction of inventory and only $30 is counted as a sale.

Why Plan Reductions as a Part of the Merchandise Budget? Reductions must be planned and accounted for so the retailer will have sufficient BOM inventory to make planned sales.

Assume that reductions for the spring season in the department are planned at 8 percent or $1,320 ($16,500 seasonal sales × .08). Figure 9-8 could be used to allocate the reductions by month (e.g., February would be $1,650 × .08 or $132, and March would be $3,300 × .08 or $264). Reductions normally vary by month.

Planned Purchases

Up to this point, the retailer has determined planned (1) sales, (2) stock, and (3) reductions. The next step in developing the merchandise budget is to plan the dollar amount of purchases on a monthly basis. Planned purchases are figured as follows:

A. We *need* dollars of purchases to ⟶	Make sure we have enough retail EOM inventory to "be in business" the following month. Make sure we have enough to cover our sales plan. Take care of our planned reductions.
B. We *have* dollars to contribute to the above needs in the form of ⟶	Retail BOM inventory

Stated more concretely;

Planned purchases = Planned EOM stock + Planned sales
+ Planned reductions – Planned BOM stock

To calculate planned purchases for March, look at Figure 9-8 to get the needed information.

Planned Purchases =	$10,640	(EOM March or BOM April)	(Figure 9-8)
	+ 3,300	(Planned sales, March)	(Figure 9-8)
	+264	(Planned reductions, March)	(see above)
	= $14,204	(Dollars *needs*, March)	
	−13,860	(BOM March-what you *have*)	(Figure 9-8)
	= $ 344	(Planned purchases)	

One Additional Point Purchases are planned in terms of *retail* dollars. However, when buying merchandise, the buyer must think in terms of the *cost* of merchandise. Thus, it is necessary to convert the planned purchase figure at retail to a cost figure. This conversion process will be explained in detail in Chapter 11. At this point simply remember: To convert retail dollars to cost dollars, multiply retail dollars by the complement of the initial retail markup. For example, assume that planned purchases for a given month are $1,000 at retail, and that the planned initial markup is 40 percent of retail. To convert retail dollars to cost dollars, multiply $1,000 by 60 percent, the complement of the planned initial markup. (100 percent - 40 percent = 60 percent.) Thus planned purchases at cost would be $600 ($1,000 x .60 = $600).

We have now worked through the dollar merchandise planning process. Figure 9-9 is a planning form for a typical six-month merchandise plan that includes all the factors just discussed. However, as Figure 9-2 shows, the retailer still needs to plan the width and depth factors of stock balance (points 4 and 5). The following sections of the chapter describe how to plan these parts of the merchandise budget.

Figure **9-9** Six-Month Merchandising Plan

		Department name ______			Department no. ______			
					Plan (this year)		Actual (last year)	
Six-Month Merchandising Plan		**Stock turnover**						
		Workroom costs						
		Etc.						
Spring 20—		**Feb.**	**Mar.**	**Apr.**	**May**	**June**	**July**	**Seasonal**
Fall 20—		**Aug.**	**Sep.**	**Oct.**	**Nov.**	**Dec.**	**Jan.**	**Total**
Sales	Last Year							
	Plan	1,650	3,300	2,475	2,475	4,950	1,650	16,500
	Percent of increase							
	Revised							
	Actual							
Retail Stock (BOM)	Last Year							
	Plan	7,755	13,860	10,640	10,890	15,840	11,385	70,370
	Percent of increase							
	Revised							
	Actual							
Markdowns	Last Year							
	Plan (dollars)	132	264	198	198	396	132	1,320
	Plan (percent)							
	Revised							
	Actual							
Retail Purchases	Last Year							
	Plan		344					
	Revised							
	Actual							
Percent of Initial Markup	Last Year							
	Plan							
	Revised							
	Actual							

PLANNING WIDTH AND DEPTH OF ASSORTMENTS

Now that the retailer knows how much to spend for stock, a decision still must be made on (1) what to spend the dollars for (width) and (2) in what amounts (depth). The goal here is to set up a **model stock plan** (Figure 9-2, point 6). A model stock plan is the retailer's best prediction of the assortment needed to satisfy customers.

The Width Plan

Figure 9-10 is a model stock plan for a sweaters classification in a sporting goods department. Assume that only two customer-attracting features are important—synthetic and natural fibres. Even though the illustration is simple, it shows that to offer customers only one sweater in each assortment *width* factor (in both synthetic and natural fibres), 270 sweaters (2 x 5 x 3 x 3 x 3) are needed (column 1 of Figure 9-10).

The Depth Plan

The depth plan involves deciding how many sweaters are needed in each of the five assortment factors (Figure 9-10). Assume that 800 are needed for one turnover period. (If turnover is to be 3, then 800 sweaters are needed for 4 months—12 months divided by 3 is 4.) Also remember that the retailer is planning dollars at the same time as assortments. Thus, the amount of dollars will affect support.

If the retailer believes that 90 percent of sales will be in synthetic fibres, then 720 sweaters will be needed (800 x .90 = 720). Following Figure 9-10, one sees that the retailer will have 144 of size A, 58 in colour A, 29 at price point A, and 14 in design A.

The Art of Planning

The foregoing illustration of the formulation of the width and depth (model stock in units) appears to be a rather routine approach to planning. In fact, the decisions as to the percentage relationships among the various assortment factors are based on many complex factors relating to store objectives and to the merchandising art of retailing. In planning the assortment width factors, the entire merchandising philosophy and strategic positioning of management assume critical importance. The factors would be significantly different for a classification in a unit of the Bay than for the same classification in a Zellers outlet. The Bay's merchandiser would consider the most unusual styles and fashion colours. Also, price points would greatly exceed those of Zellers.

In other words, the total image management wants the store to project and the strategy assumed to accomplish the store's objectives affect decisions on width factors and the relative importance of each. Certainly the target market of the store affects planning decisions, as do environmental conditions of the planning period. For example, as technological advances in textile fibres allowed more vibrant colourfast materials to enter the menswear industry, the width of offerings was expanded. The technology was a response to changing lifestyles, which dictated a more fashion-conscious male market for sportswear in general. In addition, changing styles of living and utilization of time for such activities as tennis and golf were reflected in sportswear offerings.

Figure 9-10 Model Stock of Sweaters

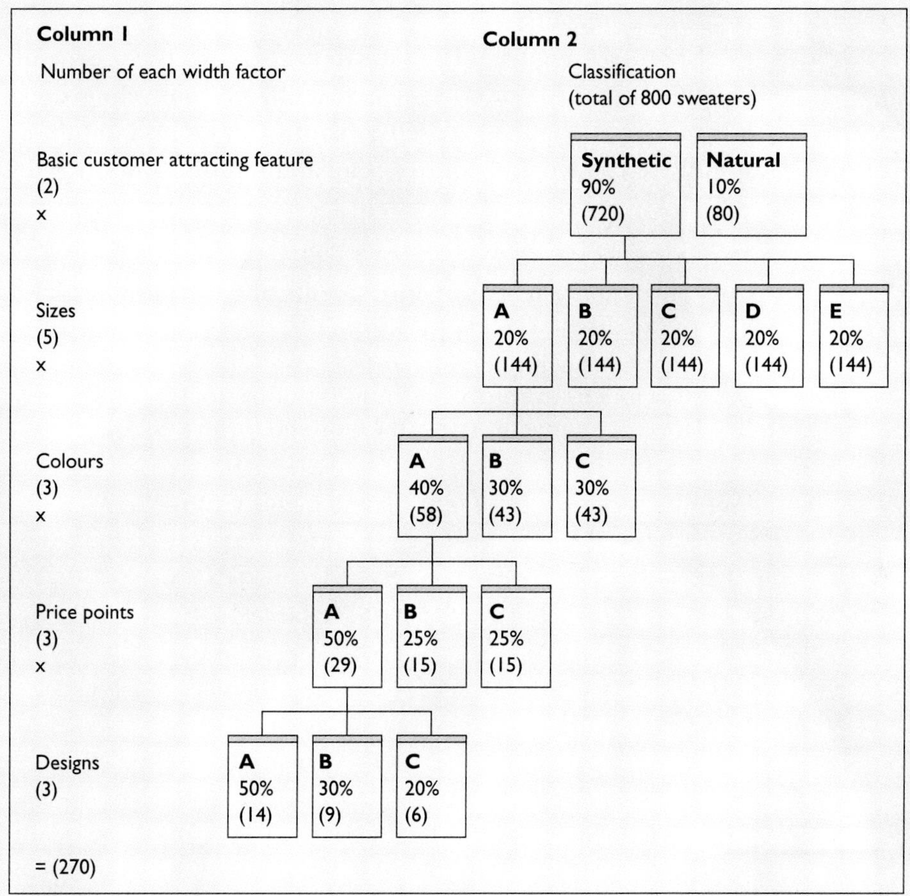

We have focused on the "how to" rather than the "what" and "why" because of the artistic and creative nature of merchandising, the variability among differing types of merchandise classifications, and especially the virtual impossibility of teaching the *art* of merchandising. Our major concern is that you appreciate how the operating and the creative aspects of merchandise planning relate.

MERCHANDISE CONTROL

The final step in merchandise management is control; the relationship between planning and control is essential, direct, and two-way. As shown in Figure 9-11, control records are needed to develop plans. Once a plan is developed, control records are needed to determine how well the retailer is doing.

The merchandise plan has been discussed in terms of developing the following: (1) dollars, (2) width, and (3) depth. A merchandise budget in dollars and a model stock were developed for planning the width and depth factors. In this section, attention is given to the systems used to control the merchandise budget. Figure 9-12 illustrates the relationships between the merchandise planning and control systems.

Note from Figure 9-12 that two systems are used for controlling the merchandise plan. **Dollar control** is the way of controlling dollar investment in inventory. **Unit control** is used to control width and depth. Figure 9-13 shows how these two types of control—dollar and unit—work together.

Dollar Merchandise Inventory Control

To control dollar inventory investments, the retailer must know the following:

1. The beginning dollar inventory.
2. What has been added to stock.
3. How much inventory has moved out of stock.
4. How much inventory is now on hand.

Figure 9-11 The Relationship Between Planning and Control

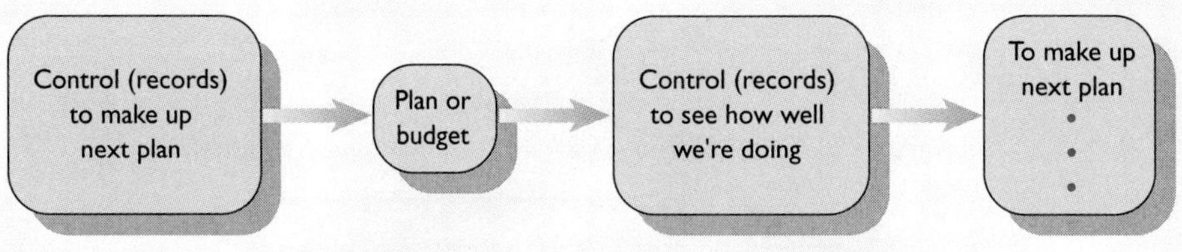

Figure 9-12 From Planning to Control

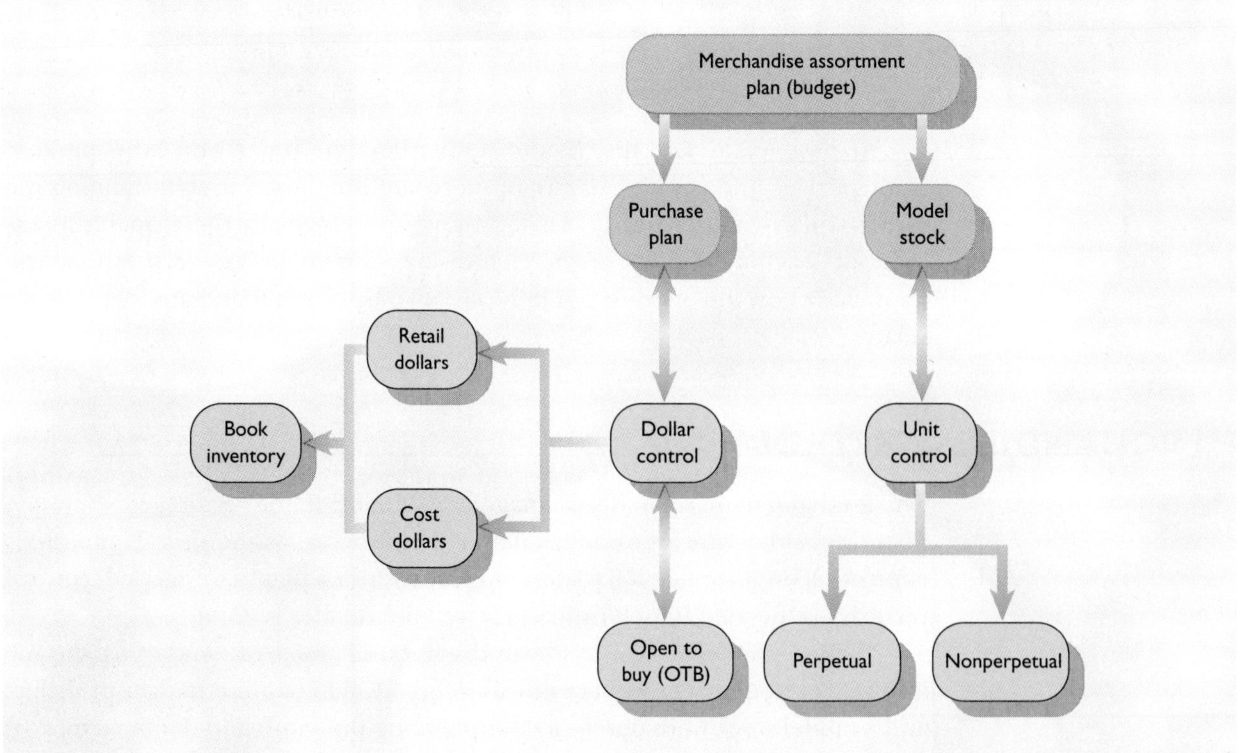

Figure 9-13 Diagram of Merchandise Planning and Control

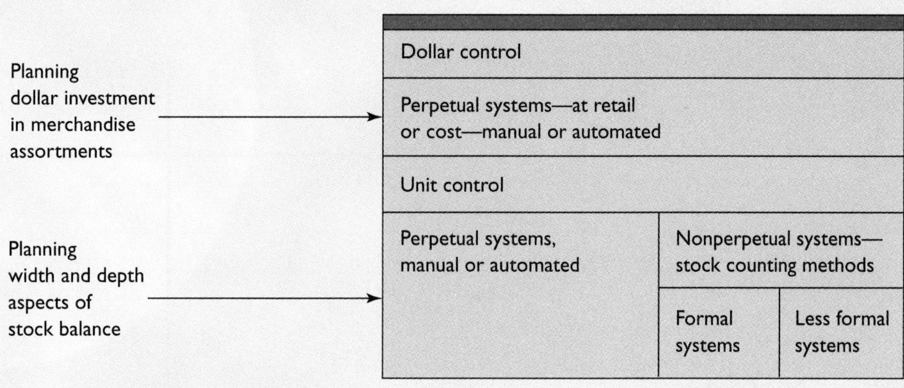

A more detailed statement appears in this section, but the following example shows the basic facts the retailer must know to control dollar inventory investments:

	1. Retail value of inventory at beginning of period	$10,000
+	2. Purchases at retail	2,000
=	Stock available for sale during period	$12,000
–	3. Total deductions from stock (sales plus markdowns)	2,500
=	4. Retail value of inventory at end of period	$ 9,500

To determine the value of inventory at the end of the period (number 4 in the example above), the retailer may (1) take a *physical inventory* (actually count the entire inventory on hand) or (2) set up a book inventory or *perpetual inventory system.* A **book inventory** is the recording of all additions to and deductions from a beginning stock figure to continually have an ending inventory figure. It is impractical to take a physical inventory every time the manager wants to know how much inventory is on hand. Thus, retailers set up a book inventory system. This enables them to know the dollar value of inventory on hand without having to take a physical inventory.

A book inventory system is needed for efficient and effective dollar control. Information must be collected and recorded continually; it can be recorded in retail dollars or in cost dollars, typically by computer.

Retail Dollar Control

Figure 9-14 includes the typical items included in a retail dollar control system. The system is a perpetual one and provides answers to the following questions:

- *What dollar inventory did the retailer start with?* The BOM (beginning of month) inventory dated 3/1 gives the answer to this question. This March BOM inventory figure is the EOM (end of month) February figure, or $10,000.
- *What has been added to stock?* The additions to stock are purchases, transfers, and additional markups that add dollars to the beginning inventory. Total additions are $2,300. The total available for sale is $12,300.

Figure 9-14 Illustration of Retail Dollar Book (Perpetual) Inventory (Sweat Suits) for Month of March

Items Affecting Dollar Value of Inventory during Month				Necessary Explanations of Certain Items	Where to Get Information
BOM inventory, 3/1			$10,000		EOM February inventory
Additions to stock:					
Purchases	$2,000				Purchase records or invoices
Less: Vendor returns	(100)			Goods go back to source	Vendor return records
Net purchases		$1,900			
Transfers in	$ 200			In multistore firm, goods transfer from one store to another	Interstore transfer forms in multi-store firm
Less: Transfers out	(100)				
Net transfers in		100			
Additional markups		300		Price increase after goods in stock	Price change forms
Total additions			2,300		
Total available for sale			$12,300		
Deductions from stock:					
Gross sales	$2,500				Daily sales report
Less: Customer returns	(100)				Return forms
Net sales		$2,400			
Gross markdowns	$ 500			Reduction from original price	Price change forms at start of sale
Less: Markdown cancellations	(100)				Price change cancellation at end of sale to bring prices back to regular
Net markdowns		400			
Employee discounts		200		Employee pays less than merchandise price	Form completed at sale
Total deductions from stock			$3,000		
EOM inventory, 3/31 (including shortages)			$9,300	A book inventory figure so actual amount is somewhat different (physical inventory necessary for actual)	Derived figure from additions and deductions from BOM inventory

- *How much inventory has moved out of stock?* The deductions from stock are sales, markdowns, and employee discounts, which reduce the total dollars of inventory available for sale. Total deductions are $3,000.
- *How much inventory is on hand now?* The EOM inventory, dated 3/31, is the difference between what was available and what moved out of stock. This is the book inventory figure or $9,300.

The explanations in Figure 9-14 should be studied carefully since it is important to fully understand the items that affect retail book inventory. This information, however, should not be confused with an accounting statement discussed in Chapter 17. The information comes from accounting data, but it is for control purposes only.

Note in Figure 9-14 the notation "including shortages" at the end of the illustration. Since these are "book" figures, a chance for error exists. The only way to determine the accuracy of the book figure is by taking a physical inventory.

The retail book figures indicate the value of on-hand inventory to be $9,300. Assume that when a physical inventory is taken, the retail value of on-hand stock is $9,000. This situation represents a shortage of $300. A **shortage** occurs when the physical inventory is smaller than the book inventory. Shoplifting, internal theft, short shipments from vendors, breakage, and clerical error are common causes of shortages. If, on the other hand, the physical inventory had indicated the value of stock on hand to be $10,000, then the retail classification has incurred an overage of $700. An **overage** occurs when the physical inventory is larger than the book inventory. In retailing, an overage situation is usually caused by clerical errors or miscounts.

Open-to-Buy

One of the most valuable outputs of a retail dollar control system is **open-to-buy** (OTB). (See Figure 9-12.) OTB exists to "control" the merchant's utilization of the planned purchases. The purpose of OTB is to keep spending in line with planned purchases. It is the amount of new merchandise the retailer can buy in a specific time period without exceeding the planned purchases for that period. Dollar control provides the essential information to set up an OTB system. These essentials are the BOM and EOM inventories.

Figure 9-15 illustrates how OTB as of February 15 can be calculated. As shown, OTB is determined by deducting from planned purchases the commitments that have been made. The two commitments are (1) merchandise on order that has not been delivered and (2) merchandise that has been delivered. Remember that planned purchases relate to one particular month (in the example, to February). So, OTB relates to only one month. If, for example, merchandise was ordered in January to be delivered in March, that amount would not be a February commitment and would not affect OTB for February.

Figure 9-15 Open-to-Buy Illustration

Planned purchases		=	$25,000	(EOM February or BOM March at retail)
		+	2,500	(Planned sales - February)
		+	600	(Planned reductions - February)
		=	$28,100	(Dollars needed)
		–	24,000	(BOM February at retail) (EOM January)
		=	$4,100	(Planned purchases)
Commitments against planned purchases during the month of February:				
On order to be delivered in February:	$1,000			
Merchandise received as of February 15:	$1,500	–	$2,500	(Commitments against planned purchases)
OTB as of February 15		=	$1,600	(Note: The $1,600 figure is in retail dollars and must be converted to cost to use as a buying guide in the market.)

From the illustration, one can see that as of February 15, the buyer has $1,600 (in retail dollars) to spend for merchandise to be delivered in February. At the beginning of any month with no commitments, planned purchases and OTB are equal. Assume, however, that by February 20 all of the OTB has been used up and that, in fact, the buyer has overcommitted by $100. This situation is called *overbought* and is not a good position to be in. This leads to another point that must be made about OTB.

OTB must be used only as a guide and must not be allowed to actually dictate decisions. A retailer, however, always wants to have OTB to take advantage of unique market situations. The system must also allow for budget adjustments. If the buyer needs more OTB for certain purposes, management approval must be obtained. This can be done by: (1) convincing management of the importance of a contemplated purchase and obtaining a budget increase for planned sales; (2) increasing planned reductions or taking more markdowns than have been budgeted; or (3) increasing the planned EOM inventory in anticipation of an upswing in the market. Each of these is a legitimate merchandising option and indicates that the OTB control system is flexible, as any budget control system must be. As well, OTB is a tool for preventing stockouts.

Figure 9-16 presents a sample open-to-buy report form. Of course, this form would vary by company based on what the retailer feels is needed for decision making. By using this form, OTB could be derived by: Line 11 + Line 7 + Line 14 - Line 5 = Planned purchases - Line 17 = OTB (Line 18). (Numbers from Figure 9-15).

Figure 9-16 Example of an Open-to-Buy Report

Open-to-buy report

Department ______________ Classification ______________ Date prepared February 15

Line				
		Last Month (January)		
1	Sales	–	Actual last year	____
2		–	Adjusted plan this year	____
3	Stock	–	Actual last year	____
4		–	Adjusted plan EOM this year	____
5		–	Actual EOM this year	24,000
6		–	Actual last year	____
7	Sales	–	Adjusted plan this year	2,500
8		–	Month to date this year	____
		This Month (February)		
9	Stock	–	Balance of month this year	____
10		–	Actual EOM last year	____
11		–	Adjusted plan EOM this year	25,000
12		–	Actual as of this report	____
13	Markdowns	–	Actual last year	____
14		–	Adjusted plan this year	600
15		–	Actual as of this report	____
16		–	Balance of month this year	____
17	On order to be received and received to date			2,500
18	Open-to-buy			1,600

Cost Dollar Control

Retail dollar control is used more often than cost dollar control. The major problem in using cost versus retail control is *costing* each sale. Costing means converting retail dollars to cost dollars after a sale has been made. When using a cost dollar control system, it is not possible to record additional markups and reductions such as markdowns and employee discounts because all the figures are in cost dollars.

Unit Merchandise Inventory Control

Unit control is the system used to control the width and depth aspects of stock balance (see Figures 9-12 and 9-13). Unit control is simpler than dollar control since fewer factors affect units than affect dollars invested. The difference is that the price changes do not affect units carried. As Figures 9-12 and 9-13 indicate, the two types of unit control are perpetual and non-perpetual (or stock-counting) systems.

Perpetual Unit Control

Perpetual unit control, like perpetual dollar control, is a book inventory. Figure 9-17 provides an illustration of perpetual unit control.

A perpetual (book) inventory for unit control is the most sophisticated of the unit systems. Because perpetual book systems require continuous recording of additions and deductions from stock, they are more expensive to operate. However, the use of point-of-sale systems reduces costs and saves time in collecting the information needed. If the system is manually maintained, sales information is recorded in the office, detaching a part of a sales ticket to be counted later, or deducting items sold from a tag on a floor sample.

Note in Figure 9-17 the notation "including shortages," which appears at the end of the illustration. As with dollar control, this is a book figure—thus, there is chance for error. Again, the only way to determine the accuracy of the book figure is to take a physical inventory. The concepts of shortages and overages apply here just as they do in dollar control. The only difference is that shortages and overages are expressed in terms of number of units rather than in dollars.

Non-Perpetual Unit Control

Non-perpetual unit control systems are also called stock-counting systems. These systems are not book inventory methods. Thus, the retailer will not be able to determine shortages or overages because there is no book inventory against which to compare a physical inventory.

Non-perpetual systems for unit control are actually a compromise. Perpetual control is better and the retailer gets more and better information. But sometimes the benefits simply do not justify the cost. Non-perpetual unit control systems include formal and less formal systems.

Formal Systems

The requirements of formal, non-perpetual systems are as follows: (1) a planned model stock, (2) a periodic counting schedule, and (3) definite, assigned responsibility for counting. Let's use a tie classification as an example. Every tie in stock might be counted once a month. The retailer might select the first Tuesday of each month for the count schedule. Based on the stock on hand, the stock on order, and the stock sold, the buyer will place a reorder as the information is reviewed each count period.

For formal, non-perpetual systems to be used effectively, the rate of sale of the items being controlled must be predictable. Further, the items controlled by formal systems should not be of such a fast-moving, fashionable nature that the retailer needs to know the status of stock more often than the periodic count schedule will permit. The alert retailer will spot check between count dates to catch any out-of-stocks that might occur. Formal systems do account for items on order (which less formal systems do not).

Figure 9-17 Illustration of Perpetual Unit Control (Sweat Suits) for Month of March

BOM Inventory			1,000
Additions to stock:			
Purchases	250		
Less—vendor returns	(40)		
Net purchases		210	
Transfers in	41		
Less—transfers out	(20)		
Transfers in		21	
Total additions			231
Total available for sale			1,231
Deductions from stock:			
Gross sales	225		
Less—customer returns	(8)		
Net sales		217	
Total deductions from stock			(217)
EOM inventory, 3/31 (including shortages)			1,014

Less Formal Systems

Some kinds of merchandise can be controlled with a less formal system. If immediate delivery of goods is possible, there is no need to account for merchandise on order. However, the retailer still must have a planned model stock and a specific time for visually inspecting the stock.

Under a less formal system, there will be a minimum stock level (e.g., shelf level or number of cases in the stockroom) below which the stock must not go. When the stock reaches that level, a reorder is placed. In the canned goods department in a supermarket, this system might be used quite effectively.

CHAPTER HIGHLIGHTS

- Merchandising management is the management component of the marketing mix and involves the planning and control of merchandising. The key to successful merchandising is to ensure that the customer is offered the right merchandise, at the right price, at the right place, at the right time, and in the right quantities (the five "rights" of merchandising).
- One of the more difficult problems facing merchants is the optimal balance between national, private, and generic brands.
- Preparing a merchandise budget is a challenging and important task. It requires managers to look at width, breadth, and total dollars.
- The following items affect profitability and are included in the merchandise budget: (1) sales, (2) inventory or stock, (3)markups, (4) reductions, and (5) purchases.

- Retailers need to monitor operating results to determine whether goals are being met. If not, corrective action must be taken to improve the situation. The monitoring process is the control aspect of merchandise and expense management.
- The relationship between planning and control is essential, direct, and two-way. Control records are needed to develop plans, and plans are evaluated by these control data.
- Two systems are used for controlling the merchandise plan: *dollar control* for controlling dollar investment and *unit control* for controlling the width and depth aspects of stock balance.
- One of the most valuable outputs of a retail dollar control system is open-to-buy (OTB), which exists to control the retailer's utilization of the planned purchase figure.
- Retail dollar control is used more often than cost dollar control because of the problems of "costing" each sale for the latter system.
- Unit control is the system used to control the width and depth aspects of assortments and is simpler than dollar control since fewer factors affect units than affect dollars invested. For example, price changes do not affect units.
- The two types of unit control are perpetual and non-perpetual (or stock-counting systems).

KEY TERMS

DISCUSSION QUESTIONS

1. By using examples, distinguish among the following: product, merchandise line, breadth, and assortment.
2. Explain "merchandise turnover" and indicate how it is useful in planning total dollars in inventory.
3. What factors must a retailer consider in deciding how many dollars to spend on inventory?
4. Discuss the following: sales planning, stock planning, reductions planning.

5. Explain the relationship between stock-to-sales ratios and turnover. How are stock-to-sales ratios used as a guide to stock planning in the merchandise budget?
6. How does a retailer plan purchases? Give an example of the process.
7. Explain the relationship between *planning* and *control*.
8. Explain open-to-buy (OTB). Why would a retailer attempt to have OTB always available? How can a retailer who has overbought make adjustments to get more open-to-buy?
9. What is the purpose of unit control? What is the difference between perpetual and non-perpetual unit control systems?

PROBLEMS

1. If net sales for the season (6 months) are $48,000 and the average retail stock for the season is $21,000, what is the annual stock-turnover rate?
2. If cost of goods sold for the first four months of operation is $127,000 and average stock at cost for this same time period is $68,000, what is the annual stock-turnover rate?
3. Given the following figures, what is the stock-turnover rate for the season?

	Retail Stock on Hand	**Monthly Net Sales**
Opening inventory	$16,000	$7,500
End of 1st month	16,450	6,900
2nd month	16,000	7,250
3rd month	17,260	6,840
4th month	16,690	6,840
5th month	15,980	6,620
6th month	16,620	7,180

4. What is average stock if the stock-turnover rate is 4 and net sales are $36,000?
5. What is the cost of goods sold if the stock-turnover rate is 2.5 and the average stock at cost is $8,700?
6. A new department shows the following figures for the first three months of operation: net sales, $150,000; average retail stock, $160,000. If business continues at the same rate, what will the stock-turnover rate be for the year?
7. Last year a certain department had net sales of $21,000 and a stock-turnover rate of 2.5. A stock-turnover rate of 3 is desired for the year ahead. If sales volume remains the same, how much must the average inventory be reduced (a) in dollar amount and (b) in percentage?
8. A certain department had net sales for the year of $71,250. The stock at the beginning of the year is $22,500 at cost and $37,500 at retail. A stock count in July showed the inventory at cost as $23,750 and at retail as $36,250. End-of-year inventories are $25,000 at cost and $38,750 at retail. Purchases at cost during the year amounted to $48,750. What is the stock-turnover rate (a) at cost and (b) at retail?

9. Given the following information for the month of July, calculate planned purchases:

Planned sales for the month	$ 43,000
Planned BOM inventory	60,250
Planned reductions for the month	1,200
Planned EOM inventory	58,000

10. Given the following information for the month of October, calculate planned purchases:

Planned sales for the month	$198,000
Planned EOM inventory	240,000
Stock-to-sales ratio for the month of October	1.2
Planned reductions for the month	3,860

11. Given the following figures, calculate planned purchases for January:

Stock on hand—January 1	$ 36,470
Planned stock on hand—February 1	38,220
Planned sales for January	21,760
Planned reductions for January	410

12. Given the following data for a certain department as of June 10, calculate (a) planned purchases and (b) open-to-buy:

Planned sales for the month	$ 47,000
Planned reductions for the month	1,500
Planned EOM inventory	52,550
Planned BOM inventory	47,800
Merchandise received to date for June	14,980
Merchandise on order, June delivery	6,850

13. The following data are for a certain department as of January 20. Calculate (a) planned purchases and (b) open-to-buy:

Planned sales for the month	$142,000
Planned BOM inventory	177,000
Planned reductions for the month	4,200
Planned EOM inventory	165,000
Merchandise received to date for January	130,000
Merchandise on order, January delivery	4,200
Merchandise on order, February delivery	2,200

14. Given the following data for a certain department as of September 20, calculate (a) planned purchases and (b) open-to-buy:

Planned sales for the month	$ 9,200
Planned reductions for the month	100
Planned BOM inventory	14,600
Planned EOM inventory	15,500
Merchandise received to date for September	9,800
Merchandise on order, September delivery	500

15. Given the following information for the month of July, calculate (a) planned purchases and (b) open-to-buy:

Planned sales for the month	$ 27,000
Planned reductions for the month	650
Planned EOM inventory	36,000
Stock-to-sales ratio for July	1.5
Merchandise received to date for July	13,800
Merchandise on order, July delivery	5,250

16. Calculate open-to-buy for March, given the following figures:

Stock on hand, March 1	$ 72,500
Planned stock on hand, April 1	80,000
Merchandise on order for March delivery	49,875
Planned sales for March	63,500

17. Given the following information for November, calculate open-to-buy (a) at retail and (b) at cost:

Planned sales for the month	$ 24,600
Planned reductions for the month	300
Planned EOM retail stock	32,300
Planned BOM retail stock	30,800
Merchandise received for the month of November	16,300
Merchandise on order, November delivery	4,000
Merchandise on order, December delivery	2,575
Planned initial markup at retail	35%

18. Given the following information for August, calculate open-to-buy (a) at retail and (b) at cost:

Planned sales for the month	$ 57,000
Planned reductions for the month	1,200
Planned EOM retail stock	72,000
Stock-to-sales ratio for the month of August	1.2
Planned initial markup at retail	42%
Merchandise received for the month of August	35,000
Merchandise on order, August delivery	16,400

APPLICATION EXERCISES

1. Attention is given in the text to formal merchandise planning. Select some stores and find out how they handle this function. How much planning? Levels of sophistication? Does the degree differ by merchandise lines? See if you can develop some generalizations from your investigations.
2. Visit two competing supermarkets and list the SKUs in one product category (e.g., laundry detergents). Analyze the lists and prepare a short paper on the two supermarkets' apparent merchandising strategies.
3. Visit a local supermarket that has "scanning" equipment at the check-out. Ask to see the manager and tell that person you are a student and want to ask him/her a few questions. Design your questions so you can find out if information received from the new equipment is being used for control. If not, what is it being used for?

SUGGESTED CASE

14. Shoes for Sports

CHAPTER 10

BUYING, HANDLING, AND INVENTORY MANAGEMENT

CHAPTER OBJECTIVES

After reading this chapter you should be able to:

1. Identify factors influencing the buying cycle.
2. Understand the major technology changes that have impacted on buying and inventory management.
3. Explain how retailers negotiate price, discounts, datings, and transportation charges.
4. Evaluate issues related to the management of physical handling activities.
5. Discuss problems associated with shoplifting and employee theft and the preventive measures available.

Technology is having a major impact on the way that Canadian retailers manage buying, handling, and inventory. With the advent of high-powered, lower cost computer systems, customized software, and electronic data interchange, retailers are reducing distribution and handling costs, improving merchandise selection for customers, and increasing inventory turnover.

A key element is the electronic link between the retailer and its suppliers. For example, Sobeys Inc. is a diversified national food distributor with approximately 150 Sobeys supermarkets located throughout Atlantic Canada, Quebec, and Ontario. It introduced Efficient Consumer Response (ECR), aimed at coordinating the operations of manufacturers, distributors, and retailers to improve efficiencies. ECR eliminated inefficient processes that added nothing to the value of Sobeys' products and services and developed programs in which the supplier, the customer, and Sobeys won. The installation of an advanced electronic data interchange with key suppliers has led to paperless transactions, an electronic inventory replenishment system, and lower operating costs. Recently, Sobeys launched the Vision 2020 Enterprise Systems project. Vision 2020 is the cornerstone of a new generation of supply chain management initiatives. All of the retail, wholesale, and food services business will be run on a single, advanced system. The system will allow Sobeys to examine each business right down to the real-time status of every item, on every store shelf, in every market. It will offer powerful benefits for their just-in-time inventory approach. It will provide category managers, those people responsible for a specific line of products—from buying to distribution to marketing and promotion—to identify and quickly respond to changes in the consumer market.

Sears Canada re-engineered its entire merchandise procurement process from the initial ordering of merchandise to the receipt of goods in the selling unit or delivery to the customer. The program improved customer service and in-stock positions, increased inventory turnover, decreased costs and overheads, and reduced merchandise procurement cycle times. Implementation included the adoption of a supplier compliance program that supported the introduction of electronic data interchange, quick response, and just-in-time ordering systems.

These two examples reflect the impact of technology and the new partnerships being formed between Canadian retailers and their suppliers. By working more closely together, the two parties can improve customer value and reduce their costs, benefiting everyone.[1,2]

The buying function is critical to the success of any retail firm. Buyers can be viewed as investment specialists and can be responsible for millions of dollars in merchandise. They must forecast demand for the merchandise, negotiate with vendors on a variety of issues such as price and transportation, and work as partners with the vendors in the sale of the merchandise. As shown above, buying relationships are changing, and as new technology makes more and better information available to retailers, it will allow them to work with suppliers in new and creative ways.

GOALS OF GOOD BUYING

Good buying involves purchasing the right merchandise for customers at the best price, in the right quantity, of the right quality, and from vendors who will be reliable and provide other valuable services. Many considerations are involved in doing this thoroughly and competently. These are all described in the buying cycle (Figure 10-1).

Figure 10-1 The Buying Cycle

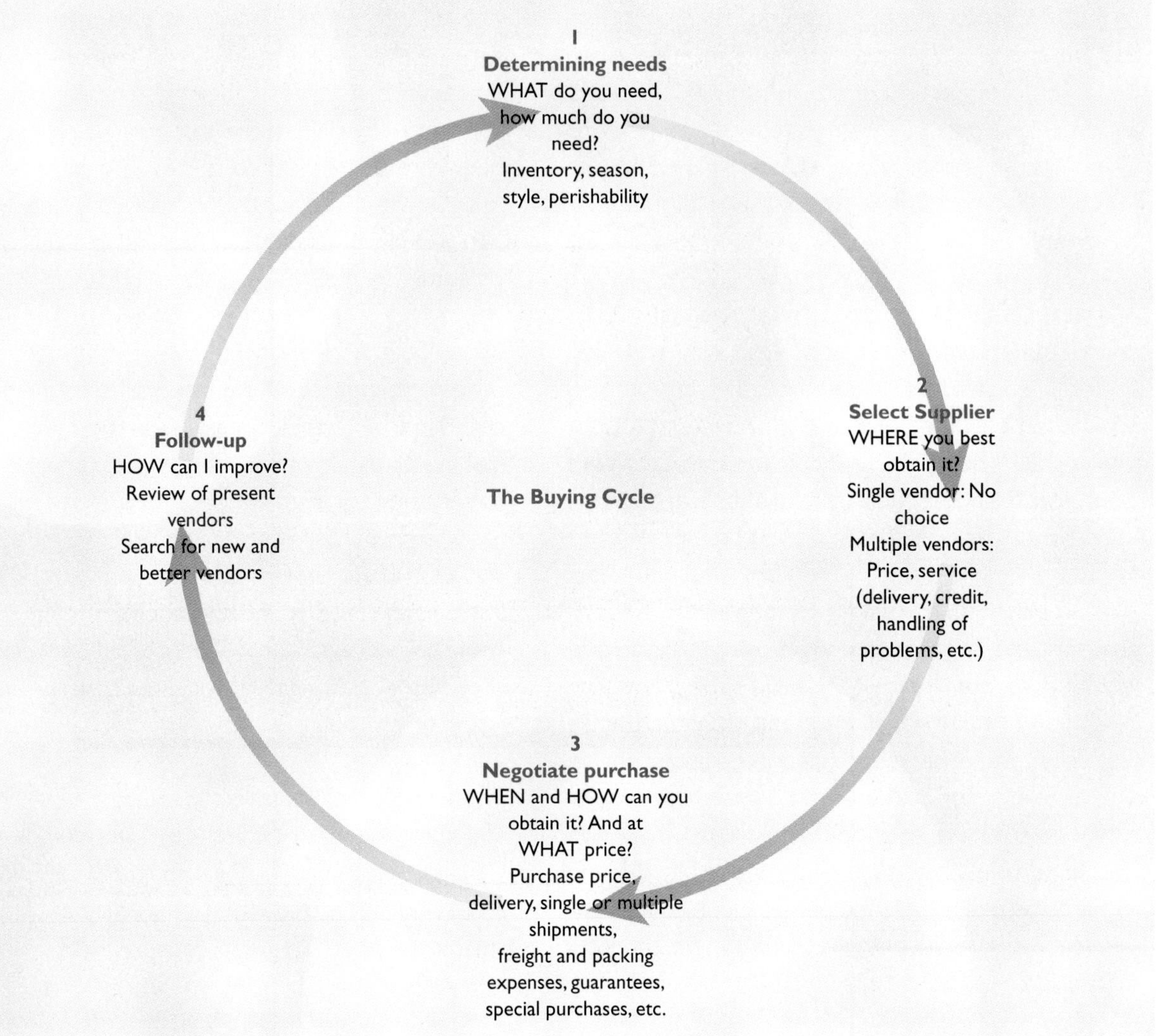
1
Determining needs
WHAT do you need,
how much do you
need?
Inventory, season,
style, perishability
2
Select Supplier
WHERE you best
obtain it?
Single vendor: No
choice
Multiple vendors:
Price, service
(delivery, credit,
handling of
problems, etc.)
3
Negotiate purchase
WHEN and HOW can you
obtain it? And at
WHAT price?
Purchase price,
delivery, single or multiple
shipments,
freight and packing
expenses, guarantees,
special purchases, etc.
4
Follow-up
HOW can I improve?
Review of present
vendors
Search for new and
better vendors
The Buying Cycle

The process of buying involves four major steps. They are:

1. *Determining needs.* The buyer must determine for each line of merchandise what will be needed until the next time the line is reviewed. Determining what is needed involves, for some items, merely looking at inventory and past sales. For other lines, it concerns risky decisions—which styles to select and how much of each to buy. One thing management does not want is a lot of merchandise in stock when a style is outmoded or the season is past.
2. *Selecting the supplier.* After determining the merchandise needs, the buyer must find vendors who can supply the merchandise. Some merchandise can be bought only from one vendor; in this case, the only decision to be made is whether to carry the line. For most merchandise lines, several suppliers are available. In these instances the buyer must evaluate price as well as service in terms of reasonable and reliable delivery, adjustment of problems, and help in emergencies and in other matters, such as credit terms, spaced deliveries, and inventory management assistance. For a

Sobeys, a leader in supply chain management

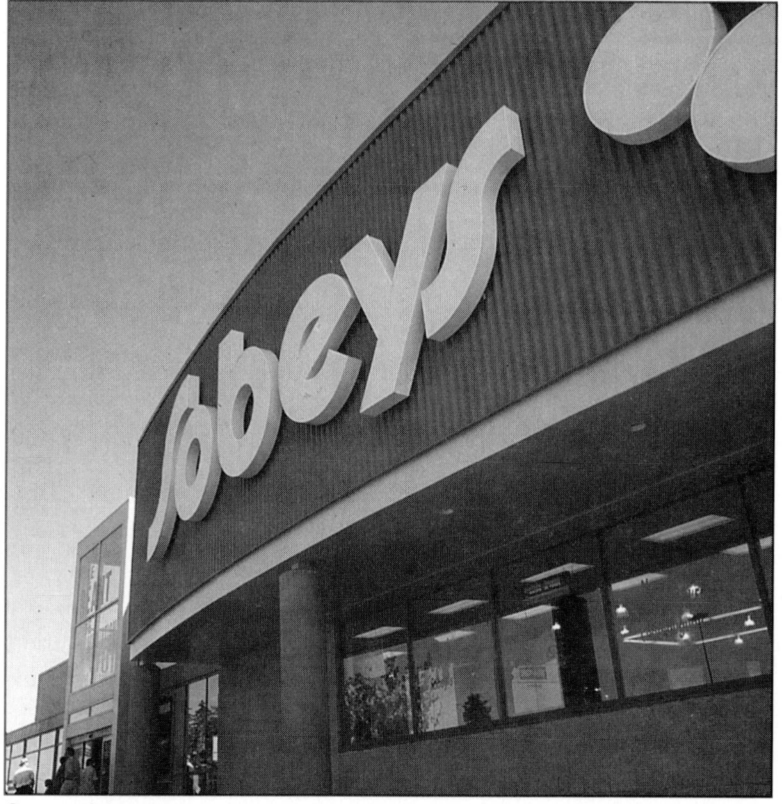

Courtesy Sobeys Inc.

retailer like Canadian Tire, supplier selection is a major task as the company deals with more than 3,000 Canadian and international suppliers.

3. *Negotiating the purchase.* This crucial third step involves not only the purchase price but also quantities, delivery dates, single or multiple shipment deliveries, freight and packing expenses, guarantees on the quality of the merchandise, promotion and advertising allowances, special offers on slightly damaged materials or sellouts, and so forth.
4. *Following up.* Finally, to improve service, the buyer must review the relationship with each vendor from time to time to determine if changes should be made.

DETERMINING NEEDS

Different types of merchandise require different techniques to determine what is needed. It is therefore important to recognize, for the various merchandise lines in the store, whether they are primarily *staples, seasonal items,* or *style* and *perishable items.*

The goal in each case is to establish or maintain inventory at the lowest possible level and still have a sufficient variety of colours, sizes, or models available from which customers can choose. Such a practice will minimize losses due to obsolescence and spoilage, while freeing capital that may be put to other uses.

Timeliness

Progressive retailers continue to refine the buying process, shorten lead times in ordering merchandise, maintain the minimum inventory level needed to meet customer needs, and have sufficient flexibility to quickly respond to changing customer tastes. By using sophisticated computer-based inventory management systems, these retailers have established faster buying than other retailers and are able to maintain less inventory than competitors, be more responsive to customer needs, and maintain higher gross margins than the norm.

Forecasting Sales

Technology has dramatically improved the methods retailers use to forecast sales. In the past, retailers would use a manual system based on a combination of factors such as past sales and a lot of judgment to determine what and how much should be ordered. As an example, Retail Highlight 10-1 outlines the capabilities of today's retail software.

A major decision faced by retailers in forecasting sales is the type of computer software system to install to aid in this decision. As noted, it depends, in part, on whether the merchandise is primarily *staples, seasonal items,* or *style* and *perishable items.*

Staple merchandise is generally in demand year-round, with little change in model or style. Basic appliances, hardware, housewares, books, and basic cloth-

Retail Highlight 10-1 The New Approach to Buying

Companies like Retail Technologies International design systems to aid retailers in managing the buying cycle. Consider the Retail Pro program for point-of-sale, merchandising, and inventory control.

- Point-of-sale—all data is captured for analysis and inventory is updated in real time. It can provide sales by SKU, returns, and taxes on a daily basis.
- Inventory control functions—a perpetual inventory system, it will show stock on hand, on order, received, and sold for each inventory item. It will calculate the minimum-maximum levels of any item based on the store's sales history to calculate scientifically what and when to reorder.
- Purchasing, receiving, and ticketing—it will automatically create purchase orders and as orders are received, by scanning LTPC codes, it will update inventory by units, cost, and retail. It produces designed or standard price tags for the quantity of goods received.
- Key statistics—turnover rates can be viewed for any item or category, days of supply by item, and gross margin return on investment. It monitors any key indicators selected by the retailer and provides an alert when any of the items or areas of inventory are above or below the designated levels.
- EDI interface—makes possible vendor-managed inventory solutions through which stock levels are automatically maintained at a defined stock level by automatic replenishment.

www.retailpro.com

Source: www.retailpro.com

ing items like underwear fall into this category. Staples, even if the store is primarily focused on seasonal fashion, generate extra profits and bring customers into the store who may then purchase some of the primary merchandise. The important characteristic of staples is steady usage. Most basic computer inventory systems can handle the buying quantity for staples by using:

- *Sales trends.* Taken from records showing how much of each staple sold during the past two or three months, and also how much sold during the same period in the previous year. From this, the system will predict future sales.
- *Profitability.* Items that bring a better return on investment in space and capital are the more desirable items to buy.
- *Discounts.* These are usually available with quantity purchases.

From this information, the buyer can devise a strategy (e.g., days of supply modified by season) and the system will scientifically calculate what and when to reorder.

Seasonal merchandise, as implied, is in demand only at certain times of the year. Obvious examples include skis, bathing suits, sunglasses, lawn equipment, holiday greeting cards, and patio furniture. Although some seasonal items can be secured during peak demand to replenish inventory, many are unavailable or cannot be obtained quickly enough at this time. Therefore, such merchandise is bought well in advance of the season. Most clothing stores in Canada would have a seasonal component to their merchandise mix, reflecting the different clothes worn in the four seasons.

Forecasting needs for seasonal items relies heavily on recording past customer demand for that item or merchandise line. These records, for each merchandise *item, group of items,* or *entire line* can then be examined on a yearly basis, enabling the buyer to identify selling trends and make buying decisions accordingly.

Accurately predicting future sales is more difficult for seasonal versus staples. Here, the computer system needs to incorporate as many of the following factors as is possible:

- Records of previous sales.
- Length of the season.
- Planned selling price.
- Planned advertising and promotion effort, including sales.
- The extent to which there is an increase or decrease in competition.
- Predictions of consumer buying from economic forecasts.

The computer system should allow the buyer to view sales history and forecasts by item (including style, colour, price range, department, cost, and vendor), groups of items, and product lines. This information plus the buyer's experience should provide a reasonable idea of the quantity of each item likely to sell during the upcoming season.

Style and perishable **items** include such merchandise as apparel and sportswear. Stylish items are usually more expensive than staples and seasonals. Because the demand for any particular style tends to increase rapidly, then drop

Figure 10-2 Sales of Different Styles

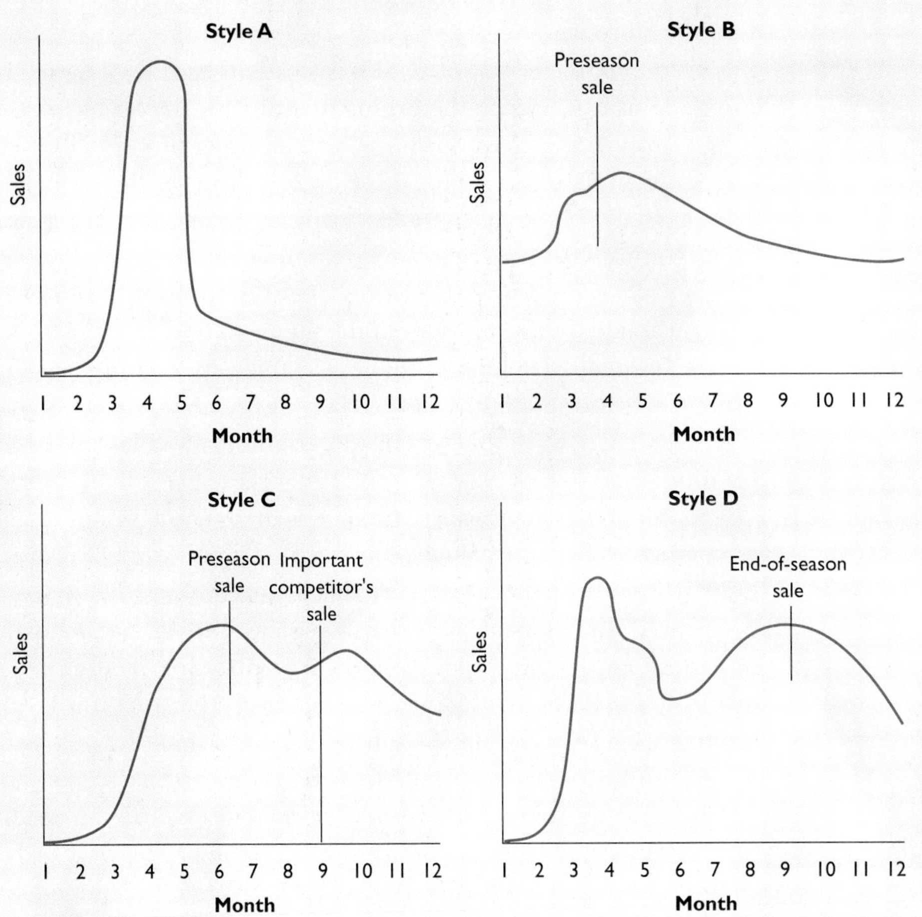

off rapidly, overbuying can have a disastrous effect on profits. Once a style is "out," it is often difficult to sell at a profit.

Le Chateau, a specialty clothing chain with over 150 stores in Canada, has an interesting approach to forecasting and purchasing fashion merchandise. Using a reporting system that provides fast information on inventory and style performance, the company can identify and react quickly to trends in clothing style and colour. It then manufactures more of the items in its Montreal-based facility and uses the information in the design and buying of the next season's collections.[3]

Perishable merchandise has similar characteristics. If management buys more than can be sold, some of it will begin to spoil and bring only a fraction of the normal price.

The computer system should allow management to plot the sales progress of different styles. A few examples of such graphs are shown in Figure 10-2. These graphs can help to predict how much to buy and when to buy.

When plotting graphs, it is important to note all special, significant events such as sales, including those of major competitors. These events also have to be planned or predicted and kept in mind when forecasting merchandise needs. These graphs may not predict sales very accurately, but they usually will narrow the amount of buying error. With styles and fashions, the computer system will aid the buyer but experience and judgment are critical in making these decisions.

Today, information partnerships between retailers and vendors are the standard way of buying merchandise.

Information Partnerships

Electronic data interchange (EDI), quick response (QR), and just-in-time (JIT) delivery are changing the way merchandise is ordered and shipped. New partnerships are emerging between retailers and vendors that are making the buying and replenishment process more timely and cost effective, as we discussed in the chapter introduction.

Ingredients

The ingredients of these emerging partnerships include the following:

Electronic Data Interchange EDI consists of software systems that allow for direct communication of standard business documents between retailers and vendors. Electronic sharing of information enables retailers and vendors to reduce reorder cycle times and speed delivery of replenishing inventory.

Just-in-Time JIT systems are designed to allow delivery of only the quantity of a specific product needed at the precise time it is needed. For example, the Bay might provide manufacturers with a six-month forecast of demand but a one-week lead time forecast of sizes, designs, and colours.

Quick Response This is an information-sharing partnership between retailers and vendors (often manufacturers) that provides retailers with timely replenishment of inventory sufficient to meet customer demand without the necessity of carrying high levels of inventory in anticipation of customer demand. These partnerships work with a strong alliance between the vendor and the retailer. The level of trust and information sharing required in such relationships is very high.

QR consists of several interrelated technologies and partner initiatives. Six factors are considered essential:

- Sharing inventory data among trading partners.
- Sharing sales and marketing data among trading partners.
- Using bar coding on packaging to track sales and inventory.
- Enabling retailers to order through EDI.
- Managing stock replenishment for key customers.
- Using automated stock replenishment systems.[4]

Although retailers such as Wal-Mart and Zellers have used it for several years, the system is now affordable and cost effective for small and medium-sized retailers and manufacturers.

Quick delivery and rapid merchandise turns provide several benefits. They can ensure both a high level of profitability and a low stockout level, the most desirable dimensions of an inventory strategy. Short lead times can also ensure that the merchandise is more likely to be fashionable and, for perishables, fresh. Shorter lead times can help the retailer influence the size, colour, and style mix closer to the fashion season.

Large companies such as Canadian Tire link their databases directly to the manufacturers of the merchandise. Small manufacturers and independent regional retailers typically link through third-party providers, such as Transcare Supply Chain Management of Toronto. Either way, the results are improved efficiency, stronger relationships, and higher profits for suppliers and retailers alike.

For suppliers, EDI provides added service to retailers—a step beyond the usual merchandising, order-taking, shipping, and billing process. It strengthens the bonds between the companies as the suppliers become more important players in the retailers' merchandising plans.

For sales reps, it eliminates the tedium of frequent order taking and paper shuffling, which in turn enables them to focus on presenting new and special products and promotions, learn more about their customers by developing stronger interpersonal relationships, meet each customer's special needs, and call on more customers.

For retailers, it provides added efficiency and effectiveness. It enables them to serve their customers better by ensuring adequate, reliable stock. It also improves profitability by increasing stock turns and minimizing stock of slow items. For small retailers, the system relieves the mathematical drudgery of estimating turnover, forecasting demand, and determining economic order quantities. Finally, it frees everyone to concentrate on business activities other than inventory maintenance. It clearly shows how improved marketing improves other business functions.

Establishing Buying Guidelines

Determining the amount of stock that should be ordered is an important decision. In some cases, product shelf life may be the deciding factor. If the grocer stocked more than a two day supply of muffins, the muffins would lose their freshness and the grocer would lose customers. Delivery is immediate. The supermarket will have a standing order with the bakery, which can be modified on a daily basis.

More often, there are many other factors to consider. The retailer needs to incorporate two basic factors into the computer inventory management system; lead time and safety stock, which influence the amount or frequency of purchase.

The length of time between order placement and receipt of goods is called **lead time**. If the lead time is two weeks, in theory it would be sufficient to establish a minimum inventory level of a two week supply. However, if anything went wrong there would be a stockout before the order was received. An unexpectedly large request from a customer might not be filled because of insufficient inventory. A strike, shipping delays, manufacturing problems, or unforeseen weather conditions could seriously delay the arrival of the merchandise so that the stockout could last for several weeks. Therefore, most businesses maintain a **safety stock** as protection against such occurrences. For many Canadian retailers who purchase merchandise from Europe and the Far East, lead times may be measured in months, not weeks. In these cases, the purchase of seasonal merchandise could be made up to six months before it is expected to go on sale.

The size of the safety stock will depend on the number and extent of the factors that could interrupt deliveries. Suitable guidelines should be based on past computer records. Additionally, many items require a **basic stock**, an amount sufficient to accommodate regular sales, offering customers a reasonable assortment of merchandise from which their selection can be made.

The buyer will then decide on a strategy for ordering items from vendors that includes lead time, safety stock, and basic stock. The computer system would then be programmed to order from a vendor automatically based on the buyer's strategy.

The system will determine when to buy based on the **order point**; the amount of inventory below which the quantity available should not fall or the item will be out of stock before the next shipment arrives. The system will determine how much to buy; which will depend on the usual time between orders, called the **order interval**. In this way, sufficient supplies are maintained so that inventories between orders average out to the desired level. Finally, a stock equal to expected sales during the order interval should be added to the order point to determine the **order ceiling**.

The following example is provided to illustrate the basic factors and concepts just discussed. The hardware store buyer would have included all these factors in the computer model for buying hammers.

The hardware store buyer wants to maintain a basic tool stock equal to one week's sales and a safety stock of one week's sales for hammers. Average weekly sales are three hammers. Lead time for order placement and delivery is two weeks. Orders are placed every four weeks.

A desirable inventory level, or order point, is then calculated as follows:

Lead time	2 weeks
+ Basic stock	1 week
+ Safety stock	1 week
= Order point	4 weeks or 12 (4 x 3) hammers

Whenever the supply of any tool drops to a four-weeks' supply or below (i.e., 12 hammers), an order should be placed.

To determine the order quantity, management must first calculate the order ceiling:

Order point	4 weeks
+ Order interval	4 weeks
= Order ceiling	8 weeks or 24 (8 x 3) hammers

Assume that an order is being prepared for hammers. Average weekly sales are 3 hammers, and the stock on hand is 10 hammers. This is below the order point of 12 (4 x 3) hammers.

The order quantity would then be calculated as follows:

Order ceiling	24
– Stock on hand	10
=Order quantity	14

The hardware store should order 14 hammers. If any are already on order, the outstanding order quantity should be subtracted. Again, the purchase orders would automatically be generated by the inventory management system and sent electronically to the vendor.

SELECTING SUPPLIERS

The first step in supplier selection is to obtain a list of those to consider. Awareness of available suppliers and their services will place the buyer in a position to choose the best one.

There are two primary ways to find suppliers. First, many vendors will contact the retailer to offer merchandise for sale. Second, the retailer can seek out suppliers; either by contacting them directly or attending merchandise shows. These shows provide an excellent opportunity to see a variety of new products and compare similar products of different manufacturers. A host of trade shows are held in Canada ranging from grocery products to children's fashion wear to hardware and home improvements.

Also available are central markets, places where a large number of suppliers concentrate. Because of the close proximity of the United States, many Canadian retailers will visit central markets such as New York for women's fashion goods and High Point, North Carolina, for furniture.

Supplier Evaluation Criteria

Factors to be considered in determining the best supplier are price and discounts, quality, reliability, services, and accessibility.

1. *Price and discounts.* Price is the most important consideration in the selection of a supplier, provided that quality and service are equivalent to that of other vendors. Price has many dimensions since it includes quantity discounts, special allowances, the chance to buy special lots, seconds, or sellouts, and dating of invoices.
2. *Quality*, and assurance of consistent quality, is almost as important as price and closely linked to it. Obviously, in selecting a supplier, buyers want to be certain that they will rarely, if ever, receive a poor quality shipment.
3. *Reliability* of delivery from a supplier is important as unreliable delivery can create problems of stockout, which result in lost sales. In addition, slow or unreliable delivery also requires the buyer to maintain larger average inventories, which results in increased carrying costs. A good supplier will be reliable when the store has a sudden emergency and needs some quick supplies and will protect the store when there are shortages of material due to a strike or disaster.
4. *Services* suppliers might provide are many and include spacing of deliveries that allows the buyer to purchase a larger quantity than the store may

immediately handle, thus giving the advantage of quantity discounts; recycling of packaging to reduce overall freight and packing expenses and to help protect the environment; providing advertising and promotional materials and displays to help promote merchandise; and giveaways, such as literature and bags for the customers.

5. *Accessibility* is another factor on which suppliers should be judged. It is often important to contact the supplier concerning special problems that may arise. A supplier who is difficult to contact is clearly not as desirable as one easy to reach.

Methods of Buying

Group Buying

Group, or cooperative, buying is the joint purchase of goods by a number of noncompeting, nonaligned stores such as independent hardware stores in different areas of a province. By combining their orders into one large order, the stores hope to get lower prices. These group arrangements can be beneficial in other ways, too, because the noncompeting buyers can share knowledge about markets, fashion trends, and so forth.

There are disadvantages to group buying. Members of the group give up some of their individuality, which they may not want to do. Fashion merchants, particularly, find cooperative buying difficult because they feel their customers are unique.

In Canada, buying groups have been formed by independent sporting goods stores (Sports Distributors of Canada), grocery and convenience stores (Distribution Canada), and drugstores (Drug Trading Company). For many of these independents, the buying groups provide the opportunity for volume discounts and are an important source of merchandise and marketing information.

Central Buying

Central buying is typically used by chains. Central buying means that one person or department handles the buying of goods for all stores in the organization.

In firms where central buying occurs, most of the authority for buying lies outside any one retail outlet. In some firms, store managers are given limited authority to purchase locally produced items. For example, in a food store, locally grown produce might be bought by the local store instead of by the central buyer.

Because they order in such large quantities, central buyers hope to get favourable prices. Zellers, with its 300-store chain, uses centralized buying to obtain excellent prices, which are necessary to support its price image. Technology is important in central buying, as the buyer must have adequate and rapid information from individual stores. Canadian Tire is in the forefront of Canadian retailers who use technology to improve their buying practices (see Retail Highlight 10-2).

Committee Buying

Committee buying is a version of central buying. It is a way to achieve the savings of central buying while having more than one person share the buying responsibility. This type of buying is common in firms selling staples, such as hardware stores.

Consignment

In consignment, suppliers guarantee the sale of items and will take merchandise back if it does not sell. University and college bookstores often purchase textbooks on this basis. The retailer assumes no risk in such an arrangement. Merchandise from an unknown supplier or a high-risk item might require such an arrangement. If a buyer has overspent the assigned budget, consignment can be attractive. But the buyer must be aware that most vendors would not offer consignment if the goods could be sold any other way.

Leased Departments

If retailers do not have the skills to operate a specialized area, they may choose to lease departments. Shoe, camera, jewelry, and optical departments, as well as beauty salons and restaurants, are often operated under lease arrangements. By leasing to an expert, the retailer can provide customers with specialized items without fear of failure caused by inexperience.

Retail Highlight 10-2 Technology Improves the Buying Process

Progressive retailers, like Canadian Tire, are linked with vendors in a computer system that allows for buying and ordering without sending "paper" through the mail or fax machines. With electronic data interchange (EDI), companies can trade and "talk" electronically and they can exchange business documents, like cheques, invoices, and purchase orders, for different transactions via computer on standard forms.

Canadian Tire has converted the majority of its vendors to its EDI system. Today, virtually all of Canadian Tire's suppliers are electronically linked to the retailer. The benefits of EDI include: (1) more efficient order processing, (2) saving time preparing and delivering purchase orders, and (3) reducing invoice errors.

Canadian Tire has more than 430 associate stores that can select and stock more than 44,000 items through EDI. With EDI, Canadian Tire has (1) reduced its inventory safety stock (saving five days lead time), (2) almost completely eliminated paper handling in its buying transactions, and (3) allowed buyers to take action immediately if there is a problem.

The EDI project leader for Canadian Tire has stated that EDI is a prerequisite for retailers and that future success will depend on how you do it, not whether. EDI facilitates their Quick Response Strategy (a program to ensure faster delivery, reduce administrative expenses, and turn inventory faster). For an initial investment of 1.9 percent of sales, and an annual cost of 0.28 percent of sales, they are realizing a savings of 5.1 percent of sales.

The Supply Chain and Information Technology team is using the EDI system to roll out a leading-edge electronic inventory forecasting and replenishment system. This will lead to fewer stockouts and lower costs across the entire supply chain.

While the benefits to the retailer are clear, suppliers also benefit. With EDI, suppliers devote fewer resources to order processing and other administrative functions, make fewer errors, do a greater volume of business using the same number of employees, and have happier customers.

Source: Canadian Tire, *Annual Report*, various years

Negotiating the Purchase

A good relationship between buyer and vendor may be one of the most important assets of the retail business. When a strong, friendly, yet professional relationship exists with suppliers, negotiations can go smoothly. In negotiations, the buyer is trying to get the best deal, while the vendor is trying to keep the price up to protect profits. Buyers normally attempt to negotiate on the following elements: list price, discounts, datings, and transportation charges.[5]

List Price

Suppliers typically provide retailers with a price list of the merchandise available for sale. These list prices form the starting point for negotiations.

Discounts

Even though identical list prices may be offered by various vendors, they may offer different discounts and different provisions as to who will be responsible for paying transportation charges. An understanding of these purchase terms is necessary to negotiate the best price.

A **trade discount** is a reduction off the seller's list price and is granted to a retailer who performs functions normally the responsibility of the seller.

A trade discount may be offered as a single percentage or as a series of percentages off list price. If the list price on a sport shirt is $14.95, with a trade discount of 40 percent, the retailer will pay $8.97 ($14.95 - $5.98). The $5.98 ($14.95 x .40) is the trade discount. The same buyer might be offered a similar sport shirt from another manufacturer at a list price of $14.95 less 30 percent, 10 percent, and 5 percent. The three discounts (30 percent, 10 percent, and 5 percent) offered by the manufacturer could be for advertising support, transportation charges, and other promotional activities. The net price in this case would be computed as follows:

List price	=	14.95	
	–	4.48	($14.95 x 0.30)
	=	10.47	
	–	1.05	($10.47 x 0.10)
	=	9.42	
	–	0.47	($9.42 x 0.05)
Net price	=	$8.95	

An alternative way of calculating the net price in the example above is to use the complement of the discount percentages. In this case, the net price would be calculated as: $14.95 x .70 x .90 x .95 = $8.95.

A **quantity discount** is a reduction in unit cost based on the size of the order. Such discounts may be noncumulative, meaning the reduction is based on each order, or cumulative, meaning the reduction is computed over the sum of purchases for a specified period of time. When deciding whether a quantity discount is worthwhile, the buyer must compare the money saved with the extra inventory carrying cost.

To determine the *value* of a quantity discount, use the following steps:

1. Determine the savings from the quantity discount.
2. Determine how much extra merchandise the store would have to carry in inventory, and for how long.
3. Multiply the average extra stock by the carrying charge (which is usually 20 to 25 percent) to obtain the additional cost of carrying the extra stock for a year.
4. Determine the additional carrying costs for the period of time it will take to work off the extra stock.
5. Compare the savings from the quantity discount with the cost of carrying the extra inventory and decide whether it is worthwhile to buy the larger quantity.

For example, if the buyer can save $500 by taking an extra $6,000 of merchandise into stock, and if it will take six months to work off the extra stock, the calculations are as shown below:

Cost savings (discount) = $500

Extra inventory would be $6,000 in the beginning and zero six months later; therefore:

Average extra inventory	= $3,000
Carrying costs of average extra inventory	= $3,000 x 25% x 1/2 year
	= $750 x 1/2 = $375
Actual savings	= Cost savings – Carrying costs
	= $500 – $375 = $125

Since the real savings from taking the discount would be only $125, this deal is worthwhile only if the store can work the extra inventory off in six months without getting stuck with any hard-to-sell merchandise.

A **seasonal discount** is a special discount given to retailers who place orders for seasonal merchandise in advance of the normal buying period.

Promotional allowances are offered by vendors to retailers as compensation for money spent in advertising particular items. This discount may also be given for preferred window- and interior-display space for the vendor's products. One form of a promotional allowance is co-op advertising. A manufacturer will pay for up to 50 percent of a retailer's advertising costs for ads that promote the manufacturer's products. For example, appliance manufacturers will allow a retailer an allowance of up to 50 percent if the retailer devotes at least 50 percent of the space or time in the ads to the manufacturer's products.[6]

A **cash discount** may be granted by the vendor for cash payment prior to the time that the entire bill must be paid. The three components of the cash discount terms are: (1) a percentage discount, (2) a period in which the discount may be taken, and (3) the net credit period, which indicates when the full amount of the invoice is due. A cash discount stated as 2/10, n/30, means that the retailer must pay the invoice within 10 days to take advantage of the discount of 2 percent. The full amount is due in 30 days.

A cash discount may be taken in addition to a trade or another type of discount. Returning to the earlier example, assume an $895 net bill for 100 sport shirts and that the invoice is dated May 22. The retailer has 10 days to take the discount. Payment is due June 1 (9 days in May and 1 in June). If the invoice is paid within this time, the retailer will remit $877 instead of $895 ($895 x .02 = $18; $895 - $18 = $877). If the retailer does not discount the invoice, the bill must be paid in full by June 21.

The 2 percent, for paying the bill 20 days early, in the example represents an annual interest rate of 36 percent. Since there are 18 20-day periods in the year (using 360 days as a year), this comes to 36 percent annually (18 x 2 percent).

Datings

The agreement between the vendor and the retailer as to the time the discount date will begin is known as dating. Technically, if the terms call for immediate payment, the process is known as **cash dating** and includes COD (cash on delivery) or CWO (cash with order). Cash datings do not involve discounts.

There are two reasons why a negotiation may include cash terms. First, the seller may have a cash flow problem and may insist on cash on delivery (or with the order) to meet the bills incurred in the processing or distribution of the goods. Second, the retail buyer's credit rating may be such that the seller will deal with the firm only on a cash basis.

There are four types of **future datings**: end-of-month, date-of-invoice, receipt-of-goods, and extra dating.

- *End of month (EOM).* If an invoice carries EOM dating, the cash and net discount periods begin on the first day of the following month rather than on the invoice date.
- *Date of invoice (DOI).* DOI, or ordinary dating, is self-explanatory. Prepayments begin with the invoice date, and both the cash discount and the net amount are due within the specified number of days from the invoice date.
- *Receipt of goods (ROG).* With ROG datings, the time allowed for discounts and for payment of the net amount of the invoice begins with the date the goods are received at the buyer's place of business.
- *Extra.* Extra datings allow the retailer extra time to take the cash discount.

Transportation Charges

The final aspect of negotiation relates to who will bear the responsibility for shipping costs. The most favourable terms for the retailer are *FOB (free-on-board) destination.* In this arrangement, the seller pays the freight to the destination and is responsible for damage or loss in transit. A more common shipping term is *FOB origin,* which means the vendor delivers the merchandise to the carrier, and the retailer pays for the freight.

Small retailers typically do not have the power to bargain with a vendor on discounts or the transportation charges. On the other hand, large retailers may be able to obtain price concessions from the supplier by bargaining on discounts even though the list price of the merchandise does not change.

FOLLOW-UP

The last step in the buying cycle is follow-up. Follow-up consists of continuous checking to find more desirable suppliers, merchandise, and buying and merchandise control practices.

Finding better suppliers can be accomplished only by getting to know existing suppliers and being alert to information sources on new ones who may come into the market. Improving merchandise selection is a matter of merchandise management, as discussed in Chapter 9.

Two tasks remain to ensure success while operating within the buying cycle. The first is to develop an effective merchandise handling system and the second is to design a good inventory management system.

An effective merchandise distribution system in a multiunit retail organization can be an important element of competitive strategy and can have a positive impact on profitability. The first part of the next section focuses on **merchandise distribution**—getting merchandise from consolidation warehouses or distribution centres to the individual stores. The second part focuses on the physical handling aspect of merchandise management, including the receiving, checking, and marking of goods.

MERCHANDISE HANDLING

Merchandise Distribution in Multiunit Organizations

Some multiunit retailers operate under a system of direct store delivery (DSD), whereby merchandise is shipped from vendors directly to the individual stores in the chain. The possibilities of direct store deliveries have received increasing attention among multiunit retailers as a result of the efficiencies of vendor marking and electronic data interchange (EDI) between vendors and retailers. With EDI and vendor marking in place, stores do not have to do any checking or ticketing of goods. Shipments arrive in floor-ready condition, so goods can flow directly from the receiving dock to the selling floor. Disadvantages to DSD for some retailers may be additional payroll costs, increased transportation costs, and lack of receiving facilities at the stores.

Many chain operations, however, employ a merchandise distribution system involving the use of consolidation warehouses or distribution centres. Merchandise is shipped from vendors to the retail chain's distribution centres and from there is redirected to the individual store units. Many of these centres are computerized and highly automated, using the most recent innovations in merchandise handling and moving equipment including automatic guided vehicles and computerized sorting systems.

Multiunit retailers, like Canadian Tire and Wal-Mart, are also using a new distribution approach called cross-docking. For example, with cross-docking, designated products on incoming trailers to Canadian Tire's main distribution

Loblaws has developed its own efficient distribution system.

Courtesy Loblaw Companies Ltd.

centre are immediately loaded onto scheduled outbound trucks taking shipments to the individual stores. Cross-docking effectively reduces handling costs by eliminating the typical storage and retrieval of goods.[7]

Advantages of using highly automated, computerized, distribution centres include more effective inventory control and merchandise reordering, more rapid movement of merchandise to increase turnover and margins at the stores, and cost efficiencies. The specific advantages resulting from retailers' implementation of distribution technology include the following benefits:

Operating Efficiencies and Cost Reduction Developing effective distribution systems can be an important factor in helping a retail firm lower its cost structure, which, in turn, leads to lower prices and higher levels of profitability.

Faster Movement of Merchandise Retailers are finding that the speed with which they respond to changes in the market—the **cycle time**—is a critical element in being more competitive. Highly automated, computerized distribution centres enable faster movement of merchandise to the individual stores, which results in higher sales and margins.

Greater Accuracy Common errors in multiunit organizations include individual stores receiving the wrong merchandise from the distribution centre, or receiving the right goods but in the wrong quantities. Chains using a computerized system allow individual stores to know exactly what is on the way from the distribution centre before it arrives at the stores. These systems not only provide greater accuracy in the movement of goods to individual stores but also lead to reduced paperwork and labour savings at the store level.

PHYSICAL HANDLING ACTIVITIES

Physical handling involves receiving, checking, and marking merchandise. Although these activities are often performed in distribution centres, the following sections focus on these activities being performed in the retail store.

The Receiving and Checking Activities

Receiving is that phase of physical handling in which the retailer takes possession of the goods and then moves them to the next phase of the process. **Checking** involves matching the store buyer's purchase order with the supplier's invoice. Today most merchandise is received and checked in using vendor electronic scanners. The vendor marks the boxes with unique identifying bar codes. The individual at the receiving dock scans the bar coded cartons and the merchandise is automatically checked in. The scanners record specific information including date and hour of arrival, weight, form of transportation, receiving number, invoice number, delivery charges, name of deliverer, amount of invoice, and department ordering the goods.

The packing cartons are inspected for damage. If there is no damage, the cartons are moved to the next stage. If damage has occurred, the cartons are opened and the contents examined to determine if the merchandise has been damaged.

In some cases, the buyer may want to conduct a check to ensure that the order matches the supplier's invoice. A quality check is conducted when the buyer wants to determine if the quality specified (e.g., 100 percent cotton shirts) is, in fact, what was shipped. A quantity check is conducted to ensure that the items ordered were delivered. The two basic methods of quantity checking are (1) the **direct check** where the shipment is checked against the vendor's invoice and (2) the **blind check** where the checker lists the items and quantities received without the invoice in hand. This system is designed to avoid carelessness associated with the direct check.

The Marking Activity

Marking is putting information on the goods to assist customers and to aid the store in the control functions. Various methods are used for establishing the price information to be marked on the goods. Goods can be marked either within the store or by a vendor. In **source marking**, the vendor rather than the retailer marks the merchandise. Source marking involves the use of codes such as the Universal Product Code (UPC). Source marking reduces store costs and reduces the time to place merchandise on the floor. A common in-store method is **preretailing**. Here, the buyer places the retail price on the store's copy of the purchase order at the time it is written. The store's markers then put the price on the item when it arrives in receiving.

The remainder of the chapter discusses various aspects of the inventory management system.

INVENTORY MANAGEMENT

To manage inventory successfully, management should maintain accurate and up-to-date records of sales and stock on hand for every item. Inventory records tell you what you have. Sales records tell you what you need. Inventory records are used for making the following decisions: (1) purchases for inventory replenishment, (2) scrapping or clearing of obsolete items that are no longer in demand, and (3) addition of new items to inventory.

Electronic Data Processing

Although some retailers may use a manual inventory control system, with the advent of inexpensive microcomputers and software packages, the vast majority of retailers use some form of electronic data processing system. The system records all transactions and keeps a continuous record of changes in inventory. The system also prepares a sales summary. This information is needed for determining the adequacy of inventories and for order preparation. The sales summary can be compared periodically with stock on hand so that items that are not showing sufficient sales activity can be cleared through price reductions, scrapped, or otherwise disposed of. In this way, space and dollars invested in inventory are available for more active and potentially more profitable items.

Physical Inventory

A physical inventory should be taken periodically to be sure that the actual quantities on hand equal those shown on the inventory records. The inventory records must then be adjusted to reflect any difference between "physical inventory" and "book inventory," the quantities shown on the inventory records. The actual quantity of each item on hand must be counted and compared with that shown on the inventory records.

Differences between book and physical inventory arise for many reasons. The most easily understood, of course, are shoplifting and employee theft. Any business naturally wants to maintain an inventory control system to detect this situation as early as possible. This is the topic of the final section of the chapter.

Other reasons for inventory shortages are somewhat subtler but equally damaging. For example, if receiving procedures are faulty, a receiving clerk may not be counting actual quantities received and comparing them with those on the vendor's packing list or invoice. Merchandise may be sold to customers without being billed to them, through oversight or carelessness.

Any of these factors can result in inventory shortages. Although most businesses take careful steps to guard against theft, relatively few adopt serious procedures for protection from inventory shortages caused by such factors as poor receiving procedures, poor billing procedures, and merchandise damage.

CONTROLLING SHOPLIFTING AND EMPLOYEE THEFT

An important aspect of inventory management is controlling for merchandise shortages. As shown by many surveys, the main causes of shortages are shoplifting and employee theft. In one survey, retailers attributed approximately 66 percent of inventory shrinkage to employee theft and customer shoplifting, and 34 percent to poor paperwork control. It is estimated that Canadian retailers lose over $2 billion to shoplifters each year.[8] The following sections will focus on shoplifting and employee theft, how they occur, and what actions can be taken to control and prevent them.

Controlling Shoplifting

Time and money are better spent in preventing shoplifting than in prosecuting the offenders. There are several areas where retailers can take action to control shoplifting.

Educate Employees Retailers know that salespeople are the most effective tool against shoplifting. Management can do a number of things to use salespeople effectively as a way of reducing shoplifting. Here are five key points:

1. *Create awareness and concern.* Managers must communicate their concern about shoplifting and keep employees constantly aware of the problem.
2. *Provide employee training.* Salespeople will respond to shoplifting only when they feel comfortable in doing so. Thus, they need to be taught to recognize shoplifters and how to respond to the situation. Retail Highlight 10-3 provides some practical advice on how to recognize shoplifters.
3. *Motivate salespeople to get involved.* Store managers should remind salespeople that shoplifters affect their jobs. Shoplifting makes the salesperson's job more difficult and diverts time from customers who are buying merchandise.
4. *Support the salesperson.* Salespeople need to know they are not alone in controlling shoplifting. Management needs to support salespeople's efforts by giving them the tools and devices they need to detect shoplifters and by providing backup assistance when needed.
5. *Show appreciation.* Salespeople need positive feedback; they need to know that their efforts are meaningful and recognized by management. Salespeople should be provided with periodic information on progress being made toward controlling shoplifting.

Plan Store Layout with Deterrence in Mind Retailers should maintain adequate lighting in all areas of the store and keep protruding "wings" and end displays low. In addition, display cases should be set in broken sequences and, if possible, run for short lengths with spaces in between. Small items of high value (e.g., film, small appliances) should be kept behind a counter or in a locked case with a salesperson on duty. Display counters should be kept neat; it is easier to determine if an item is missing if the display area is orderly.

Retail Highlight 10-3 How to Recognize Shoplifters

Be on the lookout for customers carrying concealment devices such as bulky packages, large pocketbooks, baby carriages, or an oversized arm sling.

Employees should be alert to groups of shoppers who enter the store together, then break up and go in different directions. A customer who attempts to monopolize a salesperson's time may be covering for an associate stealing elsewhere in the store. A gang member may start an argument with store personnel or other gang members or may feign a fainting spell to draw attention, giving a cohort the opportunity to steal merchandise from another part of the store.

Shoplifters do not like crowds. They keep a sharp eye out for other customers or store personnel. Quick, nervous glances may be a giveaway.

Sales help should remember that ordinary customers want attention; shoplifters do not. When busy with one customer, the salesperson should acknowledge waiting customers with polite remarks such as, "I'll be with you in a minute." This pleases legitimate customers—and makes a shoplifter feel uneasy.

Salespeople should watch for a customer who handles a lot of merchandise, but takes an unusually long time to make a decision. They should watch for customers lingering in one area, loitering near stockrooms, or other restricted areas, or wandering aimlessly through the store. They should try to be alert to customers who consistently shop during hours when staff is low.

Use Protective Personnel and Equipment Protective devices may be expensive, but shoplifting is more expensive. Electronic tags are judged by retailers to be the most effective protective device. Retailers using such devices, however, should be sure that salespeople and cashiers are diligent in their use. If an employee forgets to remove the tag and the customer is falsely accused, the retailer could be held liable. Guards are also considered by retailers to be powerful visual deterrents to shoplifters. Although mirrors are the most frequently used device, they are judged by retailers to be the least effective. The nearest runner-up in lack of effectiveness is visible TV cameras.

Apprehending, Arresting, and Prosecuting Shoplifters

To make legal charges stick, retailers must be able to: (1) see the person take or conceal the merchandise; (2) identify the merchandise as belonging to the store; (3) testify that it was taken with the intent to steal; and (4) prove the merchandise was not paid for.

If retailers are unable to meet all four criteria, they leave themselves open to countercharges of false arrest. False arrest need not mean police arrest; simply preventing a person from conducting normal activities can be deemed false arrest.

It is wisest to apprehend shoplifters outside the store. The retailer has a better case if it can be demonstrated that the shoplifter left the store with stolen merchandise. A recommended procedure is for store employees to identify themselves, then say, "I believe you have some merchandise you have forgotten to pay for. Would you mind coming with me to straighten things out?" Many Canadian retailers are taking a more aggressive stance and are prosecuting all shoplifters to reduce this cost.

Employee Theft

Employee theft is a major problem facing retailers. In Canada, employees steal over $500 million worth of merchandise annually.[9]

How Do Employees Steal?

Discount abuse is the leading form of retail theft by employees. Most frequently, employees will purchase merchandise for friends and relatives who are not eligible for a discount. The amounts of merchandise purchased often exceed limits set by company policy. Employees may purchase merchandise at a discount and then have it returned by a friend for full value. Theft of merchandise and cash can also occur.

Because of the magnitude of the problem, retailers must establish prevention and detection procedures for controlling employee theft.

Controlling Employee Theft

Some of the ideas discussed earlier for controlling shoplifting, such as use of guards and detection devices like mirrors and TV cameras, also serve to detect and prevent employee theft.

Obviously the greatest deterrent to internal theft is to hire honest people. Some retailers are using the Reed report, which consists of 90 psychologically oriented questions whose yes/no answers classify a person as prone or not prone to theft.

Another way to reduce employee theft is to run awareness programs. Such programs show how employees can hurt themselves by stealing. Through awareness programs, management points out the store's policy on dealing with employee theft and how important honesty is to job security and to a good reference when an employee changes jobs.

Other deterrents to internal thievery include use of (1) employee identification badges; (2) restriction on employee movement within the store before, during, and after selling hours; (3) regular internal audits; (4) surprise internal audits; and (5) tight controls over petty cash, accounts receivable, payroll, and inventory.

CHAPTER HIGHLIGHTS

- The buying cycle consists of determining needs, selecting suppliers, negotiating purchases, and following up after the purchase. Buyers face different problems depending on whether the merchandise bought is primarily staples, seasonal items, or style or perishable items. The goal in each instance is to establish or maintain inventory at the lowest level and still have a sufficient assortment from which customers can choose.

- The primary factors influencing the level of staples to be purchased include sales trends, profitability on various items, and discounts available. One way to establish buying levels for style and perishable items is to plot the sales of different styles in the past to see how they typically behave and use the resulting information as a guide in future purchasing decisions.
- A variety of factors determine desired inventory levels and when stock should be ordered. The length of time between order placement and receipt of goods is also important. Many businesses maintain a safety or cushion stock as a protection against variation in demand and delivery.
- Factors to be considered in determining the best supplier include prices and discounts, quality, reliability, services, and accessibility.
- Technology is having a major impact on the buyer–seller relationship, including closer relationships and more effective ordering and distribution of merchandise. Electronic data interchange (EDI) and quick response (QR) mechanisms are at the heart of the emerging retailer–vendor relationships today. The application of such techniques has led to shorter lead times in merchandise delivery, and less on-hand inventory because of rapid replenishment schedules, especially for staples.
- The physical handling process involves receiving, checking, and marking merchandise. Receiving is that phase of the physical handling process that involves taking possession of the goods and then moving them to the next phase of the process. Checking means matching the store buyer's purchase order with the supplier's invoice. Marking is putting information on the goods or on merchandise containers.
- Successful inventory management requires retailers to maintain an accurate and up-to-date record of sales and stock on hand for every item they sell. Shoplifting is a very large monetary crime in Canada. Retailers, however, can take a number of actions to detect and prevent shoplifting.
- Employee theft is also a major problem retailers face. Because of the magnitude of the problem, retailers must establish prevention and detection procedures for controlling internal theft.

KEY TERMS

basic stock	245	order point	245
blind check	254	physical handling	254
cash datings	251	preretailing	254
cash discount	250	promotional allowance	250
checking	254	quantity discount	249
cycle time	253	receiving	254
direct check	254	safety stock	245
future datings	251	seasonal discount	250
lead time	244	seasonal merchandise	241
marking	254	source marking	254
merchandise distribution	252	staple merchandise	240
order ceiling	245	style items	241
order interval	245	trade discount	249

DISCUSSION QUESTIONS

1. Discuss the roles and responsibilities of a buyer.
2. Discuss each element of the buying cycle.
3. Discuss how technology has changed the buying cycle.
4. Explain the new relationship between many retailers and their vendors.
5. Explain the types of discounts available to retailers.
6. What are the most favourable transportation terms for the retailer? Explain your answer.
7. What are the various types of shoplifters? What can retail managers do to control shoplifting? What can retail managers do to control employee theft?

PROBLEMS

1. A manufacturer of tables offers terms of 2/20, n/60. A furniture store places an order for a dozen tables at $27 each and receives an invoice dated July 2. The invoice is paid August 10. Failure to obtain the discount is equivalent to paying what annual rate of interest? (Use 360 days as a year.)
2. An invoice dated June 5 in the amount of $1,800, with terms of 3/10, n/30, EOM, and a trade discount of 20 percent, arrives with the merchandise on June 8. The invoice is paid July 2. What amount is due the vendor?
3. An invoice dated January 3 in the amount of $12,200, with terms of 2/10, n/30 ROG, and a trade discount of 10, 5, and 2 percent, arrives with the merchandise on January 10. The invoice is paid January 30. What amount is due the vendor?
4. A manufacturer of women's blouses quotes terms of 2/20, n/30, and grants retailers trade discounts of 10 and 5 percent. The list price of the blouses is $140 per dozen. A retailer receives an invoice dated July 7 for eight dozen of these blouses. The invoice is paid July 10. What is (a) the net cost per blouse and (b) the net amount of the cash discount taken?
5. A manufacturer of women's skirts quotes terms of 2/10, n/30 EOM, and grants retailers trade discounts of 10, 5, and 2 percent. The list price of the skirts is $360 per dozen. A retailer receives an invoice dated September 16 for 10 dozen of these skirts. The invoice is paid October 2. What is the net cost per skirt to the retailer?

APPLICATION EXERCISES

1. To clarify the relationships between the buyer and the supplier, the text approaches the subject from the retail point of view. It may be valuable to approach the subject from the other point of view. Make contacts with local suppliers (wholesalers or local manufacturers who sell to retailers), and see what they attempt to do to strengthen relationships with their customers. What problems do they incur in these relationships? What efforts do they make to "improve" the relationships?

2. Go on the Internet and find the retail consulting firms that offer merchandise and inventory management systems for retailers. Evaluate the software programs they offer retailers in terms of managing inventory.
3. In interviews with retailers with whom you establish good rapport, attempt to find out (a) what special problems have been encountered with vendors; (b) what kinds of special "concessions" are offered to the retailers; (c) whether any particular plans have been effective in improving relations; and (d) why vendors are dropped.

SUGGESTED CASES

15. Robson's Fashions
16. JKA Department Store

Part 4

Designing the Retailing Mix

Pricing, Promotion, and Customer Service

In *Part 4, Designing the Retailing Mix—Pricing, Promotion, and Customer Service*, the various decisions on the variables of the retailing mix other than merchandising are discussed. Determining retail prices is the topic of Chapter 11. In order to successfully promote their products or services, retailers need to: help their employees develop methods of successful selling (Chapter 12); design effective programs in the retail promotion mix, i.e., advertising, sales promotion, and publicity (Chapter 13); and instill in their employees a customer-focused culture (Chapter 14).

CHAPTER 11

PRICING STRATEGY

CHAPTER OBJECTIVES

After reading this chapter you should be able to:

1. Understand the role of price in the retailer's competitive environment.
2. Discuss the store policies, product and brand issues, consumer issues, and external factors affecting pricing decisions.
3. Understand a simple way to handle arithmetic pricing.

When Wal-Mart, the world's largest discount retailer, entered the Canadian retail market, it brought a number of retail innovations to Canada including its use of technology, its distribution strategy, and its human resources policy. One key innovation was its pricing strategy, often considered the foundation of this retailer's success.

Since it began, Wal-Mart has followed an everyday-low-pricing (EDLP) policy. Unlike many other retailers who offer regular sales (high-low), Wal-Mart only marks down merchandise to clear it out at the end of the season. EDLP at Wal-Mart is to offer very competitive prices on most of the 80,000 items it carries, which may be slightly above or slightly lower than its discount store competitors.

However, Wal-Mart is always lower on the 500 to 600 items that are price sensitive—laundry detergent, paper towels, motor oil—products that consumers frequently purchase and know a bargain when they see one. On these items Wal-Mart will not be beaten and store managers are free to drop prices when they see a competitor underselling them.

Many consumers feel that everything is cheaper because the most frequently purchased products are discounted. When shoppers are asked which discounter has the lowest prices, over 75 percent say Wal-Mart. As one retailing expert states, "The battle is won on perception. Most people perceive that Wal-Mart is a lot lower. It's a subtle thing: In Wal-Mart stores, prices are posted in black and yellow, the colour combination retail studies have shown to be the most eye-catching. Customers never have to pick up a product and search for a price tag."

Although pricing is just one element of Wal-Mart's strategy, it is critical to its success. Pricing is also critical for its major competitors. Wal-Mart's entry into Canada led to retailers like Zellers and Canadian Tire lowering prices on thousands of products to maintain a competitive price image. Whether the competitors can master the Wal-Mart approach to pricing remains to be seen, but it will be a major weapon in the continuing battle for market share.[1]

The Wal-Mart example illustrates that its managers understand the important role price can play in a firm's competitive strategy and the need to make price decisions that support that strategy. Price decisions must be compatible with the overall marketing strategy for the firm.

Wal-Mart reinforces its lowest price image with effective advertising.

Courtesy Wal-Mart

PRICING STRATEGY

A retail pricing plan should start from explicitly defined objectives. For example, management must decide whether financial goals will be achieved by higher margins on merchandise and thus perhaps lower turnover, or lower margins and higher turnover. Various trade-offs are in order for such decisions. For instance, if management's objectives are short-run profit maximization, pricing should maximize cash flow. A policy of strengthening market position, on the other hand, probably would call for prices that are not above those of the market leader.

The absence of a distinct pricing policy often reflects a lack of strategic focus. For example, traditional department stores are being squeezed from both above and below their traditional market segments. They are being squeezed at the lower end by discount chains such as Zellers and Wal-Mart and at the higher end by specialty chains such as Holt Renfrew. In response, in the early 1990s Eaton's emphasized its everyday prices to be as good as or better than its competitors—even their sale prices. Eaton's used the slogan "Why Wait for Sales" to focus on its competitive prices. This strategy was abandoned in the mid-1990s because consumers expected department stores to have sales and Eaton's returned to its previous strategy of using sales to attract customers. The Bay, concerned about lower margins because of all its sales, dramatically reduced its price promotions in late 1998. The result was substantially lower

Retail Highlight 11-1 Eaton's and the Bay Try to Cut Back Promotions

Eaton's and the Bay constantly struggled for market share in a declining department store market. Both announced (more than once) that they would cut back the amount of special sales—scratch and save, fill the bag at 25 percent off, one day only—as these sales impacted on the bottom line. Here are some views from experts on their strategies:

- Shoppers are overdosed with sales promotions and can hardly tell one department store's blitz from the next. If these stores have off-price sales every weekend, this isn't exactly the way they want to be perceived.
- It's naive on the part of department stores to think they can discount themselves out of the issues of poor customer service and other problems.
- Both the Bay and Eaton's are overly promotional – scratch and saves are risky because they usually apply to all items in the store, rather than just the items the retailer wants to get rid of. It can eat into your margins a lot more than it appears.

Both the Bay and Eaton's planned to be more selective on sales but it was noted that when Eaton's was promoting a lot of sales, the same-store sales increased. Same-store sales are a monthly comparison of the sales by a store from one year to the next and are a key measure in retailing.

[In the fall of 1999 Eaton's declared bankruptcy and went out of business.]

Source: Marina Strauss, "Eaton's to Scale Back Discount Sales," *The Globe and Mail*, April 19, 1999, p. B5.

sales as shoppers went elsewhere. The Bay, like Eaton's, returned to more price promotions (Retail Highlight 11-1). In spite of price promotions and many other strategic moves, Eaton's went bankrupt in the fall of 1999.

Everyday Low Pricing Versus High-Low

These examples illustrate the two opposite pricing strategies; everyday low pricing (EDLP) and high-low pricing. Many of the U.S. retailers who entered the Canadian market including Wal-Mart, Home Depot, and Office Depot use an EDLP strategy; maintaining prices at a level somewhere between a regular price and a deep discount price. At any time, a competitor may offer a sale price that is lower than an EDLP firm. The advantages to EDLP include creating a competitive price image in consumers' minds, reducing price wars, lowering distribution costs, reducing stockouts, and possibly increasing profit margins.

With a high-low strategy a retailer may have prices that are above their EDLP competitors, but they offer frequent sales, often on a weekly basis, to attract customers to their stores. The high-low strategy creates interest, helps move merchandise, appeals to many customers, and may create a competitive image.

Both strategies have their shortcomings. EDLP has difficulty attracting shoppers who expect sales; high-low has problems with sales items that stock out and customers who wait until the merchandise goes on sale. While retailers typically pursue one of the strategies, the EDLP retailers will offer some sales and the high-low retailers are attempting to cut back on sales.[2]

The remainder of the chapter will discuss the factors a retailer should consider in setting prices: (1) store policies, (2) product issues, (3) consumer issues, and (4) external factors. Then, the arithmetic of retail pricing will be presented.

STORE POLICIES AFFECTING RETAIL PRICING

Price-Lining Policy

Retailers practising **price lining** feature products at a limited number of prices, reflecting varying merchandise quality. A price-lining strategy can be implemented either in the context of rigid **price points** or more flexible **price zones**. Using suits as an example, the retailer might establish a limited number of price points to indicate quality difference between merchandise. The "good" suits might be priced at $275, the "better" suits at $325, and the "best" suits at $400. Alternately, the retailer may decide to use "price zones" instead of rigid price points. For example, prices for good suits might fall between $275 and $350.

Price lining makes shopping easier for consumers, since there are fewer prices to consider. The merchant can offer a greater assortment of depth and width with fewer price points. In addition, inventories can be controlled more easily. With price lining the salesperson can more easily become familiar with the merchandise. Also it is much easier to explain differences between the merchandise when it is carefully planned and priced to show differences. In addition, the retail buyer may reduce the number of suppliers needed to provide merchandise in specific retail price ranges.

Certain disadvantages do exist in price lining. The retailer may feel "hemmed in" by the price line and lose some flexibility. Also, selection may be limited. If manufacturers' prices rise and fall rapidly, it may be difficult to maintain rigid price points. This is a reason for the use of price zones.

Leader Pricing Policy

In **leader pricing** the retailer takes a less-than-normal markup or margin on items to increase store traffic. Some call this loss-leader pricing, implying a loss of the normal amount of markup or margin. In using leader pricing, the retailer is trying to attract customers to the store who will also purchase items carrying normal profit margins. Canadian supermarket chains, like Loblaws, Sobeys, and Safeway, use leader pricing to attract customers with the objective of having customers purchase all their grocery needs at the store. If customers only buy the "leaders," the retailer is in trouble. Thus, in selecting the leader item, retailers should choose products that will stimulate purchases of other, perhaps complementary, goods. For example, a supermarket may lower the price of ribs, which, in turn, might stimulate the sale of barbecue sauce, charcoal, starter fluid, and food products typically eaten with barbecued ribs. In a department store, using dresses as leaders might stimulate the sale of shoes, jewelry, and other accessories.

Price Discount Policy

Retailers may offer various discounts, such as cash discounts and frequent shopper discounts, to attract and retain customers.

Cash Discounts

Cash discounts can be profitable if retailers have (1) a high proportion of credit sales, (2) a high proportion of credit customers who are willing to pay by cash or cheque as a result of a discount, and (3) large ticket items or large volume purchases.

A variation of cash discounts is offered by Canadian Tire. If a customer pays cash or uses a Canadian Tire credit card for payment, the customer receives Canadian Tire "money" in proportion to the purchase. The "money" can be used to purchase merchandise at Canadian Tire stores. This tactic encourages customers to pay cash instead of using a Visa or MasterCard credit card, draws traffic to the stores, and provides an incentive for customers to return to the store and spend their Canadian Tire "money."

Frequent-Shopper Discounts

Some retailers are experimenting with frequent-shopper discounts, much like the frequent-flyer programs offered by the airlines, to generate greater sales volume and customer loyalty. Shoppers' cumulative purchases are tracked throughout the year and bonuses are offered after shoppers reach a specified dollar volume of purchase. Additional bonuses are sometimes given to stimulate shopping on slow days

Shoppers are attracted to Zellers for many reasons including prices, products, and Club Z.

Courtesy Hudson's Bay Company—Corporate Collection

or to clear out slow-moving merchandise. Zellers' frequent-buyer program has over six million members and Club Z is one of the most successful customer loyalty programs in North America. Sears Canada also has a large customer loyalty program with over four million members in its Club. In an interesting twist on customer loyalty programs, the Loyalty Management Group started the Air Miles program. Over 64 percent of Canadian households have joined the program and accumulate points when they purchase goods and services from more than 100 retailers, including Shell, the Bay, Safeway, Pro Hardware, and Sport Chek. The points can be used for air travel or other merchandise including movie passes and free long distance.[3]

PRODUCT ISSUES

Retailers' pricing decisions are affected by type of products and brands carried.

Type of Products

One product issue affecting pricing decisions relates to whether the products offered are primarily convenience, shopping, or specialty goods. If products are viewed by consumers as convenience goods, prices do not vary greatly from store to store. Consumers do not believe it is worth their time to shop around for a better price (or quality) for convenience items because the savings are not likely to be worth the extra effort of comparison shopping. The retailer has only a little latitude in the pricing of convenience goods. A retailer has more leeway in setting prices for shopping goods. These are items for which consumers carefully compare price and quality differences before making a purchase decision. Finally, the retailer has the greatest latitude in pricing specialty goods. Specialty items are products consumers know they want and are willing to make an effort to acquire because they will not accept a substitute. To them, price is not particularly important.

Type of Brands

Another product-related issue concerns the extent to which a retailer carries private brands and generics in addition to manufacturers' brands. Many retailers, such as Sears Canada, Canadian Tire, the Bay, Zellers, and Loblaws have their own private brands (also referred to as dealer brands). Private brands are owned by the retail firm, rather than by a manufacturer. Only the owner or the owner's designee may carry a private brand. A manufacturer's brand (often referred to as a national brand) may be carried by anyone who buys from the manufacturer of the brand. President's Choice is a private brand of coffee owned by Loblaws; Maxwell House, a manufacturer's brand, is owned by General Foods.

If private brands are featured, the retailer may offer them at prices lower than national brands and still make a good profit. This is possible because the retailer can pay less for the private brand merchandise than for comparable manufacturer brands. Consequently, the retailer has more freedom in pricing private brand items.

Department stores, grocery chains, and some specialty retailers are increasingly turning to private brand merchandise as a source of competitive advantage, especially in the face of the challenges posed by EDLP retailers. Private brands, such as Mastercraft at Canadian Tire and President's Choice at Loblaws, are not subject to the price cutting that may occur with national brands.

The question of generic merchandise and pricing is also important. **Generics** are "no-name" goods. For example, if a supermarket offers generic paper products, the identification might read paper napkins. Customers may be willing to accept lower quality in some types of goods in return for lower prices. More profits may be made on generics than on private brands, because even though generics are priced lower, they cost less to manufacture. Typically generics are produced at a lower cost than private brands or national brands because of economies of scale in manufacturing, lower quality ingredients that reduce manufacturing costs, and reduced packaging costs. Generics are strongest in low-involvement merchandise such as paper products and other staples.

CONSUMER ISSUES AFFECTING RETAIL PRICING

A variety of consumer issues affect pricing decisions in retail operations. The following sections will focus on—the issues of consumer demand and price sensitivity, price perceptions, and psychological pricing.

Consumer Demand and Price Sensitivity

Retailers must consider consumer reactions to different prices. In general, consumers will purchase more of a product at a lower price than at a higher price. Thus, the retailer needs to understand the effects of different price levels on consumer demand. Known as **price elasticity**, or the elasticity of demand, it is the ratio of the percentage change in the quantity demanded to a percentage change in price:

$$\text{Price elasticity} = \frac{\text{Percent change in quantity demanded}}{\text{Percent change in price}}$$

Elastic demand is a situation where the change in price strongly influences the quantity demanded (consumers are sensitive to price changes). For example, demand for many convenience products like soap and toothpaste is elastic; consumers will stock up on these items at a lower price. Inelastic demand is a situation where the change in price has little influence on the quantity demanded (consumers are relatively insensitive to price changes). For example, demand for gasoline tends to be inelastic because consumers typically do not increase or decrease their driving if the price of gasoline decreases or increases. Retailers should understand which products are sensitive, or not, to price changes (Retail Highlight 11-2).

Price Perceptions

Consumer perceptions are important factors in establishing prices. For example, consumers have ranges of acceptable prices for products: prices outside the acceptable range—whether too low or too high—are objectionable. Demand provides not only an upper constraint on pricing decisions—pricing what the market will bear—but also a lower constraint. Cost-plus pricing may thus lead to a pricing error even if the price satisfies the cost and competition requirements. Below certain price points, which vary widely from category to category, there is no elasticity of demand; lowering prices further does not have the classic effect of adding sales.

Retail Highlight 11-2 Sam Walton on Pricing

Sam Walton, called America's most successful merchant, built the Wal-Mart chain into a retail dynasty, based on a number of simple but powerful concepts like price elasticity. In his own words talking about his early days in retailing: "Here's the simple lesson we learned—which others were learning at the same time and which eventually changed the way retailers sell and customers buy all across America. Say I bought an item for 80 cents. I found that by pricing it at a dollar I could sell three times more of it than by pricing it at $1.20. I might have made only half the profit per item, but because I was selling three times as many, the overall profit was much greater."

Source: "Sam Walton in His Own Words," *Fortune*, June 29, 1992, p. 100.

Consumer price perceptions tend to be imprecise about exact amounts, though reliable within well-defined ranges. Price-conscious shoppers perceive prices more accurately than do less-price-conscious shoppers. The number of stores shopped and frequency of shopping trips also affect price perception accuracy.[4]

Retailers need to understand consumer sensitivity to price discounts. A price discount of less than 10 percent appears to have only a limited effect on consumer response. The reason, in part, is that consumers consider price differences in percentage terms (e.g., 10 percent) rather than absolute terms (e.g., $100). Small percentage differences may not be noticed by consumers.[5] One study of Canadian consumers' reactions to retail "price-offs" found that consumers thought the "best deal in town" was more likely when substantial savings were announced (for example, 50 percent off), and depended on the particular store doing the advertising (for example, a discount store).[6]

Psychological Pricing

A retailer can price merchandise too low. A blouse might not sell at $25; but marked up to $37, it might. The reason for this phenomenon is that, for some goods, customers believe that price reflects quality (or value).[7] This situation may occur when the consumer has difficulty judging the quality of the product (e.g., fashion merchandise).

Odd price endings are believed by many to have psychological value. Odd ending prices are set just below the dollar figure, such as $1.99 instead of $2.00. Although the phenomenon is not verified, retailers practising odd pricing believe that consumers perceive odd-ending prices to be substantially lower than prices with even endings, despite the fact that the prices are only slightly lower in actual dollar terms. Odd pricing may suggest that the price has been established at the lowest level possible.

EXTERNAL FACTORS AFFECTING RETAIL PRICES

A variety of external (environmental) factors affect retail price setting. The following sections focus on the issues of economic conditions, government regulations, the Internet, and the level of competition.

Economic Conditions

Retailers must be conscious of economic conditions and their impact on pricing decisions. During periods of low economic growth or recessions, consumers become more concerned about prices because of the fear of job loss and their future. Retailers will typically use more price competition during these times to appeal to these concerned consumers and maintain their share of a declining or low growth market. For example, prices of many grocery products decrease during these times due to the extensive price cutting that many of these retailers are using just to remain in business or to meet competitive prices.

Government Regulations

Retailers are restricted from certain kinds of pricing actions, most of which are covered by the federal Competition Act. Chapter 2 presents a full discussion of the legal impacts on pricing.

The Internet

In the past, consumers had to expend time and effort to compare products and prices. Now, with the Internet and e-commerce, consumers can easily compare products and prices—it's just a "click" away. This will create increased pressure on retail prices as consumers gain more knowledge and power through the Internet (Retail Highlight 11-3).

Level of Competition

The degree of competition in the market will greatly affect pricing decisions. If little competition exists, pricing decisions are easier than if there is a great deal of competition. For example, a retailer with an "exclusive" on a brand in a market can probably price with greater freedom. In addition, competitors' actions in the pricing area must be monitored. A good retailer is aware of prices being charged by competitive outlets.

When competition is severe, retailers must run efficient operations as their prices need to reflect the competitive nature of the market. The entry of the giant United States warehouse clubs, Price Club and Costco, to the Canadian market created tremendous competition in the grocery trade and the home improvement business. With the entry of Wal-Mart and Home Depot, the com-

Retail Highlight 11-3 Retail Pricing and the Internet

As more consumers use the Internet, pricing products and services will become more challenging for retailers. Consumers can readily find the best deal; they can quickly compare products and retailers almost anywhere and they can demand better service. With Internet commerce the balance of power is shifting to the buyer. The buyer has instant choice (if they can't find the book at Chapters, they can go to Indigo), can do comparison shopping (CompareNet offers detailed information on more than 100,000 products), can increase purchasing power (consumers can group together), and can shop globally.

As well, some manufacturers are reaching consumers directly; cutting out the intermediaries and offering the consumer lower prices. In fact, new intermediaries have arrived on the Internet. These infomediaries (like GoldFish) will "shop" for consumers and find the best deals for them online.

The implications for the traditional retailer are that price will start to dominate consumer decisions and that new ways of differentiating will have to be discovered. Many retailers will have to lower operating costs to survive in this new environment.

Source: Robert D. Hof, "The Buyer Always Wins," *Business Week e.biz*, March 22, 1999, pp. EB 26-27.

petition intensified even further. Canadian supermarket chains responded by opening up their own warehouse type outlets (Loblaws), matching Price/Costco's prices (Loeb, IGA), and modifying the merchandise selection in existing outlets (Oshawa Group). Canadian Tire, Sears Canada, and Zellers reduced prices on thousands of items to remain competitive. Chapters, with its big box stores and aggressive pricing, has forced independent booksellers to lower prices and increase services to survive.

Possibly the most difficult struggle has occurred at Zellers, which has continually revised its strategy to adapt to the intense price competition from Wal-Mart. The two discount chains engaged in a price war that led to dramatic results (Retail Highlight 11-4).

Retail Highlight 11-4 Retail Price Wars: The Battle for the Low Price Image: Wal-Mart Versus Zellers

In 1994, when Wal-Mart came to Canada with their "Everyday Low Prices ... Always" campaign, it was the beginning of a real price war that hammered a number of retailers, led to substantial changes in strategy for some retail chains, and pleased consumers who benefited from lower prices. Zellers, with its "Where the Lowest Price Is the Law," responded with aggressive price cutting on thousands of items in its 300-store chain. Paul Walters, Zellers' president, felt that Zellers could not give up its position as the lowest price retailer to Wal-Mart and survive. In the second half of 1995, Zellers took its price-matching strategy a step further and significantly undercut Wal-Mart prices on key items sparking a price war that escalated through the Christmas season. Wal-Mart continued to match Zellers with the following dramatic results:

- Zellers' president, Paul Walters, resigned in March 1996, in part because of a consolidation of some Zellers' operations with the Bay (both are owned by the Hudson's Bay Company), and in part because of a change in strategic direction for Zellers (an easing of its price cutting strategy). For the year ending January 31, 1996, Zellers' operating profit fell to $106.7 million from $215.6 million for the previous fiscal year.
- Wal-Mart Canada replaced its president in early 1996, and although operating results were not known, it was rumoured that sales and profits were considerably below expectations. In the spring of 1996, Wal-Mart changed its slogan from "Everyday Low Prices ... Always" to "Where Every Day Costs Less."
- In early 1998 the Hudson's Bay Company purchased K mart Canada, which had been losing money and market share for three years. It quickly closed 40 K mart stores, merged the remaining stores with the Zellers chain, and replaced the president of Zellers.
- In the summer of 1998, the new president of Zellers, George Heller, abandoned the price war with Wal-Mart and began remodeling the stores, introducing new private brands, and moving to a more upscale position. To quote Mr. Heller: "We finally realized that if we kept at Wal-Mart's game of gun slinging on price, we were going to get whacked. The landscape is littered with casualties of Wal-Mart."
- In early 1999 Mr. Heller became president of the Bay, which had considerable problems including declining profits and market share. Zellers continued to introduce new private labels and focus on exclusive brands with more fashion appeal.
- Industry experts feel that Zellers will continue to lose market share in spite of its new upmarket approach.

Sources: John Heinz, "American to Run Wal-Mart Canada," *The Globe & Mail*, January 31, 1996, p. B17; Paul Brent, "Bay Shakes up Zellers," *Financial Post*, March 15, 1996, pp. 1–2; John Heinz, "Did Zellers Discount the Wal-Mart Threat?" *The Globe & Mail*, March 28, 1996, p. B9; Marina Strauss, "Hudson's Bay Appoints New Head," *The Globe and Mail*, February 27, 1999, pp. BI, B2; and Zena Olijnyk, "The Wal-marting of Canada Gathers Speed," *Financial Post*, March 26, 1999, pp. CI, C2.

THE ARITHMETIC OF RETAIL PRICING

This section presents information to help you understand the arithmetic of pricing. Every retailer is faced with the issues explained in this section.

Concepts of Price and Markup

To begin, several terms need to be defined. First, as shown in Table 11-1, the **original retail price** ($1,000) is the first price at which an item (or a group of items) is offered for sale. The **sales retail price** ($800) is the final selling price, the amount the customer paid. Before the item was sold, a reduction or markdown ($200) occurred. (In a classification of merchandise, reductions also include employee discounts and shortages or shrinkage. See the section "Reductions Planning" in Chapter 9 for a review of these concepts.)

Table 11-2 shows that markup can be viewed in two ways. **Initial markup** is the difference between the cost of the merchandise and the original retail price ($1,020 – $800 = $220). Initial markup as a percentage of the original retail price is 21.6 percent ($220/$1,020). The concept of initial markup is used when planning a total classification or department (as discussed in Chapter 9).

Maintained markup, shown in Table 11-2, is the difference between invoice cost and sales retail price ($1,000 – $800 = $200). In percentage terms, maintained markup is related to sales retail price ($200/$1,000 = 20 percent).

Maintained markup covers operating expenses and provides the retailer with a profit. Maintained markup and initial markup differ by the $20 reduction. For purposes of the present discussion, maintained markup can be considered the same as gross margin.

Planning Markup Goals

Retailers must determine the initial markup to be placed on merchandise as it goes on the sales floor. Some retailers do not use a planning process to establish initial markup percentages. They simply add a fixed percentage to their costs. If the goods do not sell at that price, the retailer marks them down. This approach is not likely to maximize sales or profits. Most retailers use a planning process to establish initial and maintained markup goals. As part of this planning procedure, the retailer develops projected figures for sales, operating expenses, reductions, and profits for the operating period. These figures can then be used to calculate the initial markup percentage (Table 11-3) that should be placed on merchandise as it comes into the store.

Table 11-1 Price Concepts

Original retail price	$1,000
Less reductions	– 200
Sales retail price	$ 800

Table 11-2 Markup Concepts

The Concept of Initial Markup

Original retail price	$1,020
Less invoice cost	– 800
Initial markup	$ 220

The Concept of Maintained Markup

Original retail price	$1,020
Less planned reductions	– 20
Sales retail	1,000
Less invoice cost	– 800
Maintained markup	$ 200

Assume that management has forecast sales of a merchandise line at $100,000, expenses of $15,000, and a profit return of 5 percent of sales or $5,000, and reductions as 2 percent of sales ($2,000). As shown in Table 11-3, a planned initial markup of $22,000, or 21.6 percent ($22,000/$102,000), is necessary to maintain a markup of $20,000, or 20 percent ($20,000/$100,000).

Of course, a retailer cannot expect to have a uniform initial markup policy. This kind of policy would suggest that every item brought into a department would carry the same initial markup. Too many external factors and store policies exist for a uniform markup to make sense. As one example, retailers should consider consumers' sensitivity to prices (price elasticity of demand) when setting markups. When consumers are very sensitive to price, retailers should consider lower markups. When consumers are less sensitive to price, retailers should consider higher markups.

Table 11-3 Planning Markup Goals

$$\text{Initial markup percentage} = \frac{\text{Expenses + Profit + Reductions}}{\text{Sales Retail + Reductions}}$$

$$= \frac{\$15{,}000 + \$5{,}000 + \$2{,}000}{\$100{,}000 + \$2{,}000}$$

$$= 21.6\%$$

$$\text{Maintained markup percentage} = \frac{\text{Expenses + Profit}}{\text{Sales retail}}$$

$$= \frac{\$15{,}000 + \$5{,}000}{\$100{,}000}$$

$$= 20\%$$

Pricing Computations

Every merchandiser needs practice in computing some routine relationships among cost, initial markup, and the original retail price. There is no need to memorize formulas, simply remember that *Cost + Initial markup = Original retail price.* Before working specific problems, let's first look at the ways markup percentages can be expressed.

Expressing Markup Percentages The initial markup percentage can be expressed as a percentage of the cost of the item or as a percentage of the retail selling price. To illustrate, assume that a colour television set costs the retailer $500. The original retail selling price is set at $800. The dollar amount of the markup is $300. The initial markup percentage based on cost is 60 percent ($300/$500). Based on retail, the markup is 37.5 percent ($300/$800). Remember that the markup percentage on cost = $ markup/$ cost, and the markup percentage on retail = $ markup/$ retail.

In working with pricing, the buyer is often faced with the need to convert a markup on retail to a markup on cost or vice versa.

Conversion of Markup on Retail to Markup on Cost Assume that a supplier quotes an initial markup of 42 percent on retail. What is the equivalent markup on cost? The formula is shown below:

$$\text{Markup percentage on cost} = \frac{\text{Markup percentage on retail}}{\text{100 percent} - \text{Markup percentage on retail}}$$

If the retail markup is 42 percent, then retail is 100 percent and cost must be 58 percent. So, markup as a percentage of cost is .42/.58 = .724 or 72.4 percent. In other words, 42 percent markup on retail is the same as 72.4 percent on cost. Clearly, markup on cost will always be larger than markup on retail, because the cost base is smaller than the retail base.

Conversion of Markup on Cost to Markup on Retail Suppose a vendor quotes an initial markup of 60 percent on cost. What is the equivalent markup on retail? Use the following formula:

$$\text{Markup percentage on retail} = \frac{\text{Markup percentage on cost}}{\text{100 percent} + \text{Markup percentage on cost}}$$

If the cost markup is 60 percent, then cost must be 100 percent, and retail has to be 160 percent. So, markup on retail base is .60/1.60 = 37.5 percent. Or, 60 percent markup on cost is the same as 37.5 percent on retail.

Pricing Problems The following problems illustrate the various types of pricing decisions made by retailers.

1. A chair costs a retailer $420. If a markup of 40 percent of retail is desired, what should the retail price be? If 60 percent = $420, then 100 percent = 420/0.60, or $700, the retail price needed to achieve the desired markup of 40 percent on retail.
   Formula: Whenever the retail price is to be calculated and the dollar cost and markup percentage on retail are known, the problem can be solved with the following equation:

$$\$\ \text{Retail} = \frac{\$\ \text{Cost}}{100\ \text{percent} + \text{Markup percentage on retail}}$$

2. A dryer retails for $300. The markup is 28 percent of cost. What was the cost of the dryer? If 128 percent = $300, then 100 percent = $300/1.28, or $234.37, the cost that is needed to achieve the desired markup of 28 percent on cost.
   Formula: Whenever the cost price is to be calculated and the dollar retail and markup percentage on cost are known, the problem can be solved as follows:

$$\$\ \text{Cost} = \frac{\$\ \text{Retail}}{100\ \text{percent} - \text{Markup percentage on cost}}$$

3. A retailer prices a jacket so that the markup amounts to $36. This is 45 percent of retail. What is the cost of the item and its retail price? If 45 percent = $36, then 100 percent = $36/0.45, or $80. If retail is $80 and markup is $36, then cost is $80 – $36 = $44.
   Formula. Whenever the dollar markup and the retail markup percentage are known, the retail price can be determined as follows:

$$\$\ \text{Retail} = \frac{\text{Retail markup}}{\text{Markup percentage on retail}}$$

PRICING ADJUSTMENTS

In practice, retailers typically adjust prices, primarily through markdowns on selected products at some time during the year.[8]

Markdowns

A **markdown** is a reduction in the original selling price of an item. Most retailers take some markdowns, since this is the most widely used way of moving items that do not sell at the original price. Other things a retailer might do instead of taking markdowns are: (1) give additional promotion, better display, or a more visible store position to an item; (2) store the item until the next selling season; (3) mark the item up (discussed in "Psychological Pricing"); or (4) give the goods to charity.

Markdowns are taken for a variety of reasons including purchasing errors, selling issues, and external factors. Retailers may purchase styles, colours, and sizes of merchandise that its target customers do not want. It may purchase too much merchandise or purchase it at the wrong time. In these instances, the retailer needs to mark down the merchandise because it is taking up floor space that could be better used to sell merchandise that its target wants. As well, merchandise gets damaged, shopworn, and dirty. Again, markdowns can be used to move this merchandise.

Selling issues include pricing merchandise too high. Here the target market does not see value in the product because these consumers perceive the price to be too high for the quality of the product. Markdowns can also stimulate sales, attract customers to the store, and match competitors' prices in the short term.

External factors include a shift in market tastes where today's fad is tomorrow's markdown. New popular items can also have an effect on existing items, even those that are less prone to fashion cycles.

Markdowns should be handled with care. If an item is marked down too often, the customer may come to view the markdown as the "normal" price and will not buy the item at the "regular" price. Consumers normally do not expect large markdowns on luxury items. Customers may question product quality if prices are slashed too much. Seasonal, perishable, and obsolete stocks are exceptions. Further, excessive markdowns should be avoided. If markdowns are too high, the retailer should find out the reason. As noted, the causes can come from buying, selling, or pricing errors. A plan should be worked out to correct the errors once they have been determined.[9]

CHAPTER HIGHLIGHTS

- Price must be set to support the retailer's competitive strategy. A major decision is whether the retailer will pursue an everyday low pricing strategy or a high-low pricing strategy.
- All stores have pricing policies that are often based on industry practices. Examples include a price-line policy, a leader pricing policy, and a price discount policy.
- A variety of consumer issues affect price decisions in retail operations. Such issues include consumer demand and price sensitivity, price perceptions, and psychological pricing.
- A variety of external (environmental) factors affect retail price setting. Examples include economic conditions, the Internet, and the level of competition.
- Retailers must understand the arithmetic of pricing. In addition to planning markup goals, they must be able to perform a variety of mathematical calculations involved in making pricing decisions.
- In practice, retailers make pricing adjustments, called markdowns, after they have made the original pricing decisions.

KEY TERMS

generics	270	price elasticity	271
initial markup	275	price lining	267
leader pricing	268	price points	267
maintained markup	275	price zones	267
markdown	278	sales retail price	275
original retail price	275		

DISCUSSION QUESTIONS

1. Discuss the two basic price strategies available to a retailer. Give an example of a type of retail organization that follows each of the strategy options.
2. Illustrate price lining and evaluate the concept.

3. Discuss the concept of leader pricing.
4. How does a retailer's flexibility in setting prices depend on the extent to which he or she is selling primarily convenience, shopping, or specialty goods? How can a retailer offer private brands and generics at prices below manufacturer brands and still make a good profit?
5. What is meant by the concept of price elasticity of demand? Explain how a retailer can determine whether demand is elastic or inelastic by studying the directional changes in price and total revenue. How does the nature of demand elasticity affect retailers' pricing decisions?
6. Summarize the information presented in the text concerning external factors affecting retail price setting.
7. Define the following terms: original retail price, sales retail price, initial markup, and maintained markup.

PROBLEMS

1. If markup on cost is 36 percent, what is the equivalent markup on retail?
2. If markup on cost is 44 percent, what is the equivalent markup on retail?
3. If markup on retail is 18 percent, what is the equivalent markup on cost?
4. If markup on retail is 41 percent, what is the equivalent markup on cost?
5. A suit costs a retailer $36.80. If a markup of 43 percent on cost is required, what must the retail price be?
6. A lamp is marked up $168. This is a 61 percent markup on retail. What is (a) the cost and (b)the retail price?
7. The retail price of a ring is $7,800. If the markup on retail is 78 percent, what is the cost of the ring to the retailer?
8. The retail price of a picture is $48.50. If the markup on cost is 38 percent, what is the cost of the picture to the retailer?
9. Men's wallets may be purchased from a manufacturer for $300 per dozen. If the wallets are marked up 28 percent on cost, what retail price will be set per wallet?
10. Women's scarves may be purchased from a manufacturer at $81.60 per dozen. If the scarves are marked up 16 percent on retail, what is the retail price of each scarf?
11. Determine the (a) initial markup percent and (b) the maintained markup percent in a department that has the following planned figures: expenses, $7,200; profit, $4,500; sales, $28,000; employee discounts, $450; markdowns, $1,200; and shortages, $225.
12. Sales of $85,000 were planned in a department in which expenses were established at $26,000; shortages, $2,200; and employee discounts, $600. If a profit of 6 percent of sales were desired, what initial markup percent should be planned?
13. Department Z has taken $600 in markdowns to date. Net sales to date are $22,000. What is the markdown percentage to date?

APPLICATION EXERCISES

1. Devise a questionnaire to get consumer reaction to raising the price of goods already on display. Also get consumers' reaction to the fact that UPC codes allow supermarkets to change prices immediately even if old stock is still on the shelves. Do consumers feel these practices are fair or unfair? Why? Allow room for individual consumer comment on your questionnaire.
2. Assume that you are a management trainee for a major supermarket chain. Select a market basket of products that are available in all stores and easily comparable (for example, no private brands), and compare prices (including specials) in a conventional supermarket, a "warehouse-type" outlet, and a convenience store (a Mac's Milk). Keep your record over a period of time, present your data in an organized format, and draw conclusions about the pricing philosophy of the different types of food operations.
3. Health and beauty aids are carried in many different kinds of retail establishments, for example, conventional drugstores, supermarkets, discount drugstores, warehouse clubs, and department stores. Often, each type of establishment promises lower prices, better assortments, and so on, to establish a differential advantage. List selected items available in each store and group stores by type. Compare and contrast the items among the various types of stores. See what you find to be the "real" strategy of the competing stores in the market. Why is the lowest priced store able to price as indicated? What are the specials? Are they similar for all stores?

SUGGESTED CASE

17. Classic Shirts

CHAPTER 12

SUCCESSFUL RETAIL SELLING

CHAPTER OBJECTIVES

After reading this chapter you should be able to:

1. Describe the types of selling needed in retailing.
2. Understand the steps in the selling process.
3. Describe ways to increase sales force productivity.
4. Understand the need for sales training programs.
5. Understand how to help people in buying.
6. Understand the opportunities for motivating retail salespersons.

Many retailers seem to have forgotten about serving the customer. The good news, of course, is that there are some fine salespeople out there who make buying a pleasure. They know how to make you feel comfortable when you spend your money. These good salespeople know that investing money and time in a customer is far cheaper than finding a new one. Look at the following examples:[1]

- Lucy, a legal secretary, went to a store during her lunch break. There she found blouses on sale for $14.99. She selected a few blouses and went to the change rooms at the back of the store. Before she could use one, the salesperson brought another customer and let her in one of the change rooms. She asked the salesperson if she could try the blouses. Her answer was: "Come back later." Lucy could not understand, and the salesperson repeated: "Come back after the lunch hour." Asked why, she said: "So people can try on regularly priced clothing. Those blouses are only $14.99." Needless to say, Lucy never set foot in that store again.
- The Elbow Room Café in Vancouver has taken the "bad service" philosophy as a parody and developed an atmosphere of (jokingly) insulting their clientele (who know it is a game). So the waiter would say to a customer asking for coffee: "If you want more coffee, get it yourself." Or to another who complains about the slow service: "If you're in a hurry, you should have gone to McDonald's." Customers come in to have a good laugh (to be insulted of course) and a good lunch.

A high quality sales force can generate "plus" sales for a retail outlet. Consumers are increasingly frustrated over the poor quality of service they receive in retail outlets. One way to create strong customer loyalty is by offering a superior quality sales force as a complement to good merchandise and strong price/value relationships. Creative selling differs dramatically from the image of the huckster or "sales clerk," which too many people have in their mind when they think of retail sales.

To the customer, the salesperson often is the business. The salesperson is the only person with whom the customer has contact. The salesperson encourages the customer to buy or, through a hostile or indifferent attitude, drives the customer away—forever. Salespersons can act as "sales prevention managers" by their rudeness or indifference.[2]

BUILDING SALES AND PROFIT

Salespeople can help build a business for greater sales and profit. They can:

- Sell skillfully to realize maximum sales and profit from each customer attracted to the firm.
- Provide customers with useful selling suggestions that will build sales and improve customer satisfaction.
- Assure that customers' needs are met so that returns are held to a minimum.
- Develop a loyal following of customers who will return to the store and will send their friends.
- Follow store policies and procedures so that losses through billing oversights, failure to secure credit approvals, and acceptance of bad cheques are held to a minimum.

Retail Highlight 12-1 Finding the Right Merchandise Is Not Always Easy

It was an impossible request. One of Jan Dawe's regulars was begging her to find a certain pin-striped jacket made by American designer Donna Karan, an item last seen on Barbra Streisand in the March issue of *Us* magazine. Dawe, who manages the designer sportswear department at Holt Renfrew's flagship store in Toronto, did some research. Alas, the jacket for Streisand was one of a kind. Undaunted, Dawe found an equally attractive Karan blazer. The customer approved.

This is just one example of what makes Jan Dawe an excellent salesperson. Lynn Joliffe, Holt Renfrew's general manager, says: "Jan exemplifies what good service should be. She is sincere, hospitable and truly wants to assist customers." To Holt Renfrew's emphasis on superior service, Jan Dawes adds her own rule: "Never high-pressure sell. Never put something on a customer that does not look right on her. Give the customer your undivided attention—you can't just stare off into a corner."

Source: Jared Mitchell, "I Can Sell You Anything," *Report on Business Magazine*, June 1992, pp. 48–49.

Personal selling in retailing is essentially matching customers' needs with the retailer's merchandise and services. In general, the more skillfully this match is made, the better the personal selling. If salespeople make a good match, not only is a sale made, but a satisfied customer is developed (or maintained), as the Retail Highlight 12-1 illustrates. Thus, a long-term, profitable relationship can be established.

In retailing, the top producers far outsell the average. The more top producers in a store, the more profitable it will be. Retailers cannot expect salespeople to become top producers by accident. There is no magic wand to wave or button to push to make this happen. However, there are a number of positive actions retailers can make to attract people with potential and, once hired, develop that potential so that maximum performance is achieved.

BASIC ISSUES

When Are Salespersons Needed?

The nature of the merchandise sold in the store is a factor affecting the extent to which salespeople are needed. For example, stores selling primarily convenience goods emphasize self-service. However, if the merchandise is expensive (such as jewelry) or technically complex (such as personal computers) and customers have little knowledge about the product, salespeople are needed. In such cases, consumers generally desire detailed information before making a purchase decision and expect to find knowledgeable salespeople to provide that information.

The overall strategy of the store affects the role assigned to salespeople. For example, in discount operations customers do not expect a fully staffed store. Of course, even discounters will assign salespeople to certain departments, such as those carrying more expensive, technically complex products (such as stereos and cameras) and merchandise that must be displayed in locked cabinets (such as gold jewelry). On the other hand, customers shopping in upscale, above-the-market retail stores expect high levels of customer service and expect personal selling to be emphasized.

What Are The Types of Retail Selling?

Several types of selling occur in retailing. A different type of person and different skill levels are needed for each type.[3]

Transaction Processing

The easiest selling task is **transaction processing**. Employees simply serve as checkout salespersons or cashiers and do little selling. Typical examples are personnel in discount department stores or supermarkets. Even though such employees do not sell in the sense of presenting merchandise and relating how merchandise can fill needs, transaction processors can affect consumers' perceptions of a store and their eagerness to shop in that store. As a result, transaction processors should be trained to smile and pleasantly greet customers as they go through the checkout line, to ask whether they found everything they

Suggestion selling requires product knowledge and good selling skills.

Courtesy Sears Canada

were looking for, and to thank them for shopping in the store. Such simple actions as these can do much to create a positive attitude among customers.

Routine Selling

Routine selling involves more product knowledge and a better approach to the sales task. Often, people in routine selling are involved in the sale of nontechnical items such as clothing. These salespeople assist the shopper in buying by giving them confidence in their judgment and answering simple questions.

Personnel involved in routine sales should also be trained in the techniques of suggestion selling. For example, a salesperson might suggest a shirt and tie to go with the suit a customer is trying. They should then be monitored closely to make sure they practise the concepts they have learned. Such techniques may increase sales by 10 percent or more, and additional sales are almost pure profit since they add little, if anything, to the cost structure of the firm. Retailers such as McDonald's consistently practise suggestion selling when the salesperson asks: "Would you like french fries or a Coke with your order?"

Creative Selling

Creative selling is a type of higher level selling in which the salespeople need complete information about product lines, product uses, and the technical features of products. They are often called sales consultants and may, for example, work as interior designers in a furniture store. Creative selling occurs when the product is highly personalized, and the primary selling activities revolve around determining customers' needs or problems and creatively helping them meet those needs.

Regardless of the type of selling involved, salespeople have a key role in the communications plan for a firm. Many extra sales can be made by creative sales efforts. The cost of retail selling is high, in spite of the low wages paid to sales personnel, and these costs must be offset by high productivity. A well-trained sales force can be a major advantage for a firm. Competing firms may duplicate price cuts and promotion, but may have difficulty in developing a quality sales

Table 12-1 Types of Personal Selling in Retailing

Criteria for Comparison	Transaction Processing	Routine Selling	Creative Selling
Purpose	Assist at check-out counter	Suggestion selling	Creative selling
Training required	Clerical training	Sales training	In-depth product knowledge
Source of sales	Impulse purchases	Maintain sales volume plus "add on" accessories	Creation of new sales volume
Type of products	Simple convenience items	Standardized with new options	Complex and customized
Primary activity	Order processing	Suggestion selling	Creative problem solving

force. The main differences in the three types of selling are summarized in Table 12-1.

AN OVERVIEW OF PERSONAL SELLING

A basic concept in retail sales is that a sale must first occur in the mind of the buyer. The job of the salesperson is to lead the customer into a buying situation. A successful salesperson should think of selling as a process consisting of the steps shown in Figure 12–1.

Figure 12-1 The Selling Process

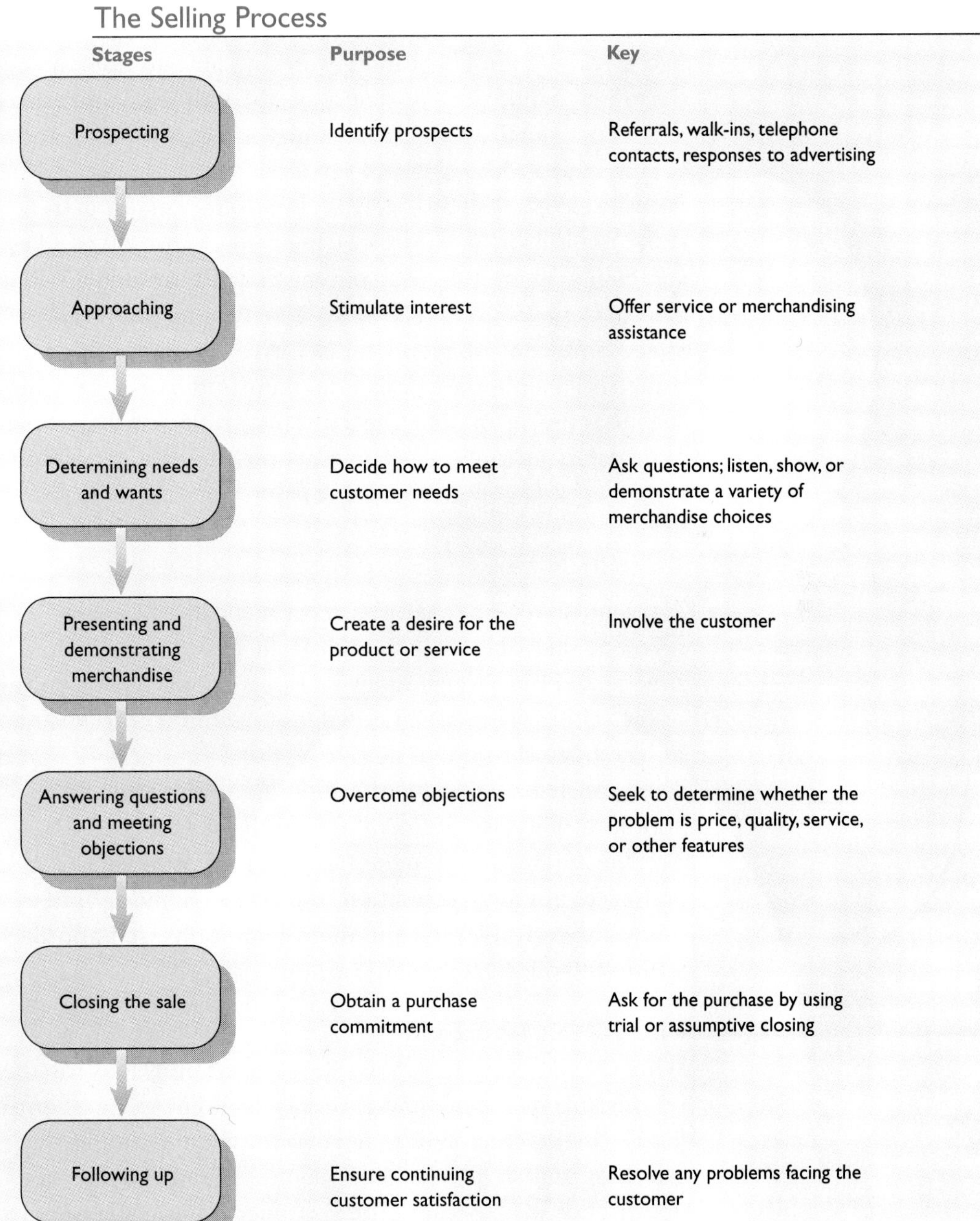

Stages
Purpose
Key
Prospecting
Identify prospects
Referrals, walk-ins, telephone contacts, responses to advertising
Approaching
Stimulate interest
Offer service or merchandising assistance
Determining needs and wants
Decide how to meet customer needs
Ask questions; listen, show, or demonstrate a variety of merchandise choices
Presenting and demonstrating merchandise
Create a desire for the product or service
Involve the customer
Answering questions and meeting objections
Overcome objections
Seek to determine whether the problem is price, quality, service, or other features
Closing the sale
Obtain a purchase commitment
Ask for the purchase by using trial or assumptive closing
Following up
Ensure continuing customer satisfaction
Resolve any problems facing the customer

Prospecting

Prospecting involves identifying and qualifying possible customers. Promotional, telephone, and direct mail programs often attract potential customers to the firm. Likewise, word of mouth can be effective when satisfied customers refer friends to the store.

Salespeople should try to know as much about their customers as possible before approaching them. This may seem difficult at first, but the concept of market segmentation discussed earlier may aid in identifying customers. The type of promotion program featured by the store is also a key. For example, most customers shopping at Zellers expect good price/value relationships and normally buy on the basis of price. These customers are often presold on products through national-brand advertising and do not expect many services. On the other hand, the customers of an exclusive store, such as Holt Renfrew, expect personalized attention, a high level of product knowledge by the salesperson, and a wide variety of services.

Salespeople can also play an important role in getting customers into the store. Some firms keep lists of their good customers' likes and dislikes, measurements, as well as past purchases as illustrated in Retail Highlight 12-2. Salespersons, as in the Harry Rosen example, often call these customers when a new shipment of merchandise arrives. Some salespeople, however, dislike using the telephone to call customers and worry that they will be bothering their customers or that the customers will think they are being too pushy. Management should teach salespeople the proper techniques of telephoning customers and encourage and reward them for doing so.

Approaching the Customer

A recent survey revealed that more than three-fourths of the 800 salespeople surveyed said that what they disliked most about their job was approaching strangers.[4] Even though many salespeople may feel negatively about this aspect of the selling process, the initial approach is a crucial variable affecting a sale. Research has shown that salespeople who exhibit poor approach skills also perform poorly on subsequent selling tasks. Similarly, those exhibiting excellent approach skills also perform well on the selling tasks that follow.[5]

The approach is designed to gain the customer's attention, create interest, and make a smooth transition into a presentation. Various approaches to customers are possible, but the most commonly used approaches are the service approach and the merchandise approach.

The Service Approach

With a **service approach**, the salesperson simply asks whether he or she can be of assistance to a potential customer by asking a question such as "Can I help you?" The greeting is especially useful if the customer has apparently made a selection and simply needs someone to ring up the sale. However, such an approach is weak because the customer is given the opportunity to quickly say

Retail Highlight 12-2 Generating Sales Through Good Customer Service

According to Harry Rosen, CEO of the menswear chain of the same name, good service does not mean having someone friendly standing by your elbow, ready to do your bidding, it's also knowing about the product and individual customer needs. And, adds Rosen, "it's imparting knowledge to the customer so that he can make an informed decision on his purchases."

In order to provide this level of service, all 24 Harry Rosen stores across Canada have been linked with a computer database. "Whenever a customer returns to one of our stores," says company president Bob Humphrey, "a sales associate can call up his name on a computer terminal and receive a detailed accounting of all his past purchases. In this way, we can ensure that our customer's wardrobe is kept well-rounded, that no duplications are made, and that he can always get the proper size and fit."

Source: Leslie C. Smith, "Dressing up customer service," *The Globe & Mail*, June 11, 1992, p. D1.

"No." It is better to approach by saying "Hi, if you need my help, let me know."[6] Even though it is weak, the "Can I help you?" approach was found to be the most frequently used approach based on observations of salespeople in both specialty and department stores. Thus, this greeting is useful when (1) the customer has apparently made a selection, (2) the customer clearly needs a salesperson to explain something about the merchandise, or (3) the customer needs someone to ring up a sale. Above all, sales personnel should always make the customer feel welcome. The customer needs to know that the salesperson is willing to serve him or her, and that the salesperson is knowledgeable about the merchandise.

The Merchandise Approach

The **merchandise approach** begins with a statement about the merchandise or an open-ended statement related to the merchandise. Questions such as: "The style you are looking at is very popular this year," or "For this style blouse, what size do you need?" The salesperson begins talking to the customer about the merchandise without asking whether he or she would like to be waited on. Such an approach is especially effective in making a smooth transition to the next stage of the selling process—determining customers' needs and wants.

Determining Customers' Needs and Wants

Salespeople should quickly discover the customer's needs and wants after the greeting. Good questioning and listening skills are the key. Once the salesperson has the customer's attention and understands his or her needs, the salesperson can quickly move the customer into the interest and desire stage and on to the buying stage. Motives for buying generally are either emotional or rational.

Getting a customer to talk is important because it is the only way to find out his or her special problems, interests, and needs. Then, when making the sales presentation, the salesperson is in a position to stress the things that are important to the customer and to talk specifically about the situation. One way to develop information on customer needs and desires is to ask the customer about his or her planned use for the merchandise. This knowledge will help the salesperson better understand the buying problem and how the merchandise can help solve the problem. Such information can also provide insight into the price, styles, and colours that a customer may prefer.

Good listening is more than giving the other person a chance to talk. It means giving the person your undivided attention. Getting a prospect to talk is important because it is the only way to find out the person's special problems, interests, and needs. Then, when making the sales presentation, the salesperson is in a position to stress the things that are important to the prospect and to talk specifically about the situation.

Knowing the *importance* of listening and actually doing it are two different things. Many salespeople keep planning what to say next instead of listening. A salesperson who is wrapped up in the sales pitch cannot hear the prospect. A good listener concentrates on what is being said. A good salesperson learns the attitudes and problems the customers have. Learning what is important to the individual may be important in selling to the individual.

By visualizing the person's problems, the salesperson understands. Eye contact is important. The salesperson should make a special effort to be attentive, not letting the mind wander to other subjects. To keep the prospects talking, salespeople should acknowledge that they are listening by prompting with nods, or commenting with "I see" or "I understand." Asking a question now and then helps. Salespeople should not worry about what to say next. If they listen carefully, their next move will usually be obvious. It is not easy to be a good listener, but it is important. Top salespeople listen to a prospect, show that they understand, and remember what is said.[7]

Presenting and Demonstrating Merchandise

Effective questioning and listening helps determine which merchandise to show the customer and which features of the merchandise will help solve the buying problems the customer faces. For example, if a salesperson discovers that a customer is buying apparel for a trip abroad, the salesperson might point out items that are lightweight, that do not wrinkle easily, and that are most appropriate for the area of the world where the customer will be travelling.

Good salespeople have a mental outline they follow when presenting the merchandise. This mental outline differs from a canned sales presentation in which the salesperson repeats exactly the same statements to each customer. The salesperson is free to deviate from a fixed statement but still keeps key points from the outline in mind as a checklist. A mental guide should include the following points:

- *Begin with the strongest features of the product.* These features might be price, durability, performance, and so forth.
- *Obtain agreement on small points.* This helps the salesperson establish rapport with the customer.
- *Point out the benefits of ownership to the customer.* Salespersons should try to identify with the customer in making these points.
- *Demonstrate the product.* A demonstration helps the customer make a decision based on seeing the product in action.
- *Let the customer try the product.* Good salespersons get the customer involved as much as possible. The involvement pushes the customer toward the sale.

Other useful techniques include testimonials of customers who have used the product, discussion of research results, and discussion of product guarantees and case histories.

Answering Questions and Meeting Objections

Customers may object to a point during the sales process. When that occurs, the salespersons should try to find the real reason for the objection, which may be based on price, quality of the product, service available, or various other reasons. The salespersons should try to get the customers to see the situation in a different way. They should acknowledge that they can understand why the customers hold a particular view. But they also should try to provide information that can overcome the objection. For example, an objection to a high price might be overcome by pointing out that the purchase is really an investment. Also, the salespersons might point out that the price of the product has not gone up any more than other items the consumers have recently purchased.

Good listening skills are key to discovering customers' needs and wants.

Courtesy Hudson's Bay Company–Corporate Collection

Table 12-2

Overcoming Objections

Knowing when to answer an objection is almost as important as being able to answer it.

Timing is crucial! In general, it's wise to answer as many objections as you can *before* the prospect brings them up.

Putting the answers to objections into the sales talk saves time. But more important, when a salesperson, rather than the prospect, mentions an objection, the issue seems less important. It also makes the customer feel you're not trying to hide anything.

Sometimes a customer may hesitate to bring up a particular objection because he doesn't want to embarrass you. You can save the day by getting it out in the open, showing the customer you understand his or her concerns.

Another reason for discussing as many obvious objections as possible is that you avoid an argument. If the prospect brings up an objection, you may have to prove he's wrong in order to make the sale. That's a situation to avoid if you possibly can.

On the other hand, what if the customer does bring up an objection before you get to it? If you can give a satisfactory reply without taking attention away from your sales point—answer it immediately.

Sometimes you should delay your answer to a customer's objection. For example, you may not even need to answer if there's a good chance the objection will diminish in importance as you continue your presentation.

It's also best to delay answering if you would seem to be flatly contradicting the prospect. Rather than do this, wait and let the answer become clear as you proceed with your presentation. This gives the prospect a chance to save face.

There are some objections that it's best not to answer at all. If the prospect's statement is simply an excuse or a malicious remark, don't bother trying to answer. This will only put you on the defensive.

Having good answers to objections and presenting them to the customer's satisfaction is important. But so is timing.

Choosing the right time and the right way to handle objections keeps you in control of the selling process.

Source: *On the Upbeat*, June 1982, pp. 11–13.

Above all, the salespersons should consider a customer's question as an opportunity to provide more information about the product or service. They should welcome objections as providing a way for overcoming obstacles to a sale. The key to handling objections is *timing*, as explained in Table 12-2.

Closing the Sale

Salespersons often have a problem with the close. Based on observation of 122 salespeople in specialty stores and 164 in department stores, a researcher discovered that only 24 percent of the specialty store salespeople and only 32 percent of the department store salespeople attempted to close the sale.[8] These findings support the commonly held perception that few retail salespeople attempt to close the sale. They would rather wait passively for the customer to volunteer to purchase.

Customers, however, often give signals to alert salespeople that a buying decision is at hand. Such signals may include questions about the use of the item, delivery, or payment. Facial expressions may also indicate that the customer is close to the buying stage. More frequently, it's up to the salesperson to bring up the closing question. An easy way to approach the close is through use of a trial close.

Trial Close[9]

A **trial close** is a question that is asked to determine the prospect's readiness to buy. The following is an example of such a question: "Are you satisfied that our product will help you reduce your maintenance costs?" If the answer is negative, the salesperson can reemphasize how the product reduces maintenance costs or can ask the prospect to be more specific about the cause of his or her doubt.

Seeking Agreement If the prospect agrees with the salesperson on a series of points, it becomes difficult to say no when the salesperson asks for the order. However, the prospect who disagrees on a number of points will probably defend this position by also saying no when the salesperson asks for the order. The salesperson should **seek agreement** on a number of points such as:

- "Don't you think the self-defrosting feature of this refrigerator is a real convenience, Mr. Baker?"
- "You probably need a larger refrigerator than your present one, don't you?"

The salesperson probably knows the points to which the prospect will agree. The idea is to summarize them and ask them consecutively to establish a pattern of agreement, one that will make it difficult for the prospect to say no when the salesperson asks for the order.

Above all, salespersons should:

- Not make exaggerated claims.
- Use honest facts and figures to back up the claims they do make.
- Demonstrate and prove their points whenever possible.
- Use solid, legitimate testimonials that the prospect can check.
- Not promise what they cannot deliver.
- Back promises in writing and in performance.
- Show sincere interest in every customer's problems.
- Consistently and conscientiously put the customer's interest ahead of their own.[10]

Salespersons should not be pressed to act too quickly or make exaggerated claims because of potential legal consequences. Five categories of careless statements with potential legal consequences are: (1) creation of unintended warranties, (2) dilution of the effectiveness of existing warranties, (3) disparagement of competitive offerings, (4) misrepresentation of the firm's own offerings, and (5) unwarranted interference with business relationships.

Table 12-3 summarizes the critical skills needed and common errors to avoid in the personal selling process.

Table 12-3 Critical Skills and Common Errors in Personal Selling

Critical Skills

Good listening to establish needs and to develop basic information
Demonstrating how a product or service can meet an identified need
Establishing good rapport with customers
Skillfully handling objections or negative attitudes
Summarizing benefits and actions required in closing the sale

Common Errors

Talking instead of listening
Not seeking critical information from a customer by failing to ask crucial questions
Failing to match customers' needs with product benefits
Failing to handle objections
Not knowing how or when to close the sale

Benefit Summary Another effective trial close is the **benefit summary**, which is a statement that summarizes **product benefits**, such as the following:

> Ms. Perkins, I think you'll find that the Brand X washer has everything you're looking for. A partial load cycle saves you water, energy, and money. Temperature controls protect your fabrics. And Brand X's reputation for quality assures you that this machine will operate dependably for a long time with little or no maintenance.

Closing Techniques

Now let us look at the most vital factor in the selling process—actually closing the sale. All previous steps have been taken with one purpose in mind—to close the sale and to get the prospect to buy. A variety of techniques can be used to close the sale. The best approach often depends upon the salesperson's individual selling style, the prospect, the product or service that is offered, and the salesperson's earlier success in convincing the prospect of the advantages of the product and the benefits that it offers.

Direct Close The **direct close** assumes that the prospect is ready to buy. In closing, the salesperson asks a direct question such as the following:

- "We can deliver your sofa next week. What is the address that we should ship to?"
- "You want this in green, don't you?"
- "Will this be cash or charge?"
- "Would you like to put this on a budget plan?"

Assumptive Close The **assumptive close** is a modification of the direct close. The salesperson assumes that the prospect is ready to buy, but asks less direct questions, such as:

- "Which colour do you prefer, red or green?"
- "Which model do you prefer, the standard or the deluxe?"

- "Have you decided where you would like the machine installed?"
- "Shall I call an electrician to arrange the installation?"

Open-ended Close In the **open-ended close**, the salesperson asks open-ended questions that imply readiness to buy, such as:

- "How soon will you need the sofa?"
- "When should I arrange for installation?"

The prospect's answer to these questions leads to an easy close. If the prospect needs the sofa in three weeks, the salesperson can respond, "Then I'll need an order right away, to assure you of delivery on time."

Action Close The salesperson takes some positive step toward clinching the order (**action close**), such as:

- "I'll write up the order right now and, as soon as you sign it, we can deliver."
- "I'll call the warehouse and see if they can ship immediately."

Urgency Close The salesperson advises the prospect of some compelling reason for ordering immediately (**urgency close**), such as:

- "That's a pretty tight schedule. I'll have to get an answer from you very quickly if we are going to be able to meet it."
- "That item has been very popular, and right now our inventory is running pretty low."
- "Our special price on this product ends the 15th of the month."

Dealing with Delay Not all closing attempts are immediately successful. The prospect may delay, unable to make a decision. If so, the salesperson should ask the reason for the delay. The reason will often help the salesperson plan the next course of action in reestablishing the presentation of the product or service.

For example, the prospect might say: "I think I'll stick with my present machine a while longer." If the salesperson has properly qualified the prospect earlier she or he might respond: "But didn't you say that repair costs were running awfully high? Isn't it worth a few dollars to know that you will save on maintenance costs and not have to worry about a breakdown at a critical time?"

The choice of the closing technique will depend on the salesperson, the salesperson's style, the customer, and the facts. Regardless of the technique chosen, the most important thing to remember is to pursue some closing technique and not avoid this critical step.

Following Up

A note or telephone call to a customer after the sale is an important part of the selling process. Through such communications, the salesperson can again thank the customers for their patronage. They can provide additional information on the product purchased and assure the customers they have made wise product choices. For certain kinds of merchandise, such as major appliances and furniture, salespeople should make sure that the merchandise is delivered on time, that it arrived in good condition, and that installation, if needed, was satisfactory. Such communications can also be used to suggest other merchandise in which the customer might be interested and to invite him or her to visit the store again soon.

Retail Highlight 12-3 Following Up Is Showing Customers That You Care

Stan Rich gave up his coal-mining job to become a car salesman at Halifax's Colonial Honda. During his first 18 months, he moved 150 automobiles, a phenomenal achievement during a recession. According to Rich, the key to his success is showing customers that you care about their needs. Before hitting the sales floor each day, Rich consults index cards to see which of his previous customers he is scheduled to telephone. "How is the car?" he'll ask them in his Cape Breton drawl one week after they have driven away a new Prelude, Accord, or Civic. He'll do the same thing in a month's time, then in three months' time and every six months after that, trouble-shooting where necessary, but always reminding customers that Stan Rich cares.

Source: Jared Mitchell, "I Can Sell You Anything," *Report on Business Magazine*, June 1992, p. 50.

Above all, the salespeople should think back over the sale to determine what they learned that will help them in their future sales efforts. Also, they should think about why some sales were not made and what might have been done to overcome the lack of a sale. Salespersons should always be seeking to identify ways of achieving future sales by satisfying their customers, as the Retail Highlight 12-3 demonstrates.

INCREASING SALES FORCE PRODUCTIVITY

Productivity of the sales force can be generally defined as total sales divided by employee costs. More precise measures can be tailored to each type of salesperson. The cost of retail selling is high, in spite of the low wages sometimes paid to sales personnel. However, these costs can be offset by developing a quality sales force and increasing its productivity. For example, management should know how many salespeople are needed at a given time and avoid overscheduling. They should avoid having too few personnel available at periods such as lunch time and think about split schedules to cover these busy periods. Management should consider having less overtime and hiring more part-time personnel. Keep in mind that salespeople should be used for selling; such tasks as gift wrapping and shelf stocking should be done by nonselling personnel. The following sections discuss how better employee selection, effective training programs, appropriate compensation, and effective performance evaluation lead to increased sales force productivity.

Employee Selection

Finding good salespeople is a problem for large and small retailers alike. What retailers fail to realize is that much of the problem is of their own making. They may not define clearly what they mean by "good" salespeople or specify what qualities they are seeking.[11] Therefore, to do a better job in finding and hiring salespeople, firms are doing several things.

First, many retailers are realizing that customers have more confidence in salespeople who are like themselves. As a result, some firms are attempting to hire salespeople that parallel as much as possible the firm's target customer. Firms that are doing so find that the result often leads to a rather diverse sales force.

Retailers should also develop *job descriptions* as discussed in Chapter 6. A job description is a written statement, often no longer than one or two paragraphs, spelling out the requirements for a particular job. The job description forces the retailer to be more explicit about what a job requires and provides a guide for appraising the capabilities of prospective employees. For example, since the job discussed above emphasizes big-ticket items, the retailer should look for people who have this kind of experience. There are many instances of salespeople who can do an excellent job on low-unit-value merchandise but have trouble closing sales on the big-ticket items. Job specifications help to avoid such problems.

Job Orientation

A job description and job specification can simplify the process of providing an orientation, or introducing a new employee into the business. An orientation will make the new employee feel at ease and better able to begin work. It is important to note, however, that a job orientation only explains the job to the employee and does not train her or him to do it. A typical job orientation checklist is shown in Table 12-4.

Table 12-4

Job Orientation Checklist

- Explain background:
  Company purpose
  Company image
  Kind of clients catered to
- Introduce to other employees and positions
- Explain relationship between new employee's position and other positions
- Tour the building:
  Working areas
  Management office
  Rest facilities
  Records
  Employee locker room or closet
  Other relevant areas
- Explain facilities and equipment
- Review the duties and responsibilities of the job from the job description
- Introduce to emergency equipment and safety procedures
- Questions and answers

After the periods of formal job training and orientation are completed, management still faces the task of helping the salesperson perform successfully. One way to do this is a program of **management by objectives** that helps the person work to achieve tangible goals.

Sales Training Programs

Many people wonder why training salespeople is necessary, since their turnover is often so high. But effective training can increase employee sales levels, lead to better morale, and produce higher job satisfaction and lower job turnover. Training or retraining gives employees more knowledge about the items they sell and may make them feel more a part of the firm. Much training occurs on the job for the purpose of skills enhancement.

Retailers should budget dollars for training just as they budget dollars for hiring staff members, since training is a way to increase sales. Most people really want to succeed but no one can succeed without adequate training. Customers will show their appreciation by increased levels of buying. And add-on sales as a result of employee training are almost pure profit since they add little or nothing to expenses.[12]

Unfortunately, when the word *training* is mentioned, the retailer typically associates it with formalized programs conducted by large department stores and national chains. However, sales training by smaller retailers does not have to be a formal and structured program. Actually, any conscious effort the retailer makes to improve the basic skills needed for effective retail selling is a form of sales training.

Sales Training Methods

Some of the frequently used retail sales training methods are: (1) role playing, (2) sales meetings, and (3) seminars.

Role Playing **Role playing** is an excellent method for developing a salesperson's skills at learning customer needs. In role playing, one person plays the part of the customer, while the other plays the part of the salesperson. Next time around, they reverse the roles. Role playing enables salespeople to see various sales situations from the customer's point of view. The skill necessary to quickly "size up" customers (learn about their needs) is rapidly sharpened through role playing.

Sales Meetings Knowledge of the merchandise and service can be improved with regularly scheduled *sales meetings*. Sales meetings offer an excellent opportunity to discuss the features of new products, changes in store policies, new merchandising strategies, or other matters relating to the store's merchandise and services. Sales meetings do not have to be formal and precisely scheduled events. Instead, they can be conducted right on the sales floor during slack periods or shortly before the store opens for business. What is important is that management holds the meetings regularly and frequently and each has a specific theme or focus. For example, at one meeting management might discuss the features of a new line of products the store is now carrying and how to introduce them to the customer. The next meeting might focus on changes in the store's merchandise return policy. At another meeting, management might talk about the sales strategies for the upcoming inventory clearance sale.

Seminars Training aimed at improving the ability to convince customers that a store's merchandise and service offering is superior is perhaps the most difficult. Some people believe that an individual either has this skill naturally or does not, and hence training makes little difference. While there may be some truth in this position (people do differ in their natural communication abilities), training can still make a difference. Training can range from encouraging salespeople to take a formal course in salesmanship, to informal *sales seminars* organized by the store. These seminars may be no more elaborate than sitting down with salespeople for half an hour over a cup of coffee and discussing ways that merchandise and service offerings can be better communicated to customers.

If conducted informally (but regularly), these sessions may foster a constructive interchange of ideas about selling. For example, a salesperson may have developed a good argument that can be used successfully to close a sale when it looks as if the customer is ready to walk out.

What Should Training Include?

Information about the Company and Its Products Who started the company? How long has it been in business? What lines of merchandise are sold? What are their main characteristics, uses, etc.

Expectations of the Salesperson A training program should outline such things as dress code, job skills expected, goals to be met, and how performance will be measured.

Basic Training in Selling Techniques Will the personnel need special technical skills? Management should also help employees to understand their nonselling duties.

The Company's Promotion and Fringe-Benefit Policies Management should explain promotion opportunities. Does the company pay for education for the employees? What are the sick leave and annual leave policies? What benefits such as health and life insurance does the company provide?

Training in Telephone Selling Salespersons may call a list of regular and preferred customers when new merchandise arrives.

Equipment Use Nothing is more frustrating for a customer than to stand at the cash register for what seems an eternity, waiting for the salesperson to figure out how to use the cash register. Before being placed on the sales floor, sales associates should be trained thoroughly in how to operate such equipment as cash registers, credit card machines, and sensor tag removal machines.

Teaching Selling Skills[13]

Teaching selling skills consists of the three following steps:

- *Customer communications.* Developing a courteous approach to greeting customers and discussing their buying needs. This permits the salesperson to assist customers in their product selection and describe products in terms that show how they fulfill the customers' buying needs.

- *Feature-benefit relationship.* Understanding the reasons why customers buy, relating products or services to those reasons, and describing the products or services to the customers accordingly.
- *Suggestion selling.* Using customers' original purchase requests to develop suggestions for related or additional sales in which the customers might be interested.

Customer Relations

Customer relations is the foundation of a successful selling effort, not simply because a courteous approach to selling is "nice," but because it can build sales and profit. In small businesses, it is particularly important because the customers of small retailers generally expect more personal service than they find in a major department or discount store. The personal service could be advice on the colour, quality, or use of certain products. Or it might be just a friendly greeting and the confidence that comes with knowing that they are buying from people who are interested in them and their business, as the Retail Highlight 12-4 demonstrates.

The salesperson should try to know as much about the customer's buying interest as possible. This is done by asking questions such as:

- "Are you looking for a fall or a winter coat?"
- "How long has your daughter been playing tennis?"
- "How often do you do home renovations?"

The answers to these questions will help the salesperson direct the customer to the right product—perhaps the winter coat, the expert model tennis racket, or the appropriate tools. The salesperson will be performing a service

Retail Highlight 12-4 Showing Customers That They Are Important

Of all the 24 Walters Jewellers stores, the one in Barrie, Ontario is the best, thanks to Karen MacPherson's selling skills. Once, when a necklace that a customer had brought in for repair failed to return from the factory a few days before an important wedding, MacPherson took the customer to the jewelry case and asked her to pick out a piece she could borrow for the big day. The woman chose a gold piece valued at $2,000. A few days after the wedding she came back to say that she'd received so many compliments about it that she'd decided to buy it.

Another time, MacPherson took 15 minutes to explain diamonds to a customer who admitted he knew nothing about gems. When he went to another jewelry store and started using the information to ask detailed questions, the saleswoman said she did not have a clue as to what he was talking about. When he told her he had just received a crash course in diamonds at Walters, the salesperson sniffed, "We don't do things like that here." This superior attitude was more than enough to persuade the man to hightail it back to MacPherson and buy a ring.

Source: Jared Mitchell, "I Can Sell You Anything," *Report on Business Magazine*, June 1992, p. 48.

for the customer by matching the customer's needs to the right product and will be increasing the chances of closing the sale.

As in the hiring interview, the most effective questions are those that cannot be answered "Yes" or "No." Instead, the salesperson should try to use open-ended questions that require a more complete answer. These are usually questions that begin with "Why," "What," "How," or offer a choice for the customer to make.

Even an apparently negative response can be useful. The customer who likes the style of a skirt but dislikes the colour can be shown another skirt in a colour she may prefer. The customer who objects to the price of an appliance can be shown a lower priced model, or can be shown how the particular appliance justifies the apparently high price. Unless the salesperson is aware of the customer's objections, nothing can be done to overcome them.

Salespeople are responsible for *selling* products and services. Customers have no responsibility to buy them. It is up to the salesperson to find out what the customer wants and match a product or service to those wants.

Feature-Benefit Relationship Whenever a salesperson describes the product or service to a customer, it should be described in terms of the **feature-benefit relationship**.

Features and benefits are defined as follows:

- A *feature* is any tangible or intangible characteristic of a product or service.
- A *product benefit* is the customer's basic buying motive that is fulfilled by the feature.

For example, a salesperson says, "These all-leather hiking boots have waterproof seams. They are our highest priced line, but the leather will last a long time, look good, and keep you dry even on wet trails." The salesperson mentioned two features, "all leather" and "waterproof seams." The benefits that the owner can expect to derive from these features were also mentioned as follows:

- "Last a long time."—Although they are higher priced, they represent value because they won't have to be replaced frequently.
- "Look good."—People want things that they wear to look good.
- "Keep you dry."—People are naturally interested in comfort and in preserving their health.

People's buying motives vary widely, as noted earlier. In fact, two people buying the same product might be looking for altogether different benefits. One man buys an expensive suit because of the status it confers upon him. Another man buys the same suit because its superior tailoring will make it more durable and long-lasting. A third buys it because he likes the styling.

The following are some typical benefits that people seek from the things they buy:

- *Safety.* The desire to protect their lives and property.
- *Economy.* Not just in the initial purchase price but in long-run savings through less frequent replacement or, in the case of certain products, lower maintenance and operating costs.

- *Status.* People buy things to be recognized. The woman buying an evening dress may consider the designer's name all-important. A 12-year-old boy might consider the brand of blue jeans or the autograph on a baseball bat to be equally important.
- *Health.* People buy exercise equipment, athletic equipment, and outerwear because they wish to preserve their health.
- *Pleasure.* People attend theatres, go to athletic events, eat at restaurants, and buy books and objects of art because they expect to derive personal pleasure from these pursuits.
- *Convenience.* People buy many things to make the routine chores of life easier. For example, the cook buys a cake mix because it is far more convenient than mixing the individual basic ingredients.

The list could go on indefinitely. The important question to consider is the customer benefits that are provided by the goods or services to be sold. Knowing these benefits, salespeople can describe products to customers in terms of the benefits that the customers can derive from them. Relatively few customers are interested in the technical or design details of a product. Customers are primarily interested in what the product will do for them. The principal reason for a salesperson to describe features of a product or service is to prove the benefits that the person can expect from it. For example, a salesperson might describe insulating material to a customer as follows: "This insulating material creates a thermal barrier." Impressive words, perhaps, but the statement tells the customer little or nothing about the reasons for buying.

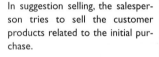

In suggestion selling, the salesperson tries to sell the customer products related to the initial purchase.

Courtesy Hudson's Bay Company—Corporate Collection

Suggestion Selling In **suggestion selling**, the salesperson tries to build upon the customer's initial request in order to sell additional or related merchandise. For example, the salesperson might suggest that a woman buy two blouses to take advantage of a weekend special. If a man buys a dress shirt, the salesperson should suggest a complementary tie. With a tablecloth, a salesperson might suggest napkins that go well with it. With a stereo receiver, a skilled salesperson could suggest a pair of speakers matched to the output of the receiver.

The opportunities for suggestion selling are endless. Frequently, the benefit that a customer might derive from one product could be used to develop suggestions for others. Young parents buying one safety product for a baby would be interested in seeing others. Or the man who buys a designer necktie for status reasons could be persuaded to buy a belt, shirt, or eyeglass frames from the same designer.

Even a "no sale" or a return can become a sales opportunity through suggestion selling. The customer who is looking for a shirt to buy as a gift may not find the right shirt but could be persuaded to buy something else, perhaps a necktie or a sweater. The man who returns a raincoat because it doesn't fit properly still needs a raincoat and could be sold one if the salesperson takes advantage of the opportunity for a suggestion sale.

Involvement and Feedback[14] When training people in sales skills, it is relatively easy to get their involvement and the feedback needed to evaluate their progress to better shape the training needed. Instead of telling salespeople how you would sell a certain product, ask them how they would do it, and what they would say to a customer.

After management hears their presentation, they can explain any other features that should have been mentioned and any other benefits that are important. Then let the person try again, perhaps reviewing the basic technique of features and benefits if necessary.

Similarly, management can list a number of products that the store offers and have the salesperson write down a related product that he or she would suggest to every customer. In so doing, management will be gaining the trainee's active involvement and secure necessary feedback so they can see where review or correction is necessary. Management will also learn of the employee's strengths and weaknesses so they can perform their supervisory job more effectively.

Criteria for Successful Training

Regardless of the training method used, there are two key elements for success. These are as follows:

Trainee Participation The training process should directly involve the trainee. Listening to a person talk has little value. Few can absorb it. The passive role of reader or listener is seldom helpful in understanding and remembering. Reading a book or hearing a speech is fine for entertainment or intellectual stimulation, but these activities are seldom effective in a training environment. People learn by doing things. When new personnel are taught how to prepare an invoice or credit memo, it is not enough to tell them how or show them how. It is far more important to have them do it.

Feedback Feedback is what a person learns by testing the employee's understanding of the facts that are being taught. It permits the trainer to measure the employee's progress at each step. Through feedback, management can recognize problems when they arise. Through early recognition of misunderstandings, they can correct them as soon as possible so that training can progress.

Feedback helps direct training efforts since management then knows those things that give the employee particular difficulty, such as arithmetic or trade terminology. In the remainder of the training effort, management can then be particularly careful and painstaking in teaching anything that involves trade terminology or arithmetic skills.

Compensation Systems

The appropriate method of payment for a salesperson (for example, straight salary, straight commission, salary plus commission, or other options) depends on a number of factors. Because we discussed these factors in Chapter 6, we will not repeat the information here. However, an issue that is quite relevant today is the extent to which increasing numbers of retailers are attempting to link pay to performance.

Retailers must remember that incentive pay plans that work provide benefits for the company, the sales force, and customers. A proper balance must be struck between motivating employees and good customer service.

Performance Evaluation Systems

A well-designed performance evaluation system can result in improved customer relations and sales force productivity. In developing such a system, management must generate a set of standards against which sales associates' performance is to be measured. Actual performance should be compared to standards to determine areas where a salesperson is performing well versus those areas where improvement is needed. Management should personally meet with salespeople to give feedback. These sessions should be viewed as a mechanism for helping salespeople perform more effectively for their own benefit as well as that of the company. Thus, a well-designed performance evaluation system not only provides an objective way of evaluating and improving performance but also is often useful in helping management discover content areas where training programs need to be conducted.[15]

CHAPTER HIGHLIGHTS

- The trend today is toward more self-service. Improved signing, displays, packaging, and store layouts all make self-service possible. But retailers still need salespersons to answer customers' questions about the technical dimensions of products, to reassure customers about items of fashion apparel, and to help customers fit items such as shoes.
- The key to a good sales force is the right interaction between the merchandise, the customer, and the salesperson. A salesperson is needed when cus-

tomers have little knowledge about the merchandise they plan to buy, when price negotiation is likely, and when the product is complex.

- The easiest type of selling is transaction processing. This means that employees simply serve as checkout salespersons or cashiers and do little selling. Routine selling involves more product knowledge and a better approach to the sales task. Creative selling requires the use of creative sales skills by salespersons who need complete information about product lines, product uses, and technical features.
- The job of the salesperson is to lead the customer to a buying situation. Successful salespersons normally think of selling as a process consisting of the following steps: prospecting (preapproaching), approaching, determining needs and wants, demonstrating and handling merchandise, answering questions and meeting objections, closing, and following up.
- The most vital step in the selling process is closing the sale. Techniques include the direct, the assumptive, the open-ended, the action, and the urgency closes.
- Developing a strong sales force is not a matter of luck. Training is needed; adequate incentives must exist to motivate personnel to high levels of performance; and supervision is necessary. Above all, management of the sales force means planning for increased sales. Sales per person can be increased by: better employee selection, training, and supervision; improved departmental layout; more self-selection by customers; streamlining sales processing; improved merchandising and promotion; making sure salespersons are fully knowledgeable about the products they're selling; and following up where necessary after the sale (for example, with the service department).
- Retail sales managers should set up performance standards and let salespersons know what they are. Nonselling activities should be included if they are also expected to be performed by the employee. Finally, management should decide how to reward employees who exceed the established standards.

KEY TERMS

action close	295	productivity of sales force	296
assumptive close	294	prospecting	288
benefit summary	294	role playing	298
creative selling	286	routine selling	286
direct close	294	seeking agreement	293
feature-benefit relationship	301	service approach	288
management by objectives	298	suggestion selling	303
merchandise approach	289	transaction processing	285
open-ended close	295	trial close	293
product benefit	294	urgency close	295

DISCUSSION QUESTIONS

1. What are the various types of retail selling? How do the skills required vary by type of selling? What is the difference between the service approach and the merchandise approach?

2. Under what conditions is the presence of sales personnel most essential in a retail store?
3. What are the various ways a salesperson can determine customer needs and wants?
4. Comment on the following statement: The best way for a salesperson to deal with a customer objection is simply to ignore it and continue with the sales presentation.
5. In closing a sale, how does an assumptive close differ from that which might be used during a special-sale event?
6. Why is sales force productivity so important? How can it be increased? Why are self-selection and self-service becoming more common in retailing?
7. Assume that you have been asked by a retail store manager to describe what an effective sales training program should include and what sales training methods can be used. How would you respond?
8. Why should performance standards be established for sales personnel? List examples of performance standards for salespersons.

APPLICATION EXERCISES

1. Visit with the human resources manager of the leading department store in your community and discuss briefly their training programs for salespeople. Find out their major problems with sales personnel. Do the same thing with the manager of a fast-food franchise. Be prepared to discuss the differences you find.
2. Interview 10 to 15 of your student friends and find out their overall impression of salespersons in your community. Are they satisfied? If yes, why? If not why not? Get their thoughts on what can be done to improve the quality of service in retail outlets. Now, talk to several of your friends who have worked for or are working as part-time salespersons. Prepare a report based on their experiences. Get them to talk about their reaction to most customers in the stores where they work, their likes and dislikes about their jobs, and what could be done to make their jobs easier.
3. Visit three of the new car dealers in your community and act as a serious buyer. Develop a list of questions ahead of time about such things as kilometres per litre of the auto, service requirements, and warranty and safety features. Compare and contrast the results you get in talking to the different salespersons about each of these points. Find out if they have what you consider the needed knowledge for selling the product. Do they conduct themselves in the way you would expect from persons who are selling items valued at $15,000–$25,000? If not, make suggestions for improving their quality of service to customers.

SUGGESTED CASES

10. Martin's Department Store
18. Travel Agencies—A Variation in Service

Courtesy Chapters

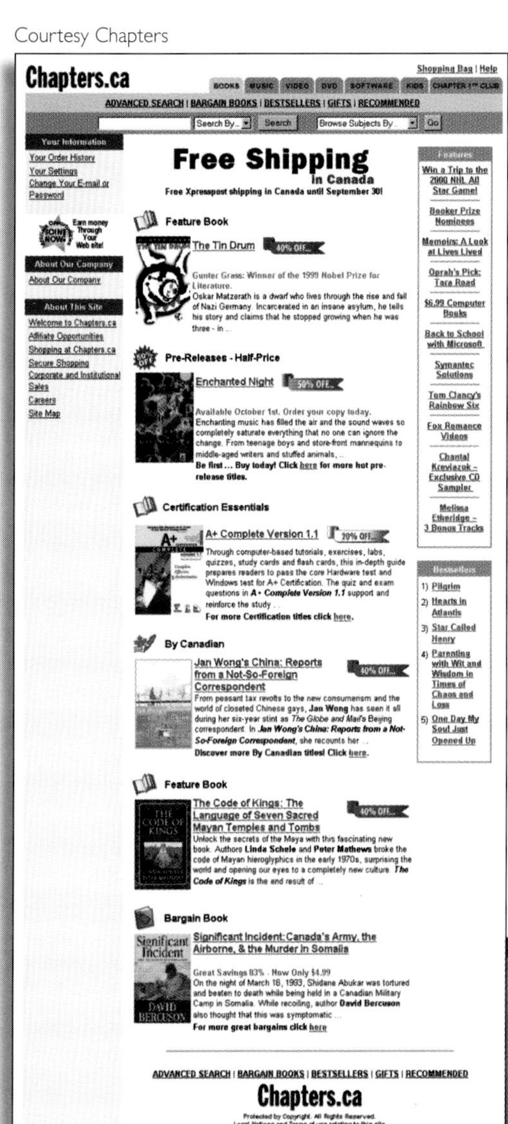

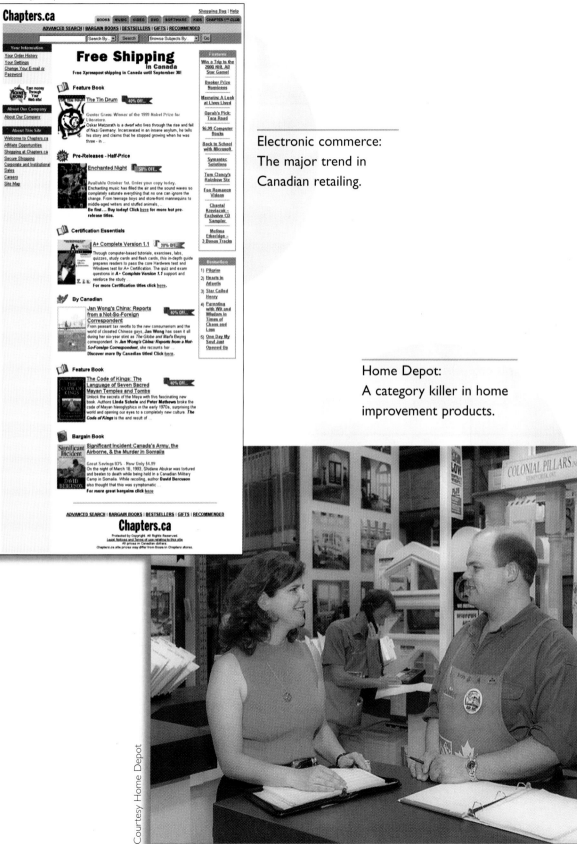

Electronic commerce:
The major trend in
Canadian retailing.

Home Depot:
A category killer in home
improvement products.

Courtesy Home Depot

Benetton: Satisfying customer needs with global lifestyle products.

Photos: Rodney C. Daw

Timber Creek Lodge provides a complete dining experience – food, atmosphere, and fun times.

Courtesy Loblaw Companies Ltd.

Private brands are a successful part of Loblaws' pricing strategy.

Courtesy Hudson's Bay Company – Corporate Collection

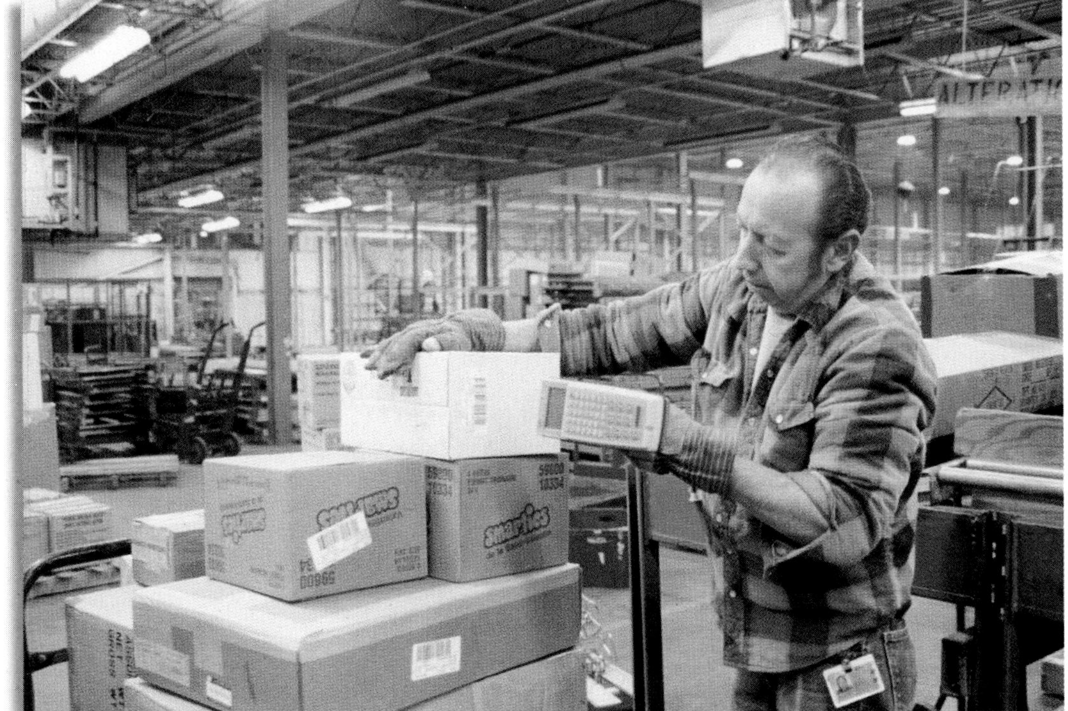

New technologies improve the accuracy of inventory management.

Courtesy Hudson's Bay Company – Corporate Collection

An exciting merchandise line with a well-known "brand name" – Wayne Gretzky.

Photo: Anne Laroche

Birks: Classic store design creates a strong image and attracts the store's target market.

Courtesy Cookstown Outlet Mall/Photo: Kalloon Photography

Cookstown Outlet Mall: Manufacturers sell goods directly to consumers, who are drawn by perceived value and one-stop shopping.

Courtesy Future Shop

Future Shop: To provide the service that consumers demand, retailers must focus on product knowledge and excellent training.

Photo: Rodney C. Daw

Mountain Equipment Co-op: A vision and strategy that matches a target market's needs.

CP Picture Archive (Dan Loh)

McDonald's: A global franchise and the world leader in the fast-food business.

Courtesy CompareNet Inc.

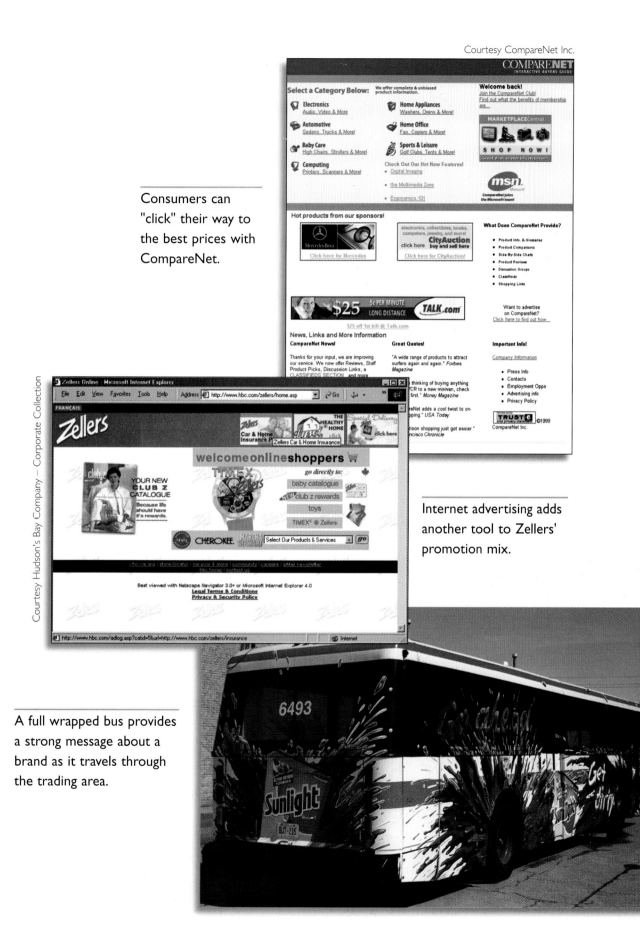

Consumers can "click" their way to the best prices with CompareNet.

Internet advertising adds another tool to Zellers' promotion mix.

Courtesy Hudson's Bay Company – Corporate Collection

A full wrapped bus provides a strong message about a brand as it travels through the trading area.

Courtesy Club KO

Joining the Kids Only team has been much more fulfilling
an I could have imagined! I have had a wonderful time
eeting other "Moms", sharing and swapping stories and
aving a night out (a fun one too!) Club KO has helped to
utfit my two girls and myself in fabulous, quality fashions.
has enabled me to spend more time at home and
ovided a creative outlet for me. I love what I sell and I
ve what I do! KO has enriched my life. I never dreamed
could be this successful!"
Karen Dinsmore, Vancouver, BC
7212
HOODED JACKET
004 red
021 lemon
BRUSHED FLEECE
12M 18M 24M
$38
7225
PRINT PANTS
218 geckos
519 jade stripe
COTTON SHEETING
12M 18M 24M
$26
7035
PULL ON PANTS
001 jade
004 red
019 navy
021 lemon
COTTON INTERLOCK
12M 18M 24M
$24
35
EVAN 33"
SIZE 18 M
PATRICIA 32"
SIZE 18 M
KARRY 31"
SIZE 18 M
JONAH 32"
SIZE 18 M
GOODYEAR

Kids Only: Nonstore retailing with an interesting product category.

Sympatico

MY SYMPATICO · SITE INDEX · COMMUNICATE · SHOPPING · SEARCH

Shopping > Computers + Electronics

Meeting the needs of your business — Sympatico Small Business

Shopping

- Stores + Services
- Advisories + FAQ's
- Forums
- Add Your Store

- Buyer's Guide
- Compare Prices
- Credit Cards
- Currency Converter
- Present Picker
- Product Reviews
- Service Charges

- Appliances
- Computers
- Garden Tools
- Music

Or enter a keyword

SEARCH

"Buy books online in Canada. Visit Indigo.ca"

Computers + Electronics

	prices in CDN$	ships from Canada
Business Depot	✓	✓
Electronics Boutique		✓
Future Shop	✓	✓
Megadepot	✓	✓
Programmer's Paradise	✓	✓

Suggestions or comments? EMail Us!

Find another shopping category:

Auction go!

HOME and Family on Sympatico

Sympatico Travel

Book a flight

HOT DEALS

Vista 350 - low price!

Look cool in Sympatico gear!

Online business? Get listed!

Courtesy Bell Canada

A new form of advertising: Banner ads on the Sympatico Web site.

CHAPTER 13

RETAIL PROMOTION MIX

CHAPTER OBJECTIVES

After reading this chapter you should be able to:

1. Describe the communication process in the context of retail promotions.
2. Explain the role of advertising in attracting, informing, and motivating consumers.
3. Explain how to establish and allocate a budget.
4. Evaluate and select appropriate media alternatives for retail messages.
5. Understand how to determine the effectiveness of media.
6. Outline the stages involved in developing creative retail messages.
7. Explain how to measure the results of advertising.
8. Determine when to use an advertising agency.
9. Describe the role of sales promotion and publicity in the retail firm.

Advertising, sales promotion, and publicity are key ingredients of the integrated marketing communications strategy of many successful retailers. Consider the following example:

On January 2, 1998, Burger King launched their new french fries by giving them away for free on "Free FryDay!" More than half a million Canadians lined up for the giveaway, and sales of Burger King increased by 20 percent, as customers bought other products with the free fries. Traffic increased by 40 percent nationally and by 60 percent in Toronto.

The advertising showed a claymation character called Mr. Potato Head who introduced the new product in a press conference. In addition to television, the same strategy was used in print, outdoor, and in-store promotions. For radio, the French Friars sang the praises of the new entry.

Media coverage was widespread, with news items, interviews of Burger King managers, and even impromptu taste tests by television stations.

This is part of the overall strategy by Burger King to continue expanding into the Canadian market and doubling the number of outlets to 500 by 2003.[1]

This example illustrates the role of integrated marketing communications in conveying to a target market the retailer's strategy. Retailers use promotion as a major source of communication with consumers. **Promotion** includes the creative use of advertising, sales promotion, and publicity in providing information to customers. The purposes of communication may be to inform the consumers of short-term price promotions, to help establish and maintain the desired image, or a variety of other tasks. The processes of developing promotion plans, establishing budgets, and evaluating the effectiveness of promotions are critical issues in the success of any retail firm. Retailers, such as Mega Movies, are constantly seeking new and creative ways of communicating with the consumer.

Promotion is an integral part of a firm's total merchandise process. If promotion efforts are not in harmony with decisions on pricing and other elements of the retail mix, the outlet will project a confusing and distorted image. Developing and maintaining store identity thus become the cornerstones of most retailers' promotion plans. Think about the successful positioning strategies these retailers promoted through their campaigns:

- Your money's worth ... and more—Sears Canada.
- From tune-ups to tires, Goodyear takes you home.
- We do chicken right—Kentucky Fried Chicken.
- You deserve a break today—McDonald's.
- Where's the beef?—Wendy's.
- For the seafood lover in you—Red Lobster.

A sound promotion plan can be developed only in the context of the firm's marketing strategies. All promotion efforts should seek to tap the buying motivations of the target market groups selected by management. Sophisticated retailers develop promotion plans similar to those of leading nonretail firms. Each element of the retail plan should be supportive of the targeting and positioning of the firm. For example, media choice is affected by target market selection. Radio station audiences can be segmented on the basis of whether they appeal to teenagers, ethnic groups, or car drivers. Similarly, magazines can be chosen to reach boaters, hunters, tennis players, or the prospective bride. University or college newspapers are appropriate to reach students.

Promotion objectives may be either strategic or tactical. *Strategic objectives* are long-term, broad based, and designed to support the overall competitive strategy of the retailer by developing and maintaining a favourable identity or image. *Tactical objectives* are short-run and designed to achieve specific measurable goals that support the strategic objectives, for example, to liquidate last year's inventory and launch a new line.

THE COMMUNICATION PROCESS

One role of retail communication is to *inform,* by providing information on store hours, brands carried, services available, and so forth. Retailers may also seek to *persuade* individuals to do a variety of things such as to make a purchase during a sale. A third role of advertising is to *remind* customers of the retailers' products and services.

A Theoretical Model of Communication

A theoretical model of communication is shown in Figure 13-1. Communication takes place only when the individuals to whom the retailer is sending a message attach a meaning to the message similar to that intended by the retailer.

Figure 13-1 A Theoretical Model of the Communication Process

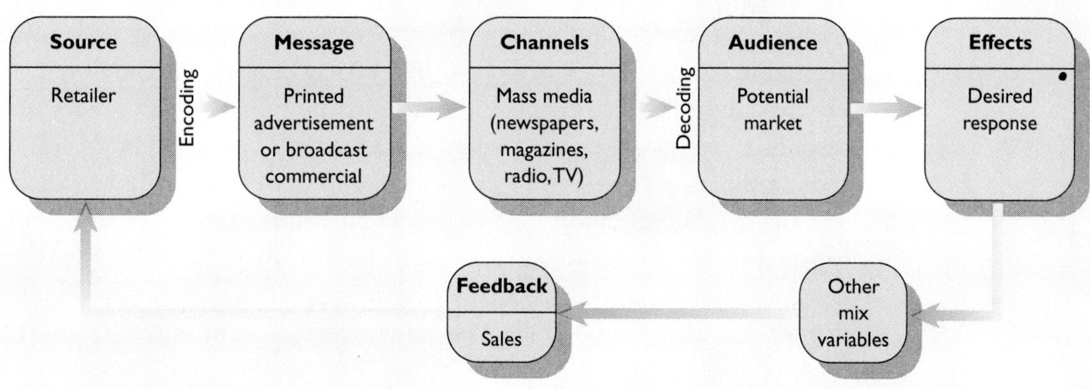

Source: Adapted from René Y. Darmon and Michel Laroche, *Advertising in Canada*, Toronto: McGraw-Hill Ryerson, 1991, p. 15.

The **source** in the communication process is the originator of the message, normally the retailer. The retailer selects words, pictures, and symbols to present the message to the targeted audience. Composing the message is known as *encoding* and refers to putting together the thoughts, information, or ideas in a symbolic form that is familiar to and understood by the target audience.

The **message** is the idea to be transmitted. It may be either oral or written, verbal or nonverbal, or a symbolic form or sign as in the case of McDonald's golden arches. Often, the impression or image created by the advertisement is more important than the actual words.

The next decision after message content selection is the *channel* to be used to communicate the message to the receiver. The nature of communication may be either personal or nonpersonal. Personal channels such as salespeople include face-to-face contact with target individuals or customers. *Word-of-mouth communication* by conversations with friends or associates is also a powerful source of information for consumers.[2] *Nonpersonal channels* of communication include mass media such as radio, television, newspaper, direct mail, or other means of message transmission.

The intended *receiver* is the target audience. Market segmentation plays a particularly important role in this process because segmentation ensures that the message is targeted to a relatively homogeneous audience. *Decoding* occurs when the receiver transforms and interprets the sender's message as part of the thought process. The process of decoding is influenced by the individual's experience, attitudes, and values. Active communication is most likely to occur when a common ground exists between the sender and the receiver.

Unplanned distortion in the communications process is known as *noise.* Noise may occur because of a lack of common experience between the sender and receiver or a failure to properly encode messages, such as the use of signs, symbols, or words that are unfamiliar to the receiver or that have a different meaning than the one intended.

The *desired response* after seeing, hearing, or reading the message depends on the purpose of the promotion program and may include immediate sales, requests for further information, or success in establishing or reinforcing a desired image. Feedback can occur in a variety of ways. The potential customer may ask the salesperson specific questions or in some way reflect nonverbal responses by gestures or facial expressions. Customer inquiries, coupon redemptions, and reply cards are also examples of information feedback.

Market segmentation plays a particularly important role in the communication process because segmentation assures that the message is properly designed and is targeted at a relatively homogeneous audience. Retailers cannot be all things to all people. They must segment their messages, markets, and merchandise. Understanding the customer is the key in all such decisions. For example, the Bay has successfully used Quebec singing superstar Céline Dion in its advertising, all across Canada, singing: "I'm gonna make you love me." These commercials are not only liked by consumers all across the country, but they are motivating them to purchase the advertised goods.[3]

Developing the Promotion Plan

Developing the **promotion plan** requires starting with the goals of the firm. Retailers must decide (1) who they want to reach, (2) the message they want to get across to these customers, and with what effect, and (3) when and how often their message should reach this audience.

We will begin our discussion of promotion by starting with advertising, followed by sales promotion, and public relations.

ADVERTISING: OBJECTIVES AND BUDGETS

The American Marketing Association defines advertising as "any paid form of nonpersonal presentation and promotion of goods, ideas, and services by an identified sponsor."

Goals of Advertising

The basic goals of advertising can include:

- Communicating the total character or image of the store.
- Getting consumer acceptance for individual groups of merchandise.
- Generating a strong flow of traffic.
- Selling goods directly.

These goals can be combined with merchandising and store image objectives into the following framework:

How much to spend ——> advertising budget
What to advertise ——> merchandise
When to advertise ——> timing
Where to say it ——> media
How to say it to achieve
a campaign objective ——> copy
Whom to reach ——> audience
How to provide balance ——> planning

Communicating the total character of the store is known as **institutional advertising**, and the corresponding advertising campaign is called **image campaign**. Neither specific merchandise nor prices are featured. Rather, institutional advertising is designed to enhance the image of the outlet and to communicate targeting and positioning strategies to consumers. *Direct response advertising,* in contrast, induces consumers to take a specific action such as purchase particular merchandise, increase the volume of store traffic, or participate in some type of contest or giveaway. The corresponding advertising campaign is called an **event campaign**.

Campaign Objectives

In determining the particular objective of an advertising campaign, the retailer must understand that consumers respond to advertising according to various stages. Such a framework is called a **hierarchy of effects model**. The simplest such model is the **AIDA model**: this is, attract **A**ttention, develop **I**nterest, arouse **D**esire, and get **A**ction.

A more useful model is described in Figure 13-2. According to this model, the retailer must decide if the campaign objective is either one of the following, and then decide the type of campaign that must be developed:

- to increase **awareness** of its name, and develop an attention-getting campaign;
- to increase *knowledge* about the store's assortment, location, services, etc., and develop a campaign that provides information;
- to increase *liking* of the store, and develop arguments to that effect;
- to increase *preference* for the store, with an aggressive campaign to attract new customers and convert them into loyal customers;
- to increase *conviction* by keeping current customers loyal to the store, with reminder advertising;
- to increase *purchase* through event advertising.

Developing the Advertising Budget

A budget helps retailers plan their promotions. This step alone can go a long way toward better campaigns. Why? There are at least three reasons: (1) a budget forces retailers to set goals so they can measure the success of the promotions; (2) retailers are required to choose from a variety of options; and (3) budgets are more likely to result in well planned ads.

Figure 13-2 The Hierarchy of Effects Model

Behavioural Dimension	Campaign Objective	Target Audience	Type of Advertising Campaign
Cognitive– the realm of thoughts; ads provide information and facts	AWARENESS ↓	All potential customers	*Attention-getting* (teasers, slogan, jingle, humour)
	KNOWLEDGE ↓	Potential customers aware of store	*Learning campaign* (description, demonstration, repetition)
Affective— the realm of emotions; ads change attitudes and feelings	LIKING ↓	Knowledgeable potential customers	*Competitive campaign* (reason why, endorsements, soft argumentation)
	PREFERENCE ↓	Customers of competitors	*Aggressive campaign* (comparative, testimonials, status, strong arguments)
Conative— the realm of motives; ads stimulate and direct desires	CONVICTION ↓	Present customers	*Reminder campaign* (image, reinforcements, new ideas)
	PURCHASE	Customers and potential customers	*Value-oriented campaign* (specials, price deals, rebates, direct-mail)

Source: Adapted from René Y. Darmon and Michel Laroche, *Advertising in Canada*, Toronto: McGraw-Hill Ryerson, 1991, p. 280.

What Should Be in the Budget?[4]

Promotion is a completely controllable expense, and the function of the budget is to control expenditures. By comparing the budget with actual financial reports coming from business activities of the firm, it is possible to compare planned activities with actual events.

What retailers would like to invest in advertising and what they can afford are seldom the same. Spending too much is obviously an extravagance, but spending too little can be just as bad in terms of lost sales and reduced visibility. Costs must be tied to results. It is necessary to be prepared to evaluate goals and assess capabilities and a budget will help do this. The budget can help retailers choose and assess the amount of advertising and its timing. The budget also will serve as a benchmark for next year's plan.

Methods of Establishing a Budget[5]

There are three basic methods of establishing an advertising budget: *(1)* percentage of sales or profits, *(2)* unit of sales, and *(3)* objective and task. Management needs to use judgment and caution in deciding on any method or methods. The first two methods are "naive" in the sense that sales, in effect, help determine the advertising budget, while logically it should be the other way around. The third one is more in keeping with the logic that advertising affects sales, but is more difficult to apply.

Percentage-of-Sales or Profits A widely used method of establishing an advertising budget is to base it on a percentage of actual sales. Advertising is as much a business expense as the cost of labour and should be related to the quantity of goods sold for a certain period.

The **percentage-of-sales method** avoids some of the problems that result from using profits as a base. For instance, if profits in a period are low, it might not be the fault of sales or advertising. But if retailers base the advertising budget on profits, they will automatically reduce the advertising allotment when profits are down. There is no way around it: 2 percent of $10,000 is less than 2 percent of $15,000.

If profits are down for other reasons, a cut in the advertising budget may very well lead to further losses in sales and profits. This in turn will lead to further reductions in advertising investment, and so on.

In the short run, it may be possible to make small additions to profit by cutting advertising expenses. But such a policy could lead to a long-term deterioration of profits. By using the percentage-of-sales method, it is possible to keep advertising in a consistent relationship with sales volume. Sales volume is what advertising should be primarily affecting. Of course, gross margin, especially over the long run, should also show an increase if advertising outlays are being properly applied.

Table 13-1

Some Canadian Retailers That Advertise Heavily

Rank in 1993*	Retailer	Spending (000)	Revenues (000)	A/S† (%)
7	Sears Canada	46,582	4,009,100	1.2
14	McDonald's Restaurants of Canada	35,476	1,520,363	2.3
22	Cineplex Odeon	28,884	549,270	5.3
23	Canadian Tire	28,558	3,232,836	0.9
32	Leon's Furniture	21,388	277,975	7.7
33	Brick Warehouse	21,209	N/A	N/A
39	Royal Bank of Canada	16,504	11,676,000	0.1
45	Canada Safeway	14,556	4,456,600	0.3
62	F.W. Woolworth	11,880	2,143,355	0.6
66	Le Mouvement Desjardins	11,115	411,000	2.7
74	Bank of Montreal	9,321	8,706,000	0.1
77	Majestic Electronic Stores	8,776	39,634	22.1
80	Multitech Warehouse Direct	8,735	N/A	N/A
82	Dylex	8,483	1,940,627	0.4
84	K mart Canada	8,238	1,235,072	0.7
91	Toronto Dominion Bank	7,309	6,366,000	0.1
94	20th Century Theatres	7,178	N/A	N/A
96	Rodale Books	7,136	N/A	N/A

* Based on the top 100 advertisers (the other ranks are non-retailers).
† In interpreting these figures, one must remember that some companies have large wholesale or commercial sales.
Source: Adapted from "Canada's Top 100 Advertisers of 1993," *Marketing*, May 2, 1994, pp. 21–22; *The Globe and Mail: Report on Business*, July 1994.

What percentage? The choice of a percentage-of-sales figure can be based on what other similar retailers are spending. This can be done since these percentages are fairly consistent within a given category of business. The information may be found in trade magazines such as *Marketing*, association publications, and reports published by financial institutions such as Dun and Bradstreet. It can also be purchased from companies such as Elliott Research (and its subsidiary Media Measurement).

Table 13-1 presents some of the retailers that are among the top 100 companies in advertising spending. Knowing the ratio for a particular industry helps retailers put their spending into a competitive perspective. Then, depending on the situation, retailers can decide to advertise more than or less than their competition. For example, compare Sears Canada, Canadian Tire, and Woolworth, both in terms of advertising expenditures and advertising-to-sales ratios. It may be necessary to out-advertise competitors and forgo short-term profits. Growth requires investment.

Retailers should not let any method bind them. The percentage-of-sales method is quick and easy, and ensures that the advertising budget is not out of proportion for the business. It may be a sound method for stable markets. But if retailers want to expand market share, they may need to use a larger percentage of sales than the industry average.

Which sales? The budget can be determined as a percentage of past sales, of estimated future sales, or as a combination of the two:

1) *Past sales.* The base can be last year's sales or an average of a number of years in the immediate past. Consider, though, that changes in economic conditions can make the figure too high or too low.

2) *Estimated future sales.* The advertising budget can be calculated as a percentage of anticipated sales for next year. The most common pitfall of this method is an optimistic assumption that the business will grow. General business trends must always be kept in mind, especially if there is the chance of a slump. The directions in the industry and in the firm must be realistically assessed.

3) *Past sales and estimated future sales.* Future sales may be estimated conservatively based on last year's sales. A more optimistic assessment of next year's sales is to combine both last year's sales with next year's estimated sales. It is a more realistic method during periods of changing economic conditions. This method allows management to analyze trends and results thoughtfully and predict more accurately.

Unit of Sales In the **unit-of-sales method** retailers set aside a fixed sum for each unit of product to be sold. This figure is based on their experience and trade knowledge of how much advertising it takes to sell each unit. For example, if it takes two cents' worth of advertising to sell a case of canned vegetables, and the object is to move 100,000 cases, management will plan to spend $2,000 on advertising. If it costs X dollars to sell a refrigerator, management will need to budget 1,000 times X to sell a thousand refrigerators. Managers are simply basing the budget on unit of sale rather than dollar amounts of sales.

Some people consider this just a variation of percentage-of-sales. The unit-of-sales method, however, does permit a closer estimate of what should be planned to spend for maximum effect. This method is based on a retailer's experience of what it takes to sell an actual unit, rather than an overall percentage of the gross sales estimate.

The unit-of-sales method is particularly useful where product availability is limited by outside factors, such as bad weather's effect on crops. The owners estimate the number of units or cases available to them. Based on a manager's experience, they advertise only as much as it takes to sell the products. The unit-of-sales method works reasonably well with specialty goods, where demand is more stable. But it is not very useful in sporadic or irregular markets or for style merchandise.

Objective and Task The most difficult method for determining an advertising budget is the **objective-and-task method.** Yet this method is the most accurate and best fulfills what all budgets should accomplish. It relates the appropriation to the marketing task to be achieved.[6] This method relates the advertising spending to the volume of expected sales. To establish a budget by the objective-and-task method it is necessary to have a coordinated marketing program. This program should be set up with specific objectives based on a thorough survey of markets and their potential.

The percentage-of-sales or profits method first determines the amount retailers will spend with little consideration of a goal. The task method establishes what must be done in order to meet company objectives. Only then is the cost calculated.

It is best to set specific objectives, not just "increase sales." For example, a retailer wishes to "sell 25 percent more of product X or service Y by attracting the business of teenagers." First, the manager determines which media best reaches the target market. Then the retailer estimates the cost to run the number and types of advertisements it will take to get the sales increase. This process is repeated for each objective. When these costs are totalled, the projected budget is available. As this description indicates, applying this method requires an excellent knowledge of media planning principles, often not the case among retailers. The media representatives of each medium, an advertising agency, or a media buying service may often be of assistance to a retailer.

Of course, retailers may find that they cannot afford to advertise as they would like to. It is a good idea, therefore, to rank objectives. As with the other methods, managers should be prepared to change plans to reflect reality and the resources available.

Allocating the Budget

Once the advertising budget has been determined, management must decide how to allocate the advertising dollars. A decision to use institutional (image) advertising, or promotional (sales) advertising must be made. After setting aside money for the different types of advertising, retailers can allocate the promotional advertising funds. Among the most common breakdowns are: (1) departmental budgets, (2) calendar periods, (3) media, and (4) trading area.

Departmental Budgets The most common method of allocating advertising to departments is on the basis of their sales contribution. Those departments or product categories with the largest sales volume receive the biggest share of the budget. In a small business, or when the merchandise range is limited, the same percentage can be used throughout. Otherwise, a good rule is to use the average industry figure for each product. By breaking down the budget by departments or products, those goods that require more promotion to stimulate sales can get the required advertising dollars. The budget can be further divided into individual merchandise lines.

Calendar Periods Most executives usually plan their advertising on a monthly, or even a weekly, basis. Even a budget for a longer planning period, however, should be calculated for these shorter periods as well. This permits better control. The percentage-of-sales methods are useful to determine allocations by time periods. The standard practice is to match sales with advertising dollars. If February accounts for 5 percent of sales, it might get 5 percent of the budget. Sometimes, retailers adjust advertising allocations downward in heavier sales months in order to boost the budget of poorer periods. This is done only when a change in advertising timing could improve slow sales, as when competition's sales trends differ markedly from those of the firm.

Monthly percentages of annual sales differ by store type and region. Also, economic conditions can affect budget plans. Other ways for allocating funds focus on the traffic-drawing power of some items or on the growth potential of key lines. Sales variations by month normally have the largest effect on advertising. Almost three-fourths of the advertising budget by boating retailers for example, is spent during March to July. In contrast, over 20 percent of the advertising budget for jewelry is spent in the month of December. Garden supplies retailers spend over 50 percent of their advertising budget during March to June. December is the largest advertising month for appliance dealers, bookstores, department stores, retail furniture dealers, hardware dealers, music stores, and shoe stores.

Media The amount of advertising that is placed in each advertising medium—such as direct mail, newspapers, or radio—should be determined by past experience, industry practice, and ideas from media specialists. Normally, retailers use the same sort of media that competitors use, because it is most likely where potential customers will look or listen.

Trading Area Retailers can spend their advertising dollars in established trading areas or use them to try to stimulate new sales outside the primary trading area. It is wise to do the bulk of advertising in familiar areas. Usually, it is more costly to develop new markets than to maintain established ones.

Maintaining Budget Flexibility

Any combination of these methods may be employed in the formation and allocation of the advertising budget. All of them—or simply one—may be needed to meet the retailer's advertising objectives. However management decides to plan the budget, they must make it *flexible,* capable of being adjusted to changes in the marketplace.

The duration of the planning and budgeting period depends upon the nature of the business. If management can use short budgeting periods, they will find that advertising can be more flexible and that they can change tactics to meet immediate trends. To ensure advertising flexibility, management should have a contingency fund to deal with specials available in local media, or unexpected competitive situations.

Management should be aware of competitors' activities at all times. They should not blindly copy competitors, but analyze how their actions may affect business—and be prepared to act.

Cooperative Advertising

Cooperative advertising is a situation in which a manufacturer pays part of the retailer's advertising costs under specific conditions. Many manufacturers and wholesalers state that a significant part of the reserves they set up for cooperative advertising are not used by their retailers. It has been estimated that $600 million of the $1.5 billion in co-op funds available to Canadian retailers goes unclaimed, and the reason is that many retailers do not know about these programs or are unsure of how they operate.[7] This is surprising. Cooperative advertising substantially lowers the cost for the retailer, since manufacturers or wholesalers pay part of the advertising cost.

For their own legal protection and to ensure the greatest return from their investment, manufacturers set up specific requirements to be observed in cooperative advertising. The retailer should consult each vendor about the requirements that must be met to qualify. The retailer must also be aware of the procedures to follow to apply for and receive payment. Some vendors relate cooperative dollars to the amount of the retailer's business. Others figure on a percentage basis. The amount and rules for payment of cooperative dollars are at the discretion of the vendor. For more details and examples, see Retail Highlight 13-1. Cooperative advertising as a percentage of total advertising is approximately 50 percent for department stores, shoe stores, and clothing stores, and approximately 75 percent for food stores and electrical appliance stores.[8]

Retail Highlight 13-1 Understanding Co-op Advertising Programs

When Gary Kugler decided to get more aggressive about promoting his camera store in Ottawa (Focus Centre), he increased the advertising budget by 100 percent. Through co-operative advertising, Kugler's suppliers shared the costs of his newspaper and radio ads. In return, their products got greater exposure in the local market—and everyone benefited. As his co-op relationships developed, Kugler saw his annual sales increase by 20 percent. Adding a photofinishing centre, he marked the expansion with a two-page insert in the *Ottawa Citizen*, for which most of his 20 suppliers contributed co-op funds. The ad cost $13,000, and Kugler's share amounted to $2,000.

In many co-op programs as in the previous example, retailers earn co-op dollars based on a percentage of purchases made from a distributor or manufacturer: between 2 and 5 percent, although they can go as high as 10 percent. For example, if Kugler buys $10,000 worth of Canon cameras, his supplier will give him 5 percent of that, or $500, to be spent in advertising Canon. The supplier then pays for a portion of advertising Canon cameras, up to the amount of co-op dollars his dealer accumulates. Most suppliers pay 50 to 75 percent of the cost for any one campaign (in some cases, they pay the full amount).

The suppliers' sales representatives are very important sources of information for these programs. Every manufacturer has different rules, from logo size to placement of the ad in the media. They can also provide ready-made ads or help the retailer create his or her own. Local media can also help. About 68 percent of co-op dollars are spent on newspaper advertising. In order to generate more co-op business, many newspapers handle much of the co-op paperwork, such as billing agreements. Finally, co-op dollars can also be used for a wide variety of promotions, such as direct mail or sales promotions.

Source: Jennifer Pepall, "Co-op advertising builds strength from numbers," *Profit*, November 1990, pp. 53–54.

ADVERTISING: EVALUATING MEDIA OPTIONS

Each medium has its strengths and weaknesses. Retailers normally use a media mix to give them the strengths of each. The characteristics of each medium are shown in Table 13-2. Other specialized forms of promotion are also available, and discussed later in the chapter.

Three general questions can help an advertiser evaluate media:

- Is the audience of the medium appropriate for the advertising campaign?
- Among the available media, which provides the largest audience at the lowest cost?
- Can the medium effectively communicate the sales message?

Advertising can be tricky. However, by establishing specific goals, analyzing various media, and using proven techniques, a retailer can successfully promote merchandise.

Media Information Sources

For most media, information about rates charged to national advertisers and ad agencies (called **national rates**), as well as various conditions offered by the media, is published monthly in ***Canadian Advertising Rates & Data (CARD)***.[9] However, the rates charged directly to retailers (called **retail or local rates**) are not published in CARD, but in an individual Retail Rate Card that the retailer obtains directly from the local medium. For example, a quick phone call to the sales office of the local newspaper will get you the retail rate card for that newspaper. Or check the Web site for the medium for which you need retail rates (check, for example, the site for *The Globe and Mail*: www.globeandmail.com, and click on the Media Kit).

www.globeandmail.com

Some of the reasons for charging different rates are: (1) the medium does not pay the 15 percent commission to advertising agencies on retail rates, since most retailers do not use an advertising agency (because of a small budget and tight schedules); (2) retailers do not normally need the total audience of a medium, as their trading area is more restricted.

Most retail advertising in Canada is spent on daily newspapers, followed by radio (Table 13-3) because it effectively reaches geographic targets. Table 13-4 provides an example of media budget allocation for a retailer.

Table **13-2** Advantages and Disadvantages of Various Advertising Media

Medium	Advantages	Disadvantages
Newspapers	Good flexibility Timeliness Good local coverage Broad acceptance High believability	Short life Poor reproduction quality Small pass-along audience
Magazines	Good geographic and demographic selectivity Good credibility and prestige High-quality reproduction Long life Good pass-along readership	Long production lead time Some waste circulation Poor position guarantee
Radio	Mass audience Good geographic and demographic selectivity Low cost	Audio presentation only Lower audience attention than TV Nonstandardized rate structure Fleeting exposure
Television	Appeals to many senses Commands high attention levels High reach	High absolute cost High clutter Fleeting exposure Less audience selectivity Long production lead time
Direct mail	Best audience selectivity Good flexibility No clutter Good personalization	Relatively high cost Sometimes poor image
Outdoor	Good flexibility High repeat exposure Low cost Low competition	Poor audience selectivity Limited creativity
Internet	Fully interactive Very low operating costs Excellent audience selectivity Easy to research exposure Available 24 hours a day Allow in-home/comparison shopping	Currently limited to text/pictures/sounds Perceived risks for payment Low reach Exposure under audience control

Table 13-3

Retail Advertising for Each Medium, and Share of Retail Advertising per Medium

Medium	Retail Expenditures (Millions)	Distribution (%Total Retail)	Retail Share (%Total Medium)
Television	$ 388	14.8%	18.5%
Radio	647	24.7	76.2
Daily Newspapers*	1,017	38.9	65.8
Weekly Papers	564	21.6	89.0
Total Retail	**$2,616**	**100.0**	**51.0**

* Excludes classified advertising.
Source: *The Canadian Media Directors' Council Media Digest*, 1999/2000, p. 12.

Media Terminology

Before discussing the various media available to a retailer, a few definitions would be useful:

- **Reach** is the number of different persons exposed at least once to a message during an ad campaign. Reach is often expressed as a percentage of the total audience.
- **Frequency** is the average number of times a person will be exposed to a message during the advertising period.
- **Cost per thousand (CPM)** is the cost of reaching 1,000 members of a desired audience with one or several ads.
- **Selectivity** is the ability of a medium to reach only specific audiences, minimizing waste (e.g., only teenagers or men aged 24 to 45).
- **Spot advertising** refers to commercials shown on local (radio or television) stations, whereby the negotiation and purchase of time is made directly with the individual station. Network television advertising done by national advertisers during the prime time period is called **prime time advertising**.

Table 13-4

Example of Media Budget Allocation for Sears Canada

Medium	Sears Canada (in $000s)	%
Television	13,144	28.2
Daily Newspapers	26,185	56.2
Magazines	4,735	10.2
Out-of-Home	3	0.0
Radio	2,515	5.4
Total	*46,582*	*100.0*

Source: "Canada's Top 100 Advertisers of 1993," *Marketing*, May 2, 1994, p. 21.

Radio

Radio follows the listener everywhere: in the home, at the beach, and on the highway. Almost every Canadian owns at least one radio. There are currently 346 AM stations and 564 FM stations in Canada.[10] Radio advertising is characterized by comparatively low rates, little or no production costs, and immediacy in scheduling. Retailers spend about 24.7 percent of their advertising dollars for radio (Table 13-3), and radio stations depend on retail advertisers for 76.2 percent of their revenues.

Basic rates depend on the number of commercials contracted for, the time periods specified, and whether the station broadcasts on AM and/or FM frequencies. Usually, FM broadcasting is more localized and offers wider tonal range, for technical reasons.

Strengths of Radio. Radio allows retailers to (1) direct ads to large target audiences; (2) have the ability to reach people at home, in their cars, on the beach, and almost anywhere else; (3) advertise at relatively low cost; and (4) work with short lead time.

Disadvantages of Radio. These are: (1) no pictures; (2) short messages; (3) the need to use several stations in large cities to reach a large target audience; (4) production problems, since most programming is local; and (5) large, wasted audiences for small local retailers.

Radio advertising is used to convey and reinforce distinctive images that draw shoppers to retail outlets. Such advertising typically is institutional, stressing features retailers believe customers are looking for. Humour, ad-lib dialogues, catchy music, and jingles increasingly are used to create bright images in radio advertising. Retailers prefer institutional advertising over price-advertising because they believe that price/item advertising gets "lost" on air.

Buying Radio Time

Radio advertising time is typically sold in blocks of 30- or 60-second slots, with a few stations offering 15-second slots. The 60-second slots tend to be most popular. The price of advertising time varies by time of day, size of listening audience, and length of the spots.

Radio rate schedules vary by stations, as does the system of discounts. The most expensive time is known as "drive time," between 6 and 10 A.M. and 4 and 7 P.M. on weekdays. Advertising is very inexpensive between midnight and 5 A.M., since few people are listening to the station. Weekend rates often differ from weekly rates, depending on the composition of the audience.

Other factors affecting cost include the frequency of advertising during a given week, the number of weeks the ad is aired, and the time of year the spot is on the air. The station may select the air time—this is called run-of-station (ROS)—or the retailer may choose a more costly fixed time slot. If the slots are part of a package, they probably consist of different time slots and frequencies for an extended period of time.

Television

TV has the visual impact of print and the sound impact of radio, plus colour, motion, and emotion. Canadians now spend as much time viewing TV as radio, newspapers, and magazines combined, e.g., about 25 hours per week for adults, and 20 hours for children. Problems include the high cost of time and high production costs. Most people view TV at night after the stores are closed. Infrequent summer viewing is also a disadvantage as is the increasingly fragmented audience because of cable services, either part of the basic subscription such as the Youth Channel, or as pay-TV such as Cable News Network, The Sports Network, and others. Another major problem for advertisers is the high incidence of zapping and zipping, which lower the chance of the commercial being seen.

Local TV stations carry the programs of major networks. There are two English (CBC and CTV) and two French (Radio Canada and TVA) national commercial networks in Canada, eighteen regional or provincial networks, and thirty-nine specialty networks. Canadian network programs are viewed by 40 percent of the TV audience, against 21 percent for the U.S. stations (including U.S. Pay TV), 12 percent for the Canadian Independents, 14 percent for the Canadian Pay and Specialty channels, and 13 percent for the others (including VCR).[11]

The network programs include commercials bought by national retailers such as Sears Canada or the Bay. The stations sell local commercial time during station breaks. Management probably should plan on using daytime, news program times, and early evening hours before TV prime time.

TV Ads Are Costly

The cost for a 30-second spot ad in a small local market such as Red Deer (Alberta) may be between $100 and $200, and in a major market such as Toronto a similar ad may cost between $700 and $2000. The cost varies according to the time of the day, and the most expensive time is prime time (8 P.M.-11 P.M.).

Cost Per Viewer Is the Lowest for a National Audience

However, few retail firms other than the Bay, Sears Canada, and Wal-Mart have enough outlets to justify national TV ads. Use of local TV by large retailers is increasing, but about 15.6 percent of retail ad expenditures go to television. TV stations rely on local advertising for less than 19 percent of their revenues (Table 13-3).

Few retailers feel that TV is the best overall medium by which to reach their audience. However, they are more prone to use television to reach a specific target audience like youth, which has been weaned on TV. Cable penetration in Canada is very high and reached 77 percent in 1999. Pay TV, with a share of 22 percent, does not yet have a sufficiently large audience, particularly in major markets, to attract many national advertisers.[12]

Buying Television Time

Television time is normally sold in 15-,30-, and 60-second time slots, with the 30-second slot being the most popular (74 percent). The cost of television depends on the size of the audience, which can be described in terms of ratings and shares.

A **gross rating point** (GRP) is one percent of all homes with television sets in a market area. A program with a GRP of 10 is reaching 10 percent of the television homes. In contrast, a **share** is the percentage of television sets in use that are tuned to a given program. Thus, a program may have a GRP of only one, for example, at 4 A.M. on Sunday morning. But it may also have a share of 56.

Newspapers

About 39 percent of all retail ad dollars go to daily newspapers and another 22 percent go to weeklies and community newspapers (Table 13-3). Daily newspapers rely on retail advertising for about 66 percent of their revenues. The other types of newspaper depend on retail advertising for 89 percent of their revenues.

Daily Newspapers

Most markets have some type of daily newspaper, and newspaper ad supplements are a popular advertising medium. **Supplements** are preprinted pages of ads that are inserted into the papers. Sunday papers are usually full of supplements, and local department stores are heavy users. There are about 108 daily newspapers in Canada with an average daily circulation of 4.7 million copies and a penetration of 63 percent of households. Almost 8 million adults read daily newspapers and they spend about one hour reading them.[13]

Newspaper ad rates are quoted for short-term advertisers as weekly insertion rates, as monthly rates, and as yearly rates. Newspapers quote local retailers a retail rate that is below the **general rate** (charged to agencies for national advertisers). Newspaper personnel speak in terms of modular agate lines when quoting prices. A **modular agate line (MAL)** is one (standardized) column wide and 1.8 mm deep. In addition a **Canadian newspaper unit (CNU)** is a unit one column wide and 30 MALs deep. Newspapers have special rates for supplements, and rates for colour are higher than black-and-white rates.

The strengths of newspapers include: (1) broad market coverage; (2) short lead time for ads; (3) a large number of items can be advertised together; (4) wide readership; (5) high graphic potential; and (6) assistance in ad preparation (important for a small retailer).

Newspapers have their weaknesses, too. They include: (1) problems in reaching the younger market and children; (2) the chance that many readers will miss an ad; (3) accelerating ad rates; (4) limited ability to segment readers; and (5) lower suburban coverage by big-city papers.

The newspaper office can be helpful in planning the copy and layout. Many small retailers have few skills in these areas and rely on the newspaper professionals to provide the needed services.

Community Newspapers

Community newspapers are published in almost every community in Canada with the majority being published once a week. In Table 13-3, they are included with the weeklies, and they rely almost exclusively on retail advertising. Their circulation has been increasing because their editorial coverage deals principally with local issues of interest to many readers. There are over 1000 community newspapers in Canada with an average weekly circulation of 10 million.[14] They tend to be well read within the community and represent an attractive audience for local retailers, and often a very efficient buy, since there is little wasted circulation. The main drawback is the low frequency of publication.

Shoppers

Shoppers go by many names, including "shopping news," "pennysavers," or "marketplace." These papers are quite different from the traditional newspaper. They normally carry less than 25 percent editorial content. Virtually all news is syndicated feature material as opposed to local news, and shoppers are distributed on a free basis. They offer retailers the opportunity for almost total coverage of a market area. Since they are primarily an advertising medium, the people who read them are already in a buying mood and seeking specific information. Still, the fact that the papers primarily contain advertising may cause some customers not to read them, and wasted advertising can occur.

More and more merchandisers are demanding the services of shoppers, however, since they want better market coverage. Each "shopper" has its own advertising rate schedule, and costs are often quite low. However, the coverage of markets in Canada is very uneven, with the majority in Ontario, and a handful in Quebec, New Brunswick, Manitoba, and Saskatchewan. Suppliers of "shoppers" in the Toronto metropolitan area provide about ten different "shoppers." Each will cover only a selected portion of the metropolitan area, such as a specific suburban community.[15]

Special-Purpose Papers

There are newspapers for special-interest groups such as universities or community colleges (over 200), farmers (95 publications), and ethnic groups (about 200). General information about these media is also available in *CARD*, and the retail rates from the publisher. These media are especially desirable advertising outlets for retailers who are seeking to reach highly specific audiences.

Magazines

A negligible percentage of retail ad budgets are spent on magazines. Until recently, the only retailers using magazines were national firms such as Sears Canada (10.2 percent), as illustrated in Table 13-4. However, local retailers can now place ads in regional editions of such magazines as *Reader's Digest*, *Maclean's*, and *Chatelaine*. There are over 500 consumer magazines in Canada, and about 30 of them offer geographic editions.

Zellers Family magazine combines content from *Today's Parent* magazine with Zellers' advertising. Distributed free to customers, it is published four times a year.

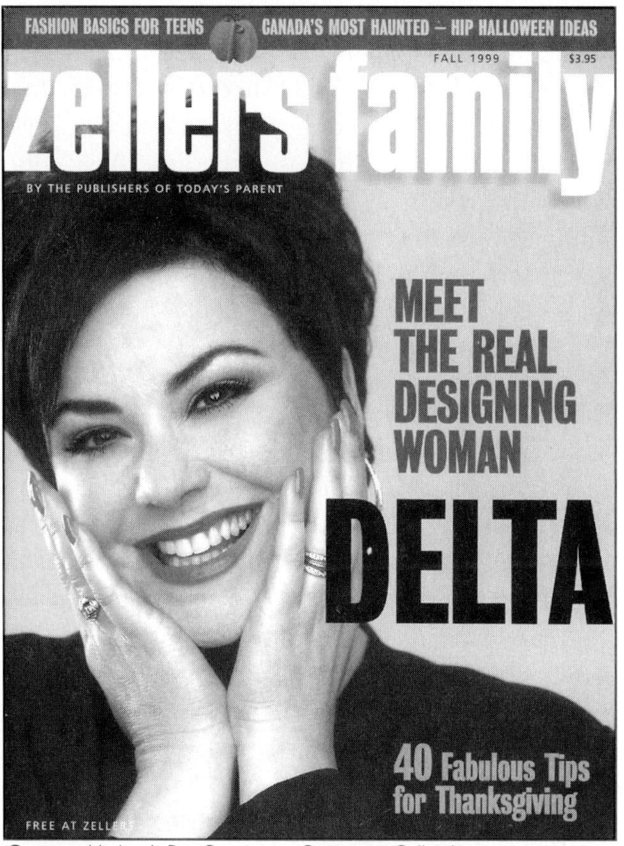

Courtesy Hudson's Bay Company—Corporate Collection

Magazine strengths include (1) carefully defined audiences, (2) good colour reproduction, (3) long ad life because they are not thrown away as quickly as newspapers, (4) low cost per thousand readers, and (5) good pass-along readership (as some magazines are read by people other than the subscribing household, such as friends and neighbours).

The primary problems are (1) high cost, (2) long closing dates (ads must be submitted several weeks before publication for monthly magazines), and (3) slower response.

Buying Magazine Advertising Space

Advertising space is typically sold in pages or fractions of pages, such as one-half or one-sixth. The rates charged depend upon the circulation of the magazine, quality of the publication, and type of primary audience. Rates are higher for magazines with higher circulation. Magazines typically offer discounts for advertising depending upon the bulk and frequency of advertising. Higher prices are normally charged for special positions in the magazine and for special formats.

Direct Promotion

Direct promotion will be covered in detail in Chapter 15. However, since direct mail is an important part of the retailer's media options, this particular form will be treated here for completeness.

Direct Mail is the most selective form of retail advertising. But the cost per person reached is high. According to retailers, direct mail is among the top three forms of retail advertising today. Most retailers use some form of direct mail. The strengths include (1) the high response rate by consumers, (2) the ability to send material to a specific person, (3) not being bound by media format (it is possible to use as much space as needed to tell the story of the product and use colours or other creative effects as the budget allows), and (4) the message does not have to compete with other editorial matter.

The weakness of direct mail is its high cost compared to other media. The cost per thousand is many times higher than for other media.

There are good reasons for the popularity of direct mail. Direct mail includes bill stuffers (which are about 70 percent of direct mail), catalogues, flyers for store openings, sales letters, and everything we normally call "junk mail." To cut costs, some retailers have resorted to hand-delivered flyers to selected targets. In addition to lower costs of printing and distribution (compared to a newspaper insert), the retailer can more effectively reach his or her customers.[16]

The Procedure for Direct Mailing

Mailing lists can be rented from mailing houses. The list can be selected according to consumer tastes on a variety of bases including, for example, model of automobile, family income, tendency to buy through mail-order companies, and FSA code (Forward Sortation Area codes are the first three digits of the postal code) or census tract. A typical mailing list will cost between $30 and $50 a thousand. An occupant list (no personalized name) of all households in a designated area may cost as little as $5 per thousand. Understandably, the more precise and well-defined the list, the higher the cost.

The frequency of mailing depends on the purpose of the campaign. However, to generate new sales leads, one consulting firm recommends one mailing every other month for continuity and long-term effectiveness, or four mailings six weeks apart for maximum short-term impact. But one annual mailing may be sufficient for a seasonal operation or for a firm that occasionally needs a limited amount of new business.

Catalogues Many merchants now operate catalogue sales departments. Sales through mail **catalogues** are growing. It is estimated that in 1994 there were about 620 catalogue firms in Canada, generating $1.8 billion in annual sales.[17] In addition, there is very strong competition from U.S. catalogue firms such as L.L. Bean, Spiegel, and Lands' End, generating more than $200 million in Canadian sales.[18]

Catalogues are a special form of direct mail promotion and are often used as an advertising medium by department and specialty stores, for example, the

Sears Catalogue or the Regal Gifts Catalogue. Most large department stores now have Christmas catalogues. Consumers like catalogues because of the convenience afforded by shopping at home, calling a toll-free number, and getting door-to-door delivery. There is even a *Catalogue of Canadian Catalogues* (Alpel Publishing). It has been estimated that about 60 percent of Canadians make a catalogue or mail-order purchase during a one-year period.[19]

The following are trends in catalogue marketing:

- New and better design/format. Upscale retailers like Holt Renfrew and Harry Rosen have developed new catalogue format, Holt Renfrew a "magalogue"[20] for men, and Harry Rosen a catalogue on CD-ROM. Launched in March 1995, the new Harry Rosen catalogue under the theme of "Get an attitude" allows customers to "try" various outfits in combination, in addition to providing the standard pricing and product information.[21]
- Emphasis on "lifestyle" merchandising, although the term itself is defined in almost as many different ways as there are catalogues.
- A stepped-up search for cost-cutting techniques, including charging a "subscription" to a series of catalogues, or offering the catalogue, via magazine advertising, at a charge to noncustomers.
- Growth of separate catalogue operations, with full responsibility for inventory and controlling direct mail business, and increasingly on-line through the Internet. For example, Sears has several catalogues that can be accessed through www.sears.com.

www.sears.com

The typical department store catalogue has a life of about six weeks. Two or three catalogues per year is not uncommon for some stores, and many are talking about 20 or more "specialogs." For example, Sears produces about 15 catalogues per year, almost like a magazine publication, and distributes 40 million copies in addition to its on-line access.[22] A few have over 1,000 pages and the others 300 pages or less. The emphasis in all of the stores is on "target mailing"—the use of catalogues to sell separate categories of merchandise. Stores are increasingly using computers to target prime customers instead of blanket mailings.

Directories

Every retail business normally advertises in one or more directories. The most common is the *Yellow Pages* in the telephone directory. Directories, however, are published by various trade associations and groups, and they reach more prospective customers than virtually any other medium. Consumers have normally already made a decision to purchase before turning to a directory for help in deciding where to buy. Also, directories have a longer life than most advertising media.

Most directories are published for a minimum of 12 months, which can serve as a drawback. Retailers do not have the option of changing the advertisement in any way until the appearance of a new directory. Thus, the advertisements can become obsolete rather quickly. But costs are reasonable for ads such as the Yellow Pages advertising in a telephone directory. A half-column display ad can vary from $20 a month in an area with 20,000 residents to $200 a month or more in an area of 1,000,000.

Internet Advertising

The medium of Internet advertising, particularly the World Wide Web, has been exploding in recent years, as the number of Canadians accessing it has surpassed 7.6 million per week.[23] On-line advertising revenues are expected to reach $100 million in 2000.[24] This number will grow as more Canadian families acquire computers and become familiar with using the Internet. As the topic of electronic retailing will be covered in detail in Chapter 16, we will briefly mention the strengths of this medium: (1) it is a fully interactive medium, and the audience can be determined by the retailer; (2) once the Web page has been constructed, the costs of maintaining it are very low; (3) the audience selectivity is very high, since it is under the control of the retailer; (4) it is available around the clock; and (5) it allows the audience to make comparisons (which favours the efficient retailer).

On the other hand, the current weaknesses are: (1) the message is limited to text, picture, and sound; (2) there are perceived risks in exchanging information, particularly credit card information; (3) exposure to the message is under the control of the audience; and (4) reach tends to be low. As the technology and its diffusion improves, some of these weaknesses will be lessened.

Out-of-Home Advertising

Retailers are in a unique position to place advertisements near their stores, or along the roads leading to their stores. There are a large variety of **out-of-home media**, with the most important being transit advertising (e.g., buses) and outdoor advertising (e.g., billboards), but there are many other minor ones available at a relatively low cost (e.g., bench advertising).

Transit Advertising

Transit advertising includes signs placed on buses, subway cars, and commuter trains, as well as advertising placed in the terminals, platforms, and stations for such vehicles. Full wrapped buses, where the whole bus is painted with the message, have become popular in the last few years, although they tend to be expensive. Transit advertising has a captive audience in the people using the vehicles. Outdoor transit advertising (also on the outside of the vehicle) is especially effective for certain types of retailers. The vehicles carrying the advertising normally travel through the business area of a community and have a high level of exposure to prospective consumers. Transit advertising is typically a media option only for retailers in large metropolitan areas. Small areas normally do not have public transportation.

Full wrapped buses make a strong statement and reach large audiences in the trading area.

Outdoor Advertising

Outdoor advertising signs are among the oldest form of advertising. Outdoor signs can be found along the roads, at the airports, in malls, and in the downtown areas of major cities. Most retailers have signs outside their business even if they don't use billboards. Outdoor advertising signs have a large number of advantages, one of which is a high exposure rate. People tend to see the same outdoor billboard many times a month because they tend to follow the same traffic patterns each day. The signs are inexpensive but are heavily read by travellers and other customers seeking specific information. The disadvantages are the relatively small amount of information that can be placed on a billboard, the large amount of display space needed, and the competition with other billboards in a community.

Buying Outdoor Advertising Outdoor billboard advertising usually is bought from companies that specialize in leasing sign space to merchants. Outdoor signs come in a variety of sizes, shapes, and locations. The typical billboard size is 3.7 metres by 7.5 metres. Outdoor advertising signs are bought in terms of a set level of GRPs. A hundred GRPs weekly in a market means that advertising space was purchased on enough posters to deliver an *exposure* level equal to 100 percent of the population in an area on the average during a week.

Nonstandard signs are normally those erected by the retailer. No standard size exists for such billboards. And the retailers arrange with each individual landowner for the space they want to lease. They have to be careful not to violate local regulations on the placement and construction of the signs, however. Billboards are becoming increasingly controversial in many communities because of concerns over quality of life and aesthetics.

Other Out-of-Home Media

Other options for retailers include aerial advertising (e.g., balloons and sky writing), bench advertising, elevator advertising, sports advertising (e.g., in hockey arenas), taxicab and truck advertising, and theatre and videoscreen advertising.

Video Tech

We discussed **video technology** in Chapter 2 and are highlighting it again as a reminder of its growing impact on promotion plans. Video involves promoting directly to the consumer by the use of cable TV or video discs. Technological advances in two-way interactive cable are making shop-at-home services more feasible. The primary drawback still is the high cost per purchase. Nevertheless, merchants are looking at the new technologies as ways of expanding their profit centres.[25]

Use of in-store audio and video promotion devices is one of the more rapidly expanding areas of opportunity for retailers. Such examples include the following:

- *Video screens.* In-store TV screens mounted at eye level, which are sometimes linked together to form a video wall for presenting brief brand and price identification messages lasting for 7 to 10 seconds.
- *Audio systems.* Messages can be placed anywhere and typically are activated by motion or body heat. The devices contain a 10- to 20-second recorded selling message calling attention to a product and are typically placed within an aisle.
- *Shopping carts.* Some shopping carts today contain a video message that can be activated by the consumer.
- *In-store kiosks.* Such devices typically are placed next to a product and can operate either on constant play or be activated by a consumer who wants to see and hear a message about the product.[26]

Promotional Products Advertising

Promotional products (formerly called specialty) **advertising** uses gift-giving to customers as the advertising medium. Examples include clothing (caps, T-shirts), fountain pens, calendars, and key chains. The gifts typically contain the name of the firm, company address, and perhaps its logo or slogan. The business endeavors to build goodwill among customers by providing useful items that will remind customers of the firm each time they use them. The promotional items chosen should match the type of merchandise sold by the firm. For example, wallpaper and paint stores often will provide a tape measure. But promotional products advertising is more useful in retaining present customers than in attracting new ones.

Visual Merchandising

Visual merchandising is often viewed as a form of non-media advertising. Good displays inform the consumer about the merchandise offered and help to entertain and delight the consumer in such a way as to differentiate the outlet from competitors. As such, visual merchandising is part of a total store focus for communicating a unified image.

Evaluating the Effectiveness of Media

Media effectiveness is usually measured in terms of (1) cost per thousand and (2) reach and frequency, in order to establish a price/value relationship between media options.

Cost per Thousand (CPM)

The most common method of evaluating the cost effectiveness of several media is the cost per thousand (CPM). The CPM is measured by dividing the cost of an advertisement (of given sizes, e.g., a full page, and options, e.g., four colours) by the number of households or persons reached within the target market. The general formula is:

$$\text{CPM} = \frac{\text{Ad cost}}{\text{Audience or circulation (in thousands)}}$$

The CPM allows comparing several different vehicles (e.g., different newspapers, magazines, radio, or TV stations) with different audiences, by standardizing the rates to the same 1000 readers, viewers, or listeners. However, this calculation does not take into account other considerations such as quality of editorial matter or clutter (both could impact on ad readership).

This formula is useful only for intramedia comparisons, that is, for comparing one newspaper to another, and using it for media planning purposes. Intermedia comparisons of radio and a newspaper are less useful.

Example For example, a 60-second spot in radio station A provides 100,000 impressions (the audience reached by each spot in the schedule) weekly and costs $500. The same size spot in radio station B provides 200,000 impressions weekly and costs $800.

The cost per 1,000 impressions is $5.00 for A and $4.00 for B.

$$\text{CPM (A)} = \frac{\$500}{100} = \$5.00 \qquad \text{CPM (B)} = \frac{\$800}{200} = \$4.00$$

Thus, B is a better buy, in addition to providing a bigger audience.

Reach and Frequency

When comparing advertising programs it is important to select the most effective balance of reach and frequency. Although separate concepts, reach and frequency are closely related, and their product is the GRP (gross rating point) concept introduced earlier:

$$\text{Reach} \times \text{Frequency} = \text{Gross Rating Points}$$

Consider a hypothetical situation as an example: an advertiser who uses magazines for an advertising campaign has two options:

- Buy one insertion in five different magazines.
- Buy five insertions in one magazine.

Assuming that each magazine has a reach of 10, and that both options have the same cost (i.e., magazine budget), both deliver the same level of GRP, i.e.,

50 GRPs (5 times 10 in both cases). However, the first option tries to reach more people by using different magazines, while the second one will reach the same people several times. The first option emphasizes reach, and the second one frequency.

A major cause of failure in advertising programs is insufficient frequency. It is far more effective to reduce the reach of an advertising campaign and add frequency than to reduce frequency and add reach. Unless a product or service is well-known and has no competition, increasing the frequency of the advertising message will increase overall effectiveness.

ADVERTISING: DEVELOPING THE COPY

Developing an effective message is as essential as using the right media, since the message is the one that has to produce results. Good messages get noticed: in surveys of advertising awareness, many ads from retailers score very highly, among them McDonald's, Sears Canada, Mr. Submarine, Canadian Tire, and Provigo. In terms of product categories, among the top ten one finds grocery stores, drug stores, department, furniture, and chain stores.[27]

Creative Strategy and Execution

The creative strategy is developed around the chosen level in the hierarchy of effects model introduced in Figure 13-2, and according to the corresponding type of campaign. Copy can be either rational (awareness or knowledge) or emotional (liking, preference, or conviction). The rational approach focuses essentially on the name of the store, merchandise, and various facts about it. The emotional appeal addresses the psychological benefits that one can obtain by visiting the store or using the product bought there.

Sometimes, a combination of the two possibilities is effective. For example, product benefits could be both rational (economy) and emotional (appearance). *Headlines* in the ad can focus on benefits, promises, or even news to attract attention and/or transmit a message. Retail Highlight 13-2 describes some sample retail campaigns that have won awards in the past, and they illustrate the role of copy in the overall advertising strategy.

The body copy of the advertisement can do many things, including: (1) stating reasons for doing something (buying the product, patronizing the store), (2) making promises or giving testimonials, (3) publicizing the results of performance tests, (4) telling a story, (5) reporting a real or imaginary dialogue, (6) solving a predicament, or (7) amusing the audience.[28] For example, in the ads on page 334, humour can help attract attention, increase awareness of the retailer, and develop some liking. If the need for the product is present, desire can be aroused, and the reader may be convinced to go and visit the store.

Illustrations are also important to convey a message to the audience, such as enhancing the prestige of the store, showing fashionable merchandise, or suggesting uses of the featured product.

Retail Highlight 13-2 Award-Winning Retail Campaigns

Every two years, the best in Canadian advertising in terms of achievement of business results are given the Cassie Awards. The winners of the 1997 Cassies are as follows (and some great retail ads are reproduced below):

- Richmond Savings: The third largest credit union in Canada needed to expand its membership and asset base, but had image problems compared to regular banks. An advertising strategy was developed around the theme: "We are not a bank, we are better." Through print, outdoor, radio and the Internet, the campaign used a fictional bank called the Humungous Bank to appeal to dissatisfied bank customers. In addition, the media provided $300,000 worth of free coverage. The Internet site was one of the hottest sites named by several search engines (www.humungous.com); it used the same humorous approach of the fictitious bank with poor service, high fees, etc., and by clicking on the emergency exit sign, the user is rescued by the Richmond Savings Bank! Advertising a fictional bank provided 25,000 new members, a 50 percent increase, as well as 100 percent growth in asset base! This campaign received the gold award in the service category.
- BMG Music Service: Introducing a new service in Canada, it received a certificate as a most innovative communications program.
- Metropolitan Toronto Zoo: A successful campaign was developed around the white lions exhibit.
- Walt Disney World: The campaign on the theme "Not just a theme park" also received a Cassie certificate.

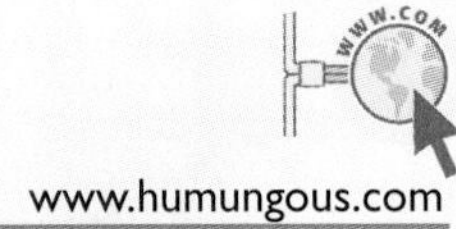

www.humungous.com

Source: "The 1997 Cassie Awards," *Marketing*, October 29, 1997.

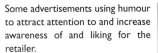

Some advertisements using humour to attract attention to and increase awareness of and liking for the retailer.

Toronto Zoo and BMG, Courtesy *Marketing Magazine*; Humungous Bank, Comstock/Comstock

Major Creative Principles

The following are some major creative principles that can be used when developing effective print advertisements or broadcast commercials.

- *Make each word count and avoid unnecessary words.* Keep sentences short, use action words, and terms the reader will understand, and do not use introductions. It is important to get right to the point of the message.
- *Make your ad easy to recognize.* Give the copy and layout a consistent personality and style. Avoid the cluttered look.
- *Use a simple layout.* The layout should lead the reader's eye easily through the message from the art and headline to the copy and price to the signature (i.e., name and logo of the store).
- *Use dominant illustrations.* Show the featured merchandise in dominant illustrations. Whenever possible, show the product in use.
- *Show the benefit to the reader.* Prospective customers want to know "what's in it for me." But do not try to pack the ad with reasons to buy—give customers one primary reason, then back it up with one or two secondary reasons.
- *Feature the "right" item.* Select an item that is wanted, timely, stocked in depth, and typical of your store. Specify branded merchandise, and take advantage of advertising allowances and cooperative advertising whenever possible.
- *State a price or range of prices.* Don't be afraid to quote high prices. If the price is low, support it with statements that create belief, such as "clearance" or "special purchase."
- *Include store name and address.* Double-check every ad to make sure it contains store name, address, telephone number, and store hours.

The Role of the Ad Agency

The function of an agency is to plan, produce, and measure the effectiveness of advertising. Larger retailers with outlets in several communities are more likely to use an ad agency's service. An agency helps them avoid the complication of having to deal with a variety of media in each community.

Advertising agencies typically earn their incomes from commissions. As an agent for the retailer, the agency will buy space in a medium. The agency then will bill the retailer for 100 percent of the cost and pay the medium, such as a newspaper, 85 percent. The 15 percent is the normal agency commission. Agencies may also take on the accounts of small retailers on a fee basis if the normal commission of 15 percent is too small to make the project worthwhile. Also in situations such as preparing direct mail advertising, the agency may charge a percent of the cost involved.

However, it is important to note that retailers are normally entitled to *retail or local rates,* which are often much lower than *national or general rates,* provided that they are the ones purchasing the space or time from the media (no commission will be paid on retail rates). This often makes it uneconomical for a retailer to use an agency. In addition, retailers have to react very quickly to events in the marketplace, and agencies tend not to provide this service. For these reasons, retailers tend not to use an advertising agency for event advertising; when they use one, it is more likely to be for developing an image campaign.

SALES PROMOTION

Sales promotion has been defined as "marketing activities other than personal selling, advertising, and publicity that stimulate consumer purchasing and dealer effectiveness, such as displays, sales and exhibits, and demonstrations."[29] Perhaps the best way to introduce the varied nature of sales promotion possibilities is to highlight trends in sales promotion activities by retailers.

What Are the Trends in Sales Promotion[30]

Couponing

Although coupon fraud and misredemption are serious problems,[31] couponing continues to be a very popular promotion device to introduce new products, stimulate trial, and increase purchase frequency.

In 1997, 15 billion **coupons** were distributed, 12 billion by retailers as in-ads coupons or in retailer booklets. Of all the coupons distributed, 260 million were redeemed, and the average face value was 80 cents. The redemption rate of coupons is about 4 percent for regular coupons, and 1 percent for retailer-initiated coupons (which have short expiry dates and are only valid at one retailer). There is still a great amount of potential since, on a per capita basis, Canadian consumers received only 15 percent as many coupons as the U.S. consumers, and they redeem only 25 percent as many coupons.[32]

Coupon Distribution Methods The most important methods of coupon distribution are:[33]

- Free-standing newspaper inserts, usually in four colours.
- Cooperative direct mail, distributed directly to households in non-addressed mail, according to selected postal codes.
- Selective direct mail, sent to specific customers.
- In/On pack, produced by manufacturers.
- Newspaper run-of-press, where the coupons are part of the newspaper advertisement.
- In-store coupons, distributed in-store through hand-outs, product demonstrations, at cash registers during checkout (e.g., Catalina coupons), in special retail booklets and calendars, on bulletin boards at the entrance (including electronic boards or kiosks).[34]
- Magazine coupons, usually in four colours, with the editorial support of the magazine, recipes, etc.

Trends in Couponing The following trends can be identified, and one can expect more creative uses to be made in the future:

- In general, more in- and on-pack coupon usage is likely, as is continued use of retailer in-ad coupons (retailer coupons paid by manufacturers), and more combination promotions with other devices—premiums, sweepstakes, and refunds.
- Double coupons: to generate additional sales, and combat cross-border shopping, some retailers such as A&P and Miracle Food Mart have experimented with success with *double coupons:* these retailers double the face value of manufacturers' coupons for brand-name products.[35]
- An increased penetration and development of interactive electronic couponing. Safeway and K mart are experimenting with electronic kiosks. Canadian-developed technology by Qponyx International of Winnipeg allows the store to dispense coupons in 15 to 20 grocery categories, valid only the same day, at this store only. In addition, a seven-second message is played while the coupon selected by the customer is being printed. Other systems are also available in Canada.[36]

More Sampling

Use of **sampling** is increasing, especially to new or nonusers. Quite a few services now provide selective sampling and there are many ways to do so effectively.[37] Retailers prefer saleable samples because they make a profit on them. Retailers don't profit from free samples. Saleable samples are good for manufacturers too because they save distribution costs.

Fewer Cents-Off Bonus Packs

Retailers generally resist these promotion devices because they necessitate additional stock-keeping units. They can also be quite costly to marketers because of the required special labelling and/or packaging. The advantages are that the benefit is passed on to the consumer, and the consumer readily sees the value in them.

More Premiums

Some retailers are lukewarm to **premium** offers. This is especially true when they are used alone, rather than in combination with other promotion devices, such as coupons. In- and on-packs, special containers, and other forms of package-related or in-store premiums are sometimes resisted because of pilferage and handling problems. Nevertheless, consumers like these types of promotions. Retailers prefer premium offers that do not require their involvement but add excitement and impact to a promotion, create consumer interest, and generate increased product movement. The general trends are toward more expensive self-liquidators, free premiums with multiple proofs-of-purchase, and brand logo premiums that are product or advertising-related.

More Selective Point-of-Purchase Material

Typical **point-of-purchase materials** include end-of-aisle and other in-store merchandising and display materials. Retailers like and want p-o-p materials, but generally feel that the material provided by manufacturers does not meet their needs. Retailers are highly selective in their use of p-o-p materials and prefer displays that: merchandise an exciting and interesting promotion theme, support other promotion devices, adapt to store-wide promotions on a chain-wide and individual store basis, harmonize with the store environment, sell related products, provide a quality appearance, install easily, are permanent or semi-permanent, and guarantee sales success. Some retailers develop and produce displays in accordance with the manufacturer's budget and guidelines. Some retailers are renting floor space to manufacturers.

More Refunds/Rebates

These devices, similar in intent and nature, continue to grow in popularity and use. Refunds and **consumer rebates** are usually handled as mail-ins with proofs-of-purchase. They are very effective promotion tools and will be used in more creative ways. Increasingly popular are rebates as charitable donations that show social concern, and higher price refunds for multiple products.

Fewer Contests and More Sweepstakes

Sweepstakes are generally more popular than regular contests. However, the Instant Win contests are growing in use and importance. Retailers like both sweepstakes and instant wins, especially when they bring traffic into the store to look at product packages and obtain entry blanks.

More Mailers and Circulars

These promotion devices have been the biggest gainers in sales promotion over the past five years. Indeed, their share of sales promotion dollars has increased from one-third to almost one-half of the total dollars during this period, with the growth coming at the expense of newspapers.

More Loyalty Programs

A loyalty program is one that encourages the customer to keep coming back to the store to accumulate stamps or points. An example of loyalty programs is Zellers' Club Z, but even a small retailer can develop an inexpensive card that would provide free items after a certain number of purchases. Another example for a small retailer is Odyssey Books and its discount stores Empire Books. Customers, for example, earn "Empire dollars," which they can use for their future purchases, and at Odyssey, they earn discount stamps on special customer cards; when the cards are complete, they can enter a monthly draw for a $25 gift certificate.[38]

Cooperative Promotions

Manufacturers also offer co-op funds for promotions in the same way they often offer advertising co-op dollars. Suppliers often advertise directly to retailers informing them about promotion allowances available for a product line. Suppliers then seek a commitment from the retailers for an increased volume of purchases, because of the accelerated promotional program for the product line.

MEASURING THE RESULTS OF ADVERTISING AND SALES PROMOTIONS

Sales response to ads can be checked daily during the ad period. The effects of image ads are harder to measure. It is not always possible to tie a purchase to image advertising. However, the message may stay in the minds of people who have heard it. Sooner or later, it may help trigger a purchase. Research is needed to measure the success of image.

Tests for Immediate Response Ads[39]

In weighing the results of the immediate response to advertisements, a number of measurements have been used in the past.

Coupons Redeemed

Usually, coupons represent sales of a product. Where coupons represent requests for additional information or contact with a salesperson, management may ask if enough leads were obtained to pay for the ad. If the coupon is dated, it is possible to determine the number of returns for the first, second, and third weeks. It is possible to design a low-cost couponing experiment to determine the profitability of retailer couponing.

Phone or Letter Inquiries

A "hidden offer" can cause people to call or write. For example, included in the middle of an ad is a statement that on request the product or additional information will be supplied. Results should be checked over periods of one week through 6 months or 12 months, because this type of ad may have considerable carry-over effect.

Testing Advertising Executions

Retailers can prepare two ad executions (different in some way that they would like to test) and run them during the same period. Management can identify the ads by the message or with a coded coupon so they can tell them apart. They can ask customers to bring in the coupon or to use a special phrase. Broadcast ads can be run at different times or on different stations on the same day with varying "discount phrases." Some consumer magazines can provide a "**split run**"—that is, to print "ad A" in part of its press run and "ad B" in the rest of the run. The responses to each can then be counted.

Sales Made of a Targeted Item

If the ad is on a bargain or limited-time offer, retailers can consider that sales at the end of one week, two weeks, three weeks, and four weeks came from the ad. They may need to make a judgment as to how many sales came from in-store display and personal selling.

Store Traffic

An important function of advertising is to build store traffic. Store traffic also results in purchases of items that are not advertised. Pilot studies show, for example, that many customers who were brought to the store by an ad for a blouse also bought a handbag. Some bought the bag in addition to the blouse, while others bought it instead of the blouse.

Testing the Effectiveness of the Advertising Campaign

When advertising is spread over a selling season or several seasons, part of the measurement job of campaign effectiveness is keeping records. Retailers' records of ads and sales for an extended time should be compared.

An easy way to set up a file is by marking the date of the run on tear sheets of newspaper ads (many radio stations now provide "radio tear sheets," too), keeping log reports of radio and television ads, and keeping copies of direct mail ads. The file may be broken down into monthly, quarterly, or semiannual blocks. By recording the sales of the advertised items on each ad or log, management can make comparisons.

In institutional (image-building) advertising, individual ads are building blocks of the campaign, so to speak. Together they make up the advertising campaign over a selling season. A problem is trying to measure the effects of the ads, since they are designed to keep the name of the store before the buying public and to position the outlet in a way that harmonizes with overall marketing strategy. In contrast to institutional advertising, product advertising is designed to cover a short period of time and increase sales.

One approach to testing is making the comparisons on a weekly basis. If a retailer runs an ad each week, management can compare the first week's sales with sales for the same week a year ago. At the end of the second week, managers can compare sales with those of the end of the first week, as well as year-ago figures, and so forth. Of course, the retailer should try to take into account other factors that may have influenced the sales, such as price reductions, advertising by competitors, or other environmental changes (e.g., a heat wave may boost the sales of fans).

PUBLICITY AND PUBLIC RELATIONS

Publicity has been defined as "any nonpersonal stimulation of demand for a product, service, or business unit by planting commercially significant news about it in a published medium or obtaining favourable presentation of it upon radio, television, or stage that is not paid for by the sponsor."[40] Publicity and public relations are known by various names. Regardless, such activities normally fit into three categories: (1) merchandising, (2) entertainment, and (3) education or community service.

Merchandising Events

Special events create publicity. Often they may be featured in the editorial section of a newspaper, may result in an interview on a talk show, or generate other free promotion. Merchandising events require careful coordination between merchandising, advertising, and publicity. Such events can include fashion shows, bridal fairs, cooking demonstrations, celebrity authors, cartoon characters, or sports heros. They can include exhibits of art, costumes, antiques, or rarities. Merchandising events may also be staged in conjunction with designers such as Lise Watier or sports figures such as Wayne Gretzky.

Entertainment

Retailers seek to build goodwill, store image, and name awareness through entertainment programs. For example, several retailers participate in such events as the Quebec City Winter Carnival, the Calgary Stampede, or Canada Day festivities across the country. The results from such activities are hard to measure. Free publicity from such events can be worth hundreds of thousands of dollars.

Education or Community Service

Retailers sometimes sponsor education or community service activities. For example, Sears Canada is extensively involved in many community activities, including support for United Way/Centraide and childhood literacy campaigns. Such activities are provided free of charge during lunch hours. Other retailers offer fashion advice, career counselling, and even cooking courses, all on the store premises. For example, Elte Carpets of Toronto runs the "University of Fuzzy Side Up," a series of Saturday-morning courses on broadloom and rugs held at its showroom. About 20 people attend each week, learning about different kinds of carpets and how they are installed.[41]

ADVERTISING REGULATION AND ETHICS

The retailer must be more and more concerned with the effects of consumer protection regulations, both at the federal and provincial levels (see also Chapter 2).

At the federal level, advertising is regulated by a number of agencies, including the CRTC, Health and Welfare Canada, and Consumer and Corporate Affairs. Among the regulations of the greatest importance to retailers are those concerning the use of false or misleading advertising resulting in "bait and switch" practices, forbidden by the Competition Act. There are also a number of codes, such as the Canadian Code of Advertising Standards. The media can also exercise judgment in refusing to carry an advertisement that they deem misleading, sexist, or in bad taste.

At the provincial level, retailers must contend with bureaus of consumers affairs, the Better Business Bureaus, and the small claims court.

CHAPTER HIGHLIGHTS

- Promotion should be viewed as a sales-building investment and not simply as an element of business expense. When promotion is executed correctly, it can be an important factor in the future growth of a business.
- Promotion is communication from the retailer to the consumer in an effort to achieve a profitable sales level. Promotion includes mass media advertising, coupons, trading stamps, premium offers, point-of-purchase displays, and publicity.
- Promotion is a key element of the marketing mix. All promotion should be in harmony with pricing, product lines, and store-location decisions (place). Otherwise a poor image for the firm can result.
- Developing promotion plans begins with the goals of the firm. Retailers must decide on who to reach, the message to get across, the number of messages to reach the audience, and the means for reaching the audience.
- After defining the goals, retailers must carefully establish their advertising budget. Typical methods include the percentage-of-sales, the unit-of-sales, and the objective-and-task methods. Such a budget must also be carefully allocated, and cooperative advertising programs should be used to stretch the impact of the budget on sales.
- Numerous options exist for retail advertising, and each medium has its strengths and weaknesses, which must be studied carefully before a choice is made. Media choices include direct mail, magazines, billboards, transit ads, newspapers, radio, television, and the Internet. The most commonly used media are newspapers, radio, direct mail and distribution, and out-of-home media. Large retail chains also use television and magazines. Nonmedia advertising includes point-of-purchase displays and specialty advertising.
- Media effectiveness is normally measured in terms of cost per thousand and reach and frequency. Results tests for immediate response ads can be in terms of coupons redeemed, requests by phone or letter referring to the ad, sales made of a particular item, or an analysis of store traffic.
- Advertising copy can be either rational or emotional. The rational approach focuses on the merchandise, while an emotional appeal focuses on the psychological benefits obtained from using the product. Headlines in an ad can focus on benefits, promises, or news.
- Some retailers use an advertising agency. The function of an agency is to plan, produce, and measure the effectiveness of advertising. Agencies earn their commissions on advertisements placed for the retailers. However, retailers qualify for very advantageous retail rates (non-commissionable), if they buy directly from the media.
- Retail sales promotions include such activities as couponing, product sampling, cents-off bonus packs, premiums, point-of-purchase materials, refunds or rebates, contests and sweepstakes, and trade-in allowances.
- Publicity includes media exposure that is not paid for by the sponsor. Such activities normally fit into three categories: merchandising, entertainment, and education or community service.

KEY TERMS

- AIDA model 312
- awareness 312
- *Canadian Advertising Rates & Data (CARD)* 319
- Canadian newspaper unit (CNU) 324
- catalogues 327
- community newspapers 325
- consumer rebate 338
- cooperative advertising 317
- cost per thousand (CPM) 321
- coupons 336
- direct promotion 327
- event advertising 311
- frequency 321
- general rate 324
- gross rating point (GRP) 324
- hierarchy of effects model 312
- image campaign 311
- institutional advertising 311
- message 310
- modular agate line (MAL) 324
- national rates 319
- objective-and-task method 315
- out-of-home advertising 329
- percentage-of-sales method 313
- point-of-purchase material 337
- premiums 337
- prime time advertising 321
- promotion 308
- promotion plan 311
- promotional products advertising 331
- publicity 340
- reach 321
- retail (or local) rates 319
- sales promotion 336
- sampling 337
- selectivity 321
- share 324
- shoppers 325
- source 310
- split runs 339
- spot advertising 321
- supplements 324
- unit-of-sales method 315
- video tech 331

DISCUSSION QUESTIONS

1. Is it possible to increase advertising expenses as a percentage of sales, yet increase the profitability of the firm?
2. Comment on the following statement: "The only goal of advertising is to increase sales and profitability."
3. Discuss the following approaches to establishing an advertising budget (be sure to include in your discussion the advantages and disadvantages of each): the percentage-of-sales method; the unit-of-sales method; and the objective-and-task method.
4. What are the reasons a retailer should consider using a multimedia mix?
5. Evaluate the following media in terms of their strengths and weaknesses: billboards, radio, television, newspapers, transit advertising, Internet, and magazines.
6. Why should a retailer consider the use of co-op advertising funds?
7. What are the various ways by which retailers can measure advertising results?
8. Comment on the use of the hierarchy of effects models for determining advertising objectives, the type of campaign to use, and the creative strategy to select. Give some examples with retail ads from your local newspaper.

APPLICATION EXERCISES

1. Imagine you work for the promotion division of a department store and have been told that you are to prepare a campaign for a new product. Select your own "new product." Plan the campaign, select the media, and prepare the message.
2. Make contacts with dealers in a specific product line (e.g., electronics), which have definite differences in product image, price, quality, and so on. Through interviews with the store managers, attempt to determine the allocation of the advertising (promotional) budget among the various media. Compare and contrast among the groups. If actual dollars of promotional expenditures are not available, then utilize percentage allocations. Additionally collect national and local ads for the same dealers/brands and evaluate the differences and similarities noted.
3. Select several automobile dealerships that seem to project differing public images. Interview management of each to determine their particular image perceptions of themselves and perhaps of their competition. Prepare a portfolio of ads of each dealership and also of the national ads of that same dealership's make of auto. Compare the images that seem to be projected by the local versus the national promotions. Attempt to reach certain strategy conclusions from your investigation.

SUGGESTED CASES

6. Clean Windows, Inc.
7. Omer DeSerres: Artists' Supplies and Computers

CHAPTER 14

CUSTOMER SERVICE

CHAPTER OBJECTIVES

After reading this chapter you should be able to:

1. Understand the meaning of "customer service" versus "customer focused."
2. Define the meaning of customer service and reasons for the gap that often exists between customer expectations and perceptions.
3. Understand the strategic role of customer support services in the retailer's overall marketing plan.
4. Describe the various types of retail credit.
5. List the various types of retail credit cards.
6. Understand the laws affecting customer support services.
7. Describe customer support activities such as shopper services, educational programs, delivery, and extended hours.

This is a true story of a customer who had just bought a new suit at Harry Rosen in Toronto especially for an important meeting and then left for the airport, leaving behind the suit he had bought in the store. Recognizing the problem, employees at Harry Rosen were able to pull out the information about the customer from its computerized database, then phone the Winnipeg store, have the store employees find the same suit, make the same alterations as in the Toronto store, and take the suit to the airport. When the customer landed in Winnipeg he was given an identical suit to the one he had left by mistake in Toronto.

What this story also deals with is what Hubert Saint-Onge, the head of the CIBC leadership centre, calls "human capital," defined as the capabilities of a company's employees to provide solutions for customers, as in the example of Harry Rosen. Human capital is different from "customer capital," the depth, breadth and loyalty of the company's franchise, but high human capital helps increase customer capital. According to Hubert Saint-Onge, "if an employee's attitude is low—if she or he does not feel ownership of the job—the customer knows that right away, and if employees are well treated by the company, this is reflected in excellent customer service."[1]

Services offer retailers the opportunity to differentiate themselves from the competition. Services are expensive, however, and many retailers do not agree on what services should be offered. Some are even reducing the number of services they offer.

Customer support services include such functions as credit, layaway, delivery, personal shopping programs, and a variety of other activities designed to attract new customers and to strengthen relationships with existing ones. Customer support services are a primary way in which retailers can differentiate their outlets from those of competitors. Many retail outlets offer essentially the same merchandise at the same price with similar merchandising programs. Services provide the opportunity to create a unique image in the minds of consumers. Retailers probably cannot eliminate all basic services if they want to stay in business. Such services include credit, repair, warranty service, and others (depending on the merchandise sold). No service should be offered, however, unless it contributes directly or indirectly to profit.

A high-fashion store such as Holt Renfrew that appeals to the upper-income shopper will usually offer more services than a discount store. Also, two different stores may offer wide variations in the same service. For example, a discount store may accept a bank credit card as the only means of payment other than cash, but a department store may also accept the store's credit card, a travel and entertainment card such as American Express, or offer a customer charge plan. Department stores may deliver large items such as furniture free of charge, whereas a warehouse furniture store such as Leon's may charge extra for delivery.

A full-service specialty outlet such as Parachute stores offers a full array of customer services, often through special promotions. In contrast, a discount outlet such as Zellers Plus may offer identical merchandise, but without supporting services, at reduced prices. The use of services is thus part of the positioning strategy by merchants in targeting key market segments, as discussed in Chapter 4.

UNDERSTANDING CUSTOMER SERVICE EXPECTATIONS

The difference between customer service expectations and experiences, if any, results in a customer expectations gap, as shown in Figure 14-1. The size of the gap depends on the difference between expectations and experiences.[2] Harry Rosen's customers have high expectations and experience excellent service. Therefore, no service gap exists. Customer assessments of retailer response depend on their perceptions—which may differ from reality. Customer service expectations are different during the busy Christmas season, for example, than during the slower times of the year. Expectations may also vary by customer.

Management can most effectively address the issue of customer support services by focusing on both customers and processes, which, in turn, translates into focusing on the outcome. Focusing on the customer means listening to his or her ideas about what constitutes satisfactory service. Focusing on the process means understanding the things necessary to meet customer expectations such as length of time waiting in line, personnel friendliness, and store cleanliness. Focusing on the outcome directs attention to the reliability of the service delivered such as accuracy in repair, delivery when promised, and so forth.

Nurturing the Customer-Focused Culture[3]

The only constant in retailing is change—in fashion, distribution channels, organization, buying patterns, customer wants and lifestyles, and in retail format. Because of these constant changes, some retailers have lost sight of their primary mission, satisfying the customer. Two of the most misunderstood words today are *customer service.* Do they refer to an attitude, a function, or a result.

Figure 14-1 Customer Service Evaluation Model

Consumer expectations	Actual consumer experience: Poor	Actual consumer experience: Excellent
Low	No gap Confirmation of low expectations 1	Large gap Pleasant surprise 2
High	Large gap Unpleasant surprise 3	No gap Confirmation of high expectations 4

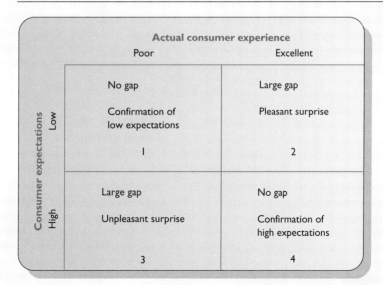

Source: Reproduced with permission from Barry Berman, "Customer Service Strategy," *The Retailing Strategist*, no. 2, 1991, p. 10.

With increased competition, many retailers are placing greater emphasis on customer service to differentiate themselves from the competitive pack. The traditional approach to customer service, however, is not broad enough to accomplish this objective or to satisfy the needs of today's customer. To find new areas of opportunity, retailers must go beyond customer service to a customer-focused culture.

Traditional Approach

Traditional customer service program objectives generally fall into four categories:

- *Integrity*—warranties, product quality, return and exchange policies.
- *Convenience and shopping ease*—store layout, convenient parking, store hours, mail- and phone-order service, etc.
- *A pleasant shopping environment*—valet parking services, decor and lighting, fitting-room privacy, music, credit account confidentiality.
- *Personal shopping services*—knowledgeable sales personnel, merchandise availability, informative product signing.

The traditional customer service approaches include a variety of organizational structures and policies aimed at making the customer "happy," as illustrated in Retail Highlight 14-1.

Organizations range from a large central customer service staff, to a service/return desk at each store, to an authorized manager at each individual point-of-sale location in department and specialty stores. Policies range from very lenient to a policy of no returns without a sales cheque to no returns at all.

Retail Highlight 14-1 Providing Good Customer Service Pays Off

Debbie Blyth had complained to head office that when she went to the Harry Rosen menswear store in Toronto, carrying her new baby, she had asked a salesman for help on selecting a shirt for her husband and he uncaringly pointed her to the display. Offended she left the store vowing never to return. Fifteen minutes after she made the call, Mr. Harry Rosen himself called Debbie. He apologized for the poor service, assured her that the manager of the store would hear from him, and assured her that this would never happen again. Impressed by the whole event, she felt better about the store. By a simple phone call, showing he cared about his customers, he made her a loyal customer.

Fortunately, there are not too many complaints about service, but for each one Harry Rosen gives his undivided attention. When he takes a customer call, "sometimes I get this silence on the other end," and the caller says "I didn't really expect to speak to you." Rosen's answer is: "I don't live in some ivory tower, I work in our stores and our customers are our greatest concern." No wonder this retailer grew to a chain grossing $135 million a year.

Source: C. Cornell, "There is Something about Harry," *Profit*, April 1999, pp. 44–50.

Customer Service

When the term **customer service** is used, it usually refers to cashing cheques, handling bill adjustment transactions, or managing complaints. Some stores handle complaints at the store level when they arise and provide no feedback to management on complaint types, volumes, and frequency. Some companies have no clearly defined responsibility for pinpointing customer service, and resolve complaints slowly. Other stores have elaborate and well-defined systems for handling complaints, including procedure manuals, time standards for resolution, performance audits, and management reporting of complaints by type, store, work centre, and merchandise area. But the customer service program is always receptive, based on some function that is not meeting the customer's expectations.

Customer Expectations

Retailers play a role in the development of customer expectations through advertising, store operations, and everyday marketing. When there are inconsistencies between what retailers say and do and what the customer expects, there is a gap, as indicated in Figure 14-1. At best, the result is customer confusion and, at worst, the loss of a customer. The situation is further complicated by the fact that customer expectations vary, not only by type of store, but also by major category of merchandise within a given store type. To make customer service proactive, retailers need to anticipate customer expectations and take action to meet or exceed them.

One simple way to identify these expectations is a customer expectation matrix by broad merchandise category. This approach identifies customer expectations of fashion, value, service, and the store facility for several types of retail store categories. It assigns a numerical value to each category as perceived by a customer. The higher the cumulative total, the higher the expectation.

A customer-focused culture means knowing customer concerns and meeting customer expectations.

Courtesy Hudson's Bay Company—Corporate Collection

Confusing the Customer

One of the most common ways retailers confuse the customer is by doing one thing and saying another, thus, creating large gaps. The following are examples of such practices:

- *Discontinuing services* such as delivery, cheque cashing, wrapping for mailing, alterations, and various repair services without offering the customer an alternative.
- Establishing *fees for support services* that are not in line with competition or that are disproportionately high for that particular service.
- Preaching customer service, but *posting restrictive negative signs* throughout the store (for example, "no cheque cashing").
- *Aisles that are narrow or cluttered with merchandise:* no natural grouping of merchandise categories, entering and exiting traffic collides, or high interior fixtures restrict visibility.
- *Department and merchandise signing is inadequate:* lack of up-to-date store directories, inadequate department signing, inadequate product information signing, using sales sign headers on nonsale merchandise, not highlighting advertised merchandise.
- *Inadequate merchandise or shelf-marking:* no price on merchandise or shelves, size information difficult to find, no standard location for merchandise tickets.
- *Advertising lacks integrity:* fictitious or overstated comparative regular prices, advertising limited quantity merchandise without a disclaimer, unstated restrictions that apply to a special-price ad.
- Merchandise is out of stock and *the customer is not helped* by calling a different store to fill the order; providing similar merchandise at the same price (even if a markdown is involved).[4]

The Customer-Focused Culture

A **customer-focused culture** is one that primarily focuses on customer concerns. Some retailers with already strong reputations for customer service are reluctant to reveal their secrets to success. Other retailers may try to remedy their customer service problems by copying their competitors, erroneously believing that they will then have joined a customer-focused culture.

They miss the point. A combination of many positive programs produces positive results, not a limited mix of them. For example:

- Knowing the particular customer of the store.
- Planning an integrated approach to customer acquisition and service.
- Developing a clear statement on customer focus that is commonly shared and committed to.
- Hiring knowledgeable, consistent, motivated employees.
- Using customer information in an effective manner.
- Monitoring and measuring the results of all the combined efforts.

As mentioned, the examples provided in the introduction to this chapter clearly reflect a customer-focused culture.

Customer Definition and Knowledge

The most critical starting point is a precise definition and in-depth knowledge of the customer base. A retailer must use both primary and secondary research on demographics, psychographics, media preferences, and purchasing. Primary research derives its information directly from potential customers, while secondary research derives its information from third parties. For obtaining research material, retailers have a variety of sources to choose from. However, a retailer's own customer information base can provide useful information if it is properly coded. The closer this information can be fine-tuned to the customer base of a given store, the better the results.[5]

A Planned Integrated Approach

A well-planned approach to customer service includes the integration of the strategies used to attract customers, serve customers, and keep customers. Strategies to attract customers generally fall into the categories of *fashion* (newness, uniqueness, broad assortments), *value* (product/service quality, convenience, price), and *dominance* (assortment, effective presentation, strong in-stock position).

Strategies to serve customers, that is, high-quality customer services include:

- Qualified sales personnel in quantity.
- In-stock position.
- Integrity—"We do what we say we will do."
- Consistent, timely handling of customer complaints.
- Support services including gift wrap, delivery, repairs, credit services, child care, package checking and consolidation.
- Clean, easy access and exit, easy flow, pleasant facilities.
- Kiosk and free-standing product information and other placement terminals.

There are many programs that when properly timed and implemented help to keep the customers you already have. One example is to make it easier for customers to shop and, more importantly, to purchase. Management might extend store hours (when it is legally possible); add mail- and phone-order services; develop bridal, pregnancy, and baby registry programs; or add various financial services. All of these conveniences will make established customers happy to return to the store; they will be able to take care of many chores in the same place at the same time.

Another way to keep them coming back is to develop programs that build self-esteem in both customers and employees. Incentive programs can be successful as can programs designed to enhance personal appearance via cosmetics. Customers will feel good when they leave the store, and employees will feel good for having satisfied the customers.

Basically, the way to retain customers is to be creative and anticipate as many of their needs as possible. Retail Highlight 14-2 indicates that a customer-focused culture can also thrive in a warehouse-type operation.

Retail Highlight 14-2 Big Does Not Have to Mean Poor Customer Focus

For women who like wearing jeans, shopping for a pair is very frustrating, since the ready-made jeans rarely fit: they may be too long (short) in the rise, too big (small) in the waist, and too long (short) in the legs. A large company like Levi Strauss cannot mass produce and distribute the huge variety of sizes to satisfy all these varied combinations.

Advances in technology have helped Levi Strauss answer this call for help. First, go to the Levi's Only Store, like the one in Mississauga, Ontario, and a fit consultant will take four key measurements: waist, hip, inseam and rise. By entering these measurements into a computer, it suggested one of 478 prototype pairs available in the store (the system is programmed for 4,200 combinations of measurements). The customer can then try one of the suggested prototypes, and the fit consultant may finalize the measurements, and offer additional options such as slim leg or boot cut, and stone-washed blue, stone-bleached blue, or white. The final act is to send all the measurements through phone lines to the Levi Strauss plant in Stoney Creek. They are first cut and sewn according to the customer's measurements, then sent to Brantford for finishing and labelling, then to the store in Mississauga, for example, within 21 days of receiving the measurements. The custom-made perfectly-fitting jeans are now ready to be picked up, or they can be delivered (for a small extra charge).

Source: Miles Socha, "Jeans that fit," *The Kitchener Record*, May 11, 1995, p. E1.

Commitment and Communication

Underlying all of these strategies is the key factor that initiates and nurtures a customer-focused culture—a statement of customer focus. That will produce the drive, incentive, and awareness and must include:

- Top management commitment.
- Clear organizational goals.
- Specifically assigned responsibilities to each area.
- A focal point for questions and problems.
- Ongoing communication and positive examples.

Once a clear "customer-focus" statement has been developed containing all of these elements, all participants will have a game plan by which to achieve the goals. For example, Elte Carpets of Toronto has a clear customer focus of staff availability to customer questions on carpets: for that goal, it set up a 24-hour hotline service that responds to customers' questions within six hours; customers may request the salesperson's home numbers written on their receipt for future queries; it also set up a shop-at-home service, staffed by two sales representatives who answer customer queries by phone, then take carpet-sample books (and sometimes full rugs) to their homes. Customers can make a selection, or ask them to return with more samples, or come into the store to look at full rugs.[6]

Customized Targeted Marketing

Another important key to developing a customer-focused culture is to effectively use marketing information. Business strategies are market driven—not product driven. Thus, one current approach toward successful marketing is to serve the needs of the customers by offering services that enhance their daily lives. The objective here is to design a shopping experience for each customer type, while offering a personal approach to the sale and handling of each individual customer. Individuality and personal preference are the hallmark of today's consumer.

The growth of the "niche" catalogues and other nonstore approaches tells us that customers welcome this type of marketing.[7] Targeted direct mail is a growing medium capitalizing on some important lifestyle trends; for example, one-stop shopping is becoming more and more desirable because consumers have far less leisure time; home delivery during off hours has become an important consideration. Chapter 15 will provide more detail about this trend to nonstore retailing.

Analysis for Action

There is a lot of consumer information available from both inside and outside the company. It is easier and less costly to sell to current customers than it is to attract new ones. With this in mind, there are several things that need to be accomplished in order to improve the use of customer information:

- Focusing on customer needs, not on merchandise department's needs.
- Developing a list of merchandise classifications that customers are not buying.
- Cross-analyzing lists to use by merchandise type.
- Merging and updating lists with external lists.
- Determining where and how a given customer buys each product. (Department stores tend to approach all products the same way. One solution is to develop stores comprised of privately owned shops.)

Anticipation—The Next Level

With improvements in the content and administration of customer databases, the next opportunity to develop a competitive edge in customer service is to anticipate what the customer wants. To successfully accomplish this goal, one must have a preplanned action based on information in the company's files. Here are some promotional ideas:

- If a customer books a vacation through the store's travel service, send a promotional package including information on camera and film, camcorder and videotape, photo finishing, luggage and accessories, etc.
- When a customer buys a carpet, automatically send information on carpet cleaning, drapery services, decorating services, etc.

Using files in this manner allows management to anticipate other related customer needs. This is where proper use of the computer can actually personalize the relationship with customers and offer additional sales opportunities.

Organizing for the Customer

Management must have a focal point by which to gather, maintain, analyze, interpret, market, and measure the use of customer service information within the company. Functions include:

- Who buys what and where?
- Share of market surveys.
- Consumer shopping panels.
- Analysis of what current customers are buying elsewhere.
- Customer lists consolidation, development, administration, and potential communication.
- Employee feedback.
- Sales-results analyses including test mailings and promotions.

STRATEGIC DIMENSIONS OF SERVICES

Given the preceding framework, services can now be analyzed on two critical dimensions—value to customers and cost. Four categories of services emerge from such an analysis: support services, disappointers, basics, and patronage builders.

Support Services

Support services directly support the sale of the retailer's merchandise. They have high value to consumers but also a high cost to the retailer. Such services include home delivery, child care, gift wrapping and personalized shopper services. Retail Highlight 14-3 provides some examples of support services.

Retail Highlight 14-3 Examples of Excellent Support Services

Helping adults and children with special needs shop

- McDonald's introduced braille and picture menus, emphasizing its commitment to serving the more than 3 million Canadians with vision, speech, or hearing impairments.
- Toys "Я" Us is distributing 175,000 copies of a 16-page brochure entitled, *Toy Guide for Differently-Abled Kids!,* featuring 50 toys assessed as helping disabled children. The guide is targeted to the parents of disabled children and is distributed at the 56 Canadian locations of Toys "Я" Us, and through agencies such as Easter Seals Canada, the Canadian Institute for the Blind, and the Canadian Down Syndrome Society.

Personalized services

Harry Rosen's 24 stores across Canada are all linked by computer, with a database of their customers that allows salespeople to know what a particular customer has bought in the past, and to assist him in selecting the proper sizes, fit, and items (to avoid duplications). This data is also used to improve the merchandise mix, so that the right items are always in stock. See how it was used in the example in the introduction to this chapter.

Source: "Face to Face: A Look at McDonald's Customer Satisfaction," *First Quarter 1992 McDonald's Shareholders Newsletter*, James Pollock, "Toys 'Я' Us reaches out to differently-abled kids," *Marketing*, October 16, 1995, p. 2; C. Cornell, "There is Something about Harry," *Profit*, April 1999, pp. 44–50.

Disappointers

Disappointers include lay-away and parcel pick-up. These services require high labour effort but return little value to the customer. They are candidates for elimination from the services offered by some retailers. An alternative possibility is to restructure them in such a way as to reduce their cost and increase their value to customers.

Basic Services

Customers take some **(basic) services** for granted. An example is free parking. Retailers often provide such services without giving much thought to their cost content, particularly if they are a competitive necessity.

Patronage Builders

Patronage builders are the services that receive the most strategic attention from retailers. They include such services as birthday reminders and gift certificates. The services have high consumer value and can be provided at nominal cost. As such, they provide the opportunity to increase the store's customer base, especially if competitors are unable to provide comparable service at the same price. Computers have allowed retailers to shift some services from the high-value/high-cost category to one of high consumer value but low cost. Computerized bridal registries, for example, can be accessed from multiple store locations and purchases can be entered on virtually a real-time basis today.

Management may want to charge for support services, eliminate disappointers, and use patronage builders as a way to expand the customer base. Regardless, management needs to periodically re-evaluate services and make sure that patronage builders do not drift into the support services category.

Services Audit

A services audit can help management evaluate the firm's services offerings relative to competition and on the basis of value to customers, as discussed above. The end result likely will be a more customer-driven services program. Identifying what services consumers really value is no simple task, partly because consumers may have difficulty articulating their preferences. Additionally, customers often form opinions about the quality and quantity of services by using competitors as a reference point.[8]

Effective implementation of the services program is critical after the completion of the audit. Services response systems should be standardized whenever possible and a pricing policy should be established in those situations where management decides to charge for various services.[9]

RETAIL CREDIT

Understandably, credit in one form or another is one of the most basic customer support services many retailers can offer. *Consumer credit* can be defined

Table 14-1 Advantages and Disadvantages of Retail Credit

Option	Advantages	Disadvantages
Maintaining in-house credit	Builds strong identification with customer. Retains customer loyalty. Facilitates customer purchase decision. When outside agency purchases credit contract, bad debt risk is transferred. Special consumers may be targeted with credit plan.	Bad debt may be incurred. Must staff and equip credit department. Clerical work involved with transaction. When credit contract is sold to outside agency, retail firm loses a percentage of credit contract.
Accepting bank cards	Attracts more diverse clientele. Outside agency may accept responsibility for collection of bad debts. Reduces pressure on sales personnel to grant credit. Loss due to bad debts accepted by outside agency. Credit offered to customers who otherwise would not qualify. Steady cash flow can be maintained. Broadens customer base. Supplements retailer's credit options.	Fees paid to third party. Clerical work involved with transaction. With large purchases liability for nonpayment may rest with retail outlet if proper authorization, signature, or both are not obtained. Depersonalizes relationship between firm and customer.
Accepting travel and entertainment cards	Attracts more diverse clientele. Cardholders are usually more affluent customers. Broadens customer base. Supplements existing credit options. Responsibility for processing applications, credit authorization, and collection rests with outside agency.	Fee charged to firm for using card. Clerical work involved with transaction. Proper authorization and/or signatures must be secured from cardholder (firm may be liable for debt if not). Depersonalizes customer/firm relationship. Types of purchases may be restricted.
Buying a private-label credit system	Bank handles details of processing, promotion of plan, credit authorization, and collections. Identity of third party is hidden because name of retail firm is on card. Customer loyalty is retained. Strong identity with retail firm is built. No additional fee beyond up-front payment to sponsoring bank.	Up-front fee paid by firm to sponsoring bank.

as sums that are borrowed, or financial obligations incurred, for a relatively short period of time. Historically, retailers have used a number of forms of retail credit to encourage patronage and purchases in their premises. The advantages and disadvantages of the various types of retail credit systems are shown in Table 14-1.

Credit is expensive, and write-offs are very costly. However, well-managed, large-scale credit operations can be very profitable. Most retailers believe that granting credit is necessary. Consumers apparently feel the same way since they often shop only in stores where credit cards are honoured.

Types of Credit

A retailer has two choices in offering credit: (1) in-house credit or (2) third-party credit.

In-House Credit

As shown in Figure 14-2, management has six choices in offering store credit: (1) instalment payments, (2) open-charge credit, (3) revolving credit, (4) deferred billing payment, (5) layaway, and (6) store-issued credit card.

Instalment credit (a monthly payment account) means that a customer pays for a product in equal monthly instalments, including interest. Automobiles and major appliances are often paid for in this way.

Open-charge credit means that the customer must pay the bill in full when it is due, usually in 30 days. Credit limits are set that the customer cannot exceed; also, part payments on the account are not allowed.

Revolving credit means that a customer charges items during a month and is billed at the end of that month on the basis of the outstanding balance. Such

Figure 14-2 Types of In-House Credit

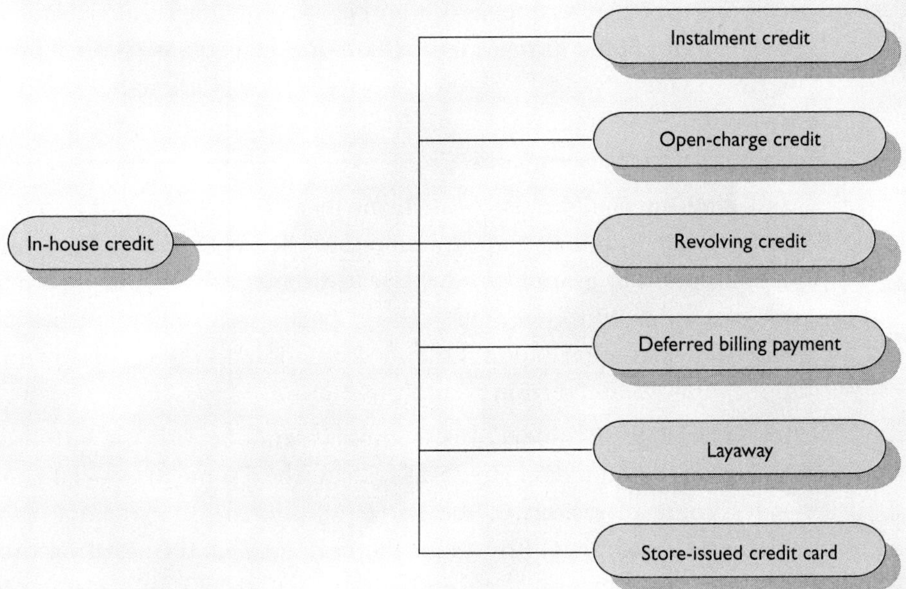

a plan allows the customer to purchase several items without having a separate contract for each purchase.

A business can also offer **deferred billing credit**. Deferred billing occurs when a retailer allows customers to buy goods and defer payment for an extended time with no interest charge. Many stores advertise during the Christmas season, touting "No down payment, and first payment not due for 90 days."

A **layaway plan** is another type of credit. This plan allows a customer to make a small deposit, perhaps two or three dollars, to hold an item. The retailer retains possession of the item until the customer completes paying for it. The advantage to the customer is not having to worry about whether the item will be in stock when it is needed. And retailers do not have to worry about collection problems.

Most larger retailers historically have offered a *store-issued credit card*. The reason is clear. Store cardholders, compared to bank card customers, spend more per year in using their card, and also are more frequent card users.[10]

Credit Cards A credit card is basically a convenient way for customers to obtain credit without having to go through the approval process. It is in fact a modern form of revolving credit. Credit cards were first introduced in 1968 by the Royal Bank as the Chargex card (which became VISA). In 1998, it was estimated that 54.2 million credit cards were in circulation in Canada (i.e., 2.3 for each adult), of which about 35 million were MasterCard and Visa cards. Credit card balances were $94 billion, accounted for by the 1 billion transactions done with MasterCard and Visa cards.[11]

Most retailers today honour some type of credit card. A retailer has two basic choices with credit cards. They can (1) have their own card or (2) participate in a third-party program.

Today, independent department stores and petroleum companies are practically the only stores that have internal credit operations (and even those are declining). These stores believe they get a strong marketing advantage from in-house credit. Many have added bank credit card plans to their programs, primarily to take advantage of out-of-town business. Others have sold their credit card business to financial institutions. Thus, in-house credit probably is on its way out for many merchants.

Managing Internal Credit Most firms issuing credit use an application form. The application requests information that allows the firm to decide whether the person should be granted credit. The forms may ask for such information as the size of savings and chequing account balances, extent of debts, and various other personal information. Often information on the credit worthiness of the applicant is obtained from a credit bureau.

Key Legislation Retailers must comply essentially with the antidiscrimination sections of the Canadian Human Rights Act and some provincial Human Rights Codes, some provisions of the Bank Act and the Interest Act, as well as the appropriate provincial Consumer Protection Act and Cost of Credit Disclosure Act. To a lesser extent, the Competition Act (section 49) and the Small Loan Act may apply to credit.

Credit Authorization The retailer also needs to decide how credit will be verified when a credit purchase is made. Most credit authorization is now done electronically. The clerk enters the account number and the amount of the sale at the cash register. The system then automatically checks the accounts receivable information stored in the computer and indicates whether a credit charge should be approved. High credit volume retailers are integrating credit authorization into POS terminals.[12]

Loyalty Programs Retailers often entice their core credit customers to remain loyal by creating purchase incentives for them. The key is adding value to the credit card.[13] Examples are:

- Zellers' Club Z program allows charge customers to accumulate 100 points for every dollar in charge purchases. Customers begin receiving benefits and rewards based on their point totals earned.
- Canadian Tire has a new program called "options," which can be used instead of receiving Canadian Tire "money" (3 percent of cash purchases). With the Canadian Tire card, customers receive 10 points per dollar in charge purchases, and they begin receiving benefits at the 3,000 point mark at the cash register, either in terms of percentage discount on merchandise or dollar rebates.
- Another successful loyalty program, called Air Miles, provides points for shopping at participating sponsors, and in 1995 there were more than 7 million Air Miles cards in circulation, in 3.7 million households, representing 37 percent of all Canadian households.[14]

Third-Party Credit

Third-party credit can consist of (1) a bank card such as Visa or Mastercard, (2) a **private-label credit card** for the store, which is issued by a third party such as a bank, (3) *travel and entertainment cards* such as American Express or Diner's Club. Bank credit cards, such as Visa, or travel and entertainment cards such as Diner's Club are not controlled by the merchant. Rather, the bank or the entertainment company receives applications and issues cards and is responsible for customer billing and collection. The firms then bill the merchants accepting the card at a flat percentage of all credit sales.[15]

Zellers' Club Z is one of the most successful loyalty programs in Canada.

Courtesy Hudson's Bay Company—Corporate Collection

In a third-party program, banks handle (1) credit applications, credit processing, and authorization; (2) customer inquiries; (3) promotion; and (4) issuing each customer a card with the name of the participating store on it.

A *co-branded card* is a dual-purpose card combining the features of a private-label card and a bank card.[16] The issuer and the retailer each have their logo on the card. Recently, Visa has gone this route and will place a store name on the face of their card. Such programs allow consumers to reduce the number of cards they carry and to use the card at outlets that might not accept bank cards. Another advantage is consolidated billing. As with other third-party cards, the retailers focus on their skills—selling merchandise and services—while financial institutions handle the consumer credit issues.

SHOPPING SERVICES

Retailers are always trying to make it possible for customers to buy goods without having to spend an extended time in the store. Shopping services thus are being experimented on by large food retailers like Provigo. The most common shopper services are (1) telephone and Internet shopping, (2) in-home shopping, and (3) personal shopping.

Telephone and Internet Shopping

Telephone and Internet shopping are pushed by retailers because many people have less time for shopping. Often, the store will mail a catalogue to the consumer. After looking at the catalogue, the customer calls the store, orders the merchandise, and charges the goods to an account or credit card. With the Internet the catalogue is viewed on-line and the order can also be placed on-line (see Chapter 16). The goods are then delivered to the shopper's home. Some retail outlets also offer toll free 800/888 service as a way of increasing sales. Harrod's Department Store in London, England was the first store in Europe to join AT&T's international 800 service. Shoppers were able to order goods during the store's post-Christmas sale by dialing direct—even before the store opened for business to Londoners.

In-Home Shopping

In-home demonstrations remain popular for such services as home decoration. Employees bring samples of draperies, carpeting, and wallpaper to a customer's home and the customer can then see how the materials look under normal lighting conditions. One such example is Elte Carpets discussed earlier.[17]

Personal Shopping Services

Personal shopping is one of the fastest-growing services. The customer goes to the store and provides a list of needed measurements, style and colour preferences, and lifestyle information. After that, the person can call the store and indicate the types of items wanted. The store personnel then assemble several choices and have them ready at the customer's convenience.[18]

OTHER CUSTOMER SUPPORT SERVICES

The customer service possibilities are almost limitless. The type and level of services vary depending on the positioning strategy of the retailer. Some are quite unique, as in the case of the "people greeters" who meet shoppers at the front doors of Wal-Mart. The people greeters are one of the most popular customer support services offered by the firm.

Warranties

A strong customer satisfaction warranty forces the retailer to provide high-quality service and merchandise. Anything less than excellence will entice the customer to invoke the guarantee, which can be an expensive process. Thus, guarantees and warranties serve a two-fold purpose: to identify problems with the quality of service delivered, and to force the organization to meet consistently high standards of customer service.[19]

Some retailers also offer an *extended warranty* or a service contract.[20] The store agrees to extend a manufacturer's warranty for a period of time, commonly a year or so. The customer does not have to pay a repair bill during the agreed period of time regardless of how much the repair service may cost. Extended warranties are common on major household appliances and television sets.

Retailers should be aware of warranty legislation, however, when offering extended warranties, in particular the Competition Act, and the appropriate provincial Consumer Protection Act. *Satisfaction guaranteed* is a phrase often heard, but today such a statement is more of a contract than a courtesy. Some laws also determine where and how warranty information must be displayed. Many retail catalogues inform consumers that warranty information is available by mail before purchasing from the store.

Delivery

Delivery can be a large expense item for big-ticket items such as furniture and household appliances. Stores are often pressured not to charge extra for delivery. Retailers can help their image as full-service retailers by having their own trucks for delivery. The delivery schedule can then be more flexible, but the cost of having delivery trucks is high.

Another method of delivery is to use parcel post and service express. Retailers may want to use these services in addition to independent delivery services. Parcel post is a good way to deliver small packages to customers who may live a long distance from the store. Mail-order retailers often arrange delivery in this way.

Extended Shopping Hours

Retailers are offering consumers longer shopping hours, either late night or 24-hour shopping. Utility charges are about the same since the equipment runs most of the time anyway. Additional sales generated by longer hours can help spread the fixed costs over a larger sales base. Merchants may do very well with such a service since in many communities only a few stores are open 24 hours a day. But retailers have to pay overtime to employees or add part-time workers. The chance of being robbed is greater, and energy bills will go up somewhat.

Automatic Bill Payment

Retailers are increasingly offering bill-payment programs that allow bills to be paid by telephone, by preauthorization, or by electronic terminals as an alternative to paying by cheque. One such system is the **debit card** introduced in Canada in 1986. The debit card works within the network of merchants signed on by the issuing bank. This type of service is now integrated with the Interac banking system, allowing customers to use their card almost anywhere, including grocery stores and even corner stores.

The advantages of such systems include (1) the elimination of bad cheques, (2) lower labour costs to the retailer, (3) lower cheque-processing fees because of a smaller cheque volume, and (4) reduced postage.

The disadvantages include (1) the loss of direct contact with the consumer, (2) the loss of the opportunity to send stuffers with monthly statements, (3) misunderstandings with consumers over the timing of the payments, which can lead to loss of goodwill, and (4) the loss of an audit trail that would help in catching dishonesty and fraud. Automated bill paying is very popular because consumers react positively to saving time by this means of payment. Also, banks are developing plans for a "smart" card that will be more efficient and will cut back on fraud.[21]

Customers with Special Needs

Special opportunities exist to meet the needs of "special" consumers, including those who don't speak English, or French (in Quebec), the aged, and the infirm (including people who are deaf, blind, or confined to wheelchairs).[22]

The federal government mandated the push toward barrier-free environments in education, employment, and nonemployment situations. Now many provinces also have legislation requiring architectural compliance in developing barrier-free environments. Some progressive stores offer programs to assist and inform handicapped and aged shoppers.

Large retailers in such metropolitan markets as Toronto, Vancouver, and Montreal, or in places popular with tourists such as Banff, Niagara Falls, or Charlottetown offer multilingual signing to attract and serve foreign tourists. They also maintain lists of employees with foreign language ability. In addition, store directories and information pamphlets are sometimes printed in foreign languages.

Registries

The Internet is giving department stores a convenience and flexibility in their registry system that was previously unavailable. The benefits these retailers have seen in an on-line bridal registry are broadbased. The most obvious advantage is in access and updating capabilities. Because a complete registry can be printed within a matter of minutes, stores on the system can provide customers with an instant "shopping list" for a betrothed couple—a list they can carry with them from department to department as they make their selections.

But perhaps of most interest to store executives is the merchandising aspect, providing buyers and merchandise managers with complete, up-to-the-minute sales information, right down to details on vendor, patterns, size, or colour of each gift purchased.

Nursery Services

Some retailers are adding nursery services as part of their customer support programs. IKEA, the Swedish-owned home furnishings chain, has been widely noted in the trade press as having an excellent child-care program to encourage parents' shopping.[23] Sears Canada has also added a play area in the Kids & More departments in its new power format stores.

RESPONDING TO COMPLAINTS

Invariably, in spite of a retailer's best efforts, complaints about the merchandise or store policies will arise. Management must strive, within reasonable limits, to retain customers whenever possible. Customer loyalty and profitability go hand in hand because it costs less to serve repeat customers than to attract new customers (see Retail Highlight 14-4).[24]

Customer service breakdowns are especially likely in the following situations: (1) when the service process involves complex scheduling; (2) when a new customer support service is being introduced; (3) when the customer support activity involves high employee turnover; (4) when front-line employees are inadequately trained; and (5) when the retailer is forced to rely on suppliers or other uncontrollable external factors such as the weather.[25]

Retailers need a policy for dealing with customer complaints. Customers are allowed to return items in most stores, and some retailers feel the customer should be satisfied at any price. Almost all retailers, while not guaranteeing satisfaction, do try to be fair to the customer.

Complaints and returns can be handled on either a centralized or decentralized basis. Stores with a *centralized policy* handle all issues at a central level in the store; in this way they can be sure that a standardized policy is followed for all departments. In a *decentralized approach,* problems are handled on the sales floor by the person who sold the item, and the customer gets greater personal attention.

Retail Highlight 14-4 The Economics of Customer Dis/Satisfaction

According to author William A. Band, each time a company loses a customer, it forfeits the investment it made in the first place. For example, if it cost the retailer a conservative $20 to acquire each customer, and the retailer lost on a national basis over 100,000 customers because of poor service, the lost business would be over $2 million annually.

Since it is at least five times more costly to acquire a new customer than to retain a current one, the retailer must develop a relationship with customers to keep them patronizing its stores. This is called *relationship marketing*.

On the negative side, research shows that 96 percent of unhappy customers never complain, and of these 91 never return; but each one of them may tell nine other people about their bad experience, and one in eight may tell at least 20 other people.

On the positive side, if the complaint is resolved satisfactorily, seven out of ten will return, and as high as nine if the complaint is resolved on the spot. That customer will then tell five other people how well the complaint was handled.

Source: Adapted from William A. Band, *Creating Value for Your Customers*, Wiley, New York, 1991; R.M. Morgan and S.D. Hunt, "The Commitment-Trust Theory of Relationship Marketing," *Journal of Marketing*, vol. 58 (July 1994), pp. 20–38; Michel Huet, "Keeping the Customer Happy", *Marketing* (June 20, 1994), p. 16.

Stores normally prefer not to give a cash refund when handling a complaint or return. Most retailers try to get the customer exchanging an item to accept a slip (or "due-bill") which allows them to purchase an item at the same price in the future. This policy is designed to keep the customer coming back to the store. Some retailers may feel, however, that the consumer should be given a refund. They believe this better satisfies customers and builds better customer relations.

Stores have to make a decision in handling complaints and returned merchandise about whether to put the emphasis on the customer or the store. Again, a cost-benefit analysis is required. Providing an elaborate system for handling complaints and returns is costly, especially when the consumer wants money instead of merchandise upon returning an item. Still, stores may be better off viewing returns primarily from the viewpoint of the consumer and generating goodwill by going out of their way to have a liberal returned-goods policy.

EVALUATING THE COST-EFFECTIVENESS OF SERVICES

All services offered cost the firm money. Employees may need to be added to offer certain services. The cost must be balanced against anticipated revenues or the loss of goodwill if the services are not offered. It is not possible to precisely determine the revenue-generating effects of each service. Also, if certain services are offered by competition, the firm may have to offer them to remain competitive.

Many factors must be considered in deciding to offer or discontinue a service. The same is true when the retailer is deciding whether to charge for a service such as merchandise returned through no fault of the retailer. Let's consider the issue of credit. Management must balance the additional revenue from additional customer sales against the cost of offering credit. For example, interest is lost because the funds are not available to management.

Other costs of credit include the discounting of receivables such as when a financial institution buys the credit accounts from a retailer at a discount. The advantage to the retailer is that the cash is immediately available and no risks of collection are assumed. Still, the discount paid to get quick access to the funds can result in lower net profit. Other outside costs include the time sales clerks spend in charging a sale to a bank credit card or a travel and entertainment card.

CHAPTER HIGHLIGHTS

- Customer service expectations vary by type of retailing. The differences between customer expectations and experiences, if any, result in a customer expectations gap.
- Management can most effectively address the issue of customer support services by focusing on both customers and processes which, in turn, translates into focusing on the outcome.
- Traditional customer service in the retail industry is no longer sufficient. A broader customer-focused culture is called for today that incorporates customer lifestyles and buying patterns into the strategy. The results can provide a wide range of creative, competitive opportunities. But using this information to the greatest advantage requires planning, commitment, a focal point, a merger of inside and outside information, communication, and careful measurement.
- Services can be analyzed on two key dimensions: value to customers and cost to retailers. Four categories of services emerge from such an analysis: support services, disappointers, basics, and patronage builders.
- A services audit can help management develop a customer-focused culture. Identifying what services customers really value is no simple task, partly because customers may have difficulty articulating their preferences.
- Retailers face a variety of decisions in deciding whether to offer credit. They can offer in-store credit or have credit handled by an outside agency such as a bank by honouring bank credit cards. They may also issue a store credit card of their own or have a card with their name on it, but have the bank handle the administrative details. Consumer pressure in favour of bank credit cards is increasing, and most stores now honour them.
- Most types of credit are offered by the retailer at a loss. However, credit normally is a necessary customer service.
- Retailers can offer a variety of other services as part of the customer support mix. These include warranties, extended hours and Sunday openings, delivery, automatic bill payment, nursery services, services to customers with spe-

cial needs, and registries. However, it is important to try to balance likely revenue against the cost of the services.

- Retailers should closely monitor the legal issues relating to many of the services they offer.

KEY TERMS

basic services	355	open-charge account	357
customer-focused culture	350	patronage builders	355
customer service	349	personal shopping service	360
debit card	362	private-label credit card	359
deferred billing credit	358	revolving credit	357
disappointers	355	support services	354
instalment credit	357	third-party credit	359
layaway plan	358		

DISCUSSION QUESTIONS

1. What might be the major reasons for a retailer to offer selected services? Why are many retailers cutting down on the number of services they offer?
2. Why should a retailer offer a store's own card for credit? What problems or disadvantages exist with a store having its own card?
3. What are some retailers doing to encourage customers to pay cash for purchases?
4. What are some retailers doing to entice customers to remain loyal?
5. What are the advantages and disadvantages of offering customers liberal merchandise return privileges?
6. Explain the concept of a debit card. Describe its advantages and disadvantages for both the customer and the retailer.
7. What are some of the things retailers are doing to be more responsive to customers who have special needs?
8. What are the advantages and disadvantages of a centralized versus a decentralized procedure for handling consumer complaints?

APPLICATION EXERCISES

1. Talk to the credit manager at a couple of the local department stores in your community and to the loan officer at a couple of banks to determine how they evaluate customer applications for credit. Try to get a copy of the forms they use, if possible. Find out what they do in order to be objective in their evaluations. Find out if they are reasonably current on the regulations about granting credit to women.
2. Interview a group of students at random and select a department store, supermarket, discount store (e.g., K mart), and national chain like Sears Canada. Develop a list of services that the stores might offer (from the text listing). Then, have each student check the services that they perceive are offered by each type of store chosen. Write a report on the findings and suggest what they mean to you in terms of the material included in the chapter.

3. Discuss with several friends complaints that they may have had against a store or stores. Describe how each was handled by (1) the customer and (2) the store. Evaluate the process that you discover in this project.

SUGGESTED CASES

4. Dave Wong—Experiences of a New Immigrant
6. Clean Windows, Inc.
18. Travel Agencies—A Variation in Service

Part 5

New Dimensions in Retailing

In *Part 5, New Dimensions in Retailing,* Chapter 15 develops two important emerging issues in retailing: the retailing of services, and the various types of nonstore retailing. Chapter 16 covers the very important issue of electronic commerce, which is expected to continue an explosive growth rate for many years to come.

CHAPTER 15

SERVICES AND NONSTORE RETAILING

CHAPTER OBJECTIVES

After reading this chapter you should be able to:

1. Cite differences between service and tangible goods firms.
2. Describe unique aspects of consumer behaviour as related to the purchase of services.
3. Discuss various decisions involved in developing competitive plans and managing a retail service organization.
4. Highlight alternative forms of nonstore retailing.

On her way to work, Sally Dubesque dropped off some dry-cleaning and bought a coffee to go from The Second Cup. During her lunch break, she bought a pair of slacks at Le Chateau, and had a quick salad at McDonald's Express. After work, she went to the Adelaide Club for an aerobics class, had dinner, and went to see a movie with a friend. Sally's activities during the day reflect what is happening in retailing; service businesses are growing rapidly in Canada and around the world. Service industries now account for over 70 percent of all business and provide most of the new jobs. Part of the reason is due to demographic shifts, such as the sharp increase in two-income families and other "time-pressed" consumers.

As well, when consumers have time they often want to spend it on leisure activities, not doing chores. The growth of firms like Molly Maid International Inc. is indicative of the trend towards a service economy. The phenomenal increase in the use of the Internet and electronic commerce is also part of consumers' desires to use services to spend time on other activities.

Molly Maid offers services that save consumers time and effort.

Used under license by Molly Maid International Inc., Trademark Owner

Because of the importance of service retail firms to the Canadian economy, this chapter is devoted to these firms. It also presents information on nonstore retailing—another segment of the Canadian economy that is experiencing growth.

SERVICES RETAILING

Services are "activities, benefits, or satisfaction which are offered for sale, or are provided in connection with the sale of goods."[1] Therefore, a service may have both tangible (high goods content) and intangible (low goods content) attributes. Depending on the combination of tangible and intangible attributes, firms may be placed along a tangibility continuum from very tangible to very intangible. At one end of the continuum would be services that are very intangible, such as Sally's exercise class and dry-cleaning, to very tangible, such as buying a pair of slacks (Figure 15-1). In order to have a better understanding of service firms, let's look at some of the differences between the more tangible goods firms and purely service firms.

Figure 15-1 The Tangibility Continuum

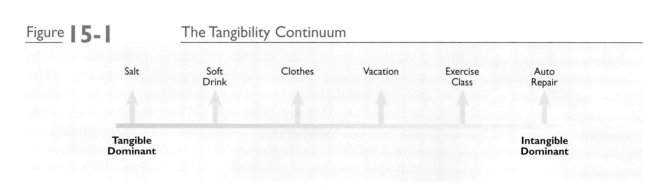

Differences Between Tangible Goods Firms and Service Firms

Understanding the differences between tangible goods firms and service firms is important in developing successful competitive strategies for service firms. The following sections highlight the important differences between the two types of firms.

Intangibility

As noted, the main difference between pure goods versus service firms is **intangibility**. In general, goods can be defined as objects, devices, or things; whereas services can be defined as deeds, efforts, or performances.[2] To a degree, all retailers have a service component but for some—for example, convenience stores—the service component is small relative to the goods component (e.g., milk, bread). Highly intangible services, like a movie, cannot be seen, felt, tasted, or touched in the same manner that goods can be sensed (e.g., bread). A pair of slacks can be evaluated before being purchased, can be taken home, and are owned by the buyer. A movie cannot be evaluated beforehand, it is "experienced," and the buyer has only a memory to take home. Thus, how consumers evaluate and buy goods versus services are different. For services, consumers often rely on word of mouth and others' experiences because of the difficulty in evaluating them before purchase. For goods, consumers can judge the physical product—the slacks—for quality, style, colour, and texture.

Perishability

Many services are essentially **perishable**. If a Four Seasons Hotel room is empty for an evening, or if an Air Canada plane leaves with empty seats, the revenue is lost forever. Dentists, physicians, attorneys, and accountants similarly cannot recover revenue lost because of an unfilled schedule. In contrast, tangible goods not sold on any given day can be held in inventory and sold at a later point to capture the revenue. With services that are perishable, the retailer needs to consider strategies that increase demand in low periods and lower demand in high periods. Pricing can be used to increase demand (e.g., movies at half price on Tuesdays) and reservations can help to reduce demand or at least smooth it in high periods.

Inseparability

With many services, the customer and the service provider must be physically together—**inseparability**—to complete the service. A haircut, a restaurant meal, most medical and many other professional services require both parties to be present. The consequence is that the customer may evaluate the service based on tangible cues (e.g., the physical surroundings) and the personal interaction skills of the service provider. For example, consumers may be more satisfied when the dental hygienist is in a uniform and is friendly and courteous rather than in casual clothes and stern.

Variability

Because many service firms are labour-intensive and because many services are offered only at the point of sale, consistency in the level of service and quality is difficult to achieve. This **variability** is caused by the interaction between the service provider and the customer and is sometimes referred to as "bad hair days." Either party may be tired, lack the appropriate communication skills to explain what they want or have, or lack the training. Fast-food operations, offering a combination of tangible goods and services, are an exception. Firms like McDonald's have been able to introduce assembly-line techniques to the fast-food business to ensure consistent quality.

Services will have varying degrees of these four characteristics. For example, a department store is close to the goods end of the tangibility continuum because it offers physical products for sale. However, department stores have intangibility aspects to their offering—the quality of service offered by the staff (e.g., friendly, courteous)—and they need to be concerned about variability. The point to remember is that there are intangible components for most retail firms.

As noted with the examples, competitive strategies of service firms are affected by the fact that they possess some unique characteristics that differentiate them from tangible goods firms. In addition, consumer behaviour differences in the purchase of services versus tangible goods affects competitive strategy development in retail service firms.

Consumer Behaviour in the Purchase of Services

Consumers view the purchasing of services differently from the purchasing of goods. For example, consumers often feel that purchasing services is frequently a less pleasant experience than buying goods and they perceive higher levels of risk in buying services than tangible goods.[3]

Consumers often face an information gap when purchasing services. A lack of reliable data on the retailer, be it a garage mechanic or bank, exists. Especially lacking is information to help consumers choose professionals such as doctors and lawyers.

Furthermore, because services are often intangible, consumers find it difficult, if not impossible, to evaluate the service before purchase and also, in many instances, even after purchase and use. This issue can be explained in terms of three types of product properties: search qualities, experience qualities, and credence qualities.[4] Tangible goods possess **search qualities**, or attributes that a consumer can see, feel, or touch and can thus determine prior to purchasing a product. Services, on the other hand, possess varying degrees of experience and credence qualities. **Experience qualities** are attributes such as taste that can be discerned only after purchasing or during consumption. Restaurants and theatres are examples of services with experience qualities. **Credence qualities** are attributes that consumers may find impossible to evaluate even after purchase and consumption, usually because they do not have the knowledge or skill to do so. Services provided by professionals such as doctors and lawyers are examples of services possessing credence qualities.

The fact that services primarily possess experience and credence qualities suggests that consumers will be seeking information to ensure they made the right decision. Service retailers should establish the evaluative criteria and provide information to help the buyer know what to look for before, during, and after the service encounter. In addition, the use of reference groups to present favourable information about the use of a service is an important surrogate for evaluative criteria.

Many other implications exist in developing competitive strategy as a result of the unique characteristics of service retailers and the buying behaviour of consumers in purchasing services. These will be addressed in the following section, which focuses on the development of competitive strategies for service retailers.

Developing Competitive Strategies

In developing a competitive strategy, the service retailer, like the goods retailer, must have a clear definition and understanding of its market and must then develop a positioning strategy to attract this market and to distinguish itself from competitive firms.

Defining and Analyzing Target Customers

Service firms take a similar approach to goods firms in segmenting and targeting customers (Chapter 4). Management must understand the characteristics of its target market and its needs, perceptions, and expectations. For example, banks are increasingly trying to build customer loyalty by bundling their services into packages targeted to segments of the population. Banks segment the market on a variety of variables including age, geographic, ethnic, financial, and lifestyle differences. Banks target consumer groups with different financial goals—ranging from students who need loans, to the elderly who need financial security, to "boomers" who are seeking investment growth. They offer an array of packages from loans to mutual funds to guaranteed investment certificates to attract these segments.

Studies on customer behaviour found that there were two major segments of banking services: those who want convenience and those who want performance from their bank.[5] Some Canadian banks, in response, have designed their branch networks to serve convenience users who do mostly basic transactions, and sophisticated users who have more complex needs. Automatic teller machines and telephone banking will serve the convenience segment, while the sophisticated users can visit "financial centres" for personal advice on how to manage their money.

The Service Offering

The **core service** of a service firm is the primary benefit customers seek from the firm. **Peripheral services** are secondary benefits sought by customers. The core service for Federal Express, for example, consists of picking up the package, transporting it overnight, and delivering it the next morning. Peripheral services include providing advice and information, providing labels and certain types of packaging, documentation of shipments, and problem solving.

Many service firms start with a single core service offered to a single market segment. Initial growth opportunities normally occur through the addition of peripheral services and expansion into new geographic markets. Some service firms have been successful following a strategy of offering new core services for existing market segments, and some have followed a strategy of moving into different, but closely related, services. Sears Canada offers both: new core services such as home services (air conditioning, carpeting, roofing), flower delivery service across Canada, and Sears Travel Service as well as different, but related services. Sears Canada continues to add to its home services and now offers duct, carpet, upholstery, and drapery cleaning and lawn care. Thus, service strategies include deciding what new services to introduce to which target markets, what existing services to maintain, and what services to eliminate. Decisions on the service offerings then set the stage for decisions on other components of competitive strategy, such as price, promotion, and distribution (delivery) strategies.

In judging a company's service offering, consumers are primarily concerned that the service provider gives consistently high levels of quality service. Customers are also concerned with tangibles, such as the appearance of physical facilities, equipment, personnel, and communication materials. The following sections focus on these and other related issues.

Service Provision One characteristic of service firms, as discussed earlier, is the important role employees play in the delivery of the service.[6] Often, customers judge the service based on *how* it was delivered, that is how courteous and responsive the employee was in the service encounter. Many of the issues regarding employee selection, training, and motivation discussed in Chapter 6 are relevant here. Service firms need to ensure that employees are providing consistently high levels of quality service to their customers. They need to carefully select and train employees and to develop programs to motivate them to offer excellent service. These firms often use both monetary and nonmonetary incentives to encourage employees to provide good service. One incentive is the employee-of-the-month award. The effectiveness of using such an award is enhanced when it is based on customer feedback.

Even the best firms sometimes fail to deliver excellent service due to the variability of the service delivery process. These firms recognize that failures will occur and design service recovery strategies to resolve the failures. A successful service recovery, which could include compensating the customer for the failure or solving the problem, helps to maintain customer loyalty and increase positive word of mouth.[7] These firms know that it can cost up to five times more to get a new customer than to keep an existing customer.

Many service firms have found that an effective way to affect customers' perceptions of reliable service is to offer a guarantee of satisfaction. Interestingly, one of the first retailers to offer a guarantee was Timothy Eaton, a goods retailer (Retail Highlight 15-1). Often, these guarantees promise complete customer satisfaction and a full refund or complete, no-cost problem resolution to dissatisfied customers. For many firms, such a guarantee has proven to be a powerful tool for building customer loyalty and market share and for improving overall service quality. Management should, however, carefully assess both the benefits and the risks of providing unconditional guarantees. Of course, such risks can be managed, but doing so requires care in the guarantee's design and implementation, as well as in achieving and maintaining high service quality.[8]

Importance of the Physical Environment As consumers often find the offerings of service firms difficult to understand and evaluate because they are largely intangible, they often look for tangible evidence to help them determine just what the offering is. Service retailers can provide such tangible evidence. For example, a hotel puts drinking glasses in clean paper bags, provides wrapped tablets of soap, and attaches "cleaned" bands across the toilets as tangible evidence that the room has been specially cleaned and prepared for the new occupant. The decor of the salon, the appearance of the staff, and the quality of the appointment cards are all tangible, surrogate product features for the basically intangible product of hairdressing.

Retail Highlight 15-1 Service Guarantees – Reduce Customer Risk and Increase Satisfaction

"Satisfaction guaranteed or your money refunded." Timothy Eaton was the first retailer to offer a service guarantee and it was critical to Eaton's success for over 100 years. Today, many firms—from Federal Express to Pizza Hut—offer guarantees to gain a competitive advantage, to reduce consumers' risk, and to signal to consumers that they stand behind their services. Clearly, the major benefit for consumers is that they know if the purchase doesn't "work out," they will get their money back. This is important for many services because, unlike many products, consumers often have difficulty in judging the quality of services before they buy them. Do guarantees work? In a study of Canadian consumers, it was found that:

- Service guarantees can increase consumers' confidence in the store.
- Consumers prefer to select stores that offer particular types of guarantees.
- Guarantees that offer a specific payout—i.e., your money back—are preferred to other types of guarantees.
- Consumers prefer guarantees that are37 easy to invoke.

Probably the major benefit of guarantees is that they provide an incentive for managers and staff to get it right in the first place.

Source: G. McDougall, T. Levesque and P. VanderPlaat, "Designing the Service Guarantee: Unconditional or Specific?" *Journal of Services Marketing*, 12, 2, 1998, pp. 278–293.

Standardization and Specialization in Service Delivery Increasingly, managers in service firms are engaging in activities to achieve greater economies and higher levels of efficiency. Such activities enable service firms to enjoy not only economies of scale but also more consistent, predictable quality in service delivery. Fast-food restaurants have introduced an assembly-line approach to what is a combination of tangible goods and services delivery in an effort to improve efficiency. Other examples of standardized consumer services range from quick auto service providers (such as oil change, muffler, and tune-up shops) to highly specialized medical services, such as centres that treat only one ailment such as hernias or cataracts. For example, Shouldice Hospital in Toronto only performs hernia operations, about 8,000 a year.[9]

Standardization of service does not necessarily mean the end of personal attention, which is often the key element the customer seeks from a service firm. For example, trade-offs are successfully being made between standardization and personal service in the chains of home cleaning services that offer routine, standardized services to customers. As noted, the banks' use of technology through ATM, Internet, and telephone banking is another way to standardize service delivery and increase efficiency.

Service Delivery

Although service retailers are less concerned with issues such as transportation, inventory, and warehousing than are goods firms, service delivery is an important element of a service retailer's competitive strategy and involves decisions on channel structure and location.

Channel Structure Many services are provided directly by the producer to the end user. Most physicians deal directly with patients, as do attorneys with their clients. Still, some indirect channels are used in service delivery. Tickets to ball games, concerts, and similar events are often sold at other locations in addition to the place of performance. Travel agencies serve as intermediaries between the airline and the consumer. Banks extend credit to customers who use the bank's credit card, so the bank becomes a third party to any credit transaction a customer has with a retail outlet.

The Importance of Location Location is an important element of the competitive strategy in a service business. Because many services are perishable, if the service is not available where and when the customer wants it, the potential revenue is lost forever. Therefore, service retailers who can obtain locations that are convenient for their target market will gain a competitive advantage. As an example, frequent air travellers are more likely to use auto rental agencies with the largest number of airport locations because such firms are most likely to have an outlet in a major airport. In some cases, the service firm comes to the customer (home cleaning and lawn care) and here the location is irrelevant. When the customer does not have to be physically present to receive the service, then location is less important.

Promoting the Service Offering

Effective use of promotion is extremely important for service retailers. Promotion is important in providing tangible "cues" for an intangible offering, in communicating the image of the firm and promoting its individual services, and in communicating with the customer after the service encounter.

Promotion plays an important role in making a service more tangible to consumers. For example, some advertisements associate the service with some tangible object to establish a psychological association between a vaguely perceived intangible and a more easily perceived tangible object. Prudential Insurance's association with the rock of Gibraltar is an example. The rock signifies the solid, unwavering security and peace of mind a consumer desires from insurance. A similar example is the association of the Royal Bank and the lion in its logo. In addition, advertisements may focus on the physical environment in which the service is to be performed in an effort to make services more tangible. As shown in Exhibit 15-1, the ad for the Four Seasons Hotels shows the various amenities, the decor, the doorman, the valet and the room service for busy and successful businesspeople.

Service marketers should also try to create a strong brand image through their promotional efforts. Many service franchise chains, including McDonald's, have created strong, tangible brand images. The quality of a store's services is an important determinant of its image and store image strongly affects shopping and patronage behaviour.

Exhibit **15-1** Advertisement for the Four Seasons Hotels, with its "Defining the Art of Service" Theme

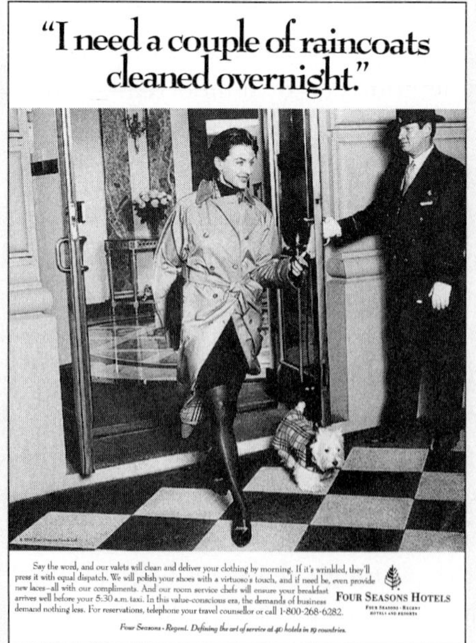

Courtesy Four Seasons Hotels

In addition, service retailers should make post-purchase communication a part of promotional strategy. This can be accomplished with postcards, surveys, telephone calls, brochures, or a variety of other devices to show customers that their input is sought and their patronage is appreciated.

Finally, many customers of service firms prefer personal sources for obtaining information. Hence, service retailers should try to stimulate positive word-of-mouth communication among present and potential customers.

Pricing

Price is a key element of a service retailer's competitive strategy. Price setting for a service firm may prove to be a challenging task because of the intangibility of services. It is often difficult for consumers to see what it costs the service provider to "produce" the service (e.g., the customer doesn't see why a plumber should charge $80 to fix a leaky faucet because the customer can't see the training, equipment, and office the plumber needs to be in business).

Consumers may often perceive a stronger relationship between price and quality for services than for goods. This, together with the difficulties that customers have in evaluating services, suggests a greater emphasis and reliance on price as an indicator of quality. It thus becomes crucial that service retailers' prices are set appropriately, something they have difficulty doing, even today.[10] To effectively price services, the retailer needs to know what its customers truly value. What the customer values can be related to satisfaction, relationship, and efficiency and can be determined by understanding the benefits customers seek from the service.[11]

Because of intense competition, slow growth, and other conditions, many service firms are focusing heavily on price as a competitive weapon. Intensive price competition has been evident, for example, in deregulated service industries such as financial services, telecommunications, and transportation. Air travellers today, for example, are faced with a bewildering array of different prices. In fact, the lowest fare may even differ from one ticketing agent to another.

NONSTORE RETAILING

Nonstore retailing has experienced rapid growth. On an annual basis, Canadians purchase more than $12 billion in goods and services from direct marketers.[12] A number of environmental dynamics explain this growth. Demographic and lifestyle changes have affected the demand for nonstore retailing. Single-person or single-parent household members lack the time to shop, as do those in two-career families. The senior segment is growing and, although many of these consumers have more disposable income, they are less mobile. Furthermore, some people are afraid to go downtown or to malls and prefer shopping in the safety of their homes. Many consumers also like the idea of shopping 24 hours a day, seven days a week. In addition, advances in the technological environment have spurred the growth of some forms of nonstore retailing: direct-mail retailing, in-home retailing, telephone retailing, electronic retailing, and vending-machine retailing.

Direct-Mail Retailing

Direct-mail retailing is a significant part of nonstore retailing. Canada Post alone delivers more than 1.5 billion pieces of addressed advertising mail each year. The catalogue industry in Canada is estimated at $2 billion annually and growing at about 5 percent per year. Catalogue merchandising in Canada is widespread with over 600 titles, selling anything from seeds to silks. Sears Canada alone distributes 40 million catalogues a year to Canadian households.[13] As well, many U.S. catalogue retailers have entered the Canadian market including Lands' End, L.L. Bean, and Spiegel. Typically, these catalogues present a tightly focused assortment of goods designed to meet the needs of a specific market segment.

In addition to focusing the content of their catalogues, companies are using consumer data and technology to develop highly targeted mailing lists. With the use of selective binding, for example, a customer and her next-door neighbour might get two different catalogues. Another option is ink jetting, which enables the company to print personalized messages within a catalogue. Techniques such as these enable a company to treat each customer as an individual. Some industry analysts believe that in a few years, the industry will be at the point where almost every catalogue will be for a specific customer. Retail Highlight 15-2 provides some examples of the use of new technologies for direct selling.

Retail Highlight 15-2 Three Examples of Direct-Marketing Methods

Tilley Endurables: The 60-page catalogue of Tilley Endurables of Toronto (www.tilley.com) can be seen around the world thanks to the Internet on the World Wide Web: it includes pictures, prices, and descriptions of its merchandise. Products can be ordered through e-mail, fax, or an 800 number.

Harry Rosen: Headquartered in Toronto, Harry Rosen has 22 stores in Canada and one in Buffalo, New York. On March 14, 1995, it launched its first CD-ROM catalogue provided free to customers. Two weeks later, it had already distributed 1,000 copies of the CD catalogue. The CD provides information and prices, but also allows customers to point and click various outfits and play with them singly or in combination to see how they would look!

Grand & Toy: This Toronto office-supply company (www.grandandtoy.com) developed a software program (OrderPoint) for its numerous commercial clients, which not only helps them order supplies but reduces the number of procedures for placing an order, and can be tailored to the needs of a client. The company catalogue is built into the software itself. Updates and upgrades are sent later.

www.tilley.com

www.grandandtoy.com

Source: Adapted from Lara Mills, "From print to bits and bytes," *Marketing* (May 22, 1995), p. 14.

Even though direct-mail retailing is experiencing growth, it is not without its critics. Environmentalists are concerned not only with disposal issues but also with the destruction of trees. Some direct-mail companies are attempting to respond to these concerns by using recycled paper and using telephone systems instead of the postal system for customer orders.

In-Home Retailing

In-home retailing is a method of distribution of consumer goods and services through personal contact (salesperson to buyer) away from a fixed business location. Major modes of personal selling include one-on-one selling and the party plan, in the home or elsewhere. The significance of direct selling is underscored by the fact that it generates about 25 percent of total nonstore sales.[14]

Two major categories of products and services are sold by direct selling firms:

1. Household products, including cookware, tableware, kitchen and decorative accessories, vacuum cleaners and other appliances, household cleaning products, and foods and beverages.
2. Personal care and beauty items, including cosmetics, fragrances, skin care items, jewelry, and clothing. Well-known firms in the cosmetics and skin care line include Mary Kay and Avon.

Of interest is the fact that many of the environmental dynamics discussed earlier that have led to an increase in demand for nonstore buying have adversely affected personal selling. With more single-person and dual-income households, there are fewer people at home. Many personal sellers are therefore attempting to reach consumers during the evening hours and at locations other than consumers' homes, such as work sites. Some are using direct mail pieces and are printing 800/888 numbers in their literature as well as on product packages to assist customers in reordering products or making contacts. Such companies are quick to point out, however, that customer orders generated by the toll-free numbers or direct mail pieces are turned over to their salespeople to fill. In an attempt to increase sales, some companies are moving into international markets. Amway, for example, has more than 100,000 salespeople in Japan. Avon is sold in more than 100 countries today and earns a substantial portion of its profit from its international operations.

Telephone Retailing

Telephone retailing, or **telemarketing**, can be either *inbound* when the retailer receives orders or requests from customers thanks to the use of 1-800 or 1-888 numbers; or *outbound* when the retailer calls customers or potential customers to sell merchandise or services.

Consumers are buying virtually every type of product and service via the telephone—from prescriptions to computers to prepared foods. Telemarketing not only gives companies a practical, cost-effective way of interacting personally with customers, but it also gives consumers a chance to ask questions and seek information about a company's offering.

Although some consumers welcome telephone selling, others view it as an interruption and an invasion of privacy. Especially objectionable to many consumers are computerized machines that automatically call and relay messages. They are concerned, for example, that some consumers must pay for calls—people with car phones and pagers are charged for every minute they use a telephone line even if they don't initiate the call.

Electronic Retailing

Electronic retailing can assume a variety of forms, including phone shopping from computerized listings, such as Comp-U-Card International Inc.; cable television programs with product and service presentations and demonstrations, such as the Canadian Home Shopping Network that claims to reach 5 million households; and electronic retailing—using the **Internet** to buy merchandise. The Internet is revolutionizing retailing and Chapter 16 examines electronic commerce in more depth.

Regardless of the format, electronic shopping has taken on increased significance as a form of nonstore retailing. Over 200 companies are experimenting with ways to use personal computers, videodisc players, and other technologies to improve customer service and provide convenient access to merchandise and product information. More than 5,000 electronic shopping systems now provide information and transaction services to consumers.

Vending-Machine Retailing

Historians believe that the first vending machine, created by Hero of Alexander in 215 B.C., was a five-drachma machine that dispensed holy water. Since that time, **vending-machine retailing** has been used to sell a wide variety of merchandise, ranging from soft drinks and snack food items to blue jeans to freshly baked pizza. Vending machines have even been used to vend names and telephone numbers of ladies of the evening.

The largest categories of products sold through vending machines are coffee, non-alcoholic beverages, cigarettes, and confectioneries. Most vending machines can be found in industrial plants, business offices, hospitals, universities, and schools.

CHAPTER HIGHLIGHTS

- The rapidly growing service sector of the Canadian economy is becoming increasingly important. There are strategic differences between tangible goods firms and service retailers. The competitive strategies of service firms must match their unique characteristics. In addition, consumer behaviour differences in the purchase of services versus tangible goods affects competitive strategy development in retail service firms.
- Service firms must develop competitive strategies just as firms selling tangible goods do. The service retailer must have a clear definition of its target market and an understanding of that market.

- An element of strategy is the decision regarding the service offering. Here, the retailer must determine not only the core service to be offered but also the peripheral services. Because of the intangible nature of many service offerings, the people involved in service delivery and the physical environment are key ingredients of a service firm's competitive strategy.
- In terms of service delivery, service retailers are involved in channel structure decisions. Although most services are provided directly by the producer to the end user without an intermediary, some indirect channels are used in service delivery. Location is also an important element of service delivery.
- Effective use of promotion is important for service retailers. Promotion is important in providing tangible "cues" for an intangible offering, in communicating the image of the firm and promoting its individual services, and in communicating with the customer after the service encounter.
- Pricing is also a critical element of a service firm's competitive strategy. Because the offering of a service firm may largely be intangible, price is often used by consumers as a surrogate for quality.
- Nonstore retailing has experienced rapid growth. Forms of nonstore retailing include direct-mail retailing, in-home retailing, telephone retailing, electronic retailing, and vending-machine retailing.

KEY TERMS

core service	374	peripheral service	374
credence qualities	373	perishability	372
electronic retailing	382	search qualities	373
experience qualities	373	services	371
in-home retailing	381	telemarketing	381
inseparability	372	telephone retailing	381
intangibility	372	variability	373
Internet	382	vending-machine retailing	382
nonstore retailing	379		

DISCUSSION QUESTIONS

1. Summarize the differences between tangible goods firms and service retailers.
2. Discuss the unique aspects of consumer behaviour in the purchase of services that affect competitive strategy development in service firms. Be sure to include in your discussion the differences between search, experience, and credence qualities of products.
3. What is the difference between core services and peripheral services?
4. What are some service organizations doing to increase service standardization? Are there any disadvantages in following such a strategy? If so, what are they?
5. Comment on the validity of the following statement: "Channel structures in service industries are always direct from producer to user."

6. Why is promotion such an important part of a service retailer's competitive strategy?
7. Discuss why pricing is an important element of competitive strategy for service retailers. What difficulties do service firms encounter in price setting?
8. How do present-day catalogues and their use differ from earlier catalogues? What controversial issues surround the use of direct mail as a form of nonstore retailing?
9. What is in-home retailing as a form of nonstore retailing? What environmental dynamics are affecting in-home retailing firms and how are these firms responding?
10. What are the advantages of telephone retailing from the perspectives of companies and consumers? What controversial issues are related to the use of telemarketing?

APPLICATION EXERCISES

1. Review the recent business press regarding the competition among hotel chains.
   a) What has motivated hotels to engage in price competition?
   b) Are there any negative repercussions from competing on the basis of price? If so, what are they?
   c) Is there any way a full-service hotel could maintain prices and promote its services when competitors are reducing and advertising price specials? Or is its only effective response to likewise lower prices?
2. Find a local direct seller in your community or by reading about that company in the library. Interview the manager of that company with respect to the following issues:
   a) What are the environmental dynamics that have negatively affected the company?
   b) What motivated the company to stay with its distribution system of direct selling rather than selling its products through stores?
   c) What are the future prospects for direct selling in this sector?

SUGGESTED CASES

4. Dave Wong—Experiences of a New Immigrant
6. Clean Windows, Inc.
8. Wing and a Prayer
18. Travel Agencies—A Variation in Service
19. The Fitness Centre

CHAPTER 16

ELECTRONIC COMMERCE

CHAPTER OBJECTIVES

After reading this chapter you should be able to:

1. Understand why consumers shop on-line.
2. Understand the key success factors in electronic commerce.
3. Understand the types of products sold on the Internet.
4. Understand how to design and maintain an effective Web site.
5. Understand the role of advertising on the Web.

A busy office manager and mother of two children saves time by buying greeting cards and getaway holidays on the Internet. Her father buys supplies for his wood-carving hobby on-line. Her niece selects gifts from the Disney Web site. As these examples suggest, the Internet is not for techno-nerds any more.[1]

By April 1999, 50 percent of Canadian households had at least one person with regular access to the Internet at home, work, school or another location.[2] This milestone reflects the importance of a new, exciting, and potentially most significant form of retailing—electronic commerce. Consider these facts, opinions, and predictions:

- The growth rate for on-line sales in the past year has ranged from 40 percent for food and wine to 340 percent for gifts.[3]
- In the first year of on-line operations, Canadian book retailers sold approximately $50 million of books over the Internet.[4]
- While predictions vary, it is estimated that e-commerce sales will increase at an annual rate of 50 to 100 percent over the next five years. By 2002 it is estimated that Canadian consumers will spend over $13 billion, up from $2 billion in 1998.

While more Canadians are shopping on-line every day, there are some concerns. In particular, 97 percent of Canadians are uncomfortable sending credit card data over the Internet and 53 percent prefer to see products before they purchase them.[5] The main reasons they shop on-line are to save money (75 percent), convenience (50 percent), and choice (48 percent).

This chapter explores this dynamic, challenging form of retailing. It will cover and address the following issues and questions:

- The Internet empowers consumers through information. How will consumer behaviour change?
- How can retailers better establish lasting relationships with customers and suppliers?
- How will advertising and the evaluation of advertising effectiveness change?
- Growth potential for e-commerce—the importance of the entertainment and social experience, ordering and getting merchandise, number of alternatives, assistance in screening alternatives, providing information to evaluate merchandise, and cost of merchandise.
- What type of merchandise can be effectively sold through e-commerce?
- The impact of e-commerce on retailing and the future, in particular, increased price comparison by consumers.
- Should the on-line site be part of the store or a separate operation?
- Channel conflict—what happens when firms like Nike sell on-line?
- Key to successful e-commerce—getting customers to come back.

A NEW DISTRIBUTION CHANNEL

E-commerce is the same as opening a new distribution channel. It needs a considerable amount of planning, particularly in making sure that the "back-end" process—the delivery, returns, and exchanges—is in place. This process is critical for success because if an e-commerce retailer doesn't fulfill the order when promised (and it has to be quick), it loses the trust of customers and they don't come back. So, it's more than just putting up a Web site.

WHY DO CUSTOMERS SHOP ON-LINE?

There are six basic reasons why consumers shop on-line (Figure 16-1).[6] Each of the **six Cs**—convenience, cost, choice, customization, communication, and control—will be discussed in turn.

Convenience Within one minute a consumer can enter a retailer's Web site and search the merchandise offered for sale. In ten minutes a consumer can compare a product or brand offered by four retailers, decide on which retailer to buy the product from, order it, and have it delivered a few days later. Increased convenience is a key trend in retailing, as consumers increasingly select retail modes based on convenience.[7]

www.sears.ca

www.ftd.com

For example, convenience is a major factor in the gift market. Consumers buying gifts for relatives and friends who live in other cities can order merchandise on-line and have it shipped directly to the recipient. E-commerce retailers who sell flowers, such as Sears Canada (www.sears.ca) and FTD.COM (www.ftd.com) have seen remarkable growth in their sales.

Figure 16-1 The Reasons Consumers Buy On-line

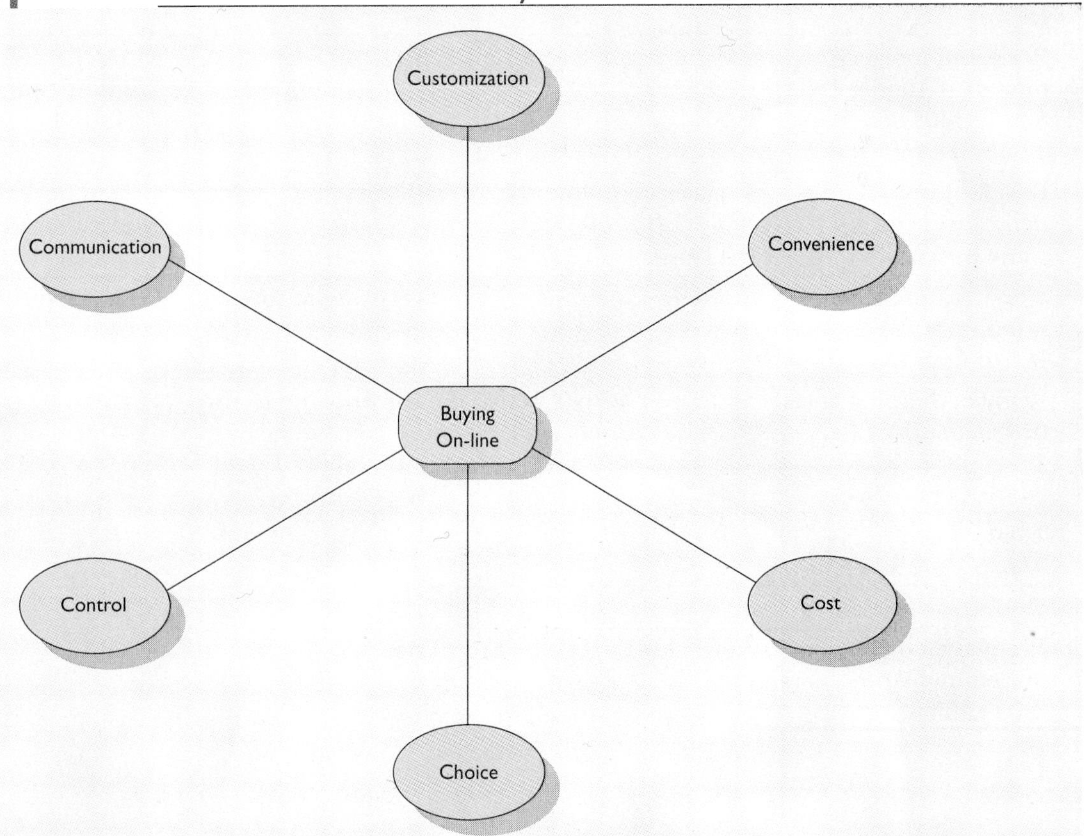

Cost The ability of a consumer to compare the prices across a number of retailers is relatively easy on the Internet. Further, Internet providers now will search a variety of sites and let the consumer know which firm offers the lowest price. However, consumers typically pay shipping and handling costs from e-commerce retailers and in a number of instances it has been found that traditional retailers offer lower prices than e-commerce retailers do. On the other hand,

Retail Highlight 16-1 Is Buying on the Internet Cheaper?

Quill and Quire magazine rated four book Web sites (two Canadian, two U.S.) on selection, price, design, and service. They searched each site for five books and bought one, Tom Wolfe, *A Man in Full.* The list price for *A Man in Full* in Canada was $42.75 but it was available at 30 percent off ($29.93) in regular bookstores. Here's what they found (all prices in Canadian dollars):

Amazon	Barnes & Noble	Chapters	Indigo Books & Music
Number of titles: Three million	Three million	More than two million	2.5 to three million
Site styling: Think K mart	Think Macy's	Think the Bay	Think Ikea
Book search results: Two out of five titles found	One out of five titles found	Four out of five titles found	Five out of five titles found
Price and delivery time of *A Man in Full:* $26.53 (40% off, 24-hour shipping)	$31 (30% off, 24-hour shipping)	$25.41 (40% off, 24-hour shipping)	$30.27 (30% off, 24-hour shipping)
Best feature: Free daily gifts with some purchases	Magazines on-line; out-of-print title database	Daily news hit	Clean design; easiest to use
Worst feature: Prices listed only in U.S. dollars	Slow, slow, slow!	Advertising at the top of every page, no reviews	Few reviews of issued books
Regular shipping costs to Canada: $6.12 + $2.98 per item, 1–12 weeks delivery	$6.12 + $2.98 per item, 2–12 weeks delivery	$6 for first one to three books, $2 for each additional book, 1–4 days delivery	$4 + $0.95 per item, 1–4 days delivery
Total cost of *A Man in Full*: $35.63	$40.10	$31.41	$35.22
Online savings: $7.12	$2.65	$11.34	$7.53
Premium over discounted store price: $5.69	$10.17	$1.48	$5.29

Source: *Quill & Quire*, "Checking Out Books Online," January 1999, p. 41.

when consumers visit a store, they have some travelling costs. Retail Highlight 16-1 provides an example of shopping on-line versus a regular bookstore—in this case the regular bookstore offers the lower price.

www.compare.net

www.bottomdollar.com

As another example of seeking the lowest price, consumers can use comparison shopping Web sites such as www.compare.net or www.bottomdollar.com to find the lowest price available for a wide range of products. These sites are designed to facilitate the search for shoppers who are seeking to obtain the lowest price possible.

www.indigo.ca

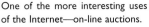

INTERNET EXERCISE: Go to the following Web sites and shop for a book. Compare the shopping experience to shopping at a bookstore. What are the advantages and disadvantages of the Internet shopping experience?

- Indigo – www.indigo.ca
- Chapters – www.chapters.ca
- Amazon – www.amazon.com

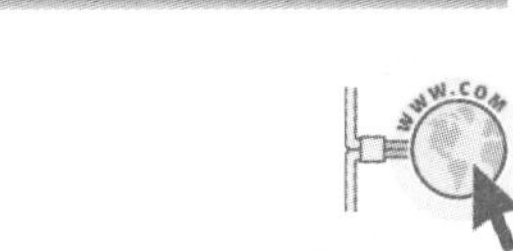

www.chapters.ca

www.amazon.com

Choice A consumer can now "shop" in stores around the world. Consumers are not bound by physical locations in terms of choice. They do not have to shop in their community or neighbouring communities. If a consumer wants an item that is available only in France or Brazil, he or she can get it with relative ease. Not only do consumers have a wide choice of stores, but they also have a wider range of merchandise choice with the wider store choice. This allows customers to select products and services that more closely match the benefits they are seeking.

One of the more interesting uses of the Internet—on-line auctions.

Courtesy Clickabid

Compare with Clickabid on previous page. Which Web site offers more convenience?

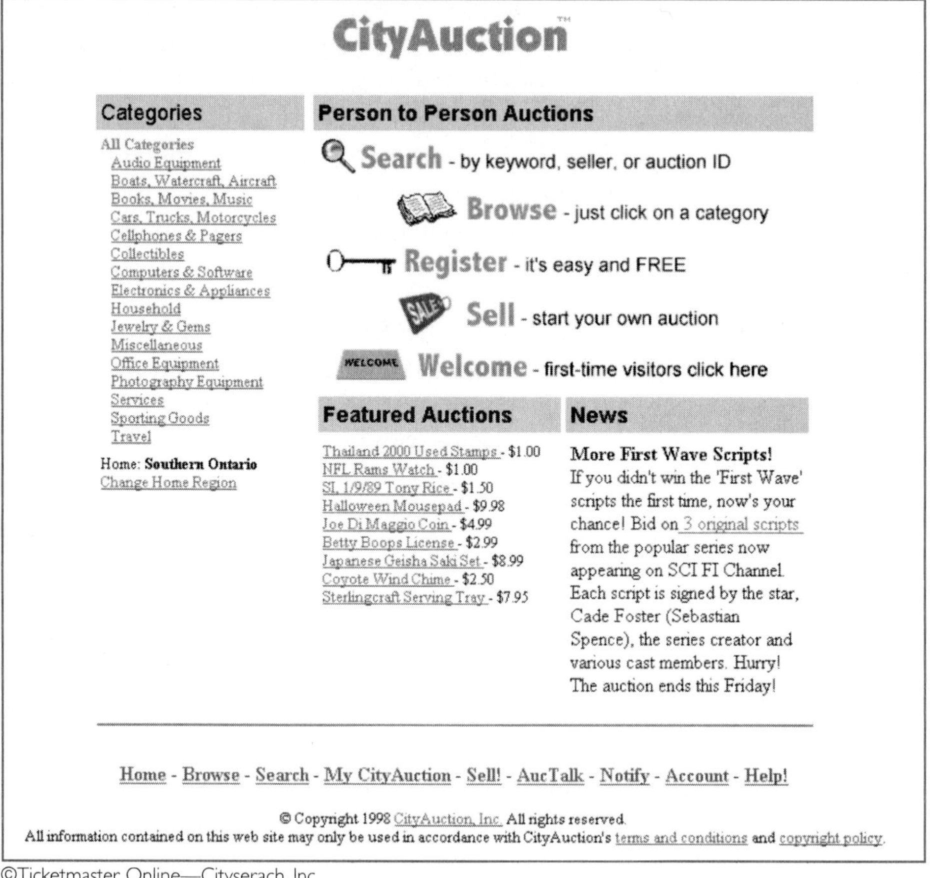

©Ticketmaster Online—Cityserach, Inc.

How much choice consumers want is up for debate. In many instances, consumers shop in only one or two stores, even for shopping goods. How much choice do they really want? Is it a real benefit? The answers to these questions will be determined as researchers gain an understanding of how much value consumers place on choice.

Customization Electronic commerce retailers will provide customers with items of interest to them by asking the customers for their preferences, then signalling them when these items are available. As an example, retailers like Amazon.com and CDNow will identify consumer preferences, either by asking them or, based on their purchase patterns, offer recommendations when they visit the site. Amazon and CDNow help consumers develop their tastes in music or books by providing them information. Possibly the best example is Dell Computers, which allows customers to specify the exact characteristics of the computer they wish to buy, then Dell builds it and ships it within five days.

E-commerce retailers have the ability to identify consumer preferences and electronically send them a catalogue that is tailored to their individual needs.

Communication Customers and electronic retailers can “talk” to each other via the Internet and many retailers have 1-800 or 1-888 numbers that consumers

www.BotSpot.com

can use to talk to the retailer. A huge variety of information is available almost instantaneously about important product information, brand attributes, prices, and suppliers. By asking questions on the Web, using either simple search engines or **intelligent agents** (called **bots**, see www.BotSpot.com), consumers can learn, see, evaluate, compare, and even make decisions to purchase on-line. The ability to quickly get vast amounts of valuable information from home, plus the use of intelligence agents to process it, makes the Internet a more powerful communication tool for on-line retail consumers.

www.jango.excite.com

www.bottomdollar.com

www.mysimon.com

www.compare.net

www.inktomi.com

INTERNET EXERCISE: Evaluate, using a table format, the following product-comparison services in terms of product information, merchants, price comparison, availability, and ease of use:

- www.jango.excite.com
- www.bottomdollar.com
- www.mysimon.com
- www.compare.net
- www.inktomi.com

Control It is generally agreed that the Internet has allowed consumers to take more control and power over the buying situation. One of the powerful marketing tools of the traditional retailer is personal selling—a persuasive medium for convincing customers to buy merchandise. With the Internet, the customer can obtain most, if not all, the information they need to make an informed purchase decision without using a salesperson. Further, the customers' ability to compare prices, products, and services across retailers allows them to make a decision that best suits their needs. It also allows customers to bargain with retailers because they may have as much, if not more, knowledge of the product, prices, and services than the salespeople of a particular retailer.

KEYS FOR SUCCESS IN ELECTRONIC COMMERCE[8]

A successful e-commerce retailer needs to have:

- A large number of visitors to the site, particularly repeat visitors.
- A broad selection of merchandise available that can be shipped quickly.
- A well-designed, entertaining, and efficient site that allows customers to easily find the products they want.
- Competitive prices.
- Customer trust and ongoing satisfaction.

The importance of branding to e-commerce retailing is critical. It brings visitors to the site, gives them confidence, and gets them to come back (see Retail Highlight 16-2). However, the e-commerce retailer must also offer service and price along with the brand in order to succeed. Thus, a strong brand is essential to bring visitors to a site but the retailer then has to "deliver" the service at a competitive price.

Retail Highlight 16-2 The Internet Debate: How Important Is Branding?

There is a critical debate regarding the importance of branding on the Internet. Consider the following:

- The Internet, where prices and services can be compared with a couple of clicks, fundamentally shifts the balance of power from the retailer to the customer. Customers will buy based on the best price, not the brand (i.e., Amazon.com, CDNow). They will buy from the lowest price Internet provider.
- But the race by all the big Internet players to get huge fast is based on the opposite assumption—that consumers will align themselves early on with one of a couple of names and stay put out of sloth and habit.
- Coke and Microsoft started with products and wrapped them in brands. Amazon.com, which sells other people's products, is almost entirely a creation of branding.
- Look at traditional markets and marketing—brands win.

Source: Peter de Jonge, "Riding the Perilous Waters of Amazon.com," *New York Times Magazine*, March 14, 1999, pp. 36–41, 54, 68, 79–81.

Bricks-and-Mortar Versus New Retailers

There are two types of e-commerce retailers: (1) the new firms with no history—like Amazon and CDNow—and (2) established retailers (referred to as bricks-and-mortar retailers) who are developing a new distribution channel—like the Bay, Chapters, and Sears Canada. While a number of new firms have created a brand, as the established retailers increase their marketing efforts on the Internet, it will become more difficult for new firms to penetrate these markets.

The amount spent on marketing costs by the new firms to create a brand is extremely high. While traditional retailers typically spend less than 5 percent of revenues on marketing, the new firms spend up to 65 percent or more of revenues on marketing.[9]

In 1999, Amazon spent about 24 percent of its revenues on marketing, which amounted to $29 per customer. At issue is whether this investment will ever pay off. It shows the stakes required to create a brand from scratch.

An advantage that traditional retailers have over e-commerce retailers is that a customer can buy the merchandise and take it home. The customer's needs are immediately satisfied. With the Internet, the retailer needs to establish a system to offer the customer relatively quick delivery of merchandise. How quick will depend on the type of merchandise. Catalogue retailers have been quite successful with delivery within a week. The speed of delivery will probably be critical for e-commerce retailers, which means they will have to establish warehouse systems.

With traditional retailers, the transformation to e-commerce should be easier on the shipping dimension because they have the inventory, expertise, and relationships with suppliers to obtain and ship merchandise.

The Technology Issue

The technology issue is challenging. The e-commerce retailer will require various technologies to develop a satisfying on-line experience for customers and deliver the order quickly. The technology required will include the ability to:

- Process and track orders—inventory database and IT systems.
- Create an efficient, pleasant shopping experience—fast, reliable Web site and systems tied to inventory and order databases.
- Have efficient inventory management—integrated systems with suppliers.
- Have customer service—phone and e-mail customer support systems.

Large catalogue firms, like Sears Canada, have many of these capabilities. These firms need to add the Web technologies. The debate is whether traditional retailers can develop these systems.

www.ibm.com

INTERNET EXERCISE: IBM (www.ibm.com) has a section on their Web site that allows a retailer to evaluate its chances of marketing success on the Internet (in IBM's site, go to e-business, then e-commerce assistant). Decide on a retailer that might be thinking of going on the net and go through the exercise. What did you learn?

TYPE OF PRODUCTS SOLD ON THE INTERNET

Products can be characterized as **atom-based** or **bit-based**.[10] Atom-based products have a physical form and presence, involve a shipping process, and are returnable and resaleable. Examples are cars, CDs, and books. Bit-based products are digital data in an electronic form that do not have a physical form and presence, even though they can be stored in a physical media. These products do not require a separate shipping process; they can be transferred to the consumer on-line. They are nonreturnable—once customers have seen them, then they have received the value of the product. Examples are on-line movies, books, software, newspapers, and other forms of information and entertainment. Bit-based products also include services that can be purchased on-line where no physical exchange is required, such as banking and insurance services.

Because they can be "shipped" on-line, sales of bit-based products are growing far more rapidly than atom-based products. As e-commerce retailers determine how to price and collect payment for "downloading" music, movies, books, and magazines, the sales will increase even more dramatically. Any traditional retailer who sells products and services that can be delivered electronically is under threat. When consumers can select and customize their services on-line and then receive them at the click of a mouse, traditional retailers will find it difficult to compete.

The growth of Internet sales of atom-based products will depend on the type of product. The main drawback of e-commerce is that "touch and feel" and, to an extent, "look and see" information is not available. The customers' ability to view fashion merchandise and determine what size to buy is limited on the Internet. Thus, the adoption rate of on-line shopping for any type of merchandise where "touch, feel, look, and see" is important will be met with some customer resistance. Where it is less important, such as merchandise that can be purchased based on specifications (e.g., computers, software), consumer acceptance rates are more rapid.

In terms of actual sales, the hot categories for 1999 were books, music, travel, videos, automobiles, flowers, and apparel. The projected future winners are office supplies, sporting goods, toys, and specialty foods.[11]

DESIGNING AN EFFECTIVE WEB SITE

Retailers are continually learning about the design and maintenance of an effective **Web site**. With this new, interactive medium the "rules" are being revised as consumers "click" on and off sites that offer value or don't. Consider the fact that there are over 100 million Web pages and of these the top 10 percent get 90 percent of the traffic. Consider as well the problem that many Canadian retailers face because many Canadian Internet users have a U.S. portal. A **portal** is a Web site that functions as the first screen seen when someone accesses the Internet (Retail Highlight 16-3). Many of these portals, including Yahoo, allow consumers to customize the Web site's content so that it only provides information that is of interest to them. This creates loyalty for the portal.

Retail Highlight 16-3 The Importance of Portals—Will Canadian E-commerce Retailers Lose Out?

A portal is a Web site that functions as the first screen seen when someone accesses the Internet. Well-known U.S. portals include AOL and Yahoo. Canadian portals include Yahoo Canada, Sympatico, Canoe, and Canada.com. When a consumer starts a search for merchandise using a portal, it will guide them to Web sites identified by the search engine of that portal. Here's the issue: If a Canadian consumer uses a U.S.-based portal (e.g., AOL), the search is likely to bypass Canadian e-commerce retailers. This has considerable implications for Canadian firms seeking to establish themselves on the Internet. The U.S. Internet industry dominates the world e-commerce scene—size matters. For example, Canoe.com is viewed about 46 million times per month; Yahoo is viewed by 167 million people each day!

It is predicted that unless Canadian portals are supported by more products and services and promoted more aggressively, the e-commerce trade gap with the U.S. will continue to grow. Most of the billions that Canadian consumers will spend on the Internet will go south.

Source: Jack Fuerstenberg and Jordan Worth, "Canadian E-commerce Faces Death of a Thousand Clicks," *Financial Post*, May 11, 1999, p. C7.

To illustrate how a portal creates traffic and loyalty, Yahoo is regarded as a master of building "stickiness;" figuring out which services will encourage on-line consumers to register with the portal, stay and check out many Web pages, and visit again and again. For any retailer seeking to market to consumers, getting "sticky" is critical. Yahoo has created an image of fun and discovery, added personalized features that consumers value (e.g., free e-mail, a home page with the consumer's own stock quotes, a card on his or her birthday, news item updates of interest) and created virtual "clubs" that allow people with similar interests to chat and share ideas.[12]

Basic marketing and retailing principles are used in building an effective Web site. For example, the retailer needs to consider the sales and marketing cycle and address the following issues:[13]

- **Customer:** Who are your target customers and what do they need? What advertising and awareness strategies will be used to get customers to the store the first time? How will you get them to come back? Table 16-1 provides some shopper types using the Internet.
- **Merchandising:** What products will you offer and how will you position and display them to your customers?

Table 16-1

Shopper Types Using the Internet

Shopper	Definition
Directed shoppers	Know what they want and like to shop quickly. Believed to be the majority of today's on-line shoppers.
Category shoppers	Customers who tend to purchase certain categories frequently to the exclusion of others.
Gift givers	In the business of buying gifts; visit flower and specialty gift sites often.
"Gotta have it" impulse buyers	Typically buy the latest and greatest, though few sites have made this feature and respective functionality fun for shoppers.
Browsers	"Just visiting" mindset where merchants must look to turn browsers into buyers.
Bargain hunters	Those price-sensitive shoppers in the market for a bargain. Sales shoppers permeate the Web culture and, according to studies, many people believe products should be less expensive on-line.
Information seekers	"Hungry for information" consumers head on-line due to lack of information at retail. The trick here is converting these browsers into buyers on-line where the cost savings for merchants can be significant and upscale a true reality.

www.shop.org

Source: The e.guide, www.shop.org.

- **Sales service:** How will you answer customers' questions and solve their problems?
- **Promotions:** How will you promote merchandise and services to give customers incentives to make purchases?
- **Transaction processing:** How will you handle orders, tax, shipping, and payment processing?
- **Fulfillment:** How will you pass orders to the fulfillment centre?
- **Post-sales service:** How will you provide customer service and answers to order-status questions after the sale? Some recommendations for customer service are provided in Table 16-2.
- **Marketing data and analysis:** What information about sales, customer, and advertising trends will you gather? How will you use it to make decisions?
- **Brand:** How will you communicate with customers during each of these interactions in a way that reinforces your unique company image?

The answers to these questions will assist the retailer in designing the Web site. With respect to the actual Web site, the retailer has the choice of doing it from scratch, using existing software to create the site, or hiring a professional firm. There are considerable choices in available software including Intershop ePages, iCat Lemonade Stand, and Yahoo Stores, which are "ready to go" programs. More sophisticated solutions that integrate much of the sales and marketing cycle include Microsoft Site Server Enterprise and IBM Net.Commerce. Many retailers have chosen to develop their sites in partnership with these software firms.

Table 16-2

Customer Service Recommendations

- First time visitor icons are a great way to welcome new users by giving them that in-store salesperson feeling that help is just around the corner.
- Provide easy to locate 800/888 customer service phone number, fax number, and customer service hours.
- Make user registration an option, not a requirement.
- Ensure that the shoppers can purchase on their first try, as time is of the essence.
- Specify bill to and ship to on the order form at the beginning of the process, so that the customer doesn't have to go back and redo it.
- Be sure to include item price, shipping/handling charges, all taxes, gift wrap costs, and the grand total for quick read, as the order summary is part of the order process.
- Deliver a real-time order confirmation so the customer has a confirmation number at the end of the order process.
- Send an e-mail confirmation including relevant shipping and/or order status.
- Make gift wrapping a service as opposed to another step in the process, as harried, last minute shoppers are especially fond of this service.
- Be sure the shipper includes a return label, a gift card (if applicable), and return information as instructions to facilitate good customer service.

www.shop.org

Source: Lauren Freedman, "The e-tailing Group's Top 10 Customer Service Recommendations," The e-guide, www.shop.org

The e-commerce retailer that has created a model that many others are attempting to follow is Amazon.com (Retail Highlight 16-4).

The design of the actual Web site will depend on the type of product offered.[14] Considering gifts and impulse items, consumers often don't know what they want until they see it. A site that offers impulse buys should be easy and entertaining to explore, and should offer advice and ideas.

www.sympatico.ca

www.ca.yahoo.com

www.canoe.com

www.canada.com

INTERNET EXERCISE: Sympatico, Yahoo Canada, Canoe, and Canada.com are four on-line search engines that feature news and information about Canada and search capabilities. Search each site for a flower shop that will send flowers to a friend in Halifax. What are the advantages and disadvantages of using these search engines versus phoning a florist to send the flowers?

- Sympatico – www.sympatico.ca
- Yahoo Canada – www.ca.yahoo.com
- Canoe – www.canoe.com
- Canada.com – www.canada.com

Types of Products

Commodity Products Commodity products, like CDs and books, are low risk purchases. Here, the merchant has to have them in stock at a good price. E-commerce retailers that offer these products differentiate based on price, selection, and availability. But these companies cannot compete only on price—margins are too low. They focus on adding value through customer service and convenience. For example, they extend search capabilities to help customers find items based on song lyrics or word phrases. By adding this value, the customers keep coming back.

Retail Highlight 16-4 Amazon.com—The "Killer" Site on the Internet

Amazon.com is the leading consumer e-commerce Web site in the world. It leads because of its:

- Wide product selection
- Easy-to-navigate site
- Excellent use of e-mail for marketing and customer service
- Skill at tailoring product recommendations to individuals

But there is more. What sets it apart is its ability to innovate—to come up with novel ideas to work with customers and keep ahead of its competitors. Amazon learns from its customer information and preferences and then invents things that it thinks customers want. These innovations include one-click shopping, best-seller lists, and auctions. The results are that more than 60 percent of Amazon's sales are to repeat customers and it has a growth record that is unmatched in e-commerce.

Source: Eryn Brown, "Nine Ways to Win on the Web," *Fortune*, May 24, 1999, pp. 112–125.

Shopping Products With shopping goods—like electronic products, cars, and software—customers want to compare different models and features to reduce their risk and make a "good" decision. Here, the site has to allow for easy comparison across brands and features. It is likely that customers will visit sites, like CompareNet and mySimon, which offer side by side comparisons of different products.

Specialty Products Customized products, like computers, need to have Web sites that enable the customer to design their own product (e.g., Dell, Apple).

The design of a Web site clearly depends on the retailer's target market, the type of products offered, and the retailer's strategy. Recognizing that these factors will determine the specific design of the Web site, there are some basics, or rules, that good Web site designers follow. Here are a number of suggestions from Web site designers:[15]

- Keep it simple. The power of good design is in its simplicity. When the final design seems too simple for the amount of work you've put in, then you know you're done. Less is more.
- Don't be seduced by form versus content. The designer concerned with content will make a more meaningful contribution. Users are completely uninterested in learning anything about how your site works. They came for content. Give it to them—fast and simple. More speed, less interactivity. Content is king.
- Make sure that you clearly identify the problem that needs solving and that you are not simply icing the cake. The final appearance is only the icing; it's the bigger, more difficult process of problem solving that matters.
- The most important aesthetic consideration is transmission speed. If it takes too long to download, go back to the drawing board. You have 30 seconds to load everything on a screen. And that's probably a liberal estimate—it's actually more like 15 seconds. Be very fast. If it "ain't" 100 percent product usable within 10 seconds, you failed. Shoot for 5 seconds.
- When laying out text, actually read it! Think about how someone with even less interest than you would look at it. Also, short sentence length is a good thing.
- Learn the structure of **HTML** and why it works like it does. Design in ways that take advantage of what HTML can do well, and route around what it cannot.
- Learn and think about your audience, then learn and think about computers, then think about your audience again.
- Think about this—people hate to wait. People hate to scroll. People hate to read. People would rather scroll than wait. People would rather wait than read. People are not necessarily rational or consistent, but sometimes they are.
- Think about the first screen as the front page of a newspaper. Really important stuff goes on the front page, and the most important stuff goes at the top or "above the fold" as newspaper folks say.

Retail Highlight 16-5 On-line Marketing—Personalized Selling—One to One

An important aspect of successful e-commerce retailing is the ability to market on a one-to-one basis. This means developing a Web site that allows individual recommendations to be made based on the customer's preferences. Here's what Net Perceptions, a Web design firm, can offer its e-commerce retail clients:

- Dynamic segmentation—creates segments of one customer based on that customer's wants, needs, and tastes.
- Continuous learning—automatically learns from each customer's behaviour and keeps learning at every point of interaction.
- Predictive—predicts matches between individual customers and products.
- Operates in "real time"—customers interact with the site and it responds.

Net Perceptions states that the results of using its system will turn browsers into buyers, increase sales per transaction, build customer loyalty, and leverage data the firm already has.

www.netperceptions.com

Source: www.netperceptions.com

- People read left to right and top to bottom. They almost always look at the upper-left corner first, which is a good place to put something really important. If one of your goals is to get people to call your 800 number, you know where to put it.

The ability to customize a Web site to appeal to individual consumer's tastes can lead to considerable business if done properly (Retail Highlight 16-5).

ADVERTISING ON THE WEB

Retailers can use the Internet to promote their products through either **banner ads** (which can be placed at various sites), or through the design of an effective Web site, as just covered. The objectives of advertising on the Web can go from providing information about the retailer's products and services, to creating or enhancing an image, to stimulating trials by providing electronic coupons.

Web advertising in Canada has been growing very rapidly, with half of the revenues coming from banner advertising in 1998, and half of the retail store chains reporting advertising on the Web.[16]

The advantages of advertising on the Internet are: more precise targeting, better and interactive messages that can be designed to appeal to various customer groups, ability to generate immediate sales, and high potential for creativity.

The disadvantages of advertising on the Internet are: current technical problems leading to Websnarl (long time to access a site), increased clutter, potential for deception, and production costs.

www.egateway.com

www.iabcanada.com

INTERNET EXERCISE: Check the following sites to research advertising on the Web, and write a small report on the subject, with recommendations to retailers:

- e-marketer's gateway—www.egateway.com
- IAB Canada—www.iabcanada.com
- AIMS—www.aimscanada.com
- AC Nielsen—www.acnielsen.com
- BBM—www.bbm.ca
- ComQUEST—www.comquest.ca

THE FUTURE OF E-COMMERCE

www.aimscanada.com

www.acnielsen.com

www.bbm.ca

www.comquest.ca

It is clear that e-commerce is evolving and the future will bring many changes. Currently, computer specialists are creating artificial intelligence systems that are "intelligent enough and lifelike enough that consumers will feel that they're dealing with another person."[17] Referred to as virtual sales agents, these systems will make Web sites warmer, more inviting places to shop. The systems can be programmed to ask how the customer is doing and remember what the customer "said" and bought from one visit to the next. The forecast is that the Web will be populated by virtual humans that people will interact with because that's the most natural way for humans to interact.

Other predictions for the future include continued rapid growth of e-commerce as more consumers gain experience with this mode of shopping, a trend to capture greater market share by e-commerce retailers who deliver what target markets want, and more traditional retailers losing sales and going out of business. Whatever happens, the future of e-commerce, like retailing in general, will continue to be exciting, dynamic, and challenging.

Canada's oldest retailer adopts the newest form of retailing—electronic commerce.

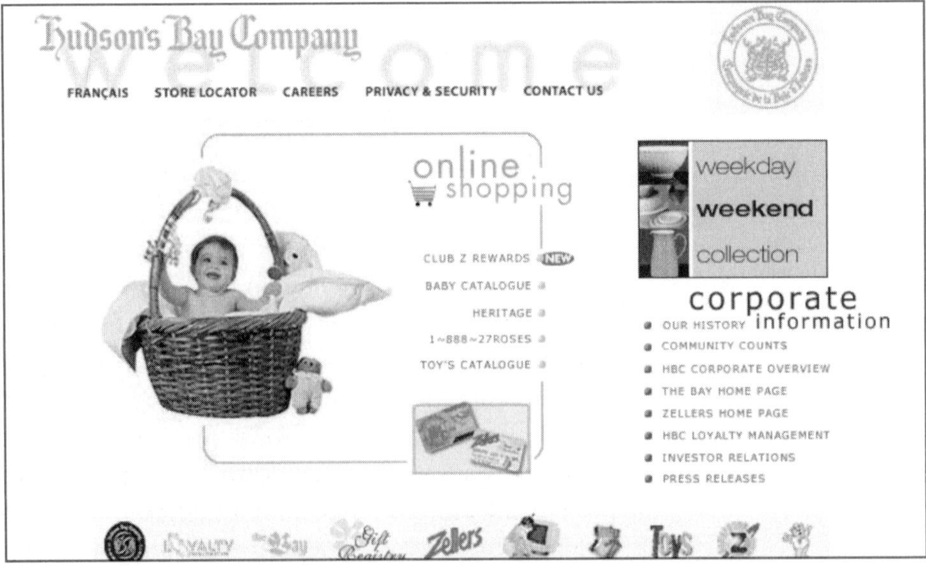

Courtesy Hudson's Bay Company—Corporate Collection

CHAPTER HIGHLIGHTS

- Consumers buy on-line for more convenience, lower costs, bigger choice, more customization, and better communication and control.
- To be successful, retailers must attract visitors to their site, have good selection, competitive prices, customer satisfaction, and a well-designed, entertaining Web site.
- Products can be characterized as atom-based or bit-based.
- Designing an effective Web site is critical to the retailer's success: first, a portal must be designed to generate traffic and loyalty; Internet shopper types as well as product types must be understood and taken into account; and good customer service is essential.
- The Internet allows the retailer to communicate directly with its customer, design an ad that is effective, and use the interactivity to generate a dialogue. Advertising can be done by using a banner ad or being incorporated within the Web site.
- E-commerce ensures that the future of retailing will continue to be exciting, dynamic, and challenging.

KEY TERMS

atom-based product	393	HTML	398
banner ad	399	intelligent agent	391
bit-based product	393	portal	394
bots	391	six Cs	387
e-commerce	386	Web site	394

DISCUSSION QUESTIONS

1. Briefly explain the six Cs of on-line customer behaviour, and give an example of each.
2. Explain how a bricks-and-mortar retailer can develop a program of selling through the Internet.
3. What are the most important factors in designing a Web site?
4. Describe briefly the profile of each Internet shopper type, and identify a retailer that might appeal to each one.
5. In your opinion, what are the characteristics of a successful banner ad?

APPLICATION EXERCISES

1. Find a retailer in your community that would like a Web page designed. Use free Web page design software (e.g., Web Wizard, Netscape Communicator, or Microsoft Web Publishing Wizard) for this assignment. Design the Web site.
2. As a class project, we will examine whether or not shopping on the Internet is easier than shopping at a store. While many people claim it is easier, there is little actual evidence to support the claim. Break the class into four groups, have each group shop for a different item both on-line and in a physical retail store. The four items are: a compact disk, a book, an item of clothing

(either a shirt or blouse), and flowers. Pretend you are purchasing the item as a gift for a friend. As you do your "shopping," think about how Internet shopping compares with shopping in physical retail stores. How easy is it to evaluate products? How easy is it to find and evaluate retailers? How do your search time and costs compare between the two channels?

The assignment:

a. First, shop in as many stores as you normally would until you find the store and price that you want. As you shop, think about the information you used to evaluate the product. Keep track of the following:
   i. Total time spent in travelling to and from the store(s), searching for and evaluating the product, and time spent paying for the product.
   ii. Price of the product (including taxes) and the name of the store you decided to "buy" from.
   iii. Evaluation of your shopping experience from 1 to 10 (1 being worst, 10 being best).
b. Now "shop" on-line for the same product. Think about how this shopping experience compares to shopping at a physical retail store in terms of ease of finding retailers, searching for and evaluating products, and "making" the purchase. As above, record:
   i. Total time spent in getting to the computer and starting the Web browser, finding the product at the Internet retailers you searched, and checking out and "paying" for the product.
   ii. Price of the product (including taxes) and the name of the store you decided to "buy" from.
   iii. Evaluation of your shopping experience from 1 to 10 (1 being worst, 10 being best).
c. Compare your shopping experiences in terms of:
   i. The advantages and disadvantages of the Internet over regular shopping.
   ii. The differences between Internet competitors.

Keep your answers short—your whole answer should fit on one page.

SUGGESTED CASES

20. TeleGrocer—A Virtual Retailer
21. The Natural Group
22. Treasure Toys

Part 6

Evaluating Retail Performance

In *Part 6, Evaluating Retail Performance,* the tools used to determine how well the retail strategy is doing are explained in Chapter 17. Internal evaluation is critical to the retail manager, including the elements involved in the evaluation of the performance of the firm.

CHAPTER 17

EVALUATING RETAIL PERFORMANCE

CHAPTER OBJECTIVES

After reading this chapter you should be able to:

1. Review the key financial statements of a retailer.
2. Use the strategic profit model (SPM) as a framework for evaluating performance.
3. Examine the problems that management faces in determining the cost and value of merchandise inventory.
4. Understand the two approaches to costing for performance evaluation.

Firms such as Mark's Work Wearhouse, the Canadian retail chain, strive for success by devising effective strategies to attract customers and to compete, and also by monitoring and evaluating performance to determine whether their strategies are being implemented effectively and whether changes in strategy and operations are needed. Mark's Work Wearhouse has annual objectives for the company, its senior managers, and store managers. At a company level, some of its operational goals for 1999 were:

- Sales per average retail square foot of $270 (actual was $251)
- Gross margin return on investment of 1.9 times (actual was 1.5)
- After-tax profit on sales of 2% (actual was 1.4%)
- Return on average equity of over 15% (actual was 11.5%)
- Current ratio of not less than 1.5 to 1 (actual was 1.7 to 1)

For senior managers, the goals included:

- The President – pre-tax profit of $17.9 million or greater (actual was $11 million)
- The VP merchandising – inventory turnover rate of 2.2 turns (actual was 1.9 turns)

For store managers, a number of targets were set including sales per store, store performance rating, staff performance rating, and average dollar amount per transaction.

Every year, Mark's sets objectives and evaluates performance against these objectives. By constantly monitoring performance and making the appropriate strategy adjustments, the targets are attainable.[1]

Mark's Work Wearhouse evaluates performance against objectives on an annual basis.

Courtesy Mark's Work Wearhouse

This chapter focuses on monitoring and evaluating performance. The tools presented here help retailers assess their effectiveness in implementing strategy and provide a framework for determining shortcomings and identifying areas that need improvement.

KEY FINANCIAL STATEMENTS AND RATIOS

The balance sheet, the income statement, and the various ratios derived from them give management the information needed to evaluate the effectiveness of strategy in financial terms.

The Balance Sheet

The **balance sheet** is a snapshot of a firm's financial health on a specific date. Table 17-1 lists the components of the balance sheet—**assets** (**current** and **fixed**), **liabilities**, and **net worth** (the owners' investment or equity). The simplest expression of the balance sheet equation is: assets = liabilities + net worth.

Table 17-1

Balance Sheet December 31, 20—

Assets			
Current assets:			
Cash	$15,000		
Accounts receivable	34,000		
Merchandise inventory	84,000		
Total current assets		$133,000	
Fixed assets:			
Building	$85,000		
Furniture and fixtures	23,000		
Total fixed assets		$108,000	
Total Assets			$241,000
Liabilities and Net Worth			
Current liabilities:			
Accounts payable	$20,000		
Payroll payable	26,000		
Notes payable	32,000		
Total current liabilities		$78,000	
Fixed liabilities:			
Mortgage payable	$75,000		
Total fixed liabilities		$75,000	
Total liabilities		$153,000	
Net Worth:			
Capital surplus	$80,000		
Retained earnings	8,000		
Total net worth		$88,000	
Total Liabilities and Net Worth			$241,000

The Income Statement

The **income statement** shows operating results over a period of time and indicates whether investments in assets and strategy have been successful and profitable (Table 17-2). The income statement indicates net sales, **gross margin** (the difference between net sales and cost of goods sold), total expenses, and after-tax profit. Cost of goods sold is computed as follows:

Beginning inventory
\+ Purchases
= Goods available for sale
– Ending inventory
= Cost of goods sold

Table 17-2

Income Statement Year Ending December 31, 20—

Gross sales	$208,600			
Less returns and allowances	16,300			
Net sales			$192,300	100.00%
Cost of goods sold:				
Opening inventory	$21,650			
Net purchases	113,500			
Goods available for sale		$135,150		
Less closing inventory		$28,495		
Cost of goods sold			$106,655	55.46
Gross margin			$85,645	44.54
Expenses:				
Total expenses			$70,655	36.74
Profit before taxes			$14,990	7.80
Income tax			4,950	2.57
Net profit after taxes			$10,040	5.22%

In general, the income statement is a valuable tool for measuring the results of operations. For example, if expenses are higher than in the past and higher than in similar stores, the manager may decide that corrective action is needed.

Ratio Analysis

Retailers, like Mark's Work Wearhouse, establish ratio goals as part of their financial plan. They can then compare performance with objectives. Comparison over time is valuable, as is comparison of performance ratios with trade data for similar firms. Monitoring selected financial ratios can help determine whether problems are developing.

Table 17-3 presents a summary of key financial ratios, their methods of calculation, and the information they show. Two of the ratios—return on total assets (net profit after taxes divided by total assets) and the current ratio (current assets divided by current liabilities)—can often predict the success or failure of retail firms. Too high a current ratio and the inability to make a profit, as reflected by return on assets, can lead to the failure of a retail business.

We also call your attention to leverage ratios. **Leverage** is a situation in which a business unit acquires assets worth more than the amount of capital invested by the owners; the higher the ratio, the higher the amount of borrowed funds in the business. Leverage can be measured in various ways. Regardless of how it is measured, too high a leverage ratio can be dangerous, especially in periods of economic instability and high interest rates.

Table 17-3 A Summary of Key Financial Ratios, How They Are Calculated, and What They Show

Ratio	How Calculated	What it Shows
Profitability Ratios:		
1. Gross profit margin	$\frac{\text{Sales} - \text{Cost of goods sold}}{\text{Sales}}$	An indication of the total margin available to cover operating expenses and yield a profit.
2. Operating profit margin (or return on sales)	$\frac{\text{Profits before taxes and interest}}{\text{Sales}}$	An indication of the firm's profitability from current operations without regard to the interest charges accruing from the capital structure.
3. Net profit margin (or net return on sales)	$\frac{\text{Profits after taxes}}{\text{Sales}}$	Shows after-tax profit per dollar of sales. Subpar profit margins indicate that the firm's sales prices are relatively low or that its costs are relatively high, or both.
4. Return on total assets	$\frac{\text{Profits after taxes}}{\text{Total assets}}$	A measure of the return on total investment in the enterprise.
Liquidity Ratios:		
1. Current ratio	$\frac{\text{Current assets}}{\text{Current liabilities}}$	Indicates the extent to which the claims of short-term creditors are covered to cash in a period roughly corresponding to the maturity of the liabilities.
2. Quick ratio (or acid-test ratio)	$\frac{\text{Current assets} - \text{Inventory}}{\text{Current liabilities}}$	A measure of the firm's ability to pay off short-term obligations without relying on the sale of its inventories.
Leverage Ratios:		
1. Debt-to-assets ratio	$\frac{\text{Total debt}}{\text{Total assets}}$	Measures the extent to which borrowed funds have been used to finance the firm's operations.

Table 17-3 A Summary of Key Financial Ratios, How They Are Calculated, and What They Show (continued)

2. Debt-to-equity ratio	Total debt / Total stockholders' equity	Provides another measure of the funds provided by creditors versus the funds provided by owners.
3. Times-interest-earned(or coverage) ratio	Profits before interest and taxes / Total interest charges	Measures the extent to which earnings can decline without the firm becoming unable to meet its annual interest costs.
Activity Ratios:		
1. Inventory turnover	Sales / Avg. inventory (in retail dollars)	When compared to industry averages, it provides an indication of whether a company has excessive or inadequate inventory.
2. Average collection period	Accounts receivable / Total sales/365	Indicates the average length of time the firm must wait after making a sale before it receives payment.

THE STRATEGIC PROFIT MODEL

An important purpose of this section is to use the **strategic profit model (SPM)** as a framework for monitoring performance results. The SPM is derived from information obtained in the balance sheet and the income statement. The SPM provides the essential ratios for performance evaluation needed here, as illustrated in Figure 17-1.

The objective of all retailers is to make a profit, but exactly what does "making a profit" mean? Perhaps the most common way to describe profit is net profit after taxes—the bottom line of the income statement. Profit performance is often evaluated in terms of sales volume—that is, profit as a percentage of sales. For strategic purposes, the most valuable way to view profit, however, is in terms of a return on investment (ROI).

The two ways of looking at ROI from a strategic point of view are: (1) return on assets (ROA) and (2) return on net worth (RONW). The ROA reflects all funds invested in a business, whether they come from owners or creditors. The RONW is a measure of profitability for those who have provided the net worth funds—that is, the owners.

Figure **17-1** The Strategic Profit Model Process

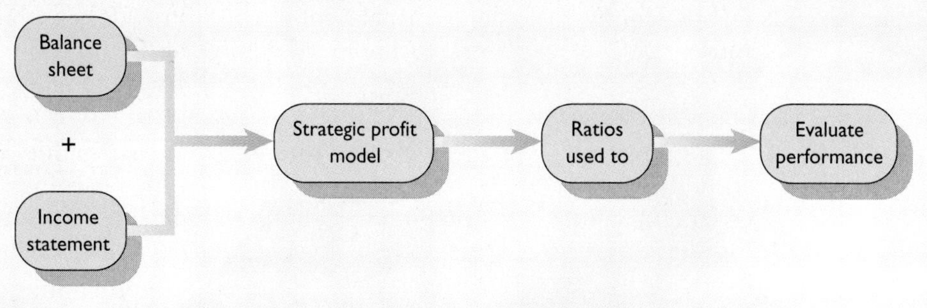

Figure **17-2** The Strategic Profit Model

Margin management

(1) Net profit margin

Net profits / Net sales

Measures amount of net profit produced by each dollar of sales

X

(2) Rate of asset turnover

Net sales / Total assets

Measures dollars of sales volume produced by each dollar invested in total assets of business

=

Asset management

(3) Rate of return on assets (ROA)

Net profits / Total assets

Measures for managers of return on all funds invested in business (by both owners and creditors)

X

Leverage management

(4) Leverage ratio

Total assets / Net worth

Dollars of total assets that can be acquired or supported for each dollar of owners' investment

=

(5) Rate of return on net worth (RONW)

Net profits / Net worth

Measures of profitability for owners who have provided net worth funds

$$\left(\frac{\text{Net profits}}{\text{Net sales}} \times \frac{\text{Net sales}}{\text{Total assets}}\right) = \frac{\text{Net profits}}{\text{Total assets}} \times \frac{\text{Total assets}}{\text{Net worth}} = \frac{\text{Net profits}}{\text{Net worth}}$$

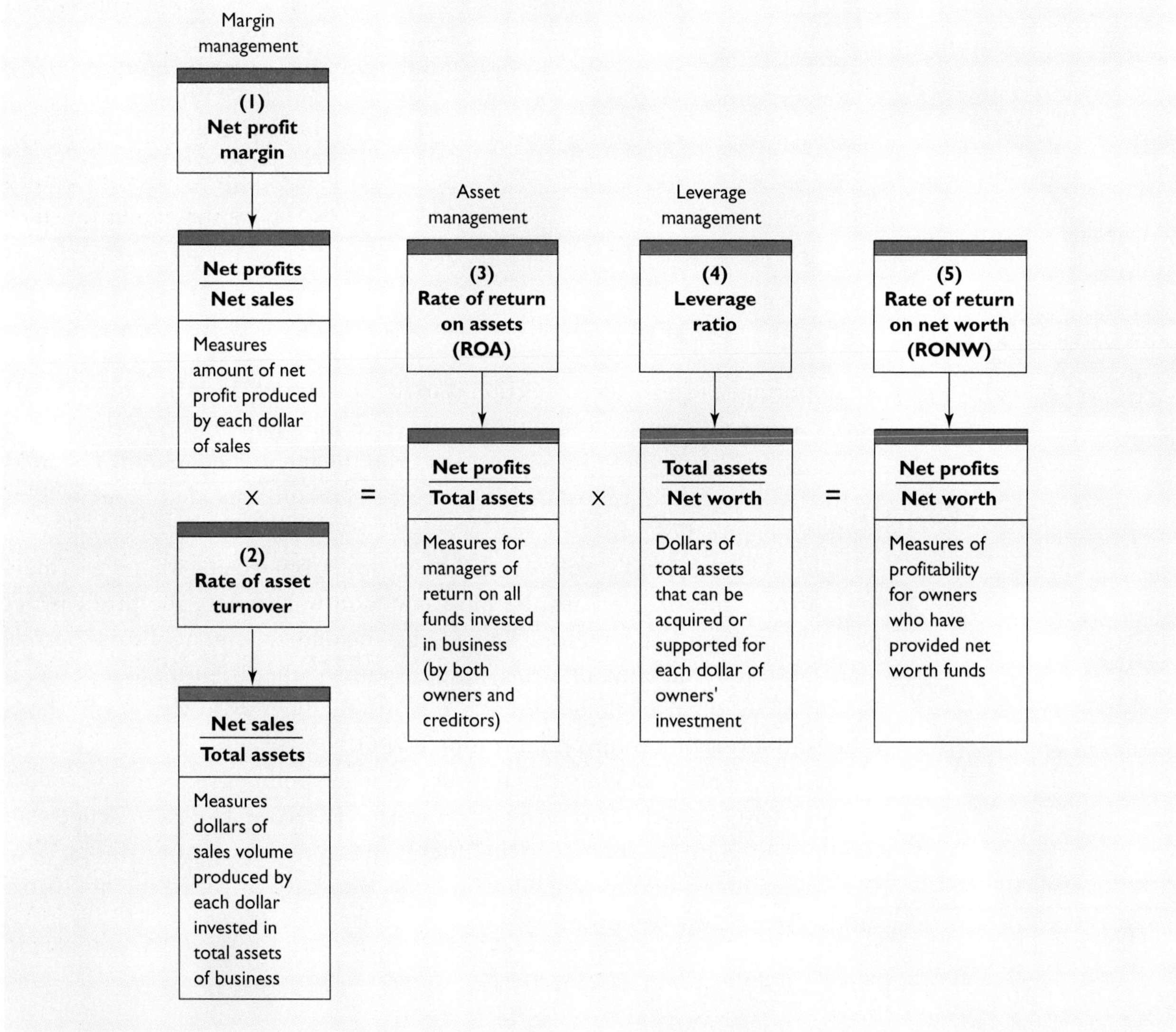

Purposes of the SPM

Figure 17-2 diagrams the SPM. Boxes 1 through 5 provide the basic ratios (derived from the key financial statements) that comprise the model. A simple algebraic representation of the model would look like this:

$$\underset{(1)}{\frac{\text{Net profit}}{\text{Net sales}}} \times \underset{(2)}{\frac{\text{Net sales}}{\text{Total assets}}} = \underset{(3)}{\frac{\text{Net profit}}{\text{Total assets}}} \times \underset{(4)}{\frac{\text{Total assets}}{\text{Net worth}}} = \underset{(5)}{\frac{\text{Net profit}}{\text{Net worth}}}$$

Figure 17-2 also indicates the various paths to profitability and indicates what each component of the model measures. Specifically, the purposes of the SPM are as follows:

1. To emphasize that a firm's principal financial objective is to earn an adequate or target rate of return on net worth (RONW).
2. To provide an excellent management tool for evaluating performance against the target RONW and high-performance trade leaders.
3. To dramatize the principal areas of decision making—margin management, asset management, and leverage management. A firm can improve its rate of RONW by increasing its profit margin, raising its rate of asset turnover, or leveraging its operations more highly.

Please note that in the SPM, leverage is calculated differently from the methods shown in Table 17-3. The ratio in the SPM is another way of calculating leverage; this ratio enables management to determine the extent to which debt is being used to support the asset base of the firm. Figure 17-3 provides an example of the SPM in action for a Canadian fashion retailer.

DETERMINING THE VALUE OF INVENTORY

The focus of this section is on the importance of merchandise inventory in performance evaluation and the problems that arise in determining its value. Retailers can either value inventory at cost, what was paid for the merchandise—its cost price—or at retail, what the merchandise is sold for—its selling price. Because merchandise inventory is typically the largest current asset on the balance sheet, how it is valued has a major impact on the financial statements. The value of ending inventory is used to calculate cost of goods sold—a figure reported on the income statement. An error in determining the inventory figure will cause an equal misstatement of gross profit and net income in the income statement. The amount of assets noted on the balance sheet also will be incorrect by the same amount.

Because retailers invest large sums of money in merchandise, they must know the value of this inventory investment. The information is needed for tax reasons, to compute gross margins as measures of performance, and to make day-to-day decisions. The two main ways of placing a value on inventory are the cost method and the retail method.

Figure 17-3

The Strategic Profit Model in Action—Canadian Fashion Retailer

1. Information

Income Statement (in 000's)		Balance Sheet (in 000's)			
		Assets		Liabilities and Net Worth	
Net sales	$150,200				
Cost of goods sold	96,000				
Gross margin	54,200	Current	$37,300	Liabilities	$22,500
Operating expenses	48,800	Fixed	27,200	Net worth	42,000
Net profit	5,400	Total	$64,500	Total	$64,500

2. Calculation

$$\frac{\text{Net profit}}{\text{Net sales}} \times \frac{\text{Net sales}}{\text{Total assets}} = \frac{\text{Net profit}}{\text{Total assets}} \times \frac{\text{Total assets}}{\text{Net worth}} = \frac{\text{Net profit}}{\text{Net worth}}$$

$$\text{Profit margin} \times \text{Asset turnover} = \text{Return on assets} \times \text{Financial leverage} = \text{Return on net worth}$$

$$\frac{5{,}400}{150{,}200} \times \frac{150{,}200}{64{,}500} = \frac{5{,}400}{64{,}500} \times \frac{64{,}500}{42{,}000} = \frac{5{,}400}{42{,}000}$$

$$.036 \times 2.32 = .0837 \times 1.54 = .129$$

$$3.6\% \times 2.3\text{x} = 8.4\% \times 1.5\text{x} = 12.9\%$$

3. Comments

- Canadian Fashion Retailer (CFR) has a profit of 3.6%, low by industry standards for a fashion retailer. To increase the profit margin, CFR needs to increase prices (or reduce sales promotions), or increase sales without increasing expenses, or maintain sales while reducing expenses.
- Asset turnover is 2.3, which compares favourably to industry standards. CFR is effectively using its assets.
- Return on assets is 8.4%, low by industry standards. The problem is the low net profit.
- Financial leverage is 1.5, due to the high owner equity at CFR. It has the opportunity to increase the leverage of its operations.
- Return on net worth is 12.9%, low by industry standards. CFR needs to examine the factors contributing to the low net profit.

The Cost Method

The cost method provides a book evaluation of inventory and the system uses only cost figures. All inventory records are maintained at cost. When a physical inventory is taken, all items are recorded at actual cost. The major advantage of the cost method is that it is easy to understand. The limitations of the cost method are: difficulty in determining depreciation; difficulty for large retailers with many classifications and price lines; daily inventory is impractical; and costing out each sale and reducing markdowns to cost are extremely difficult. The cost method is appropriate in operations with big-ticket items, where there are few lines and few price changes, where the rate of sale is rapid, and/or where management has very sophisticated computer expertise.

A major problem in determining inventory cost arises when identical units of a product are acquired over a period of time at different unit costs. This can occur during inflationary periods or when there are fluctuations in the exchange rate and the retailer is importing merchandise. One of the two costing methods, FIFO or LIFO, may be adopted to address the problem of inventory costing.

FIFO

The assumption of the **first-in, first-out (FIFO)** method of costing inventory is that costs should be charged against revenue in the order in which they were incurred—that is, the first items purchased (e.g., shirts) are the first ones sold. Thus, the inventory remaining at the end of an accounting period is assumed to be of the most recent purchases. FIFO is generally in harmony with the actual physical movement of goods in a retail firm. Thus, FIFO best represents the results that are directly tied to merchandise costs.

LIFO

The costing method known as **last-in, first-out (LIFO)** assumes that the most recent cost of merchandise should be charged against revenue. Thus, the ending inventory under LIFO is assumed to be made up of earliest costs.

When costs of items are increasing, FIFO yields the lower cost of merchandise sold and thus yields higher gross margin and net income as well as higher inventory figures on the balance sheet. On the other hand, LIFO yields a higher figure for cost of goods sold and lower figures for gross profit, net income, and inventory. For income determination purposes, Revenue Canada accepts FIFO but LIFO is not accepted.

With thousands of inventory items, Loblaws uses the retail method of inventory costing.

Courtesy Loblaw Companies Ltd.

The Retail Method

Because of the limitations with the cost method, the retail method of inventory costing is more widely used. The retail method is a logical extension of a retail book (perpetual) inventory utilized for dollar control (see Chapter 9). These steps, illustrated in Table 17-4, are described in the following section. The retail method is in actuality an income statement that follows certain programmed steps in the final determination of net profits.

Steps of the Retail Method

1. *Determine the total dollars of merchandise handled at cost and retail.* As indicated in Table 17-4, we start with a beginning inventory that we assume is an actual, physical inventory from the end of the previous period. To this figure we add purchases (minus vendor returns and/or allowances) and transportation charges (at cost only). The price change, which is a part of step 1, is additional markups. Wholesale costs have increased since the delivery and we calculate an additional markup of $1,500 to accommodate the price increase. Summing all the items that increase the dollar investment provides the total merchandise handled at cost and retail ($270,000 and $435,000, respectively).

2. *Calculate the cost multiplier and the cumulative markup.* The computation of the cost multiplier (sometimes called the cost percentage or the cost complement) is derived by dividing the total dollars handled at cost by the total at retail (that is, $270,000/$435,000 = 62 percent). This is a key figure in the retail method and in fact involves the major assumption of the system. This cost multiplier says that for every retail dollar in inventory, 62 percent or 62 cents, is in terms of cost. The assumption of the retail method is that if cost and retail have this relationship in goods handled during a period, then that same relationship exists for all the merchandise remaining in stock (that is, the ending inventory at retail).

   The cumulative markup is the complement of the cost multiplier (that is, 100.00 – 62.07 = 37.93) and is the control figure to compare against the planned initial markup. (See Chapter 11 where this planned figure is discussed.) For example, let's assume that the planned initial markup is 38 percent. If our interim statement shows, as ours does, that our cumulative markup is 38 percent, then management will consider that operations are effective, at least as they relate to the planned markup percentage. The initial markup is planned so as to cover reductions (markdowns, employee discounts, and shortages) and provide a maintained markup (or gross profit or margin) at a level sufficient to cover operating expenses and to assure a target rate of profit return.

3. *Compute the retail deductions from stock.* Step 3 includes all the retail deductions from the total retail merchandise dollars handled during the period. Sales are recorded and adjusted by customer returns to determine net sales. Markdowns are recorded as they are taken.

   As an example, let's assume that during this period a group of 900 sport shirts retailing for $25.95 each are put out for a special sale at $15.95. We would thus take a markdown of $9,000 before the sale. Employee discounts are included as deductions because employees receive, for example, a 20 percent discount on items purchased for personal use. If a shirt retails for $19.95, the employee would pay $15.96. If the discount were not entered as a separate item in the system, the difference between the retail price and the employee's price would cause a shortage. Recording employee discounts as a separate item gives management a good picture of employee business obtained and affords a measure of control over use of the discount. Next, we include in our retail deductions from stock an estimated shortage figure ($2,250), which would give us as accurate a figure as possible for total deductions, and thus a figure for closing book inventory at retail.

Table **17-4** Statement of Retail Method of Inventory

Calculations	Step	Items	Cost	Retail	Percent
	1	Beginning inventory	$60,000	$105,000	
		Net purchases	205,500	328,500	
		Transportation charges	4,500		
		Additional markups		1,500	
		Total merchandise handled	270,000	435,000	
($270,000/ $435,000)	2	Cost multiplier/ cumulative markup			62.069/ 37.931
	3	Net sales		300,000	
		Markdowns		10,500	
		Employee discounts		1,500	
		Shortages (estimated)		2,250	
		Total retail deductions		314,250	
($435,000– $314,250)	4	Closing book inventory at retail		120,750	
($120,750× 0.62069)		Closing inventory at cost	74,949		
($270,000– $74,949)	5	Gross cost of goods sold	195,051		
($300,000– $195,051)	6	Maintained markup	104,949		35.0
		Less: Alteration costs	(3,000)		
		Plus: Cash discounts	6,000		
($104,949+ $3,000)		Gross margin	107,949		36.0
		Less: Operating expenses	(75,000)		25.0
		Net profit	32,949		11.0

4. *Calculate the closing book (and/or physical) inventory at cost and retail.* The statement thus far has given us a figure for the dollars at retail that we had available for sale ($435,000) and what we have deducted from that amount ($314,250). Thus we are now able to compute what we have left ($435,000 – $312,000), or the ending book inventory at retail—$120,750. The key to the retail method, as noted, is the reduction of the retail inventory to cost by multiplying the retail value by the cost multiplier ($120,750 x 0.6207). In our illustration, we get a value of $74,949. We can now go to the next step with this figure.
5. *Determination of gross cost of goods sold.* Since we know the amount of the merchandise handled at cost ($270,000) and know what we have left at cost ($74,949), we can determine the cost dollars that have moved out of stock ($195,051).
6. *Determine maintained markup, gross margin, and net profit.* Gross cost of goods sold is deducted from net sales to determine maintained markup ($300,000 – $195,051). Alteration costs (or workroom expenses) are traditionally considered in retailing as merchandising, non-operating expenses and are offset by cash discounts earned (non-operating income). The net difference between the two is added or subtracted from the maintained markup to derive the gross margin ($104,949 – $3,000 + $6,000 = $107,949), from which operating expenses are deducted to calculate net profits before taxes ($107,949 – $75,000 = $32,949). The various percentages appearing on the statement are all based on net sales (with the exception of the cost percentage and the cumulative markup).

Evaluation of the Retail Method

The retail method of inventory valuation offers the retailer many advantages:

1. The method is easily programmed for computer systems, and accounting statements can be drawn up at any time.
2. Shortages can be determined. The retail method is a book inventory, and this figure can be compared to the physical inventory. Only with a book inventory can shortages (or overages) be determined. This reason, as well as the one previously mentioned, are advantages that exist because the retail method is a perpetual, book inventory method. The following two advantages are uniquely related to the system of the retail method of inventory.
3. The physical taking of inventory is easier with the retail method. The items are recorded on the inventory sheets only at their selling prices, instead of their cost and retail prices.
4. The retail method gives an automatic, conservative valuation of ending inventory because of the way the system is programmed. This means that the retail method gives a valuation of ending inventory at cost or market, whichever is lower.

Even though there are many advantages to using the retail method of inventory it has been criticized. A major complaint is that it is a "method of averages." This refers to the determination of the cost multiplier as the "average relationship" between all the merchandise handled at cost and retail, and the application of this average percentage to the closing inventory at retail to determine the cost figure. Such a disadvantage can be overcome by "classification merchandising," breaking departments into small subgroups with similarity in terms of margins and turnover. The technology in point-of-sales systems affords unlimited classifications and thus allows the similarity necessary for implementation of the retail method, giving management a good measure of the actual effectiveness of operations.

DEPARTMENTAL PERFORMANCE EVALUATION

Individual departments within a retail firm must be analyzed to evaluate performance and to determine whether changes need to be made in any aspect of the departments' operations. An important component of departmental evaluation is the assignment of costs to the individual departments. But before discussing approaches that may be used to assign costs to departments, we direct your attention to the types of costs in a retail operation.

Types of Costs

Direct costs are costs directly associated with a department. Such costs would cease to exist if the department were eliminated. An example of a direct cost is advertising in support of products sold in a given department. **Indirect costs** are costs that cannot be tied directly to a department. An example is the store manager's salary.

In conducting a departmental performance evaluation, management must first redefine costs from natural accounts to functional accounts. **Natural accounts** are company-wide accounts defined by the accounting department and include such categories as salaries, rent, promotion, and cost of supplies. **Functional accounts** reflect the retailing function involved. An example would be the allocation of salaries to administrative support, sales personnel, and so forth. Management must then determine which of two approaches (the contribution margin approach or the full costing approach) will be used to assign costs to individual departments.

Cost Allocation Approaches

In the **full costing approach**, both direct and indirect costs are assigned to departments (see Table 17-5). Each department's direct costs and its allocation of indirect costs are deducted from the department's gross margin to determine its net profit or loss. The store's indirect costs can be allocated to departments in several ways, including equal allocation to all departments or allocation based on the sales volume of each department. Advocates for the full costing approach argue that all the costs of operating a department should be included so that management has an accurate picture of how each department contributes to the overall profitability of the firm. However, the approach has been criticized because of the arbitrary bases sometimes used to assign indirect costs to departments and because it can lead managers to erroneous conclu-

Table 17-5 Example of the Full Costing Approach

		Department A		Department B		Department C
Sales		$20,000		$10,000		$15,000
Cost of goods sold		5,000		5,000		3,000
Gross margin		$15,000		$5,000		$12,000
Expenses:						
Direct	$5,000		$3,000		$5,000	
Indirect	6,000		5,000		3,000	
Total expenses		11,000		8,000		8,000
Net profit		$4,000		($3,000)		$4,000

sions about whether a department should be abandoned or deleted. Let's look at the issue of deleting a department in more detail.

As shown in Table 17-5, the full costing approach shows that Department B is operating at a loss. Management's initial reaction might be to delete the department. However, several factors should be considered before making such a decision. First, Department B is covering all its direct costs and is contributing $2,000 toward the coverage of store indirect costs. If Department B were deleted, the initial costs currently being allocated to the department would have to be reallocated between Departments A and C, which would negatively affect their profit pictures. Thus, management might want to consider to what extent equitable bases are being used to allocate indirect costs to the departments. For example, Department B may be receiving a disproportionate share of indirect expenses. Several other factors should be considered in deciding to delete a department. For example, some departments are important because of their traffic drawing ability. Their profit performance may be poor but they are important in drawing customers who then make purchases in other departments. Furthermore, sales in one department often affect sales in some other department. Thus, if management were to delete a department, the action could negatively affect sales in other departments. Before deleting a department, management should carefully consider not only the accounting data but also these other factors.

In the **contribution margin approach** only direct costs are assigned to departments. The department's direct costs are deducted from its gross margin to determine its contribution to the store's indirect costs. Advocates of this approach argue that even if a department is showing a loss under the full costing approach, it may still be making some contribution toward indirect costs and thus should not be abandoned or deleted. Advocates also argue that focusing only on direct costs in evaluating departmental performance is logical because indirect costs will continue even in the absence of the department.

Let's look more closely at the process of departmental evaluation, using the contribution margin approach. Assume that sales in Departments 1, 2, and 3 of a retail store are as shown in Table 17-6. Total store sales for the three

Table 17-6

Example of the Contribution Margin Approach ($ millions)

Sales	
Department 1	16.2
Department 2	12.4
Department 3	11.6
Total	40.2
Merchandise costs	31.0
Gross margin	9.2
Expenses	
Promotion	2.6
Sales salaries	3.0
Overhead	1.2
Net profit before taxes	2.4

departments are $40.2 million, and the cost of merchandise is $31.0 million. Storewide net profit before taxes is $2.4 million. The natural accounts of merchandise costs, promotion costs, and sales salaries (all of which are direct costs) must be transformed into functional accounts in order to assign the costs on a departmental basis. All costs except overhead, which is an indirect cost and thus not assignable to the departments, are assigned to the three departments, as shown in Table 17-7.

A departmental performance evaluation can now be conducted for each department, as shown in Table 17-8. Department 1 contributes $4.3 million towards coverage of indirect costs and thus is responsible for the majority of the contribution margin. Even though Department 3 contributes $800,000, it is not a strong department in comparison to Department 1 and may need an evaluation to check where improvements could be made. Department 2 is showing a negative contribution margin and, thus, is in serious need of a detailed evaluation. Salespeople might need retraining, advertising and sales promotion efforts and expenditures may need to be reevaluated, and alternative vendor

Table 17-7

Transformation of Natural Accounts to Functional Accounts ($ millions)

		Functional Accounts			
Natural Accounts	**Total**		**Dept. 1**	**Dept. 2**	**Dept. 3**
Merchandise costs	31.0		10.0	11.3	9.7
Salaries	3.0				
		Sales personnel	0.8	1.0	0.6
		Administrative	0.2	0.3	0.1
Promotion	2.6				
		Department signing	0.1	0.2	0.1
		Newspapers	0.8	0.9	0.2
		Radio	—	0.2	0.1

relationships may need to be established. Management may even consider deleting Department 2; however, before doing so, it should carefully consider the issues discussed earlier in this section.

Table 17-8 Contribution Margin Analysis by Department ($ millions)

Department 1	
Sales	16.2
Merchandise costs	10.0
Gross margin	6.2
Direct expenses	
Salaries	1.0
Promotion	0.9
Contribution to indirect costs	4.3
Department 2	
Sales	12.4
Merchandise costs	11.3
Gross margin	1.1
Direct expenses	
Salaries	1.3
Promotion	1.3
Contribution to indirect costs	(1.5)
Department 3	
Sales	11.6
Merchandise costs	9.7
Gross margin	1.9
Direct expenses	
Salaries	0.7
Promotion	0.4
Contribution to indirect costs	0.8
Summary	
Contribution	
Department 1 contribution to indirect costs	4.3
Department 2 contribution to indirect costs	(1.5)
Department 3 contribution to indirect costs	0.8
Less overhead (shown in Table 17-6)	(1.2)
Net profits before taxes (as shown in Table 17-6)	2.4

SPACE EVALUATION

The final performance evaluation issue we will discuss is that of space within the store. Effective use of space translates into additional dollars of profit. Retailers must therefore evaluate whether store space is being used in the most effective way. Management can use a variety of measures to evaluate space utilization, but we will discuss the gross margin per square metre method to illustrate one method retailers can employ.

Table 17-9 shows the calculations involved in evaluating space utilization by the gross margin per square metre method. Sales per square metre less cost of merchandise sold per square metre yield the gross margin per square metre figure.

With this figure, management can compare departments of various sizes selling different types of goods. Such an analysis can show management which departments are doing well, which are not, which might improve if expanded, and which can be reduced in space allotment.

For example, based on the calculations shown in Table 17-9, management might be tempted to decrease the selling space allocated to Department A in order to increase the selling space devoted to Department B. However, the decision to reallocate space is not a simple one. Advertising and selling costs for a department may rise when its selling space is increased. After the reallocation, the merchandise mix may change, which can result in either higher or lower gross margins. Management thus needs to stimulate the likely changes in the variables used in the calculations as a result of possible shifts in space allocation and determine whether reallocations are likely to increase the overall profitability of the firm.

Table 17-9

Calculating Gross Margin Per Square Metre

Three calculations are involved in figuring gross margin per square metre:

1. $\frac{\text{Total sales}}{\text{Total square metres}}$ = Sales per square metre
2. $\frac{\text{Cost of merchandise sold}}{\text{Total square metres}}$ = Cost of merchandise sold per square metre
3. Sales per square metre – Cost of merchandise sold per square metre = Gross margin per square metre

Example

	Department A	**Department B**
Sales	$50,000	$70,000
Cost of merchandise sold	$30,000	$35,000
Square metres of space	500 square metres	700 square metres
Sales per square metre	$ 100	$ 100
– Cost of merchandise sold per square metre	60	50
= Gross margin per square metre	$ 40	$ 50

CHAPTER HIGHLIGHTS

- The balance sheet, the income statement, and various ratios derived from them give management information needed to evaluate the effectiveness of strategy in financial terms.
- The strategic profit model (SPM) emphasizes that a firm's principal financial objective is to earn an adequate or target rate of return on net worth (RONW) and dramatizes three areas of decision making (margin management, asset management, and leverage management) for improving RONW.
- Merchandise valuation is an important factor in performance evaluation. One of two methods—first-in, first-out (FIFO) and last in, first out (LIFO)—may be adopted to determine the cost value of inventory. According to the conservative rule, however, inventories should be valued at the lower of cost or market.
- In terms of accounting practices that assist management in inventory valuation decisions, retailers may use the cost method or the retail method. The cost method provides a book evaluation of inventory in which only cost figures are used. However, because of the limitations of the cost method, the retail method is more widely used.
- Individual departments within a retail firm must be analyzed to evaluate performance and to determine whether changes are needed in any aspect of the departments' operations. In evaluating departments, management may use either the contribution margin approach or the full costing approach.
- Effective use of space can translate into additional dollars of profit. Thus, retailers must evaluate whether store space is being used in the most effective way. The gross margin per square metre method is one method retailers may use.

KEY TERMS

DISCUSSION QUESTIONS

1. Distinguish between the balance sheet and the income statement. Illustrate an advocated format for each.
2. Explain the problems related to defining the terms *profit* and *investment.*
3. What are the significant purposes of the strategic profit model (SPM)?
4. Discuss the practical value of the strategic profit model.

5. Discuss your reaction to the following statement made by the manager of a large, full-line department store: "I am very pleased that my store had a 3.6 turnover rate for last year."
6. Why is it difficult to determine cost of ending inventories? How do (a) FIFO and (b) LIFO relate to this problem? Explain the assumptions of and contrast the two methods.
7. Describe the cost method of inventory valuation. What are the limitations of the cost method? Under what conditions would this method be more appropriately used?

PROBLEMS

1. Use the retail method of accounting. Prepare a well-organized statement and determine for each of the three problems the following sets of figures:

   a. Cumulative markup percentage.

   b. Ending inventory at retail.

   c. Ending inventory at cost.

   d. Maintained markup in dollars and percent.

   e. Gross margin of profit in dollars and percent. Net profit in dollars and percent.

I.	Item	Cost	Retail
	Beginning inventory	$20,000	$ 35,000
	Gross purchases	72,000	115,000
	Purchase returns and allowances	3,000	4,700
	Transfers in	1,000	1,600
	Transfers out	200	400
	Transportation charges	1,216	
	Additional markups		700
	Additional markup cancellations		400
	Gross sales		111,000
	Customer returns and allowances		11,000
	Gross markdowns		4,500
	Markdown cancellations		1,000
	Employee discounts		500
	Estimated shortages, 0.4 percent of net sales		
	Cash discounts on purchases	1,600	
	Workroom costs	800	
	Operating expenses	16,000	

2.

Item	Cost	Retail
Additional markup cancellations		$620
Estimated shortages, 0.05 percent of net sales		
Gross markdowns		8,000
Workroom costs	$500	
Sales returns and allowances		12,000
Transportation charges	2,094	
Beginning inventory	44,000	64,000
Purchase returns and allowances	2,200	5,200
Markdown cancellations		1,200
Gross purchases	65,600	105,240
Gross additional markups		2,480
Gross sales		102,000
Employee discounts		1,400
Cash discounts	1,500	
Operating expenses	11,000	

3.

Item	Cost	Retail
Gross sales		$27,200
Beginning inventory	$14,300	20,100
Sales returns and allowances		200
Gross markdowns		2,200
Gross additional markups		650
Transportation charges	418	
Purchase returns and allowances	830	1,720
Employee discounts		500
Gross purchases	17,200	27,520
Markdown cancellations		300
Operating expenses	3,800	
Cash discounts on purchases	200	
Additional markups cancelled		150
Alteration and workroom costs	300	
Ending physical inventory		16,500

2. Given below are the balance sheet and the income statement for a retail firm. Use this information to work Problems a and b.

Balance Sheet

Assets		Liabilities and net worth	
Current assets	$342,000	Current liabilities	$252,000
Fixed assets	300,000	Long-term liabilities	170,000
Total assets	$642,000	Total liabilities	$422,000
		Net worth	$220,000
		Total	$642,000

Income Statement

Net sales	$752,000
Cost of goods sold	480,000
Gross margin	$272,000
Operating expenses	182,000
Profit before taxes	$ 90,000
Taxes	30,000
Profit after taxes	$60,000

a. Calculate the current ratio.

b. Using the strategic profit model (SPM) format, calculate the (i) net profit margin, (ii) rate of asset turnover, (iii) rate of return on assets (ROA), (iv) leverage ratio, and (v) rate of return on net worth (RONW).

3. Given the following information, calculate each department's gross margin per square metre:

	Department A	Department B
Sales	$56,000	$43,800
Cost of goods sold	39,200	31,200
Selling space	54 square metres	30 square metres

APPLICATION EXERCISE

www.marks.com

1. Obtain an annual report of a retail firm (most can be obtained via the Internet, for example, Mark's Work Wearhouse is at www.marks.com) and construct (to the best of your ability) an SPM for that organization.

SUGGESTED CASES

6. Clean Windows, Inc.

23. Sears Canada—Financial Performance Analysis

APPENDICES

Appendices

APPENDIX A

CAREERS IN RETAILING

Retailing has been, and will continue to be, an important sector in the Canadian economic scene. Retailing offers many career opportunities for those interested in a dynamic, ever-changing field. As well, there are opportunities available for retail entrepreneurs. Budding entrepreneurs should consider the field of retailing as a likely, long-term choice for one's own business. We hasten, however, to encourage all students not to go into retailing immediately following an educational experience. We are strong believers in "making mistakes for someone else" before investing one's own capital in any business, especially retailing.

This appendix addresses the concerns of the average student who will probably go into the job market to seek a job with someone else. Consequently, the purposes of this appendix are to:

1. Focus your attention on career orientation.
2. Review the characteristics of retailing careers.
3. Stress the job skills needed to succeed in retailing.
4. Offer tangible tips on job search.
5. Offer suggestions for career planning and progress.

Students considering retailing as a career possibility may not realize where the jobs really are. Department stores, although highly visible, are just one source of entry-level opportunities. Retailing takes place in many kinds of operations—specialty stores (Future Shop, Business Depot) and off-price (BiWay); the national chains (Sears Canada and the Bay); national, regional, and local food organizations (Safeway, Loblaws, and Sobeys); the specialty chains (Toys "Я" Us); and many other types of firms. Students interested in retailing careers may also consider shopping centre developers and managers (Cambridge); mail-order firms (Eddie Bauer); and services retailing (Century 21 and the Toronto Blue Jays). This is quite a list, though still incomplete, to add to Wal-Mart and Zellers.

The skills gained in retailing can be transferable to other fields. Retailing can be a good experience for anyone who enjoys buying and selling merchandise. If you are excited about "making your day"—seeing how well you did compared to the same day in the previous year—retailing can be a challenge.

Not everyone who studies retail management wants a career in the field. For those of you who are curious about retailing opportunities, however, this appendix can help you discover what to expect after graduation.

Career Development

Students are at various stages of career development. The continuum below suggests the degrees of career development or orientation that you may be experiencing. You probably have friends who are at each phase. A student who is "career disoriented" may not have given any thought to the future; the student may be less disoriented than unconcerned. This apparent casual attitude may seem immature, and indeed this may be the case. Career development is, after all, part of total human development:

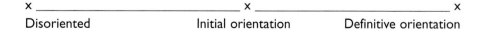

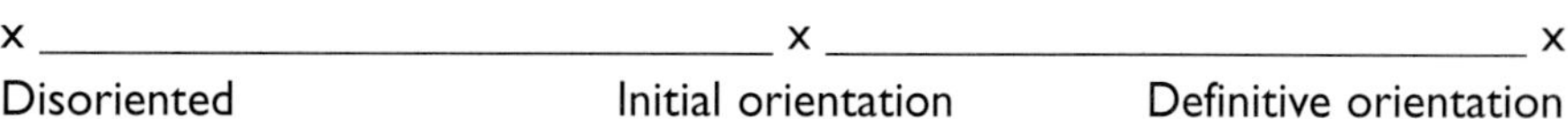

We encourage you to seek career counselling at all phases of your career development, especially when a concern about careers surfaces. Also, don't confuse "getting a job" with "career development." We suspect that a great deal of early attrition in first jobs results from both a desire to get a job simply to earn money and uncertainty about a career. A job without a career direction is likely to prove unsuccessful in the long run.

The following sections offer information on careers in retailing and in general to assist you in finding the right direction for your career.

CHARACTERISTICS OF RETAILING CAREERS

Employment in retailing exceeds 1.4 million people in Canada. The diversity of opportunities is staggering and can fulfill almost every kind of ability, ambition, and desire. Retail establishments are located in the smallest village and the most sophisticated metropolitan area.

Security

Security in a job is important to many people. Traditionally, even during periods of economic stagnation, retailing usually suffers fewer employment declines than manufacturing or wholesaling. Consumers must continue to buy goods and services regardless of the state of the economy. However, with the low growth of the Canadian economy and the number of retail bankruptcies, job security is less certain than in the past.

Decentralized Job Opportunities

No matter where they live, people must purchase goods and services on a regular basis to maintain their standards of living. This means you can have a successful career in retailing even if you do not want to move far from home. On the other hand, people who want to move frequently can find the opportunity for employment in retailing wherever they go.

Opportunities for Advancement

Many executive positions exist because of the large number of retail establishments in Canada. Even in a low-growth economy, successful retailers continue to expand, and positions in management are created in these firms.

Reward for Performance and Entrepreneurship

Retailing offers a daily performance measure because sales and profits can be evaluated daily. For high performers, such tangible measures are a delight; for the non-performers, each day is painful. Obviously, not everyone is right for retailing (and the same can be said for all career options). A graduate who performs may become a buyer for a high-dollar-volume department in a large department store organization within two or three years. As a buyer responsible for producing a profit in the department, such an achiever will really be acting as an entrepreneur in the security of an established firm.

Salaries in Retailing

Starting salaries for graduates entering retail training programs vary widely—from $17,000 to $40,000 annually. The contrast in starting salaries reflects the variation in training programs, location, cost of living, and the competitive market for trainees.

Non-Monetary Rewards

A person's ability and effort—or their absence—are quickly recognized in retailing. The position of store manager appeals to people with the ability to organize and direct the activities of others. As store manager, you set your own sales and profit goals as well as control expenses, compensate employees, and perform other vital management functions. In effect, you have the opportunity to manage your own business with someone else's money. A management career in retailing also offers the opportunity to work with ideas. Managers create ways of increasing sales and profit through imaginative use of the retail mix.

JOB SKILLS IN DEMAND

Mention retailing and many people think of selling or working as a cashier. Yet these positions make up only a small portion of total job opportunities. Consider the need for fashion experts, accountants, advertising and personnel specialists, market researchers, and lawyers. Go even further and think in terms of public relations, engineering, data processing, real estate analysis, and physical distribution. Think beyond the people you typically see when making purchases. Visualize the complex organization behind most retail outlets. Consider the increasing role of technology, which has opened up career opportunities that simply didn't exist a few years ago. Retailing today is high tech.

TANGIBLE CAREER TIPS

For this discussion to be meaningful, we must assume that you have moved along the career orientation continuum to at least the initial orientation phase. We also want to note here that this section is rather "generic." We think the tips herein are valuable even if retailing is not your career objective.

Job Search Plan

We urge you to develop a job search plan; Exhibit A-1 provides a seven-step plan.

Questions To Ask in an Interview

If you really want the job, you ask probing, intelligent questions. The following questions are suggested:

How was this position created?
Will I be able to work with the person I am replacing?
What kind of training will be provided?

How much responsibility will I be given in this position?
What is the first task I would be undertaking?
Does the company promote from within?
Can you tell me about the organization's training policies/incentives?
In your opinion, what is the most difficult part of this job?
How would you describe the work atmosphere in this organization?
What do you like about working here?
Does the company have any plans for expansion?

Exhibit A-1

Job Search Plan

Here are seven steps that will help in your job search:

1. Who Am I Really?

If you do not know where you are going, any road will take you there. In a job search, it is crucial to determine what you want from a position, as well as what you have to offer an employer, before you take any other steps. To do this, remove all labels (e.g., Teacher, Psych Grad, Music Major) and, instead, examine the skills you have acquired from past experiences, the interests and values you possess, how your personality might fit in with the position and organization, and your preferred working environment. Only after you have developed a list of your abilities and needs should you start looking for employment.

2. The Paper Chase

With your self-assessment completed, you should have a range of prospective areas to investigate; the idea here is to find the environments that would offer conditions similar to those you have identified as "ideal." It is most important, at this stage, to start with a sense of what you want to *do*, rather than what you want to *be*. You will have more scope and depth to your search, and more options from which to choose.

Now, begin your research—use libraries and your school's career placement office to learn about the occupations and companies that are of interest to you. When you have zeroed in on some possible career choices, information on the companies you might like to work for can be found in business magazines, annual reports, newspaper articles, the Internet, and directories.

3. Getting First-Hand Knowledge

Although some very good, basic information can be gleaned from libraries (written, video, and audio materials), the most valuable information comes from talking to people. Meeting with people who are in the field or occupation that interests you can provide information on the advantages and drawbacks to the field, the type of entry-level positions and who offers them, and inside "tips" on how to get started in the field.

4. Preparing to Job Search

If you really dislike the thought of looking for work, you are not alone. Job search is hard work; it's a full-time job. In many ways, it's a gamble. Therefore, we need to learn how to improve our odds and take control of the parts we can control. There will be rejection, so build it into your plan—expect it, so it doesn't catch you off guard. Perseverance is critical to

Exhibit A-1 **Job Search Plan (continued)**

move you, step by step, closer to that YES. Be positive and realistic. Two books that can help with this phase are:

- *What Color Is Your Parachute,* by R.N. Bolles.
- *Guerilla Tactics in the New Job Market,* by Tom Jackson.

Finally, a very important tool in conducting a successful job search is a well-prepared résumé and cover letter. A good résumé and cover letter probably will not get you a job, but they could lead you to the most important phase—the job interview (see Exhibit A-2 for an example of a résumé).

5. Looking for Work

The three main techniques in looking for work are reactive, on-line, and proactive. Reactive job search strategies target positions that are advertised in some form. The job opening exists, and job seekers respond to the request for applications. On-line computer search strategies use the Internet to identify employment opportunities and job postings. Finally, a proactive job search strategy involves contacting firms that you think best suit your skills and experience and where hiring opportunities may exist. The outcome of step 5 is an interview (see Exhibit A-3).

6. Follow-Up

An organized follow-up program is essential to a successful job search. Always keep a detailed log, recording all information in one place so you can easily monitor the process of your search. Make note of each time you contact an employer and flag each organization for future contact. Follow-up is critical in a number of situations:

- After an informational interview, always send a thank-you note.
- After submitting a résumé or broadcast letter, follow up with a telephone call seven to ten days later.
- After a job interview, it is wise to write a brief follow-up letter expressing your pleasure at having had the opportunity to meet with the interviewer(s). Refer to some topic of interest discussed during the interview, and reiterate your interest in the position/organization.
- After receiving a rejection letter, contact the employer to indicate your desire to be considered for future positions. Also ask for feedback on your interview presentation and your qualifications, as well as advice on your job search.

7. The Job Offer

Your creativity, perseverance, determination, and efforts have finally paid off—you receive one or more job offers. Take some time to analyze whether or not accepting this job is the best move for you. Does this position meet most of the needs you addressed in your original self-assessment? If not, have your priorities changed, or should you reject this offer? Can you realistically expect to find something that better meets your needs in an acceptable time frame? This is a major decision for you, so take some time to reflect before saying yes or no.

Exhibit A-2 Example of a Résumé

Julie K. Ashman
215 Old Post Road
Prairie City, Saskatchewan
S4S 0K7
(306) 588-1234

HIGHLIGHTS AND QUALIFICATIONS

- Served two years on Board of Directors for U. of P. Students' Union
- Attentive to detail, with strong analytical skills
- Able to work effectively with a wide variety of people

EDUCATION

Bachelor of Business Administration, The University of the Prairies, Prairie City, Saskatchewan (199_–200_) Relevant courses: Retailing, Industrial Marketing, Marketing Strategy

RELATED EXPERIENCE

Small Business Consultant, Small Business Consulting Service, The University of the Prairies, Prairie City, Saskatchewan (Summer 199_, Part-time 199_–200_)

- Designed, administered, and analyzed market research survey for two retail stores
- Developed an advertising plan for a small manufacturer
- Performed a feasibility study for a restaurant
- Interviewed prospective clients and prepared written reports
- Presented a seminar to a group of local citizens

Sales Clerk, Stereo Warehouse, Regina, Saskatchewan (Summer 199_, Part-time 199_–199_)

- Received two awards for outstanding monthly sales
- Provided customers with comparative technical information about television and stereo components
- Corresponded with suppliers and other dealers in the chain

OTHER EXPERIENCE

Cashier, J and L Supermarket, Regina, Saskatchewan (Summers and part-time 199_–199_)

- Operated computerized cash register

UNIVERSITY ACHIEVEMENTS

Student Senator (199_–200_)

- Participated in decisions related to academic policies
- Member, Varsity Ski Team (199_–200_)
- Attended regular practices and entered annual slalom races

SKILLS

Software: Word, Lotus 1-2-3, Quattro Pro, CorelDraw

Languages Spoken: English, French

REFERENCES

Available upon request.

Have a Good, Up-to-date Résumé

Check with the placement office for ideas, but above all, make sure that the résumé is neat, has no spelling errors, and points out your skills and work-related background. Focus on the jobs you have held and on your skills, talents, and interests. Exhibit A-2 shows you the organization of a typical résumé for a person in college seeking retailing employment. Exhibit A-3 provides some ideas on the job interview.

Exhibit A-3

The Job Interview

The job interview is critical, as it is the final stage in the job search process. It is a time during which both you and the employer are exchanging information relating to employment, and it requires both interpersonal and information presentation skills.

The interview should meet *your* objectives to:

1. Market your transferable skills, experience, interests, and personality to meet the requirements of the employer.
2. Assess the appropriateness of the position and the employer in relation to your career goals.

It should also meet the *interviewer's* objectives to:

1. Assess the knowledge, abilities, self-confidence, motivation, initiative, teamwork, and communication skills you possess to fulfill the employment needs of the organization.
2. Promote his/her organization to you, the applicant.

To prepare for the interview, first, you need to research yourself (know your abilities, interests, goals, skills, experience, and personality and your strengths and weaknesses in each of these areas). Second, you need to be informed about the occupation you are interested in; and third, you need to research the organization you are interviewing (products and services offered, history, future plans, etc.).

In the interview, you should present information in a coherent, sequenced, and dynamic manner. In preparation, decide what information you want your interviewer(s) to have about you at the close of the interview. Plan your comments and examples accordingly. As questions are asked, you can respond using this material.

Source: *The Interview*, Wilfrid Laurier University, Career Services booklet.

TRAINING PROGRAMMES AND CAREER PATHS

Thus far, this appendix has focused on career orientation, the characteristics of retailing careers, the job skills needed to succeed in retailing, and some generic, tangible career tips. This concluding section is concerned with training programmes and career paths.

Training Programmes

Training programmes involve rotation among the various departments/functions within a firm until the trainee is familiar with the operations. Programmes vary in detail and reflect the philosophy of the particular retail organization.

Career Paths

A career path can be thought of as the route taken within a particular company. The progression through a retailing organization depends at least in part on the organizational structure. For example, in a highly centralized structure, more executive-level opportunities exist in the corporate or division headquarters. In a more decentralized operation, where most of the necessary functions are at the local level, additional opportunities may exist in the individual stores. A career path can also be viewed as a lifetime pattern of advancement. This longer time frame will undoubtedly involve multiple organizations, different industries, and apparent total changes in direction.

Conclusions

We do not believe our role is to sell you on a retail career. Retail career paths are definable and can result in high-level performance for the right person. Retailing offers many excellent training programs. Evaluate them in terms of your own career aspirations. Consider retailing as a career possibility—we ask no more.

APPENDIX B

RETAILING RESEARCH

In today's highly competitive environment, the need for better information becomes essential to the success of retail strategy. Retail managers need information on consumer market trends, competitive actions, and customer perceptions of each element of the firm's and competitors' retail strategies.

INFORMATION NEEDS OF RETAILERS

Retail managers need information to add to their intuition and experience as they make decisions within the firm's external and internal environments. The **external environment** consists of the political, social, technological, and economic forces surrounding the organization. The **internal environment** consists of forces at work within the organization. *Internal information* is information generated within the retail business. *External information* is information about outside factors that may affect the business on a regular basis. The key external factors on which information may be needed include technological trends, legislative trends, work force availability, and the actions of potential competitors. Examples of internal information include financial resources, company strengths and weaknesses, and merchandise quality.

Information needs vary widely within an organization because of the various responsibilities of managers. The level of detail needed in data analysis, the frequency of data use, the need for updating, and the source and uses of data differ depending on the purpose of the activity. A chief executive officer needs one type of data when making high-risk, strategic decisions; while lower-level management requires different kinds of data to make detailed, practical, policy-based decisions.

Sources of Information

Internal Data

Internal data is probably the least expensive type of data. Internal data can be developed from a number of sources, including: (1) financial/accounting records, (2) salespersons, and (3) customer feedback.

Financial/Accounting Data Financial and accounting data can reveal a wealth of useful information. Such information can include sales trends over time by merchandise lines, profitability by merchandise lines and departments, frequency of maintained markup by merchandise line, and information on merchandise turnover.

Information from Salespersons Salespersons have the closest continuing contact with customers. They are in the best position to recognize shifts and trends in consumer demand. Salespersons can be especially important in providing information on missed sales opportunities because of merchandise that was out-of-stock or that the firm does not carry. Many retailers require salespeople to complete "want slips" each time a customer requests merchandise the retailer does not stock. Managers also have regular meetings, some even daily, with salespeople to generate suggestions, criticisms, and feedback that are not easily communicated by a written system.

Customer Feedback Customer feedback can include information obtained based on product returns, warranty cards, coupon redemptions, or customer service records. Customer correspondence, such as complaint letters, can also provide useful information on product quality and service problems. Customer records are essential as part of database marketing. *Database marketing* is the use of customer-specific information to allow retailing programs to be narrowly targeted to specific groups of customers.[1]

Secondary Data

Secondary data is information published by various sources and used by management to determine what is going on outside the firm. Information is available from (1) syndicated services; (2) government reports; (3) guides, indexes, and directories; (4) trade associations; and (5) computerized searches.

Syndicated Services **Syndicated services** specialize in collecting and selling information to clients, either financial or market information.

Financial Data. Dun & Bradstreet provides average operating ratios of various companies. *The Financial Post* annually publishes its Survey of Markets, and the *The Globe and Mail Report on Business* publishes the Top 1000 Companies in Canada.

Market Data. Such information may be in the form of store audits, warehouse withdrawal services, or consumer purchase panels. One of the most widely known firms providing such information is the A.C. Nielsen Company. Nielsen-type data on product movement is tracked by retailers to determine which merchandise is most popular with various consumer market segments.

Other new services also promise retailers greater insight into the hearts and minds of consumers. During the past decade, new research tools, such as the categories developed by Compusearch, Goldfarb, VALS (Stanford) or Thompson and Lightstone, have been introduced to track changes in consumer attitudes and lifestyles.

These methods, which track shifts in consumer lifestyles, are providing information about consumer behaviour that has made it easier to implement market segmentation strategies based on lifestyles, as described in Chapter 3. The emphasis on these services is on the "nonrational, emotional aspects of decision making, as well as the kind of information that can be obtained from such techniques as trade-off modelling and conjoint analysis. The services have emerged as retailers began to realize that there is more to understanding the consumer than just demographics and turned to lifestyle and psychographic information to 'explain some of the things that previously weren't explainable' by demographic analysis."[2]

Government Reports Provincial and federal governments maintain detailed information on many aspects of the economy that can be useful to management. Among the censuses conducted by Statistics Canada are the Census of Canada, as well as surveys covering many areas, including retail trade. Examples of those publications of interest to retailers are *Family Expenditures in Canada, Retail Trade, Operating Results* (various categories), and *Direct Selling in Canada.* Results of these and other studies are available in virtually every library. The *Marketing Research Handbook* also contains such information in capsule form, including average sales per square metre for various categories of retailers.

Provincial agencies typically publish similar information at the provincial level.

Guides, Indexes, and Directories Other valuable sources of external information include guides, indexes, and directories. Guides such as the *Canadian Periodical Index* provide complete references by subject matter to articles in a wide array of journals. Specialized indexes such as the *Financial Post Index* or the *New York Times Index* provide information for those specialized sources only and are available as computerized databases. Finally, the *Canadian Trade Index* is an index for information on specific companies and industries, particularly useful to reporters. Directories are often helpful in identifying diverse sources of information. For example, the *Fraser's Canadian Trade Directory* is organized by industrial sectors. Some useful Internet links are listed in Table B-1.

Trade Associations Most retailers belong to trade groups that collect and publish data for association members. Such information can be useful for comparing the retailer's performance to industry averages. Associations may also publish annual industry forecasts that can be used as a guide to firms making their own forecasts. As well, the Retail Council of Canada is an association that actively promotes the interests of retailers to governments, the public, and manufacturers.

Table B-1 Useful Internet Links

Business Researcher's Interests	www.brint.com
Canadian Corporate Information	www.corporateinformation.com
Canadian Information	www.canadainfo.com
Canadian Job Source	www.irus.rri.uwo.ca/-jlaw
Canadian Online Explorer	www.canoe.com
The Globe and Mail	www.theglobeandmail.com
Hoover's Online (companies)	www.hoovers.com
Industry Canada	strategis.ic.gc.ca
Industry Week	www.industryweek.com
International Retailing	www.msu.edu/~hed/internationalretailing
Investment research	www.quicken.ca
Marketing library	www.marketinglibrary.com
SEDAR (Canadian companies)	www.sedar.com
Statistics Canada	www.statcan.ca
The World Bank	www.worldbank.org
United Nations	www.un.org

www.brint.com
www.corporateinformation.com
www.canadainfo.com
www.irus.rri.uwo.ca/-jlaw
www.canoe.com
www.theglobeandmail.com
www.hoovers.com
strategis.ic.gc.ca
www.industryweek.com
www.msu.edu/~hed/
internationalretailing
www.quicken.ca
www.marketinglibrary.com
www.sedar.com
www.statcan.ca
www.worldbank.org
www.un.org

Computerized Searches The required information is often available through library on-line searches, Internet searches, or CD-ROM searches (e.g., Canadian Business and Current Affairs, ABI/Inform, and Statistics Canada's CANSIM).[3]

Primary Data Collection

When management cannot find what it needs to know from any existing source, it must generate first-hand information. For example, among the research projects Sears Canada conducts at the corporate level are studies of credit, public relations, and home installations. Similarly, Sears Canada's corporate research department conducts economic research to track economic trends and help evaluate sales trends, and consumer research to determine consumer attitudes and buying habits. Large retailers such as Sears Canada conduct new-product research with the same vigour as manufacturers do. Advertising is also subject to the same intensive scrutiny.[4]

In this section the focus is on **primary data** gathering activities. Primary data collection can take many forms: observation, exploratory research, surveys, or experimentation.

Observation

Observation can be an accurate method of collecting certain information. Competitors, for example, will not volunteer information on their prices, in-store displays, and other promotional efforts. Observing competitors is the only way to collect such information. Also, observation may be the least expensive way to collect certain types of data.

Exploratory Research

Management may not be able to carefully specify the problem about which it is concerned. In such situations, exploratory research is needed to help define the problem. **Exploratory research** *is characterized by flexibility in design and the absence of a formal research structure.* Management, in seeking to more carefully define a problem, may obtain some qualitative information from three major sources:

1. Evaluate data either internal or external to the firm. Internally, there may be reports and sales analyses that may assist the manager in more clearly defining the problem. Externally, some secondary sources may contain information bearing on the situation faced by the manager.
2. Talk to knowledgeable people about the issue. These may include some suppliers, other retailers and even customers. A **focus group** is often used because it is a quick and inexpensive way to obtain qualitative information.[5]
3. Observe the behaviour of consumers who may be making purchase decisions.

Once the problem has been defined, a formal research design may be necessary to collect the data on which to base a decision. Such efforts may involve survey research or experimental designs for determining the presence of cause-and-effect relationships.

Survey Research

Survey research often includes the collection of information on the opinions or perceptions of persons in a market segment of interest to management. The process can be quite complex. For example, developing a questionnaire, normally the first step in survey research, is an art one can best learn by experience. Many different decisions have to be made. Survey research is probably the most frequently used method of data collection by management.

The major steps in survey research must answer the following questions:[6]

- *Objectives:* What are the objectives of the survey?
- *Questionnaire:* What information should be collected to meet these objectives?
- *Sample:* From whom will the information be obtained?
- *Survey method and organization:* How will the information actually be collected?
- *Analysis and reporting:* How should the data be prepared for analysis, and how should the data be analyzed and the findings reported?

Questionnaire Development

The **questionnaire** used for the survey must respond as closely as possible to the information needed by the retail manager. In developing a questionnaire, a number of decisions must be made:

Question Format Questions can be either *open-ended,* in which the respondents are simply asked to give their opinions without a formal response structure, or *close-ended,* in which response choices are prespecified.

Open-Ended Questions. An example of an **open-ended question** is:

What is it that you like most about shopping at Loblaws?

____

Close-Ended Questions. Close-ended questions may use one of five popular formats:

- *Dichotomous,* which pose yes or no answers, for example:

  Do you shop at the Bay at least once a month?

  YES ___ NO ___

- *Multiple choice,* which allow a respondent to choose from among several predetermined answers, for example:

  At which of the following stores do you shop most often for your shoes?

  Bata ___ Kinney's ___
  Ingledew's ___ Other ___

- **Likert scale**, which allows respondents to express their level of agreement or disagreement with various statements, for example:

Canadian Tire offers the best selection of bicycles in this city.

Strongly Disagree	Disagree	Neither Agree Nor Disagree	Agree	Strongly Agree
___	___	___	___	___

- **Semantic differential scale**, which allows respondents to select the point representing the direction and intensity of their feelings between two bipolar words, for example:

  How would you describe Harvey's restaurants?:

  Clean ___ ___ ___ ___ ___ ___ ___ Dirty

  Friendly ___ ___ ___ ___ ___ ___ ___ Unfriendly

- *Importance scale*, which allow the respondents to indicate the level of importance they attach to an attribute, for example:

  When I go grocery shopping, free parking is:

Extremely Important	Very Important	Somewhat Important	Not Very Important	Not at All Important
1	2	3	4	5

Data Collection

The next step is a decision on how the data is to be collected. The **sample** is the group of respondents selected to provide these data. The four primary methods of contact with respondents are (1) personal interviews, (2) telephone interviews, (3) mailed questionnaires, and (4) computer interviews.

Personal Interviews Personal interviews are expensive and time-consuming but allow interviewers to get more information than do the other methods. Personal interviews often are the only way to collect data if researchers need to demonstrate merchandise or to use visual aids.

Telephone Interviews Telephone interviewing is the quickest of the four methods. However, the amount of time the respondents are willing to spend on the telephone often is limited, the questioning process must be kept simple, and the use of visual aids is not possible.

Mailed Questionnaires Mailing questionnaires, the slowest of the four methods, is the least expensive. A major drawback, however, is the lack of control over who responds to the questionnaire. Researchers may want responses from adult males over 18 years of age. A mailed survey gives researchers no assurance that such an individual actually responds to the questionnaire. Response rates are also low, often less than 20 percent.

Computer Interviews Computer technology also has made possible in-store survey research by means of electronic push-button questionnaires or touch-screen computer (also called interactive kiosks)[7] for a fraction of the cost and time of personal interviews in malls or households. This technology allows management to measure consumer perceptions of retail service performance, store image, and advertising effectiveness. The equipment is positioned in a prominent location in an outlet. Signs invite customers to express their viewpoints on the issues of interest to management. The machine can tabulate customer responses by count, computer averages, and cross tabulations. The result can be a fairly sophisticated analysis of the data.

Experimental Methods

Some issues on which management wants information may not be resolved easily by survey research. Experimental research may be the only way to answer such questions as: What is the effect of a reduction in price on sales levels? Which of several advertising themes is most preferred by customers?

Experimental designs allow management to infer cause-and-effect relationships in variables of interest. Thus, management seeks to rule out explanations for changes in a variable such as sales (a dependent variable) other than those caused by changes in such variables as price or advertising (independent variables). For example, a field experiment can answer the question: how does a small retailer measure the profitability of a couponing promotion?

ETHICS AND USE OF INFORMATION

Ethics should always be the foremost issue when management is collecting and utilizing research-based information. Some of the ethical issues involve the question of confidentiality of the respondents, the use of surveys as a disguised means of selling, misrepresentation of results, and truthfulness in advertising.

In addition to the moral aspects of questionable behaviour, adverse publicity will almost always affect the profits of the firm.

APPENDIX HIGHLIGHTS

- The transition from a merchandising to a marketing orientation increases the need for quality information ranging from data on consumer market trends and competitive actions to market share measurement and measurement of consumer perceptions.
- The data sources of a retail decision support system include internal data, secondary data, and primary data.
- Internal information is probably the least expensive source of data and can be developed from customer feedback, by feedback from salespeople, by analysis of charge accounts, by the use of consumer panels, and by analysis of internal financial data.
- Frequently used secondary sources of information include information available from syndicated services, government reports, guides, indexes and directories, trade associations, and computerized bibliographic searches.
- Primary data collection can take many forms, including observation, exploratory research, survey research, and experimental research.
- Survey research is the collection of information on the opinions or perceptions of market segments of interest to management. The process includes questionnaire development, sample selection, data collection, and field work.
- Experimental methods allow management to make inferences about cause-and-effect relationships in data.

KEY TERMS

experimental design	444	open-ended question	442
exploratory research	441	primary data	441
external environment	438	questionnaire	442
focus group	441	sample	443
internal data	438	secondary data	439
internal environment	438	semantic differential scale	443
Likert scale	442	survey research	442
observation	441	syndicated services	439

DISCUSSION QUESTIONS

1. What is the difference between primary and secondary data?
2. What are some internal sources of information available to retailers?
3. What secondary sources are available to retailers?
4. How does exploratory research differ from survey and experimental research?
5. Discuss the advantages and disadvantages of telephone interviews, personal interviews, mailed questionnaires, and computer interviews as methods of contact with respondents.
6. Explain the differences among the five most popular types of close-ended questions. Under what conditions should each one be used?

APPLICATION EXERCISES

1. Visit the library and list all of the indexes or directories. Note the kinds of information contained in each. Project this exercise into the future and predict how you might use each index or directory in a specific kind of work with a retailing company.
2. Work with your university or college bookstore (or some other retailer with whom you or your instructor have a good relationship) and identify an "image problem" the outlet experiences. Define the problem; devise a questionnaire to seek answers (assuming it is a problem for which a survey may be helpful) or an observation sheet for in-store research; collect and analyze your data; write up your findings; and present conclusions to the retailer.
3. Interview a retailer in each of the major "kinds" of businesses, such as grocery and department stores. Determine the "image" that person perceives of retailing as a career opportunity. Summarize the perceptions; generalize your findings; present conclusions and recommendations.

APPENDIX C

STARTING YOUR OWN RETAIL BUSINESS

Many people dream of owning their own business in spite of the long hours, the financial risks, and the fierce competition in retailing. The odds of being successful are low—in fact, only about 20 percent of all small businesses survive for more than five years. Among the specific reasons for failure are a lack of research before starting the business, no break-even analysis conducted, no business plan completed, and poor inventory management skills. Businesses that survive for more than three years are more likely to have a business plan, to start with higher levels of capital, and to run the business full-time as opposed to hiring a manager. So you can increase the odds of being successful by planning. A business plan allocates resources and measures the results of your actions, helping you set realistic goals and make logical decisions.[1]

THE IMPORTANCE OF PLANNING

In starting a new business, proper planning is the most important ingredient in success. Effective planning will do more than anything else to help avoid failure. Success and planning go together. The owner/manager should:

1. Plan together with partners/associates.
2. Make performance expectations clear to everyone.
3. Provide for feedback on progress to keep plans on track.
4. Make plans goal-oriented (i.e., what is to be accomplished) rather than activity-oriented (i.e., the tasks involved).
5. Remember that hard work is vital to success, but this should be accompanied by efficient work.

Five "Friends" Who Can Help Make It Go

The retailer can improve the chances for success by securing the services of these professionals: lawyer, accountant, banker, insurance specialist, and professional consultants. In planning the business, some basic questions also need to be considered:

- Why am I entering retailing?
- What business am I entering?
- What goods or services will I sell?
- What is my market and who are my customers?
- Who is my competition?
- Can I compete successfully with my competition?
- What is my retail strategy?
- What marketing methods will I use?
- How much money is required?
- Where will the money come from?
- What technical and management skills do I need?
- Can I make just as much money working for someone else?

Answering the above questions honestly and objectively will help assure the new businessperson is well on the way to building a successful business plan.

A well-prepared business plan can be important in many ways:

- It provides the retailer a path to follow. It sets out goals and steps that allow the retailer to be in better control of steering the firm in the desired direction.
- It allows one's banker, accountant, lawyer, and insurance agent to know clearly what the business is trying to do. A plan will give them insight into the situation so that they can be of greater assistance to the business.
- It can help the owner communicate better with the staff, suppliers, and others about operations and objectives of the business.

Table C-1

Contents for a Business Plan

1. Summary of the mission of the retail firm—a few paragraphs on what the owner is doing, and the plans for the future.
2. The retail industry in the community as a whole, the company, and its products or services. A paragraph on each.
3. Market research and analysis.
   (a) Consumers
   (b) Market size and trends
   (c) Competition
   (d) Estimated market share and sales
4. Marketing plan
   (a) Overall marketing strategy
   (b) Merchandise and services
   (c) Pricing
   (d) Sales tactics
   (e) Advertising and promotion
5. Management team
   (a) Organization
   (b) Key management personnel—who are they and what will they do?
   (c) Ownership and compensation
   (d) Board of directors
   (e) Any supporting services
6. The financial plan (you may need accounting help)
   (a) Profit and loss forecasts
   (b) Pro forma cash flow analysis
   (c) Pro forma balance sheets
7. Proposed company offering
   (a) Desired financing
   (b) Capitalization
   (c) Use of funds
8. Overall schedule of activities for the next three years.

- It can help the owner develop better management skills and abilities. It can help management consider competitive conditions, promotional opportunities, and what situations are most advantageous to the new business. In short, a business plan will help the owner to make sound business decisions.

There are no set requirements as to the contents of the plan. The contents depend on the type and size of the business being started. The most important consideration is the quality of the plan, not its length. The plan should include all aspects of the proposed business. Any possible problem areas in starting the venture should be listed with possible methods of dealing with them. Bankers, and other prospective lenders, would rather know the problems before the

Retail Highlight C-1 Key Information Sources for Starting a Retail Business

A wealth of information is available for individuals who want to start a retail business. Here are five sources:

1. Canadian Business Service Centres (www.cbsc.org)
   Provides practical and pragmatic advice for preparing a business plan, sources of financing, and guides on advertising, pricing, market research, and selecting suppliers. Identifies the key questions in preparing a business plan.
2. Idea Café (www.ideacafe.com)
   Offers details on starting and running the business, financing, services and supplies, marketing, sales and advertising, and worldwide business information.
3. Business Owner's Toolkit (www.toolkit.cch.com)
   Provides information of starting, planning, financing, marketing, and running a small business. Has a number of planning tools and checklists that can be downloaded.
4. *Starting A Successful Business in Canada* (J. D. James, Self-Counsel Business Series)
   Now in its 14th edition, offers a wealth of practical information on starting and running a small business.
5. *Start and Run a Profitable Student-Run Business* (D. Schincariol, Self-Counsel Business Series)
   Another in the Business Series from Self-Counsel Press, offers practical information for starting and running low cost businesses.

www.cbsc.org

www.ideacafe.com

www.toolkit.cch.com

business is started than later where possible solutions may be limited. In fact, the major Canadian banks, including Scotiabank, provide information on how to start a new business and how to prepare a business plan. The banks provide software, such as Scotiabusiness Plan Writer, to help the individual prepare the plan. Suggested contents for a business plan are provided in Table C-1. Each plan will be different, but these suggestions will at least help to get started. Some key information sources for starting a retail business are provided in Retail Highlight C-1.

OPERATING CAPITAL NEEDED

After the business plan is developed, sources of capital must be obtained. The main thing is to avoid an early shortage of funds. Therefore, retailers need to begin by estimating the capital needed to open a business. Many have a tendency to underestimate the needed opening capital.

Retailers need to plan for two categories of costs: (1) *opening costs*, which are one-time costs, such as the cost of fixtures and decorating; and (2) *operating expenses*, which are the estimated ongoing expenses of running the business for a designated time period. Examples of these costs are shown in Table C-2.

Table C-2 Opening Costs and Operating Expenses for a Typical Retail Business

Opening Costs	Operating Expenses
Inventory	Rent (including one month's deposit)
Fixtures and equipment	Taxes, licences, and permits
Leasehold improvement (wiring, plumbing, lighting, air conditioning)	Advertising and promotion
	Legal and accounting fees
Security system	Wages (including owner's)
Exterior sign	Utilities
	Supplier
	Depreciation
	Insurance
	Maintenance and repair
	Auto expenses
	Miscellaneous

Developing a Cash Flow Forecast

Cash flow projections are helpful in planning for the opening and preparing for unforeseen difficulties, and they are a necessity when approaching a bank or other lender about loans.

A cash flow forecast is designed to predict when the firm will receive cash and when payments need to be made. Cash inflow and outflow vary by type of retailer; especially for those that are seasonal and that stock merchandise based on varying seasonal sales levels.

Management can use a cash budget, as shown in Table C-3, to help estimate cash flow. Negative cash flow (when outlays exceed income) should be funded with the initial capital developed for the new venture. Retailers can base the projections on experience, an estimate published in trade magazines, and information from their banker. A retailer should ideally know approximately what the operating costs and the cash inflow will be before opening the business. A person should have enough money to cover all expenses for about six months. Management should be conservative if it is uncertain about how much money is needed. They should borrow too much rather than too little, in order to avoid having to come back later for additional funds.

As an example, in Table C-3, anticipated sales for a restaurant in the first three months of operation are $53,000, $58,000, and $66,000 per month. Average monthly sales based on a sales forecast of $750,000 are $62,500 ($750,000 divided by 12). Management expects a $200 loss at the end of the first month, to break even at the end of the second month, and to show a profit at the end of December.

Table C-3

Projected Cash Flow Budget for a Restaurant for Three Months Ending December 20—

	October	November	December
Anticipated cash receipts:			
Payment for credit sales	$53,000	$58,000	$66,000
Cash sales	2,000	4,000	4,500
Total receipts	55,000	62,000	70,500
Anticipated payments:			
Cost of food and beverages	27,500	31,000	32,250
Payroll	15,500	18,200	18,200
Promotion	5,200	5,800	7,600
Loans to be repaid	1,500	1,500	1,500
Rent	4,500	4,500	4,500
Utilities	600	600	700
Outside accounting and legal fees	400	400	400
Total	55,200	62,000	65,150
Expected surplus at end of month	(200)	—	5,350
Desired cash operating balance	2,000	2,000	—
Short-term loan needed	2,200	2,000	—
Cash available	—	—	5,350

Sources of Funds

Having prepared a business plan, including a cash flow projection, the prospective retailer typically has three potential sources of funds for the business; equity, suppliers, and financial institutions, including government agencies. Equity is the amount the prospective owner can invest plus the amount that can be raised from others who are willing to invest in the business. The investors typically share in any profits generated by the business.

Suppliers will often provide merchandise based on terms of sale such as net 30 (invoice must be paid within 30 days to maintain a good credit rating). Negotiating skills are important for the prospective owners in dealing with suppliers when starting their business, as the owners have no track record.

Depending on the business plan, prospective owners can obtain loans from banks to assist in financing inventory and accounts receivable as well as some fixed assets. The federal government offers the Canada Small Business Financing Program, a loan guarantee plan, to assist small businesses. At the provincial level, a number of provinces have established small business development departments, which may also provide assistance.[2]

Once the business is up and running, future sources of financing can be obtained either from internal or external sources. The major way to generate capital inside the firm is from profitable operations. The external sources of capital have been discussed above, except that once the business is profitable, a further option is to issue stock or perhaps bonds if the business is a corporation.

In starting a retail business, an individual needs to prepare and execute a business plan. He or she needs to consider both the present and the future when putting the plan into action. The ability to understand consumers and competitors today and tomorrow, and to be proactive, will increase the odds for success in retailing.

CASES

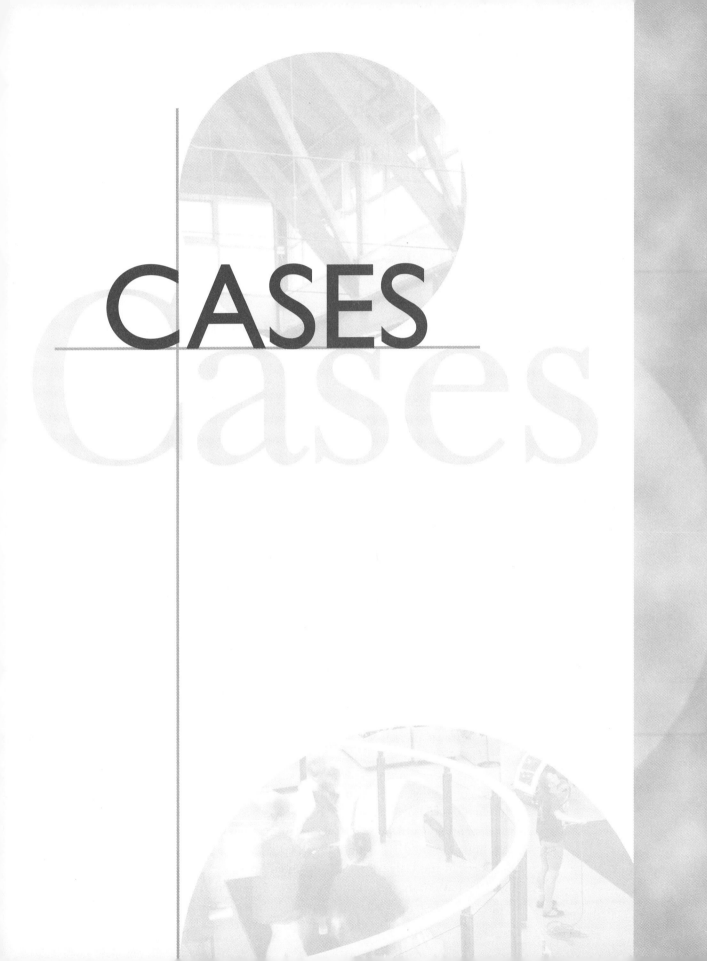

1. THE INDEPENDENT BOOKSTORE

Survival is the major issue for independent book retailers in Canada. With the introduction of Chapters superstores into the Canadian market, a large number of independent book retailers and smaller book retail chains have gone out of business and it appears that more are to follow. Consider the following:

- Chapters, including both its superstores and traditional bookstores, now has approximately a 30 percent market share (of the $2 billion Canadian retail book market). Chapters is a "category killer," a store that has a wide and deep selection of a specific set of products (i.e., books) that offers the reader choice and convenience that is very difficult for an independent bookstore to match.
- In the space of three years Chapters launched 57 superstores and plans to have 75 by the end of 2000.
- Chapters' superstores are approximately ten times larger than traditional bookstores at 2,000 to 4,000 square metres, carry up to 200,000 titles, offer substantial discounts on bestsellers (up to 40 percent off), and, in most stores, feature a Starbucks coffee café.
- Chapters launched www.chapters.ca featuring over 3,000,000 book titles as well as music CDs, videos, and DVDs.

www.chapters.ca

- Another book superstore chain, Indigo Books and Music, currently has ten stores in Canada and plans to open fifteen more in the next three years.
- The results of Chapters growing dominance in the Canadian market has led to the following:
  - Duthie Books, a Vancouver landmark, filed for bankruptcy in mid 1999. The six-store chain fell victim to the highly competitive environment (Chapters has two stores in Vancouver) and e-commerce.
  - Other Canadian bookstores that have gone out of business in the past three years include well-known stores such as Britnells in Toronto, Sandpiper Books in Calgary, Bollum's Books in Vancouver, Printed Passage in Kingston, and Edwards Books in Toronto.
  - The three largest book retailers in Quebec merged in the summer of 1999 in a bid to end the intensive price competition and take on the more financially secure national chains like Chapters and Indigo. By joining forces the trio feels they can develop the critical mass needed to develop in the evolving market.

This competitive activity in the market raises a fundamental question: can an independent bookstore survive or is it close to the end of its retail life cycle? An independent bookstore in Calgary thinks that it can survive and prosper. Pages Books, owned by Peter Oliva and Maria Caffaro, face four Chapters superstores in the Calgary area, but the competition doesn't faze them. Says Oliva, "We have more fun, and we get more interested readers and more interesting writers, if we just focus on what we do best." So far, it's worked; sales have increased by 34 percent in each of the past two years.

Before they opened the bookstore they researched the retail book business (neither had any experience in retailing), and the Calgary market (they both were from the area), and found that Kensington was the city's most heavily trafficked neighbourhood. As well, it was an upmarket area where people had money to spend on arts, crafts, and books. They found a great site in Kensington, a 300 square metre, two-storey building and opened the store five years ago.

The key to their success appears to be that they have identified a niche in the market and tailored both their titles and store activities to serving that market. They offer approximately 70,000 titles that their customers are interested in—literary fiction, high-end non-fiction, and a large selection devoted to the craft of writing. The staff, many of whom are writers, are required to not only ring up sales but to remember customers' specific tastes and order books that match their tastes. They have also taken retail initiatives, such as a frequent buyer discount card. As well, they co-sponsor a reading series with the Calgary Public Library.

However, the key to Pages' success, according to Caffaro, is in good customer service and creating an atmosphere where a customer can come in looking for a book, vaguely remembering something about it (but not the title or author), and walk out with the book in hand. They work on perfecting the most intangible consumer incentives. This means one-to-one relations with the customer and interesting conversations about books. It keeps the customers coming back.

While Pages has had short-term success, retail experts might argue that it is just a matter of time before category killers, like Chapters, completely dominate the market and the independents will be forced to close their doors. The experts would argue that Chapters has knowledgeable staff, a wider selection of books, better prices, and an atmosphere that encourages browsing. Further, because of its size, Chapters has greater buying clout and can get greater discounts on books from the publishers; it has a more efficient distribution system, which allows it to get the right books to the right stores at a lower cost; and its advertising keeps the store in the customers' minds. In summary, Chapters will "win" the market because they offer many segments in the market—including the serious book buyer—a better value than does the independent bookstore.

QUESTIONS

1. Can independent bookstores, like Pages, compete, in the long-term, with category killers like Chapters? Why or why not?
2. What strengths does a store like Pages have over the superstores like Chapters? What weaknesses? Before answering this question, visit Chapters Web site (www.chapters.ca) and consider what strengths Chapters has over independents.
3. Suggest further retail strategies and tactics that Pages could pursue to continue to be successful in the market.

2. RALPH'S OPTICAL*

Maurice Jones, a marketing consultant, arrived at Ralph's Optical to pick up his new glasses. Ralph Smith, the owner, greeted him: "Maurice, your glasses are ready. Try them on and I'll make the final adjustments. Now look at yourself in the mirror, these new glasses help convey your image as a successful consultant." Ralph then went on to say; "Maurice, I need some advice about a threat that my business is facing. If you have some time we could have a coffee in my office and I will tell you about my problem."

The following contains the major issues raised by Ralph during the conversation.

I have been an optician for almost 30 years and, with hard work, I built a successful business and now earn a good income. I take pride in the fact that over the years I was able to successfully adjust to the major changes affecting my business. For example, there have been technical changes such as the introduction of contact lenses, shatterproof lenses, and graduated bifocals. My staff and I periodically attend seminars and courses so that we are knowledgeable about the latest innovations.

Other kinds of changes have been more difficult for me. Over time, major optical firms such as Lens Crafters and Sears entered the market. These chains emphasize heavy promotion and low prices. In addition, Lens Crafters offers the customer the convenience of having the new lenses ready in an hour.

The share of the market held by independent opticians such as my store is declining as the price-sensitive segment of the market increases. In spite of the lower market share, my sales are growing because the overall market is increasing, thanks to the aging baby boomers. As people age, usually starting in their 40s, they tend to need reading glasses or glasses for distance. Even people who wear contact lens often require reading glasses for close work. There is also evidence that as some people age they are less likely to wear contacts for long periods of time.

To protect my business against the large, price-oriented competitors I took the following steps. First, I upgraded the type of frames that I carried. Instead of carrying a large selection of low and medium price frames by unknown manufacturers we have upgraded and placed an emphasis on well-known, quality designs such as Fendi, Gucci, Hugo Boss, Alfred Sung, and Givenchy. It is not uncommon for a person to pay between $300 and $450 for a new pair of glasses at my store. This is very different from the chains where I think the average price would probably be between $100 and $150 a pair.

Secondly, my staff and I are very careful to give the customer as much time as needed to find the proper frames, to fully answer questions, and to explain any technical differences between the options. We never rush a customer's deci-

The author acknowledges the cooperation and assistance of Denise Villeneuve and Greta Auerbach.

sion. In fact, many of our customers have been dealing with us for years, and if possible, we try to greet them by name and acknowledge the fact that we recognize and appreciate their on-going business. Based on statistics the average pair of glasses lasts two years. However, some of my fashion-conscious customers buy new frames more often.

Third, I implemented a print and radio advertising program. Although my budget is modest compared to the major chains I make an impact by concentrating my promotion in periodic short bursts when I feature a special item or a sale.

Although all opticians sell products that improve sight, my product is different in that I not only help clients see better but look better and convey the image that they want. Frames make a statement on your face, and the statement changes from style to style. To support the fashion orientation of my business I purchased a camera and television device that allows a person to more objectively see how he/she looks in the frames. In addition, I subscribe to magazines such as *Vogue* and *Elle* to see what frames are being shown by the fashion leaders.

Everybody who sells glasses is basically in competition with everybody else. However, some of us are licensed as opticians and others are optometrists. Opticians specialize in selling glasses, optometrists are permitted to sell glasses but they are also trained to diagnose eye disease and to prescribe corrective lenses. Ophthalmologists, on the other hand, are medical doctors who specialize in eye diseases. They prescribe corrective lenses, but most do not sell glasses or contact lenses.

Because I don't prescribe lenses, it is important to me to be located close to ophthalmologists' offices and to hospitals with eye clinics, so that it is convenient for clients to come to my store after they receive a new vision prescription. As you know, the location of my store is excellent because it is close to a large number of busy ophthalmologists and two major hospitals.

The aggressive chains sell their products on different variations of price. For example Price Club charges substantially less than you might expect to pay for contact lenses and bifocals. Their prices on frames also tend to be good value. However, because Price Club is a volume business, their customer service is not as good as mine. In addition, their selection of frames is oriented to more popular price points and, although the frames tend to be reasonably fashionable, they are designed for the mass market. They don't sell the same frames that I do. Price Club does not advertise or run promotions. Their promotion is mainly through word-of-mouth advertising and a large membership who appreciate the Price Club philosophy of low markup and low or no-frills service.

Another pricing technique used by some competitors is the famous 2-for-1 sale. Some of these 2-for-1 sales offer really good value for the shopper. Because of the high markup on frames and glasses, the retailer can actually make some money on a true 2-for-1 sale. However, some 2-for-1 sales are designed to offer you a deal on part of the purchase, but you must pay full price on the rest. For example, the sale may be 2-for-1 for the lenses, but you pay full price for the frames (or vice versa). Sometimes, any additional features that you select, such as scratchproof or UV coating, are charged at full price for both pairs.

Because of the multitude of brand names and styles, it is very difficult for most customers to know what is a fair price for a pair of frames and lenses. Because customers lack this expertise, they have to take the seller's word for quality and price. The sale boils down to which seller(s) does the buyer trust.

Let me show you some information. About three months ago, I participated in an omnibus marketing research study and I asked people why they prefer to do business with a specific retailer for their glasses. (A sample of the type of responses given is provided in Appendix A.)

As a final point, I read in yesterday's newspaper that Price Club, an aggressive discounter of vision products, is planning to open a new outlet about 8 km from my store. I need to know what kind of changes I should make to my operation, (I think you call it a marketing mix), so that I will not lose a lot of business to this competitor.

APPENDIX A

Respondent Quotes—Omnibus Study

Ralph's

I spend thousands of dollars each season on designer clothes. Why should I risk hurting my appearance by wearing inexpensive glasses or glasses that are not in fashion?

I want distinctive frames. I do not want to see many people wearing the same style of frames.

The first thing that people notice is your face. If I have to wear glasses, they should help to convey a very positive first impression of who I am.

I trust Ralph and his staff. The frames and the lenses that they have recommended have always been excellent.

I like their service, never rushed, always helpful. One thing that 1 especially like in today's impersonal world, they greet me by name.

A friend told me how satisfied she was with Ralph's selection of frames and his service. She was right. In the last six years, I bought five pairs of glasses from Ralph's.

Price Club

My insurance company allows me to spend up to $100 for a pair of glasses. I try to find a deal so that I do not have to pay anything out of my pocket.

I usually wear contacts. I need an inexpensive pair of glasses for the occasional time when I can't wear my contact lenses.

I am on a tight budget; if I can save money and still get a quality product, I am especially happy.

I have been shopping at Price Club for many years. I trust their pricing. In addition, I like being able to shop for eyewear at the same time I shop for other things.

When I go to another optician, a member of the staff wants to help me select my frames and gives me an opinion of how he/she thinks I look in the frames. I prefer to browse and make up my own mind as to how I look. At Price Club, there is no pressure to buy.

Glasses are glasses.

QUESTIONS

1. Identify the major trends that are impacting on Ralph's Optical. Which provide opportunities and which are threats?
2. Evaluate how well Ralph is responding to these trends.
3. What recommendations would you make to Ralph to improve his business?

3. THE BAY—A QUESTION OF SURVIVAL

The job from Hell. That's how the May 29, 1999 issue of *Canadian Business* described being President of the Bay, the position that George Heller had just been appointed to. The article goes on to state the following:

- The Bay has had three presidents within the past twelve months (all of them with great reputations).
- The Bay had a disastrous financial year in 1998 and the stock price has declined dramatically.
- The Bay is a chain that has no clear direction and there is no apparent solution to the problems it faces.
- The Christmas shopping season makes or breaks a retailer—and in 1998 it almost broke the Bay—earnings in the last quarter for '98 were down 86 percent from the same quarter in '97.

The problems are long-standing beginning in the late '80s when then president, George Kosich, slashed jobs (which lowered customer service), let stores get old and decrepit (which made the Bay a less attractive place to shop), made no investment in new distribution systems (which meant that it cost more to get the merchandise to stores), and had unexciting marketing (which led consumers to shop elsewhere). As if that wasn't enough, Wal-Mart entered Canada in 1994 and changed the face of department store retailers with its lower cost structure, great distribution system, and everyday low price strategy.

The previous presidents, according to retail analysts, were strong on planning but less so on implementation. For example, Bill Fields (who had been the number two man at Wal-Mart) was hired in 1997 and used the "scattergun approach." This involved trying out a whole bunch of retail ideas, seeing what worked, and giving up on the failures. Many of the ideas didn't work (for example, the HBC Outfitters lifestyle and adventure store has cost the Bay a considerable amount of money). The experiments generated confusion and avoided solving the basic problem—determine a simple focused strategy for the Bay.

A second major shift was to emphasize fashion and get out of a number of product categories including sporting goods and electronics. Here's what one retail analyst said about that strategy (which was also followed by Eaton's until it's demise): "The fundamental problem with the Bay and Eaton's is the same: they've taken the departments out of department stores. They were one-stop shops; now they are apparel stores. But you can't take a 90,000-square metre store and run it on an apparel basis—there's not enough people in any Canadian market, including Toronto, to support that concept." Along with that, a recent survey found that 56 percent of clothing purchases in Canada are at a sale price; for department stores, an earlier survey in 1993 found that 55 percent of clothing was purchased on sale, by 1998 that was up to 69 percent. One of the major causes of this change was the Bay, which offered special promotions, scratch and save days, no GST days, and many other deep discount specials. Then Eaton's did the same thing and 1998 was a bonanza for consumers shopping for clothes.

The other major criticisms of the Bay deal with the basics—can't find staff, poorly signed departments, poor layout, and poor presentation of merchandise. One study revealed that when consumers ranked stores from which they bought particular types of merchandise, the Bay was not the first choice in any category. In both men's and women's clothing it ranked fourth, behind Zellers, Sears Canada, and Wal-Mart.

As well, retail experts point to a host of external factors that do not bode well for the Bay. These factors include a general downward trend in department store sales in the past few years, the increase in competition in many product categories—like women's fashion clothing, the shift in shopping to specialty stores and category killers, the low income growth of Canadian households, and changing demographics.

So George Heller now has the job from Hell. Mr. Heller has had a successful retail career—he came from Zellers where he went upmarket to move away from Wal-Mart by adding private brands (Martha Stewart linens and towels, Cherokee casual wear, and Truly, a line of household products). These initiatives have worked well and Zellers is on the road back to more positive returns. He also has a solid reputation in the retail industry. As one expert commented: "George knows the business and he knows the people. It should be easier to make the Bay work than to reposition Zellers."

QUESTIONS

1. What are the major changes in the Canadian environment that are threats for the Bay? Opportunities for the Bay?
2. What are the major strengths and weaknesses of the Bay?
3. What would you recommend to improve the Bay's performance?

4. DAVE WONG—EXPERIENCES OF A NEW IMMIGRANT*

After graduating from college in Hong Kong in 1980 Dave Wong started his own business. After some up and down years, by the late 1980s, his trading company benefited considerably from the booming regional economy and Dave became a millionaire. However, as 1997 was approaching, Dave decided to immigrate and came to Canada as an investor (a specific category of immigration). Unlike most other immigrants from Hong Kong, he chose Montreal (rather than Vancouver or Toronto) as he liked the city and believed that Quebec offered considerable potential for the development of his trading business.

As a new immigrant, Dave had to go through a lot of hassles; getting his social insurance card, medical card, driving licence, and, of course, choosing a bank for his personal finance and trading business. Upon his friends' recommendations, he decided to open three different accounts—a term deposit, a saving, and a chequing account—at the Place d'Armes branch of the Country Bank. Since Dave did not know where he was going to live (he was temporarily staying in a downtown apartment hotel) and work, he therefore chose the nearest branch to Chinatown, a place where he expected to visit frequently. At the branch, he deposited a large portion of the $500,000 he brought from Hong Kong into the three accounts.

In Hong Kong, whenever a customer opened a saving or chequing account, s/he would sign on the inside cover of the bank book. The signature was then sealed by a special device and could only be seen under an ultraviolet light in the bank. As a result, customers were able to perform all kinds of transactions with their accounts at any branch of the bank and, with the signature on the bank book, no personal identification of any kind was required. Dave expected that degree of flexibility in Canada. As soon as he realized that his bank book did not carry his signature, he was a little concerned and asked the teller whether he would be able to withdraw money from the other branches of the Country Bank. The answer he got was a simple "Yes, certainly." After one week, Dave wanted to withdraw some money from his saving account and he went to a branch near the Guy metro station:

TELLER: Do you have any personal identification like your social insurance card, medical card, or driving licence?

DAVE: I am sorry. Since I'm a new immigrant, the only personal identification I have is my passport.

TELLER: That's fine. If you bring your passport here, we will give you the money.

Dave went back to the branch the next day with his passport and withdrew \$1,000 from his account. Meanwhile, Dave passed his driving test and received his medical card. In the following month, he did not have any trouble in withdrawing money from his account at various branches of the bank by presenting his driving licence. One afternoon, he was back in the Guy metro branch:

DAVE: Please deposit this cheque into my account and then withdraw \$1,000 from it. Here is my personal identification (he showed his driving licence to the teller).

TELLER: I'm sorry sir, we don't accept a driving licence as a piece of personal identification. Do you have any other identification?

DAVE: Yes, here is my medical card.

TELLER: Sorry sir, you haven't signed your medical card. We require a personal signature to appear on any valid personal identification.

Dave was prepared to sign his medical card but then he discovered that a signature on the card means that he is willing to donate his organs after death. He tried to explain this to the teller:

DAVE: I have no problem in donating my organs, but not for the reason that I want to get back my own money.

TELLER: In that case, I can't process the transactions. By the way, with your ATM card, you can use the machines outside to deposit and withdraw money.

DAVE: I haven't received my card. They told me it will take about one month but it has been almost two months since I opened my account. Anyway, I am prepared to sign my medical card now. Does it mean that I can get my money?

TELLER: No, sir. We require two pieces of personal identification.

DAVE: Two pieces of personal identification? But last time I was able to withdraw money from you with only one piece of identification, just my passport.

TELLER: It was not me. That must be another person.

DAVE: Can I see your manager?

The teller then asked the branch manager to come to the counter.

DAVE: I was able to withdraw money from the other branches with my driving licence; why can't I do it here? Also last time, I was able to withdraw money from you with only one piece of identification, why do you require two this time?

MANAGER: No, sir. I don't care what the other branches have done. We require two pieces of identification and a driving licence is not considered to be a valid identification.

The branch manager then showed Dave a document from the bank's head office. The bank did in fact require two pieces of valid identification—passport, social insurance card, medical card, citizen card, and/or an ATM card.

DAVE: Okay! I don't want to withdraw money now. But can you deposit this cheque into my account?

TELLER: No, sir. We need two pieces of personal identification.

Dave got very frustrated and left the branch. The same afternoon, Dave received his social insurance card. He went back to the Guy metro branch the next morning for the same transactions. Another teller served him and he was asked to present a single piece of personal identification. He showed the teller his social insurance card and the transactions were done in one minute. However, this did not make him a happier customer and when he came out from the branch, he decided to write a complaint letter.

QUESTIONS

1. What factors contributed to Dave's dissatisfaction?
2. Dave was so upset with the bank that he decided to write a complaint letter. What other actions might Dave take?
3. Suppose you were the customer service manager of the Country Bank, what could you do to improve the service quality of the bank?

5. BILL GREENE BUYS GOLF EQUIPMENT*

May 1998 was coming to an end. Bill Greene suddenly recalled that last fall, when he and his wife Mary had met their friends, Paul and Jackie Swinger, in Victoria, they had agreed to play golf the next time they met in Vancouver.

Bill and Mary were conscious of the benefits of regular physical exercise. They realized that often they were experiencing a kind of lethargy that they attributed to a lack of exercise. Bill did not like sports very much, except for cross-country skiing. The two of them had tried to play tennis, but after two summers they had abandoned that. Insofar as indoor sports were concerned, these did not interest them at all because they liked nature and preferred outdoor activities.

During their last encounter in Victoria, Jackie mentioned that she and Paul had taken up playing golf again regularly. Even though it was a quiet, relaxing sport, she found that after 18 holes she felt as if she had had a good workout.

Bill had laughed and said, "I remember that several years ago when I played in the golf tournaments of companies where I was working, I always won the prize for the worst player," and he had added: "However, today I admit that I would seriously like to take up golf again and learn to play well. Look, I promise you, the next time we meet we'll have a game of golf."

"Sure," Paul and Jackie had replied smiling.

Before inviting their friends, Bill and Mary decided to take a few golf lessons, to get some practice, and to buy a second set of golf clubs. Bill had a set of golf clubs he had won in a draw more than 20 years before. It consisted of seven clubs and a golf bag.

A complete set of clubs is composed of fourteen clubs, but sets of eleven clubs are the most widely sold. Sets of seven clubs are often used by beginners. In short, an eleven-club set includes three woods for long distances, seven irons for precision shots and one putter to get the ball in the hole when the player is on the green; a seven-club set includes two woods, four irons, and one putter.

At the time, Bill's colleagues indicated that the set he had won was a good quality one. He and Mary decided to keep the old set of clubs for her and to buy a new one for him. Since they were about the same height and weight, the clubs would be suitable for Mary to use at this stage.

Bill and Mary did not know what they should be looking for in buying golf equipment, and they had no idea about prices or brands available.

One day in June, when Bill was in a Canadian Tire store, he walked over to the clearance corner and noticed golf clubs on special for $10 each.

"That's a bargain," he thought.

He examined the clubs and noticed they all were different brands. He chose enough for a set of seven but was missing the putter.

"I could buy the two woods and the four irons on sale and then buy the putter separately," he said to himself.

Bill walked over to the sports equipment section to verify the price of a putter. At the regular price they varied between $23.99 and $36.99. A set of clubs cost between $75.99 for seven clubs and $399.99 for a set of eleven clubs. Bill calculated that if he bought a putter for $23.99 and the other six clubs on sale, the whole set would cost approximately $83.99, which would be more expensive than a set of seven at the regular price!

He wondered why the clubs were sold at that price. He returned to the clearance corner and asked a clerk why these clubs were reduced.

"These are clubs for left-handed people, and the sets are not complete. Also, the clubs are a mix of different brands," replied the clerk.

Bill not only felt disappointed but also embarrassed to realize how little he knew about golf equipment. He was right-handed himself!

As time went on, Bill and Mary continued to practise their shots on the driving range. The more Mary and Bill practised the more they liked this sport. However, they never made any real effort to purchase a second set of golf clubs.

As the summer was coming to an end, the Greene family decided to wait no longer and invited their friends from Victoria in September. They would rent a second set of clubs at the golf course for this occasion.

Bill told his friends that he and Mary had already started to play golf but they had not purchased their second set yet because they were not sure of the brand nor what a reasonable price would be.

Paul advised him: "To play golf well, two things are important: a good technique and good equipment. Regarding the equipment, there are several technical factors to be considered and last, but not least, your budget."

"For a beginner like you, I think it would be preferable, to start with, to purchase a seven-club set of a medium quality. You do not have to play at this stage with the full eleven clubs. Once you have played for some time you will develop a technique and you will start to appreciate the characteristics of the equipment required for more advanced players."

The Greene couple listened very attentively to these suggestions.

"And according to you how much should we pay?" asked Bill.

"It is difficult to pinpoint an amount; but I would say somewhere between $150 to $200 for a seven-club set, but that's only a ballpark figure," replied Paul.

"And, in your opinion, which brands should I look at?" asked Bill.

"Ah, that's a good question, my dear friend. As far as brands are concerned, I would not want to commit myself, there are so many on the market. You'll have to look around and see what is being offered," answered Paul.

"By the way, what's the brand of your clubs?" asked Bill.

"I have a Spalding set and Jackie's is a Wilson. They are good quality clubs. We did a lot of shopping around before buying our clubs and as you can see we chose different brands because we each had our own purchase criteria," answered Paul.

The four players had an enjoyable day on the golf course. After this meeting with their friends, Bill decided to learn more about golf. He bought a guide to learn how to play golf and he found in the chapter on equipment some information on this subject. To his surprise, he noticed there were numerous factors to be taken into consideration in the purchase of golf clubs as Paul had indicated. In short, the swing weight, total weight, shaft flexibility, length of clubs, loft, lie, the texture and quality of shafts, the grip, all of them had to be evaluated.

"Gee! it's not an easy purchase," he said to himself. He also took a look at *Golf* magazine and read the ads and the technical descriptions. He also learned that the woods were not always made out of wood but rather of new synthetic materials, such as graphite; there were many combinations and the choice was very complex.

"It's really too technical!" he said to himself.

The following week, towards the end of September, Bill looked at the Canadian Tire catalogue that he had at home. It advertised a Spalding eleven-club set, Executor Plus model, at $399.99, as well as some other less expensive brands such as Northwestern for which a seven-club set was advertised at $75.99.

With this information, Bill decided in October 1998 to visit the sports section of the large department stores. Bill was reluctant to go to a golf pro shop because he feared these stores sold mainly high quality equipment for professionals and that the salespeople, noticing his limited knowledge on the subject, would try to talk him into buying a set far too expensive for his level of skills.

He started by visiting a department store not far from his house. There he found a wide selection of brands and models with prices ranging from $79.89 to $399.99. After spending considerable time looking at all the models, he left the store somewhat disappointed.

On a nice day in November, he went to a *Sports-Experts* store where he saw a Spalding eleven-club set, Centurion Stainless model at $499.99, and a Dynatour seven-club set at $149.00. He looked closely at the latter and was going to ask some questions but the salespeople were so busy with other customers (it was the sales period for the beginning of the winter season) that he decided to come back another day when the store would be less crowded.

Bill realized that it was very difficult to compare the price of the models because even though each store sold the same brands, the models were always different. Faced with such a quantity of brands, models, and prices, Bill became more and more confused. He decided then to keep an eye on the end of season sales. Perhaps he could find a well-known brand such as Wilson or Spalding at a lower price.

The time passed and one day in January 1999, his wife noticed in the weekly circular from Sears, which was distributed door to door, reductions of 25 percent on all sports equipment, including golf sets.

"I'm going today to be among the first ones!" said Bill.

In the sports department of Sears, Bill looked at the equipment on sale. There was a choice of six models from brands such as Spalding, Campbell, and Augusta and the prices ranged from $125.00 to $549.00, less 25 percent.

While he was looking at the golf equipment, a salesman approached him. Bill told him that he was a beginner and that he wanted to buy a seven-club set of a medium quality in the range of $125 to $200. Bill then asked him what was the difference between the least expensive model of eleven clubs at $125.00 and the next one, a seven-club set from the Campbell brand, Stylist model, at $159.00.

The salesman described to him the different characteristics of each set. The Campbell model appeared to be better than the Northwestern model.

The salesman told Bill that he was a golfer himself and, in his opinion, the purchase of a set of golf clubs at too low a price was not recommended if he planned to play very often. As he became more experienced in the sport he would soon notice the benefits of a better quality club and he would have to purchase other clubs sooner than expected in order to better enjoy the game. He would therefore recommend starting with better equipment. The salesman described the various characteristics of the different clubs on sale, without being too technical. He seemed to have a good knowledge of the sport. Bill asked him his opinion on the Stylist model from Campbell.

"It's good quality equipment and it is on sale because we are reducing inventories to make room for new merchandise," replied the salesman.

Bill took a club and tried a swing. He studied the weight and the grip. The salesman evaluated the length of the clubs and told him that they appeared to fit him adequately.

"It's a good buy at such a price," said the salesman.

Bill hesitated a while, studied each club, and finally said: "O.K. I'll buy it!"

The salesman asked him if he needed a golf bag because they were on sale too.

"Yes, I need one." Bill compared the five models on display.

The salesman advised him: "For a beginner it's better to have a light bag because if you do not use the carts on the course you must be able to carry the bag on your shoulder without difficulty for several hours."

Bill decided to purchase a very light model at $45.99 less 25 percent, totalling $34.50.

"Do you need golf balls too?" asked the salesman.

"No, thank you. I have a good supply at home because I lose a lot of them on the course," replied Bill.

The salesman cleaned a small dirt spot on one of the clubs and carefully wrapped the set.

"Here they are, and I wish you lots of fun," said the salesman.

One day in February, the idea came to Bill to compare the new golf set with that of his wife. He was quite surprised to learn that the clubs he had recently bought were the same brand (Campbell), but a different model (Swingdale Deluxe). He concluded that the clubs he had purchased were of a good quality too.

"It's funny, I had never paid too much attention to the brand of our clubs; I thought that brand didn't exist any more. In the end, I think I made a good purchase."

QUESTIONS

1. What needs was Bill trying to satisfy in buying a set of golf clubs?
2. How did Bill conduct his search and evaluation leading to the purchase of the golf clubs?
3. Evaluate the role and behaviour of the salespeople in the initial stages and in the the final decision stage.
4. What marketing implications might Bill's purchase behaviour have for retailers of golf equipment?

6. CLEAN WINDOWS, INC.*

It was January 1995 and Terry Gill and John Kelly, partners of Clean Windows, Inc. (CW), were contemplating a marketing strategy for expanding their operations in the window cleaning market. Both were full-time students in the second year of their programs at the University of New Brunswick. They were committed to their studies and realized that their chosen strategy must allow them to complete their programs within the next two years.

They were optimistic that CW had the opportunity to grow very rapidly. Their optimism appeared justified, given the growth they had experienced in both residential and commercial contracts since they commenced operations in July 1994 (Figure 1). Mr. Kelly attributed this growth to the current lack of serious competition in the greater Fredericton area.

When questioned about balancing schoolwork and the responsibilities of his business, Mr. Gill commented:

> We know we have a really great concept here, but our study schedule could result in a lack of attention to customer demands and administrative details. I think that we can pull it off, but we need to make the right choices and develop an appropriate marketing strategy. John and I even considered franchising as our means of growth because we have to grow to maximize profitability.

*This case was prepared and revised by Professor E.S. Grant, University of New Brunswick, assisted by G.T. Clarke and K. Dunphy. Copyright ©1995.

Figure 1 Monthly Cleaning Gross Revenue

Month	Residential	Commercial	Total
July	$1,377	$ 37	$1,414
August	2,175	45	2,220
September	1,990	1,423	3,413
October	1,402	2,509	3,911
November	315	1,021	1,336
December	0	896	896

Source: Company records.

INITIAL STRATEGY

Operations commenced June 20, 1994, with enough equipment for two cleaners. Initially, all labour activity was completed by Mr. Gill and Mr. Kelly. Business was relatively slow for the first two months (Figure 1), as most of the owners' time was spent cleaning windows, not marketing and management activity. Advertising in these months was limited to the purchase of business cards and a direct mail campaign. The business cards were an important asset for business contacts, but the mailout resulted in limited success. It was thought that this was due to poor timing.

One thousand five hundred photocopied flyers were distributed just prior to a long weekend in July. Both partners and employees delivered the flyers to private residences in the downtown area and to a few upscale neighbourhoods.

By the end of July a display ad was run in the business directory section of the local newspaper and free air time was received on a local radio station interested in promoting student businesses. Unfortunately, neither of these two media proved successful. Lawn signs and T-shirts displaying the company logo and phone number were purchased. These media, combined with word of mouth, accounted for close to 85 percent of all new cleaning contracts.

The promotions were responsible for business growth in August and September. With this additional business, the need for extra staff became apparent. By August, six cleaners were employed. An increase in demand through September and October was experienced, but it became difficult for both partners to cope with the increased volume as university commenced in September. By then, CW had only two full-time employees, who were responsible for reducing the partners' workload.

In early November, Mr. Gill and Mr. Kelly realized that the two employees were not working out as anticipated and the decision was made to lay them off. This left only the partners to resume the labour-intensive duties of window cleaning. This was very difficult, since both maintained a rigorous cleaning schedule in addition to a full course load at the university.

Now, in January 1995, both partners agreed that this strategy would have to be reconsidered.

COMPETITION

When questioned about the competition, Mr. Kelly commented:

> There is only one firm that cleans residential windows, but we don't see them as a serious competitor. We know that they do have some business, but they cannot have much. We have phoned them several times, but our calls were never returned. There are two firms that service only commercial accounts. One of these firms cleans high-rise buildings only, but they operate out of Moncton, which is more than a two-hour drive. The other is a local firm; they are not equipped to clean high-rises but they have a very significant share of the local commercial market. We are certain that we can compete with them; almost all of our commercial clients have experienced their service and have expressed relief that there is now an alternative available.

Mr. Kelly had obtained information on all three of these competitors (Figure 2). Fredericton also had a number of maid and janitorial service companies, most of which cleaned windows. However, none cleaned external window surfaces, and they cleaned interior window surfaces on an irregular basis.

Although Fredericton offers only a relatively small potential market size, both partners were certain that there was an attractive opportunity in both the residential and the commercial market.

Many customers have indicated they would use CW's service again. One customer stated that she had seen the lawn sign and then decided to request CW's service. Unable to find the phone number (a business number was obtained in September), she claimed to have driven more than 80 kilometres before finding the lawn sign that she needed to find the number.

Mr. Gill believed that the most profitable opportunity would be to service what he calls high-rise buildings (all those that require staging). He estimates that there are more than 350 such buildings in the Fredericton area.

Figure 2

Competition in Fredericton Window Cleaning Market

Company	Customer Type*	Bonded	Liability Insurance	Estimated Price
City Window Cleaners	Residential	?	?	?
Mr. Windows	Commercial	Yes	Yes	\$15/hr
Gormay Cleaners	Commercial: high-rise buildings only	No	Yes	\$40/hr
Other (janitorial and maid services)	Commercial† and residential†	N/A	N/A	N/A

* Residential customers are defined as single dwellings only, all other accounts are defined as commercial.
† Clean only interior window surfaces.
? = unavailable.
Source: Telephone directory and telephone enquiries.

COST DATA

Cost data are provided in Figures 3 and 4. All costs for 1994 (Figure 3) were actual, based on the costs incurred to date. Costs for 1995 (Figure 4) have been estimated by the partners. Transportation costs have been excluded. A small van belonging to Mr. Kelly's father had been used and John was confident that this vehicle would be available for at least another year. Although CW incurs no rental fee for the use of this van, fuel would have to be purchased.

All estimated costs were believed to be reasonably accurate. However, the pricing of window contracts had been much more arbitrary. Mr. Kelly saw the pricing decision of key importance to CW's long-term profitability. To date, prices had been based on an estimated completion time for each potential contract.

The time estimate was multiplied by a charge-out rate of $15/hour per cleaner. Mr. Kelly confessed that the decision to use $15 per hour was arbitrary; however, he was confident that it was competitive and fair. This was thought to be the same charge-out rate used by Mr. Windows (Figure 2). Mr. Kelly had difficulty deciding what to charge in the future. Although he believed their price was competitive, he had a hunch that many customers expected a lower charge-out rate given their status as students. He believed it was a serious issue and realized that many customers selected CW because of the altruistic satisfaction they received from supporting a student venture.

Enough equipment (ladders, staging, buckets, etc.) to operationalize three two-person crews had been acquired. It was estimated that additional equipment would cost $300 per crew, but it was uncertain whether or not it would be necessary to hire additional crews.

Additional investment would be necessary in order to clean high-rise buildings. Staging that would allow one person to safely manoeuvre up and down the side of a high-rise would cost approximately $4,500.

Figure 3

Actual Costs—1994

Variable Costs	**Per Hour**	
Wages		
One two-person crew	(2 x $5.50 each)	$11.00/hour
Supplies		
Fuel	$ .75	
Cleaning fluids	.50	
Cleaning materials	.90	2.15
Total variable costs		$13.15
Fixed Costs	**Per Month**	
Insurance (liability)	$ 15.00	
Telephone	55.00	
Advertising	110.00	
Bank charges	25.00	
Equipment depreciation	10.00	
Total fixed costs	$215.00	

Source: Company records.

Figure 4

Estimated Costs—1995

Variable Costs	**Per Hour**	
Wages		
One two-person crew	(2 x $5.70 each)	$11.40/hour
Supplies		
Fuel	$ .80	
Cleaning fluids	.50	
Cleaning materials	.90	2.20
Total variable costs		$13.60
Fixed Costs	**Per Month**	
Insurance (liability)	$ 20.00	
Telephone	60.00	
Advertising	200.00	
Bank charges	30.00	
Equipment depreciation	20.00	
Total fixed costs	$330.00	

Source: Company estimates.

THE MARKET

Mr. Gill had evaluated the Fredericton market and concluded that it was sizable enough to allow CW to realize satisfactory profits. He had collected selected statistics at the university's library (Figure 5). Although Mr. Gill was uncertain how many households and commercial customers were likely to use his services, he was certain that his competitors were not satisfying the current demand.

In the past, CW's window contracts were largely concentrated within a small geographic area. Both partners were uncertain why this phenomenon existed. Mr. Kelly wondered, "Is this because our lawn signs were displayed more often in this area? Are these people different, or is it related to other, undetermined causes?"

Figure 5 Selected Characteristics—Fredericton, NB

Dwelling characteristics	
Single detached house	10,230
Apartment, five or more storeys	275
Movable dwelling	50
All other types	5,890
Total number of occupied private dwellings	16,445
Population characteristics	
By industry division	
All industries	24,095
Primary industries (SIC divisions A,B,C, and D)	440
Manufacturing industries (division E)	1,290
Construction industries (division F)	1,160
Transportation, storage, communication, and other utility industries (divisions G and H)	1,895
Trade industries (divisions I and J)	950
Finance, insurance, and real estate industries (divisions K and L)	950
Government service industries (division N)	4,565
Other service industries (divisions M,O,P,Q, and R)	9,365
Not applicable	480
Total labour force 15 years and over	24,570

Source: Statistics Canada, Cat. 94-107 and 108, 1986.

THE FUTURE

The partners faced a number of important decisions. They had to decide whether or not their current strategy was appropriate for the situation. If it was not, they would have to agree on appropriate changes. These changes would have to be made in light of both partners' commitment to expansion. They believed they could create a student-owned franchise operation similar to College Pro Painters and University Painters. However, they were uncertain how they should proceed.

They would need to make some decisions very soon. Exams finished in April, and they anticipated that April and May would be extremely busy months, given that many people plan to clean their homes and businesses in the spring. They realized there would be little time available for analysis and strategic planning after late March. Time would be spent hiring employees, selling, cleaning, and perhaps even studying for final exams.

QUESTIONS

1. How can the market (commercial and residential) for window cleaning be segmented?
2. What types of promotional activities would you suggest CW, Inc. use? How can the firm encourage repeat usage of its service?
3. How feasible is the venture?
4. Would you recommend that the partners attempt to sell franchise agreements? Explain.

7. OMER DESERRES: ARTISTS' SUPPLIES AND COMPUTERS*

FROM HARDWARE TO ARTISTS' SUPPLIES

Omer DeSerres was 26 years old when he opened his first wholesale and retail hardware store on St. Laurent street in Montreal in 1908. The store specialized in plumbing and heating supplies for both individual consumers and businesses. In the mid 40s, Omer DeSerres' son, Roger, took over the operations. Under his leadership, the company expanded as he added new stores and several new and diverse product lines. Customers at these stores purchased a variety of products including household appliances, gifts, renovation materials, artists' materials, and sports goods.

The company experienced sustained growth until the early 1970s. At its peak, the company owned seven outlets, five hardware stores, a sporting goods store, and a heating and plumbing supplies store. The company had about 325 employees during the peak.

During the 1970s, the company suffered several setbacks forcing Roger DeSerres to downsize its operations. First, a very aggressive wholesaler of plumbing supplies entered the market resulting in a substantial reduction in sales of these products. In 1972, Roger DeSerres closed its wholesale plumbing division and withdrew all the plumbing materials from the stores, despite the fact that 50 percent of the company's sales were generated from plumbing supplies. Second, the competition in the hardware sector intensified with the arrival of new "large store" hardware chains (i.e., Pascal, Canadian Tire and Beaver/Le Castor Bricoleur). These stores had an average selling area of 2,000 square metres compared to an average of 1,000 square metres for the Omer DeSerres stores. The Omer DeSerres stores lost customers to the new chains and sales fell substantially.

Finally, in 1974 the store located on St. Catherine Street received an expropriation notice for the construction of the Université du Québec à Montréal (UQAM) campus. As a result, the company was forced to relocate its main store, a company's landmark since 1913. The store was relocated to St. Hubert Street

*Source: Case written by JoAnne Labrecque, École des H.E.C. (affiliated with the University of Montreal).

at the corner of Bélanger Street, where the family already operated a hardware store. This outlet was poorly located to satisfy the needs of the primary and the secondary market. The 1,000-square-metre store exceeded the size required to satisfy the needs of the neighbouring area but, on the other hand, the size was not large enough to carry the selection of merchandise required to compete directly with the large chains.

Two years later, Roger DeSerres closed the hardware store on St. Hubert Street, thus ending the hardware activities he had developed during his career. Marc DeSerres, who had started working in the retail sector of the hardware store on St. Hubert Street, took over the family business. At that time the company had only a small store of 150 square metres situated on St. Catherine Street, which sold artists' and graphic arts supplies. The boutique had four employees.

THE DEVELOPMENT OF THE ARTISTS' SUPPLIES DIVISION

Marc DeSerres and the store faced an uncertain future. The store occupied a site belonging to UQAM and risked being expropriated at any time. He nevertheless went ahead and expanded its operations. In 1979, he moved the store to a larger site, still under the ownership of UQAM. He believed the site had good potential due to its proximity to UQAM, which represented an attractive target market. In 1985, the uncertainty facing the store was eliminated when the company acquired the building where the main store and head office of Omer DeSerres are currently situated, at 334 St. Catherine St. East. This choice location for the artist and graphic arts supplies store, close to UQAM and in the heart of downtown Montreal, allowed the company to rapidly increase sales in a very short time. In the mid 1980s, most of the advertising agencies and graphic artists purchased their supplies including brushes, technical rulers, and drawing tables from Omer DeSerres. The store, which had 1,000 square metres of selling space and carried 30,000 articles, could satisfy the needs of a very wide clientele including students, amateur artists, and graphic arts professionals.

GROWTH BY ACQUISITION

In the mid 1980s, Marc DeSerres began expanding operations primarily through acquiring other stores. The major product line—artists' supplies—had changed little in many years and the overall market was in the maturity stage of its life cycle. Thus, growth came through acquisitions.

In 1986, Omer deSerres acquired the Lizotte store in Old Quebec, a successful store dealing with artists' supplies. Shortly after the purchase, Marc DeSerres changed the name of the store to Omer DeSerres and made major changes to the store and to the product mix to conform to the Omer DeSerres' image of quality and product specialization. Two years later, Omer DeSerres acquired its main competitor in Quebec City, the Trottier store. Since telephone orders represented the largest proportion of sales, Marc DeSerres closed the Trottier store and concentrated all his activities in the Old Quebec area.

Exhibit 1 **Omer DeSerres Stores—1992**

Location	m²	Number of Products	Number of Employees	Delivery	Competitors
Montreal, St. Catherine Street	1,000	30,000	50	Yes	
Montreal, Stanley Street	400	15,000	7	No	
Laval	250	15,000	6	No	None
Pointe Claire	250	15,000	6	No	None
Quebec	450	20,000	20	Yes	3(Small)

In the 1987–88 period, Omer DeSerres opened two branches, one in Laval and another one in Pointe-Claire. The stores were smaller than the main store on St. Catherine Street and carried a more limited product line (approximately 15,000 items).

In 1992, Omer DeSerres acquired its Montreal competitor, Loomis & Toles, located on Stanley Street. The store layout was changed as well as the product line to conform to the distinct character of Omer DeSerres. The store had an area of 400 square metres, employed seven people and carried an inventory of 15,000 items. By the end of 1992, Omer DeSerres operated five stores in the province of Quebec (Exhibit 1).

The technological advances of the '80s revolutionized the graphic arts market. Each year, several products disappeared from the shelves as they were replaced by computer graphics packages. As these graphics packages were adopted by advertising agencies and the boutiques of graphic artists, Marc DeSerres knew that his business would suffer. As a strategic move, he expanded into the computer market and in early 1990 opened two computer stores in Montreal. By becoming an Apple dealer, Omer DeSerres was adapting to the new needs of its clients. "Since our clients were using more and more computers," said Marc DeSerres, "we had to offer that service."

Contrary to the market of artists' supplies, which had reached maturity, the world of computer graphics was continually changing. In fact, it was a difficult task to forecast the growth of the computer division of Omer DeSerres six months ahead. Omer DeSerres—Computer Graphics was positioned in the market as a specialized store selling computer equipment and offering consulting services in imagery, computerized systems, computer-aided design and manufacture, data acquisition and colour separation. Companies were its main target. According to Marc DeSerres, the future growth of the company lay in the computer division, which represented close to 50 percent of sales.

In 1993 Omer DeSerres acquired six stores specializing in artists' supplies owned by the S.P.R. RAPID-Graphic division of the CORRA group, a Dutch holding company that was well established in the French food industry. The CORRA group had set as an objective during the 1980s to penetrate new markets and had acquired ten small stores of artists' supplies in Quebec. The S.P.R. acquisition represented a turning point for Omer DeSerres. The transaction involved several stores, located in six different cities (Montreal, Quebec, Chicoutimi, Ottawa, Burlington, and Sherbrooke). The management of S.P.R. was centralized in the Montreal store, but most of the stores were poorly organized. The stores did not offer the same product mix, had different names, some of which had been changed several times (see Exhibits 2, 3 and 4). The stores employed a large number of people, 85 in total. The CORRA group had given management the freedom to manage the stores in any way they felt was appropriate. The management team, composed of four people, had considerable latitude to decide on the choice of articles, the selection of suppliers, price policies, and promotions.

Exhibit 2 Stores Acquired from S.P.R. RAPID-Graphic Division of CORRA Group

City	Store Names
Montreal	• Le Pavillon des arts (corner of St. Denis/Ontario streets)
Chicoutimi	• La spatule • RAPID-Graphic • Le Pavillon des arts
Ottawa	• Eezee-Art • RAPID-Graphic
Burlington (Ontario)	• RAPID-Blue • RAPID-Graphic
Sherbrooke	• Studio Gosselin • Rouillard • RAPID-Graphic • Le Pavillon des arts
Quebec City	• Le Pavillon des arts

Exhibit 3 Product Mix of the S.P.R. RAPID-Graphic Division

	Graphic Arts Material	Artists' Material	Crafts Material	Framing	Lettraset	Repro-graphics	Delivery
Montreal	X	X	X	—	—	—	—
Chicoutimi	—	X	X	X	X	—	X
Ottawa	X	X	—	X	X	—	X
Burlington	X	X	—	—	X	X	X
Sherbrooke	—	X	X	X	—	—	—
Quebec City	X	X	—	—	—	—	—

Exhibit 4

Some Characteristics of the S.P.R. RAPID-Graphic Stores

Location	m2	Number of Articles	Number of Employees	Delivery	Competitors
Montreal (St. Denis St.)	1,000	20,000	35	No	Omer DeSerres
Chicoutimi	1,500	15,000	10	Yes	None
Ottawa	700	15,000	12	Yes	1 (Important)
Burlington	400	10,000	10	Yes	None
Sherbrooke	150	7,000	4	No	None
Quebec City	250	15,000	6	No	Omer

Although this move would strengthen Omer DeSerres' position of leadership in the market of artists' and graphic arts supplies, Marc DeSerres knew that the purchase of the six new stores would be a challenge for a company of 130 employees and seven commercial outlets, namely five stores selling artists' and graphic arts supplies and two stores selling computers. In order to integrate these newly acquired stores into the company, Marc DeSerres started by merging the management of the two companies to avoid overlapping of administrative tasks, with the assistance of three of the four members of the S.P.R. RAPID-Graphic management. Under the new organizational structure, all the strategic decisions—promotional budget, store layout, choice of suppliers, price policies—would be made by the management. The store managers would be responsible for managing their personnel, restocking, and selecting products as per the product mix authorized by the company's purchasing agents.

Shortly after the acquisition, Marc DeSerres made major changes to the stores located in the markets he knew well, namely Montreal and Quebec. In Montreal, he changed the layout of Le Pavillon des arts, but kept the same personnel. In Quebec city, he relocated Le Pavillon des arts to be near Laval University, an important target market. Few changes were made to the other stores. On the other hand, he wonders what retail strategy should he follow for the stores located in the other cities and what commercial name should they have.

In total, the Omer DeSerres network today has 13 outlets—two computer stores and 11 artists' material stores—and employs more than 200 people. According to Marc DeSerres, sales are expected to exceed $20 million in 1995.

QUESTIONS

Following the acquisition of the S.P.R. RAPID-Graphic, Marc DeSerres wonders what retail strategy he should follow for the new stores. In particular, he would like to know what are your recommendations to the following questions:

1. Which commercial name (Omer deSerres, Pavillon, Rapid,...) should he use for the new stores in Quebec, Montreal, Chicoutimi, Ottawa, Burlington, and Sherbrooke?
2. Should he modify the product lines carried by the stores?
3. Should he use the same positioning for all the stores?
4. Would you recommend the same promotional program for all the stores?

8. WING AND A PRAYER*

Stefan Bakarich finally had found just the right name for his mobile bungee jumping operation—Wing and a Prayer. It was March, 1994, and he had eight weeks to the May Victoria Day Weekend—the first long weekend of the summer to get his operation "off the ground." If he had it figured correctly, Stefan would rent a construction crane, assemble a group of friends, and tour south-western Ontario offering bungee jumps at tourist attractions. He and his friends could earn enough money to return to university in the fall while being paid to have fun and work on their tans over the summer.

BACKGROUND

Bungee jumping started as a ritual practised by "land divers" on Pentecost Island in the New Hebrides located in the South Pacific. To cleanse themselves of wrongdoing or as acts of courage, men constructed 30 metre towers from thin trees. Climbing to the top, they dove off with vines tied around their ankles. Their heads would just touch the ground as the vine became taut. In the 1960s, a group of Oxford University students (who called themselves the Oxford Dangerous Sports Club) brought bungee jumping to the modern world. As a commercial curiosity, the sport was born in New Zealand in 1988 where ancient vines were replaced with modern man-made fibre cords tested to withstand more than 1,360 kilograms, and where bamboo pole towers were replaced with bridges spanning deep river gorges.

The sport became popular on the west coast of the United States in the late 1980s and swept across the country in the early 1990s showing phenomenal growth. In 1991, only 20 companies in the United States offered bungee jumps. In 1992, that number had grown to 200 and by 1993, more than 400 companies were in the bungee jump business. Participation in the sport had also grown. In 1992, 1.5 million Americans experienced a bungee jump spending more than $100 million for the thrill. In 1993, 2.5 million Americans participated, spending more than $125 million.

*This case was written by Marvin Ryder, McMaster University.

In Canada, the first commercial bungee operation (Bungy Zone) opened south of Nanaimo on Vancouver Island on August 4, 1990. By 1993, 30,000 people had jumped at this site. Some Bungy Zone statistics: oldest jumper 73; youngest 14; and heaviest 150 kilograms. The most paid bungee jumps by one person was 30. The typical jumper was a thrill-seeking male aged 18 to 25. Ninety-nine percent of people who paid the fee completed the jump. Ten percent of jumpers took a second jump on the same day. Participation statistics were not available for Canada but, in 1993, there were about 35 companies that arranged bungee jumps off bridges, towers, cranes, and hot air balloons. The West Edmonton Mall had introduced indoor bungee jumping and Nanaimo had even hosted bungee jumping in the nude.

Stefan had taken his first bungee jump in May, 1993. He tried to describe his experience to a friend.

> I dove straight out, in my best imitation of Superman. At first, the free-fall was exhilarating. But it was also disorienting, and after a moment I panicked. I wished there were something to grab hold of. The sound of the wind was almost deafening. The ground below rushed toward me, until everything became a blur. It was hard to believe that I was feeling 3 G's—just like air force pilots.
>
> Suddenly, the world seemed upside-down. The ground was receding, and now I was completely confused. I was up in the air again when I realized that the cord had held.
>
> I started to descend once more. This time, there was no fear, just enjoyment. I rebounded up and down four more times, with each rise becoming smaller. Finally, the bungee cord had no more bounce, and I was lowered onto the pad where my feet were untied. Friends told me I had the Look—a certain glow common to those who had just found God or had escaped the electric chair.

During the summer of 1993, Stefan took a bungee jump training course, worked for two and a half months at an amusement park in the United States and jumped 150 more times.

OPERATIONS

Stefan's experience with a crane-based company inspired him. He had taken careful notes about its operation so that he could replicate its success in Canada. For a typical jump, a patron would be taken, in a specially designed metal cage, 40 metres to the top of a crane—a ride of 60 seconds. These jump platforms were available for $500 to $1,000, though Stefan thought he could design and build one over the next eight weeks. At the top, the patron would be placed in one of two harnesses and given special instructions about jumping. One harness went around a person's ankles so that he or she would fall head first. The feet were tightly bound together with a towel and tethered to the bungee cord by a nylon strap and carabiner, a common piece of mountaineering equipment. The other harness could be strapped around a person's waist so that she or he would fall feet first. Each harness was commercially available at a cost of $150 to $300. While the patron took some time to build courage, the length of the bungee cord was adjusted to that person's weight. These "top of crane" activities could take between two and four minutes. Jumping out from the cage and away from the crane, the patron would take three seconds to fall until the bungee cord became taut and caused them to bounce. Waiting for the bounding to stop, lowering the basket, retrieving the jumper, and removing the harness would take another two minutes.

Stefan had researched potential suppliers so he had a firm estimate of costs. He would have to pay $100 per operating hour for construction crane rental, which included $1 million of liability insurance, fuel to run the generator, and a driver. Given the lack of office building construction, many companies had cranes parked in their compounds. These construction companies had been quite interested in Stefan's lease proposal. A crane operator would cost an additional $40 per operating hour. He felt the cost was justified as a skilled employee operating the crane would minimize the chances of something going wrong.

He and a jump assistant would be on the jump platform helping with instructions, adjusting the bungee cord, strapping on the harness, and communicating via walkie-talkie to the crane operator. On the ground, one person would use a microphone and sound system to speak to any crowd that had gathered and encourage them to participate. Two other people would assist on the ground by getting potential patrons to sign a liability waiver form, weighing jumpers to determine the proper bungee cord, collecting the jump fee, and talking personally with patrons in the crowd. While people under 18 could jump, a parent or guardian's signature would be required on the waiver form. Excepting the crane operator and himself, all staff would each be paid $8.00 per operating hour.

Of course, a bare crane was not very attractive so Stefan would have to invest in some cloth banners which, when hung on the crane, would also be used for promotion. Some portable tables, folding chairs, walkie-talkies, and a sound system would have to be purchased for $1,700. This cost also included portable "snow" fencing that would be used to limit public access to the crane, jump platform, and retrieval area. During less busy times, the sound system would play "hip hop," "dance," "house," and "rap" music to help attract and build a crowd. His major cost was an inflatable target pad that would be used to catch a jumper only if the bungee cord broke. Though pads came in many sizes, he felt it was a wise precaution to choose the largest size available at a cost of $12,000. As he thought the business would have a three- to five-year life, the pad and other equipment could be used year after year.

He had modelled his fee schedule on the American amusement park: $65 for the first jump and $55 for a second jump on the same day.

Realistically, the company would operate for the 110-day period from the Victoria Day Weekend in late May to the Labour Day Weekend in early September. As he did not want to be bothered with portable lighting, he would start operations no earlier than a half hour after sunrise and cease operations no later than a half hour before sunset. The company would never operate during a thunderstorm or in high winds and Stefan thought that the start of a week and overcast/rainy days would see less demand for the service.

SAFETY

Bungee jumping was not without its risks. In August 1992, a man was killed in Peterborough, Ontario, when he jumped from a crane. That same year, two people died in the United States and one in New Zealand from accidents. The Canadian Standards Association, a non-profit agency, had not determined any rules for bungee jumping so regulations varied by province. Some provinces had no regulations, but Ontario, working with the Canadian Bungee Association, had amended the Amusement Devices Act to regulate bungee jump operations starting in the spring of 1994.

In the legislature, Ontario Consumer and Commercial Affairs Minister, Marilyn Churley, said, "Operators can't just take a construction crane and set it up and have people jump off. We don't think that's safe. The government is committed to establishing and enforcing safety standards to minimize the risk to Ontarians who take part in this activity. Maintaining high standards of safety may also limit bungee operators' exposure to lawsuits and reduce the high cost of liability insurance."

Bungee jump operators were required to obtain a licence and permit ($310 fee) from the ministry prior to any jumps taking place. Before a licence could be issued, the equipment design first had to be approved by ministry engineers ($400 fee) after which a thorough on-site physical inspection of the bungee operation would be completed ($200 fee). The technical dossier of designs was to include: the jump height; a description of bungee cords including manufacturer, type of cord, and weight range of jumpers; an indication if the jump is static or portable; a description of the hoisting device including name of manufacturer, year, serial number, and safe working load; depth of water or air bag; type of harnesses to be used and types of jumps offered; wind speed restrictions; and number and function of jump personnel.

A forty-page code for bungee jumping operations was also in place. The code had been recommended by the Task Force on Bungee Jumping, a working partnership between government and the Canadian Bungee Association. The code required a number of safety features that must be in place on bungee equipment and technical specifications for the structure, platform, bungee cords, harness, and all other equipment used in the activity. It also outlined the qualifications for bungee jump employees including certificates in First Aid and Cardio-Pulmonary Resuscitation (CPR) and training specific to bungee jumping. Another requirement was a good first aid kit with a spinal board and speed splints, which would cost an operator an additional $500.

These changes were introduced to regulate careless operators and were aimed primarily at mobile bungee operations as they had less experienced staff and more failure-prone equipment because it was repeatedly set up and dismantled. Prior to the legislation, some operators had voluntarily introduced dual carabiners for ankle harnesses so there was a back-up if one failed.

Stefan planned his own set of rules. No pregnant women. No people with heart conditions. No people with high blood pressure. No people who suffered from epilepsy. No people with neurological disorders. Especially no people under the influence of alcohol and drugs. He would allow no reverse jumping (anchoring and loading the bungee cord from the ground to propel the jumper upward), no sand bagging (loading excess weight with the jumper to be released at the bottom to gain more momentum), and no tandem jumping (two or more jumpers harnessed together).

A bungee cord was made from several bound strands of latex rubber doubled back on itself thousands of times and sheathed in cotton and nylon. The cost of these cords varied from $300 to $1,000. The cord could stretch to five times its original length. For safety, most operators retired a bungee cord after 150 jumps. Prior to the popularity of jumping, these cords were used by the U.S. Air Force on aircraft carriers so were constructed to military specifications.

SOME DECISIONS

To start his business, Stefan needed capital to acquire bungee cords, harnesses, the landing pad, and his operating equipment. He was aware of two Ministry of Economic Development and Trade loan programmes. As a returning Canadian university student, he could apply for a $3,000 interest-free loan. To qualify for this loan, he had to be over 15, returning to school, and operating a business in Ontario between April 1, 1994 and September 30, 1994. Whatever loan amount he received would be payable on October 1, 1994.

He had also heard of the Youth Adventure Capital Program. It provided loans of up to $7,500 to help unemployed Canadian youth aged 18 to 29 start a business in Ontario. The interest rate on the loan would be prime plus one percent and he would be expected to make principal and interest payments each month. He would also be expected to contribute a minimum of one-quarter of the loan amount to the operating capital of the firm. This program was not intended to fund a summer job experience.

Neither program would provide him with all the capital he required. He approached his parents. While not completely sold on the venture, his parents thought it would be a good learning experience so they agreed to loan him $3,000 interest-free, though they expected to be repaid at the end of the summer.

Needing more money, Stefan shared his plan with Zach Thompson, a friend on the University waterpolo team and a recent bungee-jumping enthusiast. Zach had also worked part-time with a bungee jump operator, but he had only jumped 40 times in the last year. He would act as a jump assistant. Zach proposed a partnership and a joint application for any government loan. Profits would be split 50/50. Like Stefan, he would replace a "paid" worker on the jump crew but would not draw any hourly wages. Of all the people Stefan contacted, Zach asked the most questions.

Where would they operate the business? Stefan thought they could create a base of operations in Grand Bend, a popular beach location within an hour's drive of London, Ontario. When special events occurred, like the Western Fair in London, Ontario or the Zurich Bean Festival, they could pull up stakes and move to that location for a few days.

Would they only offer bungee jumps? Zach thought they could sell some complementary products. A colourful logo could be designed for "Wing and a Prayer" and applied to T-shirts and baseball caps. Selling for $20 and $10 respectively, these items would have a 100 percent markup on cost and could add extra revenue. Zach had also thought about selling a personalized video. That would mean purchasing a camcorder ($1,800), developing some stock footage for opening and closing credits, and somehow editing/processing on site the video footage shot so the patron could quickly get her/his tape. Zach thought they could sell the videos for $25. Building on these ideas, Stefan thought about offering a colourful poster that might be especially popular among children. To produce 1,000 posters would cost $800 but they would be sold for $4 to $6, generating a very healthy profit margin.

Would they make any money? That required some financial analysis including a break-even analysis. Zach felt they needed to assess a second scenario; the likelihood that they would make enough money to return to university in the fall. These analyses would be needed along with their marketing plan when any loans were sought.

If this was going to be their summer occupation, they needed to get started right away.

QUESTIONS

1. Based on financial analysis, how likely are the entrepreneurs to meet their profit targets?
2. Is their operational plan sound? Do you have any improvements to suggest?
3. Should they open a bungee-jumping business?

9. THE FRANCHISING EXERCISE

Assume that you have decided to start your own retail business. One of the options is to buy a franchise—it offers many advantages including a proven track record, training programs, and operating manuals that teach the retailer how to operate the business. Benefits may also include national advertising and a recognized brand name and image may already exist.

You have decided to investigate the fast-food industry and, as a preliminary step, to examine the franchises listed by the Canadian Franchise Association

www.cfa.ca

(www.cfa.ca) that have been in business for more than two years. Go to their Web site and review the following four sites (listed under "Regular Members"):

- Boston Pizza International Inc.
- De Dutch Pannekoek House
- Great Canadian Bagel Company
- Greco Pizza Donair

QUESTIONS

1. Which, if any, of the following costs are provided in the information: initial costs, franchise fee, opening costs, working capital, premises costs, site evaluation fee, royalties, and promotion costs?
2. Based on the information provided on each site, which franchise, if any would you be interested in pursuing further. That is, which franchise appears to offer promising prospects.
3. Before you went further, what additional information would you like to obtain?

10. MARTIN'S DEPARTMENT STORE

After being hired by Martin's, a chain of discount department stores located in Ontario and Quebec, Roger Bennett went through 13 weeks of intensive training in Martin's junior executive training programme. After completing his training, he was assigned as the manager of the fashion fabrics department in a Montreal store that catered to French-Canadian families and first-generation families of primarily Italian heritage. Martin's sales associates were expected to speak French, English, and Italian, but in actuality most of them spoke only two of these languages. The sales associates were hired from the neighbourhood and those of French and Italian extraction spoke their mother tongues.

Roger was from a small town in Northern Manitoba and had attended university in Halifax. Finding himself in this environment was different, to say the least. He considered his initial training quite good. He had learned systems; he had acquired a good grasp of the company's target market (although he believed that there were some problems with the many varied types of micro-markets in which stores were located); and he had trained with good store managers and buyers.

His first assignment as the department manager in fashion fabrics had provided him with some of the best training possible. But the composition of his department and the policies he inherited were causing him some problems. He had two full-time salespeople: one person who worked three-quarter time (Bettina), and three part-time women who worked the busy hours during the week. Bettina was the only person in the department who spoke English, French, and Italian. Her hours had been worked out with the store manager some years ago, and they were the hours when the store did most of its business. She was the only person in the department on a straight commission plan. The two full-time employees were on a salary plus 1 percent commission on net sales; the part-time employees were on straight salary.

Roger had been in the department for three weeks when the two full-time salespeople asked for a meeting. During the meeting, they were angry, and made the following complaints:

- "Bettina 'hogs' all sales and ties up a dozen customers at a time, and we can't make an extra loony for our commissions." (Roger was not sure whether they knew of the straight commission arrangement, but he certainly was not going to open that up for discussion.)
- "Bettina speaks all the languages, so she is able to say things we don't understand, and we know she's talking about how good she is and how inefficient we are—she's careful to speak the 'other' language when one of us is around."
- "The stock work in a fabrics department is tremendous: you always have to be folding bolts, straightening remnants, and so on. Bettina folds only her own sales and won't straighten out anything else, so we're always doing stock work while she's grabbing customers."
- "Bettina sells so much that we look bad. Even the commissions she 'steals' from us don't bother us as much as how we must look to you and others."
- "Bettina is so 'sweet' when any of you are around, but when it's just us and customers, she's a real witch."

Roger left the meeting very concerned and realized he was in a difficult position. He wondered what he should do next and how he could resolve this problem.

QUESTIONS

1. Is Bettina so valuable that her reactions must be considered?
2. Is it typical to find varying compensation plans within a single department?
3. Are the salespeople's complaints legitimate or emotional?
4. What should Roger do?

11. ARIZONA RESTAURANT*

Ted Barker, the co-owner of a successful restaurant in the west end of Montreal, had, for some time, been considering the possibility of opening a second restaurant. The restaurant, Arizona, offered a variety of Tex-Mex dishes in a 'Santa Fe' setting and was very popular among the 18–34 age group and families. Recently Ted heard that the conversion of the original Montreal Forum had resumed, and he considered this location offered considerable potential as a location for a second restaurant.

The 74-year-old Montreal Forum had remained vacant since the Montreal Canadiens hockey team moved to their new facilities at the Molson Centre in 1996. Since then, businesses in the area had suffered economically, but the opening of the new centre would certainly contribute to revitalizing the area.

The new centre was scheduled to open in July 2000, as a mega entertainment complex consisting of 30 movie screens, a 400-seat giant screen theatre, bars, restaurants including a two-storey Rainforest Café, boutiques, arcades and free shows, in a one-of-a-kind total destination experience.

The construction of the mega centre had been delayed two years as the developers tried to secure the major tenants required for the project to be viable. However, by August 1999, the developers had rented 90 percent of the centre and the construction was well underway. The centre, anchored by the world's largest multiplex cinema, AMC, was touted as the "largest cinema and entertainment complex in the world."

When the project was in its initial stages, Ted had tentatively inquired about rental space and had identified a suitable location within the mega centre. He figured that to capitalize on the expected increased volume of traffic that would be generated by the mega centre, his location would have to be in the centre itself or in the immediate vicinity. The site inside the new entertainment complex consisted of 500 square metres and was located in a restaurant area. The yearly rental was $900 per square metre including heating, air conditioning, and common maintenance fees.

While scouting the area, he found another possible site in the nearby Alexis Nihon Plaza, and two other possible sites on St. Catherine Street (see Figure 1).

Figure | Map of the Area

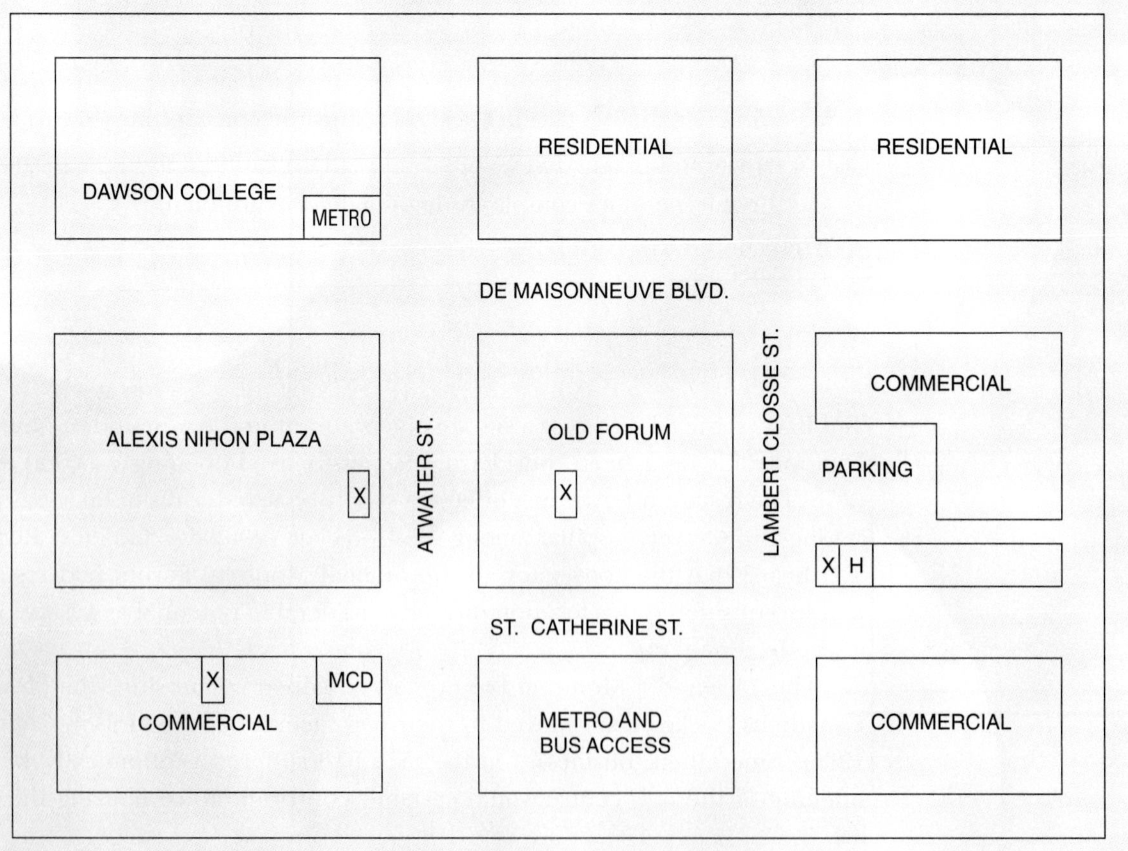

Alexis Nihon Plaza was a 21-storey office and commercial complex situated on Atwater Street opposite the mega centre. The retail section of the building was spread over three floors. The underground floor connected directly to the Metro subway and contained a Zellers department store, a three-screen movie theatre, a deli restaurant, a barbecue restaurant, and 42 stores. The ground floor at street level contained a Canadian Tire store, an IGA supermarket, a Pharmaprix, and 25 stores and stands. The next floor, one level up, contained a health club, 28 stores and a fast-food common area with 12 outlets. The remaining floors contained two levels of parking and offices above. People traffic in the plaza was estimated at 900,000 per month. The available site was located just inside the entrance at street level on the east side facing the new mega centre. The site size was 200 square metres and the annual lease cost was $1200/square metre including heating, air conditioning, and common maintenance costs.

One of the sites on St. Catherine Street was situated diagonally to the mega centre on the northeast corner of the street. It was formerly the site of the Texan Restaurant, popular during the days of the Montreal Forum. This site was 250 square metres and the lease was $15,000 per month. Ted estimated that heating and air conditioning costs would amount to approximately $10,000 per year and electricity about $200 per month. A Harvey's outlet was located next to this site.

The second location on St. Catherine St. was situated opposite Alexis Nihon Plaza. The monthly rent for 400 square metres was $8,500, including utilities. A McDonald's was situated nearby on the southwest corner at the intersection of St. Catherine and Atwater streets. Both street locations would require a large exterior illuminated sign at an approximate cost of $10,000.

The street locations benefited from a fair amount of pedestrian traffic, primarily commuters coming from the Metro station and the 13-bus transfer terminal across the street from the new mega centre. Exits of two main highways were a few blocks away. The proximity of the Alexis Nihon Plaza and other street level shops also attracted many pedestrians. Ample parking was available in the area. There were a number of residential and office towers and a CEGEP college in the area.

QUESTION

1. Evaluate the sites. What location would you recommend? Why?

12. A VIDEO RENTAL STORE LOCATION*

Jeff Coleman, a young professional, had recently moved to an apartment building in downtown Montreal, a block away from his office. After settling in, he realized that whenever he wanted to watch a video, he had to walk 15 to 20 minutes to the nearest video store, Starvideo.

It appeared to him that given the large concentration of apartment buildings in the neighbourhood, the potential existed for a video store. He noticed that in the apartment complex where he lived, a large retail space in the basement was for rent. The basement area contained a small grocery store and a dry cleaner. A well-known restaurant was located in the same building at street level.

Every time Jeff had to walk to Starvideo to rent movies and return them—rain, shine, or snow—he could not help thinking that he was missing out on a business opportunity. While talking one day with a relative, Fred, about this opportunity, Fred expressed an interest in joining Jeff in exploring this possibility.

Dorley Street, where the apartment complex was situated, consisted mainly of apartment buildings, as did the two parallel streets on the east and west sides. Dorley St. was bound on the north end by an avenue bordering a park and a few apartment buildings. On the south end it was bound by a busy street containing office buildings, hotels, and shops. It was here where the business and commercial sector of the downtown core began.

Jeff conducted a preliminary assessment of the demographics of the area, by obtaining data from Statistics Canada (Table 1). The census tract for the primary area contained dwellings situated between five to ten minutes walking distance from the potential location. The secondary area, on the west side of the primary area, comprised dwellings located within a 10 to 20 minute walk from Dorley St.

From Statistics Canada Jeff also learned that in 1996, 84 percent of Canadian households owned a video cassette recorder (VCR) and that they spent an average of $92 a year on videotape rentals compared with $74 a decade earlier. Videotape rentals were most popular among couples with children; four-fifths of such households rented videotapes, spending on average $138 per year. Couples with children accounted for half the consumer market for videotape rentals, although they made up only one-third of all households. Rentals of videotapes and videodiscs accounted for 17 percent of all the entertainment services consumer market. Although this share was virtually unchanged from a decade ago, spending increased 54 percent to just over $1 billion, primarily because the proportion of households renting videotapes increased from 42 percent in 1986 to 61 percent in 1996.

Besides the competition from the nearby video rental store, competition also existed from cable TV, television, and movie theatres. According to Statistics Canada, in 1996, almost half of consumer spending on entertainment services was on cablevision, an 80 percent increase from a decade earlier; movie theatre attendance accounted for 11 percent of the total entertainment services market, down from 17 percent a decade earlier. However, there were signs that this was changing as statistics for 1997 showed an increase of 4 percent in the number of visits to movie theatres over the previous year. Television viewing was higher in Quebec than in any other province; Quebecers on the average spent 25.8 hours per week watching television, while the national average was 22.7 hours. Jeff also wondered if Montreal downtown dwellers would be more likely to participate in the street life that defined this city, especially in the spring and summer with the numerous festivals, outdoor cafés, and restaurants.

Table | Demographic Statistics For Primary and Secondary Trading Areas

	Primary	Secondary
Total population (1996)	4,090	3,875
Male	1,915	1,820
Female	2,175	2,055
Total number of private households	2,510	2,325
by size:		
1 person	1,450	1,230
2 persons	750	840
3 persons	165	155
4 persons or more	135	100
Total population by age groups		
Less than 9 years	130	125
10–19 years	265	175
20–29 years	1,000	780
30–39 years	605	560
40–49 years	495	490
50–59 years	630	590
60 years and over	965	1,155
Average household income	$53,046	$74,155
All census families	855	910
Average family income	$85,062	$101,892
Total population by home language		
Single responses	3,840	3,695
English	2,020	2,195
French	1,075	1,090
Non-official languages	745	410
Multiple responses	250	175
English and French	100	80
Population 15 years and over in private households		
with no children at home	3,315	3,170
with children at home	570	505
with children under 6 years only	140	90
with children 6 years and over only	410	365
Total population 15 years and over by highest level of schooling		
University	2,595	2,390
Without degree	795	595
Without certificate or diploma	430	265
With certificate or diploma	365	330

Source: Statistics Canada, 1996 Census, Cat. 95-199, *Profile of Census Tracts in Montreal*, March 1999.

Next, Jeff inquired about the basement space for rent in the apartment tower. The site was accessible from two entrances, one from street level by walking down the steps to the basement passing by the grocery store, the other entrance was through the building off the main lobby, past the elevators and down to the basement, passing by the dry cleaner. Jeff learned that the space had been vacant for quite some time. The site did not have any outside exposure but the city bylaws allowed outside signs to be installed in the area. The site was large, 200 square metres, including a small office area and two washrooms. No indoor parking was available and parking at the back of the building was limited. However, the City of Montreal allowed parking on both sides of the street. The landlord appeared interested in having a video store as a tenant since it would be complementary to services already available to residents—the grocery store and the dry cleaner. He found out that a five-year lease could be negotiated with incremental rates as follows:

First three months free and $1,200/month thereafter for year 1
$1,500/month for year 2
$2,000/month for year 3
$2,200/month for years 4 and 5

The above figures included heating and air conditioning and estimated municipal taxes and the installation of an exterior illuminated sign. Electricity was estimated to cost around $100 per month. In the prime commercial and business area nearby rentals were considerably higher and vacancies were virtually non-existent. The apartment complex had three towers with a total of 610 apartments. Jeff calculated that Dorley Street alone had approximately 850 apartment units.

Table 2

Survey Results

	Yes		*No*		
Q1. Do you rent videos regularly? (1)	65.6%		34.4%		
Q2. If Yes, how many times per week? (1)	*None*	*1–2*	*3–4*	*5+*	*N/A*
	4.8%	39.2%	18.5%	3.2%	34.3%
Q3. What is the average walking distance to your video store(minutes)? (2)		16.2			
Q4. Would you rent from a video store that is closer? (2)	*Yes*	*No*	*Indif.*	*N/A*	
	75.1%	3.2%	5.8%	15.9%	
Q5. In which language? (2)	*French*		*English*		
	15.9%		84.1%		
Q6. What is your age? (1)	*15–25*	*26–35*	*36–50*	*51+*	*N/A*
	20.6%	13.2%	29.6%	27.5%	9.1%

Notes:
N/A = Did not answer.
(1) Based on the total number of respondents.
(2) Based on the number of respondents who replied Yes to Q1.

After having gathered all this information to evaluate the market size, Jeff needed to know if there was an interest in this venture among the area residents. He decided to conduct a survey among residents of the 610 apartments in the complex. After obtaining authorization from the landlord to survey the residents, Jeff prepared a brief questionnaire that he distributed to the occupant of each apartment asking residents to drop the completed questionnaires in a box located in the lobby. He received 189 responses. Table 2 shows the results of the survey. Jeff felt that the residents in the three towers would be representative of the neighbourhood.

He also evaluated Starvideo. This large store was situated on a major commercial artery, six blocks west from Dorley Street. On several occasions, he counted the number of videos that were missing from the shelves and multiplied the average number by seven. He then scaled down the figures by 30 percent to account for poor housekeeping, pilferage, overdue videos, etc., and arrived at a rough estimate of a weekly total of 4,400 rentals, of which 55 percent were for new releases.

After collecting this data, Jeff decided to consult a marketing expert. In particular, he needed to know if the trading area for this location could generate enough volume of rentals to sustain a profitable business. He estimated that the cost of opening the store, including renovation, shelves, office equipment, and video inventory, would be between $75,000 to $100,000. To run the store, one employee would be required.

QUESTION

1. Evaluate the location and assess its viability. What would you recommend to Jeff?

13. TODAY'S SUPERMARKET

James Alexander was puzzled by the design layout he had just received for his new supermarket (Exhibit 1). He was very uncomfortable with it, but could not quite say why, and if it needed to be changed, what should be done.

James Alexander is a young entrepreneur. He graduated five years ago from the University of Alberta with a bachelor of commerce. He started working for a supermarket chain in Penticton, British Columbia. However, he soon realized that he did not like working for a large corporation, and that he really wanted to be his own boss. With money lent to him by his father, and a bank loan, he had rented a corner location in a newly built shopping mall in a mixed working-middle class neighbourhood of Calgary. The mall had rented all 18 stores. Today's Supermarket was the only supermarket in the mall. There was also a small department store, and several small boutiques, but no pharmacy, bank, or post office. The mall had a 100-car parking lot.

James Alexander decided to use a store design consultant to help in planning the layout for the new supermarket. He asked the designer to consider a

Exhibit I Proposed Layout for Today's Supermarket

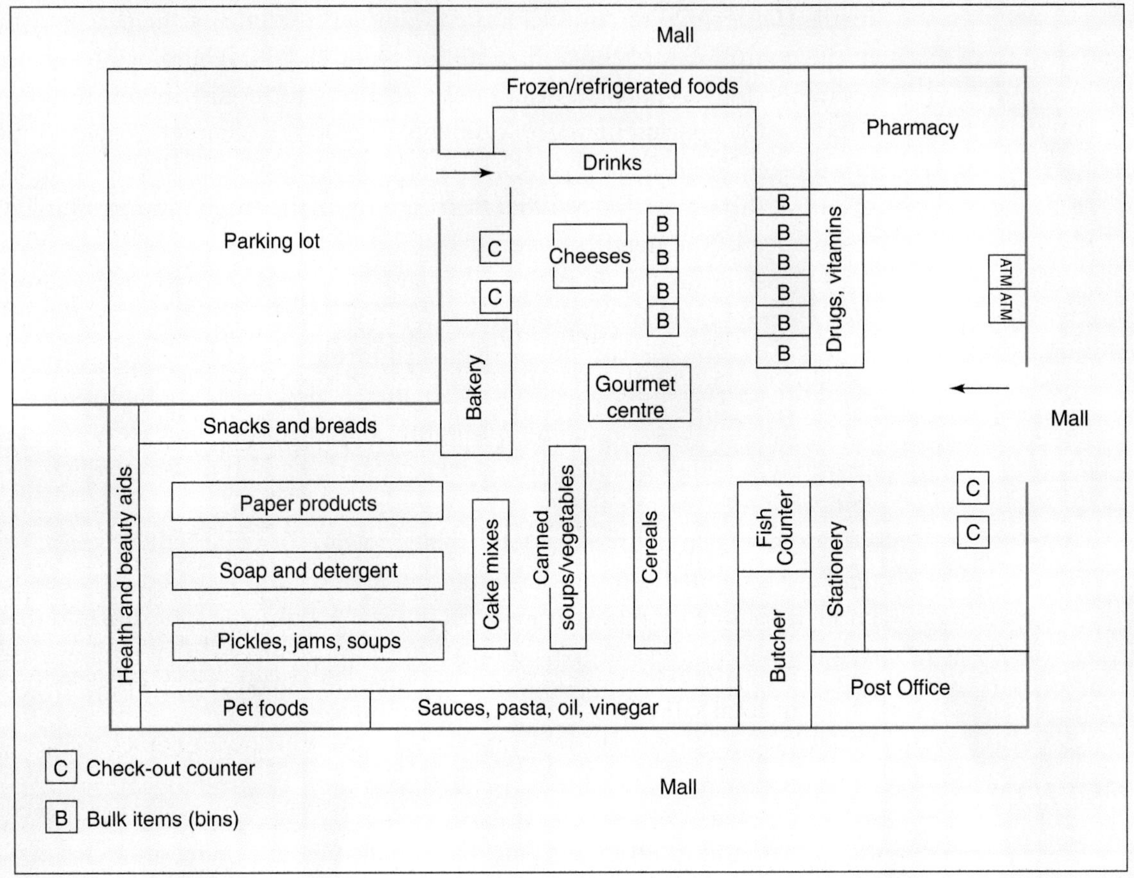

number of current trends that he found in various newspaper and magazine articles:

- The trend toward more bulk items (i.e., loose unpackaged items, such as nuts, cereals, and candy);
- the trend toward more items that are not damaging to the environment, as well as organic foods;
- the trend toward gourmet items, as well as freshly baked breads, muffins, and pastries;
- the trend toward fresh fish, seafood, and specialty cuts of meat;
- the trend toward adding non-food items in supermarkets;
- the trend toward adding departments such as a pharmacy, a postal station, and bank ATMs.

The designer has just brought a first draft of her work, and James Alexander needed to approve the layout before work could start. He was bothered by a number of decisions the designer had made, including the location of check-out counters, the placement and sizes of the different departments, and the flow of traffic in the store. He also has to decide on the interior design of the store, i.e., what kind of atmosphere and image does he want to create inside his supermarket.

QUESTIONS

1. Evaluate the design proposed by the consultant.
2. What changes, if any, would you recommend? Why?

14. SHOES FOR SPORTS

Mark Lucas, the owner of Shoes For Sports, was preparing the merchandising plan for the store for the spring season (February–July). Shoes For Sports is a specialty store that sells only sports shoes (e.g., running, tennis, and aerobics) and is located in Moncton, New Brunswick. As a first step, Mark filled in the previous year's sales, stock, markdowns, and purchases as well as this year's targets (initial markup, gross margin, etc.) on the Six-Month Merchandising Plan (Exhibit 1 on page 494). He then reviewed the information he had that included:

- The planned sales increase for the upcoming season was 25 percent.
- The planned markdown rate was 20 percent.
- April was a record cold month last year and sales were down 20 percent from the previous year. Mark felt this sales decline was due to the weather.
- A new line of aerobic shoes would be available in late April from a leading manufacturer. Mark had seen the shoes at a trade show and thought they would generate great interest and sales (up to a 30 percent increase in total sales for the next three months).
- Last year the store's major clearance sale was held in June. Mark planned to shift the sale to July this year.

With this information in mind, Mark began preparing the merchandising plan.

QUESTIONS

1. Prepare the merchandise plan for the next six months.
2. Provide a rationale for each month's planned sales increase or decrease.

Exhibit | Merchandising Plan Form

Six-Month Merchandising Plan	Shoes For Sports		
		Plan (This Year)	Actual (Last Year)
	Initial markup (%)	48.0	47.5
	Gross margin (%)	42.0	41.7
	Cash discount (% cost purch.)	7.9	7.8
	Season stock turnover (rate)	3.0	2.8
	Shortage reserve (%)	1.6	1.7
	Advertising expense (%)	3.5	3.0
	Selling salaries (%)	8.4	8.6

Spring 200_		Feb.	Mar.	Apr.	May	June	July	Season Total
Sales	Last Year	80	90	80	130	160	150	690
	Plan							
	Percent of Increase							
	Revised							
	Actual							
Retail Stock (BOM)	Last Year	250	275	270	320	275	220	250
	Plan							
	Revised							
	Actual							
Markdowns	Last Year	15	20	20	15	35	20	125
	Plan (dollars)							
	Plan (percent)							
	Revised							
	Actual							
Retail Purchases	Last Year	120	105	150	100	140	202	815
	Plan							
	Revised							
	Actual							

NOTE: All dollar figures in $000s.

15. ROBSON'S FASHIONS

Ms. Helen Picton, the merchandise buyer for Robson's Fashions, was faced with an interesting buying decision—which manufacturer to select for an order of up to 10,000 or possibly more ladies blue blazers for the upcoming fall and winter season. Robson's, a 47-store chain with outlets in eight provinces, specialized in middle- and high-end fashion merchandise for professional women. It had a loyal customer base due to its wide merchandise selection and excellent customer service.

The blazers were one of the more important product lines carried by Robson's as they were very popular with their customers. The blazers, priced at $475, had a classic look design and could be worn by women in a variety of settings, including work and social occasions.

For the past seven years Ms. Picton had been purchasing the blazers from Pascale Clothing, a Montreal manufacturer, and had been satisfied with the quality, pricing and delivery. However, an incident occurred in the past year that had caused Ms. Picton to consider alternative suppliers. Approximately 5 percent of the blazers shipped by Pascale had a defect; when dry-cleaned they faded. Robson's customers who had purchased these blazers were naturally disappointed when they returned them. About half the customers asked for their money back and the remainder took a replacement blazer. In all cases, Robson's sales staff were apologetic, accepted the blazers with no questions asked, and did their best to satisfy the customers.

When Ms. Picton approached Pascale Clothing about the problem, they too were concerned, immediately replaced the blazers at no charge, accepted all responsibility, identified where the problem occurred, and told Ms. Picton that the problem had been fixed.

As a result of this incident, Ms. Picton decided to explore other suppliers for the blazers. While she had no real intention of switching suppliers, she felt it was appropriate to ensure that she was getting the best merchandise for her customers. In her search, Ms. Picton was impressed with a Hong Kong manufacturer, Wong Clothing. The contact person, Vivien Wong, had provided samples within two weeks of receiving the enquiry. Ms. Picton examined and conducted quality tests on the blazers. Both the stitching and styling were first rate (equal to and possibly slightly better than the Pascale blazer) and the fabric was a quality grade higher than that offered by Pascale (wool was objectively graded based on worldwide standards). In checking further on Wong Clothing, she found that they had supplied blazers to a clothing chain in the United States and the buyer was satisfied with the product and delivery.

Ms. Picton then reflected on the two possible suppliers. The terms of the agreement with Pascale Clothing were as follows: Robson's placed an annual order for 8,000 units with the understanding that up to 3,500 additional units might be purchased, depending on demand. Pascale would ship these units within one week of the order being placed. This was an important factor because Ms. Picton did not want any stockouts during the selling season. In either case, payment was required within 30 days of the shipping date. Sales of the blue blazers in the past three years were 10,500, 11,000, and 9,000 respectively. Blazers that were not sold in the current season would be inventoried and sold in the next season. The price was $230 per unit including all transportation charges.

Wong Clothing would require a single order and would not be able to ship any additional blazers during the selling season. The price was $175 per unit, plus customs duty on the shipments of 10 percent of the price, plus estimated freight charges of about $8,000 (assuming a shipment of 10,000 units). The payment would be required within ten days of the order being placed (a lead time of three months was required to ensure delivery for the start of the season). Robson's typically had a line of credit with its bank at an interest rate of 10 percent.

QUESTIONS

1. What's the difference between the two suppliers in terms of potential profits? Note any assumptions made in calculating the difference.
2. What would you recommend Ms. Picton do and why?

16. JKA DEPARTMENT STORE

In his estimation, George Baker had the opportunity of a lifetime. George was an assistant buyer in the flagship store of a major full-line department store in Canada. His boss, Clarence Adams, senior buyer of home goods, was en route to the Orient for an extended buying trip. Adams had left George in charge—up to a point. George knew that if any really difficult problem arose, he should consult with Finus Cooke, the division's merchandise manager for fashions and all home goods.

George was quite comfortable working with dollar control and open to buy (OTB) data, as he and Adams discussed their position weekly. Thus George knew, as of October 15, that the department was virtually overbought for the month. He also knew that it was important to keep some OTB available for fill-ins for the remainder of the month.

On October 18, a sales representative from one of the major suppliers of table linens called George to offer a remarkable lot of goods amounting to approximately $50,000 at retail. The merchandise could be sold, with a full markup, at half price. George was positive that it would be a terrific promotion. He had to let the sales representative know by the end of the day, as the offer would then be made to a competitor.

George went to his computer to recheck the store's OTB. No change—no dollars available to spend. The promotion had not been planned, but George knew linens would walk out of the store, and a real profit would be made.

QUESTIONS

1. Should George go to the divisional merchandise manager and try to get more open to buy? Why or why not?
2. Assuming that George does go to the divisional merchandise manager to try to get more open to buy, what arguments could he present?

17. CLASSIC SHIRTS

Classic Shirts is a six-store chain with locations in Halifax (three stores), Fredericton (two stores), and Charlottetown (one store). The chain, which sold a wide range of high quality men's shirts, had gained a strong reputation for having a wide selection of up-to-date fashion and dress shirts and offering excellent customer service. The chain carried four well-known national brands and its own private label brand, which was virtually equivalent in quality to the national brands.

The owner, James Ashman, was considering if he should change the pricing strategy because he was interested in increasing the profitability of the chain. For some time Mr. Ashman had been concerned about whether or not his pricing strategy was appropriate. The national brands had an average retail price of $100 per shirt with a margin of $50. The private (store) brand had an average retail price of $70 and a margin of $30. Across the four stores, 70 percent of sales were national brand shirts and 30 percent were the private brands. Twice a year (each time for a two-week period) both the national and private brands were sold at 30 percent off the regular price. During that time period, total sales on a unit basis increased by 20 percent (average total unit sales for the rest of the year were 1,000 per week). The units sold during these sales were national brands (80 percent) and private brands (20 percent).

Mr. Ashman was considering four options regarding increasing the chain's profitability:

a. Reducing the regular price of the private brand shirts to $60 to generate greater sales.
b. Having three two-week sales per year, instead of two.
c. Reducing the markdown offered during the sales from 30 percent to 20 percent.
d. Increasing the markdown offered during the sales from 30 percent to 40 percent.

QUESTIONS

1. Evaluate each option using both quantitative and qualitative factors.
2. What other options might Mr. Ashman consider?
3. What further information would you like before you make your recommendations?
4. What would you recommend?

18. TRAVEL AGENCIES—A VARIATION IN SERVICE*

It was January and already the winter was severe with freezing rain accompanied by strong gusts of wind sweeping down upon Halifax. Looking out the window, Mary Muldoon gave a sigh and exclaimed: "Wouldn't it be nice to be under the sun on warm sand on a day like today!"

Her husband Paul looked up and replied, "You said it. I think we ought to take our two weeks of vacation soon. The thought of having to bear three more months of winter depresses me. But this time I want to go to a place I've never been to before."

"Sure. We could leave at the end of February, but we must act quickly to plan this vacation," Mary stated.

The Muldoons were DINKs (Dual Income, No Kids) and both were 35 years old. Paul was an accountant in a large company, and Mary was a paralegal in a law firm. In the past they always went to Florida for their holiday. They knew it well, but it was time for a change. Motivated by images of sunny, tropical beaches surrounded by lush vegetation, the Muldoons decided to plan a trip. On Monday, Mary went to a travel agency to pick up some travel brochures. Over the weekend they talked and looked at the various destinations offered in five different brochures on vacation packages that the travel agency had to offer.

For several destinations, there were two types of packages, one with everything included and the other called regular. The former included accommodation, transfers, air travel, meals, drinks, and tips; whereas the latter usually included only air travel, land transportation, and hotel accommodation. Paul and Mary decided to focus on the regular packages. Although the all-inclusive resort made it possible to take a vacation with few worries, they found that their objective was not only to relax but also to make excursions, try different restaurants, and explore the vicinity as they had done in Florida. But they were not the type to go to exotic destinations in remote islands. They preferred places that catered to tourists, making it easy to get around and feel comfortable and safe. Two of their most important criteria were a fine beach and a good hotel. They also were looking for a country that was politically and socially stable. So they came to choose the West Indies in the Caribbean.

Leafing through the brochures, Paul said: "This morning I read an article about St. Lucia in the travel section. It said the scuba diving is excellent, the water is crystal clear for viewing marine life and vegetation. That would be great!"

"But from what I read in these brochures, St. Lucia doesn't seem to have many shops or places to visit. You can go scuba diving just about anywhere! I don't want to spend all day on the beach watching you dive," Mary retorted. "I have to have clear water for scuba diving, and for sailboarding I don't want big waves," replied Paul.

Paul was not a winter sports enthusiast. Water sports were what he liked. He was a good swimmer, and in the summer he went sailboarding and water skiing. When he went south, scuba diving was one of his favourite sports.

Mary was not interested in sports. One of her favourite pastimes was to shop, which she spent a lot of time doing. She would buy items not only for Paul and herself but also souvenirs for their respective families. She also liked to visit different tourist attractions, like museums and historical landmarks. Paul disliked shopping and preferred doing sports while his wife strolled through shopping centres and boutiques.

Looking through the brochures, Paul remarked, "It looks to me as if going to the Caribbean is much more expensive than going to Florida."

"But, Paul," Mary responded, "when you take a vacation you shouldn't think like that! What difference does it make if it costs \$200 or \$300 more if the place is worth it?" "The difference could pay for several other diversions at a less expensive place," retorted Paul.

"Come on, Paul, we take a vacation only once a year!" Mary implored. "By the way," she continued, "someone at the office told me about going to St. Maarten recently. On one half of the island, they speak French, and on the other they speak Dutch. It's like visiting two different islands! She thought the beaches were magnificent, and the shopping in the duty-free boutiques was excellent."

"That sounds very interesting," said Paul. "Let's look at what the brochures have to offer in St. Maarten."

Mary noticed from the brochures that wearing a swimsuit on the beach was optional. Frowning, she said to her husband, "You know, I don't think I would feel comfortable on that kind of beach for two weeks." Mary had grown up in a conservative environment, and although she did not consider herself prudish, public nudity was something she did not accept.

"As you wish. There are plenty of other islands," Paul said.

Each other destination boasted about its fine sandy beaches and exceptional hotels. After having evaluated several places from different angles, they chose Barbados and Jamaica. They believed them to be long-established vacation spots well-organized for tourists. As a result, these islands offered a variety of activities. They seemed to have not only beautiful beaches and good facilities for water sports but also many restaurants, shopping centres, and a lively nightlife.

Finally Paul suggested going to a travel agency. Surely a travel agent would be able to give them more specific information on hotels. The following Thursday night they went to the travel agency that was located in a nearby shopping centre. They arrived at six o'clock and had to wait to be served. Thirty minutes passed before a travel agent motioned them over to her desk.

"What can I do for you?" she asked them.

Paul and Mary explained that they wanted information about excursions to Barbados from February 20 to March 1. The agent asked them if they had chosen one hotel in particular. Paul answered, "No, can you recommend some?"

"Let's look at the brochures. How much do you want to spend?" asked the travel agent.

"We're looking for a good hotel on a fine golden sand beach," answered Paul.

The agent showed them listings of several hotels with their rates and said, "The price indicates the quality of the hotel. The higher the price the more luxurious it is." Paul and Mary chose a deluxe hotel that cost a bit more than the other hotels. The agent called to check on availability of flights and rooms on the dates specified.

"There is no more room on the flight for those dates. Perhaps, other tour operators have space," said the travel agent turning to another agent and asking, "Gladys, do you know who else goes to Barbados?" "Try Miramar Tours," the other agent answered.

The agent called Miramar Tours who told her that their Barbados flights for those dates were full. "I am sorry," said the agent. "I could put you on the waiting list, but that will not guarantee your getting on that flight. Would it be possible for you to change your dates?"

"No, we can't change them. We'll have to think this over. Thanks anyway for your help," said Paul.

They had the distinct impression that the travel agent lacked experience. Paul suggested to Mary that they go right over to Sun Travel whose advertisement he had seen in Saturday's paper. Arriving at this agency, Paul and Mary waited a while before being able to see an agent. When one was available, Mary explained to her that they wanted to go to Barbados but that apparently there was no more space on flights on February 20 and March 1.

"Yes, that's right. They told me today that all those flights were full, but are there other destinations that interest you?" asked the agent.

"Yes, perhaps Jamaica," replied Mary.

"There you will have better luck because more wholesalers fly to Jamaica. That's a good choice," said the agent.

"In Jamaica," she continued, "there are three main tourist spots: Montego Bay, Negril, and Ocho Rios. Which do you prefer?"

"What is the difference among the three?" asked Mary.

"Montego Bay is the main seaside resort, and it is very lively. Negril has the most beautiful beaches, and Ocho Rios is the quietest with the most attractions however."

"I like to shop and make excursions," said Mary.

"And I like water sports," replied Paul.

"In that case you would be better off near Montego Bay. The beaches are beautiful and have lots of facilities while being near the centre of activity. Both Negril and Ocho Rios are located approximately 70 km from Montego Bay. And what kind of hotel do you want?"

"We'd like to stay in a good hotel on the beach that offers water sports. It doesn't have to be a luxurious hotel as long as it is fully equipped," said Paul.

"In that case, I can suggest the Sea Castles or the Holiday Inn, which are both located on the beach about 20 minutes from Montego Bay. The former is a deluxe apartment complex and the Holiday Inn is a luxury resort," said the travel agent.

A studio at the Sea Castles overlooking the ocean cost $1,690 per person for two weeks including service charges, and a superior room at the Holiday Inn cost $1,785 including service.

"I'm tempted to choose the Holiday Inn," Mary said.

Comparing rates Paul exclaimed, "But it's more expensive, and from what I see in the brochure the rooms don't have T.V.!"

"Oh, we could get along without T.V. for two weeks. I prefer a hotel in an international chain. To make up for it, I promise I'll economize on my shopping," Mary replied playfully.

"Under that condition, I agree," said Paul.

The travel agent called the tour operator and reserved the flight immediately. Then, she asked Paul and Mary if they also needed travel insurance.

"Of course," they replied.

A few days later, Mary told her brother that they were going to Jamaica in February. Her brother told her that on some islands you have to be careful because he had heard that the locals were not friendly and sold drugs on the street. Mary was shocked and decided to call the travel agent immediately to ask her if that were true about Jamaica.

She replied: "Oh, no, Mrs. Muldoon, that's no longer the case in Jamaica. In the eighties, there were some problems, but they've been settled. Tourism is far too important for them not to take action. Don't worry, there are more than one million tourists who go there every year. People like Jamaica and they keep going back there often."

Mary felt reassured and began to count the remaining days before departure.

QUESTIONS

1. What needs were Paul and Mary attempting to satisfy in buying a vacation package to the Caribbean?
2. Analyze the risk reduction strategies followed by Paul and Mary in their choice of destination and a hotel.
3. What is your interpretation of the roles and behaviour of the salespeople (travel agents) in the initial and final stages of the purchase?
4. What conclusions in terms of service quality for travel agencies can be derived from this case?

19. THE FITNESS CENTRE

"There are almost as many members going out the door as coming in," Leah Kirby said to Robert Hill. "We're going to have to do something. We can't go on like this." Leah, the co-owner of The Fitness Centre, was very concerned as she looked at the latest monthly figures of new members versus nonrenewals. She continued to discuss the issue with Robert, the other co-owner of the club. "In the past six months the story has been about the same, we get about 100 new members signed up each month and every month about 90 people don't renew their membership. It costs us a lot in marketing costs to get them in the door, then we spend time with them setting up an exercise or training program, they are enthusiastic to begin with, then they stop coming to classes or exercise, then they don't renew when their membership comes up." Robert replied, "I agree, we have to figure out a way to keep them enthused and show that the club offers them value to stay. Let's come up with a plan."

THE FITNESS MARKET

The fitness market in Canada was growing at approximately 6 percent a year due to a number of factors including demographic changes (baby boomers were increasingly interested in maintaining a good level of physical fitness), attitude changes (more Canadians recognizing the importance of a healthy life style), and marketing (increasing numbers of health/fitness clubs).

Current estimates were that about 10 percent of the Canadian population belonged to a health club. However, there was considerable "churning" (the percentage of members lost in a month or year) as many Canadians had good intentions and joined a club, only to leave at the end of their membership for a variety of reasons. The reasons included: decline in interest, took too much time, too hard, and didn't like the club. It was estimated that, on an annual basis, the average health/fitness club in Canada lost between 32 and 35 percent of its members and gained between 37 and 43 percent new members.

Another reason for the high average churn rates was that many clubs, referred to as "factories," did not take a professional approach in managing their operations. Typically, these "factories" would be owned by a sports personality (e.g., a retired hockey player), offer low initial memberships to get people into the club, have few trained instructors, have frequent equipment breakdowns, and poor facilities maintenance. These clubs often failed within a year or two, leaving customers with a valid membership and no facility.

THE FITNESS CENTRE

Leah and Robert had met when they were working on their kinesiology degrees at the University of Waterloo. They kept in touch after graduation because both were interested in opening a health club after they had gained some experience. Both worked in the health club industry for five years, continued talking about opening a club, and in late 1997 found a "factory" club, Jackson Health Club, that had just gone bankrupt in a great location in downtown Toronto. With the help of a venture capitalist, they took over the lease, renovated the interior, contacted all the previous members by mail informing them that they would honour their existing membership and offered ex-members a renewal at 40 percent of the annual fee of $600. They also advertised the opening of The Fitness Centre and within six months had 1,000 members.

The Centre had a combination weight/aerobic exercise room that had Nautilus and free weights, Stairmasters, Treadmills, Lifecycles, Versa Climbers, and rowing machines. It had a separate room for group exercise programs that included step, low and high impact, and body conditioning. Leah and Robert hired qualified instructors for these programs and selected them based on their qualifications and outgoing personalities. However, some of the instructors had minimum qualifications because the highly qualified instructors usually worked for the top clubs, which paid higher salaries. Most of the Fitness Centre instructors also served as personal trainers for any member who wanted a program designed for their specific needs. Depending on the program, a personal trainer would cost between $25 and $55 per hour. The club also rented lockers and towels for members.

The Centre offered three membership options: a full membership with an annual fee of $600, which included use of all the facilities and any of the exercise programs; a three-month trial membership of $200, which again included use of all facilities and programs; and a limited membership of $400 annually, which included only use of the facilities and not the exercise programs. Of the 1,500 current members, about 50 percent had a full membership, 30 percent a trial membership, and 20 percent a limited membership.

An analysis on the churn rates of the members revealed that, on an annual basis, the club signed up about 1,200 new members. Of these, 20 percent selected the full membership and typically 80 percent renewed for another year. Seventy percent selected the trial membership and 35 percent typically renewed (some for another three months, some for a full year membership—there was considerable variation in the proportion who renewed for each membership). Ten percent selected the limited membership and typically 50 percent renewed for another year. Taking into consideration both the new and existing members, Leah and Robert estimated the club had about a 46 percent churn rate; that is they "lost" about 46 percent of their members on an annual basis.

FURTHER INFORMATION

Prior to deciding what action to take, Leah and Robert evaluated two clubs that were also located in the downtown Toronto area. The Adelaide Club was regarded as the premier health club in Toronto. It had extensive facilities including squash courts, a number of exercise rooms, lounges, café, excellent fitness equipment, and well-qualified instructors (over 70 fitness classes were offered each week) and personal trainers. It offered both corporate and individual memberships and targeted professional businesspeople working in downtown Toronto. An individual membership cost $500 (the initiation fee) plus a monthly fee of around $90, depending on the type of membership. The estimated membership of the club was around 3,500 and, based on some casual conversations with fitness experts, Leah estimated that the club had a churn rate of around 30 percent.

The Wellington Club was also regarded as a very good, high-quality club with extensive but smaller facilities, compared to the Adelaide Club. It had an individual initiation fee of $275 and monthly fees of around $100, depending on the level of membership. It targeted the same group as the Adelaide Club, had a membership of around 2,300, and an estimated churn rate of 25 percent.

Leah and Robert also found some information on the GoodLife Fitness Clubs, Canada's largest health club chain. It currently had 42 clubs, sales of over $40 million, 100,000 members, and was growing at about 30 percent a year. The franchise chain had built its business on highly trained staff, innovative programming, and reinvesting in its facilities. The club's strategy had been to raise the bar of service excellence and professionalism in the health and fitness industry. GoodLife developed a niche below the expensive, well-established clubs, like the Adelaide and Wellington Clubs, and above the poorly run "factory" clubs. It offered a monthly membership fee between $30 and $50, qualified staff who receive ongoing training, and specialized training programs depending on the composition of any particular club's members. As an example, some clubs were for women only and the programs included daycare, tanning facilities, and individual change rooms. It was estimated that the overall churn rate at the GoodLife Clubs was 32 percent.

In reviewing their own operations, Leah and Robert were not sure why the club had a high churn rate. They suspected that staff issues might account for some of the churn. Some of the fitness instructors had lower level qualifications and may not have been able to communicate with members as to the types of programs that were most beneficial. As well, staff turnover was about 30 percent a year, which was typical for many clubs in the industry. Second, while the club had an excellent location in downtown Toronto, some members who had not renewed worked more than four blocks away. Third, in spite of their best efforts, Robert and Leah knew that on a few occasions, the club had some maintenance problems. These problems included occasionally running out of towels, lack of regular cleaning in the locker/shower rooms, and sometimes no staff person on the front desk.

During their review, Leah and Robert realized that they hadn't asked lapsed members why they didn't renew. Renewal notices were sent out to members, followed by a second reminder, but if the member didn't renew, there was no followup. All current and lapsed members were contained in a database, but nothing was ever done with the information other than reporting number of members (and nonrenewals) by type of membership. "We've been so busy running the club, that maybe we've forgotten some basics," said Robert. "I agree," said Leah, "we should think about asking some of our ex-members why they left. Maybe there are some other things we should ask as well. Whatever we do, we need to figure out a plan for the future. Our livelihood is at stake."

QUESTIONS

1. What are the possible reasons for the high churn rates in the fitness club industry and for the Fitness Centre?
2. What would you recommend that Leah and Robert do? Why?

20. TELEGROCER—A VIRTUAL RETAILER

In early 1996, a test pilot of TeleGrocer, a virtual retailer, was started in Ottawa. Based on the information gained in that trial, the entrepreneurs launched TeleGrocer. The basic concept is straightforward—using the Web, customers can contact TeleGrocer on-line and have them buy and deliver their groceries. From a retailing perspective, the major issues are: is the basic concept viable, is there a large enough target market, and is the Web site user friendly?

The following paragraphs are excerpts from their Web site.

Introduction

Welcome to TeleGrocer, Canada's first and only virtual retailer. Friends, I want to ask you a question. Are you tired of standing in supermarket lineups? Do you believe that your time is better spent doing something you enjoy? With TeleGrocer, having more time to spend with your family, time to complete that all-important project, or maybe just having some time for yourself, is just a mouse click or phone call away.

Are you exasperated with that lazy old Web page that takes forever to download? Are you ready for a truly interactive, real-time, no nonsense shopping experience? Do you want it now, not two years from now?

We have designed a low-cost on-line shopping system that our supermarket partners can use to provide you with a truly intelligent virtual shopping experience.

TeleGrocer provides clients like yourself with the convenience of purchasing your groceries from the comfort of your home. We have entered into a strategic partnership with your local retailer. As well, we have invested heavily in leading edge technology. This allows us to deliver a cost-effective virtual shopping environment right into your living room, all at a reasonable price.

A Brief History

Since September 1996, we have been running a test pilot in Ottawa, Ontario, servicing only our non-computer clients. Although this was considered uninspiring by those professing the awesomeness of the Internet, it provided us with a deeper insight into the preferences and shopping habits of our client base. These insights were then funnelled back into the software, optimizing it for maximum usability, the benefits of which our Internet clients will be reaping.

How It Works

TeleGrocer allows member-clients to order their domestic consumables, such as groceries, prescriptions, dry-cleaning, photo-finishing, and video rental from the comfort of their homes. Clients contact TeleGrocer by phone, fax and the Internet.

TeleGrocer does not warehouse its own products. We form strategic alliances with your local supermarket retailers. Orders that we receive are sent to the fulfillment supermarket where it is shopped and assembled by our team of personal shoppers.

We then deliver the products to your door at which time you pay the delivery personnel by cash or cheque (applicable to clients with credit approval). We are able to process your order within four hours of placement.

What It Costs

The fee for using TeleGrocer is less than you think. We have several options based on how your order is placed.

With full membership, shopping fees are $4.95 plus 5 percent of your total order. Therefore, if you spend $100 on groceries, your shopping charge would be $9.95. Membership is $36.00 per year.

We have a 30-day trial membership during which no membership fees are charged. Trial membership shopping fees are $5.95 plus 5 percent.

To place an order by phone or fax you must be a full member. Shopping fees for phone and fax orders are $6.95 plus 5 percent.

Now friends, is that reasonable or is that reasonable?

TeleGrocer provides its members with software that allows them to order over the Internet. The company also provides a catalogue that its members can use to order groceries. TeleGrocer offers its services in 14 Canadian cities including Toronto, Montreal, Ottawa, and Vancouver.

QUESTIONS

www.telegrocer.com

1. As part of this case, you need to visit TeleGrocer's Web site (www.telegrocer.com) and evaluate it. In particular, what are the Web site's apparent strengths and weaknesses, who do you think is their target market, how could it be improved, how many customers do you think they have?
2. Finally, after reading the case and visiting their Web site, would you invest in this venture?

21. THE NATURAL GROUP*

Five years ago, four physicians opened a clinical practice, The Natural Group, in Calgary offering both traditional and homeopathic medical services. Although the practice has been successful, the doctors feel that their potential is limited by the size of the Calgary CMA (census metropolitan area).

In their last regular business meeting, one of the partners, Dr. Lupp, suggested that they capitalize on the interest in natural herbal remedies by extending their services to offer consultations over the Internet. The partners' response was immediately and overwhelmingly negative. "We have established a well-respected practice. In no way do I want to be associated with those doctors

 This case was prepared by Mary Ann Cipriano, Concordia University, with the assistance of Isabelle Miodek.

practising medicine and prescribing prescription drugs without having seen the patient," said Dr. Ardat. "Look at all the bad publicity they're getting in the media. It's only a matter of time until the government cracks down on them," said Dr. Grey. "It's one thing to use the Internet," said Dr. Knowl, "but, I don't feel I know enough to operate a business over it, who's going to run it, and what will happen to our clinic practice?" "I think you misunderstand me," said Dr. Lupp, "I'm not proposing we practise medicine over the Net, but rather offer information and advice on products available without a prescription in drug and food stores, the same way we do for many of our patients right now. I've gathered some industry trends and drawn up a proposal for the concept, at least let's just take a few minutes to look at them before rejecting the idea."

INDUSTRY OVERVIEW

In 1998, the alternative medicine industry in Canada was estimated to be between $2.0 billion and $3.8 billion and was projected to expand at a rate of 20 percent per year. (Alternative medicine includes chiropractic, acupuncture, massage therapy, herbal remedies, and homeopathy.) Almost 50 percent of adult Canadians used one or more forms of alternative therapies, up from just 10 percent in 1994. The uses of alternative medicine varied across Canada, 84 percent of British Columbians were most likely to have used such therapies during their lifetime, compared to 66 percent in Quebec, and 72 percent in Ontario. Income did not play a role in the use of alternative medicine, but education did. People with post-secondary education were more likely to use it at 53 percent, compared to less than 40 percent by those with less than a high school education.[1]

In 1998, the alternative therapies industry in the U.S. was estimated to be between $27.0 and $34.4 billion (U.S.$), broken down as follows: herbal products, $5.1 billion; high dose vitamins, $3.3 billion; professional services, between $12.2 to $19.6 billion; therapy-specific books, classes, etc., $4.7 billion; diet products, $1.7 billion.[2] The average consumer spent $500 a year on out-of-pocket alternative medicine expenses. Women used alternative therapies more frequently than men and the highest incidence of alternative medicine use was by people aged 35–49, college graduates, and those with incomes above $50,000. Herbal medicine, megavitamins, and homeopathy were among the alternative medicine uses with the largest increases. In 1997, American consumers spent more than $12 billion on natural supplements, nearly double the amount spent in 1994, and sales were expected to grow more than 10 percent in 1998.[3]

In Canada, alternative therapies are not covered by public health insurance. However, more private health insurance plans are adding coverage for alternative medicine. With consumer interest rapidly spreading, there is a trend now to refer to alternative medicine as 'complementary medicine.'

[1] *Toronto Sun*, March 12, 1999, p. 29.
[2] *Employee Benefit Review*, May 1999, p. 32.
[3] *Time*, November 23, 1998, p. 58.

Competition

With the increasing number of consumers embracing alternative medicine, herbal remedies and natural nutritional supplements (once sold primarily in health food stores) are now also found in pharmacies and grocery stores. Some pharmacies in Canada and the U.S. have started to set up educational and counselling centres. The expansion of the market has prompted large pharmaceutical firms with large ad budgets and vast distribution channels to enter the field. Manufacturers of trusted brands like Bayer's One-A-Day, Sudafed, and Centrum have launched packaged lines of herbal remedies.

Government Regulations

Herbal medicines and nutritional supplements are not regulated or monitored as thoroughly as drugs are. Government regulations regarding their quality, labelling, and promotional requirements are not standardized and can vary from country to country. In Canada, the federal government has been studying how to best regulate the alternative health industry. The arrival of large pharmaceutical companies into this industry may, in the long run, bring more testing and standardization.

THE PROPOSAL

The idea that Dr. Lupp had in mind consisted of setting up a Web site to offer three different types of services:

1. Disseminate free information about herbal remedies and nutritional supplements via hyperlinks to reputable publications and manufacturers' sites as well as general advice on what to look for and how to choose a specific brand.
2. Sell customized consultations regarding which products would be suitable as remedies for specific conditions as well as answering consumers' specific questions. Examples of the types of questions that would be responded to include: "Can I take St. John's Wort if I'm allergic to ...?","What are the risks in taking ...?","I'd like to improve my memory, what kinds of products should I take? in what strength? etc." Before the questions would be answered the consumer would be required to register with the site by filling out a form detailing his or her medical history. Each customer would be assigned a client number and password so that, when future inquiries are made, the responding physician could access the client profile and history before responding. The first consultation and registration would be one for a fee of $10 Canadian. Subsequent inquiries would be billed to the client's credit card for $3 per inquiry.
3. Provide a list of doctor recommended publications and products for the Internet user to purchase. The user would place his/her order on the Web site. The group would then, through an e-business account, debit the customer's credit card and relay the order to one of a number of distributors, who would then ship the order. On average the group would take a 15 to 30 percent markup on cost.

THE REACTION

The doctors all listened to the proposal with varying degrees of interest and apprehension. Finally, Dr. Knowl said: "I guess that I still don't know enough about this type of thing. I heard that sites are really expensive, that you need to have years of experience on computers. Also an article I read recently pointed out that most sites end up losing money, even though they have a lot of advertising because most people just don't buy things yet ..." Dr. Grey interrupted: "Hey, a golfing partner of mine used the Net to expand his business last year and he is doing very well. He used a marketing consulting firm who had a specialist on staff to develop and co-ordinate the start-up. I think the firm was called Nobel Marketing. Why don't I talk to them about this proposal?" Dr. Ardat replied: "I agree. That is a really good idea. If we can get a consulting firm that is familiar with this type of operation to look at the concept, I would feel a lot more comfortable with investing time and money in the proposal."

After agreeing to contact the consulting firm, the doctors developed the following preliminary list of objectives they would like to see the consultation accomplish:

1. Analyze and evaluate the Internet-based proposal as a mechanism for expanding the homeopathic portion of their clinic. Are there other alternatives? What are the pros and cons of each alternative? How much competition is there likely to be? Should they provide all the services internationally, and if so are there any restrictions and how could they acquire distributors in other countries? Should they only provide the consultation portion of the service internationally and restrict sales to North America?
2. How can they proceed and how much financial and human resource investment would be required for a start up?
3. Address the issue of health information privacy.

QUESTIONS

Assume that as the e-commerce expert from Nobel Marketing you have been assigned to the project.

1. Prepare a report that addresses the doctors' concerns and objectives and evaluates the feasibility of the project in its current form.
2. Outline a retail mix and recommend a plan of action for the doctors to pursue.

22. TREASURE TOYS*

Terry Martin, a retired elementary school teacher, had made educational toys, games, and puzzles out of wood for the last 30 years. First it started as a hobby and a way to give his own children, Paul and Lisa, a special heirloom. Then the toys were so popular among neighbourhood children, he made them as gifts. As his own children grew up, the puzzles and games became increasingly com-

 This case was prepared by Mary Ann Cipriano, Concordia University.

plex, until he had a full range of designs for children from three years through adolescence. Upon taking early retirement four years ago, Terry noticed many of his early designs were still popular with his grandchildren, so he decided to open a small retail shop called Treasure Toys. Treasure Toys is located in a popular tourist area of Ottawa, opposite the National Gallery and the Canadian Mint.

Treasure Toys appeals to both local consumers, who tend to purchase the toys for their own children and as gifts, as well as to the tourist trade, who primarily purchase during the summer months. During peak times both his wife and his children help out in the store. During the off-season months, Terry keeps limited store hours as he needs time to produce inventory in his home in Nepean for the Christmas and summer peak selling times. Given enough advance notice, Terry would take orders for personalized games and toys, for example, a rocking chair or rocking horse with the child's name carved on it or a puzzle with a person's name integrated as part of the design. Standard items range from $12 to $400 depending on the complexity of the design and size.

Treasure Toys' advertising is limited to local papers during the Christmas rush and selected issues of Ottawa tourist guides during the summer. Terry has also placed sample puzzles and games in six nearby restaurants to keep patron's children occupied before and after the meal. A limited inventory of each sample toy is available in each restaurant for purchase, and a small sign near the display cabinet in the entrance features additional toys and the location of the store. Since starting the restaurant program a year ago, Terry's sales have increased almost 30 percent to a total of $76,000. The advertising expenses amount to $4,000 and the cost of the sampling program (50 games in each of the six restaurants) around $2,600 per year, including breakage and pilferage. The cost of running the store totals $19,000 per year and the cost of goods sold this year is estimated at $16,000.

Tourists who purchase from Treasure Toys often write or phone the store asking if there is a catalogue from which they could order additional toys. One customer even inquired if Terry would consider granting a franchise in the Vancouver area and supplying the product.

Paul, who is finishing his MBA at the University of Ottawa this year, is convinced it is time to expand the business, and has proposed three options to his father.

Option I

Develop a catalogue of designs to be given to customers who request it, and also to be sent to Ontario elementary schools and day-care centres. Paul would take over the store after graduation and oversee the catalogue business so that Terry could concentrate on production.

Option 2

Develop a Web site on the Internet to appeal to children and adults alike. Once again Terry would concentrate on production, while Paul would handle the store and Web site.

Option 3

A combination of the above.

Although Terry is pleased with his son's enthusiasm, he is concerned that Paul lacks business experience, and that his proposals are premature.

QUESTIONS

Assume that as a retail marketing consultant, Terry has asked you to do the following:

1. Evaluate Paul's proposals and suggest any other options you consider appropriate.
2. Recommend a retail mix.
3. Develop preliminary designs for your recommended promotional vehicles.

23. SEARS CANADA—FINANCIAL PERFORMANCE ANALYSIS

Between 1996 and 1998 Sears Canada dramatically improved its performance while its major department store competitors, with the exception of Wal-Mart, had performance declines. Here's part of Sears' strategy for its improved performance:

- It launched a dramatic cost cutting program during the recession of the early '90s that created a lean, efficient firm.
- When consumers started spending again, Sears Canada renovated its stores to make them even more productive and appealing.
- It reached its customers through a variety of channels including full-line department stores in suburban and small city malls, separate furniture and appliance stores in lower rent locations (which offered a better display of goods), and a thriving catalogue business.
- It moved to target women through the "softer side of Sears."
- Sears Canada's greatest strength lies in markets outside the major urban centres—places like Barrie and Kitchener. It is in the malls where Sears Canada is finding the Canadian consumer.

Here's what Paul Walters, Chairman and Chief Executive of Sears Canada, said in early 1999: "We've invested more capital in the business in the last two years than the previous ten. We've doubled our inventory position, we've increased our employees by 5,000, and we've invested hundreds of millions in advertising to support the increased inventory."

The financial results of Sears Canada's efforts over these three years are provided in Exhibits 1 and 2.

Exhibit 1

Sears Canada Income Statement ($000,000)

	1998	1997	1996
Net sales	4,967	4,587	3,956
Less: Cost of merchandise sold, operating administrative and selling expenses	4,612	4,283	3,845
Less: Interest expense	86	86	86
Total expenses	4,698	4,369	3,931
Net profit (before taxes)	269	215	25
Less: Taxes	123	99	16
Net profit after tax	146	116	9

Exhibit 2

Sears Canada Balance Sheet ($000,000)

	1998	1997	1996
Current assets			
Cash	190	68	188
Accounts receivable	1,100	1,225	1,033
Merchandise inventory	739	640	491
Total current assets	2,029	1,933	1,712
Fixed assets			
Building, equipment, etc. less depreciation	868	825	821
Other fixed assets	301	249	201
Total fixed assets	1,169	1,074	1,022
Total assets	3,198	3,007	2,734
Current liabilities	1,193	1,017	1,007
Long-term liabilities	841	948	778
Total liabilities	2,034	1,965	1,785
Net worth	1,164	1,042	949
Total liabilities and net worth	3,198	3,007	2,734

QUESTIONS

1. Prepare strategic profit models for Sears Canada for each of the three years using the data in the two exhibits. What were the major factors in the dramatic improvement in Sears Canada's performance?
2. What ratios also help in identifying the underlying reasons for the improved performance?

ENDNOTES

Chapter 1

1. Rom J. Markin and Clovin P. Duncan, "The Transformation of Retailing Institutions: Beyond the Wheel of Retailing and Life Cycle Theories," *Journal of Macromarketing*, Spring 1981, pp. 58–66; Stephen Brown, "The Wheel of Retailing," *International Journal of Retailing* 3, 1, 1988, pp. 16–37; and Stephen Brown, "Variations on a Marketing Enigma: The Wheel of Retailing Theory," *Journal of Marketing Management* 7, 1991, pp. 131–55.
2. Thomas J. Maronick and Bruce J. Walker, "The Dialectic Evolution of Retailing," *Proceedings: Southern Marketing Association*, (Atlanta: Georgia State University, 1975), pp. 147–51.
3. A.C.R. Dressmann, "Patterns of Evolution in Retailing," *Journal of Retailing* 44 (Spring 1968), pp. 64–81.
4. For more information on the evolution of retail institutions, see Adam Finn and John Rigby, "West Edmonton Mall: Consumer Combined-Purpose Trips and the Birth of the Mega-Multi-Mall?" *Canadian Journal of Administrative Sciences*, June 1992, pp. 134–45.
5. Wendy Evans and Henry W. Lane, "The War of 1998," *The Globe and Mail*, December 18, 1998, p. C2.
6. Hudson's Bay Company, *Annual Report*, 1994.
7. Sean Silcoff, "Boutique Z," *Canadian Business*, May 8, 1998, pp. 62–65.
8. Stephen J. Arnold, Jay Handelman, and Douglas J. Tigert, "The Impact of a Market Spoiler on Consumer Preference Structures (or What Happens When Wal-Mart Comes to Town)," *Journal of Retailing and Consumer Services* 5, 1, 1998, pp.1–13.
9. Kenneth G. Jones and Michael J. Doucet, "The Big Box, the Big Screen, the Flagship and Beyond: Impacts and Trends in the Greater Toronto Area," Centre for the Study of Commercial Activity, Ryerson Polytechnical University, Research Report 1998–9.

Chapter 2

1. Sean Silcoff, "Buy Now, Pay Later," *Canadian Business: Economic Outlook*, February 1999, pp. 36-37.
2. David K. Foot and Daniel Stoffman, *Boom, Bust & Echo 2000*, (Toronto: Macfarlane, Walter & Ross, 1998).
3. Leonard Kubas, "Grey Power," *Retail Directions*, November/December, 1988, pp. 10, 11, 30. For more information on retailing to the 50-plus age group, see Marina Strauss, "Retirees Have Big Bucks to Spend," *The Globe and Mail*, March 17, 1992, p. B7.
4. Andrew Clark, "How Teens Got the Power," *Maclean's*, March 22, 1999, pp. 42–46.
5. Based on estimates from the *1996 Census*, Statistics Canada.

6. Stephen J. Arnold, Jay Handelman, and Douglas J. Tigert, "The Impact of a Market Spoiler on Consumer Preference Structures (or What Happens When Wal-Mart Comes to Town)," *Journal of Retailing and Consumer Services* 5, 1, 1998, pp. 1–13.

7. Erik Heinrich, "Going for the Gold," *Infosystems Executive*, September 1998, pp.10–15.

Chapter 3

1. Richard Wright, "Great X-pectations," *Canadian Banker*, January/February 1999, pp. 11–15; John MacKie, "What's in the Future for Generation Why?" *Calgary Herald*, November 9, 1998, p. B8; E. Carey, "It's Generation Y: Teens born to shop," *The Toronto Star*, November 15, 1995, p. A1.

2. "The Marketing Report on the Chinese Market," *Marketing*, September 18, 1995, pp. 17–24; J. Lynn, "Approaching diversity," *Marketing*, July 3/10, 1995, p. 11.

3. B.J. Babin, W.R. Darden and M. Griffin, "Work and/or Fun: Measuring Hedonic and Utilitarian Shopping Value," *Journal of Consumer Research*, vol. 20 (March 1994), pp. 644–656.

4. "Shoppers want to have fun while they spend," *The Globe and Mail*, August 4, 1998, pp. B1, B6; M. MacKinnon, "Toys really are us," *The Globe and Mail*, December 7, 1998, pp. B1, B4; D. Gilmor, "Groceryland," *Report on Business Magazine*, October 1998, pp. 121–126.

5. L. Lee, "Background Music Becomes Hoity-Toity," *Wall Street Journal*, December 22, 1995, p. B1.

6. W.R. Swinyard, "The Effects of Mood, Involvement, and Quality of Store Experience on Shopping Intentions," *Journal of Consumer Research*, vol. 20 (September 1993), pp. 271–280.

7. William A. Band, *Creating Value for Your Customers*, Wiley, New York, 1991.

8. D.W. Rook and R.J. Fisher, "Normative Influences on Impulsive Buying Behavior," *Journal of Consumer Research* 22 (December 1995), pp. 305–313.

9. L. Festinger, *A Theory of Cognitive Dissonance*, Stanford: Stanford University Press, 1957.

10. G. McDougall and T. Levesque, "The Measurement of Service Quality: Some Methodological Issues," in *Marketing, Operations and Human Resources Insight into Services*, ed. P. Eiglier and E. Langeard, Aix, France: I.A.E., 1992, pp. 411–431; G. LeBlanc, "The Determinants of Service Quality in Travel Agencies: An Analysis of Customer Perceptions," in *Marketing*, vol. 11 (ed. J. Liefeld), ASAC, 1990, pp. 188–196.

11. G.L. Fullerton and T. Navaux, "A Profile of the Cross-Border Shopper: Some Preliminary Findings," *Marketing*, vol. 15 (ed. B. Smith), ASAC, 1994, pp. 75–84; E.R. Bruning, L. Lockshin and G. Lantz, "A Conjoint Analysis of Factors Affecting Intentions of Canadian Consumers to Shop in U.S. Retail Centres," *Marketing*, vol. 14 (ed. A. Carson), ASAC, 1993, pp. 12–21.

12. "Cross-border shopping trend reversed by weak C$," *The Financial Post*, February 21, 1995, p. 16; G.L. Fullerton and T. Navaux, "A Profile of the

Cross-Border Shopper: Some Preliminary Findings," *Marketing,* vol. 15 (ed. B. Smith), ASAC, 1994, pp. 75–84.

13. W. Weitzel, A. Schwarzkopf and E.B. Peach, "The Influence of Employee Perceptions of Customer Service on Retail Store Sales," *Journal of Retailing* 65 (Spring 1989), pp. 27–39.

14. "Department stores spend millions on improvements," *The Kitchener Record,* November 13, 1995, p. D3.

15. M. Fishbein, "The Relationships Between Beliefs, Attitudes and Behaviour," in *Cognitive Consistency,* ed. S. Feldman (New York: Academic Press, 1966), pp. 199-223.

16. "Department stores spend millions on improvements," *The Kitchener Record,* November 13, 1995, p. D3.

17. Ibid.

18. K. Riddell, "Reaching Consumers In-Store," *Marketing,* July 13/20, 1992, p. 10; K. Riddell, "Couponers Show Record Year," *Marketing,* February 10, 1992, p. 2.

19. S. Cohen, "One-stop Shopping for Dinner," *Marketing,* February 1, 1999, pp. 10–12.

20. Statistics Canada, *Profile of Census Divisions and Subdivisions,* Cat. 95-186-XPB (March 1999), Table 1, p. 50.

21. F. Taylor, "More choosing to be childless," *The Globe and Mail,* July 8, 1995, p. A3.

22. J. Gadd, "From monster home to white elephant," *The Globe and Mail,* November 10, 1995, p. A8.

23. H.L. Davis and B.P. Rigaux, "Perception of Marital Roles in Decision Processes," *Journal of Consumer Research,* vol. 1, June 1974, pp. 51–62.

24. F. Taylor, "More choosing to be childless," *op. cit.,* p. A3; H. Filman, "Baby Books Benefit from Echo Boom," *Marketing,* March 30, 1992, p. 30.

25. Statistics Canada, "Labour Force 15 Years and Over," *www.statcan.ca/census96,* Cat.93F0027XDB96007 (Nations Series); J. Gadd, "Women gain more of employment pie," *The Globe and Mail,* August 9, 1995, p. A1.

26. Cohen, "One-stop Shopping for Dinner;" S. Steinberg, "Check this out," *Canadian Business,* March 27, 1998, pp. 61–65.

27. J.J. Marshall, L. Duxbury and L. Heslop, "Grocery Shopping and Food Preparation in Dual Income Families: Implications for Marketing," *Marketing,* vol. 15 (ed. B. Smith), ASAC, 1994, p. 41.

28. J. Marney, "Measuring the Macho Market," *Marketing,* October 14, 1991, p. 22.

29. J. Meyers-Levy and D. Maheswaran, "Exploring Differences in Males' and Females' Processing Strategies," *Journal of Consumer Research,* vol. 18, June 1991, pp. 63–70.

30. G.S. Kindra, M. Laroche and T.E. Muller, *Consumer Behaviour: The Canadian Perspective,* Toronto: Nelson Canada, 1994, Chapter 12.

31. "Advisers vie for a piece of the wealthy," *Financial Post,* May 25/27, 1996, p. 44; "Nestlé taking lick of premium ice cream," *Marketing,* July 7, 1997, p. 1.

32. A. Joy, C. Kim and M. Laroche, "Ethnicity as a Factor Influencing Use of Financial Services," *International Journal of Bank Marketing,* vol. 9, 1991, pp. 10–16.

33. S. Rasula, "Beyond clothes," *Marketing,* May 10, 1999, pp. 16–17.

34. Reproduced with permission from "New VALS 2 Values and Lifestyles Segmentation," *Stores,* 1989, p. 37. Copyright © The National Retail Federation. All rights reserved.

35. Statistics Canada, *Report on the Demographic Situation in Canada, 1997* (June 1998), p. 121; A. Mitchell, "Affair with divorce shows signs of cooling," *The Globe and Mail,* March 23, 1992, pp. A1–2.

36. Statistics Canada, *Education in Canada,* 1997, Cat. 81-229-XPB (April 1998), pp. 35, 108.

37. J. McElgunn, "Foot Puts Boot to Current 'Life-Cycle' Trends," *Marketing,* June 15, 1992, p. 7.

38. M. Strauss, "Retirees will have big bucks to spend," *The Globe and Mail,* March 17, 1992, p. B7.

39. "Torlée Targets Marketing in the 1990s," *Marketing,* December 9, 1991, p. 6.

40. John Nesbitt and Patricia Aburdine, *Megatrends 2000* (New York: William Morrow, 1990), p.18.

Chapter 4

1. Diana Luciani, "The Bed Magee Made," *Marketing,* November 18, 1998, pp. 10–12, and personal correspondence with Christine Magee, President, Sleep Country Canada.

2. Danier Leather, *Annual Report,* 1998. For more examples of winning retail strategies, see L. N. Stevenson, M. R. Pearce, and J. C. Shlesinger, *Power Retail: Winning Strategies from Chapters and Other Leading Retailers in Canada* (Toronto: McGraw-Hill Ryerson Ltd., 1999).

3. Mark's Work Wearhouse, *Annual Report,* 1998.

4. Shawna Steinberg, "Have Allowance: Will Transform Economy," *Canadian Business,* March 13, 1998, pp. 59-71.

5. Mikali Folb, "Totally Girl," *Marketing,* January 14, 1999, pp. 10-12.

6. Zena Olijnyk, "Zellers' Truly Launch Likened to Explosion," *Financial Post,* March 10, 1999, p. C9.

7. The Gap, *Annual Report,* 1998 and Nora Munk, "Gap Gets It," *Fortune,* August 3, 1998, pp. 68–82.

8. Wendy's, *Annual Report,* 1998.

9. Sears, *Annual Report,* 1998.

10. Loblaws, *Annual Report,* 1998.

11. Mark's Work Wearhouse, *Annual Report,* 1998.

12. Zena Olijnyk, "The BiWay Difference," *Financial Post,* September 15, 1998, p. 11.

Chapter 5

1. Based on material provided by M&M Meat Shops and John Southerst, "M&M Meat Shops Chain Bolsters Weaker Links," *The Globe and Mail*, March 30, 1999, p. B7.
2. Richard Behar, "Why Subway is the Biggest Problem in Franchising," *Fortune*, March 16, 1998, pp. 126–134. For further franchise problems, see John Lorinc, "The Sure Thing," *Report on Business Magazine*, December, 1998, pp. 86–91.
3. Kim Hanson, "Former Franchisees Sue ICI," *Financial Post*, January 26, 1999, p. C4.
4. Information on franchising in Canada from the federal government is available at www.strategis.ic.gc.ca. For more information on evaluating franchises, see www.cbsc.org. This Web site from the Business Information Source provides a checklist for franchisees.
5. Information on franchising in Canada from the major banks is available from their Web sites.
6. David Thomas, "Franchise Advisory Councils Can Be Good for Business," *Financial Post*, February 17, 1995, p. 20.
7. www.mbe.com.
8. John Southerst, "Experts Serve Up Hot Trends for '99," *The Globe and Mail*, December 29, 1998, p. B7.
9. Scott Shane and Chester Spell, "Factors for New Franchise Success," *Sloan Management Review*, Spring 1998, pp. 43–50.

Chapter 6

1. Angus Reid Group, *Consumer Behavior and Customer Service, Summary Report* (December 2, 1997).
2. R. Corelli, "Dishing out rudeness: Complaints abound as customers are ignored, berated," *Maclean's Special Report* (January 11, 1999); R. Williamson, "Motivation on the menu," *The Globe and Mail*, November 24, 1995, p. B7.
3. P. Waldie, "Canadian retailers warned: Shape up or face extinction," *The Globe and Mail*, October 18, 1995, p. B11; J. Abend, "Personnel Strategies," *Stores*, September 1990, p. 42.
4. The material on job analysis, job descriptions, and job specifications is reproduced, with modifications, from *Job Analysis, Job Specifications, and Job Descriptions, a self-instructional booklet*, No. 1020 (Washington, D.C.: U.S. Small Business Administration).
5. This material is reproduced, with modifications, from Walter E. Green, "Staffing Your Store," *Management Aid*, No. 5.007 (Washington, D.C.: U.S. Small Business Administration).
6. R.M. Hodgetts, K.G. Kroeck, and M.E. Rock, *Managing Human Resources in Canada*, (Toronto: Dryden, 1996, pp. 94–96).

7. R. Henkoff, "Finding, Training and Keeping the Best Service Workers," *Fortune*, October 3, 1994, pp. 110–122.

8. *Canadian Human Rights Act*, paragraph 2, subsection (a). See also Hodgetts, Kroeck, and Rock, *Managing Human Resources in Canada*, Chapter 3.

9. Henkoff, "Finding, Training and Keeping the Best Service Workers."

10. Henkoff, "Finding, Training and Keeping the Best Service Workers"; "Training Programs Must Reflect Today's Environment," *Chain Store Age Executive*, June 1989, pp. 60–61.

11. R. Williamson, "Motivation on the menu," *The Globe and Mail*, November 24, 1995, p. B7.

12. This material is condensed from J.F. Scolland, "Setting Up A Pay System," *Management Aid*, No. 5.006 (Washington, D.C.: U.S. Small Business Administration.)

13. See, for example, "System Boost Productivity—Immediate Feedback on Job Performance," *Chain Store Age Executive*, June 1992, p. 42.

14. This material is condensed from J.B. Hannah, "Changing Employee Benefits," *Management Aid*, No. 5.008 (Washington, D.C.: U.S. Small Business Administration); *Managing People, Retailing's Prime Resource*, Retail Council of Canada (1988).

15. Williamson, "Motivation on the menu."

16. For further reading, see L. Berry and P. Parasuraman, *Marketing Services: Competing Through Quality* (New York: The Free Press, 1991, pp. 167–69).

17. Williamson, "Motivation on the menu"; D.E. Bowen and E.E. Lawler, III, "The Empowerment of Service Workers: What, Why, How and When?" *Sloan Management Review*, Spring 1992, vol. 33, no. 2, pp. 31–39.

18. F.N. Sonnennberg, "A Strategic Approach to Employing Motivation," *Journal of Business Strategy*, May/June 1991, p. 41.

19. S. Nolen, "It's Far Better than Being Laid Off," *The Globe and Mail*, August 13, 1993, p. A12.

20. Statistics Canada, *1996 Census*, table 93F0030XDB96004.

21. B. Brennan, "Employers try to show they care," *Kitchener-Waterloo Record*, July 9, 1992, p. E8.

22. G.S. Day, *Market Driven Strategy* (New York: The Free Press, 1990, pp. 360–361).

23. M.T. Leenders and D.L. Blenkhorn, *Reverse Marketing: The New Buyer-Supplier Relationship* (New York, The Free Press, 1988).

24. Based on W.F. Loeb, "Unbundle or Centralize: What Is the Answer?" *Retailing Issues Letter* 4, no. 3, May 1992, pp. 1–4.

25. Hudson's Bay Company, *Annual Report*, 1994.

Chapter 7

1. S. Bourette, "Sears expanding in rural markets," *The Globe and Mail,* November 10, 1995, p. B3; K. Swoger, "Mega-mall spins off benefits," *The Montreal Gazette,* December 4, 1998.
2. S. Bourette, "Sears expanding in rural markets," *The Globe and Mail,* November 10, 1995, p. B3.
3. "Wal-Mart seen taking bigger bite of market," *The Montreal Gazette,* December 24, 1998, p. E3.
4. *Canadian Markets, 1999,* Toronto: The Financial Post Information Service, p. 15.
5. *Canadian Markets, 1999,* Toronto: The Financial Post Information Service, pp. 8, 18.
6. *Canadian Directory of Shopping Centres, 1999,* Vol. 2, p. 15.
7. W.J. Reilly, *Methods for the Study of Retail Relationships,* Research Monograph #4, University of Texas Bulletin #2944 (Austin: University of Texas Press, 1929).
8. P.P. Yannopoulos, "Salient Factors in Shopping Centre Choice," in *Marketing,* vol. 12 (ed. Tony Schellinck), ASAC, 1991, pp. 294–302; A. Finn and J. Louviere, "Shopping-Centre Patronage Models," *Journal of Business Research,* Vol. 21, 1990, pp. 259–275.
9. D.L. Huff, "A Probabilistic Analysis of Shopping Centre Trade Areas," *Land Economics,* Vol. 39. Copyright © 1963 by the Board of Regents of the University of Wisconsin System, p. 86.
10. D.L. Huff, and L. Blue, *A Programmed Solution for Estimating Retail Sales Potential* (Laurence, Kansas: Centre for Regional Studies, 1966).
11. Statistics Canada, *Family Expenditures in Canada,* Cat. 62-555, Ottawa: Information Canada.
12. J.R. McKeever, "Factors to Consider in a Shopping Centre Location," *Small Marketers Aid,* #143 (Washington, DC: Small Business Administration).
13. An interesting approach can be found in A. Finn and J. Louviere, "Shopping-Centre Patronage Models," *Journal of Business Research,* Vol. 21, 1990, pp.259–275.
14. *Canadian Directory of Shopping Centres, 1999,* vol. 2, Maclean Hunter, pp. 212–213.
15. Statistics Canada, *Sales per Selling Area of Independent Retailers,* Cat. 61-522, Ottawa: Information Canada, Appendix I.
16. *Canadian Directory of Shopping Centres, 1999,* vol. 2, pp. 20–21.
17. Statistics Canada, *Sales per Selling Area of Independent Retailers.*
18. *Canadian Directory of Shopping Centres, 1999,* vol. 1, p. 600.
19. K. Swoger, "Mega-mall spins off benefits."
20. S. Silcoff, "Retail That Rocks," *Canadian Business,* November 27, 1998, pp. 48–58.

21. Statistics Canada, *Sales per Selling Area of Independent Retailers.*

22. *Canadian Directory of Shopping Centres, 1999,* vol. 1, p. 545.

23. A. Finn and J. Rigby, "West Edmonton Mall: Consumer Combined-Purpose Trips and the Birth of the Mega-Multi-Mall," *Canadian Journal of Administrative Sciences,* Vol. 9, June 1992, pp. 134–145; Sean Silcoff, "Retail That Rocks," *Canadian Business,* November 27, 1998, pp.48–58.

24. Based on R. O'Neill, "What's New in Shopping Centre Positioning," *Monitor,* May 1990, pp.68–70.

25. S.A. Forest, "I can get it for you retail," *Business Week,* September 18, 1995, pp. 84–88.

26. "Outlet malls: Do they deliver the goods?" *Consumer Reports,* August 1998, pp. 20–26.

27. A. Faircloth, "Value Retailers Go Dollar for Dollar," *Fortune,* July 6, 1998, pp. 164–166.

28. K. Shermach, "Niche malls: Innovation or an industry in decline," *Marketing News,* February 26, 1996, pp. 1, 2.

29. S. Lagerfeld, "What Main Street Can Learn from the Mall," *Atlantic Monthly,* November 1995, pp. 110–120.

30. Statistics Canada, *Sales per Selling Area of Independent Retailers.*

31. J. Heinzl, "Zellers steps up discount war," *The Globe and Mail,* November 9, 1995, p. B1; M. Socha, "Triple the pleasure: Sears Canada opens giant free-standing furniture store," *The Kitchener Record,* August 26, 1995, p. B4.

32. J.R. Lowry, *Using a Traffic Study to Select a Retail Site,* (Washington, DC: Small Business Administration).

Chapter 8

1. D. Gillmor, "Groceryland," *Report on Business Magazine,* October 1998, pp. 121–126; E. Ransdell, "Adventures in Retail," *Fast Company,* vol. 12, p. 182 (www.fastcompany.com/12)

2. G.H. Condon, "Retailing as entertainment," *Canadian Grocer,* July/August 1998, p. 13.

3. K. Pocock, "Supermarket Makeover," *Canadian Grocer,* September 1994, pp. 37–40.

4. J. Margolis, "Windowonderlands," *The Globe and Mail,* December 8, 1994, p. D11.

5. W.R. Swinyard, "The Effects of Mood, Involvement, and Quality of Store Experience on Shopping Intentions," *Journal of Consumer Research,* vol. 20, No. 2 (September 1993), pp. 271–280.

6. J. Baker, M. Levy and D. Grewal, "An Experimental Approach to Making Retail Store Environmental Decisions," *Journal of Retailing,* vol. 68, No. 4 (Winter 1992), pp. 445–460.

7. G. Levitch, "Memories of Versailles," *The Globe and Mail,* November 30, 1995, p. D4.

8. K. Pocock, "Supermarket Makeover," *Canadian Grocer*, September 1994, pp. 37-40; J.A. Bellizzi and R.E. Hite, "Environmental Colour, Consumer Feelings and Purchase Likelihood," *Psychology and Marketing* 9, September-October 1992, pp. 347-363.

9. "Office Depot Puts Spotlight on Its Goods," *Chain Store Age Executive*, September 1991, p. 94.

10. C. Jones, "Grocers pump up the Muzak," *The Montreal Gazzette*, July 17, 1998.

11. J. Baker, M. Levy and D. Grewal, "An Experimental Approach to Making Retail Store Environmental Decisions," *Journal of Retailing* 68, No. 4, Winter 1992, pp. 445–460.

12. E.R. Spangenberg, A.E. Crowley and P.W. Henderson, "Improving the Store Environment: Do Olfactory Cues Affect Evaluations and Behaviors?" *Journal of Marketing*, vol. 60, 2 (April 1996), pp. 67–80; C. Miller, "Scent as Marketing Tool," *Marketing News*, January 18, 1993, pp. 1–2.

13. G. Robins, "The Logistics of Overseas Expansion," *Stores*, April 1990, p. 22.

14. M. Kuntz, K. Naughton, G. DeGeorge and S.A. Forest, "Reinventing the store," *Business Week*, November 27, 1995, p. 86; A. Salomon and S. Hume, "Hot Fast-Food Ideas Cool Off," *Advertising Age*, September 30, 1991, p. 42.

15. A. Willis, "Canadian Tire goes flat for investors," *Financial Times*, June 1, 1992, p. 1.

16. J. Pellet, "The Power of Lighting," *Chain Store Age Executive*, July 1992, p. 90.

17. F. Brookman, "Fixtures Add Flexibility to Product Display," *Stores*, May 1992, pp. 84–85.

18. B. Cohen, "How Micromerchandising Can Work for Big Chains," *Chain Store Age Executive*, February 1992, p. 58.

19. C. Duff, "Nation's Retailers Ask Vendors to Help Share Expenses," *Wall Street Journal*, August 4, 1993, p. B4; K. Deveny, "Displays Pay Off for Grocery Marketers," *Wall Street Journal*, October 15, 1992, p. B1.

Chapter 9

1. www.futureshop.com

2. www.canadiantire.ca

3. www.loblaw.com

4. The term *variety* can also be used to describe the number of different merchandise lines that a store carries.

5. The men's furnishings department would include all shirts, ties, underwear, etc. The planning can be in terms of classifications, or subdepartmental units, or for a small department; but for illustration we will look at the sport shirt classification only as we are illustrating a procedure.

6. Obviously, dollars invested in inventory relate to width and support. In fact, the dollars planned become the controlling decision. How many dollars the retailer has will determine investment in SKUs.

7. Stock-to-sales ratios designate the amount of inventory necessary to support sales for a particular period of time (e.g., a month). This discussion assumes a going concern with last year's figures available. In a budget process for a new store, estimates/projections based on trade figures and/or experience are particularly valuable.
8. Readers may wonder why 4.7 times more dollars of inventory than sales are needed. This relates to the support factor. An example can help illustrate this point. If customers were individually predictable—that is, if retailers needed only one jacket to satisfy each customer's demand—then they might get by with a one-to-one ratio. But people want to select from many colours, designs, fabrics, and so on. Thus, retailers need many more SKUs to support planned sales. The more fashion oriented (or the less stable) the merchandise, the more stock is needed to support sales.

Chapter 10

1. Empire, *Annual Report,* 1998; and Sears Canada, *Annual Report,* 1998.
2. For more on channel partnerships, see Robert D. Buzzell and Gwen Ortmeyer, "Channel Partnerships Streamline Distribution," *Sloan Management Review,* Spring 1995, pp. 85–96.
3. Chateau Stores of Canada, *Annual Report,* 1998.
4. For more on quick response systems, see J.H. Hammond, "Quick Response in Retail/Manufacturing Channels," in S.P. Bradley, J.A. Hausman, and R.L. Nolan, *Globalization, Technology, and Competition* (Boston: Harvard Business School Press, 1993), pp. 185–214.
5. For more on negotiation, see Shankar Ganesan, "Negotiating Strategies and the Nature of Channel Relationships," *Journal of Marketing Research* 30, May 1993, pp. 183–203.
6. For more on sales promotions, see John P. Murry, Jr. and Jan B. Heide, "Managing Promotion Program Participation within Manufacturer-Retailer Relationships," *Journal of Marketing* 62, January 1998, pp. 58–68.
7. For more on Wal-Mart's use of cross-docking, see C.K. Prahalad and Gary Hamel, "The Core Competencies of the Corporation," *Harvard Business Review,* May-June 1990, pp. 79–97, and George Stalk, Philip Evans, and Lawrence E. Shulman, "Competing on Capabilities: The New Roles of Corporate Strategy," *Harvard Business Review,* March-April 1992, pp. 57–69.
8. Peter Cheney, "Heavy Lifting With Light Fingers," *The Globe and Mail,* February 27, 1999, p. A12.
9. Peter Cheney, "Heavy Lifting with Light Fingers," p. Al2.

Chapter 11

1. Sources include Mark Stevenson, "The Store to End All Stores," *Business,* May 1994, pp. 20–29; Wal-Mart, Laurier Institute Case Study, 1994; Stephen J. Arnold, Jay Handelman, and Douglas J. Tigert, "The Impact of a Market Spoiler on Consumer Preference Structures (or What Happens When Wal-Mart Comes to Town)," *Journal of Retailing and Consumer*

Services 5, 1, 1998, pp.1–13; and Zena Olijnyk, "The Wal-Marting of Canada Gathers Speed," *Financial Post*, March 26, 1999, pp. CI, C2.

2. For more information on everyday low pricing see Stephen J. Hoch, Xavier Droze, and Mary E. Purk, "EDLP, Hi-Lo and Margin Arithmetic," *Journal of Marketing*, October, 1994, pp. 16–27.

3. www.airmiles.ca

4. For more information on how consumers perceive prices, see Gerald E. Smith and Thomas A. Nagle, "Frames of Reference and Buyers' Perception of Price and Value," *California Management Review*, Fall 1995, pp. 98–116; Donald R. Lichtenstein, Nancy M. Ridgeway, and Richard G. Netemeyer, "Price Perceptions and Consumer Shopping Behavior: A Field Study," *Journal of Marketing Research*, May 1993, pp. 234–45; and Valarie Folkes and Rita D. Wheat, "Consumers' Perceptions of Promoted Products," *Journal of Retailing*, Fall 1995, pp. 317–28.

5. Referred to as the Weber-Fechner Law, the law proposes that buyers perceive price differences in proportional terms rather than in absolute terms. The implication of the law is that there are thresholds (often referred to as just noticeable differences) above and below a product's price at which price changes are noticed or ignored. For more information, see Smith and Nagle, "Frames of Reference and Buyers' Perception of Price and Value," *California Management Review*, Fall 1995, pp. 98–116.

6. For more on retail price promotions, see George S. Bobinski, Jr., Dena Cox and Anthony Cox, "Retail Sale Advertising, Perceived Retailer Credibility, and Price Rationale," *Journal of Retailing*, Fall 1996, pp. 291–306; Abhijit Biswas and Edward A. Blair, "Contextual Effects of Reference Prices in Retail Advertisements," *Journal of Marketing*, July 1991, pp. 1–12; Abhijit Biswas, Elizabeth J. Wilson, and Jane W. Licata, "Reference Price Studies in Marketing: A Synthesis of Research Results," *Journal of Business Research*, July 1993, pp. 239–56; and Kiran W. Karanda and V. Kumar, "The Effects of Brand Characteristics and Retail Policies on Responses to Retail Price Promotions: Implications for Retailers," *Journal of Retailing*, Fall 1995, pp. 249–78.

7. For more information on the price-quality issue, see Valarie A. Zeithaml, "Consumer Perceptions of Price, Quality, and Value: A Means-End Model and Synthesis of Evidence," *Journal of Marketing*, July 1988, pp. 2–22; Kent B. Monroe and William B. Dodds, "A Research Program for Establishing the Validity of the Price-Quality Relationship," *Journal of the Academy of Marketing Science*, Spring 1988, pp. 151–68.

8. For more information on price changes, see Peter R. Dickson and Joel E. Urbany, "Retailer Reactions to Price Changes," *Journal of Retailing*, Spring 1994, pp. 1–21 and Reed K. Holden and Thomas T. Nagle, "Kamikaze Pricing," *Marketing Management*, Summer 1998, pp. 31–39.

9. For more on price-value, see Timothy Matanovich, Gary L. Lilien and Arvind Rangaswamy, "Engineering the Price-Value Relationship," *Marketing Management*, Spring, 1999, pp.48–53 and Hermann Simon and Robert J. Dolan, "Price Customization," *Marketing Management*, Fall 1998, pp. 11–18.

Chapter 12

1. R. Corelli "Dishing Out Rudeness," *Maclean's Special Report* (January 11, 1999).

2. M. Morris, A. Gold, and A. Camara, "Creating a Company," *Retailing Issues Letter* 4, March 1992, pp. 1, 3–4.

3. This material is adapted from B. Rosenbloom, *Improving Personal Selling* (Washington, DC: Small Business Administration), pp. 1–3.

4. T. Kabachnick, "Is Salesmanship the Dinosaur of the '90s?" *Retailing Issues Letter* 3 (May 1991), p. 2.

5. L. Dawson, B. Soper, and C. Pettijohn, "The Effects of Empathy on Salesperson Effectiveness," *Psychology & Marketing* 9, July-August 1992, pp. 297–310.

6. M. Cartash, "Catch a Falling Store," *Profit,* December 1990, p. 22.

7. Dawson, Soper, and Pettijohn, "The Effects of Empathy on Salesperson Effectiveness"; S. Castleberry and C.D. Sheppard, "Effective Interpersonal Listening and Personal Selling," *Journal of Personal Selling and Sales Management* 1, Winter 1993, pp. 35–50.

8. L.B. Chonko, M.J. Caballero, and J.R. Lumpkin, "Do Retail Salespeople Use Selling Skills?" *Review of Business and Economic Research* 25 (Spring 1990), p. 41.

9. The material on closing the sale is adapted from *Marketing Strategy*, self-instructional booklet 1989 (Washington, DC: Small Business Administration).

10. Dawson, Soper, and Pettijohn, "The Effects of Empathy on Salesperson Effectiveness."

11. R. Henkoff, "Finding, Training and Keeping the Best Service Workers," *Fortune,* October 3, 1994, pp. 110–122; R. Henkoff, "Service is Everybody's Business," *Fortune,* June 27, 1994, pp. 48–60.

12. R. Williamson, "Motivation on the menu," *The Globe and Mail,* November 24, 1995, p. B7; D.E. Bowen and E.E. Lawler, III, "The Empowerment of Service Workers: What, Why, How and When," *Sloan Management Review* 33, 3, Spring 1992, pp. 31–39.

13. This material is adapted from *Managing Retail Salespeople,* self-instructional booklet No. 1019 (Washington, DC: Small Business Administration).

14. The material on involvement and feedback and criteria for successful training and job orientation is adapted from *Job Analysis, Job Specifications, and Job Descriptions,* self-instructional booklet no. 120 (Washington, DC: Small Business Administration).

15. B. Dalglish, "Snoops in the shops," *Maclean's,* December 19,1994, pp. 28–29.

Chapter 13

1. C. MacAuley, "A better tasting promo," *Marketing*, April 13, 1998, p. 23.
2. J. McElgunn, "Study says nothing beats word of mouth," *Marketing*, May 1, 1995, p. 2.
3. M. Strauss, "Vive la différence," *The Globe and Mail*, November 2, 1995, p. B13.
4. O. Riso, "Advertising Guidelines for Small Retail Firms," *Small Marketers Aid*, No. 160 (Washington, DC: U.S. Small Business Administration), p. 4.
5. The material on establishing and allocating the budget is based on S.H. Britt, "Plan Your Advertising Budget," *Small Marketers Aid*, No. 164 (Washington, DC: U.S. Small Business Administration).
6. G. Cestre, M. Laroche, and L. Desjardins, "Current Advertising Budgeting Practices of Canadian Advertisers and Agencies," *Canadian Journal of Administrative Sciences*, vol. 9, December 1992, pp. 279–293.
7. J. Pepall, "Co-op advertising builds strength from numbers," *Profit*, November 1990, pp. 53–54.
8. Pepall, "Co-op advertising builds strength from numbers."
9. *Canadian Advertising Rates & Data (henceforth referred to as CARD)* is a monthly publication of Maclean Hunter. For each medium the date for which the information was updated is indicated in the corresponding listing. For more complete information, you should request the General Rate Card from the medium itself.
10. *Canadian Media Directors' Council Media Digest, 1999/2000 (henceforth referred to as CMDCMD)*, p. 27.
11. *CMDCMD, 1999/2000*, p. 16.
12. *CMDCMD, 1999/2000*, p. 24.
13. "NADbank '95, the past, the present and the future," *Advertising Supplement to Marketing Magazine, 1995*, p. 4; *CMDCMD, 1999/2000*, p. 30.
14. *CMDCMD*, p. 37.
15. *CARD*, April 1999, pp. 62–63.
16. R. Scotland, "Resurgence in home shopping boosts catalogue sales," *The Financial Post*, March 23, 1995, p. 19.
17. J. Pollock "Lists of Opportunity, " *Marketing*, May 22, 1995, pp. 14–15; "U.S. apparel catalogue debuts in Canada," *Marketing*, November 6, 1995, p. 1.
18. G. Blackwell, "Just what the armchair shopper ordered," *The Globe and Mail*, July 18, 1992, p. B22.
19. Ibid.; J. Pepall, "Selling by the book, " *Profit*, December 1990, pp. 40–41.
20. Z. Olijnyk, "Retailers turn to 'magalogues'," *Financial Post*, January 29, 1999, p. C8.
21. L. Mills, "From print to bits and bytes," *Marketing*, May 22, 1995, pp. 14–15; R. Scotland, "Menswear ads tailored to tradition and high-tech," *The Financial Post*, April 4, 1995, p. 13.

22. R. Scotland, "Resurgence in home shopping boosts catalogue sales," *The Financial Post*, March 23, 1995, p. 19.

23. *CMDCMD*, p. 50.

24. "Web ad revenues on the rise," *Marketing*, July 19/26, 1999, p. 30.

25. J. Sinclair, "The new media: Are high-tech innovations likely to bring rapid change?" *Marketing*, January 2/9, 1995, p. 14; "Windows on the Interactive Future," *Stores*, April 1995, pp. 57–58.

26. K. Riddell, "Reaching Consumers In-Store," *Marketing*, July 13/20, 1992, p. 10.

27. J. Lipman, "Consumers' Favoured Commercials Tend to Feature Lower Prices or Cuddly Kids," *The Wall Street Journal*, March 2, 1992, p. B1.

28. R.Y. Darmon and M. Laroche, *Advertising in Canada*, Toronto: McGraw-Hill Ryerson, 1991, pp. 308–317.

29. Committee on Definitions, *Marketing Definitions*, Chicago, IL: American Marketing Association, 1963.

30. W. Mouland, "Coupons and loyalty cards," *Marketing*, October 23, 1995, pp. 29–30; W. Mouland, "How couponing can boost brand sales," *Marketing*, July 3/10, 1995, p. 21.

31. D. McClellan, "Desktop Counterfeiting," *Technology Review*, February/March 1995, pp. 32–40.

32. "Coupons save consumer more money in 1997," *Canadian Grocer*, March 1998, p. 13.

33. Darmon and Laroche, *Advertising in Canada*, pp. 196–199.

34. Riddell, "Reaching Consumers In-Store."

35. K. Riddell, "Double Coupons Perform Well for Miracle," *Marketing*, February 24, 1992, p. 7.

36. Riddell, "Reaching Consumers In-Store."

37. D. Mudie, "The Sampling Menu," *Marketing*, August 18/25, 1997, p. S3.

38. M. Cartash, "Catch a Falling Store," *Profit*, December 1990, p. 27.

39. This material is condensed, with modifications, from E. Sorbet, "Do You Know the Results of Your Advertising?" *Management Aid*, No. 4020 (Washington, DC: U.S. Small Business Administration).

40. Committee on Definitions, op. cit.; M.A. Charlebois, "Putting a Value on Your Program," *Marketing*, October 23, 1995, p. 16; J. McElgunn, "Study says nothing beats word of mouth," *Marketing*, May 1, 1995, p. 2.

41. Cartash, "Catch a Falling Store."

Chapter 14

1. C. Cornell, "There is Something about Harry," *Profit*, April 1999, pp. 44–50; G. Pitts, "The vision of Saint Hubert," *Report on Business*, May 30, 1995, p. B10.

2. D.E. Headley and B. Choi, "Achieving Service Quality through Gap Analysis and a Basic Statistical Approach," *Journal of Services Marketing* 6, 1 (Winter 1992), pp. 5–14.

3. This section on customer service versus customer-focus is reproduced with permission from R. Burns, "Customer Service vs. Customer-Focused," *Retail Control,* March 1989. Copyright © National Retail Merchants Association. All rights reserved.

4. "Their Wish Is Your Command," *Business Week/Quality,* 1991, pp. 126–127.

5. L.C. Smith, "Dressing up customer service," *The Globe and Mail,* January 11, 1992, p. D1.

6. M. Cartash, "Catch a Falling Store," *Profit,* December 1990, p. 29.

7. Z. Olijnyk, "Retailers turn to 'magalogues'," *Financial Post,* January 29, 1999, p. C8.

8. G.H.G. McDougall and T. Levesque, "The Measurement of Service Quality: Some Methodological Issues," in *Marketing, Operations and Human Resources Insight into Services,* ed. P. Eiglier and E. Langeard, Aix, France: I.A.E., 1992, pp. 411–431; J.J. Cronin, Jr. and S.A. Taylor, "Measuring Service Quality: A Reexamination and Extension," *Journal of Marketing* 56, July 1992, pp. 55–68.

9. A. Markowitz, "Technology Fills Multitude of Roles in Improving Customer Service," *Discount Store News,* May 3, 1993, pp. 48–49.

10. "Store Card Still Strong," *Stores,* January 1991, p. 169.

11. "Credit Card Interest Charges," *Information* (February 1999), Industry Canada, p. 2 (also check strategis.ic.gc.ca/BC).

12. G. Robins, "Wireless POS Systems," *Stores,* February 1994, pp. 47–48.

13. P. Gill, "Added Value: Relationship Marketing Is One Way for Retailers to Build Loyalty," *Stores,* October 1991, pp. 39–40; M. Strauss, "The downside of cultivating loyalty," *The Globe and Mail,* June 29, 1995, p. B4.

14. *Database Marketing* 3, 2, February 1995, p. 7.

15. D. Del Prete, "Credit Card Companies to Retailers: Use Us," *Marketing News,* March 4, 1991, pp. 1, 6.

16. "Co-Branding on the Rise," *Stores,* February 1992, p. S7; D. Alaimo, "Wegmans to Use Co-Branded Credit Cards," *Supermarket News,* February 25, 1991, p. 15.

17. M. Cartash, "Catch a Falling Store," *Profit,* December 1990, p. 29.

18. Smith, "Dressing up customer service."

19. C.W.L. Hart, J. Heskitt, and E. Sasser, *Service Breakthroughs* (New York: The Free Press, 1990), p. 89.

20. L. Freeman, "Service Contracts and Warranties Impact Bottom Line," *Stores,* January 1992, pp. 122, 124; D. Del Prete, "Looks Like A Hot Summer for Extended Car Warranties," *Marketing News,* August 8, 1991, p. 9.

21. R. Blackwell, “Canada leads way in Visa credit card fraud,” *The Financial Post,* March 12, 1998, p. 6; R. Blackwell, “Visa plans ‘smart’ cards,” *The Financial Post,* February 14, 1995, p. 8.

22. “Face to Face: A Look at McDonald’s Customer Satisfaction,” *First Quarter 1992 McDonald’s Shareholders Newsletter*; J. Pollock, “Toys“Я” Us reaches out to differently-abled kids,” *Marketing*, October 16, 1995, p. 2.

23. “Caring IKEA Sets the Pace,” *Stores,* November 1990, pp. 54–55.

24. Hart, Heskitt, and Sasser, *Service Breakthroughs*, p. 31.

25. Ibid.

Chapter 15

1. C.H. Lovelock, *Services Marketing*, 3rd Edition (Englewood Cliffs: Prentice-Hall, 1996.)

2. L.L. Berry, *On Great Service* (New York: Free Press, 1995.)

3. V.A. Zeithaml and M. J. Bitner, *Services Marketing*, (New York: McGraw-Hill, 1996).

4. Ibid.

5. G.H.G. McDougall and T.J. Levesque, “Benefit Segmentation Using Service Quality Dimensions: An Investigation into Retail Banking,” *International Journal of Bank Marketing* 12, 2, 1994, pp.15–23.

6. For more, see B. Schneider and D.E. Bowen, *Winning the Service Game*, Harvard Business School Press, Boston, 1995.

7. G.H.G. McDougall and T.J. Levesque, “The Effectiveness of Recovery Strategies After Service Failure: An Experiment in the Hospitality Industry,” *Journal of Hospitality & Leisure Marketing* 5, 2/3, 1998, pp.27–50.

8. J. Wirtz, “Development of a Service Guarantee Model,” *Asia Pacific Journal of Management*, 15, 1998, pp. 51–75.

9. J.L. Heskett, W.E. Sasser, Jr. and C.W.L. Hart, *Service Breakthroughs: Changing the Rules of the Game* (Toronto: The Free Press, 1990), pp. 43 & 51.

10. L. L. Berry and M. S. Yadav, “Capture and Communicate Value in the Pricing of Services,” *Sloan Management Review*, Summer, 1996, pp. 41–51.

11. L. L. Berry and M. S. Yadav, *op. cit.*

12. J. Heinzl, “Direct marketers push the envelope,” *The Globe and Mail,* May 7, 1998, p. B15.

13. J. Heinzl, *op. cit.*

14. Statistics Canada, *Direct Selling in Canada*, 1997, cat. 63-218 (December 1997), p. 9.

Chapter 16

1. R.O. Crockett, "A Web That Looks Like the World," *Business Week*, March 22, 1999, pp. EB46–47.
2. Simon Tuck, "Internet Milestone Set as 50% Connected in Canada," *The Globe and Mail*, May 1, 1999, pp. B1, B11.
3. Patricia Sellers, "Inside the First E-Christmas," *Fortune*, February 1, 1999, pp. 70–73.
4. Mikala Folb, "Online Book Boom," *Marketing*, January 25, 1999, pp. 15–16.
5. "Shopping Online: Not as Scary as you Think," Ernst & Young Media Café, March 30, 1999.
6. Based on an idea provided by Roger A. Kerin.
7. D.A. Griffith and R.F. Krampf, "Emerging Trends in U.S. Retailing," *Long Range Planning*, Vol. 30, June 1997, pp. 847-852.
8. This section is based, in part, on M. Charles, "E-commerce Retailing Business Strategy," paper prepared for E-commerce and Marketing course, Sloan School of Management, March 17, 1999.
9. Patricia Sellers, "Inside the First E-Christmas," *Fortune*, February 1, 1999, pp. 70–73.
10. Arvind Sahay, Jane Gould, and Patricia Barwise, "New Interactive Media: Experts' Perceptions of Opportunities and Threats for Existing Business," *European Journal of Marketing* 32, 7/8, 1998, pp. 616–628.
11. The e.guide, www.shop.org.
12. Eryn Brown, "Nine Ways to Win on the Web," *Fortune*, May 24, 1999, pp. 112–125.
13. The e.guide, www.shop.org.
14. Kevin Hakman, "E-commerce Tutorial," *Webmonkey/e-business*, www.hotwired.com/webmonkey.
15. "Hot Tips—Design" *Webmonkey/e-business*, www.hotwired.com/webmonkey.
16. Canadian Media Directors' Council, *Media Digest*, 1998–99, pp. 13–17.
17. Patrick Allossery, "Softening E-commerce with Virtual Sales Agents," *National Post*, June 4, 1999, www.nationalpost.com.

Chapter 17

1. Mark's Work Wearhouse, *Annual Report*, 1999.

Appendix B

1. "A Potent New Tool for Selling: Database Marketing," *Business Week* (September 5, 1994), pp. 56–62.
2. J.J. Louviere and R.D. Johnson, "Reliability and Validity of the Brand-Anchored Conjoint Approach to Measuring Retailer Images," *Journal of Retailing* 66, 4, Winter 1990, pp. 359–382.
3. E. Campbell, "CD-ROMs Bring Census Data In-House," *Marketing News*, January 6, 1992, pp. 12, 16.
4. "Using Computer to Divine Who Might Buy a Gas Grill," *Wall Street Journal*, August 16, 1994, pp. B1, B6.
5. S. Kelman, "Consumers on the Couch," *Report on Business Magazine*, February 1991, pp. 50–53.
6. Ibid., pp. 150–58.
7. A. Kryhul, "You ought to be in kiosks," *Marketing*, June 6, 1994, pp. 11-12.

Appendix C

1. Small Business Guide—Business Plan for Retailers, Canada–Ontario Business Service Centre, 1999.
2. For more information, see Canada Small Business Financing Program at www.strategis.ic.gc.ca.

GLOSSARY

Achievers Successful career- and work-oriented people who like to, and generally do, feel in control of their lives.

Action close A sale closing technique, where the salesperson takes a positive step toward clinching the order, such as immediate delivery.

Action-oriented consumers Consumers guided by a desire for social or physical activity, variety, and risk-taking.

Actualizers Successful, sophisticated, active, take-charge people with high self-esteem and abundant resources.

Adaptive behaviour A theory about retail institution change based on the premise that institutions evolve when environmental conditions are favourable.

AIDA model A simple hierarchy of effects model in advertising, where consumers move from attention to interest to desire and action.

Ambience The quality of design that expresses the character of a store, resulting in an institutional personality immediately recognized by consumers.

Anchor tenants The major tenants in a shopping centre that serve as the primary consumer attracting force.

Assets, current Primarily cash, accounts receivable, and inventory. They are in varying states of being converted into cash within the next 12-month period.

Assets, fixed Used in the operation of the business; they are not intended to be resold. They include real estate, leasehold improvements, machinery, equipment, and vehicles.

Assortment The number of different choices available within a particular merchandise line.

Assumptive close A sales closing technique that asks a question about preferred colours, method of payment, or type of delivery that can help the salesperson to quickly determine whether a customer is ready to make a purchase.

Atmospherics see **Ambience**

Atom-based product A product sold through the Internet that has a physical form and presence, involves a shipping process, and is returnable and resaleable.

Autonomous decision A decision within the family that is made over time independently by the husband and the wife.

Awareness In advertising, the percentage of consumers who have learned a brand or store name.

Baby boomers Individuals born between 1946 and 1964, they comprise the largest population segment today.

Balance sheet The financial statement that expresses the equation: Assets = Liabilities + Net worth. (Net worth is the owners' equity or claim to the assets of the business.)

Balanced tenancy A term that means that the types of stores in a planned shopping centre are chosen to meet all of the consumers' shopping needs in the trading area.

Banner ad A small advertisement placed within a particular Web site.

Basic services Services that customers expect to have available at all retail outlets. An example is free parking.

Basic stock The amount and assortment of merchandise sufficient to accommodate normal sales levels.

Believers Conservative, conventional people with concrete beliefs and strong attachments to traditional institutions.

Benefit summary A transition to the close technique, where the salesperson summarizes the product benefits to demonstrate that it is the right one for the customer.

Benefits Holidays and paid vacations, insurance, health care, pensions, social security, disability payments and various other forms of support for employees.

Big-box store A huge store with a large variety and quantity of merchandise organized in one floor.

Bit-based product A product sold through the Internet in digital format that has no physical form or presence, is transferred on-line, and is nonreturnable.

Blind check A checking method in which the checker lists the items and quantities received without the invoice in hand and then compares the list to the invoice.

Book inventory Recording of all additions to and deductions from a beginning stock figure to continually have an ending inventory figure. (Also called perpetual inventory.) The book inventory must be compared to the actual physical inventory to determine shortages or overages.

Boomers See **baby boomers.**

Bots Internet programs (also called intelligent agents) that allow consumers to evaluate and compare on-line several brand offerings in a product category.

Boutique layout Merchandise classifications are grouped so that each classification has its own "shop" within the store.

Breadth (or **width**) The number of different merchandise lines carried.

Browser A software program used to view WWW documents.

Canadian Advertising Rates & Data (CARD) A monthly publication providing updated general rates and other information for most media in Canada.

Canadian Human Rights Commission An agency of the federal government with the responsibility to eliminate discrimination on the basis of race, national or ethnic origin, sex, colour, age, religion, or other variables in job hiring, retention, and promotion.

Canadian newspaper unit (CNU) A unit of measure of newspaper space that is one standardized column wide and 30 MALs deep.

Cash datings Payment terms that call for immediate payment for merchandise. Cash datings include COD (cash on delivery) and CWO (cash with order). Cash datings do not involve cash discounts.

Cash discount A premium granted by the supplier for cash payment prior to the time the entire bill must be paid.

Catalogue Book containing items for sale by a retailer.

Category killers Merchants offering great depth and breadth in one line of merchandise accompanied by low prices and good quality.

Census tract A permanent small census area established in large urban communities of 50,000 or more population; the population of a census tract must be between 2,500 and 8,000 people.

Central business district The area of the central city that is characterized by high land values, high concentration of retail and service business, and high traffic flow.

Chain A retail organization consisting of two or more centrally owned units that handle similar lines of merchandise.

Checking A phase of the physical handling process that involves matching the store buyer's purchase order with the supplier's invoice (bill), opening the packages, removing the items, sorting them, and comparing the quality and quantity of the shipment with what was ordered.

Cognitive dissonance A feeling whereby, consumers, when making a major purchase, are afraid that they may have spent their money foolishly.

Community newspapers Local newspapers that are usually published once a week.

Community shopping centre A shopping centre in which the leading tenant is a variety store or junior department store. The typical leasable space is 15,000 square metres, and the typical site area is 40,000 square metres. The minimum trade population is 40,000 to 150,000.

Compensation The amount of salary and fringe benefits to be paid for a particular job.

Consumer cooperative A type of retail store owned by consumers and operated by a hired manager.

Consumer-dominated information sources Information sources over which the retailer has no influence. Examples include friends, relatives, acquaintances, and others.

Consumer rebates A situation in which a manufacturer pays the consumer a sum of money in the form of a price reduction when a purchase is made.

Contribution margin approach An approach to departmental evaluation in which only direct costs are assigned to departments.

Convenience goods Frequently purchased items for which consumers do not engage in comparison shopping before making a purchase decision.

Cooperative advertising Promotional programs in which wholesalers or manufacturers pay a portion of the retailer's advertising cost under specified conditions.

Core service The primary benefit customers seek from a service firm.

Cost per thousand (CPM) A measure of the relative cost of advertising that is determined by the number of households or persons reached.

Coupon A sales promotion technique consisting of a certificate offering a given price reduction for a given item or service.

Creative selling A type of higher-level selling in which the salesperson needs complete information about product lines, product uses, and the technical features of products.

Credence qualities Attributes consumers may find impossible to evaluate even after purchase and consumption, perhaps because they do not have the knowledge or skill to do so.

Credit scoring A method used by retailers to screen credit applicants based on various types of personal information about the applicant.

Cross-border shopping A form of outshopping, where Canadians travel to the United States to make purchases on a regular basis.

Culture A set of values, attitudes, traditions, symbols, and characteristic behaviour shared by all members of a recognized group.

Customer-focused culture An integrated approach to dealing with customers that incorporates customer lifestyles and buying patterns into the overall strategy of the retail firm.

Customer service Additional services provided to customers such as cashing cheques or managing complaints.

Cycle time The time period (or speed) within which retailers respond to changes in the market.

Debit card A bank-issued card that allows, with the help of special terminals attached to the cash register, for a customer to pay for purchases by having an electronic transfer of funds from the client's to the retailer's bank account.

Deferred billing credit A payment plan in which a retailer allows customers to buy goods and to defer payment for an extended period of time with no interest charge.

Demand merchandise Merchandise purchased as a result of a customer coming into the store to buy that particular item.

Departmentalization An organization principle that determines how jobs are grouped.

Depth The number of items carried in a single merchandise line.

Destination centres See **power centres**

Dialectic process A theory of change in retail institutional structure based on the premise that retailers mutually adapt in the face of competition from "opposites." When challenged by a competitor with a differential advantage, an established institution will adopt strategies and tactics in the direction of that advantage, thereby negating some of the innovator's attraction.

Direct check A checking method whereby the shipment is checked against the vendor's invoice.

Direct close A sale closing technique, where the salesperson takes the position that the customer is ready to buy.

Direct costs Costs associated with a department; such costs would cease to exist if the department were eliminated.

Direct product profitability Reflects a product's gross margin (selling price minus cost of goods sold), plus discounts and allowances, less direct handling costs.

Direct promotion A form of promotion of the store and its merchandise directly to customers through the use of direct mail or catalogues (printed or electronic).

Disappointers Services offered by a retailer that have a high labour content and that return little value to the consumer. An example is layaway.

Disintermediation Ability of the Internet to allow companies to bypass traditional channel intermediaries to deal directly with their customers.

Diversification A strategy of developing new lines of business unrelated to current markets or current customers.

Dollar control A system for controlling the dollar investment in inventory. To work, the system must record the beginning dollar inventory, what has been added to stock, how much inventory has moved out of stock, and how much inventory is now on hand. Involves perpetually recording additions and deductions at retail or cost.

Drawing account A payment arrangement in which a cash advance is made available to retail salespeople at predetermined intervals.

Electronic commerce Selling through the Internet (also called e-commerce).

Electronic retailing See **Electronic commerce**

Employee compensation Wages or salary, commissions, incentives, overtime, and benefits.

Energy costs Include carrying packages, fighting traffic, and waiting in line.

Enumeration area A small federal electoral area of about 100 to 200 households, the smallest geographic unit for which census data are available.

Event advertising An advertising campaign to promote a very specific sale, during a specific period (e.g., after-Christmas sale).

Exclusive dealing A situation in which a supplier prohibits a retailer from selling the product of a competitor.

Experience qualities Attributes such as taste that can only be discerned after purchase or during consumption.

Experiencers People who are young, vital, enthusiastic, impulsive, and rebellious.

Experimental design A type of research design that allows management to make inferences about cause-and-effect relationships in variables of interest.

Exploratory research A research process characterized by flexibility in design and the absence of a formal research structure.

Extensive problem-solving behaviour A thought process that consumers experience when faced with a first-time purchase in an unfamiliar product category.

External data Previously published data gathered by other groups or organizations and made available to the firm.

Factory outlet centre Shopping centres occupied by manufacturers selling directly to the public.

Family life cycle It reflects the various stages individuals go through as they get married, have children, and so on until retirement.

Feature-benefit relationship Understanding the reasons why customers buy, relating products to those reasons, and describing the products or services to the customers.

FIFO (first-in, first-out) An inventory costing method that assumes that costs should be charged against revenue in the order in which they were incurred; in other words, the first items purchased are the first ones sold. The method is generally in harmony with actual movement of goods.

Financial risk The monetary loss from a wrong decision.

Fixed-payment lease A rental agreement in which rent is based on a fixed payment per month.

Flextime A system by which workers arrive to work on a variable schedule.

Focus group A type of exploratory research, where a group of 8 to 12 suppliers, customers, or noncustomers gather around a table to talk informally around the issue, with the assistance of a trained interviewer.

Forward integration A situation in which a manufacturer establishes its own wholesale and retail networks.

Franchise contract A legal document that enables an independent businessperson to use a franchiser's operating methods, financing systems, trademarks, and products in return for the payment of a fee.

Franchisee An individual who pays a fee for the right to use a franchiser's product, service, or way of doing business.

Franchiser An organization that has developed a unique product, service, or a way of doing business and allows another firm to use the product, service, or business concept in return for payment of a fee.

Free-flow layout Merchandise and fixtures are grouped into patterns that allow an unstructured flow of customer traffic.

Frequency The average number of times a person will be exposed to a message during an advertising period.

Fulfilleds Mature, satisfied, comfortable, reflective people who value order, knowledge, and responsibility.

Full-costing approach Both direct and indirect costs are assigned to departments.

Functional accounts Reflects the retail function involved (e.g., allocation of salaries to administrative support and sales personnel).

Future datings A type of dating other than cash dating; includes DOI (date of invoice), ROG (receipt of goods), EOM (end of month), and extra datings.

General rate The advertising rate charged to agencies for national advertising.

General salary increases Increases granted to employees to maintain real earnings as required by economic factors and in order to keep pay competitive.

Generation X The group of individuals born between 1965 and 1976.

Generation Y The group of individuals born between 1977 and 1986, i.e., the children of the baby boomers.

Generics Unbranded merchandise offerings carrying only the designation of the product type on the package.

Gravity models Methods for trading area analysis that are based on population size and driving time or distance as the key variables in the models.

Grid layout Merchandise is displayed in straight, parallel lines, with secondary aisles at right angles to these.

Gross margin The difference between net sales and the cost of goods sold.

Gross rating point One percent of all homes with television sets in a market area.

Hedonic consumption Facets relating to the multisensory and emotional aspects of shopping and consuming.

Hierarchy of effects model A type of model often used in advertising where consumers respond to advertising according to various sequential stages. The simplest one is called AIDA (for attention-interest-desire-action).

High involvement Consumer's shopping characterized by a high level of search in an effort to obtain information about products or stores.

Home improvement centres Centres featuring a concentration of home improvement or hardware specialty retailers.

HTML Language used to develop WWW documents.

Husband-dominant decision A decision within the family that is made most of the time by the husband.

Image The way consumers "feel" about a store or merchandise.

Image campaign An advertising campaign by a retailer for the sole purpose to improve its image.

Impulse merchandise Merchandise bought on the basis of unplanned, spur-of-the-moment decisions.

Income statement Operating results of a period indicating if investments in assets and strategy have been successful and if a profit has resulted.

Indirect costs Costs that cannot be tied directly to a department, such as the store manager's salary.

In-home retailing A method of distribution of consumer goods and service through personal contact away from a fixed business location.

Initial markup The difference between the cost of merchandise and the original retail price.

Inseparability For some services to be performed, both the customer and the service provider must be physically together (e.g., haircut).

Instalment credit A payment plan in which a customer pays for a product in equal monthly instalments, including interest.

Institutional advertising An advertising campaign to communicate the total character or image of the store, and no merchandise or prices are featured.

Intangibility The characteristic of a service that indicates that a service cannot be seen, touched, smelled, or handled.

Intelligent agent see **Bots**

Internal data Data that helps management systematically determine what's going on in the firm.

Internal environment Forces within the organization that affect the activities of the firm.

Internet A computer network that allows computers to communicate with each other.

Intertype competition Competition between different types of retail outlets selling the same merchandise.

Intratype competition Competition among retailers of the same type.

Job analysis A method for obtaining important facts about a job.

Job classification Comparing jobs with the aid of a scale that evaluates job complexity and the length of time the respective responsibility and qualifications are utilized during an average workday.

Job description The part of a job analysis that describes the content and responsibilities of a job and how the job ties in with other jobs in the firm.

Job evaluation A method of ranking jobs to aid in determining proper compensation.

Job ranking Ranking jobs on the basis of how valuable they are to the organization and the complexity of the job.

Job sharing A situation whereby two workers voluntarily hold joint responsibility for what was formerly one position.

Job specification The part of a job analysis that describes the personal qualifications required of an employee to do a job.

Layaway plan A situation in which a customer can make a small deposit which assures that the retailer will hold the item until the customer is able to pay for it.

Lead time The length of time between order placement and receipt of goods.

Leader pricing A policy in which merchandise is sold at less than the normal markup in an effort to increase store traffic.

Leveraging When assets worth more than the amount of capital invested by the owners are acquired. Leveraging is the ratio of total assets to net worth. The higher the ratio, the higher the amount of borrowed funds in the business.

Liabilities What is owed by the business.

Licensing A tool of marketing in which the licenser or owner of a "property" (the concept to be marketed) joins with a licensee (the manufacturer of the licensed product) and attempts to sell to retail buyers.

Life cycle The stages through which retail institutions evolve, including innovation, growth, maturity, and decline or stagnation.

Lifestyle A person's pattern of living as reflected in the way merchandise is purchased and used.

Lifestyle cluster Shopping urban areas that cater to a specific lifestyle with a combination of food stalls, specialty shops, and restaurants.

Lifestyle segmentation Dividing consumers into homogeneous groups based on similar activities, interests, and opinions.

LIFO (last-in, first-out) An inventory costing method that assumes that the most recent cost of merchandise should be charged against revenue. LIFO yields a higher figure for cost of goods sold than FIFO and thus lower figures for gross profit, net income, and inventory. LIFO is popular during inflationary periods.

Likert scale A type of scale that allows respondents to express their level of agreement or disagreement with a statement.

Limited problem-solving behaviour Shopping situations in which the consumer is already familiar with the class of product or service and makes a choice between brands or outlets.

Low involvement Consumer's shopping characterized by a very low/no effort to compare products or stores; the product that will satisfy the consumer's needs will be purchased at the most convenient outlet.

Maintained markup The difference between invoice cost and sales retail.

Makers Practical people who have constructive skills and value self-sufficiency.

Management by objectives Goals established with salespersons that give direction to their efforts and that permit them to evaluate their progress.

Margin The percentage markup at which inventory is sold.

Markdown A reduction in the original selling price of an item.

Market development A strategy option that focuses either on attracting new market segments or completely changing the customer base.

Market penetration A strategy option whereby retailers seek a differential advantage over competition by a strong market presence that borders on saturation.

Market saturation A situation that occurs when such a large number of stores are located in a market that low sales per square metre, compared to the industry average, are the result.

Marketer-dominated information sources Sources of information under the control of the retailer. Examples are advertising, personal selling, displays, sales promotion, and publicity.

Marketing The process by which individuals and groups obtain what they need and want through creating and exchanging products and value with others.

Marking A phase of the physical handling process that involves putting information on the goods or on merchandise containers to assist customers and to aid the store in the control functions.

Merchandise approach A retail sales approach that begins with a statement about the merchandise.

Merchandise budget A plan of how much to buy in dollars per month by classification based on profitability goals.

Merchandise distribution An aspect of merchandise management in multiunit organizations related to getting merchandise from consolidation points/distribution centres to the individual stores.

Merchandise line A group of products that are closely related because they are intended for the same end use, are used together, or are sold to the same customer group.

Merchandise management The management of the product component of the marketing mix.

Merchandise planning Includes all the activities needed to plan a balance between inventories and sales.

Merit increases Pay increases granted to recognize superior performance and contributions.

Message The development of an idea in transmittable form.

Mission statement A statement that describes what a firm plans to accomplish in the market in which it will compete for customers it wants to serve.

Model stock plan A fashion merchandiser's best judgment about what demand will be at specific times of the year.

Modular agate line (MAL) A unit of measure of newspaper space that is one standardized column wide and 1.8 mm deep.

Money costs Costs of goods purchased and costs of travel.

Motivation Getting people to do what is best for the organization.

Multiattribute model A model that explains how attitudes toward stores are formed based on a number of attributes, their stated importances, and beliefs by consumers.

National brands The brands of a manufacturer such as Procter and Gamble that are sold through a wide variety of retail outlets.

National rates Advertising rates applicable to national (non-retail) firms.

Natural accounts Company-wide accounts such as salaries, rent, promotion, and costs of supplies.

Neighbourhood shopping centre A shopping centre in which the leading tenant is a supermarket or drugstore. The typical leasable space is 5,000 square metres and the typical site is 20,000 square metres. The minimum trade population is 7,500 to 40,000.

Net worth The owner's investment or equity.

Neutral sources of information Sources of information such as government rating agencies and state and local consumer affairs agencies that consumers perceive as trustworthy.

Niche mall A type of mall targeted to a very specific group of customers, e.g., the Chinese or working women.

Nonperpetual unit control (Also called stock-counting methods.) This is *not* a book-inventory method. A nonperpetual unit system requires the retailer to have a planned model stock, a periodic counting schedule, and definite, assigned responsibility for counting. The beginning and ending inventories are counted and the differences are the sales (and shortages).

Nonstore retailing The sale of merchandise other than through retail stores. Examples include mail order, telephone shopping, door-to-door (direct selling), and vending machines.

Nonstore shopping The purchase of merchandise by use of catalogues, telephone, or ways other than physically entering an outlet.

Objective-and-task method A method of setting the advertising budget that relates the dollar appropriation to the advertising goals to be achieved.

Objectives Statements of results to be achieved.

Observation A type of primary data collection, where the behaviour of customers or competitors is monitored and analyzed.

Open charge account A charge account in which the customer must pay the bill in full when it is due, usually in thirty days.

Open-ended close A sale closing technique, where the salesperson asks open-ended questions that imply readiness to buy.

Open-ended question A type of question, where the respondents are simply asked to give their opinions without a formal response structure.

Open-to-buy A control system devised to "control" the retailer's utilization of the planned purchase figure. Dollar control provides the essential component of the system. OTB records the commitments made against the planned purchases amount.

Opinion leader A person whose product-specific competence is recognized by others.

Order ceiling A level of stock sufficient to maintain a minimum order point level of stock and one sufficient to cover sales between ordering intervals.

Order interval The amount of time between merchandise orders.

Order point The level of stock below which merchandise is automatically reordered.

Original retail price The first price at which an item is offered for sale.

Out-of-home advertising All the advertising media that are physically outside the home, such as outdoor, transit, aerial, bench, taxicab, etc.

Outshopping Traveling out of one's local area to make purchases.

Overage The physical inventory (either in dollars or units) is larger than the book inventory.

Patronage builders A classification of services that provide high customer value and that can be provided by the retailer at nominal cost. An example is a computerized bridal registry.

People care programs Programs by some retailers to give employees paid time off to deal with personal matters such as taking a driving test, applying for a mortgage, or doing volunteer work in the community.

Percentage of sales A method of establishing an advertising budget based upon a percentage of retail sales.

Performance risk The chance that merchandise purchased may not work properly.

Peripheral services Secondary benefits customers seek from a service firm.

Perishability The characteristic of a service that indicates that a service is lost forever if not consumed within a specific period.

Perpetual unit control Is a book inventory.

Personal motives Reasons for shopping that result from the internal needs of the consumer, distinct from other needs fulfilled in purchasing a good or service.

Personal shopping service A situation in which a retailer will assemble wardrobes for men and women at their request and have the items ready for inspection when the customer comes to the store.

Physical handling Activities involved in receiving, checking, and marking merchandise.

Physical risk The likelihood that a purchase decision will be injurious to one's health or will likely cause physical injury.

Planogram A visual plan for standardized in-store merchandise presentation showing the ideal physical location of products within a merchandise grouping.

Point-of-purchase material A sales promotion technique that includes end-of-aisle and other in-store merchandising and display material.

Point-of-sale (POS) A point-of-sale terminal that records a variety of information at the time a transaction occurs.

Portal First screen of a Web site seen when someone accesses the Internet.

Positioning Is the design and implementation of a retail mix to create an image of the retailer in the customer's mind relative to its competitors.

Power centre An oversized strip centre typically anchored by destination-oriented retailers or superstores (e.g., Toys "Я" Us).

Predatory pricing Setting prices to deliberately drive competition out of business.

Premiums A sales promotion technique that offers something free or at a minimal price to induce sales.

Preretailing The practice of determining merchandise selling prices and writing these prices on the store's copy of the purchase order at the time it is written.

Price discrimination Varying the prices charged to different retailers for identical merchandise without an economic justification for doing so.

Price elasticity The ratio of the percentage change in the quantity demanded to the percentage change in price.

Price lining Featuring products at a limited number of prices that reflect varying levels of merchandise quality. Price lining may occur either in the context of rigid price points or price zones.

Price points Offering merchandise at a small number of different prices. For example a merchant might price all "good suits" at $175, all "better" suits at $225, and "best" suits at $350.

Price zones Pricing strategy in which a merchant establishes a range of prices for merchandise of different quality. For example, prices for "good" suits might be between $175 and $200, while prices for "better" suits might be between $225 and $275.

Primary data Needed information that is unavailable either internally or externally to the firm and that must be collected especially for the purpose at hand.

Primary trading area The area around the store that includes the majority of the store's customers, who live within a certain range of the store.

Prime time advertising Advertising that takes place during the prime time segments of television and radio programming.

Principle-oriented consumers Consumers guided in their choices by beliefs or principles, rather than by feeling, events, or desire for approval.

Private brands Brands of merchandise that retailers develop and promote under their own label.

Private label credit card A credit card that is imprinted with the name of the issuing retail outlet but for which the administrative details of the credit transaction are handled by a third party such as a bank.

Product A tangible object, service, or idea.

Product benefit A customer's basic buying motive that is fulfilled by a product feature.

Productivity of salesforce Total sales divided by employee costs.

Promotion Any form of paid communication from the retailer to the consumer.

Promotion plan A written document detailing the complete promotional program, including communication goals, targets, budgets, media, and messages.

Promotional allowance A discount from list price given by suppliers to retailers to compensate them for money spent on promoting particular items.

Promotional increases Salary increases given to employees assigned a different job and a higher pay level.

Promotional products advertising Advertising that uses gifts to customers as an advertising medium (e.g., calendars, pens, or T-shirts).

Prospecting The first step in the selling process that involves identifying and qualifying possible customers.

Psychographics Ways of defining and measuring the lifestyles of consumers.

Psychological risk The probability that the merchandise purchased or the store shopped will be compatible with the consumer's self-image.

Publicity Any non-personal stimulation of demand for a product, service, or business unit by planting commercially significant news about it in a published medium or obtaining a favourable presentation about it on radio, television, or in other ways that are not paid for by the sponsor.

Quantity discount A reduction in unit cost based on the size of an order.

Questionnaire A sequence of questions that elicit from respondents the information that should be collected to meet the objectives of the survey.

Racetrack layout A store layout that encourages customers to visit several departments by providing a major aisle that loops through the store.

Reach The number of persons exposed at least once to a message during an ad campaign.

Rebates The refund of a fixed amount from the purchase price.

Receiving A phase of the physical handling process that involves taking possession of the goods and then moving them to the next phase of the process.

Reductions Anything other than sales that reduce inventory value, including employee discounts, shortages, and markdowns.

Reference group Any group for which the consumer is a "psychological" participant, one with which she or he will identify and accept its norms or judgment.

Regional dominance A location strategy whereby a retailer decides to compete within one geographic region, for example, the Maritimes.

Regional shopping centre A shopping centre in which the leading tenant is one or more full-line department stores. The typical leasable space is 40,000 square metres, and the typical site is 120,000 square metres. The minimum trade population is 150,000 or more.

Resale price maintenance A situation in which manufacturers set minimum prices at which their products must be sold.

Retail accordion A theory about institutional change based on the premise that retail institutions evolve from broad-based outlets with wide assortments to specialized narrow lines and then return to the wide-assortment pattern.

Retail format development Strategy of introducing a new retail format to existing customers.

Retail rate Rate given by the media to retailers and that are considerably lower than for a national advertiser or an ad agency.

Retail saturation The extent to which a trading area is filled with competing stores.

Retail structure The structure comprising all retail outlets through which goods and services move to the ultimate consumer.

Retailing Consists of all activities involved in the sale of goods and services to the ultimate consumer.

Retailing mix Those variables—product, price, presentation, promotion, personal selling, and customer services—that can be used as part of a positioning strategy for competing in chosen markets.

Reverse marketing A situation where the buyer works very closely with the seller to develop a mutually beneficial relationship.

Revolving credit A customer is billed at the end of a month on the basis of an outstanding credit balance.

Role playing A sales training situation in which one person plays the part of the customer, while another person plays the part of the salesperson.

Routine selling A type of selling that involves the sale of non-technical items.

Routinized response behaviour Situations in which consumers, because they are familiar with the product class, do not engage in external information search before making a purchase.

Safety stock The level of stock sufficient to maintain adequate inventory for accommodating expected variations in demand and variations in supplier delivery schedules.

Sales productivity Sales by square metre of selling space.

Sales promotion Marketing activities other than direct selling, advertising, and publicity that stimulate consumer purchasing. Examples include displays, sales, exhibits, and demonstrations.

Sales retail price The final selling price, or the amount the customer pays for the merchandise.

Sample A selected group of respondents in a survey.

Sampling A sales promotion technique where the product is provided free or at nominal cost for trial.

Search qualities Attributes a consumer can see, feel, or touch and can thus determine prior to purchasing a product.

Seasonal discount A special discount given to retailers who place orders for seasonal merchandise in advance of the normal buying period.

Seasonal merchandise Merchandise in demand only at certain times of the year.

Secondary data Secondary data is existing data that has been previously collected for its own purposes.

Secondary market expansion Development of retail outlets in communities with under 50,000 population.

Secondary trading area The area around the store, beyond the primary trading area, that includes the majority of the store's customers who live within a certain range of the store (the rest is called the fringe trading area).

Seeking agreement A transition to the close technique, where the customer is made to agree with the salesperson on a number of points, leading to making the order.

Selectivity The ability of a medium to reach only specific audiences, minimizing waste (e.g., only teenagers or men aged 24 to 45).

Self-orientation The patterns of attitudes and activities that help people reinforce, sustain, or modify their self-image.

Semantic differential scale A type of scale that allows respondents to select the point representing the direction and intensity of their feelings between two bipolar words.

Service Activities, benefits, or satisfaction offered for sale, or provided in connection with the sale of goods.

Service approach A weak approach in personal selling in which the salesperson simply asks if they can be of assistance to a potential customer.

Share The percentage of television sets in use that are tuned to a given program.

Shoppers Newspapers that carry primarily advertising and very little news. They are distributed free to the homes of consumers.

Shopping goods Merchandise for which consumers will make comparisons between various brands in a product class before making a purchase.

Shortage The physical inventory (either in dollars or units) is smaller than the book inventory.

Situational analysis An assessment of internal strengths and weaknesses and external threats and opportunities.

Six Cs The six major reasons customers shop on-line: customization, communication, control, convenience, cost, and choice.

Social classes Divisions of society that are relatively homogeneous and permanent, and in which individuals or families share the same values, lifestyles, interests, and types of behaviour.

Social motives Reasons for shopping that reflect the desire for group interaction of one sort or another.

Social risk The likelihood that the merchandise or store will not meet with peer approval.

Solo location A location with no other retail stores nearby.

Source The originator of the promotion message.

Source marking The practice of the vendor rather than the retailer marking the goods.

Span-of-control A principle of organization that addresses the question of how many persons should report to a supervisor.

Specialization A principle of organization that states that the content of individual jobs should be narrowly defined.

Specialty goods Products that consumers know they want and for which they are willing to make a special effort to acquire.

Split runs A service offered by some print publications whereby the retailer can have two different ads in alternate copies of the same publication at the same time.

Spot advertising Advertising shown on local stations whereby the negotiation and purchase of time is made directly with the individual station.

Staple merchandise Items of merchandise generally in demand year round, with little change in model or style.

Status-oriented consumers Consumers heavily influenced by the actions, approval, and opinions of others.

Stockkeeping units (SKUs) One or more units of a distinctive item.

Stock-to-sales ratios Used in planning monthly stocks in relation to expected sales for the month.

Store design Refers to the style or atmosphere of a store that helps project an image to the market.

Store layout Planning of the internal arrangement of selling and sales-supporting departments, and deciding on the amount of space for each department.

Store planning Includes exterior and interior building design, the allocation of space to departments, and the arrangement and location of departments within the store.

Strategic planning Defining the overall mission/purpose of the company, deciding on objectives that management wants to achieve, and developing a plan to achieve those objectives.

Strategic profit model (SPM) A model from the basic ROI model that focuses on the firm's primary profit paths—margin, assets, and leverage.

Strivers People who seek motivation, self-definition, and approval from the world around them.

Strugglers Individuals who are chronically poor, ill-educated, low-skilled, and lacking strong social bonds.

Style items Products that are strongly influenced by fashion (e.g., apparel and sportswear).

Suggestion selling Using a customer's original purchase decision as a basis for developing suggestions about related or additional items in which the customer might be interested.

Supermarket retailing A type of retailing characterized by self-service and self-selection, large-scale but low-cost physical facilities, strong price emphasis, simplification and centralization of customer services, and a wide variety and broad assortment of merchandise.

Supplements Preprinted pages of ads that are inserted into newspapers.

Support services Services offered by a retailer that directly support the sale of the retailer's merchandise. Examples include home delivery or gift wrapping.

Survey research Collection of data on the opinions or perceptions of persons in a market segment by the use of a structured questionnaire.

Syncratic decision A decision within the family that is made jointly by both spouses.

Syndicated services Services offered by firms that specialize in collecting and selling information to clients.

Target markets The markets that management decides to serve.

Telemarketing Selling using the telephone (inbound or outbound).

Telephone retailing See **telemarketing**.

Tenure increases Pay increases given to employees for time worked with the company.

Test market A selected testing area that allows the retailer to help decide on whether to make changes in the merchandise mix, decor, store layout, or similar variables.

Theme or festival centres Shopping centres characterized by common architectural themes that unite a wide range of retailers who repeat the theme in their spaces.

Third-party credit A situation in which a customer uses a card such as Visa or Mastercard to charge merchandise purchased at a retail outlet.

Time loss risk The likelihood that the consumer will not be able to get merchandise adjusted, replaced, or repaired without loss of time and effort.

Trade discount A reduction off the seller's list price that is granted to a retailer who performs functions normally the responsibility of the vendor.

Trading area The area from which a store primarily attracts its customers.

Traffic count A method used to determine the character and volume of traffic (both vehicular and pedestrian) passing a particular site.

Transaction processing A situation in which employees serve as check-out clerks or cashiers and do little selling.

Trial close A transition to the close technique, where a question is asked to determine the customer's readiness to buy.

Turnover The number of times the average inventory is sold, usually in annual terms.

Unit control System used to control the width and support aspects of stock balance. The system records (perpetual) beginning inventory and all additions and deductions to stock to obtain the ending inventory. (See **Nonperpetual unit control** for the other system in use.)

Unit of sales A method of establishing an advertising budget whereby retailers set aside a fixed dollar amount for each unit of the product to be sold.

Unity-of-command A principle of organization that states that no person should be under the direct control of more than one supervisor in performing job tasks.

Universal transverse mercator (UTM) A system that provides the coordinates of every location in Canada.

Urban arterial development Shopping areas usually found in an older part of the city.

Urgency close A sale closing technique.

VALS A trademark program, Values and Lifestyles, developed by Stanford Research International that places emphasis on the psychological underpinnings of consumer behaviour.

Value and entertainment-oriented megamall A new type of mall providing shoppers with several additional functions, such as entertainment, recreation, eating, drinking, socializing, working, and sightseeing (e.g., West Edmonton Mall).

Values Beliefs or expectations about behaviour shared by a number of individuals and learned from society.

Variability A characteristic of services, the inability to maintain consistent levels of service quality.

Variable-payment lease A situation in which the retailer makes a guaranteed monthly rental payment to the landlord in addition to a specified percentage of sales.

Variety The width of a store's selection of merchandise.

Vending machines Mechanical dispensers of goods or services placed in strategic locations.

Video tech Reaching consumers with cable TV, teletext, and video discs.

Visual merchandising Technique of displaying merchandise in harmony with the customers' lifestyles.

Warehouse-style store See **big-box store**.

Web site An address on the Internet for a supplier of information, products, or services.

Wheel of retailing A theory about institutional structure change based on the premise that institutional innovations in retailing penetrate the system on the basis of price appeal and gradually trade up over time in terms of store standing, quality, store services, and prices.

Width See **breadth**.

Wife-dominant decision A decision within the family that is made most of the time by the wife.

Work sharing A situation that occurs during economic recessions where employees are required to cut back on their work hours rather than face layoffs and are paid accordingly.

COMPANY AND NAME INDEX

SUBJECT INDEX

URL INDEX